Author of Over 220 Books

THE EARLY CHRISTIAN COPYISTS OF THE NEW TESTAMENT

The Making and Copying of the New Testament Books

EDWARD D. ANDREWS

THE EARLY CHRISTIAN COPYISTS OF THE NEW TESTAMENT

The Making and Copying of the New Testament Books

Edward D. Andrews

Christian Publishing House
Cambridge, Ohio

Copyright © 2018, 2024 Edward D. Andrews

All rights reserved. Except for brief quotations in articles, other publications, book reviews, and blogs, no part of this book may be reproduced in any manner without prior written permission from the publishers. For information, write, support@christianpublishers.org

THE EARLY CHRISTIAN COPYISTS OF THE NEW TESTAMENT: *The Making and Copying of the New Testament Books* by Edward D. Andrews

- **ISBN-10:** 1945757841
- **ISBN-13:** 978-1945757846

Table of Contents

Book Description 6

Preface 8

Introduction 10

CHAPTER 1 The Making of New Testament Books 12

CHAPTER 2 The New Testament Copyists and Their Materials 40

CHAPTER 3 The Book Writing Process of the New Testament: Authors and Early Christian Scribes 54

CHAPTER 4 The Production of New Testament Manuscripts . 92

CHAPTER 5 Most Important Manuscripts (100 – 400 C.E.) ... 174

CHAPTER 6 Dating the Earliest Manuscripts of the New Testament 380

CHAPTER 7 The Nomina Sacra (Sacred Name) in New Testament Manuscripts 407

CHAPTER 8 Textual Variants in the Greek New Testament .. 429

CHAPTER 9 Modern Theories and Methods of New Testament Textual Criticism 469

CHAPTER 10 How Scribes Influenced the Text of the New Testament 522

Bibliography 537

Edward D. Andrews

Book Description

This authoritative work delves into the meticulous and often understudied world of the early Christian copyists who played a pivotal role in the formation and preservation of the New Testament texts. From the first century onward, these scribes not only copied sacred texts but also shaped the future of Christian doctrine through their decisions and scribal practices.

Spanning ten comprehensive chapters, the book begins by exploring the initial stages of the New Testament's composition in **Chapter 1: The Making of New Testament Books**, which sets the historical and theological context for the texts' creation. **Chapter 2: The New Testament Copyists and Their Materials** examines the tools and materials that were essential to the craft of these early scribes, revealing how the physical means of production influenced the textual transmission.

Chapter 3: The Book Writing Process of the New Testament offers insights into the collaborative efforts between authors and scribes, while **Chapter 4: The Production of New Testament Manuscripts** provides a detailed look at the actual processes involved in the creation of these enduring documents. **Chapter 5: Most Important Manuscripts (100 – 400 C.E.)** and **Chapter 6: Dating the Earliest Manuscripts of the New Testament** present a critical analysis of the key manuscripts and discuss methodologies for dating these invaluable texts.

The exploration deepens in **Chapter 7: The Nomina Sacra (Sacred Name) in New Testament Manuscripts**, which investigates the treatment of divine names and their significant role in scribal practices. **Chapter 8: Textual Variants in the Greek New Testament** addresses the complexities of textual variation and its implications for biblical scholarship.

Chapter 9: Modern Theories and Methods of New Testament Textual Criticism brings the discussion into contemporary scholarly debates, highlighting the evolution of textual criticism over the centuries. Finally, **Chapter 10: How Scribes Influenced the Text of the New Testament** synthesizes the findings from previous chapters to demonstrate the profound impact scribes had on the New Testament text.

Each chapter is meticulously researched, drawing on the latest academic studies and archaeological findings to provide a rich narrative that is both scholarly and accessible. This book is an essential resource for theologians,

THE EARLY CHRISTIAN COPYISTS OF THE NEW TESTAMENT

historians, biblical scholars, and anyone interested in the origins and transmission of the New Testament. It offers a rare glimpse into the lives and labors of the early scribes whose contributions have helped to preserve one of the world's most influential religious texts.

Edward D. Andrews

Preface

Welcome to a journey through the meticulous world of the early Christian copyists, the unsung architects behind the text of the New Testament. This book, "THE EARLY CHRISTIAN COPYISTS OF THE NEW TESTAMENT: The Making and Copying of the New Testament Books," arose from a desire to shine a light on these vital yet often overlooked figures in Christian history. It aims to bridge the gap between the known authors of the New Testament and the anonymous scribes who played a crucial role in preserving their writings.

The task of a scribe in the early Christian era was formidable. Armed with nothing more than papyrus, parchment, ink, and a profound sense of duty, these individuals undertook the painstaking work of copying texts that were not only complex but also held sacred. Their efforts were fraught with challenges—technological, linguistic, and theological. Each decision they made, from the choice of a word to the handling of a textual discrepancy, carried weight and consequence. Through their labors, the textual foundation of what would become a global faith was laid down with care and reverence.

In preparing this manuscript, I delved into ancient libraries and modern databases alike, consulting a wide range of sources to paint as complete a picture as possible of these early custodians of the Christian message. The chapters that follow unfold the story of the New Testament from its physical creation to the intricate processes that governed its transmission. We will explore not just the how but also the why behind the copyists' choices, looking at how doctrinal, cultural, and practical considerations shaped the text.

This book is structured to guide readers through an understanding of the initial composition of New Testament texts, through the detailed examination of the materials and methods used by the copyists, and into the deep implications of their work. The chapters are crafted to build upon one another, culminating in a comprehensive understanding of New Testament textual criticism.

It is my hope that this book will serve as both an academic resource and a source of inspiration. For scholars, it offers detailed analyses and a synthesis of recent research; for lay readers, it provides a clear explanation of how the texts that form the basis of Christian faith have been transmitted across centuries.

THE EARLY CHRISTIAN COPYISTS OF THE NEW TESTAMENT

As we turn the pages of history to uncover the stories of these early scribes, we also turn the pages of this book, eager to learn and understand the depth of their devotion and the breadth of their impact. Let us begin.

Edward D. Andrews

Author of 220+ books and Chief Translator of the Updated American Standard Version

Edward D. Andrews

Introduction

The New Testament, a cornerstone of Christian faith, has been preserved, studied, and cherished across millennia not solely through divine providence but also through the meticulous efforts of countless scribes whose names have long been forgotten. This book seeks to uncover and narrate the complex, often arduous processes these early copyists undertook to transmit the texts from generation to generation, ensuring the survival and integrity of the Christian scriptural canon.

In the vast landscape of Christian documents and scholarly research, the role of the scribe has been somewhat overshadowed by theological debates and doctrinal discussions. Yet, without these diligent individuals, the words of the New Testament might not have reached us in the form they have. From the initial drafting of the gospels and epistles to the careful copying of these texts onto scrolls and codices, each phase in the life of these documents was fraught with challenges and required decisions that had long-lasting implications.

This introduction sets the stage for a deeper exploration into the world of these early Christian copyists. We will explore not only who these individuals were—often monks, clergy, or learned laypersons—but also the historical and cultural contexts in which they worked. What were the physical conditions like for a scribe in the early centuries of Christianity? How did the political and theological climates of their times influence their work? These questions are essential for understanding the complexities involved in the transcription process.

Moreover, we will delve into the technologies available to them, from the making of papyrus and parchment to the development of ink and the evolution of script styles. Each technological advancement brought changes to how texts could be copied, stored, and distributed. The invention of the codex, for example, represented a significant shift in manuscript culture, influencing everything from the way texts were read to how they were preserved.

As we move through the chapters of this book, we will trace the journey of the New Testament writings from their origins as scattered letters and narratives through their compilation into the codices that laid the foundation for the modern Bible. We will examine case studies of key manuscripts, decipher the markings of anonymous hands, and uncover the reasons behind textual variations.

By reconstructing the efforts of these early scribes, this book aims to provide a comprehensive understanding of the crucial role they played in the formation of the New Testament. Their contributions were not merely clerical but were acts of profound religious devotion and intellectual labor that shaped the transmission of Christian thought and practice.

Thus, as we embark on this exploration, we are not only uncovering the physical processes of ancient bookmaking but also engaging with a deeply human story woven into the fabric of one of the world's most influential religious texts. Let us appreciate the art, the science, and the faith that guided these early Christian copyists as they preserved for posterity the teachings that continue to resonate with millions around the globe.

Edward D. Andrews

CHAPTER 1 The Making of New Testament Books

As Luke, Paul, Peter, Matthew, James, or Jude handed their authorized text off to be copied by others, i.e., published, what would it have looked like? What is the process that the New Testament writers would have followed to get their book ready to be published, copied by others? Once they were prepared for publication, how would they be copied throughout the centuries, up until the time of the printing press of 1455 C.E.?[1] As we open our Bible to the Gospel of Matthew, or the letter to the Romans, or any of the 27 books of the New Testament, how can we have confidence that what we are reading is a reflection of the original in our language? If we were to bring home from a bookstore a copy of the KJV, ASV, RSV, ESV, CSB, LEB, NASB, NLT, NIV, NRSV, UASV, or any of the other one hundred and fifty plus English translations, could we have confidence that what we are reading is, in fact, the Word of God? Some translations have footnotes throughout that say, "Other ancient MSS[2] read .... What exactly does that

---

[1] B.C.E. means "before the Common Era," which is more accurate than B.C. ("before Christ"). C.E. denotes "Common Era," often called A.D., for *anno Domini*, meaning "in the year of our Lord."

[2] Manuscripts, MS would be singular manuscript, while MSS will refer to more than one.

mean, and which is the Word of God: the words in the main text of our Bible, or the others below in the footnote?

The science and art of textual criticism have answered these questions and more. It is a science because there are rules and principles and a method or process that is to be followed if the textual scholar is to get back to the original reading.[3] It is an art because the human agent needs to be balanced with those rules and principles. It is like driving a car. The driver needs to follow all driving rules as he stays between the lines of his side of the road to reach his destination. So too, the textual scholar needs to stay within the rules to reach his destination of establishing the original words of the original texts. However, the designers of the roads were not rigid to the point of making those two lines so narrow that there was no room for the driver to miss obstructions, which might be in his path. This extra room would help the driver to avoid objects that could result in a crash. The same holds true for the textual scholar having room within the lines of his field to prevent a wreck, causing him not to reach his desired destination, i.e., the original reading.

From ancient times until 1455 C.E., anything that was authored was done literally, by hand. A "manuscript" is a handwritten text. It did not matter if it were a poem, letter, receipt, book, or marriage certificate; it would still have been produced and copied by hand. In addition, it would mostly have been done one copy at a time in the early decades of Christianity. In the second century C.E., it may have been copied in a scriptorium, i.e., a room in a monastery for storing, copying, illustrating, or reading manuscripts. In the scriptorium, there would have been a lector (reader) who would have read aloud slowly as multiple scribes or copyists took down what he was saying.

The modern-day young person is far removed from the 1920s to the 1980s where people actually used physical paper, pens, pencils, and envelopes to write letters. The same material was used for homework in school. Today, everything is digital: Microsoft Word Docx, PDFs, laptops, tablets, social media, and smartphones. A twenty-year-old today would likely find it challenging to write a letter with merely pen and paper. He would find it tedious and physically taxing. His lack of practice in writing would make it more difficult to be proficient in making the letters, and it would not be

---

[3] When we use the term "original" reading or "original" text in this publication, it is a reference to the exemplar manuscript by the New Testament author (e.g. Paul) and his secretary, if he used one (e.g. Tertius), from which other copies were made for publication and distribution to the Christian communities.

aesthetically pleasing. The hand, wrist, and forearm would get very tired to the point where he would need to take a break.

In early Christianity, manually copying a Bible text would be far more arduous than what was just described. There would be many different physical and mental tasks involved in the process of Tertius copying the book of Romans as the apostle Paul dictated to him, which would have been laborious and strenuous. The same would be even more true of the copyists who would then use Romans' original copy to make other copies. He would not have had the luxury of having the words dictated, and he would have to look at the exemplar back and forth thousands of times as he made his copy that contained 7,000+ words. Imagine if he were copying the entire Greek New Testament of 138,162 words.

Additionally, far more was involved than simply reading the exemplar and writing a word or phrase in the copy. The material that was being written on was papyrus or parchment. Papyrus was a material prepared in ancient Egypt from the pithy stem of a water plant, used in sheets throughout the ancient Mediterranean world for writing. Parchment was a stiff, flat, thin material made from the prepared skin of an animal and used as a durable writing surface in ancient and medieval times. More on this later.

When the materials used and the working environment are understood, we will fully appreciate why ancient people hired secretaries (scribes). The scribe would lay out a layer of strips that he had cut from the papyrus plant. The pithy juices of the plant would be put in the strips. Another layer would have been placed at right angles over top of the first layer. Something flat and heavy would be placed on the papyrus sheet so the two could be bonded by pressure, which would have produced what we would consider a sheet of papyrus paper. It was no easy task writing on the surface of this papyrus sheet, as the material was rough and fibrous.

The scribe could be seen sitting on the ground with his legs crossed, a board laying over his knees. He would be hunched over, holding the exemplar sheet of papyrus with the fingers of, say, his left hand and his thumb of the same hand resting on the papyrus sheet he was using to make his copy.

THE EARLY CHRISTIAN COPYISTS OF THE NEW TESTAMENT

Or, if a professional scribe, he would pin his sheets of papyrus down. To the other corner of the board would be a small container of ink that he had personally made from a mixture of soot and gum. If this scribe were not experienced at making documents, or he was using below-average level materials, his calamus, or reed pen, could very well snag and tear the papyrus, or the writing could be unreadable. To the right of this scribe, we would see a sharp knife, which would have been used to sharpen his reed pen, and a damp sponge that would be used to erase any errors he might make. Since he is copying a New Testament book, he would likely be doing his level best to write every letter with the greatest of care, meaning he would be writing slowly, all of this bringing with it some difficulty. Imagine the constant sharpening of his pen with his knife and the continuous replenishing it with ink to keep the strokes even.

Working as a scribe or copyist for long hours each day can cause back, neck, and shoulder pains, headache, eyestrain, and overuse injuries of the arms and hands. When the scribe constantly bends his head forward, the muscles in his neck, chest, and **back become almost stiffened in that position**, giving him rounded shoulders and making it more challenging for him to stand upright. Bad posture from the life of a copyist can lead to bad balance. The average human head weighs almost 12 pounds (5.44 kg). This is equal to a bowling ball! When the copyist has his neck bent to 45 degrees, his head exerts nearly 50 pounds (ca. 23 kg) of force on his neck. The weight and pressure affect his breathing and mood, aside from straining joints and muscles in his neck and shoulders.

As we can mentally picture, this scribe was carrying out many simultaneous tedious tasks as he went about copying a book of the New Testament. If he had some experience or a professional in making documents and copying literature, he would have had to consider the page before him to calculate the proper word division. He would be using stichoi notations at the end of the copying process, that is, notes on how many lines were copied to get paid, which means that he had to keep track of his lines. The scribe would always have to be conscious of an imaginary upper and lower line that he sought to keep his text between. Unlike our notebooks today, papyrus and parchment sheets did not come with ruled lines. The scribe would use an unsharpened instrument to draw 25-30 pressure lines on his page to receive the text. Before he even began the above, he would have to have the ability to estimate just how many sheets would be needed for the project. This would change if he were making a copy of an individual gospel or a codex of all four gospels, or the gospels and Acts, or a copy of Paul's epistles, or even one of Paul's epistles such as Romans. He would have to determine how he would construct the codex: was it to be one gather or multiple gathers. If it were multiple gatherings, how many sheets would he need in each gathering? To estimate these things, he would have to determine the size of the letters, how many letters to a line, how big were the margins. These are just some fundamental difficulties involved as early scribes made copies of our New Testament books.

One of the Earliest New Testament Manuscripts: P⁶⁶ Papyrus

The Scroll or Roll Book

A scroll is a roll of papyrus, parchment, or other material, used for a written document. Even though it was continuous, the scroll was generally divided into pages by gluing separate sheets at the edges. Usually, the reader or lector and the writer unrolled the scroll one page at a time, leaving it rolled up on both sides of the current page that was showing. The scroll is unrolled from side to side, with the text being written or read, from top to bottom. For example, if it were Hebrew, it would be written from right to left, and one would open that scroll by rolling to the right. On the other hand, if it were Greek, it would be written from left to right, or even in an alternating direction with other languages. Boustrophedon is an ancient method of inscribing and writing in which lines are written alternately from right to left and from left to right. Usually, professional scribes would justify both sides of the pages, aligned with both left and right margins. On the papyrus scroll, Harold Greenlee writes,

> Papyrus scrolls are mentioned several times in the New Testament; references are usually translated as "book." Luke 4:17 speaks of the scroll (*biblion*) of the prophet Isaiah. John uses the same word to refer to his gospel in John 20:30. The "books" or "scrolls" mentioned in 2 Tim 4:13 may be either parchment scrolls

or leather scrolls of the Old Testament. Rev 6:14 describes the sky as vanishing like "a scroll when it is rolled up."[4]

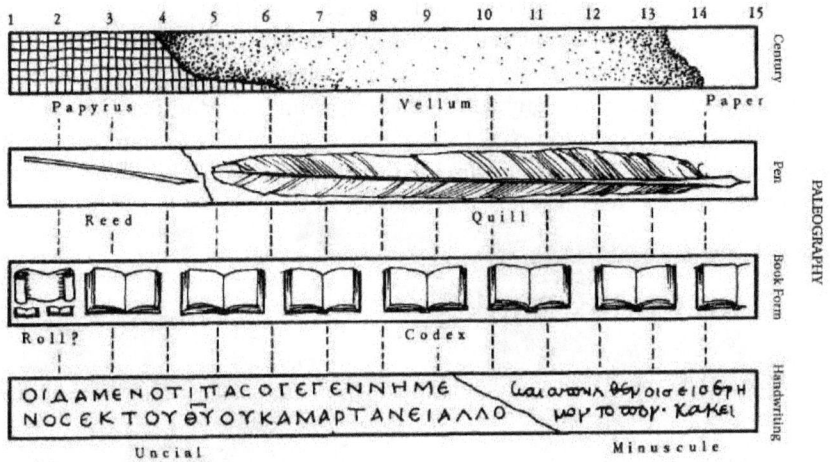

Harold Greenlee, Introduction to New Testament Textual Criticism, (p. 23)

The parchment scroll used by Moses to pen the first five books of the Old Testament; goes back to about the late sixteenth-century B.C.E. The scroll was the first form to receive writing, which was in a format that could be edited by the author or scribe and was used in the Eastern Mediterranean ancient Egyptian civilizations. The codex (bound book) got its start from Latin authors in the first-century C.E. (widely used in the second-century), some 1,500 years after the scroll. The early Christians popularized the codex in the second-century C.E. Some would even argue that the Christians invented it. However, it appears that Christians mainly began using the roll, or scroll, at least until about the end of the first century C.E. Nevertheless, from the close of the first to the third century C.E., there was a struggle between those who encouraged the use of the codex and those preferring scrolls. Traditionalists, familiar and comfortable with using the scroll, were unwilling to give up deep-rooted conventions and traditions. Nevertheless, the popularization of the codex played a significant role in the displacement of the scroll. Therefore, the scroll continued to be used for centuries.

Scrolls were used for literary works. Continuous rolls were twenty or thirty feet long and nine to ten inches high. (Psa. 40:7) The text was written in columns, which formed the pages. (Jer. 36:23) Our English word "volume" literally means *something rolled up*. Imagine being in the synagogue of Nazareth

---

[4] J. Harold Greenlee, *Text of the New Testament, From the Manuscript to Modern Edition* (Grand Rapids, MI: Baker Publishing, 2008), 13-14.

when Jesus was handed the scroll of the prophet Isaiah, where he skillfully unrolled with one hand while simultaneously rolling it up with the other hand until he reached the place he wanted to read. (Lu 4:16-17; Isa. 61:1-2) The ink used on the surface of the scrolls had to withstand being rolled and unrolled, so special ink was developed. In addition, the Jews would discard any scroll that had too many letters missing from wear and tear. It was not until about the fifth-century C.E. that the codex finally outnumbered the scroll by a ten to one margin in Egypt. When we consider the surviving examples, we also see that the scroll had almost vanished by the sixth-century C.E.

The Codex Book

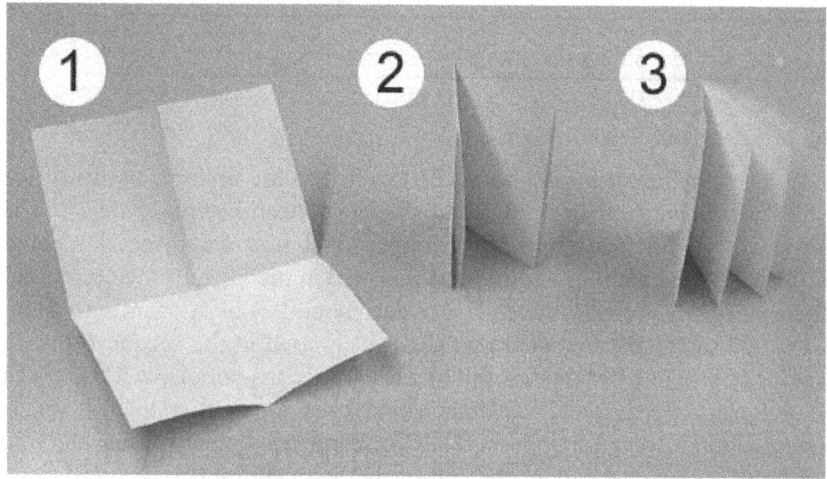

A typical four-leaf quire can be formed from a single sheet of papyrus, parchment, or paper by folding and then cutting the sheet

A codex is a collection of ancient manuscript texts, especially of the Biblical Scriptures, in book form.[5] It is made up of papyrus sheets or parchment inscribed with handwritten material, which is created by folding a single sheet of standard-sized pages, giving the scribe two leaves or four pages.

Indications of Universality

- All of the early papyrus was **in codex (book) form**. (125-400 C.E.)

---

[5] Late 16th century: < Latin, "block of wood, book, set of statutes"

THE EARLY CHRISTIAN COPYISTS OF THE NEW TESTAMENT

- The standardization of **the nominal sacra (sacred names)** very early on: God Θεός ΘΣ; Lord Κύριος ΚΣ; Jesus Ἰησοῦς ΙΣ; Christ Χριστός ΧΣ; Spirit Πνεῦμα ΠΝΑ, being in a contracted format and with a horizontal line above the letters. Eventually, it would be 15 sacred names. The following second-century manuscripts that clearly show these nomina sacra are as follows: vP4+P64+P67 dates to (150-175 C.E.), P32 dates to (150-200 C.E.), P46 dates to 150 C.E.), P66 dates to about (150 C.E.), P75 dates to about (175 C.E.), and P90 dates to (150-200 C.E.). This means that the nomina sacra for Lord, Jesus, Christ, God, and Spirit are standard by 150 C.E.
- Initially, there were some inconsistencies in the application, but universally it was soon decided to use the nomina sacra regardless of whether the referent, meaning, or context was mundane or sacred in its use.
- By the late first century, New Testament books were being collected in codex form: the Gospels or the Gospels and Acts. The early second century saw the collection of the apostle Paul's letters, which included Hebrews.
- There was the standardization of the codex size for the Gospels, like our 8.5 x 11 inches today. The standard size in the second/third centuries was 11.5-14 cm (4.5-5.5 inches) **Width** x 14.5-17 cm (5.7-6.7) **Length**. A new standard size began to develop in the third century. Just the fact that they had a standard size for the Gospels is unusual because this is not the case for Paul's letter or any other books.

The first codices were made with waxed-coated wooden tablets. The people of Greece and Rome used waxed tablets before the Christian era. Schoolboys were sometimes given waxed tablets on which the teacher had written letters in model script with a stylus. Today, we have the blackboard (UK) or chalkboard (US), initially made of smooth, thin sheets of black or dark gray slate stone. In the early part of the 20th century, schoolchildren even had smaller slate tablets. They had a reusable writing surface on which text or drawings could be made with sticks of calcium carbonate, i.e., chalk.

Roman wax tablet and stylus

To make the waxed tablets of Jesus' day, one would slightly hollow out a flat piece of wood and fill that void with wax. These tablets were also used for temporary writing like modern chalkboards. They were also commonly used for corresponding with others. Greenlee writes, "They were also used at times for legal documents, in which case two tablets would be placed face to face with the writing inside and fastened together with leather thongs run through holes at the edges of the tablets. In one of his writings, St. Augustine mentions some tablets he owned, although his were made of ivory instead of wood."[6] An example of temporary (short-term, momentary) writing is found in the Gospel of his ability to speak, was asked what name he wanted his son to have. Luke 1:63 reports, "And he asked for a writing tablet and wrote, 'His name is John.'"

Polyptychs [**pol·yp·tych** ˈpälip ˌtik] is an arrangement of three or more panels with a painting or carving on each, usually hinged together. Some were discovered at Herculaneum, an ancient Roman town near modern Naples that was destroyed along with Pompeii by the eruption of Mount Vesuvius in 79 C.E.

In time, sheets of foldable material replaced rigid tablets. The codex has been viewed as the most significant advancement in the development of the book, aside from the printing press.[7] Some of the earliest surviving codices were made of papyrus, being preserved in the dry sands of Egypt.

When we consider the thought of unrolling and using a scroll instead of the codex, we can likely think of many advantages of one over the other. The codex can contain far more written material; it is much easier to carry and more convenient. Some in the early days of the codex even mentioned these advantages. Nevertheless, some were slow to move away from the scroll's prolonged use. Again, the Christians played a significant part in the eventual

---

[6] J. Harold Greenlee, *Introduction to New Testament Textual Criticism* (Grand Rapids, MI: Baker Academic, 1995), 8-9.

[7] Colin H. Roberts; T. C. Skeat, *The Birth of the Codex*, (London, Oxford University Press, 1983), 1.

death of the scroll. Their evangelism would have been far more cumbersome without the codex.

The Codex Gigas, 13th century, Bohemia.

Compared to the scroll, the codex was also far more affordable because both sides of the pages could be written on, getting more value for one's money. Moreover, instead of having one book with each scroll, one could have the whole of the old or New Testament. The fact that one could find Bible passages far more accessible and faster, this, too, added to the codex's success. This preference for the codex was not only true for Christians but also lawyers and the like. When we think of the early Christians, we are reminded that they evangelized to the point of going from 120 disciples in the upper room on Pentecost 33 C.E. to more than one million Christians spread throughout the Roman Empire at the beginning of the second century C.E. In addition, early Christians were evangelists, who used pre-evangelism, i.e., apologetics. They could have what we now call proof texts, easily located, to make their arguments to pagans and Jews alike. Then, the fact that the codex book had a wooden cover made it more durable than the scroll, adding to its advantages. Codices were useful, sensible, and likely practical for personal reading. The Christians of the third century C.E. had parchment pocket Gospels.

Larry Hurtado, in his blog (*The Codex and Early Christians: Clarification & Corrections*), writes,

Bagnall offered figures (pp. 72-74) comparing the number of non-Christian and Christian codices from Egypt datable to the early centuries, also giving the percentages of Christian codices of the total. His own data show, e.g., that Christian codices amount to somewhere between 22-34% of the total for the 2nd-3rd centuries CE. Yet Christian books overall amount to only ca. 2% of the total number of books (codices and rolls) of these centuries. Of course, there are more non-Christian codices, but the first point to note is that Christian codices comprise a vastly disproportionate percentage of the total number of codices in this period.

The very data provided by Bagnall clearly show that Christians invested in the codex far more than is reflected in the larger book-culture of the time. That is, the early Christian *preference* for the codex is undeniable, and this preference is quite distinctive in that period. Bagnall actually reached the same judgment, stating, "Christian books in these centuries ($2^{nd}/3^{rd}$) are far more likely to be codices than rolls, quite the reverse of what we find with classical literature." (p. 74)

My second point also stands and is supported by Bagnall: the early Christian preference for the codex seems to have been especially keen when it came to making copies of texts used as scripture (i.e., read in corporate worship). For example, 95+% of Christian copies of OT writings are in codex form. As for the writings that came to form the NT, they're all in codex form except for a very few instances of NT writings copied on the back of a re-used roll (which were likely informal and personal copies made by/for readers who couldn't afford a copy on unused writing material). Here again, Bagnall grants the same conclusion, judging that, although they were ready to copy "the Christians adopted the codex as the normative format of deliberately produced public copies of scriptural texts" (p. 78), but were ready to use rolls for other texts (76).[8]

---

[8] Retrieved Thursday January 17, 2019, The Codex and Early Christians: Clarification & Corrections, https://larryhurtado.wordpress.com/2014/09/16/the-codex-and-early-christians-clarification-corrections/

The Making of a Codex

Skin of a stillborn goat on a stretcher (modern) – The J. Paul Getty Museum

Making a codex began with a dried and treated sheepskin, goatskin, or another animal hide. "The pelts were first soaked in a lime solution to loosen the fur, which was then removed. While wet on a stretcher, the skin was scraped using a knife with a curved blade. As the skin dried, the parchment maker would adjust the tension so that the skin remained taut. This cycle of scraping and stretching was repeated over several days until the desired thinness had been achieved. Here, the skin of a stillborn goat, prized for its smoothness, is stretched on a modern frame to illustrate the parchment making process."[9] The first step for preparing the pages to receive writing was setting up the quires, i.e., a bundle of parchment sheets folded together for binding into a book, especially a four-sheet bundle folded once to make eight leaves or sixteen pages. Raymond Clemens and Timothy Graham point out that "the quire was the scribe's basic writing unit throughout the Middle Ages."[10]

The Craft of the Scribe

The *recto* is the front side of a papyrus sheet or parchment sheet, while the *verso* is the back of a page. If the scribe were writing on a papyrus sheet, he would write his script on the horizontal lines of the fibers on the recto side of his sheet. If the scribe were using a parchment sheet, the manuscript had pinpricks placed in it to be ruled with lines to accommodate writing better. In some of the documents, we can still see faintly visible lines. It was similar to modern-day tablet paper, with horizontal lines running across the page to receive text, and vertical lines, which served to mark the boundaries,

---

[9] Retrieved Monday September 15, 2014 *"The Making of a Medieval Book"* The J. Paul Getty Trust. http://www.getty.edu/art/exhibitions/making/

[10] Raymond Clemens, Timothy Graham. *Introduction to Manuscript Studies*. Ithaca: Cornell University Press, 2008, 14.

justify both sides. The scribal schools had different techniques for ruling manuscripts. Sometimes, a textual scholar can identify a particular manuscript's school, based on how it was ruled, giving us the place of its origin. The parchment's hair side was darker than that of the flesh side, so scribes placed the quires so that the hair side faced the hair side of the corresponding page, making it more reader-friendly.

Study of Ancient Handwriting

The study of ancient handwriting and manuscripts is an essential skill for paleographers, but also for the textual scholar as well. The style of the characters that make up an alphabet change every fifty years or so; thus, it is essential to know the eras of different styles. Moreover, scribes use abbreviations and contractions for various reasons. Therefore, the student of ancient handwriting must know how to interpret them. For example, several contractions and abbreviations are found in our earliest manuscripts of the Christian Greek New Testament.[11] We briefly mentioned this earlier.

The abbreviations that are most relevant to this discussion are what have become known as the sacred names, or nomina sacra (nomen sacrum, singular), such as Lord ($\overline{KC}$),[12] Jesus ($\overline{IH}$, $\overline{IHC}$), Christ ($\overline{XP}$, $\overline{XC}$, $\overline{XPC}$), God ($\overline{\Theta C}$), and Spirit ($\overline{\Pi NA}$). These sacred names are abbreviated or contracted by keeping the first letter or two and the last letter. Another essential feature is the horizontal bar placed over these letters to help readers recognize that they are encountering a contraction. The early Christian writers had three different ways that they would pen a sacred name: **(1)** suspension, **(2)** contraction, and **(3)** longer contraction. The suspension was accomplished by writing only the first two letters of "Jesus," for example (ιησους = ιη), and suspending the remaining letters (σους). The contraction was accomplished by writing only the first and last letter of Jesus (ιησους = ις) and removing the remaining letters (ησου).

The longer contraction would simply keep the first two letters and the last letter (ιης). After penning the suspension or contraction, the scribe would place a bar over the $\overline{name}$. This practice of placing a bar over the name was

---

[11] It should be noted that the early manuscripts were written in what we consider all uppercase letters, known as majuscule, the large rounded letters used in ancient manuscripts. Moreover, there were no breaks between the letters, so a phrase like GODISNOWHERE could be divided as GOD IS NO WHERE or GOD IS NOW HERE.

[12] In the fourth and third centuries B.C.E., the sigma form of Σ was simplified into a C-like shape in koinē Greek.

THE EARLY CHRISTIAN COPYISTS OF THE NEW TESTAMENT

likely carried over from the typical way of scribes putting bars above contractions, especially numbers, which were represented by letters, e.g., $\overline{IA}$ = eleven.

When students of ancient handwriting know these individual letterforms, ligatures,[13] punctuation, and abbreviations, they can read and understand the text. Of course, textual scholars must learn the language of the manuscripts they are studying; in our case, Greek. They need to be an expert in the forms of the language, the various handwriting styles, writing customs, and able to identify different hands within the same manuscript and scribal notes and abbreviations. They also need to study the language development over the years and its history to better analyze the texts. As we have discussed, students of ancient handwriting must know the writing materials, which will enable them to better identify the period in which a document was copied.[14] One of the primary goals of paleographers is to ascertain the text's date and its place of origin. For these reasons alone, they must consider the style and formation of a manuscript and the style of handwriting used therein.

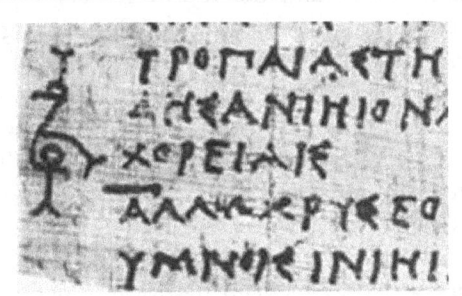

Detail of the Berlin Papyrus 9875 showing the 5th column of Timotheus' Persae, with a coronis symbol, to mark the end.

For example, with the majuscule hand, we have what is known as the **Ptolemaic Book Hand**, and how it developed is difficult to say because we have so few examples, which are not datable. It is not until we reach the third century B.C.E. that we can have confidence in the Ptolemaic bookhand era. This period's hands are stiff, awkward, and sharply defined (e.g., **E, Σ,** and **Ω**). Moreover, the letters evidenced no consistency in size. At times, there was a fineness, and pleasing subtlety attained. When we arrive at the second century B.C.E., we find the letters becoming more rounded and more uniform in size. However, one can detect a loss of unity in the first century. On this, Comfort writes, "Paleographers date the emergence of the

---

[13] A ligature is a character that consists of two or more letters joined together, e.g. "æ". We do not normally find ligatures in majuscule manuscripts. In the minuscule manuscripts, it can be difficult to determine a ligature due to the fact it is a manuscript with a running hand.

[14] Robert P. Gwinn, "Paleography" in the Encyclopaedia Britannica, Micropædia, Vol. IX, 1986, p. 78.

Roman Uncial as coming on the heels of the Ptolemaic period, which ended in 30 BC. Thus, early Roman Uncial begins around 30 BC, and the Roman Uncial hand can be seen throughout the first two to three centuries of the Christian era. The Roman Uncial script, generally speaking, shares the characteristics of literary manuscripts in the Roman period (as distinct from the Ptolemaic period) in that these manuscripts show a greater roundness and smoothness in the forms of letters and are somewhat larger than what was penned in the Ptolemaic period. Furthermore, the Roman Uncial typically displays decorative serifs in several letters, but not all. (By contrast, the Decorated Rounded style aims at making the decorations rounded and replete.)"[15]

Majuscule Hand

During the Byzantine period (300-650 C.E.), the dominant type of book-hand became known as the biblical hand. It had its earliest beginnings toward the end of the second-century C.E., being used by all, not necessarily having any connection to Christian literature. In addition, manuscripts from Egypt, of vellum or papyrus dating to around the fourth century C.E., contained other forms of script, i.e., a sloping somewhat unpolished rough hand resulting from the literary hand, which continued until about the fifth century C.E. The three early great codices, Vaticanus and Sinaiticus of the fourth century C.E. and Alexandrinus of the fifth century C.E., were penned in majuscules of the biblical hand. The hand that produced Vaticanus is the least demonstrated. The letters are characteristic of the biblical hand but do not possess the later manuscripts' heavy look, with a greater roundness to them. Sinaiticus, which was copied shortly after that, has larger, heavier letters. In Alexandrinus, we notice a development in the form, a definite distinction between thick and thin strokes.

Vaticanus, From Page Matthew 1:22-2:18

---

[15] Philip Comfort, *Encountering the Manuscripts: An Introduction to New Testament Paleography & Textual Criticism* (Nashville, TN: Broadman & Holman, 2005), 110.

Sinaiticus, From Page Matthew 2:5-3:7

Codex Alexandrinus of the fifth century, The Center for the Study of New Testament Manuscripts

Once we enter the sixth century C.E., we notice in the manuscripts, vellum or papyrus, that the heavier hand became the standard but still possessed an attractive appearance. However, there was a steady decline in the centuries to come, as the writing appears to be done artificially, i.e., as a matter of duty or custom, without thought, attention. The thick strokes became heavier; the cross strokes of **T** and **Θ** and the bottom of **Δ** were equipped with sagging spurs. This era of an unpleasant hand followed in sequence, morphing from sloping to upright.

Publishing Industry of the Ancient World

Today, most people would not imagine the ancient world's having a large publishing industry, yet this was the case. The ancient writings of famous authors were great pieces of literature that were highly sought after from the moment they were penned, much as today. Thus, there was a need for the scriptorium[16] to fill orders for both pagan and civil literature and the Bible books. There was a need for hundreds of copies, and as Christianity displaced paganism, the demand would grow exponentially.

The **Autograph** ("self-written") was the text written by a New Testament author or the author and scribe as the author dictated to him. If the scribe was taking down dictation (Rom. 16:22; 1 Pet. 5:12), he might have

---

[16] A scriptorium was a room for storing, copying, illustrating, or reading manuscripts.

27

done so in shorthand.[17] Whether by shorthand or longhand, we can assume that both the scribe and the author would check the scribe's work. The author would have authority over all corrections since the Holy Spirit did not inspire the scribe. The finished product would be the autograph if the inspired author wrote everything down as the Spirit moved him. This text is also often referred to as the **Original**. Hence, the terms *autograph* and *original* are often used interchangeably. Sometimes textual scholars prefer to distinguish, using "original" as a general reference to the text that is correctly attributed to a biblical author. This designation does not focus on the process of how a book or letter was written.

The *original* can also be referred to as the first **Authorized Text** (**Archetypal Manuscript**), i.e., the text first used to make other copies. We should also point out that some textual scholars debate whether the original or autograph of any given book was actually the first text used to make copies. And they prefer to call the latter the **Initial Text** instead, not requiring that it actually be the autograph. Conservative scholars would maintain that they are the same. Neither term should be confused with what is known as an ordinary **exemplar**, which is any authorized text of the book from which other copies were made. The original text necessarily was the first exemplar used to make copies, but additional copies of high quality were used as exemplars. We will frequently use exemplar to refer to any document that serves as a standard that a scribe employed as his text for making another copy. Usually, a scribe would have a main or primary exemplar from which he makes most of his copies and one or more secondary exemplars to compare what he found in his primary exemplar.

---

[17] "The usual procedure for a dictated epistle was for the amanuensis (secretary) to take down the speaker's words (often in shorthand) and then produce a transcript, which the author could then review, edit, and sign in his own handwriting. Two New Testament epistles provide the name of the amanuensis: Tertius for (Romans 16:22) and Silvanus (another name for Silas) for 1 Peter 5:12." Philip Comfort, *Encountering the Manuscripts: An Introduction to New Testament Paleography & Textual Criticism* (Nashville, TN: Broadman & Holman, 2005), 06.

Andrews qualifies what Comfort had to say about shorthand. There is the **slight possibility** of Tertius or other Bible author's scribes taking it down in shorthand and after that making out a full draft, which would have been reviewed by both Paul and Tertius. This is only the case if it is comparable to what a modern-day court reporter does. In some sense, they are taking down whoever is speaking down in shorthand. Imagine a courtroom where you have a witness talking fast, the prosecution interrupts, the defense jumps in with his rebuttal and the judge snaps his ruling, and the witness resumes his or her account of things. All of that is taken down explicitly word for word in shorthand, and if ever turned into longhand, it would be exactly what was said, down to the uh and um common in speech. So, if the shorthand of the day had that kind of capability; then, it is conceivable. We must remember these are the Bible author's dictated words to the scribe based on their inspiration, not the word choice or writing style of the scribe.

THE EARLY CHRISTIAN COPYISTS OF THE NEW TESTAMENT

Scribes sometimes substituted text from other exemplars for what they have in their main exemplars.

We have mentioned the **Scriptorium**, a room where multiple scribes or even one scribe worked to produce the manuscript(s). A lector would read aloud from the exemplar, and the scribe(s) would write down his words. The **Corrector** was the one who checked the manuscripts for needed corrections. Corrections could be by three primary persons: **(1)** the copyist himself, **(2)** the official corrector of the scriptorium, or **(3)** a person who had purchased the copy. While those correctors were contemporaneous with the original scribe(s), others could have corrected the text centuries later. When textual scholars speak of the **Hand**, this primarily refers to a person who is making the copy, distinguishing his level of training. Paleographers have set out four basic levels of handwriting. First, there was the *common hand* of a person who was untrained in making copies. Second, there was the *documentary hand* of an individual who was trained in preparing documents. The third level was the *reformed documentary* hand of a copyist who was experienced in preparing documents and copying literature. The fourth was the *professional hand*, the scribe experienced in producing literature.[18]

We must keep in mind that we are dealing with an oral society. Therefore, the apostles, who had spent three and a half years with Jesus, first published the Good News orally. The teachers within the newly founded Christian congregations would repeat this information until it was memorized. After that, those who had heard this gospel would, in turn, share it with others (Acts 2:42, Gal 6:6). In time, they were moved by the Holy Spirit to see the need for a written record, so Matthew, Mark, Luke, and John would pen the Gospels, and other types of New Testament books would be written by Paul, James, Peter, and Jude. From the first four verses of Luke, we can see that Theophilus[19] was being given a written record of what he had already been taught orally. In verse 4, Luke says to Theophilus, "[My purpose is] that you may know the exact truth about the things you have been taught."

---

[18] Philip Comfort, *Encountering the Manuscripts: An Introduction to New Testament Paleography & Textual Criticism* (Nashville, TN: Broadman & Holman, 2005), 17-20.

[19] Theophilus means "friend of God," was the person to whom the books of Luke and Acts were written (Lu 1:3; Ac 1:1). Theophilus was called "most excellent," which may suggest some position of high rank. On the other hand, it simply may be Luke offering an expression of respect. Theophilus had initially been orally taught about Jesus Christ and his ministry. Thereafter, it seems that the book of Acts, also by Luke, confirms that he did become a Christian. The Gospel of Luke was partially written to offer Theophilus assurances of the certainty of what he had already learned by word of mouth.

When the Son of God on Golgotha, outside of Jerusalem on Friday, Nisan 14 33 C.E. about 3:00 p.m., gave his life, Matthew, Mark, Luke, and John did not write their Gospels immediately. Matthew first wrote his Gospel in Hebrew some 12-17 years after Jesus' ascension, 45-50 C.E. Shortly after that, he translated it into Greek. Luke followed with his Gospel about 56–58 C.E. Then, Mark and his Gospel were written about 60–65 C.E. Finally, John's Gospel was written some 65 years after Jesus death in about 98 C.E. One thing few biblical scholars in the seminaries address today is how these apostles Matthew, John, and the disciples Mark and Luke were able to record the life, ministry, and death of Jesus Christ with such unerring accuracy.

The appearance of the written record did not mean the end of the oral publication. Both the oral and the written records would be used together. Many did not read the written documents themselves, as they could hear them read in the congregational meetings by the lector. This would apply to those who could read because they may not have been able to afford to have copies made for themselves. Paul and his letters came to be used in the same way as he traveled extensively but was just one man and could only be in one place at a time. It was not long before he took advantage that he could be in one place and dispatch letters to other locations through his traveling companions. These traveling companions would not only deliver the letters but also know the issues well enough to address questions that might be asked by the congregation leaders to which they had been dispatched.

In summary, the first century saw the life and ministry of Jesus Christ, the Son of God, and his death, resurrection, and ascension. After that, his disciples spread this gospel orally for at least 12-17 years before Matthew penned his gospel. The written record was used in conjunction with the oral message.

In the first-century C.E., the Bible books were being copied individually. In the late first century or the beginning of the second century, they began being copied in groups. At first, it was the four gospels and then the book of Acts with the four gospels and shortly after that a collection of the Apostle Paul's writings. Each of the individual books of the New Testament was penned, edited, and published between 45 and 98 C.E. A group of the apostle Paul's letters and the gospels were copied and published between 90 to 125 C.E. The entire 27 books of the New Testament were not published as a whole until about 290 to 340 C.E.

Thus, we have the 27 books of the New Testament that were penned individually in the second half of the first century. Each of these would have been copied and recopied throughout the first century. The copies of these

THE EARLY CHRISTIAN COPYISTS OF THE NEW TESTAMENT

copies would, of course, be made as well. Some of the earliest manuscripts that we now have indicate that a professional scribe copied them. Many of the other papyri provide evidence that a semi-professional hand-copied them, while most of these early papyri give proof of being made by a copyist who was literate and experienced at making documents. Therefore, either literate or semi-professional copyists produced most of our early papyri, with some being made by professionals.

Sadly, we do not have the autographs. Even if we did, we would have no way to authenticate them. We do, however, have copies of New Testament manuscripts that go back to the second and third centuries C.E. Over the centuries, this copying of copies continued. The authors were inspired so that the originals were error-free. However, this is not the case with those who made copies; they were not under the Holy Spirit's influence while making their copies. Therefore, these copies must have contained unintentional mistakes, as well as intentional changes, differing from the originals and each other. However, this is not as problematic or alarming as it may first sound. By far, most of the copyist errors are trivial, such as differences in spelling, word order, and such.

It is true that other copyist errors, a tiny portion, are noteworthy (significant), arising from the copyist's desire to correct something in the text that he perceived as erroneous or problematic. In an even smaller number of cases, the scribe made changes to strengthen orthodox doctrine. However, these changes have little to no effect on doctrines because other passages addressing the same beliefs provide the means to analyze and correct the copyist's "corrections." Moreover, they are easily analyzed and corrected so that we know what the original contained. Furthermore, we have enough textual evidence to know what words were in the original.

In the language of textual criticism, changes to the original text introduced by copyists are called "variant readings." A variant reading is a different reading in the extant [existing] manuscripts for any given portion of the text. The process of textual criticism is examining variant readings in various ancient manuscripts to reconstruct the original wording of a written text. These variants in our copies of the New Testament manuscripts are primarily the reason for the rise of the science of textual criticism in the 16th century. After that, we have had hundreds of scholars working extremely hard over the following five centuries to restore the New Testament text to its original state. Keep in mind that textual criticism is not just performed on the Old and New Testament texts, but in all other ancient literature as well: Plato (428/427–348/347 B.C.E.), Herodotus (c. 484–c. 425 B.C.E.), Homer (Ninth or Eighth Century B.C.E.), Livy (64or 59 B.C.E.–17 C.E.), Cicero

(106–43 B.C.E.), and Virgil (70–19 B.C.E.). However, as the Bible is the greatest work of all time, directly influencing countless Christians' lives (billions), it is the most crucial field.

Here, we should also expound more on the "criticism" portion of the term textual criticism. It may be helpful if, for a moment, we address biblical criticism in general, which is divided into two branches: lower criticism and higher criticism. Lower criticism, also known as textual criticism, is an investigation of manuscripts by those who are known as textual scholars, seeking to establish the original reading, which is available in the thousands of extant copies. Higher criticism, also known as literary criticism, investigates the restored text to identify any sources that may lie behind it. Therefore, we can say the following:

LOWER CRITICISM (i.e., textual criticism) has been the bedrock of scholarship over the last 500 years. It has given us a master text, i.e., a critical text, reflecting the original published Greek New Testament. It had contributed to the furtherance of Bible scholarship, removing interpolations, correcting scribal errors, and giving us a restored text, allowing us to produce better translations of the New Testament. However, of late, the dissecting higher criticism mindset of the 19th and 20th centuries has seeped into the field of New Testament Textual Studies.

HIGHER CRITICISM (i.e., literary criticism, biblical criticism) has taught that much of the Bible was composed of legend and myth. It claims that Moses did not write the first five books of the Bible, 8th century B.C.E. Isaiah did not write Isaiah, there were three authors of Isaiah, 6th century B.C.E. Daniel did not write Daniel, it was penned in the 2nd century BCE. Higher critics have taught that Jesus did not say all that the Gospels have him saying in his Sermon on the Mount and that Jesus did not condemn the Pharisees in Matthew 23, as this was Matthew because he hated the Jews. These are just the highlights, for there are thousands of tweaks that have undermined the word of God as being inspired and fully inerrant. Higher critics have dissected the Word of God until it has become the word of man and a very jumbled word at that. Higher criticism is still taught in almost all the seminaries. It is common to hear so-called Evangelical Bible scholars vehemently deny that large sections of the Bible are fully inerrant, authentic, accurate, and trustworthy. Biblical higher criticism is speculative and tentative in the extreme.

Constantine Von Tischendorf was a world-leading textual scholar and a renowned Bible scholar. Tischendorf was educated in Greek at the University of Leipzig. During his university studies, he was troubled by higher criticism of the Bible, as taught by famous German theologians, who sought to prove that the Greek New Testament was not authentic. He rejected higher criticism, which led to his noteworthy success in defending the authenticity of the Bible text. NT Textual scholar Harold Greenlee writes, "This 'higher criticism' has often been applied to the Bible in a destructive way, and it has come to be looked down on by many evangelical Christians."[20] The sad situation is that modern-day textual scholarship as a whole is unwittingly or knowingly moving the goalposts for some unknown reason. It is now the earliest knowable text in textual criticism, the sociohistorical approach to New Testament Textual Studies, and the newest trend to redate our earliest NT papyri to later dates.[21]

The New Testament in the Original Greek is a Greek-language version of the New Testament published in 1881. It is also known as the **Westcott and Hort** text, after its editors Brooke Foss Westcott (1825–1901) and Fenton John Anthony Hort (1828–1892). (Textual scholars use the abbreviation "**WH**") It is a critical text (Master Greek text of the NT seeking to ascertain the original wording of the original documents), compiled from some of the oldest New Testament fragments and texts discovered at the time. The two editors worked together for 28 years.

The Nestle Greek New Testament (first published in 1898) is a critical edition of the New Testament in its original Koine Greek, now in its 28th edition, forming the basis of most modern Bible translations and biblical criticism. It is now known as the Nestle-Aland edition after its most influential editors, Eberhard Nestle and Kurt Aland. Textual scholars use the abbreviation "**NA**." The NA is now in its 28th edition (2012), which is abbreviated NA[28]. Throughout the 130 years since 1881, there have been hundreds of manuscript discoveries, especially the early papyri that date within decades of the originals. One might expect significant changes been the WH text of 1881 and the 2012 NA[28] text. However, The NA[28] is 99.5% the same as the 1881 WH Greek New Testament.

In contrast, **higher criticism** (i.e., literary criticism) has attempted to provide rational explanations for the composition of Bible books, ignoring the supernatural element and often eliminating the traditional authorship of the books. Late dating of the copy of Bible books is widespread, and the

---

[20] Greenlee, J. Harold. *The Text of the New Testament: From Manuscript to Modern Edition* (p. 2). Baker Publishing Group.

[21] For defense against this redating, see THE P52 PROJECT: Is P52 Really the Earliest Greek New Testament Manuscript? Christian Publishing House (May 26, 2020) ISBN-13: 978-1949586107

historicity of biblical accounts is called into question. It would not be an overstatement to say that the effect has often challenged and undermined the Christian's confidence in the New Testament. Fortunately, some conservative scholars[22] have rightly criticized higher critics for their illogical or unreasonable approaches in dissecting God's Word.

Importance of Textual Criticism

Christian Bible students need to be familiar with Old and New Testament textual criticism as essential foundational studies. Why? If we fail to establish what was originally authored with reasonable certainty, how can we translate or even interpret what we think is the actual Word of God? We are fortunate that there are far more existing New Testament manuscripts today than any other book from ancient history. Some ancient Greek and Latin classics are based on one existing manuscript, while with others, there are just a handful and a few exceptions that have a few hundred available. However, over 5,898[23] Greek New Testament manuscripts have been cataloged for the New Testament,[24] 10,000 Latin manuscripts, and an additional 9,300 other manuscripts in such languages as Syriac, Slavic, Gothic, and Ethiopic Coptic, and Armenian. This gives New Testament textual scholars vastly more to work within establishing the original words of the text.

---

[22] Such Bible scholars as the late R. A. Torrey, Robert L. Thomas, Norman L. Geisler, Gleason L. Archer Jr., and current scholars such as F. David Farnell, as well as many others have fought for decades to educate readers about the dangers of higher criticism.

[23] While at present here in 2020, there are 5,898 manuscripts. There are **140 listed Papyrus** manuscripts, 323 Majuscule manuscripts, 2,951 Minuscule manuscripts, and 2,484 Lectionary manuscripts, bringing the total cataloged manuscripts to 5,898 manuscripts. However, you cannot simply total the number of cataloged manuscripts because, for example, $P^{11/14}$ are the same manuscript but with different catalog numbers. The same is true of $P^{33/5}$, $P^{4/64/67}$, $P^{49/65}$ and $P^{77/103}$. Now this alone would bring our 140 listed papyrus manuscripts down to 134. Then, we turn to one example from our majuscule manuscripts where clear 0110, 0124, 0178, 0179, 0180, 0190, 0191, 0193, 0194, and 0202 are said to be part of 070. A minuscule manuscript was listed with five separate catalog numbers for 2306, which then have the letters a through e. Thus, we have the following GA numbers: 2306 for 2306a, and 2831-2834 for 2306b-2306e.' – (Hixon 2019, 53-4) The problem is much worse when we consider that there are 323 Majuscule manuscripts and then far worse still with a listed 2,951 Minuscule and 2,484 Lectionaries. Nevertheless, those who estimate a total of 5,700 (Jacob W. Peterson, Myths and Mistakes, p. 63) 5,500 manuscripts (Dr. Ed Gravely / ehrmanproject.com/), 5,800 manuscripts (Porter 2013, 23), it is still a truckload of evidence far and above the dismal number of ancient secular author books.

[24] As of January 2016

THE EARLY CHRISTIAN COPYISTS OF THE NEW TESTAMENT

The other difference between the New Testament manuscripts and those of the classics is that the existing copies of the New Testament date much closer to the originals. Some of the manuscripts are dated to about a thousand years after the author had penned the book in the Greek classics. Some of the Latin classics are dated from three to seven hundred years after the author wrote the book. When we look at the Greek copies of the New Testament books, some portions are within decades of the original author's book. One hundred and thirty-nine Greek NT papyri and five majuscules[25] date from 110 C.E. to 390 C.E.

Distribution of Greek New Testament Manuscripts

- The **Papyrus** is a copy of a portion of the New Testament made on papyrus. At present, we have 147 cataloged New Testament papyri, many dating between 110-350 C.E., but some as late as the 6th century C.E.

- The **Majuscule** or **Uncial** is a script of large letters commonly used in Greek and Latin manuscripts written between the 3rd and 9th centuries C.E. that resembles a modern capital letter but is more rounded. At present, we have 323 cataloged New Testament Majuscule manuscripts.

- The **Minuscule** is a small cursive style of writing used in manuscripts from the 9th to the 16th centuries, now having 2,951 Minuscule manuscripts cataloged.

- The **Lectionary** is a schedule of readings from the Bible for Christian church services during the year, in both majuscules and minuscules, dating from the 4th to the 16th centuries C.E., now having 2,484 Lectionary manuscripts cataloged.

We should clarify that of the approximate 24,000 total manuscripts of the New Testament, not all are complete books. There are fragmented manuscripts with just a few verses, but manuscripts contain an entire book, others that include numerous books, and some that have the whole New Testament, or nearly so. This is expected since the oldest manuscripts we have were copied in an era when reproducing the entire New Testament was

---

[25] Large lettering, often called "capital" or uncial, in which all the letters are usually the same height.

not the norm. Instead, it was far more common to copy a single book or a group of books (i.e., the Gospels or Paul's letters). This still does not negate the vast riches of manuscripts that we possess.

What can we conclude from this short introduction to textual criticism? There is some irony here: secular scholars have no problem accepting classic authors' wording with their minuscule amount of evidence. However, they discount the treasure trove of evidence that is available to the New Testament textual scholar. Still, this should not surprise us as the New Testament has always been under-appreciated and attacked somehow, shape, or form over the past 2,000 years.

On the contrary, in comparison to classical works, we are overwhelmed by the quantity and quality of existing New Testament manuscripts. We should also keep in mind that about seventy-five percent[26] of the New Testament does not even require the help of textual criticism because that much of the text is unanimous, and thus, we know what it says. Of the other twenty-five percent, about twenty percent make up trivial scribal mistakes that are easily corrected. Therefore, textual criticism focuses mainly on a small portion of the New Testament text. The facts are clear: the Christian, who reads the New Testament, is fortunate to have so many manuscripts, with so many dating so close to the originals, with 500 hundred years of hundreds of textual scholars who have established the text with a level of certainty unimaginable for ancient secular works.

After discussing the amount of New Testament manuscripts available, Atheist commentator Bob Seidensticker writes, "The first problem is that more manuscripts at best increase our confidence that we have the original version. That does not mean the original copy was history ...."[27] That is, Seidensticker is forced to acknowledge the reliability of the New Testament text as we have it today and can only try to deny what it says. He also tells us of the New Testament, "Compare that with 2000 copies of the Iliad, the second-best represented manuscript."[28] Of those 1,757 copies of the Iliad, how far removed are they from the alleged originals? The Iliad is dated to about 800 B.C.E. There are several fragments of the Iliad that date to the second century B.C.E. and one to the third century B.C.E., with the rest dating to the ninth century C.E. or later. That would make this handful of

---

[26] The numbers in this paragraph are rounded for simplicity purposes.

[27] 25,000 New Testament Manuscripts? Big Deal. - Patheos,

http://www.patheos.com/blogs/crossexamined/2013/11/25000-new-testament-manuscrip (accessed November 28, 2015).

[28] Ibid

fragmented manuscripts 500 years removed and the rest about 1,700 years removed from their original.

The Range of Textual Criticism

The Importance and scope of New Testament textual studies can be summed up in the few words used by J. Harold Greenlee; it is "the basic biblical study, a prerequisite to all other biblical and theological work. Interpretation, systematization, and application of the teachings of the NT cannot be accomplished until textual criticism has done at least some of its work. It is, therefore, deserving of the acquaintance and attention of every serious student of the Bible."[29]

It is only reasonable to assume that the original 27 books written firsthand by the New Testament authors have not survived. Instead, we only have what we must consider being imperfect copies. **Why the Holy Spirit would miraculously inspire 27 fully inerrant texts and then allow human imperfection into the documents** is not explained for us in Scripture. (More on this later) Why didn't God inspire the copyists? We do know that imperfect humans have tended to worship relics that traditions hold to have been touched by the miraculous powers of God or to have been in direct contact with one of his special servants of old. Ultimately, though, all we know is that God had his reasons for allowing the New Testament autographs to be worn out by repeated use. From time to time, we hear of the discovery of a fragment possibly dated to the first century, but even if such a fragment is eventually verified, the dating alone can never serve as proof of an autograph; it will still be a copy in all likelihood.

If we ask why didn't God inspire copyists, then it will have to follow, why didn't God inspire translators, why didn't God inspire Bible scholars that author commentaries on the Bible, and so on? Suppose God's initial purpose was to give us a fully inerrant, authoritative, authentic, and accurate Word. Why not adequately protect the Scriptures in all facets of transmission from error: copy, translate, and interpret? If God did this, and people were moved along by the Holy Spirit, it would soon become noticeable that when people copy the texts, they would be unable to make an error or mistake or even willfully change something.

Where would it stop? Would this being moved along by the Holy Spirit apply to anyone who decided to make themselves a copy, testing to see if

---

[29] J. Harold Greenlee, *Introduction to New Testament Textual Criticism* (Grand Rapids, MI: Baker Academic, 1995), 8-9.

they too would be inspired? In time, this would prove to be actual evidence for God. This would negate the reasons why God has allowed sin, human imperfection to enter humanity in the first place, to teach them an **object lesson**, man cannot walk on his own without his Creator. God created perfect humans, giving them a perfect start, and through the abuse of free will, they rejected his sovereignty. He did not just keep creating perfect humans again and again, as though he got something wrong. God gave us his perfect Word and has again chosen to allow us to continue in our human imperfection, learning our **object lesson**. God has stepped into humanity many hundreds of times in the Bible record, maybe tens of thousands of times unbeknownst to us over the past 6,000+ years, to tweak things to get the desired outcome of his will and purposes. However, there is no aspect of life where his stepping in on any particular point was to be continuous until the return of the Son. Maybe God gave us a perfect copy of sixty-six books. Then like everything else, he placed the responsibility of copying, translating, and interpreting on us, just as he gave us the Great Commission of proclaiming that Word, explaining that Word, to make disciples. – Matthew 24:14;28-19-20; Acts 1:8.

As for errors in all the copies we have, we can say that the vast majority of the Greek text is not affected by errors. The errors occur in variant readings, i.e., portions of the text where different manuscripts disagree. Of the **small amount** of the text affected by variant readings, the vast majority of these are minor slips of the pen, misspelled words, etc., or intentional but quickly analyzed changes. We are certain what the original reading is in these places. A **far smaller number** of changes present challenges to establishing the original reading. It has always been said and remains true that no central doctrine is affected by a textual problem. Only rarely does a textual issue change the meaning of a verse.[30] Still, establishing the original text wherever there are variant readings is vitally important. Every word matters!

It is true that the Jewish copyists and the later Christian copyists were not led along by the Holy Spirit, and, therefore, their manuscripts were not inerrant, infallible. Errors (textual variants) crept into the documents unintentionally and intentionally. However, the vast majority of the Hebrew Old Testament and Greek New Testament has not been infected with textual errors. For the portions impacted with textual mistakes, we can be grateful for the tens of thousands of copies that we have to help us weed out the errors. How? Well, not every copyist made the same textual errors. Hence,

---

[30] Leading textual scholar Daniel Wallace tells us, after looking at all of the evidence, that the percentage of instances where the reading is uncertain and a well-attested alternative reading could change the meaning of the verse is a quarter of one percent, i.e., 0.0025%

by comparing the work of different copyists and manuscripts, textual scholars can identify the textual variants (errors) and remove those, leaving us with the original content.

Yes, it would be **the most significant discovery** of all time if we found the original five books penned by Moses himself, Genesis through Deuteronomy, or the original Gospels of Matthew, Mark, Luke, and John. However, first, there would be no way of establishing that they were the originals. Second, truth be told, we do not need the originals. **Yes, you heard me**. We do not need those original documents. What is so important about the documents? Nothing, it is the content on the original documents that we are after. And truly, miraculously, we have more copies than needed to do just that. **We do not need miraculous preservation** because we have miraculous restoration. We now know beyond a reasonable doubt that the Hebrew Old Testament and the Greek New Testament critical texts are about a 99.99% reflection of the content that was in those ancient original manuscripts.

CHAPTER 2 The New Testament Copyists and Their Materials

One of the greatest tragedies in the modern-day history of Christianity [1880 - present] is that churchgoers have not been educated about the history of the New Testament text. They are so misinformed that many do not even realize that the Hebrew text lies behind our English Old Testament, and the Greek text lies behind our English New Testament. Sadly, many seminaries that train the pastors of today's churches have also required little or no studies in the history of the Old or New Testament texts.

Textual Criticism Defined

Again, New Testament textual criticism is the study of families of manuscripts, especially the Greek New Testament, as well as versions,[31]

---

[31] A version is a translation of the New Testament into another language, such as Latin, Syriac, Coptic, Armenian, Georgian, and so on.

THE EARLY CHRISTIAN COPYISTS OF THE NEW TESTAMENT

lectionaries,[32] and patristic quotations,[33] along with internal evidence, in order to determine which reading is the original. Comparing any two copies of a document even a few pages long will reveal variant readings. "A textual variant is simply any difference from a standard text (e.g., a printed text, a particular manuscript, etc.) that involves spelling, word order, omission, addition, substitution, or a total rewrite of the text."

Again, it needs to be repeated; when we use the term "textual *criticism*," we are not referring to something negative. In this instance, "criticism" refers to a careful, measured, or painstaking study and analysis of the internal and external evidence for producing our New Testament Greek text generally called a "critical text." Today, the goal of many New Testament textual scholars is to recover the earliest text *possible*, while the objective of the remaining few, such as the author of this book, is to get back to the *ipsissima verba* ("the very words") of the original author.[34]

> Variant readings occur only in about 5 percent of the Greek NT text, and so all the manuscripts agree about 95 percent of the time. Only about 2,100 variant readings may be considered "significant" and in no instance is any point of Christian doctrine challenged or questioned by a variant reading. Only about 1.67 percent of the entire Greek NT text still is questioned at all. We may be confident that our current eclectic, or critical, Greek NT text (an eclectic, or critical text is one based on the study of as many manuscripts as possible), is far beyond 99 percent established. In fact, there is more variation among some English translations of the Bible than there is among the manuscripts of the Greek NT. God's Word is infallible and inerrant in its original copies (autographs), all of which have perished. Textual critics of the

---

[32] A Lectionary is a book containing readings from the Bible for Christian church services during the course of the year.

[33] Patristic quotations are New Testament quotations from early Christian writers, such as the Apostolic Fathers, including Clement of Rome, Ignatius of Antioch, Polycarp of Smyrna, Hermas, and Papias. There were also the Apologists: Justin Martyr, Theophilus of Antioch, Clement of Alexandria, and Tertullian, to name a few. After them came the Church Fathers, e.g. St. Augustine or St. Ambrose whose works have helped to shape the Christian Church.

[34] Dr. Don Wilkins writes. "This goal, which will be mentioned in passing throughout the book, is a philosophical difference with some implications for TC practice. Both groups of critics will arrive at what they consider the earliest form of the text, but the authors take this to be the autograph as a matter of faith. One of the implications for practice is that conjectures are not considered viable options for variant readings. Another is that every word of the autograph can be found in some extant Greek NT manuscript."

Greek NT will continue their work until, if possible, the original of every questioned reading is firmly established.[35]

An investigation of the enormous supply of Greek manuscripts and the ancient versions in other languages shows that they have preserved for us the very Word of God.

Throughout the first five books of the Bible being penned by Moses (beginning in the late sixteenth century B.C.E.), and down to the time of the printing press (1455 C.E.)–almost 3,000 years–many forms of material have been used to receive writing. Material such as bricks, papyrus sheets, animal skin, broken pottery, metal, wooden tablets with or without wax, and much more have been used to pen or copy God's Word. The following are some of the tools and materials.

Stylus: The stylus was a writing instrument used to inscribe text onto surfaces. It was typically made of metal, bone, or ivory, and was used to write on papyrus, parchment, or wax tablets. The stylus was used to make marks by either scratching or pressing into the writing surface.

In the context of early Christian copyists, the stylus was used to carefully transcribe the New Testament texts. This was a meticulous process that required a high degree of precision and accuracy. The scribes would copy the texts letter by letter, line by line, ensuring that the copied text was as close to the original as possible.

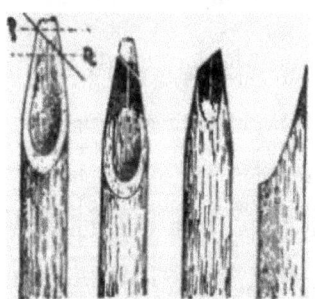

Reed Pen: The reed pen was used with ink to write on papyrus or parchment manuscripts. Καλαμος (kalamos) is the Greek word for "pen." (2 John 12; 3 John 13) The reed pen holds significant importance in the context of New Testament textual criticism, primarily due to its role in the transcription of early Christian manuscripts. This simple yet effective writing tool was crafted from a single stalk of reed,

---

[35] Charles W. Draper, "Textual Criticism, New Testament," ed. Chad Brand et al., *Holman Illustrated Bible Dictionary* (Nashville, TN: Holman Bible Publishers, 2003), 1574.

specifically from the bamboo-like plants that grow abundantly in regions like the Near East and the Mediterranean. The reed was cut and fashioned into a pen with a split tip, which allowed it to hold ink. This design facilitated a fluid, yet controlled flow of ink onto papyrus or parchment, the primary materials for writing in the ancient world.

Reed pens were widely used by scribes in the Greco-Roman world from as early as the 4th century B.C.E., continuing through the period during which the New Testament texts were first composed and copied. The durability and ease of use of the reed pen made it an indispensable tool for scribes, who were tasked with the painstaking work of copying texts accurately. The quality of the writing produced with a reed pen depended on the skill of the scribe and the condition of the pen itself, which needed to be regularly trimmed to prevent the tip from becoming too blunt or split.

The significance of the reed pen in New Testament textual criticism lies in its influence on the transmission of the text. The characteristics of the script, such as the style and size of the letters, can offer insights into the dating and geographical origin of manuscripts. Furthermore, understanding the tools and materials used by ancient scribes helps scholars in their efforts to reconstruct the original texts of the New Testament and assess the nature of textual variations.

Quill Pen: The quill[36] pen came into use long after the reed pen. The quill pen, crafted from the flight feather of a large bird, such as a goose or swan, emerged as the dominant writing instrument in the Western world from the 6th century C.E. Its prominence persisted until the 19th century C.E., when it was gradually supplanted by steel nib pens and other modern writing implements. The transition from the reed pen to the quill pen marked a significant advancement in the technology of writing, influencing the production of manuscripts, including those of the New Testament, during the latter part of this period.

---

[36] The quill pen was the principal writing instrument in the Western world from the 6th to the 19th centuries C.E.

The process of making a quill pen involved several steps. The feather had to be hardened, a process often achieved by heating the quill. Then, the end of the quill was cut into a pointed tip with a slit that facilitated the capillary action of drawing ink into the pen. This design allowed for finer control over the flow of ink and the creation of varying stroke widths, which contributed to the development of distinctive handwriting styles and calligraphic traditions in medieval and Renaissance Europe.

Quill pens offered several advantages over their predecessors. They were capable of producing finer lines and more nuanced script, which was particularly beneficial for the detailed work of copying manuscripts. The flexibility of the quill allowed scribes to create a range of stroke widths, from very fine to quite broad, by adjusting the pressure applied during writing. This capability was essential for the ornate scripts found in many illuminated manuscripts and legal documents of the period.

In the context of New Testament textual criticism, the quill pen's influence is observed in the evolution of script styles and the precision of textual transmission. The advent of the quill pen coincided with the shift from the uncial script, characterized by its rounded, capital letters, to the minuscule script, which featured smaller, more compressed letters that could be written more quickly and efficiently. This transition facilitated the copying of texts and contributed to the proliferation of Christian manuscripts during the Middle Ages.

The durability and quality of manuscripts produced with quill pens are of particular interest to textual critics. The ability to produce finer script and the enhanced control over ink application allowed for greater accuracy and detail in manuscript production. However, the quill pen also required regular maintenance; the tip needed frequent trimming, and the quality of the ink and parchment played a significant role in the longevity and legibility of texts.

Overall, the quill pen's role in the history of manuscript production, including those of the New Testament, is a testament to its significance in the development of Western literary and scholarly traditions. Its contribution to the art of writing and the preservation of texts is an essential area of study in New Testament textual criticism, providing insights into the historical context and transmission of the biblical text.

Papyrus: Papyrus was the writing material used by the ancient Egyptians, Greeks, and Romans made from the pith of the stem of a water plant. It was cut into strips, with one layer laid out horizontally and the other vertically. Sometimes it was covered with a cloth and then beaten with a mallet. Scholarship has also suggested that paste may have been used between layers, and then a large stone would be placed on top until the materials were dry. Typically, a sheet of papyrus would be between 6–9 inches in width and 12–15 inches long. These sheets were then glued end to end until scribes had enough length to copy the book they were working on. The writing was done only on the horizontal side, and it was rolled so that the writing would be on the inside. If one were to attempt to write across the vertical side, it would be difficult because of the direction of the papyrus fibers. The scribe or copyist would have used a reed pen to write on the papyrus sheets (cf. 3 John 13). Papyrus was the primary material used for writing until about 300 C.E. It was used with a *roll* or *scroll* (a document that is rolled up into itself), as well as the *codex* (book) form.

The first page of papyrus 66, showing John 1:1-13 and the opening words of v.14

Writing on the papyrus sheet, even the correct side, was no easy task by any means because the surface was rough and fibrous. "Defects sometimes occurred in the making through retention of moisture between the layers or through the use of spongy strips which could cause the ink to run; such flaws necessitated the remaking of the sheet."[37] The back pain from long periods of sitting cross-legged on the ground bent over a papyrus sheet on a board made writing letters unappealing. The dealing with running ink, the reed pen possibly snagging and tearing the papyrus sheet, having to erase illegible characters were all deterrents from personally writing a letter.

Early papyrus manuscripts, such as $P^{4/64/67}$ P^{32} P^{46} P^{52} P^{66} P^{75} $P^{77/103}$ P^{101} P^{87} P^{90} P^{98} P^{104} P^{109} P^{118} P^{137}, which date 100-150/175 C.E. Then we have P^{1} P^{5} P^{13} P^{20} P^{23} P^{27} P^{29} P^{30} P^{35} P^{38} P^{39} P^{40} P^{45} P^{47} P^{48} $P^{49/65}$ P^{69} P^{71} P^{72} P^{82} P^{85} P^{95} P^{100} P^{106} P^{107} P^{108} P^{111} P^{110} P^{113} P^{115} P^{121} P^{125} P^{126} P^{133} P^{136}, which

---

[37] Nabia Abbot, *STUDIES IN ANCIENT ORIENTAL CIVILIZATIONS* (Chicago, IL: The University of Chicago Press, 1938), 11.

date 175-250 C.E., to mention only a few. Then, the renowned Codex Vaticanus (300-325 C.E.) and Codex Sinaiticus (325-350 C.E.) were written on parchment: creamy or yellowish material made from dried and treated sheepskin, goatskin, or other animal hides.

Papyri copy - Greek Manuscript

One may wonder why more New Testament manuscripts have not survived. It must be remembered that the Christians suffered intense persecution during intervals in the first 300 years from Pentecost 33 C.E. With this persecution from the Roman Empire came many orders to destroy Christian texts. In addition, these texts were not stored in such a way as to secure their preservation. They were actively used by the Christians in the congregation and were subject to wear and tear. Furthermore, moisture is the enemy of papyrus, and it causes them to disintegrate over time. This is why, as we will discover, the papyrus manuscripts that have survived have come from the dry sands of Egypt. Moreover, it seems not to have entered the minds of the early Christians to preserve their documents because their solution to the loss of manuscripts was simply to make more copies. Fortunately, making copies transitioned to the more durable animal skins, which would last much longer. Those that have survived, especially from the fourth century C.E. and earlier, are the path to restoring the original Greek New Testament.[38]

Animal Skin: About the fourth century C.E., Bible manuscripts made of papyrus began to be superseded by the use of vellum, a high-quality parchment made from calfskin, kidskin, or lambskin. Manuscripts such as the famous Codex Sinaiticus (01) and Codex Vaticanus (03, also known as B) of the fourth century C.E. are parchment, vellum, codices. This use of parchment as the leading writing material continued for almost a thousand years until it was replaced by paper. The advantages of parchment over

---

[38] Cf. J. H. Greenlee, *Introduction to New Testament Textual Criticism* (Peabody: Hendrickson, 1995), 11.

papyrus were many, such as (1) it was much easier to write on smooth parchment, (2) one could write on both sides, (3) parchment lasted much longer, and (4) when desired, old writing could be scraped off and the parchment reused.

A 2,000-year-old Dead Sea Isaiah Scroll. It matches closely the Masoretic text and what is in the Bible today

Papyrus or Parchment?

The Hebrew Old Testament that would have been available to the early Christians was written on the processed hide of animals after the hair was removed, and the hide was smoothed out with a pumice stone.[39] Leather scrolls were sent to Alexandria, Egypt, in about 280 B.C.E., to make what we now know as the Greek Septuagint.[40] Most of the Dead Sea scrolls discovered between 1947 and 1956 are made of leather, and it is almost certain that the scroll of Isaiah that Jesus read from in the synagogue was as well. Luke 4:17 says, "And the scroll of the prophet Isaiah was given to him. He unrolled the scroll and found the place where it was written."

The Dead Sea Scroll of Isaiah (1QIsa) dates to the end of the second century B.C.E., written on 17 sheets of parchment, one of the seven Dead Sea Scrolls that were first recovered by Bedouin shepherds in 1947. The Nash Papyrus is a collection of four papyrus fragments acquired in Egypt in 1898 by W. L. Nash, dating to about 150 B.C.E. It contains parts of the Ten

---

[39] A very light porous rock formed from solidified lava, used in solid form as an abrasive and in powdered form as a polish.

[40] A Greek translation of the Hebrew Bible started in about 280 and completed about 150 B.C.E. to meet the needs of Greek-speaking Jews outside Palestine.

Commandments from Exodus chapter 20 and some verses from Deuteronomy chapters 5 and 6. It is by far one of the oldest Hebrew manuscript fragments.

Vellum is a high-quality parchment made from calfskin, kidskin, or lambskin. After the skin was removed, it would be soaked in limewater, after which the hair would be scraped off, the skin then being scraped and dried, and rubbed afterward with chalk and pumice stone, creating an exceptionally smooth writing material. Both leather and papyrus were used before the first-century Christians. During the first three hundred years of Christianity, the secular world viewed parchment as being inferior to papyrus. It was relegated to notebooks, rough drafts, and other non-literary purposes.

A couple of myths should be dispelled before continuing. It is often remarked that papyrus is not a durable material. Both papyrus and parchment are durable under normal circumstances. This is not negating the fact that parchment is more durable than papyrus. Another often-repeated thought is that papyrus was fragile and brittle, making it an unlikely candidate to be used for a codex, which would have to be folded in half. Another issue that should be sidelined is whether it was more expensive to produce papyrus or parchment. Presently there is no data to aid in that evaluation. We know that papyrus was used for all of the Christian codex manuscripts up to the fourth century, at which time we find the two great parchment codices, the Sinaiticus and Vaticanus manuscripts. Parchment of good quality has been called "the finest writing material ever devised by man." (Roberts and Skeat, The Birth of the Codex 1987, 8) Why then did parchment take so long to replace papyrus? This may be answered by R. Reed, in *Ancient Skins, Parchments, and Leathers:*

> It is perhaps the extraordinary high durability of the product, produced by so simple a method, which has prevented most people from suspecting that many subtle points are involved…. The essence of the parchment process, which subjects the system of pelt to the simultaneous action of stretching and drying, is to bring about peculiar changes quite different from those applying when making leather. These are (1) reorganization of the dermal fibre network by stretching, and (2) permanently setting this new and highly stretched form of fibre network by drying the pelt fluid to a hard, glue-like consistency. In other words, the pelt fibres are fixed in a stretched condition so that they cannot revert to their original relaxed state. (Reed 1973, 119-20)

THE EARLY CHRISTIAN COPYISTS OF THE NEW TESTAMENT

Where the medieval parchment makers were greatly superior to their modern counterparts was in the control and modification of the ground substance in the pelt, before the latter was stretched and dried .... The major point, however, which modern parchment manufacturers have not appreciated, is what might be termed the integral or collective nature of the parchment process. The bases of many different effects need to be provided for simultaneously, in one and the same operation. The properties required in the final parchment must be catered for at the wet pelt stage, for due to the peculiar nature of the parchment process, once the system has been dried, and after-treatments to modify the material produced are greatly restricted. (Reed 1973, 124)

This method, which follows those used in medieval times for making parchment of the highest quality, is preferable for it allows the grain surface of the drying pelt to be "slicked" and freed from residual fine hairs while stretching upon the frame. At the same time, any process for cleaning and smoothing the flesh side, or for controlling the thickness of the final parchment may be undertaken by working the flesh side with sharp knives which are semi-lunar in form.... To carry out such manual operations on wet stretched pelt demands great skill, speed of working, and concentrated physical effort. (Reed 1973, 138-9)

Enough has been said to suggest that behind the apparently simple instructions contained in the early medieval recipes there is a wealth of complex process detail which we are still far from understanding. Hence it remains true that parchment-making is perhaps more of an art than a science.[41]

Scroll or Roll: The scroll dominated until the beginning of the second century C.E., at which time the papyrus codex was replacing it. Papyrus enjoyed another two centuries of use until it was replaced with animal skin (vellum), which proved to be a far better writing material.

The writing on a scroll was done in 2- to 3-inch columns, which allowed the reader to have it opened, or unrolled, only partially. Although movies and television have portrayed the scroll as being opened while holding it vertically, this was not the case; scrolls were opened horizontally. It would be rolled to the left for the Greek or Latin reader as those languages were written

---

[41] R. Reed, *Ancient skins, parchments and leathers* (Studies in Archaeological Science) Cambridge, MA: Seminar Press, 1973, 172.

left to right. The Jewish reader would roll it to the right as Hebrew was written right to left.

The difficulty of using a scroll should be apparent. If one had a long book (such as Isaiah) and attempted to locate a particular passage, it would not be user-friendly. An ancient saying was, "A great book, a great evil." The account in the book of Luke tells us:

Luke 4:16–21 Updated American Standard Version (UASV)

16 And he [Jesus] came to Nazareth, where he had been brought up; and as was his custom, he went to the synagogue on the Sabbath day, and he stood up to read. 17 And the scroll[42] of the prophet Isaiah was given to him. And he unrolled the scroll[43] and found the place where it was written,

18 "The Spirit of the Lord is upon me,
   because he has anointed me
   to proclaim good news[44] to the poor.
He has sent me to proclaim release to the captives
   and recovering of sight to the blind,
   to set free those who are oppressed,
19 to proclaim the favorable year of the Lord."

20 And he rolled up the scroll[45] and gave it back to the attendant and sat down; and the eyes of all in the synagogue were fixed on him. 21 And he began to say to them, "Today this Scripture has been fulfilled in your hearing."

Codex: The trunk of a tree that bears leaves only at its apex was called a *caudex* in Latin. This name was modified to *codex* and applied to a wooden tablet with raised edges, with a coat of wax placed within those raised edges. The dried wax would then be used to receive writing with a stylus. We might compare it to the schoolchild's slate, such as seen in some Hollywood Western movies. Around the fifth century B.C.E., some of these were being used and attached by strings that were run through the edges. It is because these bound tablets resembled a tree trunk that they were to take on the name "codex."

---

[42] Or a *roll*
[43] Or *roll*
[44] Or *the gospel*
[45] Or *roll*

THE EARLY CHRISTIAN COPYISTS OF THE NEW TESTAMENT

Codex Vaticanus ("Book from the Vatican"), Facsimile, Fourth century. It is one of the earliest manuscripts of the Bible, which includes the Greek translation of the bulk of the Hebrew Scriptures as well as most of the Christian Greek Scriptures

As we can imagine, this bulky item also was not user-friendly! Sometime later, the Romans would develop a lighter, more flexible material, the parchment notebook, which would fill the need before the development of the later book-form codex. The Latin word *membranae* (skins) is the name given to such notebooks of parchment. In fact, at 2 Timothy 4:13, the apostle Paul requested of Timothy that he "bring the cloak that I left with Carpus at Troas, also the books [scrolls], and above all the parchments [*membranas*, Greek spelling]." One might ask why Paul used a Latin word (transliterated in Greek)? Undoubtedly, it was because there was no Greek word that would serve as an equivalent to what he was requesting. It was only later that the translated "codex" was brought into the Greek language to reference what we would know as a book.

The ink of ancient manuscripts was usually one of two kinds. There was ink made of a mixture of soot and gum. These were sold in the form of a bar. It was dissolved in water in an inkwell and produced a very black ink. There was also ink made out of nutgalls, which resulted in a rusty-brown color. Aside from these materials, the scribe would have had a knife to sharpen his reed pen, as well as a sponge to erase errors. With the semi-professional and professional scribe, each character was written with care. Thus, writing was a slow, tedious, and often difficult task.

'I, Tertius, Greet You in the Lord'

Tertius is among the many greetings that we find at the end of the letter of Paul to the Romans, wherein he writes, "I am greeting you, I, Tertius, the one having written this letter, in the Lord." (Rom. 16:22) Of Paul's fourteen letters, this is the only occurrence where we find a clear reference to one of his secretaries.

Little is known of Tertius, who must have been a faithful Christian, based on the greeting "in the Lord." He may have been a member of the Corinthian congregation who likely knew many Christians in Rome, which is suggested because his name is Latin for "third." Quartus for "fourth" is one of the other two who added their greetings: "Erastus the city treasurer greets you, and Quartus the brother, i.e., a member of the Corinthian congregation. (16:23b) Some scholars have suggested that Quartus could have been the younger brother of Tertius.[46] Others have suggested that Tertius was a slave or a freedman.[47] This is also suggested by his Latin name and that slaves were commonly involved in the scribal activity. From this, we could conjecture that Tertius likely had experience as a professional scribe, who became a fellow-worker with the apostle Paul, helping compile the longest of Paul's letters. It was common for Bible authors to use a scribe, as, for example, Jeremiah similarly used Baruch, just as Peter used Silvanus (Jer. 36:4; 1 Pet. 5:12). Of Paul's fourteen letters, six certainly involved the use of a secretary: Romans (16:22), 1 Corinthians (16:21), Galatians (6:11), Colossians (4:18), 2 Thessalonians (3:17), and Philemon (19).

Penning the Book of Romans

The letter of Paul to the Romans was written while he was on his third missionary journey as a guest of Gaius in Corinth, about 55-56 C.E. (Ac 20:1-3; Rom. 16:23). We know for a certainty that Paul used Tertius as his secretary to author the book of Romans. However, we cannot say with absolute certainty how he was used. Some have argued, "from evidence outside of the New Testament that it was common practice for authors to dictate their

---

[46] Chad Brand et al., eds., "Tertius," *Holman Illustrated Bible Dictionary* (Nashville, TN: Holman Bible Publishers, 2003), 1573.

[47] When the Roman Empire was in power, one who was released from slavery was called a "freedman" (Gr *apeleutheros*), while a "freeman" (Gr *eleutheros*) was free from birth, having full citizenship rights, as was the case with the apostle Paul – Ac 22:28 (Balz and Schneider 1978, Vol. 1, P 121).

letters to an amanuensis or secretary."[48] Did the secretary take that dictation down in shorthand[49] and then compose the letter, even contributing content, with the New Testament author giving the final approval? Alternatively, was the secretary used in a more limited fashion, such as editing spelling, grammar, and syntax? Otto Roller points out that for an author to dictate a letter to a scribe verbatim would require the author to speak very slowly, i.e., syllable by syllable.[50] There will be more on this later. For now, whatever method was used, the work of a secretary was no easy job. What we do know is that the sixty-six books of the Bible were "inspired by God," and "men spoke from God as they were carried along by the Holy Spirit." – 2 Timothy 3:16; 2 Peter 1:21.

---

[48] See Gordon J. Bahr, *"Paul and Letter Writing in the First Century,"* Catholic Biblical Quarterly 28 (1966): 465-77.

See also, John McRay, Paul: His Life and Teaching (Grand Rapids, MI: Baker Academics, 2003), 270.

[49] Again, there is the **slight possibility** of Tertius or other Bible author's scribes taking it down in shorthand and after that making out a full draft, which would have been reviewed by both Paul and Tertius. This is only the case if it is comparable to what a modern-day court reporter does. In some sense, they are taking down whoever is speaking down in shorthand. Imagine a courtroom where you have a witness talking fast, the prosecution interrupts, the defense jumps in with his rebuttal and the judge snaps his ruling, and the witness resumes his or her account of things. All of that is taken down explicitly word for word in shorthand, and if ever turned into longhand, it would be exactly what was said, down to the uh and um common in speech. So, if the shorthand of the day had that kind of capability; then, it is conceivable. We must remember these are the Bible author's dictated words to the scribe based on their inspiration, not the word choice or writing style of the scribe.

[50] Otto Roller, *Das Formular der Paulinischen Briefe: Ein Beitrag zur Lehre vom antiken Briefe* (Stuttgart: W. Kohlhammer, 1933), p. 333.

CHAPTER 3 The Book Writing Process of the New Testament: Authors and Early Christian Scribes

The Place of Writing

When we think of the apostle Paul penning his books that would make up most of the New Testament, some have had the anachronistic tendency to impose their modern way of thinking about him, such as presupposing where he would have written it. As I am writing this page, I am tucked away in my home office, seeking privacy from the hustle and bustle of our modern world. This was not the case in the ancient world, where Paul lived and traveled. People of that time favored a group setting, not isolation. The apostle Paul probably would have been of this mindset. Paul would not have necessarily sought a quiet place to author his letters, to escape the noise of those around him. As for myself, I struggle to get back on track if I am interrupted for more than a couple of minutes.

Most during Paul's day would have been surprised by this way of thinking, i.e., seeking quiet and solitude to focus all of one's energy on the task of writing. Those of Paul's day, including himself, would not have even noticed people talking around them, nor would they have been troubled by what we perceive as interruptions, such as others' discussions, which were neither relevant nor applicable to the subject of their letter writing.

The Scribe of the New Testament Writer

Philip W. Comfort informs us that an **amanuensis** is a "scribe or secretary. In ancient times a written document was first produced by an author who usually dictated the material to an amanuensis. The author would then read the text and make the final editorial adjustments before the document was sent or published. Paul used the writing services of Tertius to write the epistle to the Romans (Rom. 16:22), and Peter was assisted by Silvanus in writing his first Epistle (see 1 Pet. 5:12)."[51]

Dr. Don Wilkins, a Senior Translator for the NASB, also tells us that amanuensis is a "Latin term for a scribe or clerk (plural 'amanuenses'). When used in the context of textual criticism, it refers specifically to a person who served as a secretary to record first-hand the words of a New Testament book if the author chose to use a secretary rather than write down the words himself. Tertius (Rom. 16:22) is our example. The degree to which an amanuensis may have contributed to the content of any particular book of the Bible is a matter of speculation and controversy. At one end of the spectrum is the amanuensis, who merely took dictation (the position preferred here). At the other is the possibility that a New Testament author may have told his amanuensis what he wished to communicate in general terms, leaving it to the amanuensis to actually compose the book." This author would wholeheartedly disagree with the latter view, as the New Testament authors alone were inspired to give us the words of God, and the scribe was merely the vehicle for doing so.

The ancient Greco-Roman society employed secretaries or scribes for various reasons. Of course, the government employed some scribes working for chief administrators. Then, there were the scribes who were used in the private sector. These latter scribes (often slaves) usually were employed by the wealthy. However, even high-ranking slaves and freed slaves employed scribes. Many times, one would find scribes who would write letters for their

---

[51] Philip Comfort, *Encountering the Manuscripts: An Introduction to New Testament Paleography & Textual Criticism* (Nashville, TN: Broadman & Holman, 2005), 379.

friends. According to E. Randolph Richards, the skills of these unofficial secretaries "could range from a minimal competency with the language or the mechanics of writing to the highest proficiency at rapidly producing an accurate, proper, and charming letter."[52] Scribes carried out a wide range of administrative, secretarial, and literary tasks, including administrative bookkeeping (keeping records of a business or person), shorthand and taking dictation, letter-writing, and copying literary texts.

The most prominent ways that a scribe would have been used in the first century C.E. would have been as (1) a recorder, (2) an editor, and (3) a secretary for an author. At the very bottom of the writing tasks, he would be used to record information, i.e., as a record keeper. When they were needed or desired, the New Testament scribes were being used as secretaries, writing down letters by dictation. Tertius took down the book of Romans as Paul dictated to him, which was some 7,000+ words. He would have simply written out the very words that the apostle Paul spoke. Some have argued that longhand in dictation was not feasible in ancient times because the author would have to slow down to the point of speaking syllable-by-syllable. They usually cite Cicero as evidence for this argument because of his writings' numerous references to dictation. Cicero stated in a letter to his friend Varro that he had to slow down his dictation to the point of "syllable by syllable" for the sake of the scribe. However, the scribe he was using at that time was inexperienced, not his regular scribe. Of course, it would be challenging to retain one's line of thought in such a dictation process. It should be noted that Cicero had experienced scribes who could take down dictation at an average pace of speaking, even rapid speech.[53] There is evidence that scribes in those days were skilled enough to take down dictation at the average speech rate. Therefore, we should not assume that the apostles would not have had access to such scribes in the persons of Tertius, Silvanus, or even Timothy.

In fact, Marcus Fabius Quintilianus (b. 35 C.E. d. 100 C.E.) complained that a scribe who could write at the speed of everyday speech can make the speaker feel rushed, to the point of not being able to have time to ponder his thoughts.

---

[52] E. Randolph Richards, The Secretary in the Letters of Paul (Heidelberg, Germany: Mohr Siebeck, 1991, 11

[53] E. Randolph Richards, PAUL AND FIRST-CENTURY LETTER WRITING: Secretaries, Composition and Collection (Downers Grove, IL: IVP Academic, 2004), 29-30; Murphy-O'Connor, *Paul the Letter-Writer*, 9–11; Shorthand references Plutarch, *Cato Minor*, 23.3–5; Caesar, 7.4–5; Seneca, *Epistles*, 14.208.

On the other hand, there is a fault which is precisely the opposite of this, into which those fall who insist on first making a rapid draft of their subject with the utmost speed of which their pen is capable, and write in the heat and impulse of the moment. They call this their rough copy. They then revise what they have written, and arrange their hasty outpourings. But while the words and the rhythm may be corrected, the matter is still marked by the superficiality resulting from the speed with which it was thrown together. The more correct method is, therefore, to exercise care from the very beginning, and to form the work from the outset in such a manner that it merely requires being chiseled into shape, not fashioned anew. Sometimes, however, we must follow the stream of our emotions since their warmth will give us more than any diligence can secure. The condemnation which I have passed on such carelessness in writing will make it pretty clear what my views are on the luxury of dictation which is now so fashionable. For, when we write, however great our speed, the fact that the hand cannot follow the rapidity of our thoughts gives us time to think, whereas the presence of our amanuensis hurries us on, and at times we feel ashamed to hesitate or pause, or make some alteration, as though we were afraid to display such weakness before a witness. As a result, our language tends not merely to be haphazard and formless, but in our desire to produce a continuous flow we let slip positive improprieties of diction, which show neither the precision of the writer nor the impetuosity of the speaker. Again, if the amanuensis is a slow writer or lacking in intelligence, he becomes a stumbling-block, our speed is checked, and the thread of our ideas is interrupted by the delay or even perhaps by the loss of temper to which it gives rise.[54]

Therefore, again, we have evidence that some scribes were capable, skilled to the point of writing at the average speed of speech. While Richards says that this is by way of shorthand, saying it was more widespread than initially thought, where the secretary uses symbols in place of words, forming a rough draft that would be written out fully later,[55] this need not be the case. True, there is some evidence that shorthand existed a hundred years before Christ. However, it was still rare, with few scribes having the ability. Whether

---

[54] Retrieved Tuesday, February 12, 2019 (Institutio Oratoria, 10.3.17–21) http://bit.ly/2Zazw2X

[55] E. Randolph Richards, PAUL AND FIRST-CENTURY LETTER WRITING: Secretaries, Composition and Collection (Downers Grove, IL: IVP Academic, 2004), 72.

this was true of the scribes that assisted our New Testament authors is an unknown. It is improbable but not necessarily impossible.

Who in the days of the New Testament authors would use the services of scribes? Foremost would be those who did not know how to read and write. Within ancient contracts and business letters, one can find a note by the scribe (illiteracy statement), who penned it, stating he had done so because his employer could not read or write. For example, an ancient letter concludes with, "Eumelus, son of Herma, has written for him because he does not know letters."[56] It may be that they were able to read but struggled with writing. Then again, it may simply be that they wrote slowly and were unwilling to spend the time improving their skills. An ancient letter from Thebes, Egypt, penned for a certain Asklepiades, concludes, "Written for him hath Eumelus the son of Herma ..., being desired so to do for that he writeth somewhat slowly."[57]

On the other hand, whether one knew how to read and write was not always the decisive issue in the use of a secretary. John L. McKenzie writes, "Even people who could read and write did not think of submitting their readers to unprofessional penmanship. It was probably not even a concern for legibility, but rather a concern for beauty, or at least for neatness," (McKenzie 1975, 14) which moved the ancients to turn to the services of a secretary. Although the educated could read and write, some likely felt that writing was tedious, trying, tiring, and frustrating, especially where lengthy and elaborate texts were concerned. It seems that if one could avoid the tremendous task of penning a lengthy letter, entrusting it to a scribe, so much the better.

The apostle Paul had over 100 traveling companions, like Aristarchus, Luke, and Timothy, who served by the apostle's side for many years. Then, there are others such as Asyncritus, Hermas, Julia, or Philologus, of whom we barely know more than their names. Many of Paul's friends traveled for the sake of the gospel, such as Achaicus, Fortunatus, Stephanas, Artemas, and Tychicus. We know that Tychicus was used by Paul to carry at least three letters now included in the Bible canon: the epistles to the Ephesians, the Colossians, and Philemon. Tychicus was not simply some mail carrier. He

---

[56] See examples in Francis Exler, *The Form of the Ancient Greek Letter: A Study In Greek Epistolography* (Washington D.C.: Catholic University of America, 1922), pp. 126-7

[57] Adolf Deissmann, *LIGHT FROM THE ANCIENT EAST: The New Testament Illustrated by Recently Discovered Texts of the Graeco-Roman World* (New York and London. 1910). 166-7.

was a well-trusted carrier for the apostle, Paul. The final greeting from Paul to the Colossians reads,

Colossians 4:7-8 Updated American Standard Version (UASV)

⁷ All my affairs Tychicus, my beloved brother and faithful minister and fellow slave in the Lord, will make known to you. ⁸ I have sent him to you for this very purpose, that you may know how we are and that he may encourage your hearts,

Richards offers the following about a letter carrier, saying he "was often a personal link between the author and the recipients in addition to the written link.... [One purpose] for needing a trustworthy carrier was, he often carried additional information. A letter may describe a situation briefly, frequently with the author's assessment, but the carrier is expected to elaborate for the recipient all the details."[58] Many of Paul's letters deal with teachings and one crisis after another; the carrier was expected to be aware of these on a much deeper level so that he could orally explain and answer any questions. Therefore, he needed to be a highly trusted messenger who was literate.

As was mentioned, Tertius was the scribe Paul used to pen his letter to the Romans. We cannot assume that all of Paul's companions were proficient readers and writers. However, we can infer that Paul would task coworkers, who were able to carry and read letters and understand the condition of the people or congregation where they were being sent or stationed. Yes, at a minimum, these would have been proficient readers. In addition, the scribes whom Paul used, such as Tertius, would very likely have been semi-professional or professional. It would have been simply senseless to entrust the secretarial work of taking down the monumental words of the book of Romans, for example, to an inexperienced scribe. What skills would Tertius need to carry out the task of penning the book of Romans?

The ordinary coworker of Paul would likely have been able to read proficiently but likely possessed minimum writing skills. Paul would have chosen workers whose skills would have equipped them to carry out their assignments. Again, Tertius would have been the exception to the rule; most likely, he would have been a professional scribe. He would have been able to glue the sheets together if it was to be a roll or stitch the pages together if a codex. He would need to know the appropriate mixture of soot and gum to make ink and to be able to use his knife to make his own reed pen. Richards writes that a professional scribe would also "draw lines on the paper. Small

---

[58] E. Randolph Richards, The Secretary in the Letters of Paul (Heidelberg, Germany: Mohr Siebeck, 1991, 7.

holes were often pricked down each side, and then a straight edge and a lead disk were used to lightly draw evenly spaced lines across the sheet."[59] If Tertius had not been trained as a copyist of documents, he would have made many minor errors because his attention would have been on the sense of what he was penning, as opposed to the exact words, as is typical of the unconscious mind.

Porter writes, "Textual criticism has also recognized that even original authors may have **revised their work**, and these works have **gone through editions**." Stanley E. Porter (p. 35) *How We Got the New Testament*

Comfort writes, "When I speak of the original text, I am referring to the 'published' text— that is, the text in its **final edited form** as released for circulation in the Christian community."[60]

HOW do you edit the Holy Spirit? If the author was moved along by the Holy Spirit and all original Scripture is inspired, **why the need for editing?**

Some might say, "We believe that the NT authors themselves penned or dictated a one-time, single, and only version of their texts, unedited and uncorrected under the inspiration of the Holy Spirit."

However, I would pause to ponder Paul dictating the book of Romans to Tertius. Tertius was **not** inspired, so is he capable of going without making one single scribal error for 7,000+ words in his human imperfection? Are we removing the Holy Spirit in any way if Paul scratches out a few words that Tertius got wrong and wrote the correct word above it? Or is it the slippery slope to consider this possibility? If we hold fast to "I believe that the NT authors themselves penned or dictated a one-time, single and only version of their texts, unedited and uncorrected under the inspiration of the Holy Spirit," then we have to answer those kinds of questions. We have to raise them ourselves by writing, "some might ask, how is it ..." Peter said, "always being ready to make a defense to everyone who asks you to give an account." – 1 Peter 3:15.

We need to be willing to modify (or clarify) what we said above to include our qualification that Paul would edit the letter to the Romans as was described, as the amanuensis (i.e., Tertius) was not inspired. Paul would **not** change his original dictation in the process, and the outcome would be a single document, corrected, as necessary. We would also say that Paul might

---

[59] E. Randolph Richards, PAUL AND FIRST-CENTURY LETTER WRITING: Secretaries, Composition and Collection (Downers Grove, IL: IVP Academic, 2004), 29.

[60] Philip W. Comfort (p. 19), The Quest for the Original Text of the New Testament (Grand Rapids: Baker Academic, 1992)

not make the actual corrections but might direct the amanuensis to do that as Paul watched. We do not go beyond this, i.e., postulating a fresh copy made from the original before publication, etc.

Did Tertius take Paul's exact dictation, word for word?

Robert H. Mounce writes,

> The only legitimate question about authorship relates to the role of Tertius, who in 16:22 writes, "I Tertius, who wrote down this letter, greet you in the Lord." We know that at that time in history an amanuensis [scribe], that is, one hired to write from dictation, could serve at several levels. In some cases he would receive dictation and write it down immediately in longhand. At other times he might use a form of shorthand (tachygraphy [ancient shorthand]) to take down a letter and then later write it out in longhand. In some cases an amanuensis would simply get the gist of what a person wanted to say and then be left on his own to formulate the ideas into a letter.[61]

It might seem quite the task for Tertius to take down Paul's words in longhand. However, this is not to say that it was impossible, just difficult. Paul might have had to speak in a slow to normal speech rate, **but not** syllable-by-syllable. Tertius would indeed have been writing on a papyrus sheet with a reed pen, intending to be legible; however, he would have been very skilled in his trade. Then again, there is the **slight possibility** of Tertius taking it down in shorthand and after that making out a complete draft, which would have been reviewed by both Paul and Tertius. This is only the case if it is comparable to what a modern-day court reporter does. In some sense, they are taking down whoever is speaking down in shorthand. Imagine a courtroom where you have a witness talking fast, the prosecution interrupts, the defense jumps in with his rebuttal, and the judge snaps his ruling, and the witness resumes their account of things. All of that is taken down explicitly word for word in shorthand, and if ever turned into longhand, it would be precisely what was said, down to the uh and um common in speech. So, if the shorthand of the day had that kind of capability; then, it is conceivable. We must remember these are the Bible author's dictated words to the scribe based on their inspiration, not the scribe's word choice or writing style.

The last option by Mounce in the above is contrary to the attitudes that both the scribes and the New Testament authors would have had. Paul and

---

[61] Robert H. Mounce, *Romans*, vol. 27, The New American Commentary (Nashville: Broadman & Holman Publishers, 1995), 22.

Tertius knew that Paul's words were Spirit-inspired, that is, God's words. God chose to convey a message through Matthew, Mark, Luke, John, Peter, Jude, James, and Paul, not Tertius and Silvanus, Timothy, or others. We cannot say with any certainty whether Tertius or Silvanus took their authors' words down in shorthand or longhand. However, we can say that the human author was dictating the Word of God to the scribe, and in no way was it composed by the scribe. Yes, it is true that the Spirit-inspired author, who is literally moved along by the Holy Spirit, retained their style of expressing the message but not the scribe. Mark's writing style is concise, even abrupt at times. His Gospel contains rapid changes of thought. The style of writing of First and Second Timothy is the same as Titus, which adds authenticity to the letter to Titus.

Inspiration and Inerrancy in the Writing Process

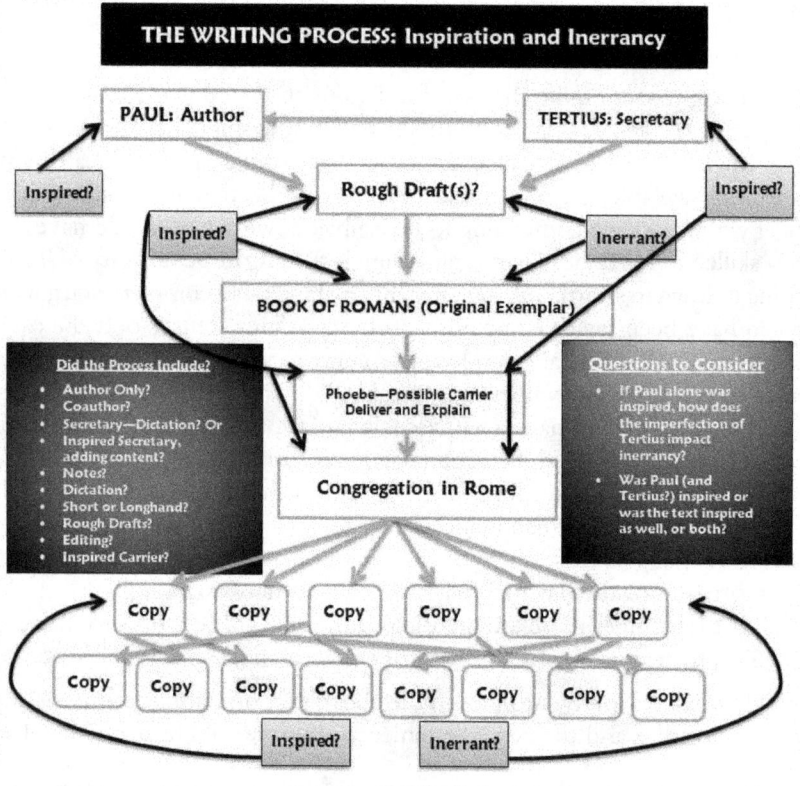

All Scripture is Inspired by God

In this context, inspiration is **the state** of a human being moved by the Holy Spirit, which results in an inspired, fully inerrant written Word of God.

Chicago Statement on Biblical Inerrancy ICBI

Article VII

We affirm that **inspiration** was the work in which God by His Spirit, through human writers, gave us His Word. The origin of Scripture is divine. The mode of divine **inspiration** remains largely a mystery to us. We deny that **inspiration** can be reduced to human insight, or to heightened states of consciousness of any kind.

Article VIII

We affirm that God in His Work of **inspiration** utilized the distinctive personalities and literary styles of the writers whom He had chosen and prepared. We deny that God, in causing these writers to use the very words that He chose, overrode their personalities. ["I would argue that if by human imperfection an author was going to choose an inappropriate word that would fail to communicate the meaning intended by God that the Holy Spirit would then override that word choice." – Edward D. Andrews]

Article IX

We affirm that **inspiration**, though not conferring omniscience, guaranteed true and trustworthy utterance on all matters of which the Biblical authors were moved to speak and write. We deny that the finitude or fallenness of these writers, by necessity or otherwise, introduced distortion or falsehood into God's Word.

Article X

We affirm that **inspiration**, strictly speaking, applies only to the autographic text of Scripture, which in the providence of God can be ascertained from available manuscripts with great accuracy. We further affirm that copies and translations of Scripture are the Word of God to the extent that they faithfully represent the original. We deny that any essential element of the Christian faith is affected by the absence of the autographs. We further deny that this absence renders the assertion of Biblical **inerrancy** invalid or irrelevant. [There is no miracle of preservation, but rather, it is preservation by restoration. Today, what we have, thanks to hundreds of textual scholars over a few hundred years, is a 99.99% restored original language text. – Edward D. Andrews]

Article XI

We affirm that Scripture, having been given by divine inspiration, is infallible, so that, far from misleading us, it is true and reliable in all the matters it addresses. We deny that it is possible for the Bible to be at the same time infallible and errant in its assertions. Infallibility and inerrancy may be distinguished, but not separated.

Inerrancy of Scripture

Inerrancy of Scripture is **the result** of the state of a human being moved by the Holy Spirit from God, which results in an inspired, fully inerrant written Word of God.

Article XII

We affirm that Scripture in its entirety is **inerrant**, being free from all falsehood, fraud, or deceit. We deny that Biblical infallibility and **inerrancy** are limited to spiritual, religious, or redemptive themes, exclusive of assertions in the fields of history and science. We further deny that scientific hypotheses about earth history may properly be used to overturn the teaching of Scripture on creation and the flood.

Article XIII

We affirm the propriety of using **inerrancy** as a theological term with reference to the complete truthfulness of Scripture. We deny that it is proper to evaluate Scripture according to standards of truth and error that are alien to its usage or purpose. We further deny that **inerrancy** is negated by Biblical phenomena such as a lack of modern technical precision, irregularities of grammar or spelling, observational descriptions of nature, the reporting of falsehoods, the use of hyperbole and round numbers, the topical arrangement of material, variant selections of material in parallel accounts, or the use of free citations.

Article XV

We affirm that the doctrine of **inerrancy** is grounded in the teaching of the Bible about **inspiration**. We deny that Jesus' teaching about Scripture may be dismissed by appeals to accommodation or to any natural limitation of His humanity.

THE EARLY CHRISTIAN COPYISTS OF THE NEW TESTAMENT

Article XVI

We affirm that the doctrine of **inerrancy** has been integral to the Church's faith throughout its history. We deny that inerrancy is a doctrine invented by Scholastic Protestantism, or is a reactionary position postulated in response to negative higher criticism.

Authoritative Word of God

The **authoritative** aspect of Scripture is that God by way of inspiration gives the words the authors chose to use power and authority, so that the outcome (i.e., originals) is the very Word of God, as though God were speaking to us himself.

Article I

We affirm that the Holy Scriptures are to be received as the **authoritative** Word of God. We deny that the Scriptures receive their authority from the Church, tradition, or any other human source.

2 Timothy 3:16-17 Updated American Standard Version (UASV)

16 All Scripture is inspired by God and profitable for teaching, for reproof, for correction, for training in righteousness; 17 so that the man of God may be fully competent, equipped for every good work.

What does this mean? The phrase "inspired by God" (Gr., *theopneustos*) literally means, "Breathed out by God." A related Greek word, *pneuma*, means "wind," "breath," life, "Spirit." Since *pneuma* can also mean "breath," the process of "breathing out" can rightly be said to be the work of the Holy Spirit inspiring the Scriptures. The result is that the originals were accurate, fully inerrant, and authoritative. Thus, the Holy Spirit moved human writers so that the result can truthfully be called the Word of *God*, not the word of man.

2 Peter 1:21 Updated American Standard Version (UASV)

21 for no prophecy was ever produced by the will of man, but men carried along by the Holy Spirit spoke from God.

The Greek word here translated "men carried along by," "men moved by" (NASB)," (φέρω pherō), is used in another form at Acts 27:15, 17, which describes a ship that was driven along by the wind. So, the Holy Spirit, by analogy, 'navigated the course' of the Bible writers. While the Spirit did not give them each word by dictation,[62] it certainly kept the writers from inserting any information that did not convey the will and purpose of God.

The heart of what the International Council on Biblical Inerrancy (ICBI) stood for is apparent in "A Short Statement," produced at the Chicago conference in 1978:

A SHORT STATEMENT

1. God, who is Himself Truth and speaks truth only, has inspired Holy Scripture in order thereby to reveal Himself to lost mankind through Jesus Christ as Creator and Lord, Redeemer and Judge. Holy Scripture is God's witness to Himself.

2. Holy Scripture, being God's own Word, written by men prepared and superintended by His Spirit, is of infallible divine authority in all matters upon which it touches: it is to be believed, as God's instruction, in all that it affirms, obeyed, as God's command, in all that it requires; embraced, as God's pledge, in all that it promises.

3. The Holy Spirit, Scripture's divine Author, both authenticates it to us by His inward witness and opens our minds to understand its meaning.

4. Being wholly and verbally God-given, Scripture is without error or fault in all its teaching, no less in what it states about God's acts in creation, about the events of world history, and about its own literary origins under God, than in its witness to God's saving grace in individual lives.

5. The **authority of Scripture** is inescapably impaired if this total divine **inerrancy** is in any way limited or disregarded or made relative to a view of truth contrary to the Bible's own; and such lapses bring serious loss to both the individual and the Church.

Questions to Consider

We have been using the book of Romans as our example, so we will continue with it. We know that Paul was the author who gave us the inspired content of Romans, Tertius was the secretary who recorded Romans, and

---

[62] Dr. Don Wilkins, Senior Translator of the NASB writes, "Exactly how the Spirit guided the writers is a mystery, and the words "thus says the Lord" in prophecy most likely do introduce a dictated message. However, those familiar with Greek can easily see stylistic differences between the NT writers which seem to reflect different personalities and rule out verbatim dictation from a single source."

Phoebe was likely the one who carried the letter to Rome or else accompanied the one who did. Thus, we have at least three persons: the author, the secretary (amanuensis; scribe), and the carrier.

What is inspiration?

Inspiration is a "theological concept encompassing phenomena in which human action, skill, or utterance is immediately and extraordinarily supplied by the Spirit of God. Although various terms are employed in the Bible, the basic meaning is best served by Gk. *theopneustos* "God-breathed." (2 Tim. 3:16) This means "breathed forth by God" rather than "breathed into by God" (Warfield)." (Myers 1987, 524) **Verbal plenary inspiration** holds that "every word of Scripture was God-breathed." Human writers played a significant role. Their individual backgrounds, personal traits, and literary styles were authentically theirs but had been providentially prepared by God for use as his instrument in producing Scripture. "The Scriptures had not been dictated, but the result was as if they had been (A. A. Hodge, B. B. Warfield)."[63]

World-Renowned Bible Scholars Define Inspiration

Benjamin B. Warfield: "Inspiration is, therefore, usually defined as a supernatural influence exerted on the sacred writers by the Spirit of God, by virtue of which their writings are given Divine trustworthiness."[64]

Edward J. Young: "Inspiration is a superintendence of God the Holy Spirit over the writers of the Scriptures, as a result of which these Scriptures possess Divine authority and trustworthiness and, possessing such Divine authority and trustworthiness, are free from error."[65]

Charles C. Ryrie: "Inspiration is ... God's superintendence of the human authors so that, using their own individual personalities, they composed and recorded without error His revelation to man in the words of the original autographs."[66]

Paul P. Enns: "There are several important elements that belong in a proper definition of inspiration: (1) the divine element–God the Holy Spirit

---

[63] Allen C. Myers, *The Eerdmans Bible Dictionary* (Grand Rapids, MI: Eerdmans, 1987), 525.

[64] B. B. Warfield, *The Inspiration and Authority of the Bible* (Philadelphia, PA: Presbyterian and Reformed Pub. Co., 1948), p. 131.

[65] Edward J. Young, *Thy Word Is Truth* (Grand Rapids: Eerdmans, 1957), p. 27.

[66] Charles C. Ryrie, *A Survey of Bible Doctrine* (Chicago: Moody, 1972), p. 38.

superintended the writers, ensuring the accuracy of the writing; (2) the human element—human authors wrote according to their individual styles and personalities; (3) the result of the divine-human authorship is the recording of God's truth without error; (4) inspiration extends to the selection of words by the writers; (5) inspiration relates to the original manuscripts."[67]

Were both Paul and Tertius inspired, or just Paul?

Only Paul and other Old and New Testament authors were inspired. First, as was stated above, **Verbal plenary inspiration** holds that "every word of Scripture was God-breathed." However, God **did not**, generally speaking, dictate the books of the Bible word by word to the Bible authors as if they were dictating machines.

As the apostle Paul states, God spoke "in many ways" to his servants before the arrival of Jesus Christ. (Heb. 1:1-2) We do have one specific circumstance: The Ten Commandments, wherein the information was divinely provided in written form. Therefore, a scribe would only have to copy them into the scrolls created by Moses. (Ex. 31:18; Deut. 10:1-5) At other times, information was communicated by verbal dictation, literally word for word. When introducing the large number of laws and statutes of the covenant with Israel, "Jehovah said to Moses: 'Write these words, for in accordance with these words I have made a covenant with you and with Israel.'" (Ex. 34:27) And on other occasions, the prophets also were frequently given precise messages that were to be delivered. These were then recorded after that, which then became part of the inspired, fully inerrant Scriptures. – 1 Kings 22:14; Jeremiah 1:7; 2:1; 11:1-5; Ezekiel 3:4; 11:5.

2 Thessalonians 3:17 Updated American Standard Version (UASV)

¹⁷ The greeting is by my hand, Paul's,[68] which is a sign in every letter; this is the way I write.

An appended note to every letter with his signature "distinguishing mark" is like a boss signing a letter that he dictated to a secretary. It is unthinkable that Paul would sign or make a distinguishing mark on anything without reading through it and, after that, making any necessary corrections or having Tertius makes the corrections. This supposes that Paul looked over all of his letters, which would also suppose that the scribe could not have been inspired because if he were, then there would have been no mistakes in the document, which means it would not have been needed to be looked over

---

[67] Paul P. Enns, *The Moody Handbook of Theology* (Chicago: Moody Press, 1989), p. 161.
[68] Lit *the greeting by my hand of Paul*

let alone corrected. So again, there would have been no need for Paul to check the work of an inspired secretary. Again, more plainly, if Tertius had been inspired, Paul would have had no need to look the text over the moment he set the pen down. There is no need to read into silence and suggest that the secretary was inspired. While Tertius was likely a professional scribe and indeed engaged in his work, they were also coworkers and traveling companions. As was stated earlier, in a small percentage of cases, information was transmitted by verbal dictation, word for word from God by way of the Holy Spirit to the author. For example, when God delivered the large body of laws and statutes of his covenant with Israel, Jehovah instructed Moses: "Write for yourself these words." (Ex 34:27) In another example, the prophets were often given specific messages to deliver. (1 Ki 22:14; Jer. 1:7; 2:1; 11:1-5; Eze. 3:4; 11:5) Additionally, the Bible authors did dictate word for word what they received under inspiration to their secretaries, i.e., amanuenses/scribes. In other words, any word choices or writing styles belonged to the Bible author.

Jeremiah 36:4 Updated American Standard Version (UASV)

⁴ Then Jeremiah called Baruch the son of Neriah, and Baruch wrote on a scroll at the **dictation of Jeremiah** all the words of Jehovah that he had spoken to him. (Bold mine)

If Paul alone was inspired, how does the imperfection of Tertius affect inerrancy?

First, we should state that just because Paul used Tertius, Peter used Silvanus, or Jeremiah used Baruch to pen the Word of God, they did not thereby detract from or weaken the authority of God's Word or the inerrancy of Scripture. The dictation that Paul gave Tertius was the result of divine inspiration as he, Paul, was moved along by the Holy Spirit. Tertius merely recorded Paul's dictation, word by word. Whether Tertius was a professional scribe[69] or had the skills of a semi-professional scribe, he must have made at least a few slips of the pen, as the epistle to the Romans was some 7,000 words, and writing conditions were challenging. Afterward, however, Paul would have reviewed the document with Tertius, correcting any errors before publishing the official, authoritative text.

---

[69] In the strictest sense, a professional scribe is one who was specifically trained in that vocation and was paid for his services.

What about Phoebe? What role did the carrier have in the process?

Those used by New Testament authors to deliver the Word of God to people or congregations would have been some of Paul's most trusted, competent coworkers. Paul had over one hundred of these. Indeed, in the case of congregations contacting Paul with questions and concerns, Paul responded with an inspired letter, the carrier would be made aware of those questions and concerns. Paul would have spoken to the carrier at length about these matters, going over what he meant by the words he had used. This would have provided the carrier sufficient knowledge; if the person or congregation had any question(s) that the carrier could address. This process is not indicated within the Scriptures. Are we to believe God and Paul, for that matter, would send a simple carrier who was left in the dark as to what he was carrying? And that no congregational leader would have follow-up questions, which God would have foreseen? Hardly.

The Publishing, Copying, and Distributing Process

In the above, we spoke of the initial aspect of the publishing process, i.e., the moment Paul decided to pen a letter to a congregation like the Romans, the Ephesians, the Colossians, or a person such as Philemon. We discussed the process that Paul went through with his secretary (e.g., Tertius), to the carrier (e.g., Phoebe, Tychicus), and the recipients (e.g., Roman congregation). Now we turn to the circulation aspect, i.e., getting the book out to more readers. Harry Y. Gamble says the following in *The Publication and Early Dissemination of Early Christian Books*:

> The letters of Paul to his communities, the earliest extant Christian texts, were dictated to scribal associates (presumably Christian), carried to their destinations by a traveling Christian, and read aloud to the congregations.[70] But Paul also envisioned the

---

[70] On the dictation of Paul's letters to a scribe, see E. R. Richards, The Secretary in the Letters of Paul (WUNT 42; Tubingen: Mohr, 1991), 169–98; for couriers see Rom. 16: 1, 1 Cor. 16: 10, Eph. 6: 21, Col. 4: 7, cf. 2 Cor. 8: 16–17. Reference to their carriers is common in other early Christian letters (e.g., 1 Pet. 5: 12, 1 Clem. 65: 1, Ignatius, Phil. 11.2, Smyr. 12.1, Polycarp, Phil. 14.1). For the general practice see E. Epp, 'New Testament Papyrus Manuscripts and Letter Carrying in Greco-Roman Times', in B. A. Pearson (ed.), The Future of Early Christianity (Minneapolis: Fortress, 1991), 35–56. Reading a letter aloud to the

circulation of some of his letters beyond a single Christian group (cf. Gal. 1: 2, 'to the churches of Galatia', Rom. 1:7 'to all God's beloved in Rome'—dispersed among numerous discrete house churches, Rom. 16: 5, 10, 11, 14, 15), and the author of Colossians, if not Paul, gives instruction for the exchange of Paul's letters between different communities (Col. 4: 16), which must indeed have taken place also soon after Paul's time.[71] The gospel literature of early Christianity offers only meager hints of intentions or means of its publication and circulation. The prologue to Luke/Acts (Luke 1: 1–4) provides a dedication to 'Theophilus', who (whether or not a fictive figure) by that convention is implicitly made responsible for the dissemination of the work by encouraging and permitting copies to be made. The last chapter of the Gospel of John, an epilogue added by others after the original conclusion of the Gospel (20: 30–1), aims at least in part (21: 24–5) to insure appreciation of the book and to promote its use beyond its community of origin. To take another case, the Apocalypse, addressed to seven churches in western Asia Minor, was almost surely sent in separate copy to each. Even so, the author anticipated its wider copying and dissemination beyond those original recipients, and so warned subsequent copyists to preserve the integrity of the book, neither adding nor subtracting, for fear of religious penalty (Rev. 22:18–19). The private Christian copying and circulation that is presumed in these early writings continued to be the means for the publication and dissemination of Christian literature in the second and third centuries. It can be seen, for example, in the explicit notice in The Shepherd of Hermas (Vis. 2.4.3) that the book was to be published or released in two final copies, one for local use in Rome, the other for the transcription of further copies to be sent to Christian communities in 'cities abroad'. It can also be seen when Polycarp, bishop of Smyrna, had the letters of Ignatius copied and sent to the Christian community in Philippi, and had copies of letters from them and other churches in Asia Minor sent to Syrian Antioch (Phil. 13). It is evident too in the

---

community, which seems to be presupposed by all the letters, is stipulated only in 1 Thess. 5: 27.

[71] This is shown for an early time by the generalization of the original particular addresses of some of Paul's letters (Rom. 1: 7, 15; 1 Cor. 1: 2; cf. Eph. 1: 1).

scribal colophons of the Martyrdom of Polycarp (22.2–4), and must be assumed also in connection with the letters of Dionysius, bishop of Corinth (fl. 170 ce; Eusebius, H.E. 4.23.1–12).

From another angle, the physical remains of early Christian books show that they were produced and disseminated privately within and between Christian communities. Early Christian texts, especially those of a scriptural sort, were almost always written in codices or leaf books—an informal, economical, and handy format—rather than on rolls, which were the traditional and standard vehicle of all other books. This was a sharp departure from convention, and particularly characteristic of Christians. Also distinctive to Christian books was the pervasive use of nomina sacra, divine names written in abbreviated forms, which was clearly an in-house practice of Christian scribes. Further, the preponderance in early Christian papyrus manuscripts of an informal quasi-documentary script rather than a professional bookhand also suggests that Christian writings were privately transcribed with a view to intramural circulation and use.[72]

If Christian books were disseminated in roughly the same way as other books, that is, by private seriatim copying, we might surmise that they spread slowly and gradually in ever-widening circles, first in proximity to their places of origin, then regionally, and then transregionally, and for some books this was doubtless the case. But it deserves notice that some early Christian texts appear to have enjoyed surprisingly rapid and wide circulation. Already by the early decades of the second century Papias of Hierapolis in western Asia Minor was acquainted at least with the Gospels of Mark and Matthew (Eusebius, H.E. 3.39.15–16); Clement of Rome, Ignatius of Antioch, and Polycarp of Smyrna were all acquainted with collections of Paul's letters; and papyrus copies of various early Christian texts were current in Egypt.[73] The Shepherd of Hermas,

---

[72] On these features see H. Gamble, Books and Readers in the Early Church (New Haven: Yale University Press, 1995), 66–81, and L. Hurtado, The Earliest Christian Artifacts (Grand Rapids: Eerdmans, 2006).

[73] For Clement, Ignatius, and Polycarp, see A. F. Gregory and C. M. Tuckett, eds., The Reception of the New Testament in the Apostolic Fathers (Oxford: OUP, 2005), 142–53, 162–72, 201–18, 226–7. For early Christian papyri in Egypt see Hurtado, Earliest Christian

written in Rome near the mid-second century, was current and popular in Egypt not long after.⁷⁴ Equally interesting, Irenaeus' Adversus haereses, written about 180 in Gaul, is shown by papyrus fragments to have found its way to Egypt by the end of the second century, and indeed also to Carthage, where it was used by Tertullian.⁷⁵

The brisk and broad dissemination of Christian books presumes not only a lively interest in texts among Christian communities but also efficient means for their reproduction and distribution. Such interest and means may be unexpected, given that the rate of literacy within Christianity was low, on average no greater than in the empire at large, namely in the range of 10–15 percent.⁷⁶ Yet there were some literate members in almost all Christian communities, and as long as texts could be read aloud by some, they were accessible and useful to the illiterate majority. Christian congregations were not reading communities in the same sense as elite literary or scholarly circles, but books were nevertheless important to them virtually from the beginning, for even before Christians began to compose their own texts, books of Jewish scripture played an indispensable role in their worship, teaching, and missionary preaching. Indeed, Judaism and Christianity were the only religious communities in Greco-Roman antiquity in which texts had any considerable importance, and in this, as in some other respects, Christian groups bore a greater resemblance to philosophical circles than to other religious traditions.⁷⁷

Artifacts, appendix 1 (209–29). The most notable case is P52 (a fragment of the Gospel of John, customarily dated to the early 2nd cent.).

⁷⁴ Some papyrus fragments of Hermas are 2nd cent. (P.Oxy. 4706 and 3528, P.Mich. 130, P.Iand. 1.4).

⁷⁵ For the A.H. in Egypt: P.Oxy. 405; for Tertullian's use of A.H. in Carthage, see T. D. Barnes, Tertullian (Oxford: Clarendon, 1971), 127–8, 220–1.

⁷⁶ The fundamental study of literacy in antiquity is still W. V. Harris, Ancient Literacy (Cambridge, Mass.: Harvard University Press, 1989); see now also the essays in J. H. Humphrey, ed., Literacy in the Roman World (Journal of Roman Archaeology, suppl. ser. 3; Ann Arbor: University of Michigan, 1991), and in W. A. Johnson and H. N. Parker, eds., Ancient Literacies (Oxford: OUP, 2009).

⁷⁷ M. Beard, 'Writing and Religion: Ancient Religion and the Function of the Written Word in Roman Religion', in Humphrey, Literacy in the Roman World, 353–8, argues that texts played a relatively large role in Greco-Roman religions, yet characterizes that role as

> If smaller, provincial Christian congregations were not well-equipped or well-situated for the tasks of copying and disseminating texts, larger Christian centers must have had some scriptorial capacity: already in the second century: Polycarp's handling of Ignatius' letters and letters from other churches shows its presence in Smyrna; the instruction about the publication of Hermas' The Shepherd suggests it for Rome; and it can hardly be doubted for Alexandria, since even in a provincial city like Oxyrhynchus many manuscripts of Christian texts were available.[78] The early third-century Alexandrian scriptorium devised for the production and distribution of the works of Origen (Eusebius, H.E. 6.23.2), though unique in its sponsorship by a private patron and its service to an individual writer, surely had precursors, more modest and yet efficient, in other Christian communities. It also had important successors, not the least of which was the library and scriptorium that flourished in Caesarea in the second half of the third century under the auspices of Pamphilus.[79] Absent such reliable intra-Christian means for the production of books, the range of texts known and used by Christian communities across the Mediterranean basin by the end of the second century would be without explanation.[80]

'symbolic rather than utilitarian', which was clearly not the case in early Christianity. The kind of careful reading, interpretation, and exposition of texts that we see in early Christianity and in early Judaism (whether in worship or school settings) provides, mutatis mutandis, an interesting analogy to the activity of elite literary circles.

[78] On the question of early Christian scriptoria (the term may be variously construed), see Gamble, Books and Readers, 121–6. Hurtado, Earliest Christian Artifacts, 185–9, rightly calls attention to corrections by contemporary hands in early Christian papyri as pointing to at least limited activity of a scriptorial kind.

[79] The role of Pamphilus and the Caesarean library/scriptorium in the private production and dissemination of early Christian literature, esp. of scriptural materials, was highlighted by Eusebius in his Life of Pamphilus, as quoted by Jerome in his Apology against Rufinus (1.9).

[80] Charles E. Hill; Michael J. Kruger, THE EARLY TEXT OF THE NEW TESTAMENT (Oxford, United Kingdom: Oxford University Press, 2012), 32-35.

Beyond the uses of Christian texts in congregational settings, there were already in the 2nd cent. some Christian circles that pursued specialized and technical engagements with texts, usually in the service of theological arguments and exegetical agendas. The 'school-settings' of teachers such as Valentinus and Justin, and a little later of Theodotus, Clement, and Origen,

THE EARLY CHRISTIAN COPYISTS OF THE NEW TESTAMENT

When we think of publishing a book today, there are some similarities to the ancient process, but it was not the same for Christian communities in the ancient world of the Roman Empire. Paul dispatched Tychicus as a carrier with a letter to the Ephesians, the Colossians, and Philemon and a potential fourth letter to the Laodiceans. Tychicus was competent, trusted, and a skilled coworker who delivered these letters hundreds of miles from an imprisoned Paul, with enough information to bring God's Word to the first-century Christian congregations. However, in the letter to the Colossians, Paul said, "When this letter has been read among you, have it also read in the church of the Laodiceans; and see that you also read the letter from Laodicea." (Col. 4:16) In other words, it was to be a circuit letter. Paul had also stated to the Thessalonians in a letter to them, "I put you under oath before the Lord to have this letter read to all the brothers." (1 Thess. 5:27) Paul encouraged the distribution of his letters.

Remember the process from the above; the book would be shared with friends of similar interests, and then the circles grew wider and wider to friends of friends and others. First, Paul's primary level of friends would be his more than one hundred traveling companions and fellow workers, some being the carriers who delivered the books. Second, the friends in the Christian congregation would have the letter read to them, who would then share it with other fellow congregations. In the secular (non-Christian) circle of friends, interested readers who wished to have a copy would have their slaves (i.e., scribes) make a copy or copies of a book. The same would have been valid within the Christian congregation. When the Laodiceans read the letter that Paul had sent to the Colossians, they would have had one of their wealthy members use his literate and trained scribe to make a copy for their congregation and maybe even a few copies for other members. The same would hold true when the Colossians received the letter written to the Laodiceans. Eventually, Paul's letters would have been gathered in one codex to circulate as a group, such as P[46]. Papyrus 46 is an early Greek New Testament manuscript written on papyrus. Its most probable date between 100 and 150 C.E. Michael Marlowe says that P[46] contains (in order) "the last eight chapters of Romans; all of Hebrews; virtually all of 1–2 Corinthians; all of Ephesians, Galatians, Philippians, Colossians; and two chapters of 1 Thessalonians. All of the leaves have lost some lines at the bottom through deterioration."

---

were Christian approximations to the kinds of literary activity associated with 'elite' reading communities in the early empire.

The scriptorium was a room for copying manuscripts, where a lector would read aloud from his exemplar, with a room full of copyists taking down his dictation. Recent scholarship has suggested that we remove the concept of the scriptorium in the time of Jesus and the apostles of the first century C.E. because this was not a practice until the fourth century C.E. Harry Y. Gamble addresses this effectively when he writes,

> It is difficult to determine just when Christian scriptoria came into existence. The problem is partly of definition, partly of evidence. If we think of the scriptorium as simply a writing center where texts were copied by more than a single scribe, then any of the larger Christian communities, such as Antioch or Rome, may have already had scriptoria in the early second century, and in view of Polycarp's activity something of the kind can be imagined for Smyrna. If we think instead of a scriptorium as being more structured, operating, for example, in a specially designed and designated location; employing particular methods of transcription; producing certain types of manuscripts; or multiplying copies on a significant scale, then it becomes more difficult to imagine that such institutions developed at an early date.[81]

Gamble goes on to inform us that Origen's scriptorium of about 230 C.E. was an exception. Just a few short years later, the scriptorium of Cyprian was a more official version of what we think of when picturing scriptoria. Then, there is the scriptorium that was attached to the Christian library in Caesarea, which we know was commissioned to produce fifty New Testament manuscripts in short order. It may even have been added in the third century when Pamphilus (latter half of the 3rd century–309 C.E.) built the library. A more official type of scriptorium could likely be found in this period at other Christian epicenters, such as Rome, Jerusalem, and Alexandria. Comfort tells us that "church history and certain manuscript discoveries from other parts in Egypt suggest that Alexandria had a Christian scriptorium or writing center."[82] Gamble adds, "It was only during the fourth

---

[81] Henry Y. Gamble, *Books and Readers in the Early Church: A History of Early Christian Texts* (New Haven, CT, New Haven University Press, 1995), 121.

[82] Philip Comfort, *Encountering the Manuscripts: An Introduction to New Testament Paleography & Textual Criticism* (Nashville, TN: Broadman & Holman, 2005), 22.

THE EARLY CHRISTIAN COPYISTS OF THE NEW TESTAMENT

and fifth centuries that the scriptoria on monastic communities came into their own, also in association with monastic libraries."[83]

While it is challenging, if not impossible, to identify a specific Alexandrian scriptorium for our early manuscripts of the second century, or even if they were produced in a scriptorium at all, we do know that professional scribes produced them. There are many possibilities: (1) the professional scribe could have produced them in a Christian scriptorium. On the other hand, (2) the professional scribe could have been a Christian who worked for a scriptorium, who then used his skills to produce copies. Then again, (3) it could have been that the scribe formerly worked in a scriptorium but now was the private scribe of a wealthy Christian who used his skills to make copies. We know that about a million Christians spread throughout the Roman Empire at the beginning of the second century (c. 130 C.E.). Therefore, the copying of manuscripts could very well have been within the Christian community, i.e., from the Christian congregation to the Christian congregation and wealthy Christians acquiring personal copies for themselves.

We have several early manuscripts that evidence that they were very likely produced in a scriptorium, even if it was simply a room attached to a Christian library, which had a handful of copyists. For example, a professional scribe undoubtedly did P46 (100-150 C.E.) because it contained stichoi marks, which are notes at the end of sections, stating how many lines were copied. This was a means of calculating how much a scribe should be paid. It is likely that an employee of the scriptorium numbered the pages, indicating the stichoi marks. Moreover, this same scribe made corrections as he went. Another example would be P66 (also c. 100-150 C.E.) according to Comfort:

> It is also fairly certain that P66 was the product of a scriptorium or writing center. The first copyist of this manuscript had his work thoroughly checked by a diorthotes [corrector], according to a different exemplar—just the way it would happen in a scriptorium. Of course, it can be argued that an individual who purchased the manuscript made all the corrections, which was a common practice in ancient times. But the extent of corrections in P66 and the fact that the paginator (a different scribe) made many of the corrections speaks against this (see description of P66 in chap. 2). It was more the exception than the rule in ancient times

---

[83] Henry Y. Gamble, *Books and Readers in the Early Church: A History of Early Christian Texts* (New Haven, CT, New Haven University Press, 1995), 121-2.

that a manuscript would be fully checked by a diorthotes. P66 has other markings of being professionally produced. The extant manuscript still shows the pinpricks in the corners of each leaf of the papyri; these served as a guide for left hand justification and right hand. The manuscript also exhibits a consistent set of marginal and interlinear correction signs. Another sign of professionally produced manuscript is the use of the diple (>) in the margin, which was used to signal a correction in the text and/or the need for a correction in the text. There are very few of these in the extant New Testament manuscripts.[84]

The production and distribution of New Testament manuscripts were carried out at the congregation and individual Christian levels in the early days of Christianity.

Moreover, this process did not negate the use of professional scribes. Just as Paul would not have used an inexperienced scribe to produce the epistle to the Romans. Congregations and wealthy Christians would have likely used professional scribes to make copies. Of course, there are exceptions to the rule, and some congregations may not have had access to a professional scribe, so they would have to have chosen to use the best person available to them. Nevertheless, if a congregation had access to a person experienced at making documents or a semi-professional or professional scribe, they would have lacked good sense or practicality not to take advantage of such a person. Think of anything we want to have done in our Christian congregation today: would we not seek a professional if we had access to one as a member, be it plumbing, wiring, teaching, or computer technology? We naturally look to the most skilled person that we can find, even if we have a clogged-up commode. Would we do any less if we were in the first century and had just received a letter from the apostle Paul, who was imprisoned hundreds of miles away in Rome?

Why Would the Holy Spirit Miraculously Inspire 66 Fully Inerrant Texts and Then Allow Variant Errors in the Copies?

Agnostic New Testament textual and early Christianity scholar Dr. Bart D. Ehrman states, "For the only reason (I came to think) for God to inspire the Bible would be so that his people would have his actual words;

---

[84] Philip W. Comfort, *New Testament Text and Translation Commentary: Commentary on the Variant Readings of the Ancient New Testament Manuscripts and How They Relate to the Major English Translations* (Carol Stream, IL: Tyndale House Publishers, Inc., 2008), 26.

but if he really wanted people to have his actual words, surely he would have miraculously preserved those words, just as he had miraculously inspired them in the first place. Given the circumstance that he didn't preserve the words, the conclusion seemed inescapable to me that he hadn't gone to the trouble of inspiring them."[85]

New Testament textual scholar Dr. Dirk Jongkind offers a brief response, "God chose not to give us exhaustive knowledge of every detail of the text, though he could have done so. Still, he has given us abundant access to his words. In other words, to say that God inspired the words of the New Testament does not mean that God is therefore under an obligation to preserve for us each and every detail."[86]

Why didn't God inspire the copyists? Some have become anxious because this question has plagued them, or some Bible critic has challenged them. Therefore, they are looking for the silver bullet to quench their personal concern or have a ready, quick response for the Bible critic. Draw comfort in that there are hundreds, if not thousands, of great responses to attacks from Bible critics that will cause them to move onto another victim in their quest to stumble God's people. However, there are good reasons, rational responses to some questions that will not be fully answered until the second coming of Jesus Christ. What lies below is the latter. Before delving into the rational, reasonable reasons why God would inspire the authors but not the copyists, let's talk a little about what we do have.

Some people have unreceptive hearts and minds. They are Pharisaical because they are not interested in an answer, and the Word of God, reason, and logic will not get through their callused hearts. Suppose I have only taught one thing in my 32 years. In that case, it is this, identify these people fast, or you will waste much of your life, giving reasonable, rational responses to then have the person reject it out of hand and move onto something else as though they never brought it up. Mind you, an angry person, a person with doubts, is not necessarily a Pharisaical person. There are reasons for some to doubt. There are reasons for some to be angry. If the person is treating you with disdain, mocking, talking down to you, these and other things are indications of a Pharisaical attitude.

Christian Bible students need to be familiar with Old and New Testament textual studies as the two are essential foundational studies. Why?

---

[85] Misquoting Jesus: The Story Behind Who Changed the Bible and Why (San Francisco: HarperSanFrancisco, 2005), 211.

[86] An Introduction to the Greek New Testament, Produced at Tyndale House, Cambridge, Crossway.

If we fail to establish what was originally authored with reasonable certainty, how are we to translate or even interpret what we think is God's actual Word? We are fortunate that there are far more existing New Testament manuscripts today than any other book from ancient history. Some ancient Greek and Latin classics are based on one existing manuscript, while with others, there are just a handful and a few exceptions that have a few hundred available. However, the New Testament has over 5,898 Greek New Testament manuscripts that have been cataloged (As of January 2021),[87] 10,000 Latin manuscripts, and an additional 9,300 other manuscripts in such languages as Syriac, Slavic, Gothic, Ethiopic, Coptic, and Armenian. This gives New Testament textual scholars vastly more to work within establishing the original words of the text.

The other difference between the New Testament manuscripts and those of the classics is that the existing copies of the New Testament date much closer to the originals. In the case of the Greek classics, some of the manuscripts are dated about a thousand years after the author had penned the book. Some of the Latin classics are dated from three to seven hundred years after the time the author wrote the book. When we look at the Greek copies of the New Testament books, some portions are within decades of the original author's book. Seventy-nine Greek papyri, along with five majuscules,[88] date from 110 C.E. to 300 C.E.

---

[87] While at present here in 2020, there are 5,898 manuscripts. There are **140 listed Papyrus** manuscripts, 323 Majuscule manuscripts, 2,951 Minuscule manuscripts, and 2,484 Lectionary manuscripts, bringing the total cataloged manuscripts to 5,898 manuscripts. However, you cannot simply total the number of cataloged manuscripts because, for example, $P^{11/14}$ are the same manuscript but with different catalog numbers. The same is true of $P^{33/5}$, $P^{4/64/67}$, $P^{49/65}$ and $P^{77/103}$. Now this alone would bring our 140 listed papyrus manuscripts down to 134. 'Then, we turn to one example from our majuscule manuscripts where clear 0110, 0124, 0178, 0179, 0180, 0190, 0191, 0193, 0194, and 0202 are said to be part of 070. A minuscule manuscript was listed with five separate catalog numbers for 2306, which then have the letters a through e. Thus, we have the following GA numbers: 2306 for 2306a, and 2831-2834 for 2306b-2306e.' – (Hixon 2019, 53-4) The problem is much worse when we consider that there are 323 Majuscule manuscripts and then far worse still with a listed 2,951 Minuscule and 2,484 Lectionaries. Nevertheless, those who estimate a total of 5,300 (Jacob W. Peterson, Myths and Mistakes, p. 63) 5,500 manuscripts (Dr. Ed Gravely / ehrmanproject.com/), 5,800 manuscripts (Porter 2013, 23), it is still a truckload of evidence far and above the dismal number of ancient secular author books.

[88] Large lettering, often called "capital" or uncial, in which all the letters are usually the same height.

Distribution of Greek New Testament Manuscripts

- The **Papyrus** is a copy of a portion of the New Testament made on papyrus. At present, we have 141 cataloged New Testament papyri, many dating between 110-350 C.E., but some as late as the 6th century C.E.

- The **Majuscule** or **Uncial** is a script of large letters commonly used in Greek and Latin manuscripts written between the 3rd and 9th centuries C.E. that resembles a modern capital letter but is more rounded. At present, we have 323 cataloged New Testament Majuscule manuscripts.

- The **Minuscule** is a small cursive style of writing used in manuscripts from the 9th to the 16th centuries, now having 2,951 Minuscule manuscripts cataloged.

- The **Lectionary** is a schedule of readings from the Bible for Christian church services during the year, in both majuscules and minuscules, dating from the 4th to the 16th centuries C.E., now having 2,484 Lectionary manuscripts cataloged.

Distribution of Papyri by Century and Type				
DATE	ALEX	WEST	CAES	BYZ
100-150/175 C.E.	7Q4? 7Q5? $P^{4/64/67}$ P^{32} P^{46} P^{52} P^{66} P^{75} $P^{77/103}$ P^{87} P^{90} P^{98} (bad shape, differences) P^{101} P^{109} (too small) P^{118} (too small) P^{137} 0189 P. Oxyrhynchus 405 P. Egerton 2	P^{104}	0	0
175-250 C.E.	P^1 P^5 P^{13} P^{20} P^{23} P^{27} P^{30} P^{35} P^{39} P^{40} P^{45} P^{47} $P^{49/65}$ P^{71} P^{72} P^{82} P^{85} P^{95} P^{100} P^{106} P^{108} P^{110} P^{111} P^{113} P^{115} P^{121} (too small) P^{125} P^{126} (too small) P^{133} P^{136} P^{141} 0220 0232	P^{29} (Metzger Western & Aland Free; too small to be certain) P^{38} P^{48} P^{69} 0171 0212	0	0

	P. Oxyrhynchus 406 P. Egerton 3	(mixed) P^{107} (Independent)		
250-300 C.E.	P^8 P^9 P^{12} P^{15} P^{16} P^{17} P^{18} P^{19} P^{24} P^{28} P^{50} P^{51} P^{53} P^{70} P^{78} P^{80} P^{86} P^{88} P^{89} (too small) P^{91} P^{92} P^{114} P^{119} P^{120} P^{129} (too small) P^{131} P^{132} too small) P^{134} 0162 0207 0231 P. Antinoopolis 54	P^{37} (Free, mostly Western)	0	0
290-390 C.E.	P^3 P^6 P^7 P^{10} P^{21} P^{54} P^{62} P^{81} P^{93} P^{94} P^{102} (too small) P^{117} (too small) P^{122} (too small) P^{123} P^{130} (too small) P^{139} (too small) 057 058 059 / 0215 071 0160 0163 0165 0169 0172 0173 0175 0176 0181 0182 0185 0188 0206 0214 0217 0218 0219 0221 0226 0227 0228 0230 0242 0264 0308 0312 P. Oxyrhynchus 4010 P. Oxyrhynchus 5073	P^{21} (mixed) P^{25} (independent) P^{112} (independent) P^{127} (independent; like no other)	0	0
4th / 5th Century C.E.	P^{11} P^{14} P^{33}/P^{58} P^{56} P^{57} P^{63} P^{105} (too small) P^{124} 0254			069 P. Oxyrhynchus 1077?

We should clarify that of the approximate 24,000 total manuscripts of the New Testament, not all are complete books. There are fragmented manuscripts with just a few verses, manuscripts containing an entire book, others that include numerous books, and some that have the whole New Testament, or nearly so. This is expected since the oldest manuscripts we have were copied in an era when reproducing the entire New Testament was not the norm, but rather a single book or a group of books (i.e., the Gospels or Paul's letters). This still does not negate the vast riches of manuscripts that we possess.

THE EARLY CHRISTIAN COPYISTS OF THE NEW TESTAMENT

What can we conclude from this short introduction to New Testament textual studies? There is some irony here: secular scholars have no problem accepting classic authors' wording with their minuscule amount of evidence. However, they discount the treasure trove of evidence that is available to the New Testament textual scholar. Still, this should not surprise us, as the New Testament has always been under-appreciated and attacked in some way, shape, or form over the past 2,000 years.

On the contrary, in comparison to classical works, we are overwhelmed by the quantity and quality of existing New Testament manuscripts. We should also keep in mind that seventy-five percent[89] of the New Testament does not require textual scholars' help because that much of the text is unanimous, and thus, we know what it says. Of the other twenty-five percent, about twenty percent make up trivial scribal mistakes that are easily corrected. Therefore, textual criticism focuses mainly on a small portion of the New Testament text. The facts are clear: the Christian, who reads the New Testament, is fortunate to have so many manuscripts, with so many dating so close to the originals, with 500 hundred years of hundreds of textual scholars who have established the text with a level of certainty unimaginable for ancient secular works.

After discussing the amount of New Testament manuscripts available, Atheist commentator Bob Seidensticker, writes, "The first problem is that more manuscripts at best increase our confidence that we have the original version. That does not mean the original copy was history …."[90] That is, Seidensticker is forced to acknowledge the reliability of the New Testament text as we have it today and can only try to deny what it says. He also tells us of the New Testament, "Compare that with 2000 copies of the Iliad, the second-best represented manuscript."[91] Of those 2,000 copies of the Iliad, how far removed are they from the alleged originals? The Iliad is dated to about 1260–1180 B.C.E. The most notable Iliad manuscripts are from the 9th, 10th, and 11th centuries C.E. That would make these manuscripts over 2,000 years removed from their original.

---

[89] The numbers in this paragraph are rounded for simplicity purposes.
[90] 25,000 New Testament Manuscripts? Big Deal. – Patheos, http://www.patheos.com/blogs/crossexamined/2013/11/25000-new-testament-manuscrip (Retrieved Monday, August 10, 2020).
[91] Ibid

The Range of Textual Criticism

The Importance and scope of New Testament textual criticism could be summed up in the few words used by J. Harold Greenlee; it is "the basic biblical study, a prerequisite to all other biblical and theological work. Interpretation, systemization, and application of the teachings of the NT cannot be done until textual criticism has done at least some of its work. It is, therefore, deserving of the acquaintance and attention of every serious student of the Bible."[92]

It is only reasonable to assume that the Old Testament's original 39 books and the 27 books written first-hand by the New Testament authors have not survived. Instead, we only have what we must consider being imperfect copies. **Why the Holy Spirit would miraculously inspire 66 fully inerrant texts and then allow human imperfection into the copies.** This is not explained for us in Scripture. We do know that imperfect humans have tended to worship relics where traditions hold to have been touched by the miraculous powers of God or to have been in direct contact with one of his special servants of old. Ultimately, though, all we know is that God had his reasons for allowing the Old and New Testament autographs to be worn out by repeated use. From time to time, we hear of the discovery of a fragment possibly dated to the first century, but even if such a fragment is eventually verified, the dating alone can never serve as proof of an autograph; it will still be a copy in all likelihood.

Pondering: If we ask why didn't God inspire copyists, then it will have to follow, why didn't God inspire translators, why didn't God inspire Bible scholars that author commentaries on the Bible, and so on? Suppose God's initial purpose was to give us a fully inerrant, authoritative, authentic and accurate Word. Why not adequately protect the Scriptures in all facets of transmission from error: copy, translate, and interpret? If God did this, and people were moved along by the Holy Spirit, it would soon become noticeable that when people copy the texts, they would be unable to make an error or mistake or even willfully change something.

Where would it stop? Would this being moved along by the Holy Spirit apply to anyone who decided to make themselves a copy, testing to see if they too would be inspired? In time, this would prove to be actual evidence for God. This would negate the reasons why God has allowed sin, human imperfection to enter into humanity in the first place, to teach them an **object**

---

[92] J. Harold Greenlee, Introduction to New Testament Textual Criticism (Grand Rapids, MI: Baker Academic, 1995), 8-9.

THE EARLY CHRISTIAN COPYISTS OF THE NEW TESTAMENT

lesson, man cannot walk on his own without his Creator. God created perfect humans, giving them a perfect start, and through the abuse of free will, they rejected his sovereignty. He did not just keep creating perfect humans again and again, as though he got something wrong. God gave us his perfect Word and has again chosen to allow us to continue in our human imperfection, learning our **object lesson**. God has stepped into humanity many hundreds of times in the Bible record, maybe tens of thousands of times unbeknownst to us over the past 6,000+ years, to tweak things to get the desired outcome of his will and purposes. However, there is no aspect of life where his stepping in for any particular point was to be continuous until the return of the Son. Maybe God gave us a perfect copy of sixty-six books. Then like everything else, he placed the responsibility of copying, translating, and interpreting on us, just as he gave us the Great Commission of proclaiming that Word, explaining that Word, to make disciples. – Matthew 24:14;28-19-20; Acts 1:8.

Reflecting: Some Bible critics seem, to begin with, the belief that if God inspired the originals and fully inerrant, the subsequent copies must continue to be inerrant for the inerrancy of the originals to have value. They seem to be asking, "If only the originals were inspired, and the copies were not inspired, and we do not have the originals, how are we to be certain of any passage in Scripture?" In other words, God would never allow the inspired, inerrant Word to suffer copying errors. Why would he perform the miracle of inspiring the message to be fully inerrant and not continue with the miracle of inspiring the copyists throughout the centuries to keep it inerrant? First, we must acknowledge that God has not given us the specifics of every decision he has made about humans. If we begin asking, "Why did God not do this or do that," where would it end? For example, why didn't God just produce the books himself and miraculously deliver them to people as he gave the commandments to Moses? Why not use angelic messengers to pen the message or produce the message miraculously instead of using humans? God has chosen not to tell us why he did not move the copyists along by the Holy Spirit to have perfect copies, and it remains an unknown. However, I would note that if we can restore the text to its original wording through the art and science of textual criticism, i.e., to an exact representation thereof, we have, in essence, the originals. This is the preservation of Scripture through the restoration of Scripture.

As for errors in all the copies that we have, however, we can say that the vast majority of the Greek text is not affected by errors. The errors occur in variant readings, i.e., portions of the text where different manuscripts disagree. Of the **small amount** of the text affected by variant readings, the vast majority of these are minor slips of the pen, misspelled words, etc., or intentional but quickly analyzed changes, and we are certain what the original reading is in these places. A **far smaller number** of changes present challenges to establishing the original reading. It has always been said and remains true that no central doctrine is affected by a textual problem. Only rarely does a textual issue change the meaning of a verse.[93] Still, establishing the original text wherever there are variant readings is vitally important. Every word matters!

It is true that the Jewish copyists and the later Christian copyists were not led along by the Holy Spirit, and therefore their manuscripts were not inerrant, infallible. Errors (textual variants) crept into the documents unintentionally and intentionally. However, the vast majority of the Hebrew Old Testament and Greek New Testament has not been infected with textual errors. The portions impacted by textual errors are the many tens of thousands of copies that we have to help us weed out the errors. How? Well, not every copyist made the same textual errors. Hence, by comparing the work of different copyists and manuscripts, textual scholars can identify the textual variants (errors) and remove those, leaving us with the original content.

Yes, it would be the most significant discovery of all time if we found the original five books penned by Moses himself, Genesis through Deuteronomy, or the original Gospels of Matthew, Mark, Luke, and John. However, first, there would be no way of establishing that they were the originals. Second, we do not need the originals. Third, we do not need those original documents. What is so important about the documents? It is the content on the original documents that we are after. And truly, miraculously, we have more copies than needed to do just that. We do not need miraculous preservation because we have miraculous restoration. We now know beyond a reasonable doubt that the Hebrew Old Testament and the Greek New Testament critical texts are a 99.99% reflection of the content in those ancient original manuscripts.

---

[93] Leading textual scholar Daniel Wallace tells us, after looking at all of the evidence, that the percentage of instances where the reading is uncertain and a well-attested alternative reading could change the meaning of the verse is a quarter of one percent, i.e., 0.0025%

How did God inspire the Bible Authors? How Were They Moved Along by the Holy Spirit? How Did Jesus Bring Remembrance to the Apostles?

Biblical inspiration is the quality or state of being moved along or by or under the Holy Spirit's direction from God.

2 Timothy 3:16 Updated American Standard Version (UASV)

16 All Scripture is **inspired by** God and profitable for teaching, for reproof, for correction, for training in righteousness;

2 Peter 1:21 Updated American Standard Version (UASV)

21 for no prophecy was ever produced by the will of man, but men **carried along by** the Holy Spirit spoke from God.

John 14:26 Updated American Standard Version (UASV)

26 But the Helper,[94] the Holy Spirit, whom the Father will send in my name, that one will teach you all things and **bring to your remembrance** all that I have said to you.

How Were the Bible Authors Inspired by God, That Is, Given Divine Direction?

Inspired By θεόπνευστος (theopneustos)

The Greek phrase "inspired by God" translates the compound Greek word θεόπνευστος (theopneustos), which literally means, literally, "God-breathed" or "breathed by God." The Greek phrase here needs to be nuanced so at not to be less than what was meant or go beyond what was meant. The Bible author was under God's influence, to the extent that he was guided or directed by God but not to the extent of dictation. To a lesser extent, Christians are guided by the inspired Word of God if they have an accurate understanding and apply it correctly in their lives. The Bible author was allowed to convey God's Word within their own writing style but would be controlled or guided to the point that he would not choose words, phrases, sentences that would miscommunicate the wrong message.

Carried Along By φερόμενοι (pheromenoi)

---

[94] Or, *Advocate*. Or, *Comforter*. Gr., *ho ... parakletos,* masc.

The Greek word φερόμενοι (pheromenoi) literally means to **cause** the Bible author to be carried along or moved along by the Holy Spirit. It means to guide, direct, lead.

Bring to Remembrance ὑπομνήσει (hupomnēsei)

The Greek word ὑπομνήσει (*hupomnēsei*) literally means to God put in the mind of the Gospel authors. God **caused** the Gospel authors (Matthew and John, Mark by way of Peter, Luke by Peter, research, and others) to recall in detail what they had formerly experienced.

The apostle Paul says that God spoke "in many ways" to his servants in Old Testament times before Christ coming. (Heb 1:1-2) The Ten Commandments were divinely provided in written form. Scribes, thereafter, would have had to merely copy it into the scrolls used by Moses. (Ex. 31:18; Deut. 10:1-5) In some very special cases, the words put into Scripture by a Bible author inspired by God, moved along by the Holy Spirit, would have been transmitted by verbal dictation, literally word for word. This would have likely been the case in situations such as the Mosaic Law given to Israel. Jehovah commanded Moses: "**Write these words**, for in accordance with these words I have made a covenant with you and with Israel." (Ex 34:27) The prophets who would author Bible books were also frequently given precise messages from God that they were to deliver, and then God put these same words in the mind of the prophetic authors. God **caused** the prophet (Isaiah, Jeremiah, Ezekiel, Daniel, and others) to recall in detail what they had formerly delivered to others, now becoming Scriptures. – 1 Kings 22:14; Jeremiah 1:7; 2:1; 11:1-5; Ezekiel 3:4; 11:5.

There are other ways that the Bible authors, such as dreams and visions. We are told, "Then the mystery was revealed to Daniel in a **vision of the night**. Then Daniel blessed the God of heaven." (Dan. 2:19) "In the first year of Belshazzar king of Babylon, Daniel saw a **dream and visions** of his head as he lay in his bed. Then he wrote down the dream and told the sum of the matter." (Dan. 7:1) Readers might not know that Bible authors were more often given visions while they were awake, fully conscious, giving the author the thoughts of God directly to his mind. "In the thirtieth year, in the fourth month, on the fifth day of the month, as I was among the exiles by the Chebar canal, the heavens were opened, and **I saw visions** of God." (Eze 1:1) "In the third year of the reign of King Belshazzar **a vision appeared to me**, Daniel, after that which appeared to me at the first." (Dan. 8:1) "And this is how I saw the horses in **my vision** and those who rode them: they wore breastplates the color of fire and of sapphire and of sulfur, and the heads of the horses were like lions' heads, and fire and smoke and sulfur came out of their mouths." (Rev. 9:17) Other visions were given to the Bible author when he was in a trance. Even though the author was clearly awake and conscious, he was extremely, deeply absorbed by what he saw, blocking out all else around him. – Ac 10:9-17; 11:5-10; 22:17-21.

Another way Bible authors received the Word of God was through angelic messengers. "For if the word spoken through angels proved reliably certain, and every transgression and disobedience received a just penalty." (Heb 2:2) "You who received the law as delivered **by angels** and did not keep it." (Ac 7:53) "Why, then, the Law? It was added because of transgressions, until the seed should arrive to whom the promise had been made; and it was **transmitted through angels** by the hand of a mediator." (Gal. 3:19) The angelic representatives spoke in God's name. Therefore, the message they delivered could therefore correctly be called "the word of Jehovah." – Gen 22:11-12, 15-18; Zech. 1:7, 9.

Regardless of how the Bible author received the Word of God, be it, dictation, God directly putting words in the minds of the author, perfect recall, dreams, visions, angelic representatives, being led along by the Holy Spirit, it was all inspired by God or "God-breathed."

Authors Evidenced Individuality That Is Still Compatible with the Bible's Being Inspired by God

The Bible authors were not merely robots who put down dictated words, literally word for word. "The revelation of Jesus Christ, which God gave him to show to his servants the things that must soon take place. He made it known by sending his angel to his servant John, who bore witness to the word of God and to the testimony of Jesus Christ, even to all that he saw." (Rev. 1:1-2) The "God-breathed" revelation was given to him through an angel, which John then conveyed in his own words. Like many things, God allowed humans to use their God's given minds, and in the case of His Word, in choosing words and expressions (Hab. 2:2), he allowed them to use their own style, but he always maintained adequate control and guided them so that the Bible book would be accurate and true. In addition, it would also be according to God's will and purposes. (Prov. 30:5-6) This concept is even conveyed in Scripture itself. "Besides being wise, the Preacher also taught the people knowledge, weighing and studying and arranging many proverbs with great care. The Preacher sought to find words of delight, and uprightly he wrote words of truth." – See also Lu 1:1-4.

This is why every Bible commentary volume explains to its reader the style of that particular author and the background of the individual author. The ones chosen to be Bible authors were not only qualified to do so but had qualities and characteristics that moved God to choose them. In some cases, God likely got them ready before having to serve this particular purpose of being a Bible author. Matthew was a tax collector before being chosen as a disciple, so we note that he makes many particular references to numbers and money amounts. (Matt. 17:27; 26:15; 27:3) On the other hand, Luke was a "physician" (Col 4:14), so we find him using unique expressions that show that he had a medical background. – Lu 4:38; 5:12; 16:20.

In many cases where the Bible speaks about the Bible author receiving "the word of Jehovah" (UASV) or things that were said, it is likely that this was given, not word for word, but rather the author was given an image in his mind of God's purpose. After that, the author would put it in his own words. This can be inferred by the author's sating he 'saw' things rather than his 'hearing' what God said or "the word of Jehovah." – Isaiah 13:1; Micah 1:1; Habakkuk 1:1; 2:1-2.

The authors of God's Word express it that "God has given me the tongue of those who are taught, that I may know how to sustain with a word him who is weary. Morning by morning he awakens; he awakens my ear to hear as those who are taught. Jehovah God has opened my ear, and I was not rebellious; I turned not backward." (Isa 50:4-5) These authors were ready and submissive to being guided by God. Isaiah was eager to do God's will and sought to be led. "My soul yearns for you in the night; my spirit within me earnestly seeks you. For when your judgments are in the earth, the inhabitants of the world learn righteousness." (Isa 26:9) In the case of Luke, he had specific objectives that he sought to carry out. (Lu 1:1-4) In many cases, Paul was writing to fill a need. (1 Cor. 1:10-11; 5:1; 7:1) God guided these authors so that their words in their style went along with his purpose. (Prov. 16:9) These men were chosen because their hearts and minds were already in harmony with God's will and purposes. In fact, they already 'had the mind of Christ.' They were not interested in human wisdom nor in "speak[ing] visions of their own minds," as was the case with the false prophets, "who follow their own spirit." – 1 Corinthians 2:13-16; Jeremiah 23:16; Eze 13:2-3, 17.

As to the being led along by the Holy Spirit, "there are varieties of activities" that would come upon these Bible authors. (1 Cor 12:6) Much information was already at the fingertips of the authors. In other words, it already existed in manuscript evidence, such as genealogies and specific historical accounts. (Lu 1:3; 3:23-38; Num. 21:14, 15; 1 Kings 14:19, 29; 2 Kings 15:31; 24:5) In the case of using historical records, the Holy Spirit would serve as a protection against inaccurate information being part of the Bible author's book. Not everything said by other persons that would end up in the Word of God was inspired by God, but the Holy Spirit guided the author to make it part of the Scriptures and record it accurately. (Gen. 3:4-5; Job 42:3; Matt. 16:21-23) We end up with clear evidence of why it is good to heed God's Word and apply it correctly in our lives. Doing or saying what we think, feel, or believe, ignoring God's Word, or being ignorant of God and his message leads to much heartache.

Then, again, there is information in the Bible that is far beyond human abilities to acquire. We can consider what happened before the creation of the heavens and the earth, as well as man. (Gen. 1:1-26) Humans are also oblivious to what happens in the spiritual heavens as well. (Job 1:6-12, etc.) Then, we have prophecies that foretell events that are to take place decades, centuries, or millenniums after the prophets penned them. We also have revelations as to what God's will and purposes are for humanity. When we think of Solomon's wise sayings, he certainly had much life experience to share. Others had vast knowledge of the Scriptures themselves, not to mention their experience at living by God's Word. They still needed to be moved along by the Holy Spirit, so that the information that they conveyed would be "living and active and sharper than any two-edged sword and piercing as far as the division of soul and spirit, of both joints and marrow, and able to judge the thoughts and intentions of the heart." – Hebrews 4:12.

There are times that Paul said things that were not taken from anything that Jesus had taught. "To the rest, I say (**I, not the Lord**) that if any brother has a wife who is an unbeliever, and she consents to live with him, he should not divorce her." (1 Corinthians 7:12-15) The first thing to notice is Paul saying, God inspires me, so I can say this and the Lord (Jesus), did not touch on this, but I am. Let us take a look at the context and historical setting. Paul says, "Now concerning virgins I do not have a command from the Lord, but I am giving an opinion as one shown mercy by the Lord to be trustworthy." (1 Cor. 7:25) "But in my opinion she is happier if she remains as she is, and I think that I too have the Spirit of God." (1 Cor. 7:40) Paul's point is clear; he, too, is inspired and moved along by the Holy Spirit. Paul's direction was "God-breathed" and so was Scripture, having the same authority as the rest of those Scriptures. – 2 Peter 3:15-16.

CHAPTER 4 The Production of New Testament Manuscripts

In the ancient world, the concept of publication vastly differed from today's understanding, encompassing both oral and written dissemination of information. This dual approach was crucial, as many individuals could not read and relied heavily on oral traditions for receiving and transmitting knowledge. However, literacy in early Christianity was not that simple.

Understanding Literacy in the Early Roman Empire

The task of defining literacy during the first three centuries of Christianity in the ancient Roman Empire and measuring the populace's literacy level is a daunting one. To aid this process, literacy can be broken down into several categories, each representing a different level of literacy.

Complete Illiteracy: Individuals at this level lack reading, writing, and basic math skills and are unable to sign their names. Their employment is typically limited to manual labor such as fruit and vegetable picking, material handling, farming, or working in large workshops producing common items like dishes or pots. Household slaves would also fall into this category.

THE EARLY CHRISTIAN COPYISTS OF THE NEW TESTAMENT

Partial Literacy: This level includes a rudimentary understanding of spoken and written words and basic math skills, enough for buying goods in the marketplace. These individuals can sign their names and are employed in manual labor positions in the marketplace, as shop assistants performing manual labor, or as soldiers.

Basic Literacy: Here, individuals have a basic understanding of spoken and written words, basic math skills, and the ability to read and write simple words. Their employment could include craftsman, marketplace worker, or soldier.

Functional Literacy: This level includes a competent understanding of spoken words, a beginner to intermediate level understanding of written words, and the ability to prepare basic documents. Individuals in this category can read and write simple sentences and are eligible for jobs such as copyists or scribes.

Advanced Literacy: At this level, individuals have a high skill level in understanding spoken words and an intermediate to advanced understanding of written words. They can prepare short texts and are trained in writing, making them eligible for jobs such as copyists, scribes, tax collectors, or clerks.

Full Literacy: This is the highest level of literacy, with individuals possessing an advanced understanding of spoken and written words. These people can prepare long texts and are professionally trained in writing. They are eligible for high-ranking positions such as copyists, scribes, tax collectors, teachers, lawyers, or clerks to senators.

The Roman Empire, much like modern-day New York City with its five boroughs, was a culturally and ethnically diverse society. Literacy levels varied widely based on factors like location and cultural background. For instance, the literacy requirements in Nazareth would not have been the same as in Rome. Similarly, the value placed on literacy would have varied, with pagans likely placing less importance on it than Jews or Christians.

Contrary to the longstanding historical belief that literacy in the ancient Roman Empire was limited to 10-20 percent of the population, evidence suggests that literacy at all levels was more widespread. The Roman Empire was overflowing with documents of different literary genres, indicating a range of literacies. The literacy level was influenced by factors such as social status, production methods, material used for writing, publication and circulation, languages, types of text, and the people who used them.[95]

Poets like Homer and philosophers such as Socrates primarily published their works through oral means, with their teachings and stories later being transcribed by followers. Similarly, Jesus Christ, a profound teacher and prophet, utilized oral publication to spread his teachings. His method of conveying the good news was through direct, oral communication, often employing parables and poetic forms to facilitate memorization among his listeners. This approach was not only strategic given the context of literacy in his time but also deeply rooted in the cultural practices of oral tradition.

The disciples of Jesus, following his example and direction, continued this practice of oral publication after his death and resurrection. The concept of kerygma, or proclamation, was central to their efforts, echoing the practices of ancient heralds who announced the decrees of kings to the people. The New Testament disciples saw themselves in a similar light, tasked with spreading the message of Jesus' teachings, death, resurrection, and the promise of salvation. Initially, this proclamation was predominantly oral, reflecting the widespread reliance on spoken communication in the ancient world.

Paul, among other disciples, played a pivotal role in this process, identifying himself as both a herald and an apostle tasked with disseminating the core Christian message. The transition from oral to written publication was gradual, driven by the need to reach a wider audience and preserve the teachings accurately for future generations. Written texts began to play a crucial role, complementing oral traditions by providing a tangible and enduring medium through which the teachings of Jesus and his apostles could be accessed and disseminated.

The Gospels and the letters of the apostles in the New Testament serve as primary examples of this transition. These texts were intended not only to document the teachings and events of Jesus' life but also to support the ongoing oral proclamation of his message. The written word, in this context, was a tool for ensuring the accuracy and integrity of the Christian message as it was taught and spread across different communities.

The apostle Paul, in particular, expanded his publishing efforts through the writing of epistles, which were circulated among early Christian

---

[95] *THE READING CULTURE OF EARLY CHRISTIANITY: The Production, Publication, Circulation, and Use of Books in the Early Christian Church* (2019) by Edward D. Andrews.

THE EARLY CHRISTIAN COPYISTS OF THE NEW TESTAMENT

communities. These letters addressed theological issues, offered guidance, and reinforced the core messages of Christianity, serving as a written extension of the oral tradition. Other apostles, including Peter and John, also contributed to the written corpus of Christian teachings, further solidifying the foundation of Christian doctrine and practice.

This blend of oral and written publication was pivotal in the early Christian church, ensuring that the teachings of Jesus and his immediate followers were preserved and circulated effectively. Without the written records, the teachings could have been subject to alteration and distortion over time. The New Testament documents, therefore, play a critical role in maintaining the authenticity and continuity of the Christian message through the ages. The early church's publishing efforts, both oral and written, were instrumental in shaping the development and spread of Christianity, providing a model of dissemination that ensured the teachings of Jesus would reach and resonate with successive generations.

Exploring the Preservation and Restoration of Scripture: A Response to Skepticism

Dr. Bart D. Ehrman, an agnostic scholar, questions why, if God miraculously inspired the Bible, He did not also miraculously preserve it without errors in its copies. He suggests that the lack of perfect preservation undermines the idea of divine inspiration. Dr. Dirk Jongkind[96] counters this by stating that while God didn't provide exhaustive knowledge of every textual detail, He ensured we have abundant access to His words, emphasizing that divine inspiration doesn't obligate God to preserve every detail for us.

The question of why God didn't inspire copyists to produce error-free manuscripts is a complex one. It's important to recognize that not all questions will have complete answers until the second coming of Christ. Some individuals, due to hardened hearts or skepticism, may not be open to any answers, displaying attitudes reminiscent of the Pharisees. It's crucial to discern these attitudes quickly to avoid fruitless debates.

Understanding the significance of Old and New Testament textual studies is vital for Christian Bible students. These studies form the foundation for accurately translating and interpreting Scripture. The New Testament, in particular, is well-documented, with over 5,898 Greek

---

[96] An Introduction to the Greek New Testament, Produced at Tyndale House, Cambridge, Crossway.

manuscripts, 10,000 Latin manuscripts, and 9,300 manuscripts in other languages, providing a rich textual history unparalleled by any other ancient work. This abundance of manuscripts, some dating back to within decades of the originals, offers a solid basis for establishing the New Testament's text with reasonable certainty.

The preservation and restoration of Scripture, despite the presence of textual variants that have now been restored to the original reading of the original texts, does not undermine its divine inspiration or authority. The meticulous care in manuscript transmission and the wealth of textual evidence available today testify to the reliability of the biblical text. This understanding helps us appreciate the depth and complexity of God's word, fostering a more profound faith and confidence in its message.

The Original Texts

In the ancient world, the process of "publishing" writings, including those that now make up the New Testament, shared similarities with modern publication practices, albeit on a much smaller scale and with significant differences in technology and dissemination methods. To grasp the early stages of the New Testament text's development, it's instructive to consider this process within the context of ancient literary culture.

The original writings or "autographs" of the New Testament were composed by their authors using the available means of writing, which could include pen and ink on papyrus or parchment. These autographs are what the authors initially produced, whether written by their own hand or dictated to an amanuensis (scribe), a secretary who would transcribe the spoken word. For example, the Apostles Paul and Peter are known to have used amanuenses for some of his letters, with Tertius being named in the epistle to the Romans (Rom. 16:22) and Silvanus (Silas) to the first letter of Peter (1 Pet. 5:12).

The process from autograph to published text in the ancient world involved several stages, akin to drafting, revising, and finalizing a text in modern terms. After composing the initial text, authors or their collaborators might revise the work to refine its content or to adapt it for a broader audience. Many scholars today would argue that this is evident in the New Testament writings. The question must be asked, 'how does one edit the Holy Spirit?' 'If the author was moved along by the Holy Spirit and all original Scripture is inspired, why the need for editing?' What we can say with certainty is that the personal involvement of the author in reviewing and authorizing the text was crucial for its authenticity and integrity. Before addressing these questions, let's define a couple of the important terms first.

The term "amanuensis" is derived from Latin and refers to a scribe or clerk. In the field of textual criticism, this term takes on a more specific role, referring to a person who served as a secretary to document the firsthand words of a New Testament book. This would occur if the author opted to use a secretary rather than writing the words themselves. Tertius, mentioned in Romans 16:22, serves as an example. The extent to which an amanuensis contributed to the content of any given book is a topic of debate and speculation. At one end, we have the amanuensis who strictly took dictation. Conversely, it's possible that a New Testament author gave his amanuensis a general idea of what he wanted to communicate, leaving the actual composition of the book to the amanuensis.

The term "autograph" refers to the text that a New Testament author wrote themselves or was written by a scribe under the author's dictation. If the scribe was taking dictation (as mentioned in Romans 16:22 and 1 Peter 5:12), they may have used shorthand. Regardless of shorthand or longhand, we can presume that both the scribe and the author would review the scribe's work. The author would have the final say over any corrections, given that the Holy Spirit did not guide the scribe. If the inspired author wrote everything himself under the movement of the Spirit, the final product would be the autograph. This text is also often referred to as the original, leading to interchangeable usage of "autograph" and "original." At times, textual critics prefer to distinguish, using "original" to refer to the text correctly attributed to a biblical author. This distinction is less strict, not focusing on the process by which a book or letter was written.

Understanding the Process of New Testament Transcription

As was mentioned, Tertius is the scribe that Paul employed to write his letter to the Romans. It's unreasonable to believe that all of Paul's companions were skilled readers and writers. Nevertheless, it is logical to deduce that Paul would delegate responsibilities to companions who were capable of carrying and reading letters, and who understood the situation of the people or congregation to which they were sent. At the very least, these individuals would have been proficient readers. Moreover, the scribes whom Paul used, like Tertius, were likely semi-professional or professional scribes. It would be impractical to delegate the critical task of recording a significant text like the book of Romans to an unskilled scribe. So, what qualifications would Tertius need to transcribe the Book of Romans?

An average colleague of Paul's would likely have been a proficient reader but probably had limited writing skills. Paul would have chosen companions whose abilities enabled them to fulfill their roles effectively. Tertius would have been an exception, most likely a professional scribe. His skills would have included binding sheets into a roll or stitching pages into a codex, concocting an appropriate mixture of soot and gum to create ink, and using a knife to craft his own reed pen. A professional scribe would also draw lines on the paper, often pricking small holes down each side and using a straight edge and a lead disk to create evenly spaced lines across the sheet. If Tertius did not have training as a document copyist, he might have made minor errors because his focus would have been on the meaning of what he was writing, rather than the exact words, a common trait of the unconscious mind.

Some textual scholars argue that textual criticism acknowledges that even original authors may have revised their work and that these works may have gone through several editions. They also suggest that when referring to the "original text," they mean the 'published' text, i.e., the text in its final edited form as it was disseminated in the Christian community.

Others may swing to the opposite extreme, unrealistically asserting, "We believe that the New Testament authors themselves wrote or dictated a one-time, single, and only version of their texts, unedited and uncorrected under the inspiration of the Holy Spirit."

The Role of Amanuenses in Scripture Writing

When considering the composition of the book of Romans, it's insightful to reflect on Paul's method of dictating his letter to Tertius. Given Tertius was not divinely inspired and being human, prone to error, the question arises: Could he transcribe Paul's words flawlessly over 7,000 words without error? This leads us to ponder whether the involvement of human imperfection, such as Paul correcting a scribal mistake, diminishes the role of the Holy Spirit in the inspiration process. This contemplation does not necessarily lead to a slippery slope but invites a deeper understanding of the divine-human cooperation in Scripture's composition. As Peter instructs in 1 Peter 3:15, we must be prepared to address these queries, suggesting a nuanced perspective on the inspired text's transmission.

THE EARLY CHRISTIAN COPYISTS OF THE NEW TESTAMENT

Clarifying Paul's Editorial Oversight

It's reasonable to consider that Paul, overseeing Tertius's transcription, might correct or clarify the text as needed without altering the original message inspired by the Holy Spirit. The process likely involved Paul dictating, with Tertius either directly transcribing or possibly using ancient shorthand methods, followed by a joint review for accuracy. This collaboration ensures the final document, though corrected as necessary, remained a faithful single record of Paul's inspired message.

Tertius's Transcription Methods

Robert H. Mounce[97] sheds light on the possible approaches Tertius might have employed in transcribing Romans. The spectrum ranges from direct longhand transcription to a more autonomous formulation of Paul's dictated ideas. While direct transcription might seem daunting, it wasn't beyond the realm of possibility, considering the skill level of a professional scribe like Tertius. The potential use of ancient shorthand (tachygraphy) could have facilitated an accurate initial capture of Paul's words, subsequently transcribed into longhand for review. This process mirrors modern court reporting, suggesting that ancient shorthand might possess the capability to accurately record speech, including its nuances and interruptions.

The Integrity of Scriptural Authorship

Mounce's speculation about Tertius's independence in formulating the letter diverges from the traditional view of scriptural authorship. The primary authors of the New Testament, such as Matthew, Mark, Luke, John, Peter, Jude, James, and Paul, were chosen by God to convey His message, not their scribes like Tertius or Silvanus. This distinction underscores that the divine message was dictated by the authors, inspired by the Holy Spirit, and not crafted by the scribes' discretion. The exact method of transcription, whether shorthand or longhand, remains uncertain. However, it is clear that the scribes' role was to faithfully record the inspired words of the biblical authors, ensuring the integrity of the divine message transmitted through Scripture.

---

[97] Robert H. Mounce, *Romans*, vol. 27, The New American Commentary (Nashville: Broadman & Holman Publishers, 1995), 22.

The Nature of Biblical Inspiration

The concept of inspiration in the Bible is unique and multifaceted. While the process of verbal plenary inspiration affirms that every word in Scripture is God-breathed, it's important to understand that the Almighty did not typically dictate the Scriptures word-for-word as if the authors were mere recording devices. The Apostle Paul, for instance, highlights that God communicated with His servants in various ways before the coming of Christ (Hebrews 1:1-2). A notable exception is the Ten Commandments, where God directly provided the content in written form, facilitating Moses's task of transcribing these commandments onto scrolls (Exodus 31:18; Deuteronomy 10:1-5). In other instances, divine messages were delivered verbally for the prophets to record, contributing to the inerrant and inspired Scriptures we have today (1 Kings 22:14; Jeremiah 1:7, 2:1, 11:1-5; Ezekiel 3:4, 11:5).

Paul's Role in the Transcription Process

Paul's personal signature at the end of his letters, as mentioned in 2 Thessalonians 3:17, served as his seal of approval, akin to a supervisor signing off on a letter drafted by a secretary. This practice implies that Paul meticulously reviewed each letter, making corrections as necessary, which suggests that the scribe, or amanuensis, wasn't inspired in the same way Paul was. If the scribe had been inspired, there would have been no need for such revisions. This detail underscores the dynamic partnership between Paul and his scribes, such as Tertius, who were not just professional assistants but also fellow laborers in the ministry.

The Distinction between Author and Scribe

The relationship between biblical authors and their scribes was marked by a clear division of roles. While the scribes played a critical role in the physical writing process, the inspiration and content came exclusively from the authors themselves, guided by the Holy Spirit. This arrangement ensured that the Scriptures remained free of human error in their original autographs, reflecting the true word of God as intended. Instances of direct divine dictation, such as the laws given to Moses or messages entrusted to the prophets, highlight the varied means by which God communicated His will to His people.

Concluding Thoughts on Scriptural Integrity

Understanding the distinction between the inspired authors of the Bible and their scribes clarifies the integrity of the scriptural texts. The Holy Spirit inspired figures like Paul to convey God's message, with scribes serving as instrumental in transcribing these revelations. This process, while involving human hands in the transcription, remained under the sovereign oversight of God, ensuring that His word was accurately and faithfully recorded for posterity. The collaborative effort between author and scribe, underpinned by divine inspiration, underscores the profound respect and reverence afforded to the sacred texts, preserving their authenticity and authority throughout generations.

Jeremiah 36:4 Updated American Standard Version (UASV)

⁴ Then Jeremiah called Baruch the son of Neriah, and Baruch wrote on a scroll at the **dictation of Jeremiah** all the words of Jehovah that he had spoken to him. (Bold mine)

The Role of Scribes and Carriers in the Transmission of Scripture

Ensuring the Inerrancy of Scripture

When considering the involvement of scribes like Tertius in the transcription of Paul's letters or Baruch in writing down Jeremiah's prophecies, it's crucial to understand this did not compromise the authority or inerrancy of Scripture. The divine inspiration guiding Paul was conveyed through his dictation, with Tertius acting as a recorder, meticulously capturing Paul's inspired words. Despite the likelihood of minor transcription errors due to the human element and the challenging conditions of writing in ancient times, any such errors were rectified. Paul, under the guidance of the Holy Spirit, would review and correct the text in collaboration with Tertius, ensuring the final manuscript remained faithful to the inspired message.

The Significance of the Carrier

The role of individuals responsible for delivering Paul's epistles, such as Phoebe, extended beyond mere physical transportation. These carriers, selected from among Paul's reliable and capable associates, were entrusted not only with the safekeeping of the letters but also with a deep understanding of their content. Given the interactive nature of Paul's correspondence with early Christian communities, carriers like Phoebe likely had comprehensive briefings from Paul. This preparation enabled them to address any immediate questions or clarify misunderstandings about the letter's contents upon its delivery. This meticulous approach underscores the importance placed on ensuring the intended message was accurately conveyed and understood, highlighting the carriers' integral role in the apostolic ministry.

The process of writing, preserving, and delivering the New Testament scriptures involved a collaborative effort between the inspired apostles, their scribes, and the trusted carriers. This system, underpinned by divine guidance, safeguarded the accuracy and authority of the scriptures as they were transmitted to early Christian communities. The meticulous care taken in every step of this process reflects the profound reverence for the Word of God and the commitment to maintaining its inerrancy and integrity throughout the ages.

From Inspiration to Circulation: The Journey of New Testament Manuscripts

In the development of the New Testament canon, the "published" version of a manuscript represents the authoritative document sanctioned for distribution among the burgeoning Christian congregations. This authorized version, meticulously transcribed by scribes, was paramount for ensuring the teachings' faithful replication across diverse communities. Although apostolic figures like Paul and Peter enlisted the assistance of secretaries for the preliminary drafting, the ultimate responsibility for the message's truthfulness and adherence to divine inspiration rested with the originating apostle or writer, affirming the conviction that these writings were guided by the Holy Spirit.

The journey of early Christian manuscripts from their inception to their adoption by faith communities underscores a meticulous and collaborative effort. The participation of individuals such as Silvanus highlights this collective endeavor, wherein adept contributors played vital roles in the articulation, preservation, and propagation of apostolic doctrines. Despite the scribes' role in the physical act of writing, the scriptural authority and inerrancy were preserved through the apostolic authors' oversight and direct contribution.

As these documents were replicated and shared, early Christian leaders were vigilant in ensuring the fidelity of the circulated texts to the original apostolic testimony. This diligence extended beyond mere transcription to defining the corpus of authoritative scripture for the faith community. The evolution from oral tradition to written scripture marked a crucial phase in early Christianity, facilitating the gospel's preservation and broad dissemination.

The differentiation between the autograph (original document) and the published text is crucial for comprehending the textual heritage of the New Testament. While the autograph denotes the initial composition, the published text is the vetted version prepared for public consumption and teaching, following a meticulous review and endorsement by the author. This vetted version became the template for subsequent transcriptions, executed with varying precision by scribes throughout the Christian domain.

The process leading to the New Testament writings' publication entailed several stages, from the original drafting or dictation to the widespread distribution of texts among Christian assemblies. This procedure was instrumental in safeguarding, authenticating, and disseminating the accounts and teachings of Jesus Christ and his apostles. Through the combined efforts of authors, secretaries, and scribes, Christianity's foundational documents were established, fostering the early Church's expansion and unity.

In the Scribe's Hand – Tracing the Autographs of the New Testament

Handwriting of the Autographs

When considering the original writings of the New Testament, it's important to acknowledge the absence of any surviving autographs or archetypal texts. Despite this, scholarly efforts and analyses of contemporary documents allow us to construct a plausible picture of their characteristics. The autographs, as initially penned texts, would likely display a variety of handwriting styles, reflecting the personal touch of their authors or the scribes employed in their creation. This variance in script would be indicative of the document's origins and the circumstances under which it was written.

Editorial Marks in the Autographs

The process of composing these sacred texts often involved some possible corrections of scribal mistakes by the author, scribe, or both, leading to the presence of editorial marks. These corrections, whether made by the authors themselves or their amanuenses, offer valuable insights into the development of the texts. Such marks could include alterations made directly on the manuscript, providing evidence of the dynamic nature of its creation. The presence of these corrections underscores the meticulous care taken in ensuring the accuracy and integrity of the writings.

Documentary Hands of the First Century

Exploring the broader landscape of first-century manuscripts reveals a spectrum of 'documentary' handwriting styles. These styles, ranging from formal to more casual scripts, offer a window into the diverse means of written communication of the time. By examining extant manuscripts from this period, scholars can gain a deeper understanding of the potential appearance and formatting of the New Testament autographs. This exploration not only enriches our appreciation of the ancient writing culture but also enhances our grasp of the textual history of the New Testament.

Insights from Specific Manuscripts

Certain extant manuscripts from the first century and slightly beyond, such as P. London 2078 and P. Fayum 110, provide concrete examples of the types of handwriting that might resemble those of the New Testament autographs. These documents, characterized by their legible yet swiftly written script, offer a glimpse into the practical aspects of manuscript production. While not polished in the sense of later, more formal publications, these manuscripts embody the authenticity and immediacy of the original writings of the New Testament.

In the absence of the New Testament autographs, the study of contemporary manuscripts and the scrutiny of editorial practices provide invaluable insights into the early Christian textual tradition. Through a careful examination of handwriting styles, correction patterns, and specific first-century documents, scholars can approximate the appearance and characteristics of the original texts. This scholarly endeavor not only deepens our understanding of early Christian writings but also highlights the meticulous care with which these foundational texts were composed and preserved.

Diverse Hands: The Amanuensis and Authorship in New Testament Autographs

The Role of Amanuenses in Ancient Letter Writing

In the ancient world, the practice of using an amanuensis, or a secretary, to draft letters and documents was widespread. This custom allowed authors to dictate their messages, which were then transcribed by skilled scribes. The final touch, typically a signature or a personal note, was often added by the authors themselves, distinguishing their direct involvement in the document. This practice ensured that the document bore the personal mark of the author, reinforcing its authenticity and authority.

Paul's Letters and Signature Authentication

The Apostle Paul's epistles provide clear examples of this ancient practice. In several of his letters, Paul explicitly mentions signing off with his own hand, a method used to authenticate the communication. This personal signature served not only as a mark of authorship but also as a deterrent against forgery and misrepresentation. By writing in his own hand, Paul imbued his letters with a personal touch that signified their importance and his direct involvement in their composition.

Script Variations and Authorial Contributions

In some of Paul's letters, there is evidence that he took up the stylus to write portions of the text himself, particularly towards the end. This transition from the handwriting of the amanuensis to Paul's own script would have been noticeable, potentially in the form of larger or differently styled script. Such changes in handwriting underscore the collaborative nature of ancient letter writing, where the roles of the author and the amanuensis intertwined to produce the final text.

The Final Greetings and Doxologies

The concluding sections of the New Testament letters, including greetings, blessings, and doxologies, likely bear the handwriting of the authors themselves. These sections, personalized by the author's own script, served to reinforce the messages contained within the letters and to provide a direct connection between the author and the recipients. The presence of such personal touches across the New Testament epistles highlights the importance of authorial involvement in the early Christian textual tradition.

John's Gospel and the Question of Multiple Authors

The question of multiple authors within a single text, such as the Gospel of John, arises from observations about stylistic changes or perceived conclusions within the narrative. However, the continuity of style and thematic elements suggests that any additions, such as the final chapter of John's Gospel, were made by the original author. The personal involvement of authors in the composition and revision of their works reflects the dynamic nature of the writing process in the ancient world.

The final chapter of the Gospel of John, chapter 21, has sparked considerable discussion among scholars regarding its authorship. Despite debates, conservative textual scholarship upholds that the style and thematic content of this chapter are consistent with the rest of the Gospel, indicating it was indeed written by John. Here are examples to illustrate this point:

1. **Use of Specific Vocabulary and Phrases**: John's Gospel is known for its unique vocabulary and recurring phrases, which are also present in chapter 21. Terms like "beloved disciple" and the specific way Jesus addresses Peter as "Simon, son of John" (John 21:15-17) mirror the intimate and personal language used throughout the Gospel. The recurrence of these terms and phrases supports the argument that chapter 21 aligns with John's stylistic signatures.

2. **Theological Themes**: The Gospel of John emphasizes themes such as love, discipleship, and the identity of Jesus as the Christ. Chapter 21 continues these themes, particularly through the reinstatement of Peter, where Jesus asks Peter three times if he loves Him, paralleling Peter's three denials. This reinstatement and the emphasis on love and following Jesus (John 21:15-19) are in harmony with the theological motifs threaded throughout the Gospel.

3. **Eyewitness Detail**: John's Gospel frequently includes detailed descriptions and eyewitness accounts, contributing to its vivid narrative style. Chapter 21 maintains this with specific details, such as the number of fish caught (153) and the distance of the boat from the shore (about 100 yards), which underscore the narrative's authenticity and detail orientation characteristic of John's eyewitness testimony.

4. **Narrative Structure and Flow**: The seamless narrative flow from chapter 20 to 21, despite 20:30-31 appearing as a concluding statement, suggests that chapter 21 serves as an epilogue rather than an addendum by another author. The transition from the proclamation of Jesus' purpose in coming to the world to the specific focus on Peter's role among the disciples doesn't disrupt the narrative structure but rather complements it, providing a practical application of the preceding theological insights.

5. **Literary Techniques**: John's use of symbolism and metaphor is evident throughout his Gospel and continues into chapter 21. For example, the miraculous catch of fish symbolizes the apostles' mission to "catch" people in their evangelistic efforts. Similarly, the specific mention of the net not breaking (John 21:11) despite the large catch could symbolize the unity and strength of the church, themes that resonate with John's overarching message.

These examples reflect the stylistic and thematic consistency of John chapter 21 with the rest of the Gospel, supporting the view that it was authored by John. This alignment in vocabulary, thematic content, narrative detail, and literary techniques reinforces the argument for a singular authorship, providing a cohesive and comprehensive conclusion to the Gospel's profound theological exploration.

Understanding the Autographs Through the Lens of Ancient Practices

The examination of handwriting variations and the role of amanuenses in the New Testament autographs offers valuable insights into the practices of ancient authorship and manuscript production. By recognizing the collaborative efforts between authors and their scribes, scholars can better understand the complexities of the textual tradition and the meticulous care taken in preserving the integrity of the Christian message. This exploration into the diverse hands that contributed to the New Testament autographs not only enriches our appreciation of these foundational texts but also underscores the importance of authorial intent and authenticity in the early Christian community.

Introduction to Textual Variations in Epistolary Conclusions

The study of the New Testament's textual history unveils a fascinating journey from the original autographs penned by the apostles and their associates to the manuscripts available today. This exploration often leads scholars to consider the nature of the epistles' conclusions, which, in several instances, appear to have been more concise in their earliest forms. The evidence, drawn from a comparison of early papyri with later manuscripts, suggests a tendency towards the expansion of closing remarks, doxologies, and blessings as the texts were copied and recopied over the centuries.

The Significance of "Amen" in Manuscript Traditions

One intriguing aspect of these textual variations is the use of the word "amen" at the end of epistles. While "amen" is commonly found in later manuscripts, its absence in the earliest documents suggests it may not have been part of the original text. The presence of "amen" in Romans, Galatians, and Jude, where it seems to be genuinely part of the original writing, contrasts with its likely addition in other epistles for liturgical purposes. This pattern indicates that the early Christian community may have adopted "amen" to conclude readings within a worship setting, reflecting the evolving use of these texts in communal practices.

Expansions in Concluding Verses

Further analysis of the epistles' closing verses reveals a pattern of expansion over time. By examining textual variants in passages like Philippians 4:23 and 2 Timothy 4:22, scholars observe how additional words and phrases were incorporated into the text, enriching the blessings and doxologies with more elaborate language. This phenomenon suggests an inclination among scribes to augment the endings of the epistles, perhaps to lend them greater weight or clarity for the benefit of their audiences.

Case Studies: Philemon and 1 Peter

Two notable instances that highlight the likelihood of shorter original endings are found in the epistles of Philemon and 1 Peter. Papyrus P87, a second-century manuscript, concludes Philemon with a succinct "Grace be with you," omitting the more detailed blessing found in later copies. Similarly,

THE EARLY CHRISTIAN COPYISTS OF THE NEW TESTAMENT

Papyrus P72, dating to the third century, ends 1 Peter with a simple exhortation to greet one another, lacking the additional peace wish present in subsequent manuscripts. These examples provide compelling evidence that the autographs of these letters likely featured more concise endings, aligning with the broader trend of textual expansion observed in the New Testament corpus.

The Evolution of Epistolary Endings through Textual Transmission

The pattern of adding to the epistles' conclusions reflects a broader process of textual transmission wherein scribes, intentionally or unintentionally, introduced changes to the documents they copied. These alterations, ranging from minor expansions to the inclusion of liturgical formulas, illustrate the dynamic nature of the New Testament's textual history. As manuscripts were copied for use in different communities and contexts, the additions to the endings of epistles served various purposes, from enhancing the text's liturgical utility to emphasizing the grace and peace bestowed upon the recipients.

Implications for Understanding the Original Autographs

The study of these textual variations not only enriches our understanding of the early Christian manuscripts but also offers insights into the practices and priorities of the communities that preserved and transmitted these texts. By examining the simpler, more streamlined endings of the earliest manuscripts, scholars gain a clearer view of the New Testament epistles' original form. This exploration underscores the importance of textual criticism in uncovering the New Testament's earliest layers, providing a window into the apostolic era and the initial stages of the Christian textual tradition.

The End of Mark's Gospel

Introduction to the Textual Dilemma

The conclusion of the Gospel of Mark presents one of the most intriguing textual puzzles in New Testament scholarship. This discussion revolves around the abrupt ending at Mark 16:8 in the earliest and most authoritative manuscripts, Codex Sinaiticus and Codex Vaticanus, and contrasts with longer endings found in later manuscripts. This variance raises questions about the original conclusion of Mark's narrative and the implications for our understanding of the Gospel's message. This image below shows the end of Mark's Gospel (1) and the beginning of Luke's account (2).

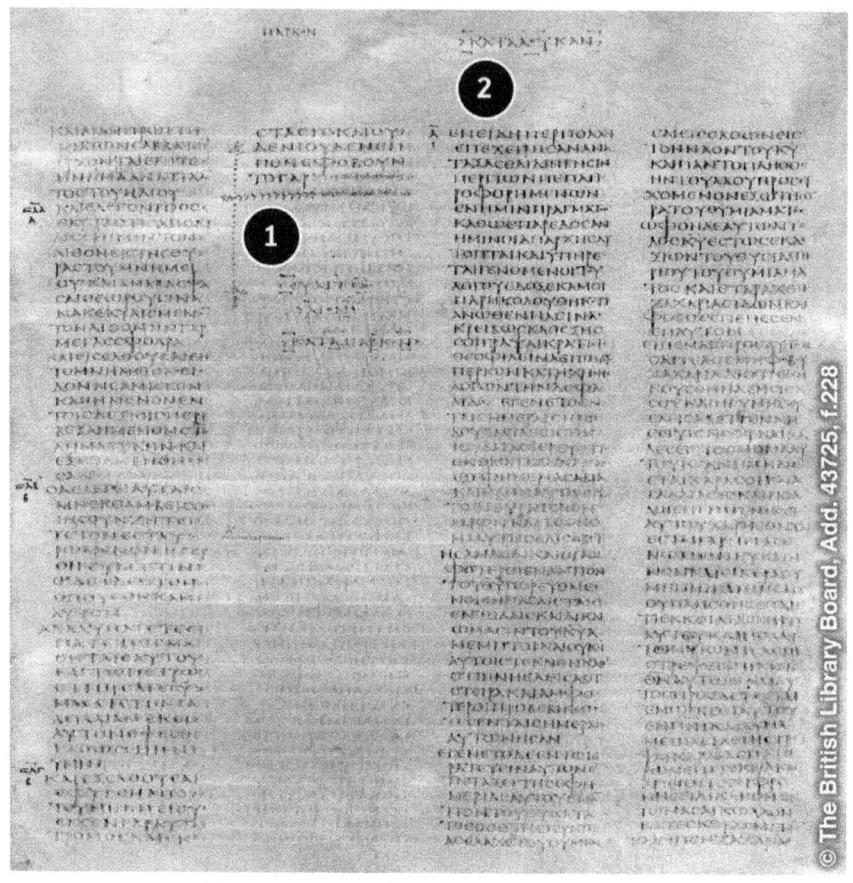

The Evidence from Ancient Manuscripts

Codex Sinaiticus and Codex Vaticanus, both dating to the fourth century C.E., end Mark's Gospel at verse 16:8, where the women flee from the tomb in fear and say nothing to anyone. This conclusion is starkly different from the longer endings present in later manuscripts, such as Codex Alexandrinus and Codex Ephraemi Syri rescriptus from the fifth century, which include up to twelve additional verses. These manuscripts introduce post-resurrection appearances of Jesus and other details not found in the earliest texts.

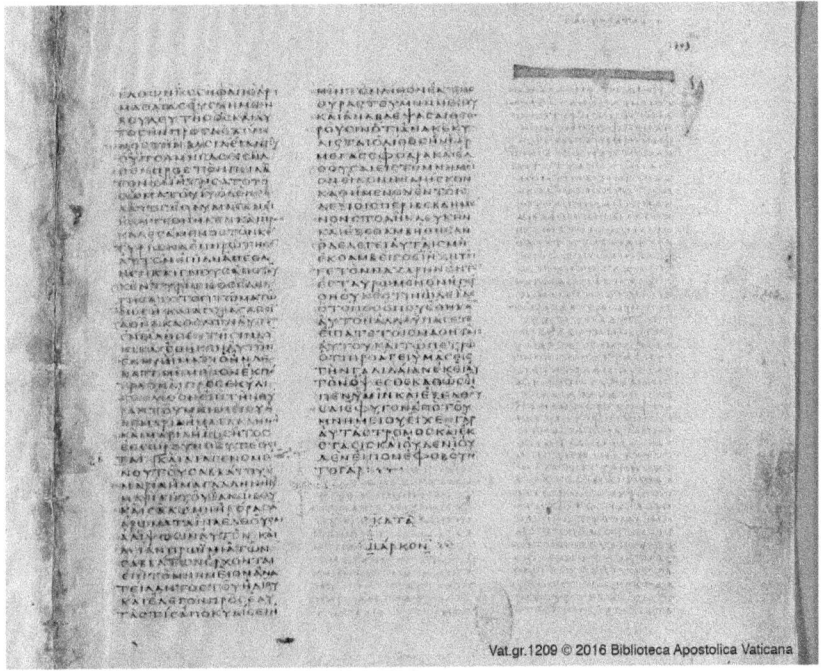

Mark's Writing Style and Historical Assertions

The argument that Mark's Gospel originally ended at verse 16:8 gains credibility when considering Mark's generally concise and straightforward writing style throughout his narrative. Additionally, early church fathers like Jerome and Eusebius affirm that the genuine ending of Mark's Gospel is at verse 8, corroborating the evidence from the earliest manuscripts. This assertion suggests that the abrupt ending, while seemingly incomplete, aligns with Mark's thematic and stylistic choices.

The Long and Short Conclusions

Beyond the earliest manuscripts, the textual tradition of Mark's Gospel includes both a long conclusion and a shorter, more terse ending, found in various manuscripts and translations from the fifth century and later. The long conclusion, which includes appearances of the resurrected Jesus and the commissioning of the disciples, appears in several significant manuscripts and translations, including the Latin Vulgate and the Syriac Peshitta. Conversely, the short conclusion, offering a brief summary post-verse 8, is found in fewer manuscripts, such as the eighth-century Codex Regius, which notably presents both conclusions with annotations regarding their questionable authenticity.

Scholarly Interpretation of the Evidence

The divergent endings of Mark's Gospel have led scholars to consider various theories about its original conclusion. The abrupt ending at verse 16:8 could reflect an intentional choice by Mark to leave the narrative open-ended, inviting the reader to contemplate the implications of the resurrection. Alternatively, some scholars speculate that the original ending may have been lost or that Mark may have intended to write a continuation that was never completed. The presence of longer endings in later manuscripts suggests an early Christian discomfort with the abrupt conclusion, prompting scribes to add to the text to provide a more conventional resolution to the Gospel narrative.

The textual variations at the conclusion of Mark's Gospel illustrate the complex process of textual transmission in the early Christian era and highlight the challenges faced by textual critics in determining the most authentic version of the New Testament texts. While the evidence leans towards Mark 16:8 as the original ending, the existence of longer endings reflects a dynamic and evolving textual tradition. This exploration into the ending of Mark's Gospel not only enriches our understanding of early Christian manuscript practices but also invites deeper reflection on the theological implications of the Gospel's conclusion.

Unveiling the Original Gospels: The Absence of Inscriptions and Subscriptions

The Tradition of Anonymity in Gospel Writing

The Gospels, as foundational texts of Christian faith, were originally penned without any direct attribution to their authors within the text itself. This practice of anonymity aligns with the broader ancient literary tradition, where the focus was more on the message conveyed than on the identity of the messenger. The lack of inscriptions or direct authorial claims in the original Gospel manuscripts underscores this emphasis, positioning the teachings and life of Jesus Christ as the central focus of these writings.

THE EARLY CHRISTIAN COPYISTS OF THE NEW TESTAMENT

The Emergence of Gospel Titles

The titles that have come to be associated with the Gospels—Matthew, Mark, Luke, and John—were not part of the original manuscripts. Instead, they were appended later, likely in the second century C.E., as evidenced by manuscript discoveries dating to the end of the second or early third century. These titles served practical purposes, offering a means of distinguishing and identifying the texts as the Christian canon began to take shape. The term "Gospel" (euaggelion), meaning "good news," was adopted to categorize these unique accounts of Jesus Christ's life and teachings, possibly inspired by the opening words of Mark's account.

The Role of Practicality in Titling

The adoption of titles for the Gospels and other New Testament writings was driven by practical needs within the early Christian communities. As the number of texts circulated among these communities grew, clear identification became essential for the use and transmission of these sacred writings. Titles such as "According to Matthew" or "According to John" provided a straightforward way to reference and discuss the texts, facilitating their integration into worship, teaching, and personal study.

The Case of the Gospel According to Mark

Mark's Gospel, with its opening declaration of "The beginning of the good news about Jesus Christ, the Son of God," may have played a pivotal role in the naming convention for the Gospel accounts. This descriptor not only highlighted the content as good news but also likely influenced the subsequent use of the term "Gospel" to describe these narrative works about Jesus Christ. Such titling reflects both the content's nature and its foundational role in the proclamation of the Christian faith.

Insights from Early Manuscript Evidence

The absence of specific inscriptions or subscriptions in the earliest Gospel manuscripts, such as P66 for John's Gospel, reinforces the notion that the titles were later additions. This practice extends beyond the Gospels to other New Testament writings, including Acts and the Epistles. For instance, the letter to the Ephesians originally circulated without a specific designation to Ephesus, as indicated by the omission of "in Ephesus" in the earliest manuscripts. This flexibility allowed for the letter's broader applicability across various Christian communities.

The Evolution of New Testament Manuscript Titling

Over time, as the New Testament canon was formalized, the addition of titles and subscriptions became a normative practice to facilitate the organization, recognition, and authoritative appeal of these texts. This development was not an attempt to alter the texts' original meaning or authenticity but rather a response to the growing need for clarity and distinction among the burgeoning Christian literature.

The original Gospels and other New Testament writings were crafted with a focus squarely on their spiritual and theological messages, without the authors' names or formal titles. The subsequent addition of titles and specific identifications served the practical and liturgical needs of early Christian communities, ensuring the texts' preservation and proper recognition within the canon. This evolution of manuscript titling reflects the dynamic interplay between the texts' sacred authority and the practical realities of their use and dissemination within the early Church.

Deciphering the Sacred: The Role of Nomina Sacra in Early Christian Manuscripts

Introduction to Nomina Sacra

In the early Christian manuscripts, a distinct scribal practice emerged that set apart certain words as sacred. This practice involved the abbreviation of specific titles and names—such as Kurios (Lord), Christos (Christ), Iesous (Jesus), and Theos (God)—into what are known as nomina sacra. These sacred names were not written in their full form but were instead represented by their initial and final letters, along with a line above to signify their sacred status. This convention is observed consistently in manuscripts dating from the middle of the second century C.E., reflecting a widespread and significant tradition within early Christian copyist practices.

THE EARLY CHRISTIAN COPYISTS OF THE NEW TESTAMENT

The Origin and Significance of Nomina Sacra

The tradition of nomina sacra may draw its origins from Jewish practices of writing the Tetragrammaton, the sacred four-letter name of God (יהוה), which was treated with great reverence. In Greek translations of the Hebrew Scriptures, like the Septuagint, this reverence was continued by substituting the Tetragrammaton with Kyrios or Theos, often in abbreviated forms. Early Christians adopted and adapted this practice, extending it to include key terms central to Christian faith and theology, thereby marking these words as sacred and set apart within the text.

English Meaning	Greek Word	Nominative (Subject)	Genitive (Possessive)
God	Θεός	Θ̄Σ̄	Θ̄Ῡ
Lord	Κύριος	Κ̄Σ̄	Κ̄Ῡ
Jesus	Ἰησοῦς	Ῑ̄Σ̄	Ῑ̄Ῡ
Christ/Messiah	Χριστός	Χ̄Σ̄	Χ̄Ῡ
Son	Υἱός	ῩΣ̄	ῩῩ
Spirit/Ghost	Πνεῦμα	Π̄ΝΑ	Π̄ΝΣ
David	Δαυῒδ	Δ̄ΑΔ̄	
Cross/Stake	Σταυρός	Σ̄Τ̄Σ̄	Σ̄Τ̄Ῡ
Mother	Μήτηρ	Μ̄Η̄Ρ̄	Μ̄Η̄Σ̄
God Bearer i.e. Mother of God	Θεοτόκος	Θ̄Κ̄Σ̄	Θ̄Κ̄Ῡ
Father	Πατήρ	Π̄Η̄Ρ̄	Π̄Ρ̄Σ̄
Israel	Ἰσραήλ	Ῑ̄Η̄Λ̄	
Savior	Σωτήρ	Σ̄Η̄Ρ̄	Σ̄Ρ̄Σ̄
Human being/Man	Ἄνθρωπος	ᾹΝΟΣ	ᾹΝΟΥ
Jerusalem	Ἰερουσαλήμ	Ῑ̄ΛΗΜ	
Heaven/Heavens	Οὐρανός	Ο̄ΥΝΟΣ	Ο̄ΥΝΟΥ

Nomina Sacra in Early Manuscripts

No New Testament manuscript discovered to date, nor any manuscript of the Christian Greek Old Testament, deviates from the practice of representing these divine titles in nomina sacra form. This consistency across manuscripts underscores the importance of nomina sacra in the early Christian textual tradition. It indicates a deliberate and uniform approach to the transcription of sacred names, reflecting the reverence early Christians held for these terms and the concepts they represented.

Theological Implications of Nomina Sacra

The use of nomina sacra had significant theological implications. By abbreviating names and titles such as Kurios, Christos, Iesous, and Theos, early Christian scribes were doing more than saving space on the parchment or papyrus. They were highlighting the divine and sacred nature of these terms, setting them apart from secular language. This practice served to reinforce the centrality of Jesus Christ and God in Christian faith, emphasizing their lordship and divinity in a visually distinctive manner.

The Presence of Nomina Sacra in Autographs

While the original autographs of the New Testament writings have not been preserved, the uniform presence of nomina sacra in all subsequent manuscripts suggests that this practice could have been established by the time the earliest copies were made. Although we cannot definitively say whether the original authors used nomina sacra in their initial compositions, the widespread adoption of this practice by the middle of the second century points to its early and rapid integration into Christian scribal tradition.

The tradition of nomina sacra is a fascinating aspect of early Christian manuscript culture, offering insights into the reverence with which sacred names and titles were treated. This practice not only reflects the religious devotion of early Christians but also serves as a marker of the sacred within the text, distinguishing the divine from the mundane. Through the study of nomina sacra, scholars gain a deeper understanding of early Christian theological perspectives and the ways in which these beliefs were manifested in the physical texts of the New Testament and other Christian writings. The consistency and care with which nomina sacra were employed underscore the reverence early Christians held for the written word and its role in the transmission of their faith.

Tracing the Script: Handwriting Styles of New Testament Archetypes

Introduction to Archetypal Scripts

The transition from the original autographs of the New Testament texts to their archetypal forms represents a fascinating area of study within New Testament textual criticism. Unlike the autographs, which were the first drafts directly penned by the authors or their amanuenses, the archetypes were polished texts prepared for broader circulation. This distinction is crucial for understanding the evolution of script styles from personal handwriting to more formalized bookhands or reformed documentary scripts used in these seminal Christian texts.

The Shift to Formalized Script

The handwriting of the New Testament archetypes likely marked a departure from the more personal and varied styles of the autographs. Professional scribes, with their training in formal script, would have produced texts that were visually consistent and legible, aiming for a quality befitting sacred scripture. This shift underscores the transition of the New Testament writings from personal correspondence or narrative accounts to authoritative texts meant for a wider audience.

Bookhand and Reformed Documentary Script

The predominant script styles for these archetypal texts were "bookhand" and "reformed documentary" script. Bookhand, characterized by its uniformity and clarity, was ideal for literary and religious texts that demanded careful reading. In contrast, reformed documentary script, while still clear and legible, retained elements of the casual style typical of everyday documents but polished for a more formal presentation. These styles not only facilitated readability but also reflected the texts' elevated status within the Christian community.

Insights from Comparative Manuscript Analysis

To approximate the appearance of New Testament archetypes, one might look to contemporaneous manuscripts such as the Greek Minor Prophet Scrolls from Nahal Hever and various Greek Old Testament manuscripts produced by early Christians. These texts exhibit the calligraphic quality and stylistic features that likely resembled the polished archetypes of the New Testament. Similarly, nonbiblical manuscripts from the mid-first century provide examples of reformed documentary script that could parallel the script style of New Testament archetypes.

The Role of Professional Scribes

Professional scribes played a pivotal role in the creation of the archetypal texts. Their expertise ensured that the manuscripts not only conveyed the sacred texts accurately but also adhered to the aesthetic and functional standards of scriptural texts. This professional involvement suggests that the earliest publications of the New Testament might have showcased the refined craftsmanship of scribes well-versed in literary and religious manuscript production.

Creative Reconstruction and Its Implications

While no extant New Testament manuscript precisely matches the mid-first-century script style, manuscripts like P52 and P104 offer glimpses into the handwriting styles of the late first or early second century. This creative reconstruction, though speculative, provides valuable insights into the possible appearance of the New Testament archetypes. Understanding these script styles helps contextualize the New Testament manuscripts within the broader landscape of ancient manuscript production, highlighting the care and reverence afforded to these texts from their earliest circulations.

The study of handwriting styles in New Testament archetypes opens a window into the meticulous process of manuscript preparation in the early Christian era. By examining contemporary manuscripts and employing creative reconstruction, scholars can gain a deeper appreciation for the evolution of script styles from the personal autographs to the polished archetypes. This exploration not only enriches our understanding of the textual history of the New Testament but also underscores the reverence and care invested in preserving these foundational texts for future generations.

From Scroll to Codex: The Early Publication of the New Testament

The Initial Publication of Individual Writings

The New Testament, a cornerstone of Christian faith, was not created in a single act of literary production but emerged through a complex process of writing, compilation, and publication. The earliest phase saw the production of individual texts, written by apostles and early Christian leaders between 49 and 90 C.E. These texts, addressing specific communities or responding to particular circumstances, laid the foundational doctrines and narratives of Christianity. Their publication, often facilitated by the authors themselves or their immediate associates, ensured the dissemination of these pivotal teachings across the burgeoning Christian communities.

THE EARLY CHRISTIAN COPYISTS OF THE NEW TESTAMENT

Compiling the Canonical Collections

Following the circulation of individual writings, the early Christian community saw the need for organizing these texts into coherent collections. This endeavor likely began in the late first century and continued into the second century C.E., marking a significant phase in the New Testament's publication history. The Pauline epistles, some of the earliest writings to be collected, were compiled by 100-125 C.E., offering a unified corpus of Paul's theological insights and pastoral guidance. Similarly, the Gospel collections, assembled by the early second century, brought together the fourfold narrative of Jesus Christ's life, teachings, death, and resurrection. This period of collection reflects the early Christians' efforts to preserve, authenticate, and standardize the apostolic witness for successive generations.

The Formation of the New Testament Canon

The compilation of the New Testament into a single entity represents the culmination of the early publication process. This comprehensive collection, encompassing all 27 books recognized as canonical, did not materialize as a unified codex until the early fourth century C.E. The inclusion of these texts alongside the Greek Old Testament in codices such as Vaticanus and Sinaiticus signifies a milestone in the textual history of Christianity, illustrating the establishment of a defined scriptural corpus. This phase not only solidified the canonical boundaries of the New Testament but also facilitated its transmission as a complete body of sacred literature.

Editorial Oversight in the Early Stages

The editorial process in the initial publication and compilation phases involved both authorial superintendence and communal discernment. Authors like Paul, actively engaged in the dissemination of their writings, might have overseen the compilation of their letters into collections. This early editorial work, grounded in the apostolic authority and aimed at preserving the integrity of the Christian message, contrasts with later editorial endeavors that sought to create a comprehensive and standardized New Testament canon. The involvement of early Christian leaders in this process underscores the careful attention given to the texts' authenticity, coherence, and theological consistency.

Distinguishing Between Early and Canonical Editions

The distinction between the early phases of New Testament publication and the later establishment of a "Canonical Edition," as proposed by scholars like David Trobisch, is crucial for understanding the evolution of the New Testament text. The initial compilations, overseen by authors or their contemporaries, focused on the pragmatic need to organize and distribute the apostolic teachings. In contrast, the concept of a Canonical Edition, emerging no earlier than the third century, reflects a more deliberate effort to define the contours of Christian scripture and to standardize its textual form for liturgical and doctrinal purposes.

The publication of the New Testament unfolded in stages, transitioning from the circulation of individual writings to the formation of canonical collections and finally to the establishment of the complete New Testament canon. This process, marked by both authorial involvement and communal discernment, highlights the early Christian community's commitment to preserving the apostolic teachings. Understanding these stages sheds light on the historical and textual dynamics that shaped the New Testament, offering insights into its development as a foundational document of Christian faith.

The Gospel's Journey: From Oral Tradition to Canonical Text

The Foundation of Gospel Transmission

The Gospels, as firsthand accounts of Jesus' teachings and activities, originate from those who were closest to Him. Unlike contemporary figures whose teachings were documented during their lifetimes, Jesus left no written records. The trustworthiness of the Gospels, therefore, relies heavily on the integrity of His disciples, akin to how Plato and Xenophon chronicled Socrates. The safeguard against fabrication was the collective memory and oversight of the early Christian community, including the Twelve Apostles, the seventy-two other disciples, and an even broader circle of followers who could attest to the teachings and events of Jesus' ministry.

The Role of the Early Christian Community

In the nascent stages of the Church, the apostolic teachings were transmitted orally, forming the bedrock of the community's faith. This oral tradition, complemented by the Septuagint, nurtured the spiritual life of the early believers. The reliance on oral recitation for the dissemination of Jesus' teachings underscores the importance of direct apostolic instruction and the communal memory in preserving the authenticity of the Gospel message.

Transition from Oral to Written Gospels

The move from oral proclamation to written documentation of Jesus' life and teachings marked a significant development in the preservation of the Christian faith. Luke's Gospel, as well as the other Gospel accounts, emerged from a desire to affirm and solidify the oral teachings received by early Christians. The written Gospels were not intended to replace the oral tradition but to serve as a tangible reinforcement, ensuring the accuracy and reliability of the teachings about Jesus for future generations.

The Publication of the Gospels

The publication of the Gospel narratives involved a formal process of dissemination, akin to the publication practices of the time. This process included the creation of a master copy, or archetype, from which further copies were made for distribution. The sponsorship of individuals like Theophilus for Luke's Gospel, and the efforts of Gospel writers such as Mark, Luke, and John, reflect the early Christian community's commitment to making the teachings of Jesus widely available. The use of the term "published" in this context indicates a deliberate and organized effort to ensure the Gospels' accessibility to a broader audience.

Apostolic Motivation and Eyewitness Testimony

The impetus behind the writing and publication of the Gospels was twofold: to provide a written testament of Jesus' life and teachings as the apostolic eyewitnesses neared the end of their lives, and to ensure that the foundational truths of the Christian faith were preserved for posterity. This motivation is particularly evident in the Gospels of Matthew and John, both of whom were apostles and could offer direct eyewitness accounts of the events they described. The assertion of eyewitness authenticity, especially in John's Gospel, lends significant weight to the historical reliability of these texts.

The Gospels' journey from the spoken word of the apostles and early disciples to the written narratives that form the core of the New Testament canon is a testament to the early Christian community's dedication to preserving the authentic teachings of Jesus Christ. The transition from oral tradition to written text, followed by the formal publication of the Gospels, reflects a thoughtful and intentional process aimed at ensuring the accuracy, reliability, and accessibility of the Christian message for future generations. This historical trajectory underscores the foundational role of the Gospels in the Christian faith and the meticulous care with which they were transmitted from the first eyewitnesses to the wider Christian community.

The Gospels: Memoirs of Faith and Foundations of Biography

The Essence of Gospel Narratives

The Gospels stand as the seminal accounts of Jesus Christ's life, teachings, and ministry, crafted by those who were either direct eyewitnesses or closely connected to firsthand testimonies. Drawing parallels with ancient practices, such as the disciples of Socrates who preserved his philosophies through their writings, the Gospel authors undertook a monumental task. They committed to parchment the deeds and sayings of Jesus, ensuring the authenticity of their accounts through the living memory of a broad witness circle. This foundational community served as both the source and safeguard of the Gospel narratives, ensuring their integrity against fabrication.

The Literary Form of the Gospels

Papias of Hierapolis and Justin Martyr, early historians and theologians, categorized the Gospels as apomenmoneumata, a term denoting memoirs or remembrances. This classification aligns the Gospels with a recognized ancient literary form, akin to Xenophon's Memorabilia, highlighting their nature as collections of teachings and events rather than comprehensive biographies. The Gospels, especially Luke's account, strive more to present Jesus' actions and teachings within a narrative framework than to offer a detailed chronology of His life.

From Oral Tradition to Written Testimony

The transition from oral proclamation to written Gospel narratives marks a pivotal moment in the preservation of Christian doctrine. Luke's Gospel explicitly aims to affirm the oral teachings received by believers, underlining the written word's role in solidifying the faith imparted through spoken testimony. This evolution from spoken to written form reflects a broader trend in ancient literature, where oral traditions formed the basis for later written records.

The Gospels within the Genre of Biography

While not biographies in the modern sense, the Gospels share similarities with ancient biographical writings, offering a narrative structure centered on Jesus' life and imbued with anecdotes, teachings, and reflections. This resemblance places the Gospels alongside other ancient biographies, such as Plutarch's Lives, yet distinguishes them through their focus on Jesus' unique life and divine mission. The didactic nature of these texts, aimed at portraying Jesus as a model of virtue, aligns with the purpose of ancient encomia, further embedding the Gospels within the biographical tradition.

Literary Techniques and Theological Aims

The Gospel authors employed various literary techniques to convey their theological messages and portray the figure of Jesus Christ. From Matthew's use of prophetic fulfillment to John's emphasis on eyewitness testimony, each Gospel writer crafted a narrative that served both literary and doctrinal purposes. These techniques underscore the Gospels' status as works of literature, designed for circulation, valuation, and use within the early Christian community.

The Divine Inspiration Behind the Gospels

The inspiration for the Gospels stemmed not only from the apostles' direct experiences with Jesus but also from the divine guidance of the Holy Spirit. This spiritual oversight ensured the accuracy and reliability of their accounts, preserving the memory of Jesus' teachings and actions. The promise of the Holy Spirit to aid in remembering Jesus' words highlights the divine foundation of the Gospel narratives, setting them apart from other historical or biographical accounts.

The Gospels, as published memoirs and biographies of Jesus Christ, represent a unique synthesis of eyewitness testimony, oral tradition, and literary composition. Their classification as apomenmoneumata underscores their foundational role in chronicling the life and teachings of Jesus, serving as a bridge between the oral teachings of the apostles and the written word of the Christian canon. Through a combination of historical authenticity, literary skill, and divine inspiration, the Gospel writers produced texts that have shaped the faith and understanding of Christian communities across centuries, offering a compelling narrative of Jesus' life that is both instructive and transformative.

The Apostolic Voice: Publishing the New Testament Epistles and Beyond

The Distinction Between Letters and Epistles

The New Testament contains a variety of writings, among which Paul's epistles stand out for their theological depth and pastoral care. Distinguishing between personal letters and epistles is crucial for understanding the New Testament's composition. Letters, as described by Adolf Deissman, are personal correspondences intended for private audiences, while epistles are stylized, literary forms aimed at broader readership. This distinction highlights the purposeful design behind many of Paul's writings, which, though personal in tone, were meant for public instruction and edification.

Paul's Publishing Strategy

Paul, an apostle with a profound understanding of the gospel's scope, initially sought to disseminate Jesus' teachings through oral proclamation. However, recognizing the limitations of physical travel and the enduring power of the written word, he adopted a strategic approach to publishing his teachings. This included sending coworkers to deliver his messages and composing epistles to be circulated among the churches. Paul's writings, known for their compelling theological insights, were crafted to ensure the gospel's reach extended beyond his spoken words, embodying the apostolic authority vested in him.

The Authority of Apostolic Writings

The early Christian community recognized the inherent authority of apostolic writings, as evidenced by the reception of the Jerusalem church council's letter recorded in Acts 15. This document set a precedent for subsequent epistles, underscoring the apostolic foundation of written teachings as authoritative and divinely inspired. Paul, in his epistles, emphasized this authority, urging the churches to receive his words as the Lord's commandments. This understanding of apostolic authority underscores the New Testament writings' role as definitive guides for doctrine and practice within the early Church.

The Role of Encyclicals and Personal Letters

Among Paul's epistles, Romans and Ephesians were designed as encyclical treatises, intended for a wide audience across multiple congregations. This contrasts with his personal letters, which, though limited in initial circulation, have been preserved as part of the canon due to their rich theological content and insight into early Christian life. The distinction between these types of writings illuminates the varied strategies employed by the apostles to address different audiences and needs within the early Church.

The Wider Apostolic Publishing Plan

Beyond Paul, other apostles like Peter and John engaged in their own publishing endeavors, crafting epistles and writings such as Revelation to instruct, correct, and encourage the dispersed Christian communities. These works, designed for public consumption, were likely produced in multiple copies to facilitate their distribution to the intended audiences. This practice of publishing and circulating apostolic writings played a critical role in the formation and unity of the early Christian Church, ensuring the widespread dissemination of core doctrines and ethical teachings.

The Apostle Paul's Ministry to the Jews and the Authorship of Hebrews

Paul, renowned as the apostle "to the nations," also held a significant ministry among the Jewish population, contrary to the perception that his work was exclusively among the Gentiles. This dual focus of his mission is underscored by the Lord Jesus' directive to Ananias, highlighting Paul's role in carrying the name of Jesus not only to the nations and kings but also to the sons of Israel. This directive aligns perfectly with the essence of the book of Hebrews, which is often debated concerning Paul's authorship due to several distinctive features.

The Question of Authorship

Critics often question Paul's authorship of Hebrews, citing the absence of his name and a stylistic departure from his other letters. However, these objections do not hold when considering the broader context of biblical writings and Paul's adaptable communication style. The practice of omitting the author's name is not uncommon in biblical texts, and Paul's ability to tailor his message to diverse audiences—including Jews, pagans, and Christians—speaks to his rhetorical skill, not against his authorship.

Internal evidence within Hebrews supports Pauline authorship. The letter's connections to Italy and Timothy, along with its doctrinal consistency with Paul's teachings, align with Paul's life and ministry. The stylistic differences can be attributed to the audience's background, as the letter addresses a predominantly Jewish readership familiar with the intricacies of the Jewish law and traditions.

The Chester Beatty Papyrus No. 2 (P46) discovery has further bolstered the case for Paul's authorship, with early manuscript tradition placing Hebrews in close proximity to Romans. Esteemed textual critics and biblical encyclopedias affirm Paul's authorship based on a comprehensive examination of external and internal evidence.

The Inspired Message of Hebrews

Hebrews stands as an inspired text, intricately weaving Old Testament prophecies and teachings to reveal their fulfillment in Christ Jesus. The letter extensively cites Hebrew Scriptures to demonstrate Jesus' superiority and the transition from the old covenant to the new. This profound connection to Jewish heritage and prophecy is pivotal for understanding the letter's purpose and its impact on the Hebrew Christian audience.

Historical Context and Date of Writing

The letter's timing is closely tied to Paul's first imprisonment in Rome, around 61 C.E. The mention of Timothy's release and Paul's anticipation of his own suggest a period of writing that coincides with the final year of this imprisonment. This timeframe is critical for appreciating the letter's immediate relevance to its original readers, who were facing intense persecution and the temptation to revert to Judaism amidst the Jewish system of things' downfall.

Addressing the Hebrew Christians

The Jewish Christians in Judea, particularly in Jerusalem, were navigating a hostile environment marked by escalating Jewish opposition.

THE EARLY CHRISTIAN COPYISTS OF THE NEW TESTAMENT

Paul, with his Pharisaical background and deep understanding of the Mosaic Law, was uniquely positioned to reinforce the Christian faith among his fellow Jews. Through Hebrews, Paul provided irrefutable arguments from the Scriptures to affirm Christ's fulfillment of the Law and the obsolescence of old covenant practices.

His comprehensive exposition on the superiority of Christ's priesthood, the new covenant, and the ultimate sacrifice of Christ over traditional offerings served not only to fortify the Hebrew Christians but also to equip them for defending their faith and witnessing to seeking Jews. The letter reflects Paul's deep compassion for the Hebrew Christians and his strategic approach to addressing their specific challenges and doubts.

Paul's ministry extended robustly to both Gentiles and Jews, with the book of Hebrews serving as a testament to his commitment to the Jewish believers. The internal and external evidences robustly support Pauline authorship of Hebrews, reinforcing its place within the canon as a bridge between the Old and New Testaments. Through this epistle, Paul adeptly addressed the unique needs of the Hebrew Christian community, providing them with theological insights and practical guidance to navigate their faith amidst persecution and societal pressures. His efforts underscored the transition from the old to the new covenant, emphasizing the centrality of Christ in God's redemptive plan for humanity.

The Book of Acts and the Gospels

Luke's Acts of the Apostles, initially published as a sequel to his Gospel, provides a narrative account of the early Church's expansion and the apostolic ministry. The separation of Acts from Luke's Gospel in later manuscript traditions does not diminish its importance as a bridge between the Gospels and the Epistles, offering a historical framework for understanding the apostolic era and the spread of Christianity.

The publication of the New Testament writings, from Paul's epistles to the broader apostolic contributions, reflects a concerted effort to preserve and proclaim the gospel message across diverse Christian communities. The strategic use of letters and epistles, the recognition of apostolic authority, and the intentional circulation of these writings underscore the early Church's commitment to maintaining doctrinal purity and fostering communal unity. Through these apostolic voices, the foundational truths of Christianity were codified, shaping the faith's trajectory for centuries to come.

Edward D. Andrews

The Scribe's Role in Ancient Manuscript Production

The ancient world relied on the meticulous labor of scribes for the proliferation of literature, including the sacred texts of the New Testament. This process was arduous, requiring a deep dedication to preserving the integrity of the texts through generations. The production of manuscript copies was a task of great significance, bridging the past with the future through the written word.

The Process of Manuscript Reproduction

In the absence of printing technology, the replication of texts was a manual endeavor, demanding both time and skill. While some popular works might be copied in a sort of assembly-line fashion with a master scribe dictating to others, the majority of texts, including those of the New Testament, were copied individually. This painstaking process involved a scribe working directly from an exemplar to create a single copy. The quality of these manuscripts varied greatly, reflecting the scribe's level of training and commitment to accuracy.

Scribe Training and Education

The education of a scribe was a rigorous affair, often beginning with an apprenticeship under a master scribe. These apprenticeships, akin to private tutoring, were widespread, even in smaller towns. This system of education ensured that scribes were well-versed in the practical aspects of their craft, from legal documents to personal correspondence. Advanced education, typically reserved for those with the means and motivation to pursue it, was available in temple schools. Here, students could delve into the sciences, literature, and more, aiming for roles as priests or scholars within their communities.

The Scribe's Toolkit

The tools of the scribe's trade were simple but effective. Writing surfaces varied from clay to papyrus, and the instruments used had to accommodate these materials. The art of writing itself was no small feat, with some writing systems comprising hundreds of signs or characters. Through rigorous practice, scribes learned to replicate these signs with precision, a skill that was fundamental to their profession.

Scribes in Biblical Times

In biblical times, the role of the scribe was multifaceted, extending beyond the mere copying of texts to encompass a variety of writing tasks. Scribes often served the public in bustling city gates or marketplaces, drafting documents for those unable to write. They also played a crucial role in religious life, copying scriptures for use in worship and teaching. Figures such as Ezra and Baruch are testament to the revered position of scribes within the Jewish community, embodying the intersection of religious duty and scholarly endeavor.

The Impact of Scribes on New Testament Manuscripts

The transmission of the New Testament texts owes much to the diligence of ancient scribes. Their efforts ensured that these foundational Christian documents were preserved for future generations, despite the challenges of manual copying and the variations in scribal quality. Through their work, scribes facilitated the spread of Christian teachings across the Mediterranean world and beyond, laying the groundwork for the faith's enduring legacy.

The ancient scribe's contribution to the preservation and dissemination of literature, particularly the texts of the New Testament, cannot be overstated. Through their dedicated efforts, these pivotal works were meticulously copied and passed down through the centuries, allowing them to reach us today. The manual reproduction of manuscripts, while labor-intensive, was a labor of love and reverence, ensuring that the words that shaped civilizations would not be lost to time.

The Evolution of New Testament Manuscript Production: A Study of Scribal Practices

The early 20th-century discovery of New Testament papyri radically altered our understanding of the texts' transmission. Initially, scholars like Kenyon viewed these manuscripts as products of non-professional, perhaps even illiterate scribes, reflective of a nascent Christian community with little concern for textual precision. This perception was based on early findings that exhibited varying degrees of scribal care, from schoolboy exercises to manuscripts laden with paraphrases and expansions.

Reassessment of Early Christian Scribes

This perspective, however, began to shift as more papyri surfaced, revealing a broader spectrum of scribal quality. Notably, Kenyon himself revised his views upon editing the Chester Beatty papyri, acknowledging a higher level of scribal proficiency in some manuscripts. This growing corpus allowed scholars to appreciate the diversity of scribal practices within early Christianity, challenging the notion that early Christian manuscripts were uniformly amateurish.

Categorization of Scribal Handwriting

Subsequent analysis by papyrologists identified four primary categories of scribal handwriting in early New Testament manuscripts: professional (bookhand), reformed documentary, documentary, and common. These classifications, ranging from formal to informal, reflect a gradation in scribal skill and intent. Professional scribes, capable of producing texts with precision and aesthetic appeal, contrast with those using a common hand, indicative of a more rudimentary level of literacy and training.

The professional or bookhand style, characterized by its clarity, regularity, and adherence to bilinearity, was the hallmark of scribes who strove for legibility and beauty in their work. These scribes operated within scriptoria or for private clients, showcasing a high degree of craftsmanship in their manuscripts. In contrast, the reformed documentary and documentary styles were faster, less polished, but still indicative of trained scribes, often engaged in legal or personal correspondence.

Professional Scribes and the New Testament Manuscripts

The variety in handwriting styles among New Testament papyri suggests that manuscripts were produced across a spectrum of contexts, from professional scriptoria to more informal settings. This diversity underscores the involvement of scribes with different levels of training and purposes, from those meticulously copying texts for communal use to individuals making personal copies. The presence of manuscripts in reformed documentary or even documentary hand does not necessarily denote non-professional work but rather reflects the adaptability of scribes to different demands and the practicalities of manuscript production.

Moreover, the evolution of scribal practices in the early Christian era highlights the complex interplay between religious devotion, textual transmission, and the socio-economic realities of the time. The engagement of professional scribes in producing New Testament manuscripts attests to the importance ascribed to these texts within the Christian community, countering earlier assumptions about their casual transmission.

The study of early New Testament manuscripts, propelled by discoveries and scholarly reassessment, reveals a nuanced landscape of scribal activity. Far from the early characterizations of these texts as carelessly produced, the evidence points to a continuum of scribal proficiency and dedication to preserving the Christian message. This evolving understanding enriches our appreciation of the early Christian community's efforts to disseminate their sacred texts, highlighting both the human element in textual transmission and the divine inspiration that guided their preservation.

The Craftsmanship of Early New Testament Manuscripts: A Closer Look at Scribal Expertise

The early New Testament manuscripts, particularly from the second and third centuries, are pivotal in understanding the textual transmission and preservation efforts of early Christian communities. Among these, a significant number exhibit characteristics of documentary and reformed documentary handwriting, pointing to a wide range of scribal capabilities and practices. Notably, a subset of these manuscripts showcases a level of craftsmanship that speaks to professional scribe work, distinguishing themselves through features that go beyond mere functionality to embrace aesthetic and structural considerations.

The Professional Bookhand in Manuscript Production

Within this corpus of early Christian texts, certain manuscripts stand out for their exceptional execution, embodying the professional bookhand style. This style is characterized by precise calligraphy, systematic text division, and the use of features such as paragraph markings and double-columns that enhance readability and textual navigation. These manuscripts not only served as vehicles for the sacred text but also as artifacts reflecting the meticulous care and reverence with which these texts were treated.

P4+64+67, a composite Gospel codex, exemplifies the high degree of professionalism in manuscript production, featuring well-executed calligraphy and punctuation, and organized into double columns. This manuscript, alongside others like P75, shares a text division system that resonates with practices observed in later significant manuscripts, suggesting a continuity and perhaps a standardized approach to manuscript preparation that transcended regional practices.

Manuscripts of Note

- **P30** showcases the Biblical Uncial script, clear and deliberate, marking it as the work of a scribe well-versed in the production of literary texts.
- **P39** stands as a beautiful example of early Biblical Uncial, its aesthetic quality underscoring the scribe's skill and dedication.
- **P46**, notable for its stichoi notations, reflects a scribe's attention to detail likely motivated by professional commitment rather than casual engagement.
- **P66**, possibly emanating from a scriptorium, represents the collaborative, professional environment in which such manuscripts were produced.
- **P75**, attributed to an exceptionally trained scribe, exhibits a level of precision and care that sets a high standard for manuscript production.
- **P77+P103** and **P95** are further examples where well-crafted calligraphy and standard text organizational features point to professional scribe work.
- **P104**, despite being a smaller fragment, shines as a testament to the skill and perhaps the devotion of its scribe.

These manuscripts collectively illustrate the existence of a professional cadre of scribes within early Christian communities, dedicated to the task of manuscript production. Their work not only ensured the transmission of the New Testament texts but also contributed to the development of a visual and structural quality that would influence later manuscript traditions.

Implications for Early Christian Textual Transmission

The presence of professionally produced manuscripts among early New Testament papyri challenges simplistic notions of how these sacred texts were copied and disseminated. It suggests a level of organizational sophistication and a recognition of the importance of these texts that prompted investment in high-quality manuscript production. This professional approach to manuscript production may also reflect early Christian communities' awareness of the need for accurate and reliable textual transmission, countering the narrative of a purely ad hoc or amateurish scribal culture.

Moreover, the use of professional bookhands and the adoption of systematic text division strategies indicate an early and deliberate effort to standardize the presentation and perhaps the reading of the New Testament texts. This effort points to a reverence for the text that goes beyond its mere content to encompass its presentation and preservation.

The exploration of early New Testament manuscripts, especially those displaying professional bookhand craftsmanship, reveals a complex and nuanced picture of early Christian scribal culture. These manuscripts serve as a bridge between the oral and written traditions of Christianity, embodying both the message they carry and the care with which that message was preserved. Through their pages, we glimpse the dedication of early Christians to ensuring that their sacred texts would endure, meticulously crafted by the hands of professional scribes who played a crucial role in the textual heritage of Christianity.

The Reformed Documentary Hand in Early New Testament Manuscripts

The early Christian manuscripts, particularly those from the second century, provide a fascinating insight into the scribal practices of the time. Among these practices, the use of what has been termed the "reformed documentary hand" stands out as a testament to the evolving nature of manuscript production within the Christian community. This style represents a significant departure from purely utilitarian scribal work, such as that found in legal documents, towards a more deliberate approach befitting the transcription of literary and sacred texts.

Understanding the Reformed Documentary Hand

The reformed documentary hand is characterized by its adaptation from the more standard documentary script, which was commonly used for everyday writing tasks, including legal and personal documents. This adaptation indicates an awareness among scribes that the texts they were transcribing held a different, more significant status. While not reaching the heights of calligraphy seen in the most beautifully crafted manuscripts, the reformed documentary hand nevertheless exhibits a level of competence and care that surpasses ordinary documentary writing.

The Role of Experienced Scribes

Scholars like Roberts and Skeat have highlighted the likelihood that scribes proficient in the reformed documentary hand were experienced and possibly received compensation for their work. This suggests a professionalization within the sphere of Christian manuscript production, where scribes, whether Christian themselves or not, were recognized for their skill and employed to produce copies of New Testament texts. Such a practice underscores the importance placed on the accurate and respectful transcription of these sacred writings.

Manuscripts in the Reformed Documentary Hand

Among the papyri predating 300 C.E., at least fifteen manuscripts have been identified as being written in the reformed documentary hand. These include:

- **P1**, featuring texts from the Gospel of Matthew, exhibits the balanced use of a reformed documentary script, suggesting a scribe's effort to ensure legibility and respect for the content.
- **P45**, one of the most significant early papyri, contains texts from the Gospels and Acts, showcasing a scribe's adeptness in handling various types of Christian literature.
- **P52**, famously known as the earliest fragment of the Gospel of John, demonstrates the application of a reformed documentary hand in a concise and precise manner.
- **P90**, another fragment of the Gospel of John, further illustrates the widespread use of this handwriting style in the transcription of Gospel texts.

THE EARLY CHRISTIAN COPYISTS OF THE NEW TESTAMENT

- **P137**, officially designated as P.Oxy. LXXXIII 5345, is a small fragment of the New Testament from the Gospel of Mark, specifically Mark 1:7-9, 16-18. This papyrus is part of the larger collection of Oxyrhynchus Papyri, an extensive group of manuscripts discovered among the ruins of Oxyrhynchus, an ancient town located in modern-day Egypt. P137 is notable for its dating; it has been dated to the early to middle 2nd century CE, making it the earliest extant manuscripts of the Gospel of Mark.

These manuscripts, along with others like P30, P32, P35, P38, P69, P87, P100, P102, P108, P109, and P110, highlight the diversity and distribution of the reformed documentary hand in early Christian manuscript production. Each manuscript, through its stylistic nuances, offers insights into the scribe's approach to the task of copying sacred texts, balancing between the functional needs of document writing and the elevated requirements of transcribing scripture.

Implications for Early Christian Communities

The prevalence of the reformed documentary hand in early New Testament manuscripts suggests a conscious effort by early Christian communities to ensure the preservation and propagation of their sacred texts. By employing experienced scribes capable of adapting their skills to the specific demands of Christian literature, these communities demonstrated a profound reverence for their scriptures. Moreover, the willingness to compensate scribes for their work reflects an understanding of the importance of professional skills in the accurate transmission of these texts.

This professional approach to manuscript production not only facilitated the spread of Christian teachings but also contributed to the standardization and preservation of the New Testament texts during a critical period of growth and development for the early Church. The reformed documentary hand, therefore, represents more than just a stylistic choice; it signifies a pivotal moment in the history of Christian manuscript production, where the sacredness of the text began to dictate the methods of its transcription.

The Scribal Hands Behind Early New Testament Manuscripts: Documentary and Common Styles

The transmission of the New Testament texts in the earliest centuries of Christianity provides a unique window into the practices and communities that shaped the preservation of these sacred writings. Among the varied styles of handwriting found in these ancient documents, the "documentary" and "common" hands represent two distinct approaches to manuscript production, reflecting the diverse backgrounds of the scribes and the contexts in which they worked.

Documentary Hand: The Transition from Business to Scripture

The documentary hand is indicative of manuscripts produced by individuals with experience in business or administrative writing rather than in the book trade. These manuscripts often lack the uniform appearance characteristic of professional scribe work, displaying features such as non-bilinear lettering and enlarged initial letters at the beginning of lines or sections. This style is closely aligned with the practical needs of document writing, where clarity and functionality outweigh aesthetic considerations.

P. Bremer 5, dated to 117 C.E., exemplifies this approach with its enlarged initial letters, a feature that finds parallels in Jewish Greek manuscripts from Nahal Hever. The use of numerical abbreviations and spaces between words or word groups, common in legal contracts, further distinguishes the documentary hand. Revelation manuscripts like P47 and P98 showcase these characteristics, underscoring the adaptability of documentary scribes to the transcription of Christian texts.

This hand was predominantly employed by church members trained in document writing, who applied their skills to the copying of Scripture for private clients or their congregations. Nearly half of the early New Testament papyri exhibit the documentary hand, evidencing the widespread involvement of these scribes in the early Christian textual tradition.

Common Hand: The Mark of the Untrained Scribe

Distinguishing between a poorly executed documentary hand and the common hand can be challenging, but the latter typically signifies the work of individuals with minimal literacy in Greek. Manuscripts like P10, which seems to be the product of a learner, and P9, containing a portion of 1 John, are prime examples of the common hand. This style is characterized by its rudimentary execution, revealing a scribe's struggle with the Greek language.

Interestingly, many manuscripts of the Book of Revelation, such as P18, P24, and especially P98, are written in a common hand. This pattern might suggest that Revelation was less frequently read in church settings, leading to its transcription by less trained individuals. The contrast with the documentary P47, another Revelation manuscript, highlights the variation in scribal involvement with this particular text.

The Scribes' Dual Roles: From Businessmen to Churchmen

The transition of scribes from business or administrative roles to religious scribal work reflects the early Christian community's pragmatic approach to preserving its sacred texts. Many of these scribes, likely serving as church lectors, were tasked with maintaining, copying, and preparing scriptures for congregational readings. Their work bridges the secular and sacred, illustrating the multifaceted contributions of these individuals to the Christian tradition.

The documentary and common hands, with their distinct characteristics, offer insights into the early Christian scribes' backgrounds and the conditions under which the New Testament manuscripts were produced. These styles not only reveal the diversity of scribal expertise but also highlight the communal effort to transmit the Christian message across generations.

The exploration of documentary and common scribal hands in early New Testament manuscripts sheds light on the complex process of textual transmission within the early Christian community. These scribal practices illustrate a broader narrative of adaptation and dedication, where the sacred task of copying scripture was undertaken by a wide range of individuals. From seasoned document writers to those barely literate in Greek, the early scribes played a pivotal role in the preservation and dissemination of the New Testament, contributing to the rich tapestry of Christian textual heritage.

The Emergence of Early Christian Scriptoria

Scriptoria in the Ancient Christian World

The early Christian church, flourishing before Constantine's era, was a period marked by the dissemination and preservation of Christian texts, including the Old and New Testaments. Scholars have long debated the existence and locations of scriptoria dedicated to the production of these sacred writings. Major cities like Alexandria, Caesarea, Antioch, Jerusalem, and Rome, along with Oxyrhynchus in Egypt, are often mentioned as potential hubs of Christian literary activity. However, concrete archaeological evidence pinpointing the existence of Christian scriptoria in these cities, with the exception of Oxyrhynchus, remains elusive.

The Alexandrian Enigma

Alexandria, known for its great library and as a center of intellectual pursuit, holds a particular interest for scholars. Despite its significance, direct evidence of Christian scriptoria within Alexandria is lacking, primarily due to historical and environmental factors that led to the destruction and deterioration of potential manuscript evidence. Yet, the historical record and manuscript findings from other parts of Egypt suggest that Alexandria likely housed a Christian scriptorium or writing center.

Alexandria's Christian Intellectual Heritage

Christianity's arrival in Alexandria during the first century intersected with a significant Jewish population that had previously produced the Septuagint, a Greek translation of the Hebrew Scriptures, for the city's famed library. This translation was embraced by Christians for its messianic prophecies, leading to its widespread use in Christian apologetics and teaching. The resultant Jewish abandonment of the Septuagint and the creation of new translations underscored the diverging scriptural paths of Jews and Christians in Alexandria.

The Didaskelion, Alexandria's catechetical school, played a pivotal role in the city's Christian intellectual life from its inception. While direct evidence of a scriptorium associated with the Didaskelion is absent, the activities of figures like Pantaenus and his successor, Origen, suggest a sophisticated engagement with Christian texts that could have included the operation of a scriptorium.

Origen's Contributions

Origen, a towering figure in early Christian scholarship, utilized a considerable team of secretaries and scribes for his extensive writings. This operation, described in detail by Eusebius, involved a coordinated effort of shorthand writers, copyists, and skilled female scribes. While primarily focused on Origen's original works, this system hints at the potential for a broader application, including the copying of New Testament manuscripts. Origen's Hexapla project, an ambitious comparative study of Hebrew Scriptures and various Greek translations, further demonstrates the capacity for organized textual production and critical study within early Christian communities.

The Significance of Ambrose's Support

Ambrose's financial and logistical support for Origen's scholarly activities is noteworthy. By providing resources for a large staff of scribes and secretaries, Ambrose enabled not only the production of Origen's writings but also their dissemination among intellectually curious Christians. This arrangement, as highlighted by scholar Harry Y. Gamble, represents an early form of Christian publishing, indicating a move towards more formalized structures for producing and distributing Christian texts.

While direct archaeological evidence of early Christian scriptoria remains scarce, the historical record suggests their existence and importance in the transmission and development of Christian literature. The efforts of figures like Origen, supported by patrons like Ambrose, point to a sophisticated network of textual production that laid the groundwork for the preservation and spread of Christian teachings across the ancient world.

The intricate web of early Christian manuscript production and dissemination is a testament to the fervent activities of ancient communities dedicated to preserving the sacred texts. Oxyrhynchus and Alexandria, two cities in Egypt, emerge as focal points in this endeavor, each contributing uniquely to the legacy of Christian scriptoria.

Oxyrhynchus: A Rural Intellectual Hub

Oxyrhynchus, while primarily known for its non-literary papyri, has yielded a significant number of Christian manuscripts, suggesting it as a potential intellectual center for rural Egyptian Christianity. C. H. Roberts' analysis posits the existence of a Christian scriptorium in Oxyrhynchus as early as the late second century, a hypothesis supported by the discovery of manuscripts like the anti-Jewish dialogue (P. Oxyrhynchus 2070) from the third century. The sheer volume of biblical texts and Christian writings unearthed here underscores the city's importance in early Christian textual history.

Alexandria's Christian Scriptorium

Despite the absence of direct archaeological evidence, historical accounts and manuscript discoveries imply Alexandria's role as a Christian intellectual and scriptorial center. The city's rich Jewish and Christian heritage, exemplified by the creation of the Septuagint and the establishment of the Didaskelion catechetical school, points to a continuity of textual scholarship and possibly the operation of a Christian scriptorium. Figures like Pantaenus and Origen, with their extensive use of secretaries and scribes for scholarly output, hint at the organized production of Christian texts, though direct evidence linking Origen's activities to New Testament manuscript production remains elusive.

The Scriptorial Practices of Oxyrhynchus and Alexandria

The manuscripts from Oxyrhynchus, characterized by their documentary or reformed documentary hands, reveal individual scribes' work rather than a unified scriptorial operation. This observation, coupled with the lack of common textual features across manuscripts, suggests a decentralized approach to manuscript production. However, the possibility that Oxyrhynchus served as a writing center, perhaps connected to Alexandria through intellectual and scholarly exchanges, remains a viable hypothesis.

The Bodmer Papyri: A Connection to Alexandria

The discovery of the Bodmer Papyri near a Pachomian monastery introduces another dimension to the network of early Christian manuscript production. These manuscripts, likely part of the monastery's library, underscore the practice of reading and memorizing Scripture within monastic communities. The diversity in craftsmanship among these manuscripts suggests that while some were locally produced, others, possibly of a more professional quality, might have originated from external scriptoria, such as Alexandria.

The Monastic Influence on Manuscript Production

The establishment of the Pachomian monastic library post-320 C.E. indicates that earlier New Testament manuscripts were sourced from outside scriptoria, potentially Alexandria, reflecting a broader exchange of texts and scholarly resources. This interaction highlights the role of monasteries not just as centers of religious life but as crucial nodes in the transmission and preservation of Christian texts.

The exploration of early Christian manuscript production through the lenses of Oxyrhynchus, Alexandria, and the Pachomian monasteries reveals a complex landscape of textual transmission. This network, characterized by its diversity in scribal practices and the interplay between rural and urban centers of Christianity, showcases the multifaceted efforts to preserve the sacred writings. While direct evidence of specific scriptoria remains elusive, the patterns of manuscript discovery and historical accounts paint a picture of a vibrant and interconnected Christian textual tradition spanning the Nile valley.

Professional Scribes and Early New Testament Manuscripts

The meticulous efforts in early Christian manuscript production reveal a sophisticated blend of religious devotion and professional scribe work. This exploration delves into the distinctive features of professional scribe work in the production of New Testament manuscripts, particularly focusing on notable examples like P46 and P66.

The Hallmarks of Professional Scribe Work

Professional scribes distinguished themselves through various practices that ensured accuracy and consistency in manuscript production. Among these, the use of stichoi notations stands out as a clear indicator of professional involvement. These notations, found at the end of several books in manuscripts like P46, were used by scribes to denote the number of lines copied, likely for purposes of compensation. This practice, alongside the presence of pagination and meticulous correction processes, underscores the professional nature of certain manuscripts' creation.

Case Studies: P46 and P66

P46 is a prime example of a manuscript likely produced in a scriptorium. Its scribe demonstrated professional expertise not only through the application of stichoi notations but also in the systematic approach to corrections, involving both the initial scribe and subsequent reviewers. This collaborative correction process, indicative of a scriptorium's quality control mechanisms, highlights the manuscript's professional origins.

Similarly, P66 showcases the characteristics of a manuscript produced under the guidance of a scriptorium or writing center. The extensive corrections made by a diorthotes (corrector) suggest a level of scrutiny and quality assurance typical of professional manuscript production. The use of pinpricks for alignment, consistent correction signs, and the application of the diple (>) for noting corrections further emphasize the professional standards adhered to in P66's creation.

The Diple: A Marker of Professionalism

The use of the diple (>) as a correction marker is a nuanced aspect of professional scribe work, evident in manuscripts such as P48 and P. Oxyrhynchus 405. In P48, the diple is utilized to signal a correction within the text, an unusual practice for New Testament manuscripts, indicating a professional level of attention to detail. P. Oxyrhynchus 405, containing a portion of Irenaeus's Against Heresies with a quote from Matthew, employs the diple to highlight textual variations. This sophisticated use of scriptorial marks demonstrates the scribes' dedication to textual integrity and the potential influence of professional standards on early Christian manuscript production.

The Role of Professional Scribes in Early Christianity

The involvement of professional scribes in the creation of New Testament manuscripts signifies a critical phase in the transmission of Christian texts. These scribes, whether operating within Christian scriptoria or applying their skills to religious texts after secular training, played a pivotal role in preserving the New Testament for future generations. Their meticulous practices, from the use of stichoi notations to the implementation of correction systems, ensured the accuracy and reliability of these foundational texts.

The examination of manuscripts like P46 and P66, with their professional production features, offers a window into the complex process of early Christian manuscript production. It highlights the blend of religious devotion and professional craftsmanship that characterized the early transmission of the New Testament. Through the efforts of these scribes, the New Testament was not only preserved but also transmitted with a degree of precision and care that underscores the sacredness of these texts to early Christian communities.

The Intersecting Paths of Jewish and Christian Manuscript Traditions

The rich tapestry of early Christian and Jewish manuscript traditions offers a fascinating glimpse into the shared practices and influences that shaped the development of religious texts in antiquity. By examining the physical features and stylistic elements of these manuscripts, we can uncover the layers of interaction between Jewish and Christian scribes, revealing a shared heritage that extends beyond theology and into the realm of textual transmission and preservation.

Shared Stylistic Features: A Testament to Cultural Exchange

One of the most striking examples of this shared tradition is the appearance of enlarged letters at the beginning of lines and sections within manuscripts. This characteristic, more prevalent in early Christian manuscripts and the Greek Old Testament, suggests a stylistic practice inherited from Jewish scribes rather than a novel Christian innovation. The presence of these enlarged initials in religious texts, but not in copies of Greek classics, points to a unique tradition that distinguished sacred writings from secular literature. This practice, as noted by scholars like Peter Parsons and C. H. Roberts, underscores the possibility that early Christian scribes were influenced by Jewish manuscript traditions, adopting and adapting these practices for their own scriptural texts.

Documentary Look: Bridging the Sacred and the Secular

The documentary appearance of these manuscripts, marked by the use of enlarged initials and specific layout features, suggests a crossover between the world of religious texts and the practicalities of everyday business documents. This intersection may reflect the social contexts in which these texts were produced and circulated, highlighting the practical aspects of manuscript production in the ancient world. It also suggests that the early Christian community, much like their Jewish counterparts, valued the accessibility and readability of their sacred texts, employing methods that would make these texts more approachable to the lay reader.

The Nomen Sacrum: A Symbolic Link

The adaptation of the nomen sacrum for "kurios" (Lord) in Christian manuscripts further illustrates the influence of Jewish practices on Christian scribes. This innovation, particularly in the use of $\overline{KC}$ to denote "LORD," mirrors the Jewish reverence for the Tetragrammaton, JHVH, in their own scriptures. Instead of incorporating the Hebrew name of God directly into Greek texts, early Christian scribes developed a unique abbreviation that honored the sacredness of the divine name while adapting it to the Greek language and scriptural context. This practice not only highlights the respect for Jewish traditions but also demonstrates the early Christian effort to create a distinct yet connected textual identity.

A Shared Manuscript Heritage

The examination of early Christian and Jewish manuscripts reveals a complex web of influences and shared practices that underline the interconnectedness of these religious traditions. The stylistic and physical features of these texts, from enlarged initials to the adoption of the nomen sacrum, reflect a deep respect for the sacredness of scripture and a practical approach to its transcription and dissemination. This shared manuscript heritage offers a window into the early centuries of religious textual tradition, showcasing the mutual respect and influence between Jewish and Christian communities in the ancient world. Through this lens, we can appreciate the profound impact of Jewish scribal practices on the development of early Christian manuscripts, highlighting a legacy of shared reverence and meticulous care in the preservation of sacred texts.

The Codex Revolution in Early Christianity

The transition from scrolls to codices marks a pivotal evolution in the history of Christian manuscript tradition. This shift not only signifies a practical adaptation for the burgeoning Christian community but also reflects a deliberate move to distinguish Christian sacred texts from those of the Jewish tradition.

The Transition from Scroll to Codex

In the nascent stages of Christianity, followers of Jesus, who were predominantly of Jewish origin, would have been familiar with the traditional scroll format for reading the Old Testament. The Gospel account of Jesus reading from a scroll of Isaiah in the synagogue underscores the prevalent use of scrolls during this period. Saul of Tarsus (later Paul the Apostle), with his Jewish background, would initially have engaged with scrolls before presumably transitioning to the more innovative codex format.

Christian Adoption of the Codex

The codex, essentially a prototype of the modern book, offered several advantages over the scroll. It facilitated the compilation of multiple texts into a single volume, which was not feasible with scrolls. This feature was particularly beneficial for early Christians who sought to consolidate the four Gospels or the Pauline epistles into cohesive collections. The adoption of the codex is believed to have been driven by the desire to establish these compilations as the authoritative canon for the Christian community. This strategic choice not only served a practical purpose but also symbolized a departure from Jewish scriptural traditions, reinforcing the distinct identity of Christian sacred literature.

The Practicality and Economy of the Codex

The codex's format—folding sheets of papyrus and binding them at the spine—allowed for writing on both sides of the page, improved access to specific passages, and facilitated the assembly of comprehensive volumes of Christian texts. This format proved to be economically and practically superior, especially for a community that was spreading its teachings and seeking efficient ways to disseminate its scriptures. The early preference for papyrus over more expensive materials like vellum or parchment further illustrates the pragmatic considerations of early Christians, who were often operating under the constraints of persecution and limited resources.

The Antecedents of the Codex

Before the codex became prevalent, other forms of notebooks, such as the tabula and membranae, served various practical purposes, including note-taking and drafting. These early versions of the codex, used by individuals such as tax collectors and lawyers for business and personal notes, may have influenced the Christian adoption of the codex format for compiling the teachings and narratives of Jesus and the apostolic letters. The transition to the papyrus codex represented a significant evolution from these precursors, offering a more versatile and accessible format for Christian scriptures.

The Codex's Role in Christian Identity

The early Christian community's embrace of the codex was a strategic and symbolic choice that facilitated the dissemination of Christian teachings and reinforced the distinct identity of Christian scripture. By consolidating multiple texts into single volumes, early Christians could more effectively spread the Gospel and Paul's teachings, laying the foundation for the Christian biblical canon. This adoption of the codex not only reflects the practical and economic considerations of the time but also signifies a deliberate effort to distinguish Christian sacred texts from Jewish traditions, thereby shaping the future of Christian manuscript culture.

Early Christian Writing Materials and the Codex Revolution

The New Testament provides intriguing insights into the writing materials and practices of the early Christian community. This exploration sheds light on the transition from scrolls to codices and offers a glimpse into the practical aspects of early Christian literary culture.

Writing Materials in the New Testament

Apostle John's reference to using "paper and ink" in his epistles highlights the use of papyrus and the reed pen, essential tools for writing in the first century. Papyrus, derived from the papyrus plant, served as the primary writing surface, while the ink was a mixture of carbon or metallic substances suitable for parchment or papyrus. These references not only illuminate the materials used but also underscore the personal and immediate nature of early Christian correspondence.

Paul's Preference for Codices

Paul's request to Timothy for "the scrolls, especially the parchments," opens a window into the apostolic use of writing materials. The term "membranas" suggests that Paul utilized codices, either as completed books or notebooks. This preference indicates a significant shift towards the codex form among early Christians, possibly driven by the practical need to compile, transport, and reference Christian texts more efficiently.

The Codex in Revelation

The description of a book in Revelation, which only the Lamb of God could open, further suggests the early Christian familiarity with the codex. The book's portrayal—having writing on both sides and being opened seal by seal—fits the characteristics of a codex more than a scroll. This depiction not only reflects the practical advantages of the codex but also symbolically represents the unveiling of divine revelations in a sequential manner, a feature uniquely accommodated by the codex format.

The Significance of the Codex for Early Christianity

The adoption of the codex by early Christians marked a pivotal development in Christian literature. Unlike scrolls, codices allowed for the compilation of multiple texts into a single volume, facilitating the formation of the Christian biblical canon. This innovation was not merely practical but also served to differentiate Christian scriptures from Jewish ones, reinforcing the distinct identity of Christian sacred texts.

Practical Implications of the Codex Adoption

The codex offered several advantages over the scroll, including the ability to write on both sides of the material, easier access to specific passages, and the capacity to bind together comprehensive collections of texts. These features made the codex an economically and practically superior choice for the dissemination of Christian teachings.

The early Christian shift towards the codex reflects a strategic adaptation to the needs of a growing religious movement. By embracing this new format, Christians were able to more effectively compile, preserve, and distribute the writings that would become the foundation of Christian doctrine and practice. This transition not only highlights the innovative spirit of the early Christian community but also underscores the codex's role in shaping the development of Christian literature and identity.

The Advent and Significance of the Early Christian Codices

The shift from scrolls to codices marks a pivotal development in the textual transmission and preservation practices of early Christianity. This transition not only facilitated the dissemination of Christian texts but also underscored the distinct identity and innovative approach of the Christian community towards scripture and literary culture.

Emergence of the Codex

The codex's introduction into Christian practice by the end of the first century C.E. represents a significant evolution in the history of written texts. Unlike the scroll, which was the predominant form for both Jewish and Greco-Roman writings, the codex offered a more versatile and user-friendly format. Its adoption by Christians is a testament to the early church's willingness to embrace and innovate within the technological and cultural contexts of the time.

Criteria for Identifying Christian Manuscripts

The identification of early Christian manuscripts, particularly those of the Greek Old Testament, relies on specific markers that distinguish them from their Jewish counterparts. One of the clearest indicators is the use of nomina sacra, a practice that involved the abbreviation and sanctification of certain names and titles within the texts. This contrasted with the Jewish tradition of preserving the Tetragrammaton, highlighting a theological and cultural differentiation in the approach to sacred writings.

THE EARLY CHRISTIAN COPYISTS OF THE NEW TESTAMENT

Cataloguing Early Christian Manuscripts

Scholars like C. H. Roberts and van Haelst have made significant contributions to the cataloguing and analysis of early Christian manuscripts. Through their work, a clearer picture emerges of the breadth and variety of Christian texts in the second century. This includes not only canonical New Testament writings but also noncanonical texts, writings of the church fathers, and theological treatises. The meticulous cataloguing of these manuscripts provides invaluable insights into the early Christian community's priorities, theological debates, and the evolution of Christian doctrine.

The Codex's Role in Early Christianity

The adoption of the codex by early Christians was more than a mere preference for a different book format. It represented a deliberate choice that aligned with the community's theological, pastoral, and missionary needs. The codex format allowed for the compilation of multiple texts into a single volume, making it easier to disseminate the teachings of Jesus, the apostolic letters, and other foundational texts. This facilitated not only the spread of Christianity but also the establishment of a unified Christian doctrine and practice.

The codex also enabled early Christians to assert their distinct identity from Judaism and the surrounding Greco-Roman culture. By adopting a book form that was relatively rare in their time, Christians could physically manifest their separation from Jewish scriptural traditions and their innovative approach to religious texts.

The transition to the codex in the early Christian community was a strategic and symbolic act that had profound implications for the development of Christian literature, theology, and identity. This shift underscores the early Christians' adaptability and their commitment to the effective transmission of their sacred texts. Through the codex, the foundational texts of Christianity were preserved, studied, and shared, laying the groundwork for the global spread of the Christian faith. The study of these earliest Christian codices continues to shed light on the dynamic and evolving nature of early Christian belief and practice, offering a window into the lived realities of the first followers of Jesus.

Christian Old Testament Codices

1. **P.Yale 1, Genesis (H 12):** Dated approximately between 80–100 C.E., P.Yale 1 is potentially the earliest Christian manuscript, indicating the rapid adoption of the codex form for scriptural texts. Its dating to the late first century suggests an early Christian community already engaging deeply with the Hebrew Scriptures in a codex format, pointing to a significant transition in how sacred texts were interacted with and transmitted.

2. **P. Baden 4.56, Exodus and Deuteronomy (H 33):** This manuscript, placed in the second century, showcases the continuity of the Pentateuch's importance in Christian tradition. The adoption of Exodus and Deuteronomy into early Christian codices reflects the theological and moral foundation these books provided to the fledgling faith.

3. **P. Chester Beatty VI, Numbers and Deuteronomy (H 52):** Dated around 150 C.E., this manuscript underscores the early Christians' comprehensive engagement with the Torah, recognizing its foundational role in shaping Christian ethics and eschatology.

4. **P. Antinoopolis 7 and P. Leipzig inv. 170, Psalms (H 179 and H 224):** The Psalms, with their rich tapestry of lament, praise, and worship, were integral to both Jewish and Christian liturgical life. Their early inclusion in Christian codices indicates the Psalms' versatility and enduring relevance across covenantal boundaries.

5. **Bodleian Gr. Bib. g. 5, Psalms (H 151):** This manuscript, alongside others containing Psalms, illustrates the early Christian community's reliance on these texts for worship, instruction, and personal devotion, serving as a bridge between Jewish and Christian worship practices.

6. **P. Oxyrhynchus Manuscripts (656 and 1074, Genesis and Exodus):** These manuscripts, dated to the second and third centuries, highlight the early Christian interest in the Pentateuch's narrative and legal texts. Their presence in the Christian codex corpus underlines the foundational role of these texts in shaping the emerging Christian identity and theology.

7. **Chester Beatty Papyri VIII and IX (Jeremiah, Ezekiel, Daniel, Esther):** The inclusion of prophetic and apocalyptic texts in early Christian codices reflects the community's eschatological orientation

and the appropriation of Jewish prophecy in understanding Jesus' ministry and the anticipated consummation of God's kingdom.

Exploring the Early New Testament Codices: A Journey through Second Century Manuscript Evidence

The early New Testament codices provide a fascinating glimpse into the textual transmission of Christian Scriptures in the first few centuries of the Common Era. These manuscripts, pivotal for understanding the early textual history of the New Testament, offer scholars valuable insights into the scribal practices, textual variants, and the early Christian community's theological emphases. This exploration delves into the significant papyri dated to the second century, highlighting their contributions to biblical scholarship and textual criticism.

Manuscript Dating and Paleographic Analysis

The practice of dating ancient manuscripts involves paleography, a discipline that examines script styles to approximate a manuscript's age. Early New Testament manuscripts such as P52, P90, and P104, along with P98 (with some uncertainty), have traditionally been dated to the second century. However, paleographic studies have often been seen as too conservative, with recent scholarship suggesting earlier dates for several papyri. Notable manuscripts such as P4+P64+P67, P32, P46, P66, P77, P90, P98, P103, P104, and the recently identified P137, undergo rigorous examination, revealing the complexities and nuances of early Christian texts.

Significant Second Century Manuscripts

1. **P4+P64+P67 (Matthew and Luke)**: These combined manuscripts, dating to the third quarter of the second century, offer critical insights into the textual traditions of the Gospels of Matthew and Luke. Their early date underscores the wide circulation of Gospel texts within the Christian communities.

2. **P32 (Titus)**: Assigned to the second century, this manuscript affirms the early establishment of Pauline epistles within Christian canon formation.

3. **P46 (Paul's Major Epistles)**: Lacking the Pastorals, P46's probable earlier date than ca. 200 highlights the importance of Paul's writings in early Christian doctrine and community formation.

4. **P52 (John 18)**: Recognized as the earliest extant New Testament manuscript, P52's dating to ca. 115–125 provides invaluable evidence for the Gospel of John's early textual transmission.

5. **P66 (John)**: With a mid-second-century dating, P66 illustrates the textual variations and scribal practices concerning the Gospel of John.

6. **P77 and P103 (Matthew 23)**: These manuscripts, possibly part of the same codex, highlight the textual integrity of the Gospel of Matthew by the late second century.

7. **P90 (John 18–19)**: Its dating confirms the widespread distribution and authoritative status of the Gospel of John by the end of the second century.

8. **P98 (Revelation 1)**: As one of the few early witnesses to the Book of Revelation, P98's late second-century dating contributes to understanding the apocalyptic text's early reception.

9. **P104 (Unknown New Testament Text)**: Dated to the late second century, P104, despite its fragmentary nature, adds to the corpus of early New Testament manuscript evidence.

10. **P137 (Mark 1:7-9, 16-18)**: Dated to the early 2nd century CE, P137 stands as the earliest extant manuscript fragment of the Gospel of Mark, offering significant insights into the early textual tradition of the second Gospel.

Implications for New Testament Textual Criticism

The early New Testament codices, particularly those dated to the second century, are crucial for textual criticism. They offer snapshots of the New Testament's textual history, revealing variations that may reflect early Christian theological debates or regional textual traditions. The study of these manuscripts not only aids in reconstructing the original text of the New Testament but also provides a window into the early Christian community's faith, practices, and the development of the Christian biblical canon.

The early New Testament manuscripts, especially those dated to the second century, are indispensable to biblical scholarship. They not only

THE EARLY CHRISTIAN COPYISTS OF THE NEW TESTAMENT

illuminate the early stages of the New Testament's textual history but also reflect the diversity and dynamism of early Christian communities. Through meticulous paleographic analysis and scholarly examination, these manuscripts continue to contribute to our understanding of the New Testament's formation, transmission, and reception in the early Christian era.

Delineating the Early Christian Codices: Insights into Second-Century Christian Literature

The early Christian codices from the second century offer a unique window into the nascent Christian community's textual practices, theological explorations, and the emergent preference for the codex over the scroll. This examination delves into lesser-known Christian manuscripts from the period, underscoring the diversity of early Christian literature and the early adoption of the codex format for Christian texts.

Early Christian Literature Beyond the Canonical Texts

The discovery and analysis of early Christian manuscripts, not part of the traditional New Testament canon, illuminate the breadth of theological and literary activity within early Christian communities. These texts, ranging from apocryphal gospels to homilies and theological treatises, demonstrate the rich tapestry of early Christian thought and the complex process of canon formation.

1. **P. Egerton 2 (The Unknown Gospel)**: Dated to around 120–130, with the manuscript copy not later than 150, P. Egerton 2 is a pivotal find. Its resemblance to P52, the earliest known fragment of the Gospel of John, suggests the diversity of gospel literature circulating among early Christians. This text's content and form provide critical insights into the theological and literary milieu of the second century, reflecting the early Christian community's engagement with the life and teachings of Jesus outside the canonical gospels.

2. **P. Oxyrhynchus 1 (Gospel of Thomas)**: The Gospel of Thomas, with its collection of sayings attributed to Jesus, is dated by scholars to the second or possibly third century. The inclination towards an earlier date aligns with the manuscript's paleographic analysis, situating it firmly within the second-century Christian literary landscape. This text's significance lies in its contribution to understanding the diversity of early Christian beliefs and practices, as well as the development of Christian literature.

3. **P. Geneva 253 (Christian Homily)**: This late second-century manuscript, containing excerpts from the Gospels of Matthew and

Luke, highlights the use of gospel texts within the context of Christian preaching and instruction. The homily demonstrates the early integration of gospel texts into the liturgical and devotional life of the Christian community, reflecting the authoritative status these texts were beginning to hold.

4. **P. Oxyrhynchus 406 (Theological Treatise or Unknown New Testament Epistle)**: Dated to around 200, this manuscript, whether a segment of a theological treatise or an unidentified epistle, underscores the theological debates and reflections occurring within early Christianity. Its content, though largely unknown, points to the vibrancy of early Christian intellectual and spiritual life, as well as the diversity of forms in which Christian thought was articulated.

The Codex: A Christian Innovation in Textual Transmission

The overwhelming preference for the codex format among early Christians, as opposed to the scroll, marks a significant departure from Jewish textual traditions. The adoption of the codex can be seen as an early indicator of Christian identity and community cohesion. The fact that virtually all Christian manuscripts from this period are found in codex form, with the notable exception of P. Oxyrhynchus 405, demonstrates a deliberate and widespread adoption of this format. This preference not only facilitated the use and circulation of Christian texts but also reflected a collective standardization in the production and dissemination of these texts, suggesting a degree of organizational coherence within early Christian communities.

The Craftsmanship of Early Christian Copyists

The meticulous work of early Christian copyists in the second century, as evidenced through both canonical and non-canonical manuscripts, showcases a profound commitment to preserving and transmitting the New Testament texts. The transition to the codex format, the careful selection of literary forms, and the precision in textual reproduction underscore the evolving practices of these early scribes. Each manuscript, with its unique calligraphic features and textual variations, offers invaluable insights into the painstaking efforts to ensure the accuracy and integrity of the Christian Scriptures.

THE EARLY CHRISTIAN COPYISTS OF THE NEW TESTAMENT

Deciphering the Manuscripts' Narratives

The diverse collection of second-century manuscripts, from gospels and epistles to homilies and treatises, serves as a testament to the early Christian copyists' dedication. These texts reveal not just the theological concerns of the time but also the meticulous craft involved in their creation. The calligraphic details of each manuscript provide a window into the scribe's world, illustrating the technical skills, aesthetic choices, and textual challenges faced in the reproduction of these sacred texts.

Textual Criticism and the Quest for Originality

The discipline of textual criticism emerges as a crucial tool in evaluating the fidelity of these manuscripts to the original Greek New Testament. By scrutinizing the calligraphic nuances and textual variants among the manuscripts, scholars engage in a meticulous analysis aimed at recovering the most authentic form of the New Testament text. This critical evaluation not only highlights the trustworthiness of the manuscripts but also illuminates the copyists' role in the careful transmission of the text through the earliest centuries of Christianity.

The study of second-century Christian manuscripts illuminates the intricate process of textual transmission by early Christian copyists. Their work, characterized by a deep reverence for the text and a commitment to its accurate preservation, laid the foundation for the future of Christian textual tradition. Through their efforts, the New Testament text was not merely preserved but also enriched, ensuring its continued relevance and authority for future generations. The legacy of these early copyists, encapsulated in each manuscript, continues to inform and inspire the ongoing pursuit of understanding the origins and transmission of the New Testament.

The Role of the Codex in Early Christian Textual Transmission

The introduction of the codex format by early Christians marked a significant advancement in the dissemination and preservation of New Testament writings. Unlike the scroll, the codex allowed for easier access to specific passages, facilitating the use of texts in worship and study. This innovation not only enhanced the practical aspects of reading and handling texts but also influenced the early Christian community's approach to scripture compilation and organization.

Identifying Multibook Codices Among Early Manuscripts

The identification of early New Testament manuscripts that were part of multibook codices presents a unique challenge due to the fragmentary nature of surviving papyri. Despite these challenges, scholars have been able to discern evidence of such compilations through careful analysis of extant materials. Features like pagination numerals and the physical characteristics of folios provide critical clues. These clues help in understanding how early Christians organized and valued their sacred texts, revealing a preference for collecting multiple writings within a single volume.

Uncovering Combinations of New Testament Papyri

The examination of manuscript combinations is a nuanced area of New Testament textual criticism. The traditional listings, such as those found in the appendix to NA28, highlight known combinations like P33+P58 and P64+P67. However, ongoing research and scrutiny of the physical and textual characteristics of these papyri suggest a more complex picture. The inclusion of combinations such as P4+P64+P67, P15+P16, P49+P65, and likely P77+P103 into this list underscores the evolving understanding of early Christian manuscript practices. These combinations not only expand our inventory of New Testament papyri but also illuminate the methodologies of early Christian copyists in assembling their sacred texts.

Implications for Textual Criticism and the Recovery of Original Texts

The identification and analysis of multibook codices among the New Testament papyri have profound implications for the field of textual criticism. By understanding the composition and context of these early Christian texts, scholars can better assess the reliability of the transmission process and make more informed decisions in their quest to recover the original wording of the Greek New Testament. This meticulous work sheds light on the early Christians' reverence for their sacred writings and their efforts to preserve and transmit these texts accurately through generations.

The study of codices and the identification of multibook combinations among early New Testament manuscripts represent crucial aspects of understanding the early Christian textual tradition. Through the diligent examination of these ancient texts, scholars continue to uncover the depth of early Christian commitment to preserving the New Testament, offering insights into the development of the Christian biblical canon and the meticulous care of its earliest copyists.

Circulation of Individual Gospel Manuscripts

The early Christian community engaged in the practice of circulating the Gospels as standalone texts. This practice is evidenced by several manuscripts from the early centuries, showcasing how each Gospel was revered and transmitted independently. For instance, P1, containing Matthew's Gospel, and P66, a codex solely of John's Gospel, highlight the early Christians' approach to disseminating these foundational narratives. The use of pagination and folio formats in these manuscripts underscores the meticulous efforts of early copyists to organize and preserve these texts for communal use and personal devotion.

Emergence of Gospel Collections

While the Gospels initially circulated individually, a shift towards compiling them into collections became evident by the middle of the second century. This transition reflects an evolving understanding and appreciation of the Gospels' interrelatedness and collective significance. The mentions by church fathers such as Justin Martyr and Irenaeus of a fourfold Gospel collection underscore the early Christians' recognition of the need to compile these texts together, enhancing their accessibility and reinforcing their canonical status within the community.

Manuscript Evidence of Early Gospel Collections

The manuscript evidence from the second and third centuries illustrates the gradual compilation of the Gospels into collections. Notably, manuscripts like P75, which contains Luke and John, and P4+P64+P67, potentially housing all four Gospels, signify this developmental phase of Gospel transmission. These collections, some focusing exclusively on the Gospels and others including Acts, indicate a strategic approach to scripture compilation that aimed to provide a comprehensive understanding of the life and teachings of Jesus Christ.

Continuation and Expansion of Gospel Collections

By the fourth century, the practice of assembling all four Gospels into single codices had become widespread, as evidenced by significant manuscripts like Codex Sinaiticus and Codex Vaticanus. These comprehensive collections were not just about convenience; they represented the theological and liturgical acknowledgment of the Gospels' integral role in Christian faith and practice. The inclusion of all four Gospels in church codices by this time reflects a maturation in the early Christian community's approach to scripture, emphasizing the Gospels' collective authority and foundational role in Christian doctrine and worship.

The evolution from individual Gospel manuscripts to comprehensive Gospel collections marks a significant chapter in the history of New Testament textual transmission. This progression underscores the early Christian community's deepening appreciation for the Gospels' central place in Christian faith. Through the diligent efforts of early copyists and the strategic decisions of early church leaders, the Gospels were preserved, compiled, and revered, laying a solid foundation for subsequent generations to explore the depths of the Christian message.

Paul's Epistles: Circulation and Collection

Paul's letters, addressed to various early Christian communities, were more than mere correspondence; they were foundational texts for theological education and communal guidance. These letters were circulated among the early churches, facilitating a shared understanding and practice of faith. The directive in Colossians 4:16 exemplifies this practice, illustrating an early form of textual exchange and mutual edification among the churches. This method of sharing not only strengthened the interconnectedness of the early Christian community but also laid the groundwork for the compilation of these epistles into a collective corpus.

The Role of Paul and His Circle in the Compilation Process

The compilation of Paul's letters into a single collection reflects a deliberate effort to preserve and disseminate apostolic teachings. Paul's intentionality in maintaining copies of his writings, coupled with his methodical approach to authorship and distribution, suggests a forward-looking strategy aimed at ensuring the accessibility and continuity of his theological contributions. This foresight is further evidenced by his instructions to Timothy, emphasizing the importance of safeguarding the apostolic deposit entrusted to them.

Timothy's Possible Role in Assembling the Pauline Corpus

The assembling of the Pauline corpus, potentially by Timothy or another close associate of Paul, represents a critical phase in the textual history of the New Testament. This phase was marked by the strategic selection and arrangement of Paul's letters to form a coherent and authoritative body of text. The exclusion of personal letters from this collection underscores a discernment process focused on the wider applicability and relevance of the texts for the Christian community.

The Significance of the Pauline Collection in Early Christianity

The establishment of a Pauline corpus by the end of the first century signifies a milestone in the textual tradition of early Christianity. References in contemporary writings, such as 2 Peter, highlight the recognition and reverence accorded to Paul's letters as scripture. The codification of these letters into a single volume facilitated their transmission and reinforced their canonical status, underscoring the centrality of Paul's teachings in the formation of Christian doctrine and practice.

Manuscript Evidence and the Transmission of Paul's Letters

Manuscripts such as P46 provide tangible evidence of the early compilation and circulation of Paul's letters as a unified collection. The presence of these texts in codex form, alongside other scriptural writings, illustrates the evolving practices of textual preservation and dissemination among early Christians. The formation of Pauline collections in the second and third centuries, as evidenced by various papyrus codices, attests to the enduring impact of Paul's writings on the development of the New Testament canon.

The journey of Paul's epistles from individual letters to a consolidated corpus encapsulates a significant aspect of the early Christian textual tradition. This process of compilation and canonization reflects the early church's dedication to preserving the apostolic legacy and ensuring the transmission of foundational Christian teachings. Through the efforts of figures like Paul, Timothy, and their contemporaries, the Pauline letters were transformed into a cornerstone of Christian scripture, shaping the theological and liturgical life of the church for generations to come.

The Formation of the New Testament Canon Beyond Paul's Epistles

The compilation of the New Testament canon was a gradual process, with the books beyond Paul's epistles and the Gospels taking a distinctive path towards canonical recognition. This journey underscores the diverse origins and reception of these texts within early Christian communities.

The Integration of Hebrews into the Pauline Corpus

Early Christian communities, particularly in the East, embraced the Book of Hebrews as part of the Pauline writings, despite debates about its authorship. The inclusion of Hebrews in the Pauline corpus, as seen in manuscripts like P46, indicates its early acceptance and the fluid nature of canonical boundaries in the formative years of the church.

Acts and the General Epistles: A Varied Path to Canonization

The General Epistles and the Book of Acts experienced a more complex route to canonical acceptance. While the epistles of James and 1 Peter enjoyed early circulation and acceptance, other texts like 2 Peter, Jude, and John's epistles faced challenges in widespread recognition and textual preservation. The eventual pairing of Acts with the General Epistles in codices such as Codex Bezae illustrates the evolving structure of the New Testament canon and the integration of these writings into the Christian scriptural tradition.

Revelation: A Canonical Enigma

The Book of Revelation presents a unique case of canonical development, characterized by its contested status and the private nature of its earliest copies. The textual tradition of Revelation, marked by manuscripts produced outside professional scribal circles, reflects the book's peripheral position in the early church and highlights the diversity of early Christian attitudes towards scriptural texts.

The Role of Manuscripts in Shaping the Canon

Manuscripts like P46, P13, and P98 play a crucial role in understanding the formation of the New Testament canon. They offer insights into the early Christians' practices of reading, copying, and compiling texts, revealing a dynamic process of canonization that was influenced by theological, liturgical, and practical considerations.

The path to the New Testament canon was shaped by the varied reception and collection of texts across different Christian communities. The integration of Paul's epistles, the Gospels, and other New Testament writings into a recognized canon reflects a complex interplay of tradition, authority, and community practice. Through the meticulous work of early Christian copyists and the transmission of manuscripts, the foundational texts of Christianity were preserved and disseminated, laying the groundwork for the development of the New Testament as we know it today.

The Early Christian Approach to Canonization

The early Christian churches engaged in a discerning process of selecting certain texts for use in their congregations, a practice that significantly contributed to the formation of the New Testament canon. The collections of the four Gospels and Paul's epistles, including Hebrews, were foundational in this process. These texts were esteemed for their apostolic authority, reflecting the teachings and truths central to Christian faith.

Recognition of Canonical Texts

The inclusion of the book of Acts and the General Epistles, known collectively as the Praxapostolos, alongside the Gospels and Paul's letters, marks a pivotal moment in the canonization process. The book of Revelation's eventual acceptance into the canon illustrates the nuanced and gradual nature of this process, underscoring the early church's commitment to discerning the contours of their sacred writings.

The Muratorian Canon and Early Lists

The discovery of the Muratorian Canon, dating around 170 C.E., offers significant insight into the early church's perspective on canonical texts. Despite its incomplete state, this document provides a glimpse into the early Christian community's deliberations over which writings were deemed scripturally authoritative. The Muratorian Canon's reference to the now-accepted twenty-seven New Testament books, while expressing reservations about certain texts, highlights the ongoing dialogues within early Christianity regarding the canon.

The Establishment of the New Testament Canon

The fourth century represented a crucial era for the solidification of the New Testament canon. Figures such as Eusebius played a vital role in advocating for the recognition of the four Gospels and other texts as part of the canon. It was Athanasius of Alexandria's Festal Letter in 367 that articulated a clear endorsement of the twenty-seven books, marking a decisive step towards the canon's finalization. The Council of Carthage in 397 further cemented this by formally recognizing these books as the definitive New Testament canon.

Codices and the Canon

The production of codices containing all twenty-seven books of the New Testament, alongside the Greek Old Testament, from the fourth century onwards, underscores the acceptance and consolidation of the canon within the Christian tradition. Codex Vaticanus, Codex Sinaiticus, and Codex Ephraemi Rescriptus stand as monumental witnesses to this historic development, encapsulating the early church's reverence for these texts and their role in shaping Christian doctrine and practice.

The formation of the New Testament canon was a complex and iterative process, reflecting the early Christian community's dedication to preserving the apostolic legacy. Through careful selection and widespread recognition, the twenty-seven books of the New Testament were established as the cornerstone of Christian scripture, guiding the faith and practice of believers across generations.

THE EARLY CHRISTIAN COPYISTS OF THE NEW TESTAMENT

Manuscript Production in the Ancient World

The creation and dissemination of New Testament manuscripts in the early Christian era were markedly different from today's book production due to the absence of printing technology. Each manuscript was painstakingly copied by hand, a process that inherently limited the speed and volume of production. This manual copying method was the standard for all texts, with the rare exception of "mass-produced" works like Homer's epics, which were copied by multiple scribes working from a single reading.

Early Circulation of New Testament Texts

By the latter half of the first century, the New Testament texts began to circulate within the Roman Empire, primarily through the efforts of the early Christian communities. Notably, Paul's epistles and the four Gospels were among the first to be widely distributed. These texts were not circulated as commercial trade books but were shared within the church network for the purpose of edification and instruction. The spontaneous and organic nature of this distribution underscores the early Christians' dedication to disseminating the apostolic teachings.

Estimating Early Manuscript Numbers

While it is challenging to determine the exact number of manuscripts in circulation by the end of the third century, particularly for texts outside the Pauline Epistles and the Gospels, it is clear that these foundational texts were more widely available due to their importance and relevance to the early churches. The process of creating and sharing these manuscripts was driven by the needs of the Christian communities, indicating a dynamic interaction between the production of texts and the growth of the early church.

The Role of Professional Scribes and Community Copyists

Evidence suggests that both professional scribes and literate members of the Christian community were involved in copying New Testament manuscripts. The distinction between these groups is visible in the varying quality of the manuscripts, with some displaying professional "bookhands" and others manifesting a more personal or informal style of writing. This variety reflects the diverse contexts in which these sacred texts were reproduced.

The Distribution Network of Early Christianity

The movement of manuscripts among the early Christian communities relied heavily on personal delivery rather than the official Roman postal system, which was neither designed for speed nor accessibility to the general public. Key figures within the Christian community, such as Paul's associates and other early leaders, played crucial roles in hand-delivering these texts. This method of distribution ensured that the New Testament writings reached their intended audiences, facilitating the spread of Christian teachings across the Empire.

The Special Case of the Book of Revelation

The distribution of the book of Revelation provides a unique example of early Christian manuscript circulation. Contrary to some interpretations, the "anggeloi" mentioned as the recipients of Revelation were likely human messengers responsible for delivering John's apocalyptic visions to the seven churches of Asia Minor. This method of distribution highlights the strategic and intentional efforts made by the early church to ensure that this significant prophetic text was shared among the Christian communities.

The early Christian approach to the production and distribution of New Testament manuscripts was characterized by a remarkable commitment to spreading the apostolic message. Despite the technological limitations of the time, these early believers devised effective strategies to ensure that the teachings of Christ and the apostles reached a wide audience, laying the foundation for the development of the Christian canon and the faith's enduring legacy.

Growth of the Early Church

The early Christian church experienced exponential growth from its inception in 33 C.E. in Jerusalem. Starting with a modest group of 120 followers, the church quickly expanded to thousands of believers, significantly impacting Jerusalem's population. This rapid growth was further fueled by the day of Pentecost, where Peter's sermon led to the conversion of three thousand individuals, and subsequent growth continued to add thousands more to their number. Despite persecution, which caused many to flee Jerusalem, the Christian faith continued to spread across Judea, Galilee, Samaria, and beyond, reaching even the diaspora Jews and Gentiles across the Roman Empire.

The Spread of Christianity Beyond Jerusalem

The dispersion of Christians due to persecution in Jerusalem served as a catalyst for the spread of the Gospel across the Roman Empire. Believers from various regions, including Parthians, Medes, Elamites, and others present at Pentecost, took the message of Christ back to their homelands. This grassroots dissemination of the Gospel played a crucial role in the establishment of Christian communities far from Jerusalem, including the significant church in Rome, which was not founded by an apostle but grew organically from converts returning home.

The Roman Church and Its Early Challenges

By 52 C.E., the Christian community in Rome had grown significantly, evidenced by historical accounts such as Suetonius's reference to the expulsion of Jews at the instigation of "Chrestus." The Roman church faced challenges early on, including persecution and expulsion, yet continued to grow, as indicated by the presence of multiple house churches by 56 C.E. Nero's persecution in 64–68 C.E. further attests to the substantial number of Christians in Rome, described by Tacitus and Clement as a vast multitude.

Expansion to Egypt and Alexandria

The church's expansion to Egypt, particularly Alexandria, illustrates the widespread influence of Pentecost. Apollos, an Alexandrian who was already a follower of the Way before arriving in Ephesus around 53 C.E., exemplifies how Christianity spread to even distant regions such as Alexandria, which had a large Jewish population and strong connections to Jerusalem. This set the stage for the growth of a significant Christian community and the establishment of a Christian academy in Alexandria by the second century.

The Ephesian Church and Its Influence

Ephesus served as a strategic center for Paul's ministry, with the church there becoming a hub of Christian activity. The presence of structured church roles such as elders and deacons, alongside a diverse congregation that included both faithful believers and heretics, underscores the church's significant size and organizational complexity. The practice of copying Paul's epistles, as mentioned in relation to Ephesus and Colossae, highlights the importance of scripture in the life of the early church and the proactive role of communities in preserving and disseminating apostolic teachings.

Antioch of Syria: A Pivotal Early Church Center

Antioch of Syria emerged as another major center of early Christianity, attracting believers fleeing persecution and serving as the birthplace of the term "Christians." The missionary activities initiated from Antioch, coupled with the church's significant role in the early church councils, underscore its importance in the spread and development of early Christian doctrine and community life.

The early Christian church's growth from a small group of followers in Jerusalem to a widespread religious movement across the Roman Empire is a testament to the compelling nature of the Christian message and the dedication of its early adherents. Despite facing persecution and challenges, the church not only survived but thrived, establishing strong communities in major cities like Rome, Alexandria, and Ephesus, and influencing the religious landscape of the ancient world.

Private Copies of New Testament Scriptures

In the early Christian community, not only were copies of the New Testament scriptures made for church use, but many believers also made copies for private use. This practice was facilitated by the literacy levels among early Christians, both men and women, who could afford personal copies. Literacy was much higher throughout the Roman Empire than many scholars have suggested. For evidence of this see my book: THE READING CULTURE OF EARLY CHRISTIANITY: The Production, Publication, Circulation, and Use of Books in the Early Christian Church. Influential figures like Pamphilus ensured that scriptures were copied and distributed to those who could not afford them, highlighting the communal aspect of Christian scripture engagement. Encouragement for private reading and study of the scriptures was evident in the teachings of early church fathers like Irenaeus, Clement of Alexandria, and Origen. This personalized engagement with the scriptures fostered a deepened individual and communal faith experience, extending beyond the collective worship settings.

THE EARLY CHRISTIAN COPYISTS OF THE NEW TESTAMENT

Persecution and Preservation of Scriptures

The widespread distribution of New Testament scriptures caught the attention of Roman authorities, particularly during the Diocletian persecution. Diocletian's edict to demolish churches and burn Christian books aimed to eradicate Christianity by destroying its sacred texts. Eusebius, an early church historian, documented the severe actions taken against Christians and their scriptures, highlighting the intention to obliterate Christian presence through the destruction of their sacred texts.

Strategies of Resistance and Preservation

Despite the harsh persecution, many Christians found ways to preserve their sacred texts. Some complied with the Roman demands, while others resisted by hiding their scriptures or handing over non-sacred texts to protect the New Testament manuscripts. This resistance took various forms across different regions, from Alexandria to rural Egypt, where believers went to great lengths to safeguard their scriptures. The creative strategies employed by these early Christians underscored their dedication to preserving their faith's foundational texts.

The Impact of Persecution on Scripture Transmission

The Diocletian persecution, although intended to destroy Christian texts, inadvertently contributed to the preservation of several New Testament manuscripts. Instances of scriptures hidden in homes or caves, and the survival of significant collections like the Beatty and Bodmer papyri, demonstrate the resilience of the Christian community in the face of adversity. These preserved texts serve as a testament to the early Christians' unwavering commitment to their faith and the lengths they went to protect and transmit their sacred writings.

The Role of Scripture in Early Christian Identity

The early Christians' response to the Diocletian persecution reveals the central role scripture played in their identity and faith practice. The willingness to endure hardship and even martyrdom rather than surrender their scriptures highlights the profound reverence and loyalty they held towards their sacred texts. This period of persecution, while a time of great trial, also exemplified the strength and resilience of the Christian community, cementing the scriptures' place at the heart of Christian worship and individual belief.

Through these challenging times, the early Christian community's efforts to make, preserve, and protect the New Testament scriptures underscored the foundational importance of these texts in shaping Christian identity, worship, and practice. The legacy of these early copyists and believers continues to resonate, offering insights into the transmission and enduring significance of the New Testament manuscripts.

The Treasure of Oxyrhynchus

Oxyrhynchus, an ancient Egyptian city, has emerged as a pivotal site for uncovering Christian texts, yielding a remarkable number of manuscripts from the New Testament, the Old Testament, and extrabiblical literature. This discovery underscores the vibrant Christian literary activity within this community, reflecting both individual and communal engagement with Christian scriptures. The diverse manuscripts found, prepared for various readers and purposes, illustrate the widespread and varied use of Christian literature in the early centuries.

A Wealth of Manuscripts

The excavation of Oxyrhynchus has brought to light forty-six papyrus manuscripts of the New Testament, dating primarily from 200 to 400, with notable examples from the second century. This collection, expanded through decades of discoveries and publications, includes both papyrus and vellum manuscripts, each contributing unique insights into early Christian practices of scripture reading and copying. The manuscripts range from those evidently prepared for church readings, characterized by their attractive appearance and large, clear handwriting, to those likely made for private study, suggesting a nuanced landscape of scripture engagement among early Christians.

Church and Private Reading Practices

The manuscripts from Oxyrhynchus reveal a dual practice among early Christians: communal readings within the church and private study. Certain manuscripts, with their distinct calligraphy and formatting, were clearly intended for liturgical use, facilitating communal worship and instruction. Others, by contrast, seem tailored for individual contemplation and devotion, indicating a personal dimension to scripture engagement. This distinction highlights the multifaceted relationship early Christians had with their sacred texts, encompassing both collective worship and personal study.

Post-Persecution Expansion of Scripture Production

The end of the Diocletian persecution and the legalization of Christianity under Constantine marked a significant turning point in the production and distribution of Christian scriptures. Constantine's commission of fifty Bible codices for Constantinople signaled the beginning of a new era for Christian literature. The subsequent increase in manuscript production, estimated to be between fifteen hundred and two thousand in the fourth century alone, reflects the rapid expansion of Christianity and its textual foundation. This period saw a dramatic growth in the availability of scriptures, facilitating both the consolidation of Christian doctrine and the spread of Christian communities.

Theodoret's Intervention and the Circulation of Gospels

An event around 420 C.E. involving Theodoret, the bishop of Cyprus, provides further insight into the circulation and influence of Christian texts. His efforts to replace the Diatessaron with separate copies of the four Gospels highlight the ongoing process of defining and disseminating orthodox Christian teachings. Theodoret's action, resulting in the distribution of two hundred copies of the Gospels in one region, underscores the scale at which Christian scriptures were being produced and circulated by the early fifth century, reflecting the entrenched position of the New Testament within Christian communities.

The discoveries at Oxyrhynchus and subsequent historical events illustrate the dynamic and resilient nature of early Christian scripture transmission. From private devotionals to communal worship, and from persecution to legal recognition, the early Christian community's engagement with the New Testament scriptures reveals a deep commitment to preserving and propagating their faith through the written word. This legacy of early Christian copyists, through their meticulous and often perilous work, has ensured the survival and continued influence of these foundational texts.

The Role of Oral Reading in Early Christian Publishing

The journey of a New Testament book from conception to its reception by the early Christian communities involved a critical final step: oral reading to the congregation. This tradition underscores the centrality of oral proclamation in the dissemination of Christian teachings, with the written word serving to preserve and standardize these teachings across different locales. Given the literacy levels of the time, where only a small fraction of the population could read, oral reading played a pivotal role in ensuring the accessibility and continuity of Christian doctrine.

The Amanuensis: From Writing to Reading

The amanuensis, or secretary, who penned the texts as dictated by early Christian leaders like Paul, often bore the additional responsibility of delivering and orally reading these writings to their intended audience. This practice was not merely a matter of convenience but a critical means of clarifying and explaining the content of these letters, ensuring their messages were correctly understood. Such figures, possibly including Tychicus for the epistles to the Ephesians and Colossians, served as vital links between the apostolic authors and the early Christian communities.

The Practice of Oral Reading in Church Meetings

In the gatherings of the early Christian church, a model borrowed from Jewish synagogal practices, the reading of scriptures played a central role. This practice included not only the Old Testament texts but also the emerging New Testament writings. The act of reading aloud in these gatherings was a communal event, with selected individuals, known as lectors, tasked with this responsibility. These readings provided a direct encounter with the sacred texts, fostering a shared understanding and spiritual communion among the congregants.

The Impact of Scribes and Lectors on Scripture Dissemination

The intersection of the roles of scribes and lectors highlights a dynamic aspect of early Christian textual tradition. Scribes, often among the most educated members of the community, were instrumental in creating written copies of the scriptures, while lectors facilitated their oral dissemination. This partnership between scribe and reader ensured that the Christian message was not only preserved in writing but also actively engaged with through public recitation. The relationship between these roles is encapsulated in the blessings found in the manuscript P72, wishing peace upon both the scribe and the lector, emphasizing their joint contribution to the spiritual life of the community.

Lectors: The Voice of Scripture

Lectors held a crucial position within the early Christian community, bridging the gap between the written text and the congregation. Initially, any community member proficient in Greek could serve as a lector, but by the third century, this role became more formalized, though it remained a non-ordained function within the church hierarchy. The evolution of this role reflects the growing institutionalization of Christian worship practices and the increasing importance of scripture in the liturgical life of the church. Through the efforts of lectors, the words of the New Testament were brought to life, allowing the teachings of Jesus and the apostles to resonate within the hearts and minds of early Christians.

This practice of oral reading, deeply embedded in the fabric of early Christian worship, underscores the communal and inclusive nature of Christian scripture engagement, ensuring that the transformative power of the gospel was accessible to all, regardless of literacy.

Lectoral Markings in Early New Testament Manuscripts

The early Greek New Testament manuscripts, much like all Greek literary texts of the time, were written in scriptio continua, a style characterized by the absence of spaces between words. This style necessitated a certain level of reader training for effectively discerning individual words during oral reading. Contrary to some modern misconceptions, early manuscripts were not devoid of punctuation. In fact, they featured several forms of punctuation and other lectoral markings designed to facilitate reading.

The Role of Punctuation

Punctuation marks such as the midpoint, highpoint, and occasional period were common in nearly every early manuscript. These marks were strategically placed by scribes to indicate separations of thought, enhancing the reader's ability to understand and convey the text's meaning accurately. Colons, signifying semantic units and particularly popular in poetry, were also used, as evidenced in manuscripts like P13, P17, and P46, particularly within the poetic context of the book of Hebrews.

Paragraph and Section Markings

To denote new paragraphs or sections, scribes employed various methods, including leaving spaces between words or outdenting a new line by one or two spaces—a method known as ekdesis. This approach is notably observed in professionally produced manuscripts such as P4+64+67, P75, and P77, and later in the well-regarded Codex Vaticanus. The use of lines or dashes extending from the margin into the text was another technique to indicate the beginning of a new section, further exemplifying the scribes' methods to aid the reader.

Slash Marks for Thought Pauses

The presence of slash marks in manuscripts, indicative of thought pauses, reveals that these were added not by the original scribe but by a lector in preparation for oral reading. This practice, particularly observed in P46 and P66, suggests a selective approach to marking texts that were intended for public reading, highlighting the interactive relationship between the manuscript and its oral presentation in a communal setting.

Characteristics of Church Copies

Manuscripts intended for church use, distinguishable by their larger print, larger sheets, and quality handwriting, were crafted with public reading in mind. This is evident in the reduced number of lines per page and letters per line, a deliberate design choice to facilitate legibility during ecclesiastical oration. Such manuscripts, including P4+64+67 and P75, reflect the early Christian community's emphasis on making the scriptures accessible through oral dissemination.

THE EARLY CHRISTIAN COPYISTS OF THE NEW TESTAMENT

Insights on New Testament Book Popularity

The surviving manuscripts offer glimpses into the early Christians' reading preferences, particularly in Egypt before 300 C.E. The prevalence of manuscripts for certain New Testament books over others provides a snapshot of early Christian scriptural engagement. The Gospels of Matthew and John, for example, enjoyed considerable popularity, while Luke and Mark were less frequently copied. This distribution, while not exhaustive, offers valuable insights into the early Christian canon and the texts that held particular significance for those communities.

The evidence from early papyri not only sheds light on the practical aspects of manuscript production and reading practices but also on the early Christians' interaction with their sacred texts. These manuscripts, with their lectoral markings and design features, stand as testaments to the communities that valued, read, and preserved the New Testament writings, offering a window into the early transmission and reception of Christian scripture.

CHAPTER 5 Most Important Manuscripts (100 – 400 C.E.)

Exploring the Greek New Testament Papyri Manuscripts: Insights into Early Christian Copyists

The Origin and Significance of Greek NT Papyri Manuscripts

The Greek New Testament (NT) papyri manuscripts form the earliest corpus of Christian scripture texts. These manuscripts, written on papyrus, a material made from the pith of the papyrus plant, provide invaluable insights into the text of the New Testament as it was transmitted in the first few centuries C.E. The discovery of these papyri revolutionized the field of New Testament textual criticism by offering direct evidence of the textual traditions that existed closest in time to the original autographs.

THE EARLY CHRISTIAN COPYISTS OF THE NEW TESTAMENT

Transmission of the Text

The early Christian community highly valued the apostolic writings, which were meticulously copied and circulated among the churches. 2 Timothy 3:16 underscores the importance of scripture, stating, "All Scripture is inspired by God and beneficial for teaching, for rebuke, for correction, for training in righteousness." This verse reflects the early Christians' view of the NT writings as divinely inspired and crucial for instruction in faith and practice.

The process of copying these texts was labor-intensive and carried out by scribes who were either part of the Christian community or professional copyists hired for their skills. The papyri manuscripts exhibit a range of textual variations, which is indicative of the scribes' efforts to be faithful to the texts they reproduced. However, given the manual nature of copying, variations and errors inevitably crept in. This phenomenon underscores the significance of textual criticism in attempting to reconstruct the original text of the NT.

Dating the Manuscripts

The dating of the Greek NT papyri manuscripts is critical for understanding their role in the transmission of the NT text. These manuscripts are dated based on paleography, a study of ancient handwriting. The earliest papyri manuscripts, such as P5252 (Rylands Library Papyrus P52), date from around 100-150 C.E., providing a tangible connection to the time less than a century after the original writings of the New Testament.

The Papyri and Their Contribution to Textual Criticism

The contribution of the papyri to New Testament textual criticism cannot be overstated. They offer the earliest textual evidence for the books of the New Testament, thus playing a pivotal role in identifying the most authentic readings of the text. For example, P66 and P75 (dated to 100-150 and 175-225 centuries C.E., respectively) contain substantial portions of the Gospels, offering critical insights into the text that predate the major codices by several centuries.

The study of these papyri has led to a more nuanced understanding of the textual transmission and has helped scholars identify textual variants that shed light on how early Christians understood and interpreted the New Testament writings. Matthew 5:18 emphasizes the durability of scripture, saying, "For truly I say to you, until heaven and earth pass away, not the smallest letter or stroke shall pass from the Law until all is accomplished." This verse highlights the meticulous care with which the text was to be preserved, a principle that guided the early copyists in their work.

Challenges and Limitations

Despite their value, the Greek NT papyri also present challenges. The fragmentary nature of many papyri means that they often provide incomplete evidence of the text. Furthermore, the variation among manuscripts reflects the dynamic nature of the early textual tradition, challenging scholars to discern the most reliable forms of the text.

Textual Variants and Interpretative Insights

The study of textual variants among the papyri manuscripts has been crucial for understanding the development of the New Testament text. Variants are not merely errors but can offer insights into the theological interpretations and practices of early Christian communities. For instance, variations in the Lord's Prayer across different manuscripts highlight how this fundamental Christian text was adapted and used in liturgical settings.

The Role of Early Christian Copyists

The early Christian copyists played an indispensable role in the preservation and transmission of the New Testament. Their dedication and labor ensured that the text was not only copied but also disseminated across the Mediterranean world. Acts 8:4 speaks to the early Christians' commitment to spreading the word, "Therefore, those who had been scattered went about preaching the word." This missionary spirit also extended to the transmission of the written word, ensuring that the teachings of Jesus and the apostles reached far-flung Christian communities.

Moving Forward with the Papyri Manuscripts

As more papyri manuscripts are discovered and analyzed, our understanding of the early text of the New Testament continues to grow. These ancient witnesses not only enrich our comprehension of the textual history of the New Testament but also deepen our appreciation for the faith and diligence of the early Christian copyists. Their work has provided a foundation upon which the faith has been built and preserved, reflecting the enduring power and relevance of the New Testament writings through the centuries.

Unveiling the Oxyrhynchus Papyri: A Window into Early Christian Textual Practices

Introduction to the Oxyrhynchus Papyri

The Oxyrhynchus Papyri are a vast collection of manuscripts uncovered in the town of Oxyrhynchus, Egypt, offering a remarkable glimpse into the early Christian era and the transmission of the New Testament texts. Discovered by archaeologists Bernard Grenfell and Arthur Hunt at the end of the 19th century, these papyri have been instrumental in expanding our understanding of early Christian textual traditions and practices.

The Oxyrhynchus Papyri stand as a monumental discovery in the study of New Testament textual criticism, offering critical insights into the scribal practices and challenges faced in the early transmission of Christian texts. These ancient documents, unearthed from the sands of Oxyrhynchus, Egypt, encompass a wide array of writings, including significant portions of the New Testament. Their analysis reveals the intricate process of how these sacred texts were copied, preserved, and transmitted across generations.

Scribal Practices and Textual Variants

In the journey from the original autographs penned by the New Testament authors to the copies that have reached us, the role of the scribe is both crucial and complex. The original writings, inspired and inerrant, were produced without error, contradiction, or omission. However, as these texts were copied by hand, the human element of transcription introduced variations. These textual variants arose from a multitude of factors, including unintentional slips of the pen, misreadings, or deliberate adjustments made by the copyists.

The work of the scribes, while diligent and aimed at faithful preservation, was inherently subject to human limitations. Despite their best efforts to accurately copy the texts, the manual process was prone to errors. Some scribes, perhaps with intentions of clarifying or harmonizing passages, introduced changes that resulted in intentional variants. These alterations, whether accidental or purposeful, underscore the distinction between the inspired original compositions and the subsequent copies made by fallible humans.

The Restoration of the Text

Spanning approximately 500 years, a significant period of textual restoration has been undertaken by scholars utilizing the principles of textual criticism. This scholarly endeavor aims to sift through the variants and reconstruct a text that closely approximates the original writings. Through a meticulous analysis of manuscripts, including the invaluable Oxyrhynchus Papyri, textual critics have worked to identify and correct errors introduced during the copying process.

The restoration phase is marked by an unwavering commitment to precision and a deep reverence for the sacred texts. By comparing manuscript evidence, scholars discern the most reliable readings and endeavor to bridge the gap between the original autographs and the copies available today. This process, grounded in scholarly rigor rather than divine inspiration, highlights the collaboration of preservation and restoration in safeguarding the integrity of the New Testament text.

The Oxyrhynchus Papyri serve as a testament to the endeavors of early Christian copyists and the ongoing work of textual critics. These manuscripts illuminate the challenges of textual transmission and the human effort involved in preserving the New Testament. While the original authors wrote under divine inspiration, the subsequent phases of copying and restoration have been guided by human dedication to preserving and uncovering the authentic text. Through this blend of preservation and restoration, the textual tradition of the New Testament continues to be studied, understood, and appreciated in its historical and theological context.

The discovery of the Oxyrhynchus papyri by Grenfell and Hunt in the late 19th and early 20th centuries marked a pivotal moment in the field of New Testament textual criticism. Found amidst the ancient rubbish heaps of Oxyrhynchus, Egypt, these papyri fragments have provided a profound insight into the early Christian era, encompassing a wide array of written materials, including an invaluable collection of New Testament manuscripts.

Discovery and Significance

The excavation of these texts spanned from 1898 to 1907, with further explorations conducted by the Italian exploration society between 1910 to 1913 and 1927 to 1934. This remarkable endeavor unearthed nearly half of the known 115 New Testament papyri, making Oxyrhynchus one of the most significant archaeological sites for biblical scholarship.

The published fragments from these excavations, including P1, P5, P9–10, P13, P15–18, P20–24, P27–30, P35–36, P39, and P48, represent a treasure trove of early Christian textuality. Later discoveries added to this corpus with manuscripts like P51, P65, P69, P70, P71, P77, P78, P90, P100 through P116, enriching our understanding of the textual transmission of the New Testament.

Among these, notable papyri such as P1 (Matthew 1), P5 (John 1, 16), P13 (Hebrews 2–5, 10–12), P22 (John 15–16), P77 (Matthew 23), P90 (John 18), P104 (Matthew 21), and P115 (Revelation 3–12) offer critical insights into the early manuscript tradition of the New Testament, underscoring the textual diversity and the scribes' efforts in preserving these sacred texts.

The Chester Beatty Papyri: Expanding the Manuscript Tradition

The Chester Beatty papyri, acquired during the 1930s by Chester Beatty and the University of Michigan, further expanded the repository of early Christian manuscripts. Likely originating from a Christian library, scholar, or monastery, these papyri, including P45 (Gospels and Acts, ca. 175-225 C.E.), P46 (Paul's epistles, ca. 100–150), and P47 (Revelation, 200-250 C.E.), have significantly contributed to the study of the New Testament's textual history.

Their substantial content and early dates have not only influenced modern Bible translations, such as the Updated American Standard Version (UASV) but have also been recognized in critical editions of the Greek New Testament, beginning with the 16th edition of the Nestle text in 1936. The scholarly examination of these manuscripts by experts like Kenyon, Zuntz, Schofield, Schmid, Aland, Colwell, and Royse have deepened our understanding of the textual variations and the development of the Christian biblical canon.

Exploring the Bodmer Papyri: Insights into Early Christian Copyists

The Bodmer Papyri, discovered in the mid-20th century, represent a significant find in the field of New Testament textual criticism. Named after Martin Bodmer, who acquired these manuscripts through a dealer in Egypt during the 1950s and 1960s, these ancient texts offer critical insights into the early transmission of the New Testament scriptures. The discovery near Dishna, close to where the Nag Hammadi codices were found, suggests a connection to a Pachomian monastery library, indicating the communal and monastic efforts in preserving Christian texts.

The Significance of the Bodmer Papyri

The Bodmer Papyri, particularly those containing New Testament writings, are paramount in understanding the textual integrity and early transmission of Christian scripture. This collection includes pivotal manuscripts such as P66 (circa 150, containing almost all of John), P72 (200-250, having all of 1 and 2 Peter and Jude), P73 (Matthew, seventh century), P74 (Acts, General Epistles, seventh century), and P75 (Luke and John, circa 175–200). Some of these manuscripts are among the oldest and most reliable witnesses to the New Testament texts, providing valuable comparisons to later textual traditions.

P66: A Window into the Gospel of John

P66, dating to around 100-150 C.E., is a near-complete codex of the Gospel of John. Its early date makes it an invaluable resource for textual critics, offering a snapshot of the Gospel text approximately a century after its original composition. This manuscript demonstrates the care with which early Christians copied and preserved their sacred texts, despite the manual copying processes that inevitably introduced variations. The textual integrity of P66 supports the reliability of John's Gospel, affirming foundational Christian truths such as those found in John 1:1, "In the beginning was the Word, and the Word was with God, and the Word was God."

P72: The General Epistles

P72, from 200-250 C.E., contains the complete texts of 1 and 2 Peter and Jude. This manuscript is particularly significant for its inclusion of these General Epistles, offering insights into their early acceptance and use within Christian communities. The preservation of these letters in P72 attests to the early Christians' recognition of their apostolic authority and doctrinal importance, echoing the sentiments of 2 Peter 1:20-21, which speaks to the prophetic and inspired nature of scripture.

P75: Luke and John's Gospels

P75, dated to around 175–225 C.E., is critical for its early textual witness to the Gospels of Luke and John. Its close textual agreement with Codex Vaticanus, one of the most important biblical manuscripts of the fourth century, underscores the textual stability and transmission accuracy of these Gospels from the second century onwards. P75 has been instrumental in confirming the early form of the Gospel texts, supporting the historical reliability of the accounts of Jesus' life and teachings.

Scholarly Engagement with the Bodmer Papyri

The extensive study of the Bodmer Papyri by scholars such as Colwell, Fee, Kubo, Aland, Porter, and Royse, along with investigations conducted for doctoral dissertations, underscores the academic importance of these manuscripts. These studies have contributed significantly to the field of textual criticism, offering deeper understanding of scribal practices, textual variants, and the early Christian community's efforts to transmit their sacred writings faithfully.

The Bodmer Papyri and Early Christian Copyist Practices

The discovery and subsequent analysis of the Bodmer Papyri shed light on the meticulous practices of early Christian copyists. The manuscripts serve as a testament to the dedication of early Christians to preserving the scriptures, reflecting a deep reverence for God's Word and a commitment to its accurate transmission across generations. This dedication is mirrored in the scriptural admonition found in Revelation 22:19, warning against adding to or taking away from the words of the prophecy, a principle that guided early scribes in their sacred task.

Insights into Early Christian Textual Transmission

The Bodmer Papyri offer a unique vantage point into the early textual history of the New Testament, providing evidence of the texts' integrity and the early Christians' devotion to preserving their sacred writings. Through these ancient manuscripts, scholars gain invaluable insights into the early church's engagement with scripture, the textual variants that arose through the copying process, and the ongoing scholarly pursuit to understand the original context and meaning of the New Testament writings. The Bodmer Papyri thus remain a cornerstone in the study of New Testament textual criticism, symbolizing the enduring legacy of the early Christian copyists and their profound impact on the preservation of Christian scripture.

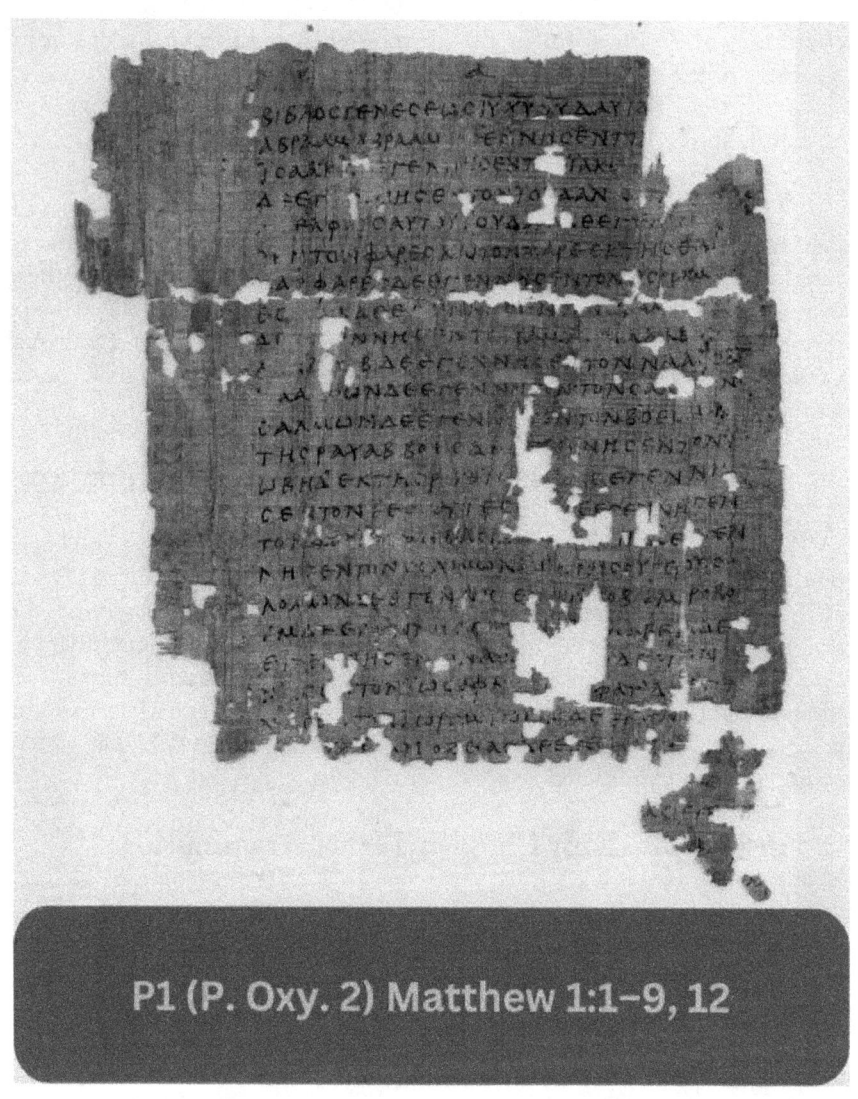

P1 (P. Oxy. 2) Matthew 1:1–9, 12

P1 (P. Oxy. 2)

Physical Description and Features of P1

P1 (P. Oxy. 2) is a single-page fragment, with one column per page, containing between 27 to 29 lines per page, and measures about 14.7 cm (6 inches) by 15 cm (6 inches). The original codex likely had two leaves bound together in a quire.

This fragment includes parts of Matthew's Gospel, specifically verses 1:1–9, 12, 13, and 14–20. The text is written in a continuous stream without any space between words. There are no accents or breathings used throughout the text, except for two instances: one smooth breathing appears on the fifth letter (ωβηδ ἐκ) in line 14 on the back side, and one rough breathing is on the fourth letter from the end (ἡ συν) in line 14 on the front side. Sacred names, or nomina sacra, are abbreviated as "IC", "XC", "YC", "ΠNA", "KΣ" and are marked with a line above them.

Content Held Within P1

P1 contains portions of the Gospel of Matthew, specifically passages from Matthew 1:1-9, 12, 14-20. This selection includes the genealogy of Jesus, setting the stage for the narrative of His life, teachings, and fulfillment of prophecy. These verses are crucial for understanding the early Christian claim of Jesus' Messianic lineage, grounding His life and mission within the broader narrative of Israel's history. The presence of such text in P1 underscores the importance placed on Jesus' genealogical record for early Christian communities, serving as a testament to His identity as the Christ.

On this Philip W. Comfort writes (Comfort & Barret, THE TEXT OF THE EARLIEST NEW TESTAMENT MANUSCRIPTS: Papyri 1-72, Vol. 1 , 2019, pp. 25-26),

Accompanying the first chapter of Matthew is a small portion of what must have been a flyleaf cover, with writing only on the outside sheet. The extant letters are written in a slightly different hand than what appears in the text of Matthew 1. Contrary to O'Callaghan's conjecture, the letters probably do not represent Matt. 2:14, because the writing is in a different hand, and the greater margin above the three broken lines distinguishes them from the text of Matthew. Rather, they may have been part of a title, as noted by Grenfell and Hunt. Or it could be conjectured that it was not so much a title as it was a kind of subhead descriptor:

εγεν[νεθη (was born; the subject being Jesus)
παρ[α (from; indicating source or origin [the Holy Spirit])
μητ[ρος αυτου (his mother [Mary])

It could have read like this:

Was born [Jesus Christ, the son of David,]

from [the Holy Spirit coming upon]
his mother [Mary, the wife of Joseph]

Dating and Paleographic Insights

The manuscript is dated to 175-225 C.E., with this dating achieved through paleographic analysis. This method involves a detailed examination of the handwriting style present in the manuscript, comparing it with other contemporaneously dated texts. The specific characteristics of the script—such as letter formation, ligatures, and text layout—contribute to placing P1 within this time frame. This period, shortly after the apostolic age, highlights the early efforts to document the teachings and life of Jesus, ensuring their preservation and transmission to successive generations.

Textual Character and Scribe Workmanship

1. **Text Type**: P1 exhibits characteristics of the Alexandrian text type, renowned for its textual fidelity and considered one of the most reliable text forms of the New Testament. This classification is significant for textual critics, as Alexandrian manuscripts often provide a closer approximation to the original texts of the New Testament.

2. **Handwriting Style**: The script of P1 aligns with the Reformed Documentary Hand. This observation suggests that the scribe, while experienced in documentary writing, exhibited a heightened level of care and uniformity in copying, aware of the manuscript's significance as a religious text.

3. **Quality of Scribe's Work**: The transcription in P1 appears to have been executed with a careful hand, aiming for clarity and accuracy. Such diligence indicates the scribe's reverence for the content and their role in its preservation.

4. **Comparative Analysis**: P1's alignment with the Alexandrian tradition affirms its textual consistency with other early and reliable manuscripts. This coherence strengthens the credibility of the New Testament's textual tradition, offering scholars a solid foundation for reconstructing the original texts.

5. **Scribal and Corrective Practices**: While specific details about the scribe or subsequent correctors of P1 are scarce, the manuscript's quality and the presence of textual variants suggest an environment of meticulous textual engagement. Evidence of corrections or

amendments within P1 would indicate an early form of textual criticism, with scribes and correctors working diligently to preserve the accuracy of the Gospel narrative.

In examining P1, scholars and believers alike are offered a window into the early Christian dedication to the written word. This manuscript not only serves as a physical testament to the early transmission of the Gospel of Matthew but also illuminates the broader efforts of early Christians to safeguard their sacred texts. Through meticulous preservation, the early Christian copyists ensured that future generations could encounter the life and teachings of Jesus Christ, rooted in the authenticity and integrity of the New Testament tradition.

P4+64+67

The manuscripts P4, P64, and P67 represent a fascinating and critical piece of early Christian history, comprising fragments of the same codex that contain texts from the Gospels according to Matthew and Luke. These fragments offer a unique glimpse into the early Christian efforts to transcribe, preserve, and disseminate the teachings of Jesus Christ.

Description and Physical Features

Crafted from papyrus, a common material for writing in the ancient world, these fragments exhibit the physical characteristics typical of early Christian manuscripts. The papyrus sheets were prepared in a manner that allowed for writing on both sides, a technique known as opisthography, which was an economical use of the material. The condition and size of the fragments vary, with each piece providing a tangible connection to the early Christian communities that valued and circulated these texts.

P4 was likely created by a professional scribe, or at the very least, someone trained in writing literary texts. It shares a striking similarity with manuscripts P75 and B. Specifically, there is a 93 percent match between the texts of P4 and P75 in the Gospel of Luke; this level of agreement also exists between P4 and B, although not for the exact same variations as with P75. P4 and P75 are identical in forty entire verses, with only five notable differences found in Luke 3:22, 36; 5:39; 6:11, 14. P64 is characterized by strong Alexandrian tendencies, aligning more closely with manuscript ℵ than with B. Meanwhile, P67 shows a significant correlation with manuscript ℵ.

Content Overview

P4 contains parts of the Gospel of Luke, P64, and P67 include passages from the Gospel of Matthew. These fragments encompass sections of the scriptures that were central to the early Christian proclamation and catechesis. The texts cover various aspects of Jesus' life and teachings, offering insights into the theological and moral foundations that underpinned the early Christian movement.

Dating and Paleographical Analysis

The dating of these manuscripts to 150-175 C.E. is established through paleographical analysis. This method involves examining the handwriting style, comparing it with other known texts from similar periods, and considering the material's form and usage. The early dating of these fragments places them within a couple of generations of the original compositions, making them among the earliest witnesses to the New Testament's textual tradition.

THE EARLY CHRISTIAN COPYISTS OF THE NEW TESTAMENT

Dating P64

Originally, Charles Huleatt, who donated the manuscript to Magdalen College, attributed a third-century date to P64. Subsequently, A. S. Hunt examined the fragments, placing them in the early fourth century. Challenging this later dating, Colin Roberts published the manuscript, dating it around 200 C.E. Carsten Thiede pushed the date even further back, suggesting the second half of the first century. This marks a trend towards progressively earlier dating for the manuscript. Hunt's fourth-century date, seen as overly conservative, was reevaluated by Roberts, who noted P64's handwriting as a precursor to the "Biblical Uncial" style of the third and fourth centuries. Roberts found similarities between P64 and P. Oxy. 843, dated around 200 C.E., despite slight differences in slant and the shape of omega. Other manuscripts like P. Oxy. 405, P. Oxy. 1620, and P. Oxy. 1819, dating from the second to third century, show similar handwriting. Thus, Roberts, supported by Harold Bell, T. C. Skeat, and E. G. Turner, dated P64 around 200 C.E., though there's justification for an even earlier date due to its style preceding P. Oxy. 843.

Thiede proposed a first-century date based on similarities in lettering with the Greek Minor Prophets Scroll from Nahal Hever, dated between 50 B.C.E. and 50 C.E. Despite some dissimilarities, Thiede observed notable similarities in several letters. He also noted resemblances with manuscripts from Herculaneum and the Greek Qumran fragment of Leviticus, suggesting an even earlier dating for P64/P67, potentially predating Matthew's gospel. Thiede's argument for an early date, possibly mid-first century, lacks additional paleographic evidence but opens the discussion for earlier dating.

Dating P67

Roca-Puig dated P67 to the latter part of the second century, observing its strong resemblance to P. Oxy. 661, dated to the same period. This similarity was confirmed through manuscript comparison. He also found parallels with P. Oxy. 224/P. Ryl. 547, indicating that P67's handwriting style aligns with late second-century examples. Given the development of this handwriting style into the third century, Roca-Puig argued that P67 could not date later than 200 C.E. He advocated for more precise dating, firmly placing P67 in the late second century.

Dating P4

The initial publication of P4 by Vincent Scheil in 1892 erroneously dated it to the sixth century due to limited understanding at the time. J. Merell, in

THE EARLY CHRISTIAN COPYISTS OF THE NEW TESTAMENT

1938, and later Kurt Aland in 1963, and C. H. Roberts in 1979, provided more accurate datings, with Roberts aligning P4 with the late second century, connecting it with P64 and P67. The provenance of P4, used as padding in a codex of Philo's treatises hidden during Diocletian's persecution, suggests its production prior to the late third century. Considering the value early Christians placed on gospel texts, P4, likely well-used before serving as padding, could date back to as early as a hundred years prior to its concealment around 250 C.E., positioning it comfortably within the second century.

The collective analysis of P4, P64, and P67 suggests a second-century origin, potentially in the third quarter of the century. Their handwriting style exhibits similarities with manuscripts such as P. Oxy. 2404, P. Oxy. 661, and P. Vindob G 29784 from the same period. Moreover, the limited use of nomina sacra in these manuscripts, compared to the expanded list in late-second and early-third-century texts, hints at an earlier phase in the development of these sacred abbreviations. This evidence collectively supports a second half of a second-century dating (150-175 C.E.), contributing to our understanding of the early transmission and preservation of New Testament texts.

Textual Character

1. **Text Type**: The textual character of P4, P64, and P67 aligns with the Alexandrian text type, known for its textual purity and considered closer to the original autographs of the New Testament. This text type is highly valued in textual criticism for its reliability.

2. **Handwriting Style**: The handwriting observed in these manuscripts suggests the work of scribes employing a Reformed Documentary Hand. This indicates a transition from merely copying documents to a recognition of the importance of accurately transcribing sacred texts, showing an increased uniformity and care in the script.

3. **Scribes' Approach**: The scriptural passages within P4, P64, and P67 were copied with diligence, as evidenced by the relatively uniform and careful handwriting. This careful approach suggests a reverence for the content, understanding its significance for the faith community.

4. **Similarities and Agreement**: These manuscripts show textual similarities with other key documents within the Alexandrian tradition, supporting their value in reconstructing the New

Testament's original text. The coherence among these manuscripts and other significant witnesses like Codex Vaticanus and Codex Sinaiticus underscores the accuracy of the early Christian textual transmission.

5. **Scribes and Correctors**: The quality of the handwriting and the textual variants present in P4, P64, and P67 suggest that these fragments were likely produced by scribes who, while not professional bookhands, exhibited a level of care and skill above that of the average documentary scribe. The presence of corrections within the text further indicates an ongoing effort to ensure the accuracy of the transcription, reflecting an early layer of textual criticism practiced by the early Christian community.

Handwriting of the Scribes/Copyists

The handwriting in these manuscripts reflects a conscientious effort by the scribes to produce clear and legible texts. While not the work of professional bookhands, the script does not descend into the irregularities typical of purely documentary hands. Instead, it exhibits characteristics of the Reformed Documentary Hand, showing that the scribes were aware of the sacred nature of the texts they were copying and endeavored to maintain a higher standard of precision and uniformity. This blend of careful transcription with an eye towards clarity and preservation underscores the early Christian community's commitment to passing down the teachings of Jesus Christ accurately and reverently.

Through the meticulous study of P4, P64, and P67, scholars and believers are offered a profound connection to the early Christian efforts to preserve the New Testament. These fragments not only serve as a testament to the historical reality of Jesus Christ and His teachings but also highlight the early church's dedication to ensuring that future generations would have access to the transformative power of the Gospel.

THE EARLY CHRISTIAN COPYISTS OF THE NEW TESTAMENT

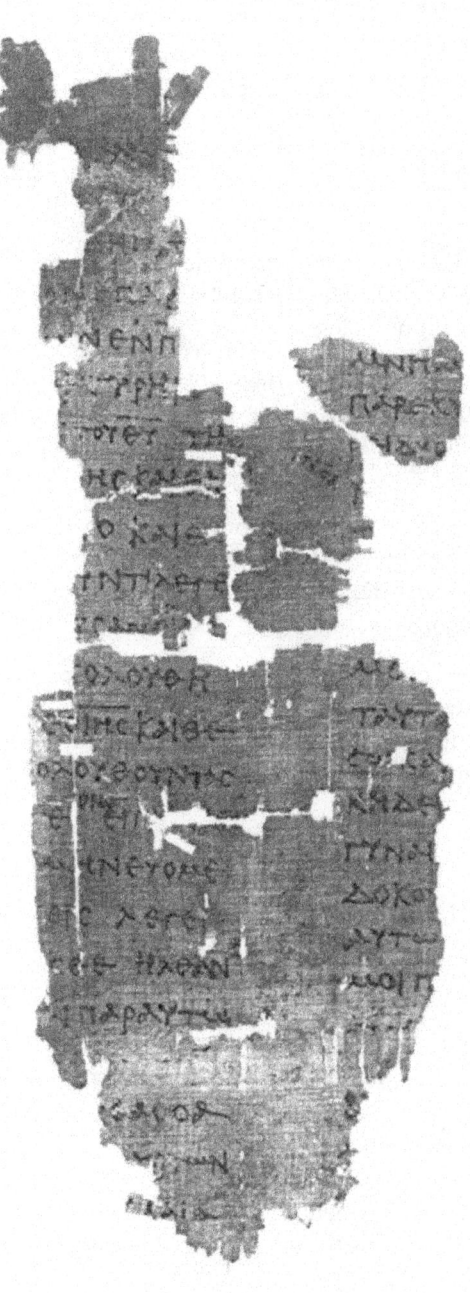

P5 (P. Oxy. 208)

Papyrus 5, identified by the siglum P5, is a significant early New Testament manuscript in Greek, specifically containing portions of the Gospel of John. Its palaeographical analysis dates it to approximately 200-250 C.E. Currently, P5 is preserved within the British Library and exists in a notably fragmentary state.

Over time, the text of P5 has undergone several reconstructions. In terms of its textual character, P5 exhibits a strong alignment with Codex Sinaiticus, albeit with notable exceptions.

The manuscript consists of fragments from three leaves, inscribed in a single column format with 27 lines per page. The extant portions of the Gospel of John include verses 1:23-31, 33-40; 16:14-30; and 20:11-17, 19-20, 22-25.

P5 was penned in a documentary hand characterized by a round, upright, medium-sized uncial script. It employs nomina sacra with standard abbreviations (ΙΗΝ, ΙΗΣ, ΠΡ, ΠΡΑ, ΠΡΣ, ΘΥ), except for the term ανθρωπος (human or person).

The scribe of P5 demonstrated a preference for conciseness, particularly by omitting non-essential pronouns and conjunctions, which aligns with the manuscript's economical use of space and materials, a common practice in ancient manuscript production.

Content

John 1:23–31, 33–40; 16:14–30; 20:11–17, 19–20, 22–25

Date

Papyrus 5 (P5) was discovered at Oxyrhynchus by Grenfell and Hunt in two distinct fragments. The first fragment includes texts from John 1:23–31, 33–40, and John 20:11–17, 19–20, 22–25, likely representing the beginning and end of a manuscript dedicated to the Gospel of John. This fragment was published as P. Oxy. 208 in the second volume of The Oxyrhynchus Papyri in 1899. The second fragment, containing John 16:14–30, was published much later, in 1922, within volume 15 of The Oxyrhynchus Papyri, and is known as P. Oxy. 1781.

Upon review, Grenfell and Hunt observed that P5 shares several unique textual readings with Codex Sinaiticus, suggesting a textual relationship between the two, particularly in several key passages. However, this initial assessment was somewhat revised after examining the second fragment, noting the relationship, while present, was not as pronounced as first thought. The papyrus is noted for its concise writing style, avoiding unnecessary words, a feature highlighted as significant by Schofield. This style aligns with what Kurt and Barbara Aland describe as a "normal" text, indicating a version of the text with a typical degree of variation and error expected from that era.

Grenfell and Hunt initially dated P5 to between 200 and 300 C.E., influenced by early beliefs regarding the advent of the Christian codex format. They described the handwriting as round and upright, of a medium size and better formed than that found in the St. Matthew fragment (P1), yet still informal and semi-literary. Considering the handwriting and other features, I suggest that P5 can be more accurately dated to the early third century, reflecting its historical and scholarly significance within New Testament textual criticism.

Physical Features

Papyrus 5 consists of two leaves, with the original dimensions being approximately 13 cm in width by 25 cm in height. Each page is arranged in a single column format, featuring 27 lines of text. The script is executed in a documentary hand, which indicates the practical, everyday use of writing in contrast to more formal or literary styles. This specific type of handwriting is characterized by its straightforward, utilitarian approach, aimed at clear communication rather than aesthetic appeal.

Textual Character

Papyrus 5 (P. Oxy. 208 + 1781) holds significant value for New Testament textual criticism, particularly in the study of the Gospel of John. Here, we refine the examination of specific textual variants and scribal corrections found within this manuscript, ensuring accuracy and current scholarly consensus.

In John 1:34, Papyrus 5 aligns with P106, ℵ (Codex Sinaiticus), b, e, ff2, and syrc, s, supporting the reading ὁ ἐκλεκτός ("the Chosen One"), which diverges from the more commonly found ὁ υἱός ("the Son") in other manuscript traditions.

In the context of John 16:17, an unusual spacing in line 7 on the recto side of the second fragment suggests the omission of additional material, inviting speculation on the original composition of this passage.

For John 16:20, the initial misspelling λουπηθησεσθε was corrected by the scribe to λυπηθησεσθε, aligning with the expected grammatical form. Similarly, in John 16:21, a correction was made from λοιπην to λυπην, and in John 16:27, Papyrus 5 uniquely omits εγω. In John 20:19, the omission of και was rectified by a subsequent superlinear addition by the scribe.

The reconstruction of John 20:16 presents challenges due to missing fragments. Grenfell and Hunt noted the impossibility of accommodating the traditional reading ο λεγεται διδασκαλε within the available space, proposing instead the abbreviation κε, drawing parallels to Codex Vercellensis and Codex Usserianus I's use of Domine. Yet, this proposed reading is not supported by any Greek manuscript tradition. Elliott & Parker's suggestion of ο λεγεται κε finds support from Peter Head, while Comfort's κε μου, though speculative and unsupported by Greek manuscripts, seeks to bridge textual gaps, referencing the reading κε διδασκαλε found in Codex Bezae and the Old Latin translation's Magister Domine or Domine.

The Greek text of Papyrus 5 is aligned with the Western text-type, considered by Kurt Aland as a "Normal text" and classified in Category I for its textual quality. Its concordance with Codex Sinaiticus, especially against Codex Vaticanus in passages like John 1:27, 34; 16:22, 27, 28; and 20:25, underscores its textual significance. However, the manuscript's condition often complicates efforts to fully discern its alignment with other textual traditions.

This analysis reflects the manuscript's nuanced role in New Testament textual criticism, where scribal habits, corrections, and the challenges of textual reconstruction offer a window into the early Christian transmission of scriptural texts.

THE EARLY CHRISTIAN COPYISTS OF THE NEW TESTAMENT

P45 (Chester Beatty Papyrus I)

Papyrus 45 (P45), identified by the siglum P45, stands as an early and significant Greek New Testament manuscript, written on papyrus. It forms part of the esteemed Chester Beatty Papyri collection, a series of early Christian manuscripts that were discovered in the 1930s. These manuscripts were acquired by the businessman and philanthropist Alfred Chester Beatty, following his purchase from an Egyptian book dealer. The publication of these manuscripts was undertaken by Frederic G. Kenyon in 1933, in his work "The Chester Beatty Biblical Papyri, Descriptions and Texts of Twelve Manuscripts on Papyrus of the Greek Bible."

The discovery of the Chester Beatty Papyri, with several being traced back to the Faiyum region of Egypt, highlights the region's significance in preserving early manuscripts, a phenomenon noted since the late 19th century. The preservation conditions in Egypt's arid climate have been instrumental in safeguarding these ancient texts.

Through palaeography, the study of ancient writing, P45 has been dated to between 175 and 225 C.E. This dating underscores its importance as the earliest known manuscript containing a collection of the four Gospels and the Acts of the Apostles within a single volume. The manuscript encapsulates fragmentary verses from Matthew chapters 20–21 and 25–26; Mark chapters 4–9 and 11–12; Luke chapters 6–7 and 9–14; John chapters 4–5 and 10–11; and Acts chapters 4–17, offering a critical window into the textual traditions of early Christianity.

P45 is primarily housed in the Chester Beatty Library in Dublin, Ireland, contributing to the library's rich collection of historical and biblical manuscripts. A single leaf of the manuscript, containing Matthew 25:41–26:39, is preserved in the Papyrus Collection of the Austrian National Library in Vienna (Pap. Vindob. G. 31974). This distribution of the manuscript between two locations underscores its historical value and the interest it holds for biblical scholarship and textual criticism.

Content

Matt. 20:24–32; 21:13–19; 25:41–26:39; Mark 4:36–5:2, 16–26; 5:38–6:3, 15–25, 36–50; 7:3–15; 7:25–8:1, 10–26; 8:34–9:9, 18–31; 11:27–12:1, 5–8, 13–19, 24–28; Luke 6:31–41; 6:45–7:7; 9:26–41; 9:45–10:1, 6–22; 10:26–11:1, 6–25, 28–46; 11:50–12:13, 18–37; 12:42–13:1, 6–24; 13:29–14:10, 17–33; John 4:51, 54; 5:21, 24; 10:7–25; 10:30–11:10, 18–36, 42–57; Acts 4:27–36; 5:10–21, 30–39; 6:7–7:2, 10–21, 32–41; 7:52–8:1, 14–25; 8:34–9:6, 16–27; 9:35–10:2, 10–23, 31–41; 11:2–13; 11:24–12:6, 13–22; 13:6–16, 25–36; 13:46–14:3, 15–23; 15:2–9, 19–27; 15:38–16:4, 15–21, 32–40; 17:9–17. New reconstructions appear in Mark 4:41; 5:2; 7:10–11; 8:11, 24; 12:1; Luke 10:29; 11:1, 24; Acts 4:36; 8:14–19, 36; 9:19, 42–43; 12:6; 13:13–14; 15:6–9, 24.

Date

Papyrus 45 (P45), ascribed to the early third century by Frederic G. Kenyon, has seen its dating corroborated by papyrologists such as W. Schubart and H. I. Bell. This dating consensus places P45 firmly within the scholarly framework utilized in modern textual criticism studies and critical editions of the New Testament.

Kenyon's analysis underlines the manuscript's adherence to early script forms, noting its simplicity—a hallmark of the Roman period. This simplicity is evident in the manuscript's execution of the epsilon and sigma characters, alongside a restrained portrayal of the upsilon and phi, all indicative of an earlier period of script development. Furthermore, the manuscript's overall sloping script and the smaller dimension of the omicron character are characteristics that align it with third-century script styles.

The assessment of P45's chronological placement benefits from comparison with similar manuscripts, notably P 110, P. Michigan 3, and P. Rylands 57. These manuscripts, dating from the late second to the early third century, provide a comparative framework that supports the dating of P45 to between 175-225 C.E.

THE EARLY CHRISTIAN COPYISTS OF THE NEW TESTAMENT

Physical Features

Papyrus 45 (P45), a manuscript from the early Christian era, presents significant challenges to textual scholars due to its damaged and fragmented condition. Initially, the manuscript likely comprised approximately 220 pages, but today, only 30 pages remain. These surviving pages include fragments from the Gospels—two from Matthew, six from Mark, seven from Luke, two from John—and thirteen from the Acts of the Apostles.

The construction of P45 utilized a codex format, an early predecessor to the modern book. This format involved arranging quires made by folding a single sheet of papyrus in half, resulting in two leaves, or four pages. The inherent structure of papyrus, created from interwoven strips of the papyrus plant, means that the inside pages of a quire have horizontal fibers facing each other, while the outer pages display vertical fibers. This V-H-H-V fiber sequence is crucial for reconstructing the original manuscript layout.

The condition of P45 is such that all pages exhibit gaps, and complete lines of text are exceedingly rare. The fragments from Matthew and John are particularly diminished, requiring careful reconstruction to approximate their original page layout. The dimensions of the original pages were roughly 10 inches by 8 inches.

A distinguishing feature of P45 is its inclusion of multiple New Testament text groupings within a single manuscript, a rarity for documents from the period of 175-225 C.E., which typically focused on singular text types such as the Gospels, general epistles, or Pauline epistles. This breadth of content suggests a unique compilation approach, employing gatherings of two leaves, or a single-quire system, in contrast to the more common methods of assembling codices either from a single block of pages folded in the middle or from several quires—groups of pages—folded and then stitched together to form a complete volume.

The binding of the codex, whether it was encased in leather or another material, remains unknown, adding another layer of mystery to the physical history of P45. This manuscript's structure, content, and state of preservation provide invaluable insights into early Christian textual practices, despite the challenges presented by its condition.

Textual Character

The examination of Papyrus 45 (P45), particularly in terms of its alignment with established New Testament text-type classifications, presents a scholarly challenge, primarily due to the manuscript's significant damage. Text-types, which categorize groups of manuscripts by shared specific or generally related readings that distinguish them from other groups, are pivotal in textual criticism for hypothesizing the original text. The main text-type groups are Alexandrian, Western, and Byzantine.

Frederic G. Kenyon postulated that the text of the Gospel of Mark within P45 might align with the Caesarean text-type, a categorization initially proposed by biblical scholar Burnett Hillman Streeter. However, this assertion has faced scrutiny, notably from Reverend Hollis Huston, who, upon reviewing Kenyon's transcription of the manuscript's partially preserved words, argued that Mark chapters 6 and 11 in P45 do not conform neatly to any established text-type, particularly not the Caesarean. This observation underscores the complexity of categorizing early manuscripts into text-types that are defined by characteristics of texts from the 4th and 5th centuries—a time postdating the Edict of Milan (313), which ceased Christian persecution and sanctioned official transcription of Christian scriptures.

This backdrop of historical context suggests that P45, predating the era of sanctioned scripture transcription, may not fit cleanly into the later-established text-type categories, reflecting the fluid and varied nature of early Christian manuscript tradition. Additionally, P45 is notable for its numerous unique readings—words or phrases not paralleled in other New Testament manuscripts at specific verses.

E. C. Colwell has remarked on the scribe's editorial style in P45, highlighting its distinctive conciseness.

> As an editor the scribe of P45 wielded a sharp axe. The most striking aspect of his style is its conciseness. The dispensable word is dispensed with. He omits adverbs, adjectives, nouns, participles, verbs, personal pronouns—without any compensating habit of addition. He frequently omits phrases and clauses. He prefers the simple to the compound word. In short, he favors brevity. He shortens the text in at least fifty places in singular readings alone. But he does not drop syllables or letters. His shortened text is readable.[98]

---

[98] Colwell, Ernest Cadman (1965). "Scribal Habits in the Early Papyri: A Study in the Corruption of the Text". In Hyatt, J. P. (ed.). *The Bible in Modern Scholarship*. New York: Abingdon Press. p. 383.

This scribe exercised a preference for brevity, omitting linguistic elements across various categories without engaging in the compensatory addition of text. This stylistic choice led to a shorter text, achieved not through the omission of syllables or letters but through the exclusion of entire words, phrases, and clauses, thereby favoring simpler expressions over compound formulations. Colwell's analysis points to a manuscript that, in its pursuit of conciseness, presents a text that is both distinct and readable, despite the absence of elements found in other New Testament manuscripts.

P46 (Chester Beatty Papyrus II)

Papyrus 46 (P46), also known in the Gregory-Aland numbering as Chester Beatty II, represents a key early Greek manuscript of the New Testament, inscribed on papyrus. As a part of the esteemed Chester Beatty Papyri collection, P46 is significant for its inclusion of texts from the Pauline Epistles, encompassing Romans, 1 Corinthians, 2 Corinthians, Galatians, Ephesians, Colossians, Philippians, 1 Thessalonians, and Hebrews.

The origins of the Chester Beatty Papyri, including P46, have been traced to various locations, with the Faiyum region being identified as the most probable source. Through paleographic analysis, a method that studies ancient handwriting, P46 has been dated to the period between 100 and 150

C.E., marking it as one of the earliest witnesses to the text of the Pauline Epistles.

The distribution of P46's leaves spans across two collections: a portion remains with the Chester Beatty Biblical Papyri, while other fragments are preserved within the University of Michigan Papyrus Collection. This manuscript's early date and broad coverage of the Pauline Epistles make it an invaluable resource for textual critics and scholars studying the development and transmission of the New Testament text.

Content

P46 contains most of Paul's epistles, excluding the Pastorals. The order is as follows: Rom. 5:17–6:3, 5–14; 8:15–25, 27–35; 8:37–9:32; 10:1–11:22, 24–33; 11:35–15:10; 15:11–16:27; Heb. 1:1–9:16; 9:18–10:20, 22–30; 10:32–13:25; 1 Cor. 1:1–9:2; 9:4–14:14; 14:16–15:15; 15:17–16:22; 2 Cor. 1:1–11:10, 12–21; 11:23–13:13; Eph. 1:1–2:7; 2:10–5:6; 5:8–6:6, 8–18, 20–24; Gal. 1:1–8; 1:10–2:9, 12–21; 3:2–29; 4:2–18; 4:20–5:17; 5:20–6:8, 10–18; Phil. 1:1, 5–15, 17–28; 1:30–2:12, 14–27; 2:29–3:8, 10–21; 4:2–12, 14–23; Col. 1:1–2, 5–13, 16–24; 1:27–2:19; 2:23–3:11, 13–24; 4:3–12, 16–18; 1 Thess. 1:1; 1:9–2:3; 5:5–9, 23–28. New reconstructions appear in Rom. 11:2; 15:10; Heb. 7:28; 1 Cor. 1:13–14; 4:10; 5:7–8; 14:15; 15:50; 16:23; 2 Cor. 4:12; 6:2; 11:21–22; Eph. 5:6; 6:18; Phil. 1:1; 3:8.

Date

The dating of Papyrus 46 (P46), also recognized as Chester Beatty II in the Gregory-Aland numbering, has been a subject of scholarly debate, primarily due to the manuscript's paleographic features. Initially, Kenyon dated the codex to the early third century, basing his assessment on the style of the stichometrical notes found at the end of several epistles, which he associated with early third-century handwriting. This viewpoint was contrasted by Ulrich Wilcken, a renowned director of the Vienna library and a pioneer in papyrus research, who argued for a second-century date, specifically around 200 C.E., after examining just a single leaf. Hans Gerstinger also supported a second-century attribution.

Young Kyu Kim proposed an even earlier dating for P46, suggesting a timeframe within the reign of Domitian (81–96 C.E.), based on six criteria, including comparisons with literary and documentary papyri known from the first century B.C. to the early second century C.E., and specific stylistic features of the manuscript's handwriting, which he argued were characteristic of early script forms.

However, upon closer examination of the manuscripts cited by Kim as parallels for the handwriting of P46, it becomes clear that while there are similarities in individual letter forms with some of these earlier manuscripts, the overall style and form do not precisely match, suggesting that P46 should not be dated as early as Kim proposes. Notably, manuscripts like P. Med. 70.01 verso and P. Oxy. 3695, among others, display elements similar to those in P46 but their overall appearance suggests they predate P46.

In contrast, manuscripts such as P. Oxy. 841 and P. Oxy. 1622, dated to the late first and early second centuries respectively, show more pronounced morphological similarities to P46. This observation supports a slightly later dating than Kim's proposal, aligning more closely with other early second-century documents.

Further analysis can be derived from comparing P46 with other manuscripts discovered alongside it within the Chester Beatty collection. For example, the comparison with P. Chester Beatty VI and other manuscripts dated to the early second century suggests that P46 likely dates to the mid-second century. This timing is consistent with the stylistic evolution from the simplicity of the best Roman hands and aligns with the appearance of other manuscripts showing close similarity to P46.

Considering the formation of the Pauline corpus, likely around 100 C.E. in Alexandria, as posited by Zuntz, a mid-second-century date for P46 allows for the development and circulation of an archetypal Pauline collection in Egypt. This period would have been sufficient for the production of a copy such as P46 for use among Egyptian Christians in Alexandria and surrounding regions. Therefore, while acknowledging the contributions of previous scholarship, my assessment concurs with a mid-second-century dating for P46, post-81–96 C.E., placing it within a critical period for the transmission and preservation of the Pauline epistles.

Physical Features

Papyrus 46 (P46) is crafted from papyrus and constructed in a single quire format. The dimensions of the folio are approximately 28 cm by 16 cm (11 inches by 6.3 inches). It features a singular column of text, with the text block measuring around 11.5 cm (4.5 inches) wide, hosting between 26 to 32 lines of text per page. Notably, the layout of P46 exhibits a gradual increase in both the width of the text rows and the number of rows per page as one progresses through the codex. The manuscript shows signs of wear, particularly at the bottom of each page where lines of text are missing—ranging from 1–2 lines in the first quarter of the codex, to 2–3 lines in the middle, and increasing to as many as seven lines by the final quarter.

A unique characteristic of P46, not commonly found in ancient manuscripts, is the numbering of each page. This could indicate a level of organizational sophistication or an early attempt at facilitating reference within the text.

In sections of Romans, Hebrews, and the later chapters of 1 Corinthians, there are observable small thick strokes or dots. Scholarly consensus holds that these marks, which are lighter in ink compared to the main text, likely originate from a reader rather than the scribe who penned the initial copy. These markings are thought to indicate sense divisions—akin to modern verse numbering systems found in contemporary Bibles—and are similarly observed in P45, suggesting a shared practice of reading within the community that possessed both codices.

Edgar Ebojo has argued that these "reading marks," whether accompanied by space intervals or not, served as aids to readers, probably within a liturgical setting. This hypothesis supports the notion that early Christian communities engaged in structured reading practices, possibly incorporating these manuscripts into their worship or communal gatherings, highlighting the interactive relationship between text and reader in early Christianity.

Nomina Sacra

Papyrus 46 (P46) exhibits a sophisticated employment of the nomina sacra, a system of abbreviating sacred names within the text. The manuscript features abbreviations for several key terms in the Christian lexicon, including κυριος (Lord) as ΚΣ, χριστος (Christ) as ΧΣ or ΧΡΣ, Ιησους (Jesus) as ΙΗΣ, θεος (God) as ΘΣ, πνευμα (Spirit) as ΠΝΑ, υιος (Son) as ΥΙΣ, and σταυρος (cross) as ΣΤΡΟΣ, each marked with a superscript line to denote their abbreviated status.

The implementation of nomina sacra in P46 has contributed to the scholarly debate on its dating. Bruce Griffin has argued against the early dating proposed by Young Kyu Kim, specifically pointing to the manuscript's comprehensive use of nomina sacra as evidence that P46 likely does not date to the 1st century. Griffin concedes, however, that the absence of a precise origin date for the nomina sacra system itself means that Kim's early dating cannot be entirely discounted.

Philip Comfort, favoring a dating of P46 to around 100–150 CE, observes that the manuscript's exemplar may have used a limited or nonexistent system of nomina sacra. This inference is drawn from instances in the manuscript where the term for "Spirit" is spelled out in full, rather than abbreviated, in contexts that traditionally would warrant the use of a nomen sacrum. This suggests that the scribe was applying nomina sacra according to the perceived theological significance of the terms, particularly distinguishing between uses of "Spirit" (with a capital S, indicating the Holy Spirit) versus "spirit" (lowercase s, indicating a general spirit), without clear guidance from the source text. Additionally, the text shows inconsistency in the abbreviation of "Christ," fluctuating between shorter and longer contracted forms.

These observations about the use of nomina sacra in P46 highlight the manuscript's place within the textual tradition of early Christianity, providing insights into the practices and theological nuances of early Christian scribes. The evidence suggests a scribe working within a developing tradition of sacred abbreviations, carefully navigating the theological implications of his textual choices.

Textual Character

The scribe responsible for Papyrus 46 (P46) appears to have been a professional, as evidenced by the presence of stichoi notations at the conclusion of several books within the manuscript, including Romans, 2 Corinthians, Ephesians, and Philippians. Stichoi notations, a practice among professional scribes, were used to indicate the number of lines copied, likely as a basis for remuneration. It is probable that an individual associated with a scriptorium, possibly connected to a church library, was tasked with the pagination of the codex and the recording of these stichoi. The original scribe made certain corrections during the transcription process, and subsequently, at least sixteen different individuals, likely members of a church or monastic community, contributed further corrections and annotations, suggesting that P46 was extensively utilized within its community.

Significantly, one annotator made extensive lectoral marks throughout Romans and Hebrews, preparing these texts for oral presentation. These marks, however, are predominantly absent beyond these books, with the exception of 1 Corinthians chapters 14 and 15, indicating selected passages deemed particularly suited for public reading. Despite these interventions, the manuscript's corrections were not executed in a comprehensive manner, indicating a document that was valued and frequently referenced, yet not meticulously maintained over time. Corrections made by the original scribe, the paginator, and a third-century corrector have been specifically identified within our analysis, aligning with Gunther Zuntz's scholarly observations.

Textually, P46 demonstrates a notable alignment with Codex Vaticanus (B), particularly in the Pauline Epistles, and exhibits similarities with the tenth-century Alexandrian manuscript 1739 and Codex Sinaiticus (ℵ). In the case of Hebrews, P46 and Papyrus 13 (P13) share a remarkably consistent text, agreeing on approximately 80 percent of textual variants. Both P13 and 𝔓46 employ double points for punctuation, and their pagination suggests a sequence where Romans precedes Hebrews, a structural choice reflecting their shared textual tradition.

Textual criticism has revealed that when P46's readings concur with those of B and the manuscripts D, F, and G, such readings are typically characterized as "Western," a term reflecting one of the major text-type classifications within New Testament textual criticism. It is important to note, however, that Westcott and Hort generally dismissed readings supported by this particular grouping. Nonetheless, several passages where P46 and B, either independently or alongside manuscripts across various text types, concur are deemed likely to represent the original Pauline text.

Despite occasional scribal errors, Zuntz regarded P46 as embodying an "early-Alexandrian type" text of superior quality. This assessment underscores the manuscript's significance in the study of New Testament textual history, illustrating its value as a witness to the early transmission and reception of Pauline writings.

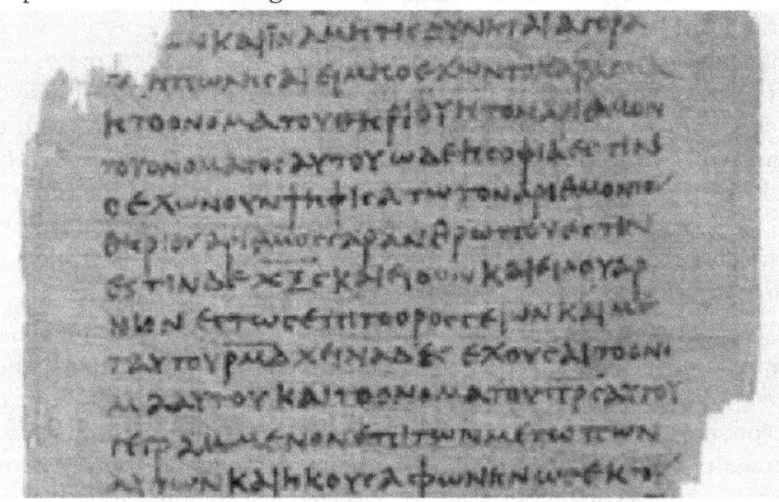

P47 (Chester Beatty Papyrus III)

Papyrus 47 (P47), identified in the Gregory-Aland system as Chester Beatty III, is a significant early Greek manuscript of the New Testament, written on papyrus. It forms a part of the Chester Beatty Papyri collection, a notable assembly of early Christian manuscripts. The most probable location of discovery for these manuscripts, including P47, is identified as the Faiyum region. Through the discipline of palaeography, which examines and compares handwriting styles, P47 has been dated to between 200 and 250 C.E.

The content of P47 encompasses excerpts from the Book of Revelation, specifically chapters 9 through 17. This manuscript offers critical insights into the early textual transmission of the Book of Revelation, providing scholars with valuable data for understanding the text's history and variant readings. P47 is preserved and accessible at the Chester Beatty Library in Dublin, under the inventory number 14. 1. 527, where it continues to be an important resource for biblical scholars and researchers studying the New Testament and the early Christian church.

Content

Rev. 9:10–11:3; 11:5–16:15; 16:17–17:2

Date

Philip W. Comfort dated P47 to the second half of the third century (200-250 C.E.) based on the formation of its letters, such as alpha, beta, epsilon, mu, sigma, and omega. This dating is supported by the manuscript's resemblance to other manuscripts of Revelation, P18 and P24, which are also dated to the late third century.

When initially examined by Kenyon, P47 was found to be closely related to Codex Sinaiticus (ℵ) and Codex Ephraemi Rescriptus (C), with Papyrus 115 (P) next in line, and Codex Alexandrinus (A) further away in textual character 56. Further study revealed that P47 is allied to ℵ but not to A or C, which are of a different text type 7. This suggests that there were distinct early groups for the text of Revelation, with P47 and ℵ forming one such group.

The dating of P47 is grounded in palaeographical analysis, which is the study of ancient handwriting. The manuscript's script has been compared to other known third-century manuscripts, and features such as a broad delta, broad theta, narrow alpha, and the finial end on the crossbar of epsilon are indicative of this period. The presence of an apostrophe between double consonants is another characteristic shared with other third-century manuscripts.

Codicology, the study of books as physical objects, also plays a role in dating manuscripts. P47 is described as a "single gathering" or "single quire" manuscript, which is an early method of codex construction. The informal handwriting and the lack of high-quality calligraphy suggest that P47 was produced in an informal setting, possibly for personal or small group use.

Physical Features

P47 is composed of ten relatively well-preserved folios, making it the earliest extensive manuscript of the Book of Revelation. It is classified as a papyrus, written with black ink on the papyrus material. The manuscript is fragmentary, containing portions of Revelation from 9:10 to 17:2.

Manuscript Features

The manuscript is a codex, an early form of a book, which was a common medium for Christian texts at the time. It was constructed as a "single gathering" or "single quire," meaning all the folded sheets were stitched together in one binding, a method typical of early codex construction. The script is described as informal, suggesting that P47 was likely produced in a non-professional setting, possibly for personal or small group use.

Scribal Characteristics

P47 exhibits several corrections and instances of scribal re-inking, which are evident throughout the papyrus. The manuscript's informal handwriting indicates it was a product of an informal, uncontrolled setting, with no pretension to high literary culture. The quality of the copyist's hand is not considered high-quality calligraphy.

Textual Character

P47 is considered a representative of the Alexandrian text-type, known for its abrupt readings, fewer words, and greater variation among the

Synoptic Gospels. The text of P47 is closest to Codex Sinaiticus (ℵ), and together they are witnesses for one of the early textual types of the Book of Revelation. However, the text in P47-ℵ is considered an inferior witness to the text of Revelation compared to that of P115-A-C.

Eclectic Nature of the Text

The textual character of P47 is described as eclectic, mixed, or unaligned. This means that while it is generally associated with the Alexandrian text-type, it also contains readings that do not align strictly with any one text-type. This eclectic nature is evidenced by the manuscript's singular readings and those supported by only a few other manuscripts.

Scribal Corrections and Variants

The scribe of P47 corrected his errors as he was copying the text, which is indicative of a careful copying process. There is no evidence of ecclesiastical control or doctrinal influence in the text's variants, which are almost entirely attributed to copyist errors. This suggests that the variations in P47 are the result of unintentional mistakes rather than intentional alterations.

Comparative Textual Analysis

Comparisons with other manuscripts, such as Uncial 0308, show that P47 shares textual variants with Codex Sinaiticus and Codex Alexandrinus in certain passages of Revelation. These comparisons help to further define the textual character of P47 and its relationship with other early Christian manuscripts.

The textual character of P47 is complex and cannot be neatly categorized into a single text-type. Its closest affiliation is with Codex Sinaiticus, and it represents an early form of the text of Revelation. The eclectic nature of P47's text, along with its scribal corrections and lack of doctrinal influence, provides a valuable witness to the early transmission of the New Testament text.

P52 (P. Rylands 457)

The Papyrus Rylands Greek 457, commonly known as P52 or the St John's fragment, is a notable artifact within New Testament Textual Criticism. This papyrus fragment is part of the extensive collection housed at the John Rylands University Library in Manchester, UK, where it is preserved under the care of the Rylands Papyri collection. The dimensions of P52 are modest, measuring approximately 3.5 by 2.5 inches (8.9 cm by 6.4 cm), making it comparable in size to a modern credit card. Despite its small size, the fragment holds significant scholarly value.

On the obverse side (recto), P52 features fragments of seven lines from the Gospel of John 18:31–33, written in Koine Greek. The reverse side (verso) similarly contains fragments of seven lines, but from verses 37–38 of the same chapter. This dual-sided inscription is characteristic of a papyrus codex, an early form of book, suggesting the fragment's origin from a codex rather than a scroll.

Since 2007, P52 has been exhibited on a permanent basis within the Deansgate building of the John Rylands University Library. Its display offers scholars and the general public alike a tangible connection to the early textual tradition of the New Testament. The preservation and study of such fragments are crucial for understanding the history of biblical texts, providing insights into the physical transmission and variant readings of scriptural manuscripts.

Content

John 18:31–33, 37–38

Date

In the field of New Testament Textual Criticism, the dating of Papyrus 52 (P. Rylands 457, hereafter P52) is of considerable interest due to its significance in early Christian studies. This papyrus fragment, which contains portions of the Gospel of John, has been subject to rigorous examination by eminent scholars including Frederic G. Kenyon, H. I. Bell, Adolf Deissmann, and W. H. P. Hatch. Their analyses, drawing upon palaeographical methods, have contributed to a consensus regarding the papyrus's date of origin.

Adolf Deissmann, in particular, argued for an early dating of P52, placing it within the reigns of Roman Emperors Hadrian (117–138 C.E.) or possibly Trajan (98–117 C.E.). His perspective was detailed in the article "Ein Evangelienblatt aus den Tagen Hadrians," subsequently translated for the British Weekly, emphasizing the papyrus's close temporal proximity to the events it describes.

The methodology for dating P52 involves comparative analysis with other early manuscripts, such as P. Fayum 110 (dated to 94 C.E.), the Egerton Gospel (130–150 C.E.), P. Oslo 22 (127 C.E.), P. London 2078 (from the reign of Domitian, 81–96 C.E.), and particularly P. Berolinenses 6845 (circa 100 C.E.), which shows the closest resemblance. P. Oxy. 2533, another manuscript exhibiting significant parallels with P52, has also been discussed. Despite its first-century characteristics, its second-century appearance led to its assignment to the second century.

The converging evidence from these comparisons supports a date for P52 within the range of 125-150 C.E. However, the close parallels to manuscripts dated closer to 100 C.E., particularly P. Berolinenses 6845, suggest a potential earlier dating, possibly near the end of the first century or early second century. This dating is especially significant in the context of the scholarly consensus on the composition date of the Gospel of John, circa 98 C.E., suggesting that P52 could have been produced as little as twenty-five years after the original text. This proximity to the original composition underscores the importance of P52 in the study of early Christian texts and their transmission, offering critical insights into the textual tradition of the New Testament during its formative period.

Physical Features

P52 is a small fragment of a papyrus codex, with dimensions measuring only 3.5 by 2.5 inches (8.9 cm × 6.4 cm) at its widest, roughly the size of a credit card.

Textual Character

Papyrus Rylands Greek 457 (P52) is critically evaluated for its textual character, despite the limited text available on the fragment. Scholars such as Bruce M. Metzger have classified the textual nature of P52 as "Alexandrian," a designation reflecting a specific, highly regarded text-type within New Testament scholarship. Kurt and Barbara Aland have described the text as "normal," indicating its conformity with the mainstream or standard text of the New Testament scriptures.

The primary significance of P52 lies not in its textual content but rather in its chronology. The papyrus is esteemed for its antiquity, providing compelling evidence for the early composition of the Gospel of John. The dating of P52 suggests that the original manuscript of John's Gospel was completed before the end of the first century. This early date is of paramount importance in textual criticism and the study of the New Testament, as it substantiates the existence and circulation of John's Gospel within a generation of the events it describes. Thus, P52 serves as a critical artifact in understanding the development and dissemination of the New Testament canon, affirming the historical reliability and early textual transmission of the Christian Scriptures.

Manuscript Form and Style

P52 was written in the form of a codex, which was a distinguishing feature of early Christian literature compared to the rolls or scrolls commonly used for pagan literature at the time . The script of P52 is described as "heavy, rounded and rather elaborate," but not the work of a "practiced scribe," indicating that it may not have been produced in a professional scriptorium . The codex from which P52 comes would have presented an appearance similar to professionally written Christian codices, despite the actual letter forms being closer to documentary exemplars .

Textual Variants and Affiliations

The textual character of P52 is not extensively discussed in the provided key points, likely due to the fragmentary nature of the manuscript. However, it is noted that the verses included in P52 are also witnessed in other manuscripts, such as Bodmer Papyrus 66, and there is some overlap with other papyri, suggesting that P52 may represent an example of the same proto-Alexandrian text-type .

P52 is a fragmentary but highly significant manuscript that provides a glimpse into the early textual character of the Gospel of John. Its form as a codex and the style of its script are indicative of early Christian manuscript traditions. The dating of P52 to the first half of the second century C.E. underscores its importance for understanding the dissemination and textual history of the New Testament.

P66 (Papyrus Bodmer II)

Papyrus 66 (P66), housing the text of the Gospel of John from 1:1 through 6:11, 6:35b to 14:26, 29-30; 15:2-26; 16:2-4, 6-7; 16:10-20:20, 22-23; and 20:25-21:9, 12, 17, stands as a paramount artifact in New Testament manuscript studies. Initially, its script was ascribed to the early third century, around 200 C.E., based on palaeographic analysis. Subsequent scholarship, notably by Herbert Hunger, proposed an earlier dating to the mid or early second century, reflecting advancements in the understanding of ancient handwriting styles. Philip W. Comfort's analysis places P66 within a narrower timeframe, approximately between 100 and 150 C.E., aligning with critical scholarly consensus on the early transmission of the New Testament texts.

P66 is particularly significant for its exclusion of the Pericope Adulterae (John 7:53-8:11), a narrative absent from the earliest and most reliable manuscripts of John's Gospel, including P45 (tentatively), P75, and the majority of New Testament uncials. This omission is indicative of the passage's later insertion into the textual tradition. Furthermore, P66 is noted for its consistent application of Nomina Sacra, a scribal practice that underscores the manuscript's liturgical and theological contexts.

Research by Karyn Berner and Philip Comfort identifies the involvement of three distinct hands in the manuscript's production and correction: the initial scribe, a professional responsible for the primary text; a thoroughgoing corrector; and a minor corrector, suggesting a complex history of transmission and revision. However, James Royse has more recently argued that except for a possible exception in John 13:19, the corrections appear to originate from the hand of the initial scribe.

The presence of the staurogram, an early christological symbol representing the crucifixion, in at least ten instances within the text (notably within chapter 19), further illuminates the manuscript's theological significance and the early Christian community's devotion to the cross. This feature, among others, establishes P66 not only as a critical witness to the text of the Gospel of John but also as a window into the early Christian practice and belief.

Content

John 1:1–6:11; 6:35–14:26, 29–30; 15:2–26; 16:2–4, 6–7; 16:10–20:20, 22–23; 20:25–21:9, 12, 17.

Date

Papyrus 66 (P66), a crucial manuscript in the study of the New Testament, has been the subject of considerable scholarly debate regarding its date of origin. In its initial assessment, Martin positioned P66 around 200 C.E., drawing parallels to P. Oxy. 1074 (Exodus), which was also tentatively placed at the beginning of the third century or potentially earlier.

Herbert Hunger, a leading figure in papyrology, revised this dating significantly. He advocated for placing P66 within the first half of the second century (100–150 C.E.), aligning it chronologically with P52 (P. Rylands 457) and the Egerton Gospel, both dated to the early to mid-second century. Hunger's reassessment was grounded in the manuscript's stylistic similarities, particularly in the use of ligatures, with other documents from the late first and early second centuries. This comparison led him to argue against dating P66 later than 150 C.E.

Conversely, Turner proposed a later date for P66, situating it within the first half of the third century (200–250 C.E.). He based his argument on specific letter forms present in P66 that he associated with third-century manuscripts. Turner's stance was partly a reaction against a trend towards earlier datings that emerged in the mid-20th century, as scholars began to recognize the codex format's origins in the late first century.

Despite Turner's arguments, evidence suggests that the handwriting characteristics of P66 can indeed be found in second-century manuscripts. Instances include the wide delta, the specific formation of the theta, and the occasional finial on the epsilon, all of which can be paralleled in documents from the second century. Moreover, the hook (apostrophe) between double consonants, another feature Turner cited, is also present in second-century papyri.

Further analysis reveals that P66 shares significant stylistic similarities with several manuscripts dated to the late first or early second century. This includes P. Oxy. 220, P. Oxy. 841 (dated to the reign of Hadrian, 120–130 C.E.), and P. Oxy. 1434 (108–109 C.E.), among others. Notably, P. Chester Beatty IX and X, dated to the second century, exhibit affinities with P66 in terms of handwriting style.

Comparative paleography, therefore, strongly supports a mid-second-century dating for P66. This is corroborated by the assessments of papyrologists G. Cavallo and R. Seider, who independently assigned P66 to the middle of the second century. Their evaluations, along with the detailed comparison of P66 to other manuscripts from the same period, underline the manuscript's alignment with second-century textual practices.

In particular, manuscripts such as P. Oxy. 1074 (Exodus), which has been closely compared to P66 and tentatively dated to the early third century by Grenfell and Hunt, exhibits characteristics that are more indicative of second-century origins. This reassessment is further supported by manuscripts like P. Lit. London 132 and P. Berolinenses 9782, both of which share substantial similarities in lettering and overall appearance with P66 and are dated to the second century.

Thus, the cumulative evidence from comparative paleography, including the analysis of ligatures, letter forms, and other stylistic features, compellingly suggests that P66 should be dated to the middle of the second century. This dating not only aligns P66 with other early Christian manuscripts but also underscores its importance in understanding the textual transmission and early reception of the New Testament writings. The meticulous examination of P66, through the lens of paleographic analysis, contributes significantly to the broader field of New Testament Textual Criticism by offering insights into the early Christian manuscript culture and the dissemination of biblical texts during this formative period.

Physical Features

P66 originally consisted of 39 sheets of papyrus, folded and arranged in quires to form 78 leaves and 156 pages. The manuscript is made up of 75 surviving leaves and 39 unidentified fragments, indicating that some portions have been lost over time. The nearly rectangular leaves measure approximately 6.4 inches high and 5.6 inches wide, which is a manageable size for a codex.

Page Layout

The number of lines of text per page in P66 varies from 14 to 25, and the number of letters in a line of text runs from 18 to 28. This variation suggests that the scribe was not strictly adhering to a uniform layout, which could be due to the content of the text or the scribe's own practices.

Handwriting and Punctuation

The handwriting of P66 is described as a good literary uncial, which is a script style characterized by rounded, majuscule letters that were commonly used in Greek manuscripts of the time. Rudimentary punctuation is present, with a high point at the end of sentences and a double point at the end of sections, aiding in the readability of the text.

Nomina Sacra and Abbreviations

Words for God, Jesus, Lord, and Christ are always abbreviated in P66, as are sometimes the words for man, father, spirit, and son . This practice of using nomina sacra, or sacred names, is typical of early Christian manuscripts and reflects a reverence for these terms.

Corrections and Scribe's Work

P66 contains 465 corrections across its pages, averaging a little over 3 corrections per page. These corrections took various forms, including erasing with a sponge, placing dots over letters, interlinear insertions, and arrows pointing to corrections in the margins. It is likely that the copyist of the manuscript is responsible for all but one of these corrections.

Preservation and Condition

The preservation level of P66 surprised scholars, with the first 26 leaves being basically fully intact, and even the stitching of the binding remained . However, some letters are missing on the right margin due to the deterioration of the edge of the papyrus sheets . To address this, some pages have a vertical strip placed on the edge to reinforce the sheet, which is a conservation measure to prevent further damage.

Papyrus 66 is a well-preserved early Christian manuscript that provides valuable information about the physical characteristics of early codices. Its size, layout, handwriting, use of nomina sacra, and correction practices all contribute to our understanding of the production and use of early Christian texts.

Textual Character

The textual characteristics of Papyrus 66 (P66) provide fascinating insights into the practices and theological orientations of early Christian scribes. The original scribe of P66 displayed a practiced calligraphic skill, adapting the size of his writing as he progressed through the codex to ensure an even distribution of text. This larger print is indicative of the manuscript's intended use for public reading within a Christian congregation, suggesting that the scribe was likely a member of such a community.

The scribe's familiarity with Scriptural texts is evident from how he harmonized certain passages in John's Gospel with those in Matthew and Luke, reflecting a deep engagement with the broader scriptural narrative. The use of specialized nomina sacra, not only for standard sacred names but also for terms like "cross" and "crucify," further underscores the scribe's Christian identity and his theological priorities.

This scribe's approach to the text was far from mechanical; it was characterized by a degree of freedom and personal engagement that led to several unique readings. While some might interpret the presence of numerous scribal errors as inattentiveness, a closer examination reveals a scribe deeply engrossed in the narrative, leading to deviations from the exact wording of his exemplar. His method of reading in semantic units rather than word by word resulted in both intentional and inadvertent alterations, which were occasionally corrected by a subsequent editor, the diorthōtēs, who focused on substantive accuracy and occasionally adjusted the text for clarity or theological emphasis.

The textual variants introduced by the original scribe often reflect an interpretive engagement with the text, such as aligning current passages with remembered or anticipated scriptural parallels. This scribe's alterations, ranging from the explicit identification of Jesus as the Son of God to adjustments that enhance narrative coherence or theological understanding, reveal an active process of reader reception and adaptation.

Moreover, the manuscript exhibits omissions that can be categorized as either inadvertent errors or deliberate redactions, with the latter suggesting an attempt by the scribe or his community to refine the text according to their theological understanding or liturgical needs. These modifications, whether inclusions or exclusions, offer valuable insights into early Christian interpretive practices and the dynamic nature of textual transmission during this period.

The case of P66 illustrates the complex interplay between textuality and theology in early Christianity, highlighting the role of scribes not merely as transmitters of a fixed text but as active participants in its ongoing interpretation and application within the life of the community.

The Correctors

The corrections made to Papyrus 66 (P66) underscore the meticulous nature of early Christian manuscript production and the rigorous efforts undertaken to ensure textual accuracy. My analysis, based on an exhaustive examination of the manuscript's corrections for my doctoral dissertation and subsequent scholarly work, builds upon and extends previous scholarly discussions by Gordon Fee, James Royse, and others. Fee's hypothesis, suggesting the use of a second exemplar for corrections, and Royse's observations on the careful nature of the manuscript's preparation, set the stage for a deeper understanding of the corrective processes applied to P66.

Further evaluation reveals that the corrective work on P66 likely occurred in stages, a view shared by other scholars such as Colwell and Rhodes. Colwell hinted at the influence of a supervisory figure or a standard guiding the correction process, reflecting a scriptorium's systematic approach to manuscript production. Rhodes elaborated on this by proposing a three-stage correction process, ranging from immediate emendations by the scribe to more comprehensive reviews for orthographic consistency and transcriptional accuracy.

Upon closer paleographic analysis, it becomes evident that the work of the second corrector aligns with the handwriting of the first paginator, suggesting a unified role in the manuscript's production and correction. Many of these corrections align the text with the Alexandrian text-type, indicating a scholarly rigor and possibly the influence of a proofreader or diorthōtēs using a distinct exemplar for guidance.

The production of P66 can thus be conceptualized in three key phases:

1. The original scribe's work, which included immediate corrections to address transcriptional errors, focusing on rectifying nonsensical readings and ensuring the text's legibility and coherence.
2. The involvement of a corrector, identifiable as the diorthōtēs, who undertook significant grammatical and substantive corrections, often aligning the text more closely with the Alexandrian tradition. This stage likely involved reference to a different exemplar, reflecting a detailed and scholarly approach to textual fidelity.
3. A final stage of correction aimed at preparing the manuscript for liturgical use, with specific attention to chapters suited for lectionary reading. This involved adding punctuation and markings to facilitate oral presentation, underscoring the manuscript's function within a worship context.

	First Hand	Second Hand	Third Hand
α	ααααααα	αααααααα	λλλλλλλ
δ	ΔΔΔΔΔΔ	ΔΔΔΔΔΔΔ	ΔΔΔ
ε	ϵϵϵϵϵϵϵϵϵ	ϵϵϵϵϵϵϵϵ	ϵϵϵϵ
ζ	ζζζζζζζ	ζζζζζζζ	ζζζζ
κ	κκκκκκκ	κκκκκκκκκ	κκ
μ	μμμμμμ	μμμμμμμ	ΜΜΜΜΜ
ξ	ξξξξξξ	ξξξξξξξ	
ρ	ρρρρρρρρ	ρρρρρρ	ρρρρρρρ
υ	υυυυυυ	υυυυυυυυ	υ

Image 1(Comfort & Barret, THE TEXT OF THE EARLIEST NEW TESTAMENT MANUSCRIPTS: Papyri 1-72, Vol. 1, 2019)

The detailed methodologies employed in these corrections—ranging from deletions indicated by dots and hooks to the use of transposition and insertion marks—reveal a complex and thoughtful engagement with the text. This engagement ensures the manuscript's utility and integrity for its intended audience. The identification and analysis of these corrective stages not only highlight the scholarly and religious care invested in P66 but also contribute to our understanding of early Christian textual practices and the transmission of the New Testament.

P72 (Papyrus Bodmer VII-VIII)

Papyrus 72 (P72, also known as Papyrus Bodmer VII-VIII) holds a significant place in the study of New Testament textual criticism. This papyrus encompasses portions of the letters of Jude, 1 Peter, and 2 Peter, marking it as an invaluable early Christian document. The texts within P72, despite being part of the broader Bodmer Miscellaneous codex, are unified in scholarly discussions due to their common scribe and content.

The handwriting of P72 has been paleographically dated to the period between 200 and 250 C.E., situating it within the early Christian era. This timeframe provides crucial insights into the textual transmission and early reception of these epistles. The fact that Jude, 1 Peter, and 2 Peter were copied by the same scribe and included within a single codex suggests a recognized canonical status or at least a specific liturgical or theological importance attributed to these texts by early Christian communities.

The inclusion of these three texts together in P72, although they do not form a continuous sequence within the codex, underscores the manuscript's significance for scholars. It offers a window into the early Christian scriptural tradition, illustrating the diversity of texts that were valued and circulated among early believers. The study of P72, therefore, not only enriches our understanding of the textual history of the New Testament but also contributes to our knowledge of early Christian practices and beliefs regarding sacred writings.

Content

1 Peter 1:1–5:14; 2 Peter 1:1–3:18; Jude 1–25

Date

Papyrus 72 (P72, Papyrus Bodmer VII–VIII) is an early Christian manuscript that has been paleographically dated to the period between 200 and 250 C.E. This dating aligns P72 with other contemporaneous manuscripts, such as P. Oxy. 1075 and P. Oxy. 4705, which are also dated to the same period. The comparison with these manuscripts not only helps in confirming the dating of P72 but also in understanding the textual practices and scribal habits of that era. This timeframe is critical for New Testament textual criticism as it offers insights into the early transmission and preservation of Christian texts. By situating P72 within this specific historical context, scholars can better assess its significance in the broader corpus of early Christian manuscripts and its contribution to our understanding of the development of the New Testament canon.

The dating of P72 to 200-250 C.E. is supported by paleographical evidence, which involves examining the handwriting style of the manuscript. The ligature forms and calligraphic features of P72, such as the effort to maintain the upper line and the form of finials at the feet of letters, are indicative of a style found in the later Ptolemaic period, suggesting a date not later than the first half of the third century. P72's calligraphic features are compared to similar literary papyri, which have been assigned to an early date. This comparison further supports the dating of P72 to the later first century or the second century C.E. Additionally, the presence of specific forms and movements of strokes in P72, when compared to other papyri of known dates, supports the conclusion that P72 was written before the reign of the emperor Domitian, indicating an early date for the manuscript. The usage of specific forms and spellings in P72, such as the εγ- form instead of the εκ-

form before compounds with β, δ, and λ, aligns with early forms found in other papyri and suggests an early date for P72.

Physical Features

P72 is made of papyrus and measures approximately 14.5 by 16 cm, a nearly square shape. This size is relatively small, which suggests that the codex may have been intended for private use rather than for liturgical purposes.

Handwriting and Script

The script of P72 is Greek, written in a documentary hand, which is a style typically used for everyday writing, such as personal letters or business documents, rather than a formal literary script. The writing is characterized by a substantially upright capital script with slight oscillations and a rather fast track without significant contrast between thick and thin strokes.

Scribes and Production

The codex was written by several hands, likely four, and the writing process is believed to have occurred from the beginning of the third century to the first half of the fourth century. This indicates that the production of the manuscript may have spanned a considerable period, possibly involving different scribes over time.

Preservation and Condition

P72 is generally well-preserved, with many pages retaining complete margins. The manuscript consists of 95 leaves, with the text arranged in a single column, featuring 14–20 lines per column. The preservation level allows for a good understanding of the manuscript's original layout and design.

Textual Character

P72 is recognized as a representative of the Alexandrian text-type, particularly in the Epistles of Peter. The text of 1 Peter shows clear Alexandrian affinities, aligning closely with Codex Vaticanus (B) and to a lesser extent with Codex Alexandrinus (A). However, the text of 2 Peter and Jude displays a more 'uncontrolled' text, with several independent readings that do not conform as closely to the Alexandrian type.

Scribes and Textual Production

The manuscript is believed to have been produced by four scribes, although another source suggests it may have been copied by a single scribe. This discrepancy could indicate either a collaborative effort or a misinterpretation of the handwriting styles present in the manuscript. The scribes' work displays both liturgical and theological tendencies, suggesting that the manuscript was used for both worship and teaching.

Linguistic Characteristics

In 1 Peter, the Greek text exhibits signs that the scribe's native language was Coptic, as evidenced by numerous misspellings and itacisms. When these are corrected, the text aligns more closely with other Alexandrian witnesses. The manuscript also contains creative pen flourishes, particularly at the end of 1 Peter, which may have served as visual markers for readers.

Textual Contents and Mixture

P72 was originally part of a larger work known as the Bodmer Miscellaneous Codex, which included a broad anthology of texts, both canonical and apocryphal. This mixture had an apologetic character and bore the marks of incipient orthodoxy, indicating its role in the early Christian community.

Papyrus 72 exhibits a complex textual character, with its content reflecting a mixture of Alexandrian and independent textual traditions. The involvement of multiple scribes, or possibly a single scribe with varied handwriting, and the presence of both canonical and apocryphal texts suggest that P72 was a multifunctional manuscript used for both private devotion and public liturgy. Its linguistic peculiarities and creative flourishes add to the rich tapestry of early Christian manuscript culture.

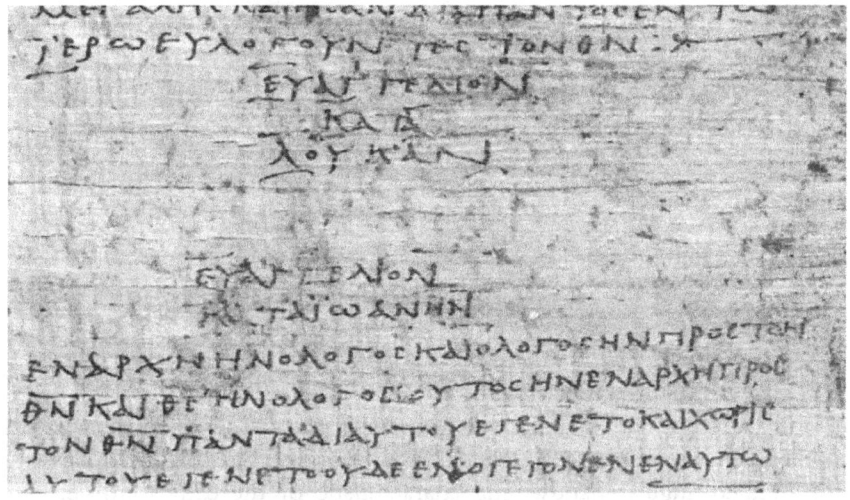

P75 (Papyrus Bodmer XIV-XV)

Papyrus 75, now known as Hanna Papyrus 1 and previously referred to as Papyrus Bodmer XIV-XV, is a critical early Greek manuscript of the New Testament, cataloged under the Gregory-Aland numbering system as P75. This manuscript encompasses substantial portions of the Gospel of Luke (3:18-24:53) and the Gospel of John (1:1-15:8), offering scholars valuable insights into the textual tradition of these Gospels in the early Christian era.

Renowned for its significance within New Testament textual studies, P75 is often regarded as one of the most pivotal papyrus manuscripts discovered to date. This prominence is partly due to its early composition, with paleographical analysis traditionally placing its creation between 175 and 225 C.E. Such an early date is crucial for textual critics, as it narrows the gap between the original autographs and extant manuscript evidence, thereby providing a closer glimpse into the original texts of the New Testament.

The value of P75 is further enhanced by its textual affinity with Codex Vaticanus (B), a fourth-century manuscript that holds a preeminent position in New Testament scholarship. The similarities between P75 and Codex Vaticanus in the text of Luke and John are particularly noteworthy, suggesting a high degree of textual stability and fidelity in the early transmission of these Gospels.

Presently, P75 resides in the Vatican Library, under the designation Hanna Papyrus 1, where it continues to be an object of intense study and veneration among scholars and theologians. Its preservation and study contribute significantly to our understanding of the textual history of the New Testament and the early Christian tradition.

Content

Luke 3:18–22; 3:33–4:2; 4:34–5:10; 5:37–6:4; 6:10–7:32, 35–39, 41–43; 7:46–9:2; 9:4–17:15; 17:19–18:18; 22:4–24:53; John 1:1–11:45, 48–57; 12:3–13:1, 8–10; 14:8–29; 15:7–8. The manuscript does not include 7:53–8:11.

Date

Victor Martin's initial dating of Papyrus 75 (P75) to the early third century was grounded in its stylistic similarities with other manuscripts, notably P. Oxy. 2293, 2322, 2362, 2363, and 2370. These manuscripts share the defined angular handwriting characteristic of the early third century, according to Martin's analysis. However, the editors of the Oxyrhynchus Papyri have suggested a slightly broader timeframe for P. Oxy. 2293, 2363, and 2370, proposing a late second century to early third century date for these texts. Notably, P. Oxy. 2293 and P. Oxy. 2452, both exhibiting close resemblance to P75, further complicate the dating process.

Additionally, Martin drew parallels between the handwriting in P75 and that found in P. Fuad XIX, a documentary papyrus dated to 145–146 C.E. This comparison, alongside the manuscript's affinities with P. Michigan 3, which has been securely dated to the latter half of the second century, suggests a potential for an earlier dating of P75 than Martin's initial proposal.

Seider's classification of P75 as "2nd/3rd century" aligns with this broader perspective, accommodating the manuscript's stylistic range. Considering these comparative analyses and the manuscript's textual characteristics, a more precise dating of P75 to the late second century, with the possibility of extending into the early third century, seems most appropriate. This timeframe not only reflects the manuscript's paleographical context but also underscores its significance in the early transmission of the New Testament, providing invaluable insight into the textual history and dissemination of the Christian scriptures during this period.

Physical Features

P75 is a papyrus codex, which means it is made from sheets of papyrus, an ancient writing material prepared from the pith of the papyrus plant. The codex format indicates that the sheets were folded and bound together, as opposed to being rolled like a scroll. The papyrus is of a smooth and fine quality, with both sides (recto and verso) nearly as smooth, giving it a texture similar to hand-woven linen.

Size and Layout

The manuscript measures approximately 27 x 13 cm, which is a typical size for a book of this period. It was constructed in a single quire format, meaning that the papyrus sheets were folded once and then bound to form a gathering or section. The codex contains 50 leaves, with the text arranged in a single column, featuring approximately 38–45 lines per column.

State of Preservation

P75 is fragmentary, with 36 folios (72 leaves, 144 pages) surviving, of which 102 pages are intact and 20 are fragmentary. Some fragments of the papyrus leaves were even found embedded in a leather cover, indicating that the codex had been rebound and repaired in antiquity.

Writing and Ink

The text of P75 is written in Greek, using an attractive vertical uncial script. This script is elegant and well-crafted, reflecting a clear and careful majuscule handwriting style. The ink used for the writing is black.

Features and Annotations

The manuscript uses a staurogram, a typographical device that combines the Greek letters tau-rho to form a monogram for the cross, in several places in the text of Luke 17. Additionally, at least two marginal notations in P75 use a 4th or 5th century majuscule hand, suggesting that the manuscript was not only used but also studied in later centuries.

Textual Character

The textual character of Papyrus 75 (P75, now Hanna Papyrus 1) reflects the work of a professional Christian scribe, evident from the manuscript's meticulous calligraphy and systematic copying method. Scholars Victor Martin and Rodolphe Kasser have described P75's handwriting as an attractive, vertical uncial script, elegant and precise, akin to the style observed in specific Oxyrhynchus Papyri. This style is recognized by paleographers as the "common angular type" prevalent in the late second to early third century, indicative of the period's scribal practices.

The scribe's Christian affiliation is discernible through the use of nomina sacra, a common practice among Christian scribes to abbreviate sacred names, and the abbreviation for "cross" (σταυρος), signaling the manuscript's intended Christian audience. Additionally, the large typeface suggests that P75 was designed for public reading within a Christian congregation, further supported by the inclusion of sectional divisions to facilitate its use by lectors.

P75 is renowned for its textual accuracy, which, prior to its discovery, challenged prevailing assumptions about the state of the New Testament text in the second and third centuries. Before P75 came to light, scholars like Sir Frederic Kenyon posited that the textual tradition during this period was characterized by significant variability, with scribes exercising considerable freedom over the text. The discovery of P75, however, revealed a close textual relationship with the fourth-century Codex Vaticanus (B), demonstrating a remarkable degree of textual stability and similarity.

This discovery has significantly influenced scholarly understanding of the New Testament's textual history. The assumption of an Alexandrian recension, a scholarly effort to collate various texts into a refined edition exemplified by Codex Vaticanus, has been reconsidered in light of P75's existence. Instead of viewing Vaticanus as the product of fourth-century editorial work, scholars now recognize that the "Alexandrian" text type existed much earlier, essentially undermining the notion of a prolonged editorial process culminating in Vaticanus.

Ernst Haenchen, upon reviewing P75, noted the early presence of "neutral" readings, arguing against the need for a prolonged editorial process to achieve the text of Vaticanus. Similarly, Kurt Aland revised his views on the nature of the second and third-century manuscripts after examining P75, acknowledging the early existence of a text closely resembling that of Codex Vaticanus. Gordon Fee further argued against the concept of an Alexandrian recension, suggesting that manuscripts like P75 and Vaticanus represent an early and "relatively pure" textual tradition.

Despite its accuracy, P75 is not without corrections, totaling 116 in the Gospels of Luke and John, reflecting the scribe's conscientious efforts to produce a faithful copy. These corrections rarely involved significant textual revision, indicating the scribe's intent to adhere closely to the source text. This disciplined approach to copying supports the view that P75, and by extension, Codex Vaticanus, reflect an early and stable textual tradition, rather than the result of a fourth-century editorial recension.

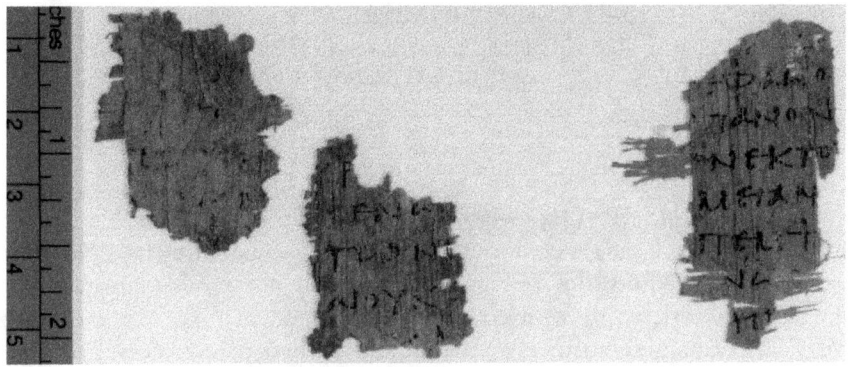

P115 (P. Oxy. 4499)

Papyrus 115 (P. Oxy. 4499), recognized in the Gregory-Aland numbering system as P115, is a significant Greek New Testament papyrus manuscript. This manuscript comprises 26 fragments from a codex that includes portions of the Book of Revelation. Through the application of comparative writing styles, known as paleography, scholars have dated P115 to the third century, specifically around 200-250 C.E.

The discovery of P115 in Oxyrhynchus, Egypt, was made by renowned scholars Bernard Pyne Grenfell and Arthur Hunt. Despite its early discovery, the manuscript remained unpublished until 2011, underscoring the meticulous and often lengthy process involved in deciphering ancient texts. Presently, P115 is preserved at the Ashmolean Museum, where it continues to be an invaluable resource for biblical scholarship and textual criticism.

The dating of P115 to the third century is particularly noteworthy, as it contributes to our understanding of the textual transmission and variant readings within the Book of Revelation. This manuscript not only enhances our knowledge of early Christian scriptural traditions but also serves as a critical witness to the text of Revelation during a formative period of Christian history.

Content

Rev. 2:1–3, 13–15, 27–29; 3:10–12; 5:8–9; 6:5–6; 8:3–8, 11–13; 9:1–5, 7–16, 18–21; 10:1–4, 8–11; 11:1–5, 8–15, 18–19; 12:1–5, 8–10, 12–17; 13:1–3, 6–16, 18; 14:1–3, 5–7, 10–11, 14–15, 18–20; 15:1, 4–7

Date

Papyrus 115 (P. Oxy. 4499), identified within the New Testament manuscript tradition, is a significant papyrus manuscript dating from the early to mid-third century. Its dating is informed by a careful comparison of handwriting styles with other contemporary documents. Notably, the script of P115 bears resemblance to that found in two manuscripts from the Heroninos Archive, specifically P. Flor. 108 and P. Flor. 259. The relevance of this comparison lies in the fact that the documents within the Heroninos Archive are dated before 256 C.E., based on documentary texts contained within the collection.

Additionally, P115's script is similar to that of P. Oxy. 1016, another document which must be dated before 234 C.E., as it contains a land register on its verso. This comparative analysis of handwriting styles places P115 securely within the third century, providing a crucial anchor for its chronological placement within the broader corpus of New Testament manuscripts.

The importance of P115 is underscored by its content, which adds to our understanding of the textual history and variance within the New Testament, specifically within the Book of Revelation. By closely examining such manuscripts, scholars are better equipped to reconstruct the early text of the New Testament and appreciate the historical context in which these documents were produced and circulated.

Physical Features

Papyrus 115 (P. Oxy. 4499) comprises 26 fragments from a codex exclusively containing the Book of Revelation. The original dimensions of each sheet were approximately 15.5 cm by 23.5 cm, accommodating between 33 to 36 lines of text per page. The physical characteristics of this manuscript suggest that the scribe worked on a pre-bound codex. This inference is drawn from the observation that the text width on even-numbered pages, which are bound on the right side, is consistently narrower compared to the odd-numbered pages, where the binding is on the left side. This variation in text width between pages indicates the practical challenges faced by the scribe when writing near the bound edge, especially on the right side of the left-hand pages, affirming the likelihood that the codex was bound prior to the scribe's engagement with the text. This detail not only informs us about the physical attributes of P115 but also provides insights into the practices and constraints of ancient manuscript production.

Textual Character

Papyrus 115 (P. Oxy. 4499) holds considerable textual significance within New Testament scholarship, particularly in the study of the Book of Revelation. Its textual character demonstrates a close alignment with Codex Alexandrinus (A) and Codex Ephraemi Rescriptus (C), both of which are esteemed for their reliable testimony to the original text of Revelation. This alignment positions P115 as a superior textual witness, offering a textual tradition that is often considered closer to the original text than that provided by Papyrus 47 (P47), which is more closely aligned with Codex Sinaiticus (ℵ). The distinction between these textual families underscores the value of P115 in textual criticism, as it contributes to our understanding of the early text of Revelation and supports the ongoing effort to reconstruct the most accurate text possible.

PAPYRUS 137 (P137): P. Oxy. 6345 The Recently Published Earliest Manuscript Fragment of Mark 1:7-8, 16-18

P137 (P. Oxy. 5345)

Physical Description and Features of P137

P137, identified as P. Oxy. 5345, emerges as a significant piece in the puzzle of New Testament textual criticism. This fragment, penned on papyrus, is a testament to the early Christian efforts in manuscript production and preservation. The quality of the papyrus, the durability of the ink, and the overall state of preservation provide a window into the material culture of early Christian communities. Despite its fragmentary nature, P137 offers crucial insights into the methods and materials used by early Christians to transcribe the texts they deemed sacred and essential for the faith community's spiritual life.

Content within P137

P137 contains a portion of the Gospel of Mark, specifically Mark 1:7-9, 16-18. This passage, which includes John the Baptist's proclamation and the calling of Simon and Andrew, is pivotal for understanding the early Christian narrative of Jesus' ministry initiation. The text underscores the continuity between John's ministry and Jesus' call to discipleship, highlighting themes of repentance, baptism, and the immediacy of Jesus' mission. The preservation of these verses in P137 underscores the significance of the Gospel narrative to early Christian identity and mission.

THE EARLY CHRISTIAN COPYISTS OF THE NEW TESTAMENT

Dating and Paleogeographical Insights

The dating of P137 to 100-150 C.E. is anchored in paleographical analysis, which examines the handwriting style to ascertain the manuscript's temporal context. This early dating situates P137 remarkably close to the Gospel of Mark's original composition, offering an invaluable witness to the text's early transmission. The paleographical evidence, coupled with the papyrus's characteristics, points to a likely origin within the broader Egyptian region, known for its pivotal role in early Christian manuscript production and preservation. This geographical and chronological setting highlights the early and widespread circulation of the Gospel texts within Christian communities.

Textual Character of P137

1. **Text Type**: P137 is aligned with the Alexandrian text type, renowned for its textual purity and critical esteem in New Testament textual criticism. This alignment underscores P137's importance in reconstructing the New Testament's earliest attainable text, offering insights into the textual tradition from which our contemporary Gospel accounts are derived.

2. **Handwriting Style**: The script of P137 is indicative of a Reformed Documentary Hand or possibly a Professional Bookhand, suggesting the involvement of a scribe who was skilled in copying literary texts. The quality of the handwriting reflects a careful and deliberate effort to produce a clear and accurate transcription of the Gospel text.

3. **Quality of Execution**: The transcription process reflected in P137 appears to have been undertaken with considerable care, indicative of the scribe's respect for the text's sacred status and the importance of its accurate transmission. The precision of the script and the effort to maintain legibility suggest a high degree of scribal professionalism and dedication.

4. **Comparative Analysis**: Although P137's fragmentary nature limits extensive comparative analysis, its coherence with the broader Alexandrian text type enhances its value as a textual witness. The manuscript contributes to the critical task of identifying textual variants and understanding the early transmission history of the Gospel of Mark.

5. **Scribes and Correctors**: The presence of corrections or annotations within P137 would indicate an editorial layer aimed at refining the manuscript, underscoring the early Christian manuscript culture's commitment to textual accuracy. While specific details of scribal corrections in P137 may be limited, the manuscript's overall integrity points to a conscientious production and review process.

Scribal Practices in P137

The creation of P137 reflects not only the technical skill of its scribe but also the broader early Christian commitment to preserving the Gospel narrative. Unlike the more rudimentary or irregular scripts associated with documentary hands, the script in P137 demonstrates a level of care and uniformity characteristic of scribes who recognized the importance of their work. Through the meticulous transcription and, where present, correction of the Gospel text, the scribe of P137 contributed to the rich textual tradition that has allowed the Gospel of Mark to be transmitted across centuries. This manuscript stands as a poignant reminder of the early Christians' dedication to the written Word, ensuring the Gospel's message remained accessible to successive generations of believers.

Significant Uncial Manuscripts

Uncial manuscripts are a category of ancient texts distinct from those written on papyrus. This distinction, however, is somewhat inaccurately named because the main difference between them lies in the material used for writing – vellum (a type of treated animal skin) as opposed to papyrus, rather than the style of writing itself. Interestingly, papyrus manuscripts are also written in uncials, which are essentially capital letters. However, when we talk about uncial manuscripts, we're usually referring to the use of large, capital lettering that became widespread in biblical texts around the fourth century, as seen in famous manuscripts like Codex Sinaiticus (א) and Codex Vaticanus (B).

This classification of manuscripts into uncials is crucial for understanding how ancient texts, especially biblical ones, were transcribed and preserved over centuries. The shift to using vellum and the distinct uncial or capital lettering style in the fourth century represents a significant development in the history of manuscript production. These materials and methods were adopted for their durability and clarity, which were essential for preserving the texts accurately for future generations. Codex Sinaiticus and Codex Vaticanus, for example, are among the most valuable ancient manuscripts because they offer insights into the textual tradition of the Bible during this period. The use of vellum and the uncial style not only marked a change in the physical appearance of manuscripts but also reflected the evolving practices of scribes who were dedicated to the task of copying texts meticulously.

ℵ (Codex Sinaiticus)

The Codex Sinaiticus, with its official designation in the British Library as Add MS 43725 and known by the siglum ℵ [Aleph] or 01 (according to the Gregory-Aland numbering system), and δ 2 (in the von Soden numbering system), stands as a monumental fourth-century Christian manuscript. This Greek Bible manuscript encompasses the vast majority of the Greek Old Testament, inclusive of the deuterocanonical books, as well as the entire Greek New Testament, complemented by the inclusion of the Epistle of Barnabas and the Shepherd of Hermas. Crafted with uncial script on parchment, Codex Sinaiticus belongs to the elite cadre of the four great uncial codices, a distinguished group originally comprising the complete texts of both the Old and New Testaments.

Positioned alongside Codex Alexandrinus and Codex Vaticanus, Codex Sinaiticus is celebrated as one of the earliest and most comprehensive biblical manuscripts, harboring the oldest complete copy of the New Testament known to date. Dated through paleographical analysis to the mid-fourth century (330-360 C.E.), this manuscript is a pivotal resource for biblical scholars, offering an unparalleled glimpse into the textual history and transmission of the biblical canon.

The significance of Codex Sinaiticus in New Testament textual criticism cannot be overstated, sharing the spotlight with Codex Vaticanus as one of the pivotal Greek texts for New Testament studies. The discovery of Codex Sinaiticus by Constantin von Tischendorf in 1844 marked a turning point in biblical scholarship, providing a critical comparative tool alongside Codex Vaticanus for the analysis and study of the biblical text.

Originally located at Saint Catherine's Monastery in the Sinai Peninsula, parts of the codex have since been dispersed across four libraries globally, though the majority of the manuscript is proudly housed and displayed in the British Library in London. The journey of Codex Sinaiticus from its monastic origins to its current status as a treasured artifact in biblical scholarship underscores its enduring value and impact on the study of Christian scripture.

Content

Codex Sinaiticus, designated by the symbol א, is a seminal ancient biblical manuscript. It encompasses the entire Old Testament and New Testament. The order of the New Testament texts in this codex is as follows: the Four Gospels, the Pauline Epistles (including Hebrews), Acts, the General Epistles, and Revelation. Additionally, Codex Sinaiticus contains two significant early Christian writings not found in the canonical New Testament: The Epistle of Barnabas and the Shepherd of Hermas. This manuscript is composed of 346 leaves of fine parchment, notable for its four-column format. The comprehensive content and meticulous arrangement of Codex Sinaiticus make it a critical resource for biblical scholarship, offering insights into the textual tradition and the canon of Scripture as understood in the early Christian era.

Notable Readings

Codex Sinaiticus, marked as א in scholarly notation, is among the most significant ancient texts of the New Testament, yet it is notable for the absence of certain passages commonly found in later manuscripts. This codex, dating back to the 4th century, provides invaluable insights into the textual history of the New Testament, reflecting an earlier form of the text that differs in several respects from that of later Byzantine manuscripts. Here are some key **omitted verses** from Codex Sinaiticus:

- **Gospel of Matthew**: It excludes passages like Matthew 12:47, where Jesus is informed that His mother and brothers are standing outside.

THE EARLY CHRISTIAN COPYISTS OF THE NEW TESTAMENT

Similarly, the verses concerning the sign of Jonah (Matthew 16:2b–3) and several others (Matthew 17:21; 18:11; 23:14) are not included.

- **Gospel of Mark**: The omission of verses such as Mark 7:16, which talks about having ears to hear, and others (Mark 9:44, 46; 11:26; 15:28) suggests a shorter version of Mark's Gospel in this codex. Most notably, the long ending of Mark (Mark 16:9–20), which contains post-resurrection appearances, is absent, aligning Sinaiticus with other early manuscripts that also lack this section.

- **Gospel of Luke**: In Luke's Gospel, Codex Sinaiticus does not include Luke 17:36, a verse paralleled in Matthew but missing here, likely due to a copying error or homeoteleuton (skipping text with similar endings).

- **Gospel of John**: The story of the angel stirring the water at Bethesda (John 5:4) and the Pericope Adulterae (John 7:53–8:11), which recounts the story of the woman caught in adultery, are both absent. Their omission is particularly significant as these passages are subjects of extensive debate regarding their authenticity.

- **Acts and Epistles**: The codex also omits several verses in Acts, such as Acts 8:37 (the Ethiopian eunuch's confession of faith), Acts 15:34 (which suggests that Judas Barsabbas and Silas might remain in Antioch), Acts 24:7, and Acts 28:29 (Paul's final words in Rome). In the Epistles, Romans 16:24, a benediction, is not present.

Codex Sinaiticus's omissions are crucial for understanding the development of the New Testament text. Its lack of certain passages that are present in later manuscripts highlights the textual variations and the dynamic nature of scripture transmission in the early Christian centuries. The study of such variations not only sheds light on how the biblical text was received and transmitted by early Christians but also helps scholars reconstruct the most probable original text of the New Testament.

Here's a look at some of the notable **omitted phrases** and variations in Codex Sinaiticus:

- **Matthew 5:44**: This manuscript omits the directive to "bless those who curse you, do good to those who hate you," emphasizing the distinctiveness of its text in comparison with other manuscripts like B, f1, 205, and others.

- **Matthew 6:13**: The doxology "For Yours is the kingdom, and the power, and the glory, forever. Amen." is not included, aligning

Sinaiticus with manuscripts such as B and D, among others, indicating variations in early Christian liturgical practices or textual transmission.

- **Matthew 10:39**: Sinaiticus uniquely omits the continuation "He who finds his life will lose it, and," illustrating the singular readings that contribute to critical textual analysis.

- **Matthew 15:6**: The phrase "or his mother" is absent, a variation shared with manuscripts B, D, and others, highlighting differences in the transmission of familial obligations.

- **Matthew 20:23**: Missing is "and be baptized with the baptism that I am baptized with," showing variance in how Christ's sacrificial role and followers' identification with Him were portrayed.

- **Matthew 23:35**: The specification "son of Barachi'ah" is included, contrasting with other manuscripts and pointing to variations in how biblical figures are identified.

- **Mark 1:1**: The title "the Son of God" is absent, reflecting early Christian debates on Christological titles and their inclusion in the Gospel narratives.

- **Mark 10:7**: Sinaiticus excludes "and be joined to his wife," highlighting differences in the textual tradition regarding marriage and unity.

- **Luke 9:55–56**: This codex includes Jesus' rebuke, emphasizing His mission of salvation over judgment, a reading shared with several other early manuscripts but omitted in others, reflecting theological emphases in early Christian communities.

- **John 4:9**: The observation "Jews have no dealings with Samaritans" is omitted in Sinaiticus's primary text but included in a correction, illustrating the complexities of textual transmission and the intersection of cultural and religious tensions.

Codex Sinaiticus's textual variations and omissions are pivotal for understanding the development of the New Testament canon. Its departures from later manuscript traditions underscore the dynamic nature of early Christian scripture transmission and the efforts to preserve, interpret, and understand the Christian message through the ages.

Some passages and phrases that were **excluded by the corrector**.

THE EARLY CHRISTIAN COPYISTS OF THE NEW TESTAMENT

1. **Matthew 24:36** - "nor the Son" is included in the original text of Codex Sinaiticus, aligning with manuscripts like B and D. This phrase was questioned by an early corrector, marked as doubtful, which mirrors the omission in several other manuscripts. However, a subsequent corrector removed this mark of doubt, reaffirming its inclusion.

2. **Mark 10:40** - The phrase "by my Father" is part of the original scribe's work, found also in manuscripts such as Θ and $f1$. An early corrector marked this as doubtful, a sentiment echoed in many other manuscripts that omit the phrase. Yet, this doubt was later removed by another corrector.

3. **Luke 11:4** - The petition "but deliver us from evil" appears in the original writing of Codex Sinaiticus, a reading supported by a wide array of manuscripts. It was initially marked as doubtful by a corrector, aligning with the omission in notable manuscripts like 𝔓75 and B. Nevertheless, this doubt was eventually cleared by a later correction.

4. **Luke 22:43–44** - The vivid description of Christ's agony at Gethsemane is included by the original scribe of Codex Sinaiticus. This inclusion was marked as doubtful by an early corrector, reflecting the omission in significant manuscripts such as 𝔓69(vid) and P75. However, this marking was removed by a subsequent corrector, reaffirming the passage's authenticity.

5. **Luke 23:34a** - Jesus' plea for forgiveness, "Father, forgive them; for they know not what they do," is initially included in Codex Sinaiticus. Despite being marked as doubtful by an early corrector, in line with the omission in manuscripts like P75 and B, this marking was later removed, indicating the passage's reinstatement.

Let's look at a couple of instances where the Codex Sinaiticus **adds content** not found in all manuscripts:

1. **Matthew 8:13 (parallel to Luke 7:10)**: In this passage, the Codex Sinaiticus tells us that after Jesus healed a centurion's servant from afar, the centurion went back to his house and discovered the servant was in good health. This specific detail, emphasizing the servant's recovery at the exact hour Jesus said he would heal him, underscores the immediacy and power of Jesus' healing words. The manuscript presents this account with the phrase, "and when the centurion returned to the house in that hour, he found the slave well," a

narrative that aligns closely with Luke's account and is supported by other manuscripts like C, Θ, and ƒ1, showing a rich tapestry of textual witness across early Christian documents.

2. **Matthew 10:12 (parallel to Luke 10:5)**: Here, Jesus instructs his disciples on how to greet a household they enter, advising them to say, "peace to this house." The Codex Sinaiticus includes this directive, though it's noted that an early corrector removed this reading, only for it to be reinstated by another corrector. This back-and-forth in the manuscript highlights the dynamic nature of early Christian text transmission and the careful consideration given to Jesus' teachings on peace and hospitality.

3. **Matthew 27:49 (parallel to John 19:34)**: In an addition that parallels John's account of Jesus' crucifixion, the Codex Sinaiticus contains a description of Jesus' side being pierced with a spear, causing blood and water to flow out. This detail, not found in all manuscripts, adds to the narrative of Jesus' suffering and crucifixion, providing a graphic image of his sacrifice. The inclusion of this passage in Codex Sinaiticus but not universally across other manuscripts showcases the complexity and diversity of the New Testament textual tradition.

Here's an overview of some of its **notable readings**:

1. **Matthew 7:22** introduces the word "numerous," suggesting a direct inquiry about the expulsion of a significant number of demons, which uniquely appears in this codex.

2. **Matthew 8:12** uses the term "will go out," a variant contributing to discussions on eschatological narratives within the gospel.

3. In **Matthew 13:54**, the manuscript uniquely refers to Jesus returning to "his own Antipatris," a reading that diverges from the more commonly known geographical references.

4. **Acts 8:5** mentions Philip going to "the city of Caesarea," offering a specific locale not typically found in other texts.

5. **Matthew 16:12** warns against the "leaven of bread of the Pharisees and Sadducees," aligning with themes of caution against doctrinal corruption.

6. **Luke 1:26** and **Luke 2:37** present unique readings regarding geographical locations and age, respectively, highlighting the meticulous detail in the narrative.

7. **John 1:28** initially mentions Bethany before a correction changes it to "Betharaba," showing the scribe's concern for accurate location details.
8. **John 1:34** labels Jesus as "the chosen one," a significant theological statement about Jesus' identity.
9. **John 2:3** gives a detailed reason for the shortage of wine at the wedding, attributing it to the completion of the wine supply.
10. **John 6:10** intriguingly notes "three thousand" before a correction updates it to "five thousand," indicating a keen interest in the number of attendees at the feeding of the multitude.
11. **Acts 11:20** interestingly uses "Evangelists," pointing to the active role of proclaiming the gospel.
12. **Acts 14:9** uniquely notes that a man had "not heard," emphasizing the miraculous nature of the healing that follows.
13. **Hebrews 2:4** uses "harvests" as a metaphor for divine interventions, a singular reading within the manuscript.
14. **1 Peter 5:13** and **2 Timothy 4:10** reference the "Church" and "Gaul" respectively, highlighting the early Christian community's geographical spread and Paul's travels.

Each variant opens a window into the early Christian world, offering insights into how the texts were read, understood, and lived by the communities that cherished them.

Date

Codex Sinaiticus is generally dated to the fourth century, with a consensus among scholars placing it in the middle of that century. This broad dating is based on the palaeographical analysis of the handwriting found within the codex.

Palaeographical Analysis

The primary method for dating Codex Sinaiticus is through palaeographical analysis, which examines the script's style and features. The handwriting of the codex is consistent with that of other known documents from the mid-fourth century.

Historical Context

Some scholars have suggested that Codex Sinaiticus may have been one of the fifty Bibles commissioned by the Roman Emperor Constantine around 330 C.E., as mentioned by Eusebius in his "Life of Constantine." However, others have dated the handwriting to a slightly later period, around 360 C.E.

Eusebian Apparatus

The presence of the Eusebian apparatus, a system of section divisions developed by Eusebius of Caesarea, within Codex Sinaiticus indicates that the codex was produced after Eusebius introduced this system, which is estimated to have been around 300-325 C.E. This provides a terminus post quem (earliest possible date) for the codex's production.

Scribe D's Notes

Milne and Skeat, two prominent scholars, believed that the notes in the codex, which exhibit occasional cursive characteristics, were copied by scribe D. They argued that these notes "certainly belong to the fourth century, and probably the first half of it." If their assessment is correct, it would support the dating of the codex to the early to mid-fourth century.

Physical Features

Codex Sinaiticus, a foundational manuscript in the study of New Testament textual criticism, represents an early transition from the scroll to the codex format, akin to contemporary books. Crafted from high-quality vellum parchment, this codex initially comprised double sheets, roughly measuring 40 by 70 cm. The majority of its construction follows a quire composition, each consisting of eight leaves (excluding a few exceptions), a design that gained popularity into the Medieval era. This method involves laying eight parchment pages atop each other, folding them in half to form a quire or folio, and binding several quires together to create the complete manuscript.

Contrary to earlier assessments by scholars like Tischendorf—who speculated an antelope origin for the parchment—modern microscopic analyses have confirmed the material primarily derives from calf skins, with sheep skins used secondarily. An estimated 360 animal hides were utilized, underscoring the significant resources invested in its creation. The codex's text is presented in four columns per page, featuring 12 to 14 Greek uncial

THE EARLY CHRISTIAN COPYISTS OF THE NEW TESTAMENT

letters per line, with a total count nearing four million letters. This layout mirrors the appearance of ancient papyrus rolls, albeit in a more evolved form.

The dimensions and proportions of the pages and text blocks were crafted with precision, reflecting an advanced understanding of typographic principles for that period. The manuscript's material, intricate scribal work, and binding collectively represent a considerable investment, equating to the lifetime wages of an individual at the time.

Within the New Testament, the scriptio continua style—writing without spaces between words—predominates, executed in a hand known as "biblical uncial" or "majuscule." The parchment was precisely ruled to guide the uniform handwriting, devoid of breathings or polytonic accents. Various punctuation forms and a few ligatures enhance the text's readability, despite its compact script.

A noteworthy aspect of Codex Sinaiticus is the consistent use of nomina sacra, a form of abbreviation for sacred names, evident throughout its texts. These abbreviations, alongside instances of itacism, indicate both the scribal practices of the time and the manuscript's theological emphasis.

Delving further into the textual characteristics of the Codex Sinaiticus, particularly within the New Testament manuscripts, we encounter a distinct scribal practice known as scriptio continua. This technique, which eschews the use of spaces between words, is executed in a handwriting style historically referred to as "biblical uncial" or "biblical majuscule." The preparation of the parchment involved meticulous ruling with a sharp point, a foundational step to ensure that the script followed a consistent trajectory across the surface. The uncial letters inscribed upon these lines do not accommodate breathings or polytonic accents—diacritical marks indicative of phonetic nuances or grammatical emphases within the Greek language. Instead, the manuscript employs various punctuation marks such as high and middle points, colons, and the diaeresis, notably on initial iotas and upsilons, to aid in textual clarity and interpretation. Additionally, the occurrence of ligatures and the distinctive practice of extending the initial letter of paragraphs into the margin (although this varies in extent) further characterize the codex's unique textual presentation. A recurrent phonetic feature within the manuscript is itacism—the substitution of the iota for the epsilon-iota diphthong in words like ΔΑΥΕΙΔ (David), ΠΕΙΛΑΤΟΣ (Pilate), and ΦΑΡΕΙΣΑΙΟΙ (Pharisees), underscoring a phonological evolution in the Greek language during the period of the codex's creation.

A notable textual feature throughout Codex Sinaiticus is the extensive use of nomina sacra, a scribal practice involving the abbreviation of sacred names, each marked with an overline. This method not only signifies the manuscript's religious reverence but also reflects a broader scribal tradition within early Christian manuscripts. Interestingly, certain terms that are commonly abbreviated in other manuscripts appear in both their full and abbreviated forms within Codex Sinaiticus. Among these, the most significant include abbreviations for key theological and ecclesiastical terms: ΘΣ (God), ΚΣ (Lord), ΙΣ (Jesus), ΧΣ (Christ), ΠΝΑ (Spirit), and others related to Christian doctrine and biblical narrative. These abbreviations, employed with strategic theological intent, encapsulate the essence of the Christian faith as perceived by the manuscript's scribes. The dual representation of certain words, alongside the consistent use of nomina sacra, not only aids in textual comprehension but also imbues the manuscript with a profound religious significance, reflecting the theological priorities and liturgical practices of early Christianity.

The meticulous approach to writing, punctuation, and the employment of nomina sacra in Codex Sinaiticus offers a window into the religious and cultural milieu of its creation. This analysis, grounded in an objective examination of the codex's physical and textual features, underscores its importance not only as a historical document but also as a testament to the complex interplay between religious tradition, textual transmission, and linguistic evolution in early Christian communities.

The surviving portion of the codex, now housed in the British Library, consists of over half of the original work, split across 346½ folios. This includes significant portions of both the Old and New Testaments, the Deuterocanonical books, the Epistle of Barnabas, and parts of The Shepherd of Hermas. Notably, the New Testament books are arranged in a distinct sequence that differs from modern canonical orders.

The condition of the manuscript varies, suggesting it was stored in multiple locations over time. While substantial portions of the Old Testament are lost, the extant sections provide invaluable insight into the textual history of the Christian scriptures.

In conclusion, Codex Sinaiticus stands as a monumental artifact in Christian history, offering critical insights into the text of the New Testament and early Christian literature. Its physical and textual characteristics not only reflect the technological and theological advancements of its time but also continue to inform contemporary biblical scholarship.

THE EARLY CHRISTIAN COPYISTS OF THE NEW TESTAMENT

Textual Character

Codex Sinaiticus is represented by the Hebrew letter aleph (א) in scholarly works. Variations within the text of Codex Sinaiticus are indicated by symbols such as א* and 2א, which denote the original scribe's text and corrections made by a later hand, respectively.

Textual Readings and Corrections

The manuscript exhibits textual variants, such as the reading ευαγγελιϲταϲ in Acts 11:20, which differs from the Textus Receptus reading of Ἑλληνιστάς. Marks above the variant indicate a textual discrepancy noted by the scribes or correctors.

Textual Families

Codex Sinaiticus is associated with the Alexandrian text-type, characterized by grammatical refinements and a tendency to prune the text by removing what was considered superfluous. It is generally in agreement with other manuscripts of the Alexandrian family, such as Codex Vaticanus and Codex Ephraemi Rescriptus, but shows some affinity with the Western text-type in certain passages, such as John 1:1–8:38.

Textual Criticism and Manuscript Analysis

Textual criticism aims to determine the most reliable reading of a text, and Codex Sinaiticus is a crucial witness in this field due to its antiquity and completeness. Variants are analyzed for their nature rather than their number, with spelling differences constituting a significant portion of the variants.

Scribe and Corrector Annotations

The text of Codex Sinaiticus has been heavily annotated by a series of early correctors, making it one of the most corrected manuscripts in existence. These annotations provide insights into the textual decisions and preferences of early Christian scribes and correctors.

Textual Order and Content

The order of books in Codex Sinaiticus is specific, with the New Testament arranged in the order of the Gospels, Pauline epistles, Acts, General Epistles, and Revelation. The manuscript also includes two other early Christian writings, the Epistle of Barnabas and part of The Shepherd of Hermas

Scribes and Correctors

In our objective and analytical exploration of the Codex Sinaiticus, a critical component to understand involves the manuscript's scribes and the subsequent corrections made to its text. Initially, Tischendorf identified four scribes (A, B, C, and D) and five correctors (a, b, c, d, and e) in his examination of the codex. He suggested that one corrector worked contemporaneously with the original scribes, while the others contributed in the sixth and seventh centuries. However, Tischendorf's assessment regarding scribe C, who he believed was responsible for the poetic books of the Old Testament formatted differently from the rest of the manuscript, was later reconsidered. Milne and Skeat's reinvestigation revealed that scribe C's existence was a misinterpretation by Tischendorf, based on the different formatting of these texts.

The contemporary consensus identifies three scribes (A, B, and D) responsible for the manuscript's content, as originally labeled by Tischendorf. It's also recognized that there were more correctors than Tischendorf identified, totaling at least seven. The responsibilities and characteristics of the three confirmed scribes are as follows:

- **Scribe A** was tasked with most of the Old Testament's historical and poetical books, nearly the entire New Testament, and the Epistle of Barnabas. Despite the significant portion of text attributed to him, scribe A, alongside scribe B, demonstrated a less reliable spelling capability, with scribe A noted for making "some unusually serious mistakes."

- **Scribe B** handled the Prophets and the Shepherd of Hermas, characterized by Metzger as "careless and illiterate."

- **Scribe D** was responsible for Tobit, Judith, a portion of 4 Maccabees, two-thirds of the Psalms, and the opening verses of Revelation. Distinguished for a relatively better spelling accuracy, scribe D carefully differentiated between sacral and nonsacral uses of terms, particularly ΚΥΡΙΟΣ.

The scribes employed nomina sacra, though their usage varied, with scribes A and B preferring contracted forms, whereas scribe D frequently opted for uncontracted versions. This variance highlights differing scribal practices and possibly differing theological emphases or levels of formality in their work.

Corrections to the manuscript are a significant aspect of its history, indicating the codex's dynamic nature through its early life and beyond. Initial corrections were made in the scriptorium before its distribution. These early modifications are marked as ℵa. Interestingly, the process of correction and modification extended into later centuries, particularly noted in the sixth or seventh centuries, with alterations marked as ℵb. These later corrections were informed by "a very ancient manuscript" corrected by Pamphylus, a martyr, suggesting a linkage to Origen's Hexapla, particularly for sections from 1 Samuel to Esther.

This analysis underscores the complexity and layered history of the Codex Sinaiticus. The efforts of its scribes and correctors reflect both the challenges of preserving sacred texts and the evolving understanding of scriptural transcription and interpretation across generations.

History of Codex Sinaiticus

The tale of the Codex Sinaiticus is not just a chapter from the annals of history but a narrative brimming with drama, discovery, and the passionate pursuit of biblical authenticity. It's a story that underlines the Codex's monumental value, not merely as an artifact of ancient times but as a crucial piece in the puzzle of biblical manuscript tradition.

Konstantin von Tischendorf, born in 1815 in Saxony, was more than just a scholar; he was a man on a mission. Educated in Greek at the University of Leipzig, Tischendorf found himself at odds with the prevailing scholarly trend of higher criticism, which aimed to question the authenticity of the Christian Greek Scriptures. Convinced that the truth lay in the manuscripts of early Christianity, he embarked on a scholarly quest that would lead him to the ends of the known academic world.

His journey, which began in the libraries of Europe, eventually led him to the remote Monastery of St. Catherine in Sinai. This fortress-like abode of monks, perched high above the Red Sea, was accessible only by a basket on a rope. Here, Tischendorf made a groundbreaking discovery: ancient parchments destined for the flames, among which were 129 leaves of a manuscript older than any he had encountered before. These parchments were parts of the Hebrew Scriptures, translated into Greek.

Despite his initial success, it was not until his third visit, years later, that Tischendorf's persistence truly paid off. On the verge of departure, he was shown more of the same manuscript, which included not only the remainder of the Hebrew Scriptures but the entire Christian Greek Scriptures. This was the Codex Sinaiticus, a manuscript of such age and completeness that it would become one of the most important biblical manuscripts known to exist.

Tischendorf's negotiation skills and dedication allowed him to take the Codex to Cairo for copying, and eventually to Russia, as a gift to the czar from the monastery. Today, this priceless treasure is housed in the British Museum, a testament to Tischendorf's life-long dedication to preserving the Word of God.

The account of the Codex Sinaiticus's rescue highlights not only a momentous chapter in the annals of biblical scholarship but also the human tenacity and dedication to the pursuit of knowledge. This manuscript's journey from the verge of destruction to becoming one of the most celebrated texts in the British Museum is a testament to Konstantin von Tischendorf's relentless dedication. His discovery underlines a significant point: often, the preservation of history relies on the curiosity, determination, and actions of individuals. Tischendorf's efforts exemplify how passion for one's work, combined with a stroke of serendipity, can lead to the safeguarding of our collective heritage. In the broader spectrum of historical preservation, it serves as a reminder of the importance of individual contributions towards saving invaluable artifacts for future generations.

A (Codex Alexandrinus)

The Codex Alexandrinus occupies a distinguished place in the annals of biblical scholarship as a principal manuscript of the Greek Bible. Catalogued in the British Library in London under Royal MS 1. D. V-VIII, it is designated by the siglum A or 02 according to the Gregory-Aland numbering system, and δ 4 in the von Soden classification. This manuscript, inscribed on parchment, has been dated to the fifth century through the discipline of palaeography, which analyzes comparative writing styles. Containing most of the Greek Old Testament and the entire Greek New Testament, Codex Alexandrinus is among the four Great uncial codices, a term denoting manuscripts that originally comprised the full corpus of the Old and New Testaments. Its peers include the Codex Sinaiticus and Codex Vaticanus, making it one of the earliest and most comprehensive manuscripts of the Bible extant.

The manuscript derives its name from Alexandria, Egypt, where it was housed for several centuries. The narrative of its relocation is steeped in the annals of ecclesiastical history: Cyril Lucaris, the Eastern Orthodox Patriarch, transported it from Alexandria to Constantinople (present-day Istanbul, Turkey). Subsequently, in the 17th century, it was bestowed upon Charles I of England. Its alphanumeric designation, A, was conferred by Bishop Brian Walton in the 1657 Polyglot Bible, a pioneering work that arrayed biblical texts in multiple languages side by side for comparative study. This designation gained formal acceptance and continued use with the standardization of the New Testament manuscript listing by J. J. Wettstein in 1751, securing Codex Alexandrinus's primacy in the sequence of manuscripts.

Before the acquisition of Codex Sinaiticus by British scholars, Frederick H. A. Scrivener, a noted biblical scholar and textual critic, lauded Codex Alexandrinus as the preeminent manuscript of the Greek Bible in Britain. Today, it is housed in the British Library alongside Codex Sinaiticus, prominently displayed in the Sir John Ritblat Gallery. For those unable to visit the British Library in person, the library provides a complete photographic reproduction of the New Testament portion of Codex Alexandrinus on its website, offering global access to this pivotal biblical manuscript.

Content

The Codex Alexandrinus, a venerable manuscript of the Greek Bible, has not come down to us intact. Of its original approximately 820 pages, only 773 remain. The vicissitudes of history and the passage of time have led to the loss of some portions of this significant biblical codex. The extant sections of Alexandrinus offer a comprehensive Greek rendition of the Old Testament, inclusive of the Apocrypha. Notably, it encompasses the entirety of the four books of Maccabees and Psalm 151, extending its canonical breadth beyond that recognized in many contemporary biblical traditions.

In addition to the Old Testament and Apocryphal books, the Codex Alexandrinus contains the majority of the New Testament's text. However, it is not without lacunae; specific passages have been lost to time, including Matthew 1:1–25:6, John 6:50–8:52, and 1 Corinthians 4:13–12:6. These missing sections underscore the manuscript's journey through the ages, marked by both preservation and loss.

Beyond the canonical texts, the Codex Alexandrinus is of paramount importance for including certain early Christian writings, most notably the First and Second Epistles of Clement to the Corinthians. These documents, attributed to Clement of Rome, are significant for their insight into early Christian thought and practice, situating the Codex Alexandrinus as a critical resource not only for biblical scholarship but for understanding the broader contours of early Christian history.

While the Codex Alexandrinus has been subject to the inevitable attrition of time, losing some of its original content, the surviving portions provide a rich tapestry of biblical and early Christian literature. Its comprehensive coverage of the Old Testament and Apocrypha, the substantial representation of the New Testament, and the inclusion of significant early Christian writings like the Clementine epistles, collectively affirm its invaluable contribution to biblical studies and the history of Christianity.

Some Textual Variants

The Codex Alexandrinus, a cornerstone in the field of New Testament textual criticism, features a plethora of unique textual variants that shed light on the intricate process of scriptural transcription and the evolution of biblical texts over centuries. This ancient manuscript, originating from the 5th century, is a treasure trove for scholars, offering insights into the textual variations that exist within the biblical canon. Here are some noteworthy textual variants found in the Codex Alexandrinus, juxtaposed with those from other manuscripts, highlighting the dynamic nature of biblical texts.

In the Old Testament, for example, the Codex Alexandrinus records Methuselah's age at 187 years in Genesis 5:25, contrasting with the 167 years noted in Codex Vaticanus. Such discrepancies extend to various books, like Deuteronomy and Joshua, where terms and actions differ (e.g., "in a pillar" vs. "in a cloud" in Deuteronomy 31:15).

Moving to the New Testament, the Codex Alexandrinus includes the longer ending of Mark (16:9–20), a passage omitted in some of the earliest manuscripts, underscoring the debates around canonical content. Similarly, in Luke 4:17, it uses "opened" instead of "unrolled," affecting the understanding of Jesus' action in the synagogue.

John 1:39 illustrates a variation in time reporting, with "about the sixth hour" in Codex Alexandrinus and "about the tenth hour" in the majority of manuscripts, potentially impacting the chronology of events. Acts 8:39 shows a divergence in describing Philip's departure, with "the Holy Spirit fell on the eunuch" in Codex Alexandrinus versus a simpler "spirit of the Lord" in the majority.

These examples highlight just a fraction of the textual variations that make the Codex Alexandrinus an invaluable asset in biblical studies. Its unique readings offer alternative perspectives on biblical events and teachings, emphasizing the diverse manuscript tradition that has preserved the biblical text through millennia. Scholars continue to study these variants to gain deeper insights into the historical, theological, and literary contexts of the Bible, ensuring the rich tapestry of biblical tradition remains vibrant and accessible for future generations.

Verses Not Included

The Codex Alexandrinus, an ancient manuscript of the New Testament, notably omits several verses found in later manuscripts, highlighting the complex history of the New Testament's textual transmission. For instance, Mark 15:28, which discusses the fulfillment of scripture through Jesus' crucifixion among criminals, is absent in this codex, as well as in other early manuscripts such as Codices Sinaiticus, Vaticanus, Bezae, and Regius, pointing to a divergence in early biblical texts.

Similarly, the emotive passage in Luke 22:43–44, detailing Christ's intense agony in Gethsemane, is not included in Codex Alexandrinus. This omission is shared with other significant manuscripts like Papyrus 75, Codices Sinaiticus, Vaticanus, and Washingtonianus, suggesting an early tradition that lacked this narrative.

The case of Acts 8:37, which provides an Ethiopian eunuch's confession of faith before baptism by Philip, further illustrates selective inclusion across manuscripts. While Codex Alexandrinus, along with the majority of manuscripts, omits this verse, it is found in Codex E and several minuscule manuscripts, revealing the textual variances that have intrigued scholars over centuries.

Acts 15:34, detailing a post-council decision, is similarly omitted in Codex Alexandrinus and the most ancient witnesses, yet appears in a handful of manuscripts, reflecting the dynamic nature of the Acts' textual history.

The absence of Acts 24:7, 28:29, and Romans 16:24 in Codex Alexandrinus aligns with the earliest manuscript evidence, challenging later textual traditions that include these verses. This pattern of omission extends to the Pericope Adultera (John 7:53–8:11), a narrative absent in Alexandrinus, with scholarly consensus suggesting there was originally no space for this passage in the manuscript.

These omissions in Codex Alexandrinus underscore the manuscript's critical role in understanding the development of the New Testament text. Its witness to an earlier form of the text offers invaluable insights into the early Christian community's scriptural traditions, emphasizing the evolution of the biblical canon through centuries of transcription, translation, and theological reflection.

Date

The dating of the Codex Alexandrinus, a cornerstone manuscript of the Greek Bible, involves a blend of historical annotation and scholarly inference. An Arabic note inscribed on the reverse of the manuscript's first volume attributes its authorship to Thecla, a martyr and distinguished figure in Egyptian Christianity. This note suggests a composition slightly subsequent to the Council of Nicaea, which convened in 325 C.E. However, the veracity and implications of this attribution warrant careful consideration.

Scholar Samuel Prideaux Tregelles offered an intriguing hypothesis linking the manuscript's commencement in the Gospel of Matthew—specifically at chapter 25, coincidentally associated with the feast day of Thecla—to a potential origin in a monastery dedicated to her. Tregelles speculated that Thecla's name might have been initially noted in the margin, later lost to trimming, leading to the tradition of her authorship. Cyril Lucaris, the patriarch who transferred the codex from Alexandria to Constantinople, also endorsed this attribution. Nevertheless, critical analysis suggests the manuscript cannot predate the late 4th century, rendering direct authorship by Thecla historically implausible.

Further anchoring the codex in time, its inclusion of Athanasius's Epistle on the Psalms to Marcellinus posits a terminus post quem (earliest possible date) of 373 C.E., given Athanasius's death in that year. Additionally, the absence of chapter divisions in Acts and the Epistles, a feature associated with Euthalius, Bishop of Sulci, not widely adopted until the mid-5th century, offers a terminus ad quem (latest possible date) for the manuscript's creation.

The presence of the Epistle of Clement within the codex hints at a period when the Christian biblical canon had not yet fully crystallized, adding another layer to its dating. The manuscript's calligraphy, characterized by relatively more sophisticated initial letters and decorative elements—though still aligned with earlier traditions—suggests a slightly later origin than the Codex Vaticanus or Sinaiticus.

Taking these factors into account, the Codex Alexandrinus is situated within a generation following the creation of the Sinaiticus and Vaticanus codices. While it may originate from the late 4th century, scholarly consensus, including that of the Institute for New Testament Textual Research (INTF), places it firmly within the 5th century. This dating not only situates the codex within a critical period of early Christian history but also reflects the evolving artistry and textual traditions of early Christian manuscripts.

Physical Features

The Codex Alexandrinus, a cornerstone of biblical scholarship, is a quintessential example of an ancient codex, precursor to the modern book, crafted with meticulous care. Comprising 773 leaves of thin, exquisite vellum, the manuscript originally contained approximately 820 pages. It is divided into four volumes, measuring 12.6 × 10.4 inches each, bound in the quarto format. This arrangement involves layering parchment leaves, folding them twice into a compact block, and stitching them together to create the codex. Historically, these folios were assembled into quires of eight, though modern rebinding has adjusted them to sets of six. The passage of time and subsequent handling have led to the pages' discoloration, particularly at the edges, with some damage inflicted by both age and at times, the oversight of modern binders, affecting the text, especially in the upper inner margins.

Frederick Scrivener highlighted the manuscript's fragility, noting the vellum's susceptibility to damage and the ink's tendency to flake, leading to restricted access to the manuscript to preserve its condition. The manuscript encompasses the Septuagint for the Old Testament, though ten leaves are lost, and the New Testament, missing 31 leaves. Notably, portions of 1 and 2 Clement are also absent, likely missing three leaves.

The text is presented in a two-column format using uncial script, with lines per column ranging from 49 to 51 and each line holding 20 to 25 letters. Early sections of each book are distinguished by red ink, and larger letters at the start of sections are marginally set, reminiscent of practices in other significant codices. Despite the absence of word division (scriptio continua), some pauses are marked with a dot, suggesting a space between words. The manuscript lacks accents or breathing marks, with minimal punctuation included by the original scribe. The Old Testament's poetical books are uniquely formatted stichometrically, and Old Testament quotations within the New Testament text are marginally annotated.

Decorative elements are sparse, limited to tail-pieces concluding each book, and there's an observed tendency towards enlarging initial letters of sentences, making Codex Alexandrinus a pioneer in this stylistic feature. The manuscript showcases iotacistic errors typical of its era, alongside occasional confusions between N and M, and the substitution of ΓΓ for NΓ, hinting at its Egyptian origins, though this is not conclusively accepted.

The manuscript evidences a stylistic shift beginning with the Gospel of Luke through to 1 Corinthians 10:8, incorporating Coptic influences in certain letters, suggesting multiple scribes' involvement. Scholars have debated the exact number, with estimates ranging from two to five, based on the analysis of handwriting differences and textual corrections.

Corrections abound within the Codex Alexandrinus, applied both by the original scribe and subsequent revisers, aligning the text with various other codices and the majority of minuscule manuscripts. These corrections vary in extent across different biblical books, with the Pentateuch seeing significant alterations and the Book of Revelation receiving minimal corrections.

The manuscript's folios are numerated in Arabic in the verso of the lower margin, a practice that provides insights into the original extent of the manuscript, as evidenced by the starting numeral in the surviving portion of Matthew.

Textual Character

The Codex Alexandrinus, a cornerstone of biblical scholarship, is a quintessential example of an ancient codex, precursor to the modern book, crafted with meticulous care. Comprising 773 leaves of thin, exquisite vellum, the manuscript originally contained approximately 820 pages. It is divided into four volumes, measuring 12.6 × 10.4 inches each, bound in the quarto format. This arrangement involves layering parchment leaves, folding them twice into a compact block, and stitching them together to create the codex. Historically, these folios were assembled into quires of eight, though modern rebinding has adjusted them to sets of six. The passage of time and subsequent handling have led to the pages' discoloration, particularly at the edges, with some damage inflicted by both age and at times, the oversight of modern binders, affecting the text, especially in the upper inner margins.

Frederick Scrivener highlighted the manuscript's fragility, noting the vellum's susceptibility to damage and the ink's tendency to flake, leading to restricted access to the manuscript to preserve its condition. The manuscript encompasses the Septuagint for the Old Testament, though ten leaves are lost, and the New Testament, missing 31 leaves. Notably, portions of 1 and 2 Clement are also absent, likely missing three leaves.

The text is presented in a two-column format using uncial script, with lines per column ranging from 49 to 51 and each line holding 20 to 25 letters. Early sections of each book are distinguished by red ink, and larger letters at the start of sections are marginally set, reminiscent of practices in other significant codices. Despite the absence of word division (scriptio continua), some pauses are marked with a dot, suggesting a space between words. The manuscript lacks accents or breathing marks, with minimal punctuation included by the original scribe. The Old Testament's poetical books are uniquely formatted stichometrically, and Old Testament quotations within the New Testament text are marginally annotated.

Decorative elements are sparse, limited to tail-pieces concluding each book, and there's an observed tendency towards enlarging initial letters of sentences, making Codex Alexandrinus a pioneer in this stylistic feature. The manuscript showcases iotacistic errors typical of its era, alongside occasional confusions between N and M, and the substitution of ΓΓ for NΓ, hinting at its Egyptian origins, though this is not conclusively accepted.

The manuscript evidences a stylistic shift beginning with the Gospel of Luke through to 1 Corinthians 10:8, incorporating Coptic influences in certain letters, suggesting multiple scribes' involvement. Scholars have debated the exact number, with estimates ranging from two to five, based on the analysis of handwriting differences and textual corrections.

Corrections abound within the Codex Alexandrinus, applied both by the original scribe and subsequent revisers, aligning the text with various other codices and the majority of minuscule manuscripts. These corrections vary in extent across different biblical books, with the Pentateuch seeing significant alterations and the Book of Revelation receiving minimal corrections.

The manuscript's folios are numerated in Arabic in the verso of the lower margin, a practice that provides insights into the original extent of the manuscript, as evidenced by the starting numeral in the surviving portion of Matthew.

Scribes and Correctors

The scholarly analysis of the Codex Alexandrinus, particularly concerning its scribes and correctors, presents a nuanced view of its textual genesis. Frederic G. Kenyon initially posited that the manuscript's transcription was the effort of five distinct scribes, whom he labeled with Roman numerals. According to Kenyon's assessment, the first two scribes were responsible for the Old Testament, while the subsequent scribes were allocated various portions of the New Testament: the third scribe copied the Gospels and part of Corinthians, the fourth was tasked with Luke-Acts, the General Epistles, and part of Romans and Corinthians, and the fifth scribe concluded the manuscript with Revelation.

Contrary to Kenyon's theory, Milne and Skeat later proposed that the entire codex was likely the work of just two scribes, identified as I and II. This simplification suggests a more streamlined approach to the codex's creation, though it acknowledges the potential for variation in the manuscript's sections.

The quality of the exemplars, or master copies, used by the Alexandrinus scribes appears to have varied significantly across the New Testament. Particularly in the Gospels, the exemplar was of a lesser quality, indicative of a Byzantine text type, which might not reflect the original text as reliably as other sources. This contrasted with the sections containing the General Epistles and Revelation, where the Codex Alexandrinus is considered a more faithful witness to the original writings.

Moreover, the scribe responsible for the New Testament content in Codex Alexandrinus did not merely copy the text verbatim but introduced his own readings into the manuscript. This practice, highlighted by textual critic Fenton John Anthony Hort, involved the substitution of synonyms within the text, suggesting a degree of interpretive freedom taken by the scribe. Such individualisms are a testament to the scribe's engagement with the text and reflect a unique characteristic of Codex Alexandrinus.

In terms of its textual witness, the Codex Alexandrinus offers a mixed representation. Within the Gospels, it aligns with the Byzantine text type, a later and more widespread text type among Greek New Testament manuscripts. Its value increases with the Epistles, where it presents a more accurate account, and it reaches its peak in the book of Revelation, where Alexandrinus is esteemed as the most reliable witness to the original text among the extant manuscripts.

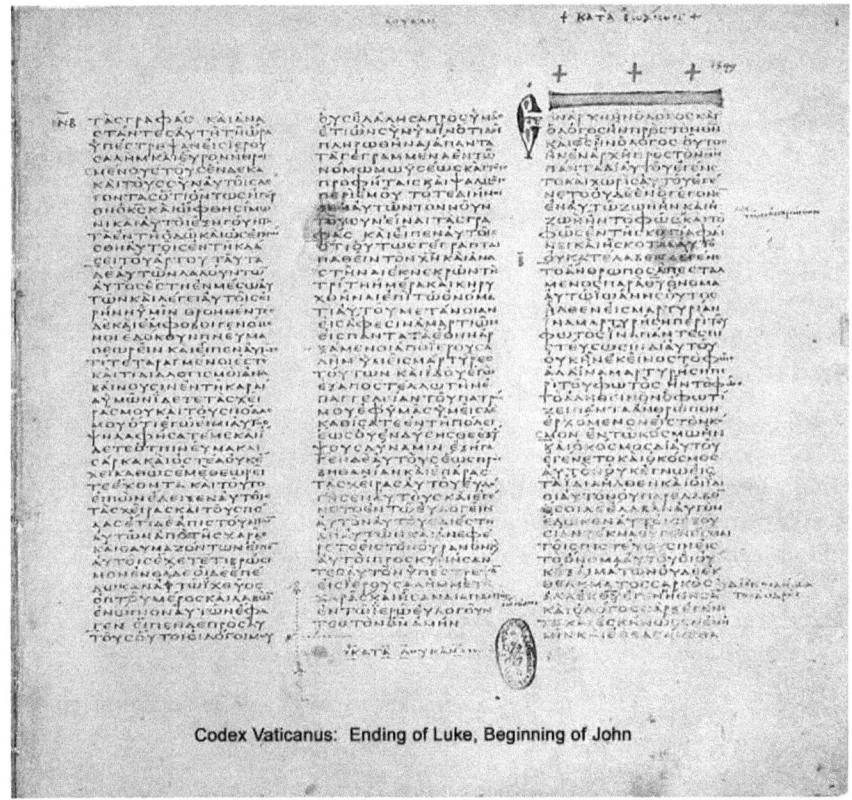

Codex Vaticanus: Ending of Luke, Beginning of John

B (Codex Vaticanus)

The Codex Vaticanus, housed in the Vatican Library (Bibl. Vat., Vat. gr. 1209) and known in scholarly circles by the siglum B or 03 (according to the Gregory-Aland numbering system), and δ 1 (in the von Soden classification), stands as a seminal Greek manuscript of the Christian Bible. This manuscript encompasses the majority of both the Greek Old Testament and New Testament, placing it among the four great uncial codices. Its significance is further underscored by its status as one of the earliest and most comprehensive biblical manuscripts, paralleled only by the Codex Alexandrinus and Codex Sinaiticus. Through palaeographical analysis, which examines comparative writing styles, the Codex Vaticanus has been dated to the 4th century, specifically around 300-330 C.E.

The Western world became acquainted with the Codex Vaticanus through the efforts of Desiderius Erasmus and Vatican Library prefects. While initial attempts to collate portions of the codex were marred by inaccuracies, these early scholarly endeavors paved the way for more rigorous 19th-century transcriptions, enhancing our understanding of its distinctiveness from the Textus Receptus and its uncertain relationship with the Latin Vulgate.

Renowned for its textual integrity, the Codex Vaticanus is attributed to the meticulous efforts of two primary scribes, designated as A and B for the Old and New Testaments, respectively. Subsequent corrections by two individuals, B1 (nearly contemporary with the original scribes) and B2 (a corrector from the 10th or 11th century who refined the text with additional accents and punctuation), attest to the manuscript's evolving accuracy over time.

Among scholars, Codex Vaticanus is revered as a paramount authority on the Greek New Testament, second only to Codex Sinaiticus. Its influence was instrumental to textual critics Brooke F. Westcott and Fenton J. A. Hort in their seminal 1881 work, "The New Testament in the Original Greek," and it continues to underpin modern editions of the Greek New Testament. Its text forms the foundation of the widely circulated Nestle-Aland editions and remains a critical benchmark for textual scholarship.

The Codex Vaticanus is distinguished by its representation of the Alexandrian text-type, offering invaluable insight into the Septuagint and New Testament texts. Its prominence in the field of textual criticism, especially for the Gospels, Acts, and Catholic epistles, is unrivaled, although its value in Pauline epistles, where it sometimes aligns with Western text-types, is viewed with slightly less esteem compared to Codex Sinaiticus. Despite its incompleteness, Kurt Aland extols the Codex Vaticanus as "by far the most significant of the uncials."

Preserved within the Vatican Library for at least six centuries, the Codex Vaticanus's enduring legacy is a testament to its pivotal role in biblical scholarship, embodying the textual history and critical study of the Christian Scriptures.

THE EARLY CHRISTIAN COPYISTS OF THE NEW TESTAMENT

Content

The Codex Vaticanus, a pivotal manuscript in the annals of biblical scholarship, was initially composed to include an almost complete text of the Greek Old Testament, or the Septuagint (LXX), with the notable exceptions of 1-4 Maccabees and the Prayer of Manasseh. Unfortunately, early portions of the manuscript, specifically the initial 20 leaves covering Genesis 1:1–46:28a and parts of Psalms (105:27–137:6b), were lost over time. These sections have since been replaced by transcriptions from the 15th century to fill the gaps. Additionally, a tear has resulted in the loss of 2 Kings 2:5–7, 10-13, further highlighting the codex's vulnerability to physical damage through the centuries.

In terms of the Old Testament's organization within the Codex Vaticanus, it begins with Genesis and continues through to 2 Chronicles, followed by 1 Esdras and 2 Esdras (Ezra–Nehemiah), marking the beginning of its divergent order from more familiar arrangements, such as that found in the Codex Alexandrinus. The codex then proceeds with the Psalms, Proverbs, Ecclesiastes, Song of Songs, Job, Wisdom of Solomon, Ecclesiasticus (Sirach), Esther, Judith, and Tobit. The twelve minor prophets are included but arranged in a unique sequence from Hosea to Malachi, with specific deviations from the traditional order. The arrangement concludes with Isaiah, Jeremiah (alongside Baruch, Lamentations, and the Epistle of Jeremiah), Ezekiel, and Daniel, underscoring the manuscript's distinctive structuring of biblical texts.

The New Testament content preserved within the Codex Vaticanus encompasses the Gospels, Acts, the general epistles, the Pauline epistles, and part of the Epistle to the Hebrews, concluding abruptly at Hebrews 9:14. Notably absent from the Vaticanus are the pastoral epistles (1 and 2 Timothy, Titus, Philemon) and the Book of Revelation. The lacunae in Hebrews and the entirety of Revelation have been supplemented by a 15th-century hand, catalogued under minuscule 1957, to provide continuity. While it remains speculative, the original inclusion of apocryphal New Testament writings or the Book of Revelation in the Codex Vaticanus is debated among scholars, with some suggesting that these texts might have been present in the manuscript's initial compilation.

In summary, the Codex Vaticanus serves as an invaluable artifact of early Christian texts, offering a unique glimpse into the textual tradition and organization of the biblical canon. Its content, both what is extant and what has been lost or supplemented, reflects the complex history of biblical transmission and the codex's enduring significance in biblical studies.

Date

Dating ancient manuscripts like the Codex Vaticanus can be quite the detective work, especially since these documents rarely come with a handy "created on" date. So, how do scholars figure out how old these manuscripts are? It's a bit like how fashion changes over time; just as you can tell roughly when a photo was taken based on what people are wearing, scholars can date manuscripts based on the style of handwriting they use.

A key style to know about is called "uncial" writing. This style features rounded capital letters that are evenly spaced out in neat lines, and it was all the rage from the fourth century for several hundred years. By comparing undated manuscripts written in uncial style with others that we know the dates of, scholars can get a pretty good calculation at when they were made.

However, this method isn't perfect. Bruce Metzger, a big name in the world of New Testament textual criticism, pointed out that because a person's handwriting doesn't really change much over their lifetime, pinning down a date to a specific year is tricky. The best scholars can usually do is give a range of about fifty years when the manuscript might have been made. Using this method, experts have come to a consensus that the Codex Vaticanus was probably created in the early fourth century C.E. This makes it one of the oldest and most valuable biblical manuscripts we have, offering incredible insights into the text of the Bible as it was over 1,600 years ago.

The dating of the Codex Vaticanus is a significant aspect of its study, placing it among the earliest and most important biblical manuscripts available to scholars. This manuscript has been dated to the early 4th century, specifically within the range of 300-330 C.E. This period is crucial in the history of Christianity, occurring shortly after the Edict of Milan in 313 C.E., which granted Christians the freedom to practice their religion throughout the Roman Empire. This era also precedes the First Council of Nicaea in 325 C.E., a pivotal event in the establishment of orthodox Christian doctrine.

The dating of the Codex Vaticanus to this specific timeframe is grounded in palaeographical analysis, a scholarly discipline that studies ancient handwriting styles to estimate the age of manuscript texts. The script used in Vaticanus, its material composition, and the stylistic features of its text all contribute to its early 4th-century dating.

This period was a time of significant transition and consolidation for the Christian Church, moving from a persecuted sect to a legally recognized religion with the patronage of the Roman Empire. The production of such a manuscript during this time suggests a context in which there was both the means and the stability necessary for the creation of elaborate and expensive biblical codices. It implies a community with significant resources and a deep commitment to the preservation and dissemination of its sacred texts.

Furthermore, the early date of the Codex Vaticanus has profound implications for biblical scholarship. Being one of the oldest extant manuscripts of the Bible, it provides critical insights into the text of the Scriptures as it existed in the early 4th century. This, in turn, helps scholars understand the development and transmission of the biblical text over time, offering a closer approximation to the original writings of the biblical authors than many later manuscripts.

Physical Features

The Codex Vaticanus, a monumental work of early Christian scholarship, represents a pivotal transition from scroll to codex, a forerunner of the modern book. This remarkable manuscript, contained in a quarto volume, is crafted from 759 leaves of exceptionally fine and thin vellum, each measuring approximately 27 cm square, although evidence suggests the original dimensions were likely larger. The textual content is inscribed in uncial letters, a script characterized by its uniformly sized, majuscule (uppercase) lettering, which contributes to the codex's legibility and aesthetic harmony.

The organization of the Codex Vaticanus is noteworthy for its use of quires—collections of five sheets or ten leaves each—mirroring the structure found in other significant manuscripts such as the Codex Marchalianus or Codex Rossanensis, yet distinct from the Codex Sinaiticus's varied sheet arrangements. The manuscript's original composition is estimated to have included 830 parchment leaves, but it currently lacks 71 leaves due to historical attrition. Presently, the Old Testament portion comprises 617 sheets, while the New Testament is preserved on 142 sheets.

Unique among New Testament manuscripts, the Codex Vaticanus employs a three-column per page format, with the number of lines per page ranging from 40 to 44 and each line containing 16 to 18 letters. This layout is consistent across the manuscript, except for the poetical books of the Old Testament, which are presented in a two-column format. Such structural decisions underscore the codex's distinctive approach to text organization and presentation.

The manuscript's text is characterized by a continuous, unbroken flow of small and neatly penned Greek letters, with no separation between words, creating the appearance of a singular, elongated word per line. Punctuation within the Codex Vaticanus is minimal, with later hands adding accents, breathings, and diaereses on initial iotas and upsilons, as well as abbreviating nomina sacra—a practice of shortening sacred names or words in Christian texts. Additionally, Old Testament citations are indicated by an inverted comma or diplai (>). Notably, the manuscript lacks the enlarged initials and punctuation marks that became common in later manuscripts, preserving a more streamlined and focused textual presentation.

The gospel texts within the codex do not adhere to the Ammonian Sections and Eusebian Canons found in later manuscripts but instead follow a unique system of numbered sections. This method parallels only two other known manuscripts, illustrating the Codex Vaticanus's singular approach to gospel organization. Furthermore, the Acts and Catholic Epistles feature two distinct division systems, diverging from the traditional Euthalian Apparatus and reflecting the manuscript's innovative structuring of biblical texts.

In summary, the Codex Vaticanus stands as a cornerstone of biblical scholarship, notable for its meticulous craftsmanship, innovative organizational structure, and the unique presentation of its textual content. Its contributions to the study of early Christian manuscripts and the textual history of the Bible are invaluable, reflecting the depth and complexity of early Christian textual traditions.

Textual Character

The Codex Vaticanus, a quintessential artifact of early Christian scripture, presents a textual character of significant variation and scholarly interest, particularly within its Old Testament component. The textual type within the Codex Vaticanus varies across different books of the Old Testament, displaying a confluence of textual traditions. For example, in the book of Ezekiel, the text aligns closely with the majority of manuscript traditions, whereas, in Isaiah, it diverges markedly. The book of Judges offers a text that substantially deviates from the majority text tradition but finds alignment with the Old Latin and Sahidic versions, as well as the writings of Cyril of Alexandria. Interestingly, the Job text within Vaticanus includes an additional 400 half-verses from Theodotion not found in the Old Latin and Sahidic versions, indicating a complex textual history.

THE EARLY CHRISTIAN COPYISTS OF THE NEW TESTAMENT

Critics such as Fenton John Anthony Hort and Emil Cornill have postulated that the Old Testament text of the Codex Vaticanus substantially reflects the textual base of Origen's Hexapla, an extensive work of biblical scholarship completed at Caesarea. This text, later issued independently by Eusebius and Pamphilus, suggests a lineage of textual transmission that Vaticanus may preserve, offering a window into the early textual tradition underpinning these biblical books.

Turning to the New Testament, the Codex Vaticanus is esteemed for its representation of the Alexandrian text-type, a textual tradition characterized by its closeness to what many scholars consider the original text of the New Testament. Its Greek text, particularly in the Gospels of Luke and John, shows remarkable alignment with the Bodmer Papyrus 𝔓75, a manuscript dated to 175-225 C.E., predating Vaticanus by at least a century. This parallelism between Vaticanus and P75, especially in these Gospels, underscores the codex's fidelity to an earlier exemplar, bolstering its scholarly reputation as a critical witness to the New Testament text. Such alignment also supports the hypothesis of its origin in Egypt, where the Alexandrian text-type predominated.

In the Pauline Epistles, however, the Codex Vaticanus exhibits a notable Western textual influence, diverging from its otherwise predominantly Alexandrian character. This mixture underscores the complex textual history and regional variations influencing the transmission of New Testament writings.

Kurt Aland's categorization of the Codex Vaticanus within Category I of his manuscript classification system further emphasizes its critical value. Manuscripts in this category are recognized for their exceptional quality and high proportion of what is presumed to be the original text of the New Testament, marking the Codex Vaticanus as a manuscript of unparalleled significance in biblical scholarship and textual criticism.

Scribes and Correctors

The manuscript production of the Codex Vaticanus, an invaluable document in the study of biblical texts, reveals a collaboration marked by meticulous scribe work and subsequent corrections. Initially, Constantin von Tischendorf posited that three scribes (A, B, and C) were involved in its creation, with two focusing on the Old Testament and one on the New Testament. This perspective was initially supported by Frederic G. Kenyon. However, T.C. Skeat, upon closer examination, refined this view, suggesting that only two scribes (A and B) were responsible for the manuscript. Skeat argued that these scribes shared the work on the Old Testament, and one of them (B) also penned the New Testament.

The division of labor was as follows:

- **Scribe A** was responsible for writing from Genesis to 1 Kings, and from Psalms to Tobias.

- **Scribe B** continued from 1 Kings through 2 Esdras and from Hosea to Daniel, as well as the entirety of the New Testament.

The manuscript also underwent corrections by at least two individuals after the initial transcription. The first corrector, B2, was contemporary with the scribes, making immediate adjustments or corrections. Another, B3, worked significantly later, around the 10th or 11th century, adding accents, breathing marks, and punctuation, which, while aimed at clarification, arguably detracted from the original script's aesthetic quality.

Tischendorf speculated on a connection between one of the Vaticanus scribes and the scribes of the Codex Sinaiticus, particularly scribe D, though this claim rests on stylistic similarities rather than concrete evidence. Skeat acknowledged the resemblance but cautioned against concluding they were the same individual, emphasizing instead a shared scribal tradition.

The later scribe who retraced the original writing not only added grammatical marks but also attempted to preserve the script's integrity, despite introducing itacistic errors—common phonetic confusions in ancient manuscripts, such as mixing ει for ι and αι for ε.

A notable feature of the Codex Vaticanus is the presence of distigmai, small double dot markings in the margins, numbering at least 795, with possibly 40 more being less certain. These markings, whose purpose was elucidated by Philip Payne in 1995, signal textual variants known to the manuscript's early correctors. Specifically, these distigmai highlight areas of textual uncertainty, suggesting an awareness of variant readings within the early Christian community.

An intriguing marginal note in Hebrews 1:3, "Fool and knave, leave the old reading and do not change it!", hints at the scribes' and correctors' ongoing struggle to maintain textual purity amidst the temptation or tendency to amend the script. This admonition underscores the complex dynamics of manuscript preservation, transmission, and the pursuit of textual accuracy within ancient scriptoriums.

The Codex Vaticanus, therefore, stands as a testament not only to the biblical texts it contains but also to the intricate process of its creation, correction, and preservation, highlighting the collaborative and corrective efforts that have shaped our understanding of sacred scripture.

In the Vatican Library

The journey of the Codex Vaticanus, known as B, to its current residence in the Vatican Library is as fascinating as the contents it holds. This ancient manuscript, believed to have been crafted between 300-330 C.E., offers a rare glimpse into the biblical texts of the early Christian era.

Originally, the Codex Vaticanus was thought to have been kept in Caesarea in the 6th century alongside the Codex Sinaiticus, as both share a unique way of organizing chapters in the Book of Acts. Its relocation to Italy likely occurred after the Council of Florence in the mid-15th century, a period of significant ecclesiastical and cultural exchanges between the East and the West.

The Vatican Library, established by Pope Nicholas V in 1448, has been the manuscript's home for centuries, possibly even appearing in the library's earliest catalog from 1475. By 1481, it was definitively cataloged, described notably for its three-column vellum Bible format.

Awareness of the Codex Vaticanus outside the Vatican emerged in the 16th century through the correspondence between Erasmus and the Vatican Library's prefects. This led to comparisons between the Vaticanus and Erasmus's own Textus Receptus, highlighting differences and sparking further scholarly interest. Despite early misconceptions aligning it more with the Vulgate than the Textus Receptus, it was later recognized for its unique textual character, distinct from both.

Efforts to study the Codex Vaticanus in detail have been met with various challenges over the centuries. Initial collations were often flawed or incomplete, and access to the manuscript was highly restricted, limiting scholarly engagement. Not until the 19th century did significant strides occur in understanding and disseminating its text. Despite initial resistance from the Vatican Library authorities, the manuscript eventually became a focal point for textual criticism, especially after the facsimile editions and comprehensive collations in the late 19th and early 20th centuries made it more accessible.

The Codex Vaticanus's history is marked by periods of obscurity and exclusivity, contrasted with moments of critical academic scrutiny and revelation. Its textual character, particularly within the New Testament, has been influential in shaping modern biblical scholarship. Esteemed for its age and textual quality, the Codex Vaticanus remains a cornerstone of Alexandrian textual tradition studies, offering invaluable insights into the early manuscript tradition of the Bible.

As technology has advanced, so too has access to this ancient treasure. The 21st century has seen the Codex Vaticanus digitized and made available online, widening its availability to scholars and the public alike, ensuring that its textual legacy continues to inform and inspire future generations.

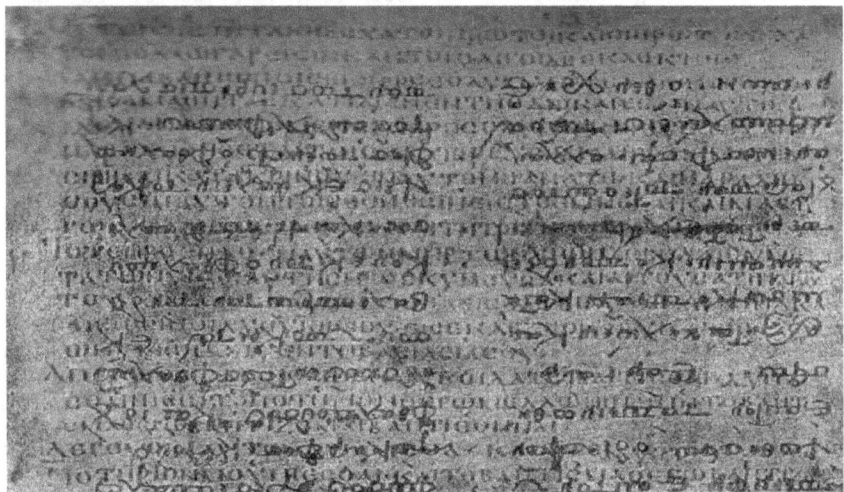

C (Codex Ephraemi Rescriptus)

The Codex Ephraemi Rescriptus, also known as C or 04 in the Gregory-Aland numbering, is a significant manuscript from the 5th century, housed in the National Library of France in Paris. It belongs to a prestigious group alongside the Codex Vaticanus, Codex Alexandrinus, and Codex Sinaiticus, making up the four major uncial manuscripts of the Greek Bible.

In the past, writing materials like parchment were rare and valuable, leading to the practice of recycling older texts. This was done by erasing the original writing to make room for new texts, creating what's known as a palimpsest, from the Greek word meaning "scraped again." The Codex Ephraemi Rescriptus is a remarkable example of such a palimpsest. Originally containing texts of the Christian Greek Scriptures, it was overwritten in the 12th century with Greek translations of 38 sermons by the Syrian scholar Ephraem. The biblical texts underneath were first noticed at the end of the

17th century, but their recovery proved challenging due to the faintness of the ink, the condition of the parchment, and the overlapping texts.

Konstantin von Tischendorf, a skilled German linguist in the 1840s, was able to decipher the manuscript thanks to his expertise in Greek uncial script and keen eyesight. By holding the parchment up to the light, he successfully uncovered the original biblical texts, a feat that had eluded others. His work, published in 1843 and 1845, significantly advanced the field of Greek paleography.

The Codex Ephraemi is notable for its size, about 12 by 9 inches, and its layout of a single column of writing per page. It contains 209 surviving leaves, with 145 covering parts of the New Testament—excluding 2 Thessalonians and 2 John—and the rest containing portions of the Old Testament in Greek.

The manuscript's origins are uncertain, though Tischendorf speculated it might have come from Egypt. Today, it is celebrated as one of the four key uncial manuscripts of the Greek Bible, offering crucial insights into the text of the Scriptures from the 4th and 5th centuries C.E. Its preservation in the National Library at Paris stands as a testament to the enduring importance of these ancient texts in biblical scholarship.

Content

Originally, this manuscript encompassed the entire Bible. However, today, it only retains sections of six books from the Old Testament and fragments of every book in the New Testament, with the exceptions of 2 Thessalonians and 2 John. Crafted in the fifth century C.E., this single-column script was later erased in the twelfth century. In its place, a two-column text was inscribed, featuring a Greek translation of sermons or discussions by Ephraem, a renowned church leader from Syria in the fourth century.

Notable Readings

The Codex Ephraemi Rescriptus, also known as Manuscript C in the world of New Testament textual criticism, contains several unique readings that diverge from or align with various Greek manuscripts or ancient translations of the New Testament. This manuscript offers a fascinating glimpse into the textual variations that exist within early Christian scriptures, underscoring the complexity and depth of biblical scholarship.

Interpolations and Variations:

- **Matthew 8:13** shows a reading that mirrors Luke 7:10, noting the centurion's servant was found healthy upon his return, a detail agreed upon by several early manuscripts and translations, yet omitted by the majority.

- **Matthew 27:49** introduces a phrase found in John 19:34 about Jesus being pierced with a spear, leading to blood and water flowing out. This insertion is supported by some manuscripts but left out by many others.

- **Acts 14:19** presents a debated statement regarding the convincing of crowds to turn away, which is included in some early texts but omitted in the majority.

Corrections Within the Text:

- **Matthew 11:2** offers variations in the preposition used, showcasing a minor yet telling example of the textual nuances scholars examine.

- **Acts 20:28** highlights differences in attributions made to the Lord or to God, with some versions adding both titles, reflecting theological emphases.

- **1 Corinthians 12:9** and **1 Timothy 3:16** illustrate adjustments over time, debating the presence or absence of phrases that could impact theological interpretation.

- **James 1:22** debates whether the text refers to the "word" or "law," a variation with significant interpretive implications.

Additional Textual Variants:

- Variations in names, places, and actions are noted throughout the manuscript, from the sons of Zebedee in **Mark 10:35** to the specifics of Paul's companions in **Romans 16:15**.

- The inclusion or omission of benedictions, as seen in **Romans 16:24**, and the precise wording used in descriptions of spiritual practices in **1 Corinthians 7:5**, are key areas of scholarly focus.

- Lastly, the numbering of the beast in **Revelation 13:18** stands out as one of the most famous textual variants, with Codex Ephraemi Rescriptus and a few others offering the number 616 instead of the traditional 666, a difference that has intrigued scholars and theologians alike.

THE EARLY CHRISTIAN COPYISTS OF THE NEW TESTAMENT

Each of these variations and corrections found in Codex Ephraemi Rescriptus contributes to the ongoing discussion about the earliest forms of the New Testament text. They represent the dynamic and evolving nature of biblical manuscripts, highlighting the meticulous work of scribes and the critical role of textual criticism in understanding the development of Christian scriptures.

Date

Early fifth century C.E.

Physical Features

The Codex Ephraemi Rescriptus is an ancient manuscript, essentially an early form of a book, written on parchment. Its dimensions are approximately 12¼ by 9 inches, with a total of 209 surviving pages. Out of these, 145 pages contain parts of the New Testament, and 64 pages are dedicated to the Old Testament. The text features medium-sized uncial letters, written in a single column format with 40 to 46 lines per page. This manuscript follows the Scriptio continua style, where words are written without spaces, and punctuation is minimal, usually just a single point similar to the practice in the Codex Alexandrinus and Codex Vaticanus. The manuscript is also characterized by larger initial letters for new sections, similar to other ancient codices.

Special attention is given to iota and upsilon, marked with a straight line above them, indicating diaeresis. Additions such as breathings and accents, which provide pronunciation guidance, were made by someone after the original writing. Sacred names and terms within the manuscript, known as nomina sacra, are often shortened into three-letter forms, deviating from the more common two-letter abbreviations.

Before the Gospels of Luke and John, there is a preserved list of chapters, suggesting that similar lists likely existed for Matthew and Mark. The manuscript doesn't seem to consistently use chapter titles at the top of pages; any titles that might have been there in red ink have either faded away or were lost if the pages were trimmed too much at the top. Marginal notes related to the Eusebian Canons, an ancient system for organizing Gospel comparisons, were probably also in red ink but have since faded, leaving no trace.

Certain biblical passages like the Pericope Adulterae (John 7:53–8:11) seem to have been absent from this codex. The specific leaves that would cover John 7:3–8:34 are missing, and calculations based on the manuscript's layout suggest there wouldn't have been enough space to include this passage. The text of Mark 16:9–20, however, is present in the manuscript.

For Luke 22:43–44, detailing Christ's agony at Gethsemane, it's unclear if it was originally included since the specific leaves are missing. Likewise, Mark 15:28 is excluded from the codex.

In summary, the Codex Ephraemi Rescriptus offers a glimpse into the textual practices and religious devotion of early Christianity, encapsulated within the physical and stylistic choices of its creation. Its preservation in the National Library of France allows scholars and the public alike to connect with one of the foundational texts of the Christian faith.

Textual Character

The New Testament within the Codex Ephraemi Rescriptus is predominantly linked to the Alexandrian text-type, a classification that indicates a certain family of manuscripts based on shared textual characteristics. However, this connection varies across different books of the New Testament. Text-types are essentially categories of manuscripts that possess similar or related readings, distinguishing them from other groups. These categories, which include the Alexandrian, Western, and Byzantine text-types, are crucial for scholars attempting to trace back to the most original form of the New Testament text.

In the Codex Ephraemi Rescriptus, the Gospel of Matthew shows a leaning towards the Byzantine text-type, while Mark displays a less pronounced Alexandrian affiliation. John is more solidly Alexandrian, and the textual character of Luke remains somewhat ambiguous. Esteemed textual critics Brooke Foss Westcott and Fenton J.A. Hort have described the manuscript as having a mixed text, indicating it doesn't fit neatly into a single category. Hermann von Soden considered it an Alexandrian witness.

Kurt Aland's analysis highlights the codex's agreement with the Byzantine text-type in several instances across the New Testament, alongside a significant number of agreements with the Nestle-Aland text, a modern scholarly reconstruction of the New Testament's original Greek text. The codex also presents numerous unique or distinctive readings. Aland placed the manuscript in Category II of his classification system, noting it contains a considerable amount of early text but also exhibits influences from later textual traditions, particularly the Byzantine.

In the Book of Revelation, the codex aligns with the textual form found in Codex Vaticanus and Papyrus 115, further illustrating its complex textual character.

This manuscript is referenced in all critical editions of the Greek New Testament due to its importance, with its various correctors' readings also being included. These correctors, identified across different centuries, have contributed to the manuscript's evolving textual character, adding accents and breathing marks among other modifications.

Bruce Metzger remarked that the text of Codex Ephraemi Rescriptus appears to be a blend of all major text types, often aligning with the Koine text of the Byzantine type, which is generally considered less reliable by scholars. The manuscript's diverse affiliations and the work of its correctors underscore its mixed textual character, making it a fascinating subject for those studying the evolution and transmission of the New Testament text.

D (Codex Bezae)

The Codex Bezae Cantabrigiensis, often referred to by its shorthand Dea or designated as 05 in the Gregory-Aland numbering and δ 5 in the von Soden numbering, stands out as a remarkable bilingual manuscript of the New Testament, written in Greek and Latin. This manuscript, penned in the early 5th century based on handwriting analysis, contains most of the Gospels and Acts, with a small part of 3 John included. It's housed at Cambridge University Library, which also offers a digital facsimile for wider access.

Théodore de Bèze, a prominent French theologian and a key figure in the early Reformation, brought this ancient text to public attention in 1562. He claimed it was found in a monastery in Lyons, France, a city that had suffered under the attacks of the Huguenots. While its exact origin remains uncertain, scholars suggest it might have come from North Africa or Egypt. Measuring about ten by eight inches, the Codex Bezae is slightly younger than other well-known manuscripts like the Sinaitic, Vatican, and Alexandrine manuscripts. It spans 406 leaves but now only includes the four Gospels and Acts, hinting it may have originally contained more biblical texts given the presence of a fragment from 3 John.

This manuscript is especially noteworthy for its bilingual format, presenting Greek text on the left page and Latin on the right, likely mirroring an earlier papyrus manuscript. The Codex Bezae's text is inscribed in bold, elegant capital letters, with lines of varying lengths indicating pauses for the reader. The Latin text intriguingly adopts Greek-style lettering, with several instances where it has been conformed to the Greek text. Conversely, the Greek text is unique and shows corrections from multiple hands, including the original scribe.

Designated as "D," the Codex Bezae is distinct from other major manuscripts, sometimes aligning with, sometimes diverging from the Sinaitic, Vatican, and Alexandrine codices. Its true value lies in how it corroborates the reliability of other significant manuscripts, despite its own textual peculiarities, including various omissions and additions. Such traits are documented in footnotes of modern Bible translations, highlighting its contributions and occasional deviations from other texts.

In essence, despite its unique readings and variances, the Codex Bezae serves as a powerful testament to the Bible's enduring preservation through the centuries, offering critical insight into the text's history and transmission.

Content

The Codex Bezae, a significant manuscript of the New Testament, showcases both Greek and Latin text. This dual-language manuscript, written in a formal and rounded script known as uncial on parchment, primarily includes the majority of the Gospels and the Acts of the Apostles, alongside a brief segment from 3 John. It stands out as a Greek-Latin diglot, meaning it contains texts in both languages, covering Matthew through Acts and a portion of 3 John, though some parts are missing.

Experts like the Alands suggest that this manuscript was crafted in Egypt or North Africa by a scribe whose first language was Latin. However, Parker offers a different perspective, proposing that it was copied in Beirut during the fifth century. Beirut was a hub for Latin legal studies at that time and was a bilingual community where both Latin and Greek were in use. This context could explain the manuscript's bilingual nature and its stylistic features.

Notable Readings

The Codex Bezae Cantabrigiensis, often called D or Codex Bezae, showcases a range of unique readings within the New Testament, making it a significant manuscript for scholars. Notably, the Codex Bezae presents variations in the text that are not supported by other manuscripts, reflecting its distinct nature.

Gospel of Matthew:

- In Matthew 1:22, where most manuscripts read "through the prophet," Codex Bezae specifies "through Isaiah the prophet," aligning with a smaller group of manuscripts.
- An unusual inclusion in Matthew 2:17 identifies the prophecy as coming "by the LORD through Jeremiah," differing from the more common reference to Jeremiah alone.
- Matthew 3:16 presents the imagery of the Spirit descending "like a dove out of heaven," a reading that varies from the majority text.
- The manuscript has a tendency for omission, as seen in Matthew 4:4, where it leaves out "proceeds out through the mouth," and in Matthew 5:4–5, where it reverses the beatitudes' order compared to the majority text.

Gospel of Mark:

- Mark's longer ending is included in Codex Bezae, presenting textual variations that add depth to the narrative.
- The manuscript is notable for its unique sequence in Mark 10, altering the order of verses 23, 25, 24, and 26.

Gospel of Luke:

- Luke 6:5 includes an additional narrative about Jesus commenting on a man working on the Sabbath, a passage not found in any other manuscript.

- In Luke 7:1, Codex Bezae's reading differs from the majority text regarding the context of Jesus' words.

Gospel of John:

- John 1:4 in Codex Bezae reads "in Him is life," contrasting with the "in Him was life" found in the majority of texts.

- The manuscript occasionally omits familiar passages, such as in John 7:8 where it lacks "yet" in Jesus' statement about going up to the feast.

Acts of the Apostles:

- Acts 20:28 is a critical passage where Codex Bezae uses "of the Lord," while other manuscripts vary between "of God" and "of the Lord and of God," highlighting the manuscript's unique textual character.

Throughout, Codex Bezae demonstrates a pattern of significant theological additions, omissions, and rephrasings, especially notable in Luke and Acts. These modifications suggest an early theological influence on the manuscript, making it a valuable witness to the Western text-type. Its varied agreement with Old Latin, Syriac, and Armenian versions further underscores its importance in textual criticism, despite the general caution among scholars regarding its reliability due to its marked independence and textual deviations.

Date

Early fifth century C.E.

Physical Features

The Codex Bezae, an ancient manuscript predating modern books, consists of 406 surviving parchment leaves, though it originally might have had as many as 534. Measuring roughly 10.2 x 8.5 inches, it's unique for having the Greek text on the left page and the Latin text on the right, written in a single column format. The text is arranged colometrically, meaning it's

THE EARLY CHRISTIAN COPYISTS OF THE NEW TESTAMENT

broken down by rhythmic units rather than by standard grammar rules, and it includes numerous gaps, known as hiatuses.

In its transcription of the Greek text, the Codex Bezae shows certain copying errors. For example, in John 1:3, the word ΕΓΕΝΕΤΟ (egeneto) is mistakenly written as ΕΝΕΓΕΤΟ (enegeto); and in Acts 1:9, ΥΠΕΛΑΒΕΝ (hypelaben) is incorrectly copied as ΥΠΕΒΑΛΕΝ (hypebalen). Additionally, the first three lines of each book are highlighted in red ink, and the titles of the books alternate between black and red ink, adding a distinct visual element to the manuscript.

Throughout its history, the Codex Bezae has been corrected by as many as eleven individuals, identified by letters G, A, C, B, D, E, H, F, J1, L, K, between the sixth and twelfth centuries. These correctors made various amendments to adjust or clarify the text.

In this manuscript, certain sacred names and terms, known as nomina sacra, are abbreviated, a common practice in ancient Christian manuscripts. Examples in the nominative case include ΙΗΣ for Ιησους (Jesus), ΧΡΣ for Χριστος (Christ), ΠΑΡ for πατηρ (Father), and ΣΤΗ for σταυρωθη (was crucified). However, other terms that are often abbreviated in similar manuscripts are spelled out in full in the Codex Bezae, such as words for mother, son, savior, man, sky, David, Israel, and Jerusalem.

This blend of unique features, from its bilingual text to the presence of both abbreviated and fully spelled sacred terms, underscores the Codex Bezae's significance in the study of ancient New Testament manuscripts. Its corrections and peculiarities provide valuable insights into the textual history and transmission of the New Testament.

Textual Character

The Codex Bezae, known for its unique and independent nature among New Testament manuscripts, presents a text that has intrigued and puzzled scholars. Parker suggests that the original scribe was more familiar with Latin than Greek, leading to an initial version that was later corrected by various scribes. The Alands highlight the Codex Bezae as particularly controversial due to its distinct departures from the typical text, including numerous additions, deletions, and modifications, especially within the books of Luke and Acts. These changes suggest the involvement of a theologically inclined individual, possibly revising an earlier version of the text to include more detailed historical, biographical, and geographical information, aiming to provide a fuller narrative context.

The Greek text of Codex Bezae is unlike any other, containing unique interpolations and notable omissions, along with a tendency to rephrase sentences. This Western text-type, aside from being represented in this Greek manuscript, is also reflected in early Latin, Syriac, and Armenian versions, making Codex Bezae a key Greek witness to this tradition.

The challenges posed by the Greek text of Codex Bezae have led to mixed views regarding its reliability in biblical scholarship. While generally treated with caution due to its unconventional readings, it gains importance when it aligns with other early manuscripts, serving as a valuable supporting witness.

Among its distinctive features, Codex Bezae includes the passage in Matthew 16:2b–3 without questioning its authenticity and offers one of the longer endings for the Gospel of Mark. It retains the passages Luke 22:43f and the story of the adulterous woman without marking them as doubtful. Notably, it omits John 5:4 and extends the text of Acts by nearly 8%, including unique stories like a man working on the Sabbath in an extension of Luke 6:4, found nowhere else.

The version of Acts in Codex Bezae is significantly different from that in other manuscripts, leading some to speculate it might represent an earlier rendition from Luke himself. Overall, Codex Bezae stands as a manuscript that, through its peculiarities and deviations, contributes to the complex tapestry of New Testament textual history, offering insights into the diversity of early Christian texts.

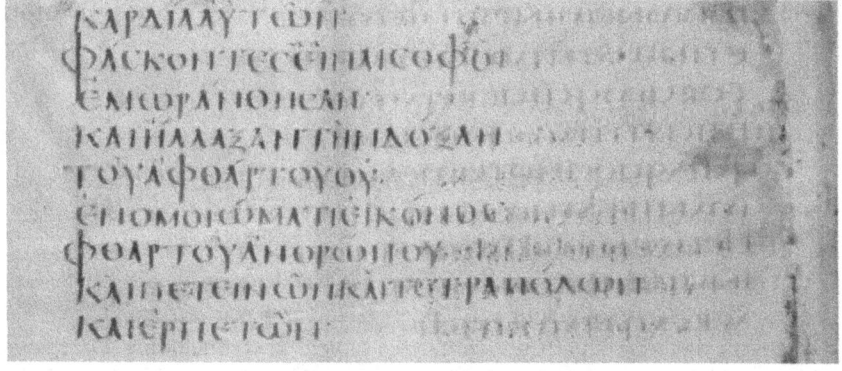

D (Codex Claromontanus)—also designated Dᵖ

Discover the Codex Claromontanus, a significant 6th-century New Testament manuscript. Learn about its historical context, contributions to textual criticism, and its role in the study of ancient biblical texts.

Codex Claromontanus, known in scholarly circles by its symbols Dp, D2, or 06, and δ 1026, stands as a Greek-Latin diglot uncial manuscript of the New Testament. Crafted with precision in an uncial hand on vellum, it features Greek and Latin texts on facing pages, mirroring the format of the renowned Codex Bezae Cantabrigiensis. This manuscript's Latin text is identified traditionally as 'd' and as '75' in the Beuron system, marking its significance in biblical manuscript studies.

Content

This manuscript is a bilingual edition, featuring both Greek and Latin, that encompasses all the Pauline Epistles, including the book of Hebrews, which is Pauline as well according to the evidence and this author. Interestingly, two of its pages were previously utilized for another purpose, faintly bearing text from Euripides' tragedy, "Phaethon." While the collection of Paul's letters is almost entirely intact, there are small portions missing: a few verses from the Book of Romans are absent in both the Greek and Latin sections, and there are also a handful of missing verses from 1 Corinthians, but only in the Latin translation.

Date

Dating of the Codex Claromontanus, achieved through palaeographic analysis, places its creation in the 5th or 6th century.

Physical Features

The Codex Claromontanus is an invaluable manuscript containing the Pauline epistles, meticulously preserved on 533 parchment leaves, each measuring 24.5 by 19.5 centimeters. The manuscript's format is notably singular, featuring a single column of text per page, with each column comprising 21 lines. This codex stands out not only for its content but also for the evidence it provides of extensive scholarly engagement, as indicated by the interventions of at least nine different correctors throughout its history. Particularly notable is the work of the fourth corrector, who, in the 9th century, enriched the manuscript with accents and breathings, adding a layer of textual nuance and aiding in its pronunciation and interpretation.

The dating of the Codex Claromontanus, achieved through palaeographic analysis, places its creation in the 5th or 6th century. This temporal attribution highlights its significance as a witness to the early textual transmission of the Pauline epistles and to the broader scriptural canon of the time.

Beyond the Pauline corpus, the Codex Claromontanus is distinguished by the inclusion of the Catalogus Claromontanus—a stichometric catalogue of the Old and New Testament canon. This catalogue, whose date remains uncertain, is a crucial artifact for understanding the development of the biblical canon. It interestingly omits certain Pauline letters (Philippians, 1 and 2 Thessalonians, and Hebrews) while including texts that modern canons do not recognize as scriptural (e.g., the Epistle of Barnabas, The Shepherd of Hermas, Acts of Paul, and Revelation of Peter). Furthermore, the catalogue uniquely categorizes the two epistles of Peter as if they were directed from Paul to Peter ("ad Petrum") and positions the Epistle to the Hebrews subsequent to these entries, offering a unique perspective on the perceived textual relationships and canonical status of these writings in the early Christian community.

Additionally, the manuscript contains two palimpsest leaves, numbered 162 and 163, which bear the texts of the Phaethon by Euripides beneath the Christian writings. These leaves, now detached and housed in the Bibliothèque nationale de France under the designation Cod. Gr. 107 B, offer a fascinating glimpse into the practice of repurposing parchment, showcasing the intersection of Christian and classical cultures.

The Codex Claromontanus, therefore, is not merely a vessel for the Pauline epistles but a complex artifact that provides insight into the textual practices, canonical debates, and cultural exchanges of early Christianity. Its contents and the layers of correction and addition it has received over the centuries reflect the dynamic and evolving understanding of Christian scripture and its interpretation.

Textual Character

The Codex Claromontanus stands as a pivotal source in the study of New Testament textual criticism, particularly for its representation of the Western text-type. This codex is celebrated for its early textual form, marked by a notable frequency of interpolations and, to a lesser extent, interpretive revisions that have been integrated as corrections over time. These features render the Codex Claromontanus a critical asset in the eclectic method of modern New Testament textual criticism. This method relies on a careful selection of readings from among the myriad variants provided by ancient manuscripts and versions, with the aim of reconstructing the most original text of the New Testament writings.

In this scholarly endeavor, the Codex Claromontanus often serves as a critical reference point or "outside mediator" in the collation of other key codices that contain the Pauline epistles, namely Codex Alexandrinus (A), Codex Vaticanus (B), Codex Sinaiticus (ℵ), and Codex Ephraemi Rescriptus (C). This role is akin to that of Codex Bezae Cantabrigiensis for the texts of the Gospels and Acts, offering an invaluable comparative perspective that aids in establishing the historical trajectory of these sacred texts.

The manuscript employs a colometric writing style, and notably, it presents the epistles to the Colossians and Philippians in a reversed order when compared to other manuscript traditions. Kurt Aland has categorized the text of Codex Claromontanus within Category II, reflecting its significant agreement with the original text, albeit with some minor variations attributable to its Western text-type characteristics.

A few specific examples illustrate the codex's textual nuances and the subsequent corrections made by its scribes:

- In Romans 1:8, the original text contains the variant περι, aligning with other important manuscripts. A corrector later amended this to υπερ, demonstrating the dynamic nature of textual transmission and interpretation.

- Romans 8:1 presents a reading that aligns with several early manuscripts, with subsequent corrections reflecting diverse textual traditions and interpretations concerning the walk in the flesh versus the Spirit.

- Romans 12:11 offers καιρω instead of κυριω, with a correction aligning it with other sources that support κυριω, highlighting the manuscript's contribution to understanding variant readings within the Pauline epistles.

- The manuscript's reading of δωροφορια for διακονια in Romans 15:31, supported by other key manuscripts, underscores its value in tracing the textual history of Paul's letters.

- In 1 Corinthians 7:5, Codex Claromontanus supports the simpler reading of τη προσευχη (prayer), as do several other early witnesses, against a more expanded reading found in other manuscripts.

- The placement of 1 Corinthians 14:34-35 after 14:40, in line with the Western text-type tradition, reflects the codex's alignment with a distinct textual family, contributing to debates on the ordering of Pauline texts.

- Lastly, its unique reading in 1 Timothy 3:1 of ανθρωπινος (human) over the more commonly found πιστος (faithful) offers insight into early Christian understandings of leadership qualities.

Through these examples, the Codex Claromontanus illuminates the intricate process of textual transmission and the ongoing scholarly quest to recover the most authentic text of the New Testament. Its contributions to the field of textual criticism are invaluable, offering a window into the early Christian textual tradition and its development over time.

Scribes and Correctors

The Codex Claromontanus, a significant manuscript in the study of the New Testament, is distinguished not only by its textual content but also by the work of its correctors. These individuals played a crucial role in the manuscript's history, contributing to its textual integrity and the broader understanding of textual variation within the New Testament tradition.

At least nine different correctors have been identified as having worked on the Codex Claromontanus over the centuries. Their contributions vary, ranging from the addition of accents and breathings to more substantial textual corrections and alterations. The work of these correctors provides valuable insights into the practices of textual transmission and correction in the early Christian era and the subsequent centuries.

The fourth corrector, active in the 9th century, is especially notable for adding accents and breathings to the text. This corrector's work reflects a scholarly concern with the pronunciation and interpretation of the Greek text, indicating an ongoing engagement with the text's readability and comprehensibility. The addition of these diacritical marks demonstrates an effort to standardize and clarify the text, a task of particular importance in a period when Greek was evolving and regional variations in pronunciation could lead to misunderstandings of the scripture.

The activities of these correctors underscore the dynamic nature of manuscript transmission. Rather than viewing the text as fixed or immutable, early Christians and later scholars approached these manuscripts as living documents, subject to revision and improvement in the pursuit of textual accuracy and clarity. Each corrector's contributions represent a layer of interaction with the sacred text, reflecting both the individual's understanding of the scripture and the broader textual traditions of their time.

The presence of multiple correctors also highlights the complexities of textual criticism, as scholars must discern not only the original wording of the New Testament writings but also understand the nature and intent of subsequent corrections. This process involves a careful examination of the manuscript's palaeography, the correctors' stylistic tendencies, and the historical context of their work. By analyzing the corrections, textual critics can gain insights into the transmission history of the New Testament, the development of the text over time, and the diverse textual traditions that have shaped the Christian biblical canon.

In summary, the correctors of the Codex Claromontanus play a pivotal role in the manuscript's history and its significance for New Testament textual criticism. Their work reflects the ongoing engagement with the text, a commitment to its preservation and accuracy, and the dynamic process of textual transmission that has characterized the history of the New Testament.

The History of Codex Claromontanus

The Codex Claromontanus, a treasure of biblical manuscript tradition, is meticulously preserved at the Bibliothèque nationale de France (Gr. 107) in Paris. This codex, named after the town of Clermont-en-Beauvaisis, Oise, in the scenic Picardy region north of Paris, owes its designation to the Calvinist scholar Theodore Beza. Beza, a figure of considerable importance in the study of biblical texts, was instrumental in bringing the Codex Claromontanus to scholarly attention after acquiring it in Clermont. His pioneering work included the examination of the codex and the incorporation of its textual readings into his editions of the New Testament, marking a significant milestone in the history of biblical scholarship.

The Codex Claromontanus has since played a pivotal role in the development of New Testament textual criticism. Esteemed scholars such as **Johann Jakob Griesbach** and **Constantin von Tischendorf** have conducted thorough examinations of its Greek text, contributing to its editorial history and enhancing our understanding of the New Testament's textual landscape. Additionally, Paul Sabatier's work on the Latin text of the codex has furthered the scholarly endeavor to comprehend the textual variations and transmission history of early Christian writings.

A notable aspect of the codex's history involves the palimpsest leaves numbered 162 and 163. Johann Gottfried Jakob Hermann, in 1821, published the underlying text of these leaves, revealing fragments of Euripides' "Phaethon." This discovery not only highlights the codex's value for biblical scholarship but also underscores the broader cultural and historical contexts in which these ancient texts were preserved, repurposed, and transmitted through the centuries.

The Codex Claromontanus stands as a testament to the intricate and multifaceted processes of textual transmission, correction, and interpretation that have shaped the New Testament's history. Its journey from the hands of Theodore Beza through the critical examinations by leading scholars of textual criticism reflects the enduring quest to access and understand the foundational texts of Christian faith with greater clarity and fidelity. The codex's legacy continues to influence contemporary scholarship, offering insights into the early Christian textual tradition and its impact on the development of biblical studies.

E (Codex Laudianus 35)—also designated Eᵃ

The Codex Laudianus, known in the scholarly world as Ea or 08, and by von Soden as α 1001, bears the name of its one-time owner, Archbishop

William Laud. This remarkable document is a bilingual manuscript, presenting the New Testament's Acts of the Apostles in both Latin and Greek. Crafted with careful attention to detail, the text is written in a distinct uncial script that dates back to the 6th century. The unique feature of this manuscript lies in its side-by-side Latin and Greek text, providing a fascinating window into early Christian scriptural traditions and the linguistic interplay between these two foundational languages of the Western Church. The preservation and study of such a manuscript not only enrich our understanding of early Christian texts but also highlight the enduring significance of these ancient works in the broader narrative of religious and cultural history.

Content

Acts (in Latin and Greek)

Date

Sixth century C.E.

Physical Features

The Codex Laudianus, also known as Ea or 35 in the catalog, stands out as a bilingual manuscript, showcasing the text of the Book of Acts in both Greek and Latin. The layout features parallel columns, with Latin taking precedence on the left side. This codex comprises 227 parchment pages, each measuring approximately 27 by 22 centimeters (10.6 by 8.7 inches), and it holds nearly the entire Book of Acts, except for a section from 26:29 to 28:26.

What makes this manuscript especially notable is its presentation of the text in columns, with each column containing 24 or more lines. However, these aren't your typical lines of text; they're exceptionally short, sometimes only stretching to one to three words. This unique arrangement, known as colonmetric writing, is structured to mirror the natural pauses in speech or thought, offering a unique glimpse into ancient reading practices. Notably, the Codex Laudianus is recognized as the oldest manuscript to include Acts 8:37, marking a significant point of interest for scholars and enthusiasts of biblical texts.

Textual Character

The Codex Laudianus, also known by its catalog number Ea or 35, holds a special place among New Testament manuscripts, especially for its presentation of the Book of Acts. Its text is a fascinating blend, showing affiliations with different ancient text-types. While it often aligns with the Byzantine text tradition, which is the most widespread among Greek New Testament manuscripts, it also contains readings that match the Western text-type, as seen in Codex Bezae (D), and occasionally the Alexandrian text-type, known for its early and often more original readings.

Kurt Aland, a renowned scholar in the field of New Testament textual criticism, analyzed the Codex Laudianus' text. He found that it matches the Byzantine text-type in 36 instances and agrees with it again in 21 cases when the Byzantine and Alexandrian texts coincide. Against the Byzantine text, it sides with the Alexandrian text 22 times. The codex also offers 22 unique readings, setting it apart from other manuscripts. Aland categorized it in Category II, indicating manuscripts of a special quality with significant early text but showing some later modifications.

One of its most notable features is the inclusion of Acts 8:37, a verse about the Ethiopian's confession of faith, which is absent in many Greek manuscripts but found in several others such as 323, 453, 945, 1739, 1891, and 2818.

The manuscript also provides unique readings in several passages:

- In Acts 12:25, it supports the reading "from Jerusalem to Antioch," aligning with a minority textual tradition as opposed to the Majority Text's "to Jerusalem."

- In Acts 16:10, the codex uses "θεος" (God), sharing this reading with significant manuscripts like P74, Sinaiticus, and Alexandrinus, while others use "κυριος" (Lord).

- Acts 18:26 is another instance where it offers a unique reading, "την οδον του κυριου" (the way of the Lord), along with a few other sources.

- For Acts 20:28, it reads "του κυριου" (of the Lord), joining an important group of manuscripts that include Papyrus 74 and Codex Ephraemi Rescriptus, among others.

These textual variations highlight the Codex Laudianus' value in understanding the diverse textual history of the New Testament, providing insights into how these sacred texts were transmitted, read, and understood in the early Christian communities.

History of Codex Laudianus

The Codex Laudianus, also known as Ea or 35, holds a fascinating spot in the annals of biblical manuscripts, particularly for its contributions to the study of the Acts of the Apostles. This ancient text, likely crafted in Sardinia during the Byzantine reign after 534, found its way into English possession before 716, utilized by the venerable Bede in his thorough examination of the Acts.

The journey of this manuscript to England remains shrouded in mystery, possibly brought over by Theodore of Tarsus, the Archbishop of Canterbury, in 668, or perhaps by Ceolfrid, the Abbot of Wearmouth and Jarrow, in the early eighth century. Its English home was likely one of the significant northern monasteries, from where it ventured back to the continent with English missionaries in the 8th century, ultimately finding a resting place in Hornbach Abbey in the Rhineland.

The tumultuous times of the Thirty Years' War saw the Codex entering the collection of William Laud, who generously donated it to the Bodleian Library in Oxford in 1636. There, under the catalog number MS. Laud Gr. 35, it remains a prized piece of the collection.

The Codex Laudianus has attracted scholarly attention over the centuries. Thomas Hearne was the first to publish its text in 1715, albeit in a form that left much to be desired. His work was followed by more accurate transcriptions from Hansell in 1864 and the renowned Constantin von Tischendorf in 1870.

Esteemed scholars like Johann Jakob Griesbach, Ropes, Motzo, Poole, Clark, Lagrange, and Walther have all examined this manuscript, each contributing to our understanding of its value and significance. Through their studies, the Codex Laudianus continues to shed light on the intricate history of biblical text transmission, offering insights into the early Christian church and the enduring legacy of the Scriptures.

F (Codex Augiensis)—also designated Fᵖ

The Codex Augiensis, known in academic circles as Fp, is an ancient manuscript crafted with care on 136 parchment leaves, each measuring 23 by 19 centimeters. This codex, while primarily a Greek document, features certain sections solely in Latin, particularly the Book of Hebrews, which is entirely absent in its Greek form. Notably, the manuscript isn't complete; it has several missing portions in the Greek text, including segments from Romans, 1 Corinthians, Colossians, and a small part of Philemon.

The layout of the Codex Augiensis is methodically organized, with the text spread across two columns on each page, and each column accommodating 28 lines of text. This structured arrangement was typical of manuscripts from its era, designed to maximize readability and the amount of text that could fit on a single page. The presence of both Greek and Latin texts within the same codex reflects the linguistic diversity and the broad audience of early Christian texts, offering insights into the historical context of biblical scripture transmission and the interaction between different linguistic and cultural Christian communities.

Content

The Pauline epistles are in Greek and Latin with Hebrews in Latin only.

THE EARLY CHRISTIAN COPYISTS OF THE NEW TESTAMENT

Date

Ninth century C.E.

Physical Features

The Codex Augiensis, also known as Fp, stands as a significant document in the study of the New Testament due to its textual characteristics. Its Greek content predominantly aligns with the Western text-type, showcasing a distinct variant of the New Testament text. According to the research by Kurt and Barbara Aland, the Codex demonstrates a particular pattern of alignment with the Byzantine text tradition: it concurs with the Byzantine standard text on 43 occasions, aligns with the Byzantine text when it shares readings with the original text 11 times, and supports the original text against the Byzantine text on 89 occasions. Furthermore, it presents 70 unique or independent readings that distinguish it from other manuscripts. This blend of textual alignments and unique readings has led the Alands to categorize the Codex Augiensis within Category II. This classification suggests that the Codex contains a text of significant quality, incorporating a considerable portion of early textual traditions but also displaying some variations characteristic of the Western text-type. This manuscript's textual diversity provides invaluable insights into the early transmission and variation of the New Testament text.

Textual Character

The Codex Augiensis, referred to as Fp, is a critical document for scholars studying the text of the New Testament. Its textual character showcases intriguing variances and alignments with other ancient manuscripts, reflecting the complex tradition of New Testament transmission.

For instance, in Romans 12:11, the Codex offers the reading καιρω ("time") instead of the more commonly found κυριω ("Lord"). This particular reading finds support from Codex Claromontanus*, Codex Boernerianus, as well as Latin translations like the Codices 5 it d,g, and commentary from early church father Origen in Latin.

In 1 Corinthians 2:4, the Codex aligns with Codex Boernerianus (in its Latin version) and manuscript 35, presenting the phrase πειθοι σοφιας, which translates to "plausible wisdom." This indicates a preference for emphasizing the persuasive power of wisdom in Paul's message, contrasting with other manuscripts that may not highlight this aspect.

Moreover, the Codex reflects a specific tradition in 1 Corinthians 7:5 by using the term τη προσευχη ("prayer") in agreement with significant manuscripts such as 𝔓11, 𝔓46, ℵ*, A, B, C, D, G, P, Ψ, and others. This is in contrast to variations that combine "fasting and prayer" or "prayer and fasting," found in manuscripts 330, 451, and others, including references by John of Damascus.

An especially notable feature of the Codex Augiensis is its arrangement of 1 Corinthians 14:34-35, which is placed after 1 Corinthians 14:40. This placement aligns with the Western text-type tradition, as seen in Codex Claromontanus, Codex Boernerianus, and several Latin manuscripts and translations. This reordering suggests early divergences in how Paul's letters were read and interpreted, offering insight into the dynamics of early Christian communities and their liturgical practices.

The Codex Augiensis, through these and other textual peculiarities, contributes significantly to our understanding of the New Testament's textual history, showcasing the diversity and richness of early Christian scriptural tradition.

Relationship to Codex Boernerianus

The Codex Augiensis, known as Fp, shares a close textual relationship with Codex Boernerianus, particularly in the Greek text where the two manuscripts are nearly identical. However, their Latin texts present notable differences. Additionally, the specific gaps or missing sections in each manuscript closely match, suggesting a connection or common source between them. This has sparked debate among scholars about their origins and relationship.

Griesbach, an influential figure in textual criticism, theorized that the Codex Augiensis was directly copied from Codex Boernerianus. Contrary to this, Tischendorf proposed that both codices were independently copied from a single, now-lost manuscript, indicating a shared ancestry rather than a direct copyist relationship. To illustrate the differences between Augiensis and Boernerianus, Scrivener meticulously documented 1982 variations between the two, underscoring the complex nature of their textual relationship.

Among scholars who study these ancient texts, there's a noticeable preference for the readings found in Codex Augiensis over those in Codex Boernerianus. This preference also extends to comparisons with Codex Claromontanus, where, despite similarities, the text of Augiensis is often favored. This preference is not merely about textual accuracy but also involves considerations of clarity, consistency, and how well the readings in Augiensis align with other ancient manuscript traditions.

The debates and analyses surrounding these manuscripts highlight the intricate process of textual criticism and the quest to trace the New Testament's textual history as accurately as possible. Each codex, with its unique features and textual variants, contributes valuable insights into the early Christian scriptural landscape, offering glimpses into how these texts were transmitted, copied, and revered through the centuries.

History of Codex Augiensis

The Codex Augiensis, also known as Fp, has a storied past that traces back to its origins at the Augia Dives monastery situated near Lake Constance. This ancient manuscript came into the possession of Richard Bentley, a renowned scholar, in 1718. Bentley, born in 1662 and passing in 1742, was notable for his contributions to classical and biblical scholarship.

The Greek text of Codex Augiensis was meticulously edited by Frederick Henry Ambrose Scrivener in 1859, bringing attention to its significant role in biblical textual criticism. Constantin von Tischendorf, another towering figure in the study of New Testament manuscripts, also examined, described, and collated this codex, further highlighting its importance. Following these scholarly efforts, E. M. Thompson brought the manuscript to a wider audience by editing a facsimile, making its contents more accessible to researchers and scholars alike.

Today, this invaluable piece of Christian heritage finds its home in the library of Trinity College, Cambridge, where it is preserved under the catalog number B. XVII. 1. Its journey from a monastic library to a treasured item in a prestigious academic collection underscores the Codex Augiensis's enduring value and the ongoing interest in its contributions to understanding the early New Testament text. Through the meticulous work of scholars and the careful stewardship of libraries, Codex Augiensis continues to be a crucial resource for those delving into the depths of biblical textuality and history.

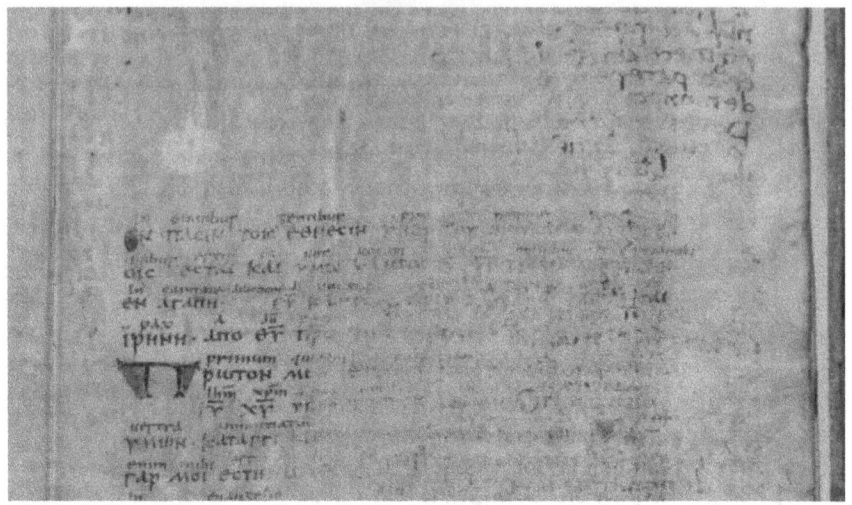

G (Codex Boernerianus)—also designated G^p

Codex Boernerianus, known in the academic community as Gp or 012 according to the Gregory-Aland numbering system, and as α 1028 in the von Soden catalog, is a significant New Testament manuscript from the 9th century. This document is primarily composed of parchment and encompasses most of the epistles attributed to the Apostle Paul. Its connection to Christian Frederick Boerner, a notable theology professor and its previous owner, is reflected in its name. Despite its importance, the manuscript is not complete and contains several gaps within its text. This artifact of early Christian writings offers valuable insight into the textual traditions of the Pauline epistles, making it a subject of ongoing study and reverence in the field of biblical textual criticism.

Content

Codex Boernerianus, known in scholarly circles as Gp has the collection of Pauline epistles, presented in Greek with a Latin translation provided in an interlinear format. This means that for each line of Greek text, the Latin translation is inserted directly above, allowing for comparative study of the two languages. Notably, after the Epistle to Philemon, there is an intriguing mention of an Epistle to the Laodiceans. However, this reference is followed by a notable absence — the text itself does not continue with the content of

THE EARLY CHRISTIAN COPYISTS OF THE NEW TESTAMENT

this mentioned epistle. This detail adds a layer of mystery and scholarly intrigue to the manuscript, inviting questions about early Christian texts and their circulation.

Date

Ninth century C.E.

Physical Features

Codex Boernerianus includes most of the letters written by Paul in the New Testament, except for Hebrews. This special book from the 9th century consists of 99 parchment pages, each about 9.8 inches by 7.1 inches in size. What makes this manuscript unique is its layout: the main text is in Greek, with a Latin translation written directly above it, making it a bilingual document. This setup is similar to another ancient book, Codex Sangallensis 48.

However, there are some parts of the text missing from this codex, specifically sections from Romans, 1 Corinthians, Colossians, and Philemon. When quoting from the Old Testament, the codex marks these references with a special symbol in the margin, and the Latin version notes where the quote is from, such as Isaiah.

Interestingly, the manuscript doesn't stick strictly to capital Greek letters; it occasionally uses smaller versions of α, κ, and ϱ, blending in elements typically seen in later manuscripts. It's also worth noting that the codex doesn't include certain standard Greek notations for pronunciation, like rough or smooth breathing marks, or accents.

The Latin portion of the text, written in smaller letters, showcases some characteristics of the Anglo-Saxon alphabet, especially noticeable in the shapes of the letters r, s, and t.

In an unusual twist, the phrase "in Rome" is replaced in Romans 1:7 with "in love" (in the Latin, "in caritate et dilectione"), and it's completely left out in Romans 1:15 in both Greek and Latin. At the end of Philemon, there's a heading for an Epistle to the Laodiceans, but, intriguingly, no text for this epistle follows, leaving us with a hint of a lost work.

Textual Character

Codex Boernerianus is a significant manuscript that contains the text of the Pauline epistles in Greek, with an intriguing characteristic: it represents what scholars call the Western text-type. This classification is part of a system that sorts New Testament manuscripts based on their shared textual characteristics, with the major groups being Alexandrian, Western, and Byzantine. Each of these groups offers insights into the historical and geographical variations of the New Testament text as it was copied over centuries.

Kurt Aland, a noted expert in the field of textual criticism, assigned Codex Boernerianus to Category III in his classification system. This category includes manuscripts that, while containing a notable number of early textual readings, also show a significant influence from the Byzantine text-type and possess unique readings from sources that are yet to be fully identified.

One of the distinctive features of Codex Boernerianus is the placement of 1 Corinthians 14:34–35 at the end of chapter 14, after verse 40. This arrangement is also observed in several other manuscripts associated with the Western text-type, such as Codex Claromontanus (Dp), Codex Augiensis (Fp), and certain Latin Vulgate manuscripts. Additionally, Codex Boernerianus is notable for the absence of the doxology typically found at the end of Romans (Romans 16:25–27). Instead, there's an empty space after Romans 14:23, suggesting that the scribe intended to include it but ultimately did not.

The Latin portion of Codex Boernerianus bears similarities to the text of the Latin lectionary manuscript, Liber Comicus (t), which contains an Old Latin version of the New Testament. This connection highlights the manuscript's role in bridging the textual traditions of the early Christian Church and providing critical insights into the development of the New Testament canon.

Notable Readings

Codex Boernerianus, known in scholarly circles as Gp, offers a unique perspective on the New Testament, especially in its presentation of the Pauline epistles. Its text often diverges from what is found in the majority of other manuscripts, showcasing variations that are noteworthy for their insight into the early Christian texts' transmission and evolution. Here are

THE EARLY CHRISTIAN COPYISTS OF THE NEW TESTAMENT

some significant examples of how Codex Boernerianus differs from the wider textual tradition:

- **Romans 6:5**: While the majority of manuscripts read "but also of the resurrection," Codex Boernerianus presents this as "simultaneously of the resurrection," hinting at a nuanced understanding of Christian eschatology.

- **Romans 12:11**: In a deviation from the common rendering "Lord," Codex Boernerianus uses "time," suggesting a focus on timeliness or opportunity in serving.

- **Romans 15:31**: Codex Boernerianus uses "gift offering" (in Greek), contrasting with the "service" found in most texts, indicating a specific type of contribution to the saints in Jerusalem.

- **Romans 16:15**: Where most manuscripts name "Julian," Codex Boernerianus mentions "Junian," indicating a possible different individual or a textual misinterpretation over time.

- **Galatians 6:2**: The manuscript encourages believers to "fulfill" one another's burdens, a directive that is more a general call to action in the majority of other texts.

- **Philippians 3:16**: Here, Codex Boernerianus expands on the idea of "following the same line," possibly emphasizing unity and conformity within the Christian community.

- **Philippians 4:7**: The text uniquely mentions "bodies" being guarded by God's peace, unlike the "minds" protected in most other manuscripts, suggesting a more holistic safeguarding of the believer.

- **Romans 8:1**: Codex Boernerianus specifies those "in Jesus" without the additional context of living "according to the Spirit" rather than "according to the flesh," found in the broader manuscript tradition.

- **1 Corinthians 2:4**: It mentions "plausible wisdom," compared to the more elaborate "words of human wisdom" in the wider text tradition, possibly indicating a simpler message of divine truth.

These deviations underscore the mixture of early Christian textual traditions and the complex history of the New Testament's transmission. Codex Boernerianus, through its unique readings, contributes to our understanding of how these sacred texts were read, interpreted, and valued in different Christian communities.

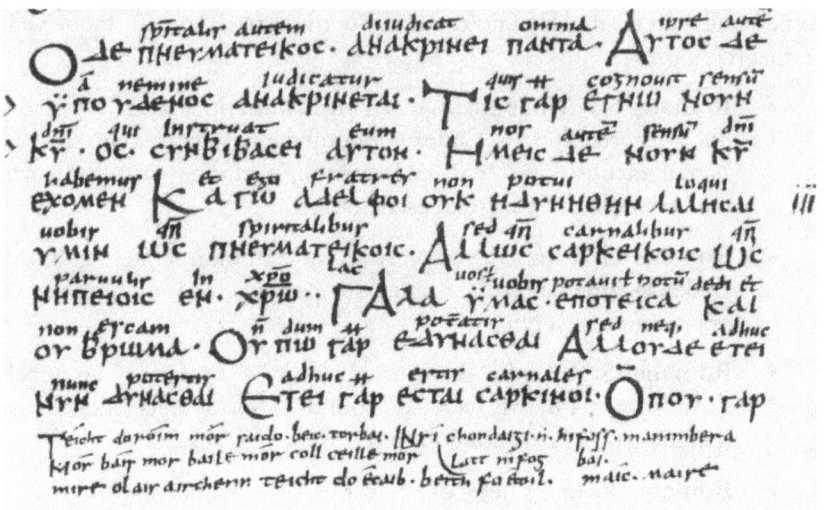

Below biblical text Irish verse (three lines)

The Old Irish Poem in the Codex Boernerianus

In the Codex Boernerianus there lies an intriguing addition on the back of the 23rd leaf — an Old Irish poem. This verse captures the reflections of a pilgrim who has journeyed to Rome, only to find the experience lacking in spiritual gain:

"Setting out for Rome,
Great effort, little profit: the King you seek there,
If you do not bring Him with you, you will not find Him.
Great death, great folly,
Great loss of sense, great madness,
Taking the road to death is certain,
Being under the displeasure of the Son of Mary."

This translation conveys the original's message: that embarking on a pilgrimage to Rome, in hopes of finding Christ, proves futile unless one already embraces Him in their heart. The poem reflects a critical stance towards the physical journey for spiritual enlightenment, emphasizing the inner spiritual journey as paramount. It's a rare and poignant reflection, suggesting that true connection with the divine transcends physical places, lodged instead within one's faith and inner life. This verse, penned by what seems to be a disenchanted pilgrim, serves as a timeless reminder of where true spiritual fulfillment lies.

THE EARLY CHRISTIAN COPYISTS OF THE NEW TESTAMENT

History of the Codex Boernerianus

The Codex Boernerianus, classified as G in the Gregory-Aland numbering, is an ancient manuscript believed to have been penned by an Irish monk residing in the Abbey of St. Gall in Switzerland sometime between 850 and 900 C.E. This conclusion is drawn from several distinctive features: the script's style, the presence of smaller Greek uncial letters, the use of Anglo-Saxon minuscule for the Latin interlinear annotations, and the practice of word separation.

The manuscript's journey through history saw it in the possession of P. Junius in Leiden by 1670. Its namesake, Christian Frederick Boerner, a professor at the University of Leipzig, acquired the codex in the Dutch Republic in 1705, bringing it into scholarly attention. Ludolph Kuster was the first to suggest the manuscript's 9th-century origins, a dating later reinforced by Johann Jakob Wettstein's designation of the manuscript with the symbol G. The codex was extensively studied and published by Christian Frederick Matthaei in 1791, who dated its creation to between the 8th and 12th centuries, a broad estimate that highlighted the challenges in pinpointing its exact age.

The theory that Codex Boernerianus and Codex Sangallensis (Δ 037) were once part of the same volume has been entertained by some scholars, including Rettig, further adding to the intrigue surrounding its history.

Tragically, the manuscript was significantly damaged by water during World War II, making the 1909 facsimile publication an essential resource for its study. Today, the Codex Boernerianus is preserved in the Saxon State Library in Dresden, Germany, ensuring its continued availability to scholars and historians interested in the textual history of the New Testament.

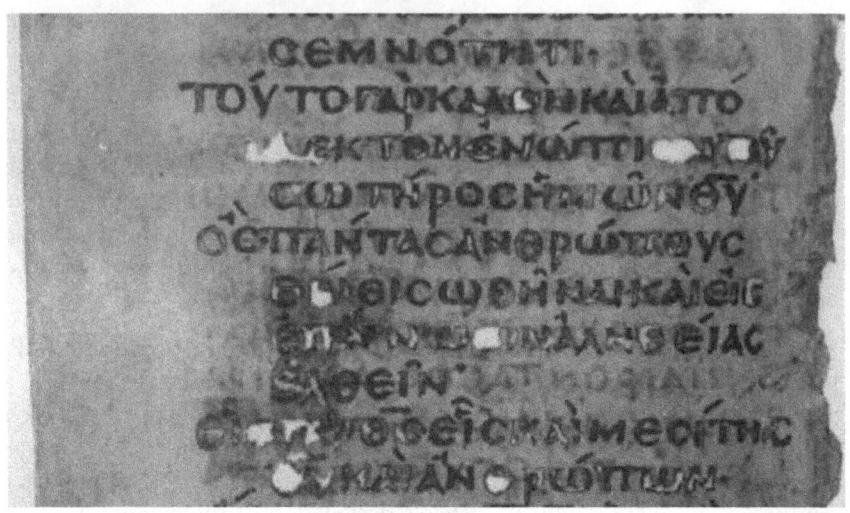

H (Codex Coislinianus)—also designated H^p

The Codex Coislinianus, also known as Hp in scholarly texts, or 015 according to the Gregory-Aland numbering system, and identified as α 1022 by Soden's classification, is sometimes referred to as the Codex Euthalianus. This ancient Greek manuscript, penned in uncial script during the 6th century, contains the Pauline epistles. What makes this document unique is the way it was written—stichometrically, meaning line by line, as opposed to in paragraphs. Additionally, it features marginal notes and a notable subscript at the conclusion of the Epistle to Titus.

This manuscript's journey through history is as fragmented as its physical state. Originally a single codex, it was later disassembled, and its parts were repurposed for new books. Its significance was rediscovered in the 18th century, thanks to the publication efforts of Bernard de Montfaucon, bringing it back into scholarly view.

Today, what remains of the Codex Coislinianus is spread across various European libraries, including prestigious ones in Paris, Athos, Saint Petersburg, Kiev, Moscow, and Turin. Despite its piecemeal existence, the Codex Coislinianus is a crucial source for biblical scholars and is referenced in all major critical editions of the New Testament, testament to its lasting importance in the study of biblical texts.

THE EARLY CHRISTIAN COPYISTS OF THE NEW TESTAMENT

Content

The Codex Coislinianus, known in scholarly circles as Hp, is a historic document containing fragmented pieces of several Pauline epistles. Specifically, it includes portions of 1 Corinthians (10:22–29, 11:9–16), 2 Corinthians (4:2–7, 10:5–11:8, 11:12–12:4), Galatians (1:1–10, 2:9–17, 4:30–5:5), Colossians (1:26–2:8, 2:20–3:11), 1 Thessalonians (2:9–13, 4:5–11), Philemon (1:7–2:13, 3:7–13, 6:9–13), 2 Timothy (2:1–9), Titus (1:1–3, 1:15–2:5, 3:13–15), and Hebrews (1:3–8, 2:11–16, 3:13–18, 4:12–15, 10:1–7, 10:32–38, 12:10–15, 13:24–25).

These texts are remnants of a collection that once included full texts of the Pauline epistles, organized according to a system developed by Euthalius, who edited the epistles in a format that groups verses into lines for easier reading. Unfortunately, significant portions of the Codex have been lost over time, including entire letters to the Romans, Philippians, Ephesians, 2 Thessalonians, and Philippians, leaving us with only these fragments of Paul's influential writings.

Date

Sixth century C.E.

Physical Features

The Codex Coislinianus, recognized in scholarly circles as Hp, is a remarkable artifact housing the writings of Paul's epistles. Originating from a period rich in religious and textual history, only 41 of its original leaves remain today. Measuring 30 by 25 cm, these leaves are a testament to the meticulous craftsmanship of its creators, featuring text inscribed on parchment in large, square uncials that span over 1.5 cm in height, arranged singularly across the page in 16 lines.

A notable feature of this codex is the later addition of breathings and accents to the text, though occasionally misplaced, revealing a layer of historical interaction with the document. It notably lacks the iota subscriptum, and demonstrates instances of itacism, such as ΙΟΔΑΙΟΙ for ΙΟΥΔΑΙΟΙ, reflecting the linguistic trends of the time. The sacred names within the text are abbreviated, preserving the reverence accorded to these terms, while some words at the line ends are contracted to fit the space.

Organizationally, the text is structured according to chapters (κεφαλαια), with their numbers noted in the margins, and includes tables of contents (κεφαλαια tables) before each book, aiding in navigation through the text.

The end of the Epistle to Titus in the codex bears a significant subscription that not only provides insight into the meticulous effort put into compiling this volume but also its scholarly verification against a revered manuscript in Caesarea, written by the hand of Pamphilus the saint. This dedication to accuracy and readability underscores the codex's value, bridging the gap between the sacred text and its readers across generations. This historical document, therefore, stands not just as a carrier of religious texts but as a witness to the rich tradition of manuscript preservation and scholarly diligence in the early Christian era.

Textual Character

The Codex Coislinianus, marked in academic circles as Hp, is an intriguing artifact from the realm of ancient biblical manuscripts, showcasing the writings of Paul's epistles. Dated to a period when meticulous transcription and preservation of texts were essential for disseminating religious teachings, this manuscript is recognized for its adherence to the Alexandrian text-type, albeit with a noticeable presence of Byzantine readings sprinkled throughout its content. Such a combination marks it as a unique testament to the diverse textual traditions that have influenced the New Testament's transmission over centuries.

Experts like Lagrange have observed its textual similarities with the renowned Codex Vaticanus, indicating a high level of textual integrity and historical importance. Its text aligns closely with what is known as the Euthalian recension of the Pauline epistles, an editorial revision aiming for enhanced clarity and readability for its early Christian audience.

Esteemed biblical scholar Eberhard Nestle hailed the Codex Coislinianus as "one of the most valuable manuscripts," a sentiment echoed by Kurt and Barbara Aland through their analytical textual profile: 71 agreements with the Byzantine standard text, 12 agreements with the original text against the Byzantine, and 3 unique readings. This profile situates the codex within Aland's Category III, indicative of a text with significant historical value and a mixture of textual traditions, primarily Alexandrian but influenced by Byzantine corrections.

The codex's textual character reveals its nuanced variance from the standard text, highlighted through specific deviations and omissions in passages from 2 Corinthians and Galatians to Colossians. These variations, from minor omissions to alternative word choices, underscore the meticulous care and scholarly rigor applied by its scribes and correctors. Through such textual analysis, Codex Coislinianus serves not only as a vital link to the early Christian scriptural tradition but also as a focal point for understanding the complex process of biblical text transmission and the evolution of scriptural interpretation in the Christian faith.

History of Codex Coislinianus

The Codex Coislinianus, also known by the symbol Hp, is a manuscript with a rich history that traces back to the 6th century. Its journey began in the Caesarea library, eventually making its way to the Great Lavra Monastery on Mount Athos. Initially, the codex's significance was not fully recognized, leading to its fragmentation; parts of its parchment were repurposed over the centuries for binding other books. By the 10th and 12th centuries, pieces of this valuable text were being used in other religious works across different regions.

The dispersion of the Codex Coislinianus fragments across Europe began when Pierre Séguier, a notable French figure, acquired 14 leaves. These leaves, known as Fragmenta Coisliniana, found their way into the Fonds Coislin collection and were stored in Saint-Germain-des-Prés, Paris. The publication of these fragments by Bernard de Montfaucon in 1715 marked the first scholarly engagement with the text, although it was not without errors, later corrected by the meticulous work of Tischendorf in the mid-19th century.

The 1793 fire at St. Germain-des-Prés led to the loss of some fragments, with only 12 of the original 14 surviving. The lost fragments had previously been moved to Saint Petersburg, Russia. By the end of the 18th century, the remaining fragments were safeguarded by the Bibliothèque nationale de France in Paris, where they reside today.

Additional fragments found their way to Moscow in 1665 and were later examined by scholar Matthaei. Porphyrius Uspensky, another key figure in the manuscript's history, managed to retrieve a leaf from Mount Athos during his travels.

Currently, the surviving parts of the Codex Coislinianus are spread across several libraries in Europe, making it a manuscript of considerable interest scattered across the continent. The most significant portions are housed in Paris, with others remaining in Mount Athos, and additional fragments located in Ukraine, Russia, and Italy.

The contributions of Henri Omont and Kirsopp Lake in the early 20th century brought further attention to the codex, incorporating it into scholarly discussions and critical editions of the Greek New Testament. Today, it is cited in major New Testament editions, recognized for its paramount importance in biblical scholarship and textual criticism. Its journey from a fragmented manuscript to a key witness in the study of the New Testament encapsulates the enduring significance of ancient texts in understanding the foundations of Christian traditions.

I (Codex Freerianus or the Washington Codex)

The Codex Freerianus, also known as the Washington Manuscript of the Pauline Epistles, is a treasured manuscript that dates back to the 5th century. It's written in Greek using an uncial script on vellum, which is a type of fine animal skin used for writing. This manuscript is special because it contains the letters written by Paul, an early Christian leader whose writings are crucial to the New Testament.

The story of how this manuscript came to be part of the Smithsonian Institution's collection is quite fascinating. It was purchased by Charles Lang Freer, a collector of art and manuscripts, during his travels in Egypt.

THE EARLY CHRISTIAN COPYISTS OF THE NEW TESTAMENT

Recognizing its significance, Freer brought it back, and it now resides in the Freer Gallery of Art in Washington, D.C., under the catalog number 06.275.

Scholars believe that the Codex Freerianus originated from the Nitrian Desert, a region known for its ancient monastic communities and a rich history of religious scholarship. This background hints at the manuscript's journey from a monastic setting in Egypt to becoming a valued artifact in a museum. Its preservation allows scholars today to study and understand more about the early Christian texts and the context in which they were written.

Content

The Washington Codex, also known as Codex Freerianus, is a remarkable 5th-century collection of parchment pages that include the writings of Paul from the New Testament. It's like a time capsule from the early Christian world, holding messages that have been shared and studied for centuries. This manuscript specifically includes portions of Paul's letters to early Christian communities and leaders, from 1 Corinthians through to Hebrews, although not all sections are complete.

Imagine flipping through ancient pages and seeing segments like 1 Corinthians 10:29, where discussions about Christian liberty unfold, or Ephesians 2:15-18, revealing messages about unity and peace. It's like a patchwork of teachings and guidance, pieced together from different letters, giving us glimpses into the early Christian faith. The codex includes practical advice for living a Christian life, heartfelt prayers, and deep theological insights, making it a treasure trove for anyone interested in the roots of Christianity.

What's fascinating is the way this manuscript bridges the past and present, showing us the concerns, hopes, and faith of early Christians. It's not just about the words themselves, while getting to the original readings of the original documents is always the goal, the journey these words have taken through history, from being carefully penned by an unknown scribe in the 5th century to being studied by scholars and believers worldwide today. Through these fragments, we're connected to the early church, its teachings, and its enduring legacy.

Date

Fourth-Fifth century C.E.

Physical Features

The Washington Codex might have had about 210 pages made of parchment, each measuring around 25 by 20 centimeters. Today, only 84 pages remain, and even these are not complete but fragmented. The layout is quite straightforward, with the text written in a single column on each page, comprising around 30 lines. The writing style is continuous, known as scriptio continua, where words and letters are not separated. This codex provides a valuable glimpse into the biblical texts of its time, housed now in the Freer Gallery of Art, part of the Smithsonian Institution in Washington.

Textual Character

The script of the Washington Codex, which follows the Alexandrian text-type, shares similarities with certain notable manuscripts like Codex Sinaiticus (א) and Codex Alexandrinus (A), suggesting a more Egyptian lineage of text. Its compilation was meticulously analyzed by H. A. Sanders in 1921, marking it as a significant exemplar of the Alexandrian family, particularly aligning with manuscripts א, A, C, and 33 more than others like P46, B, or 1739. The categorization of this codex into Category II by Aland emphasizes its association with the Egyptian text, underlining its value in textual criticism despite its incomplete condition.

A distinctive reading in 2 Timothy 1:11 demonstrates this manuscript's uniqueness, where it reads καὶ διδάσκαλος (and teacher), aligning with manuscripts like א*, A, 1175, and syrpal, diverging from the majority that includes καὶ διδάσκαλος ἐθνῶν (and teacher of nations). This particular variance not only highlights its critical role in the understanding of early New Testament texts but also points to the intricate variations that exist within the textual tradition of the New Testament. The codex's affiliation with esteemed manuscripts and its unique textual character contribute significantly to our understanding of the textual history of the New Testament, offering insights into the transmission and preservation of these ancient writings.

Double Ending of Mark

L (Codex Regius)

Codex Regius, also known as Le or 019 according to the Gregory-Aland numbering, is an 8th-century Greek uncial manuscript of the New Testament, written on parchment. Identified by its distinctive uncial script, this manuscript is significant for its content, which encompasses parts of the New Testament, despite missing several sections due to its age and condition. The importance of Codex Regius lies in its contribution to the study of the textual history of the New Testament, offering scholars a glimpse into the scriptural texts as they existed over a millennium ago.

Content

Four Gospels (nearly complete)

Date

Eighth century C.E.

Physical Features

Codex Regius stands out as an 8th-century Greek manuscript of the New Testament penned on parchment. This ancient manuscript encompasses nearly the entire text of the four Gospels, although several passages are missing due to lost leaves: parts of Matthew, Mark, and the concluding verses of John.

The physical makeup of Codex Regius includes 257 thick parchment leaves, each measuring approximately 23.5 by 17 centimeters. The Gospels' text is meticulously organized in two columns per page, with about 25 lines per column. The script, characterized by large, uncial letters, reflects a writing style that suggests the scribe may not have been thoroughly proficient in Greek, hinting at an Egyptian rather than a Hellenic background. This is evidenced by the peculiarly large size of the letter phi (φ) and the final evolutionary form of the uncial alpha (α), which hints at the scribe's possible familiarity with Coptic script.

Frederick H. A. Scrivener, a renowned textual critic, remarked on the manuscript's lack of precision, attributing it to the scribe's lack of expertise. Despite these shortcomings, Codex Regius is a treasure trove of textual features, including the use of breathing marks and accents—though often misplaced—highlighting the manuscript's phonetic considerations.

The organizational scheme of Codex Regius follows traditional methods of dividing biblical texts. This includes the kephalaia (chapters) marked in the margin and their titles (titloi) at the top of the pages. It further incorporates a comprehensive table of contents preceding each Gospel, alongside the division into Ammonian Sections with cross-references to the Eusebian Canons noted in the margins. This system facilitated navigability and cross-referencing across the Gospels. Moreover, the manuscript bears lectionary markings for liturgical use, outlining when passages were to be read throughout the ecclesiastical year.

Notably, Codex Regius lacks the Pericope Adulterae (John 7:53-8:11), a passage found in later manuscripts. It also presents two distinct conclusions to the Gospel of Mark, including a shorter ending that precedes the more widely recognized verses of Mark 16:9-20, offering a unique perspective on early Christian traditions regarding the Resurrection narrative. The shorter ending succinctly summarizes the women's encounter at the tomb and the subsequent dissemination of the message of salvation by Jesus through them, from east to west—an affirmation of the timeless and boundless nature of the Gospel's reach.

Textual Character

The Codex Regius, originating from the 8th century, is esteemed for its representation of the Alexandrian text-type, particularly in its later form. Text-types are essentially families of New Testament manuscripts that exhibit common characteristics in their readings, which can vary from one group to another. The major text-types identified are Alexandrian, Western, and Byzantine.

The Codex Regius is noted for generally aligning with Codex Vaticanus, also referred to as "B," especially in the Gospels. This alignment is an indicator of its high value in reconstructing the original text of the New Testament. Despite the presence of scribal errors, its textual integrity is considered robust, showcasing a blend of readings that mainly echo the Alexandrian tradition, yet with instances where Byzantine influences are noticeable. This manuscript falls into Category II in Kurt Aland's classification system, which denotes manuscripts of special quality that contain a significant amount of early text along with some later textual modifications.

One of the unique features of the Codex Regius is its inclusion of both endings of the Gospel of Mark, presenting a fascinating case study in the variations that exist within New Testament manuscript traditions. In the Gospel of Matthew, particularly from 1:1 to 17:26, there's a notable presence of Byzantine readings, highlighting the manuscript's textural diversity.

Several specific examples illustrate the textual character of the Codex Regius:

- It omits Matthew 12:47, a verse included in the majority of manuscripts.
- In Matthew 20:23, it shares a reading concerning baptism with a select group of other manuscripts, diverging from the majority.
- The manuscript also omits certain phrases and verses found in other manuscripts, such as Luke 9:55–56's mention of Jesus' purpose not to destroy lives but to save them, highlighting variations in manuscript traditions.

Furthermore, the Codex Regius includes certain additions and variations in verses where other manuscripts differ:

- It adds a greeting of peace in Matthew 10:12, a detail not universally preserved across all manuscripts.

- In Matthew 27:49, it contains a narrative detail about Jesus being pierced with a spear, aligning with John 19:34 but omitted in many other manuscripts.

These examples underscore the complexity of the New Testament textual tradition and the critical role of manuscripts like the Codex Regius in understanding the depth and breadth of textual variations. Each manuscript contributes to a more nuanced view of the New Testament's textual history, offering insights into how these sacred texts were transmitted, read, and interpreted in the early Christian communities.

The study of such manuscripts is not just an academic pursuit but a journey into the very heart of early Christian scripture and its transmission. The Codex Regius, with its blend of textual traditions, serves as a window into the past, revealing the care, reverence, and sometimes human error involved in the preservation of these foundational texts.

History of Codex Regius

The Codex Regius, designated as "L" in the world of New Testament textual criticism, has a distinguished history that reflects its importance in the study of biblical manuscripts. Its journey through scholarly examination and analysis over the centuries has significantly contributed to our understanding of the New Testament's textual tradition.

This manuscript was first cited by Robert Estienne, also known as Stephanus, in his notable work, the Editio Regia, where he referred to it using the Greek letter eta (η'). This early reference highlights the Codex Regius' recognition among Renaissance scholars who laid the groundwork for modern biblical textual criticism.

Further examination of the Codex Regius was undertaken by Johann Jakob Wettstein, a renowned textual critic of the 18th century, who loosely collated its text. Wettstein's work was foundational in the development of a more systematic approach to comparing New Testament manuscripts, and his attention to the Codex Regius underscores its value in these early efforts to understand the text of the New Testament more accurately.

The esteem in which this codex was held continued to grow, as evidenced by the assessment of Johann Jakob Griesbach, another pivotal figure in the field of textual criticism. Griesbach, known for his meticulous work and the development of a critical apparatus for evaluating textual variants, set a very high value on the Codex Regius. His appraisal indicates the manuscript's significance in efforts to discern the original wording of the New Testament texts.

The Codex Regius was later edited by Constantin von Tischendorf in 1846, as part of his broader efforts to document and publish ancient biblical manuscripts. This edition, included in the collection "Monumenta sacra inedita," though noted for containing some errors, further facilitated scholarly access to and analysis of the codex. Tischendorf's contributions to the study of biblical manuscripts are monumental, and his work with the Codex Regius is part of this legacy.

Today, the Codex Regius resides in the National Library of France, identified by its catalog number Gr. 62, in Paris. Its placement in this prestigious institution ensures its preservation and continued availability for study by scholars and researchers. The journey of the Codex Regius, from its early recognition by scholars like Stephanus to its current home in Paris, reflects the enduring importance of this manuscript in the quest to understand the original text of the New Testament.

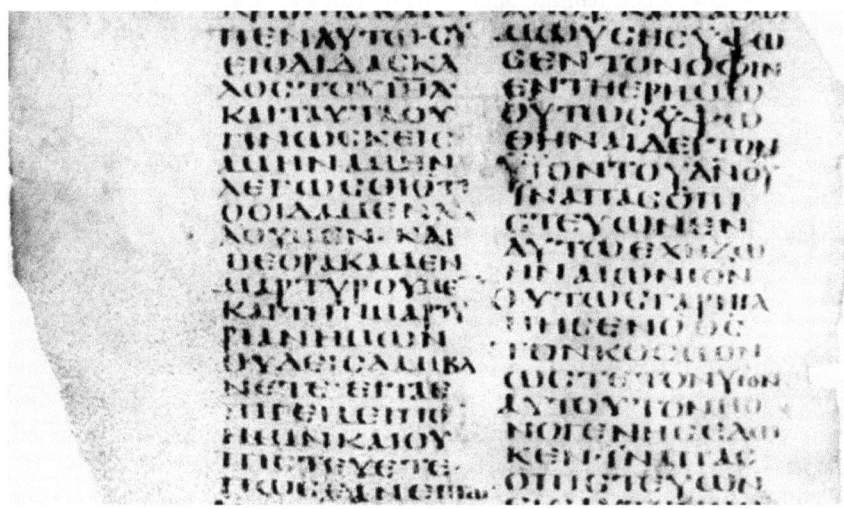

T (Codex Borgianus)

The Codex Borgianus, known within scholarly circles by the designation "T" or "029" according to the Gregory-Aland numbering system, and as "ε 5" in the von Soden classification, is a remarkable manuscript that contains the Gospels in both Greek and Sahidic Coptic. This dual-language feature makes it a unique witness to the early textual transmission of the Christian New Testament.

This manuscript is categorized as an uncial, which refers to the style of writing used in its composition. Uncial script is characterized by its large, uppercase letters, which were common in Greek and Latin manuscripts from the 4th to the 8th centuries. The use of uncial script in this manuscript helps to date it palaeographically to the 5th century, situating it within a critical period of early Christian history and textual tradition.

The name "Codex Borgianus" is derived from one of its former owners, reflecting the manuscript's journey through time and its stewardship by various scholars and collectors before finding its place in the academic study of biblical texts. The passage of such manuscripts from one caretaker to another often adds layers to their history, contributing to our understanding of their significance and the esteem in which they were held by those who possessed them.

As a Greek and Sahidic uncial manuscript of the Gospels from the 5th century, the Codex Borgianus stands as an important witness to the textual variants and the early dissemination of the Gospel texts. Its dual-language content provides valuable insights into the linguistic and cultural contexts of early Christian communities, especially those that engaged with both the Greek and Coptic-speaking worlds. This aspect of the Codex Borgianus underscores the diversity within early Christian traditions and the broad geographic spread of Christianity by the 5th century.

Content

The Codex Borgianus, recognized in scholarly circles by its Gregory-Aland designation "T" or "029," presents an invaluable resource in the field of New Testament textual criticism. This manuscript, dating back to the 5th century, is distinguished by its bilingual text, comprising both Greek and Sahidic Coptic translations of the Gospels. Specifically, it includes portions of the Gospels according to Luke and John, making it a crucial witness to the textual variations and transmission history of these New Testament books.

The Greek sections of the Codex Borgianus encompass various passages from Luke and John:

- In Luke, the Greek text includes segments from chapters 6, 18 through 24. This selection offers a glimpse into Jesus' teachings and parables, as well as the events leading up to and including his crucifixion and resurrection narratives.

THE EARLY CHRISTIAN COPYISTS OF THE NEW TESTAMENT

- The excerpts from John feature portions of chapters 1, 3, 4 through 8, covering a range of Jesus' interactions and discourses, from the testimony of John the Baptist to the early signs and teachings of Jesus.

The Sahidic Coptic portions of the manuscript provide a parallel textual tradition, covering similar passages from Luke and John but with slight variations in the extent of the text. This Sahidic Coptic translation is particularly significant, as it represents one of the earliest vernacular translations of the New Testament, offering insights into how these texts were received and understood within early Coptic-speaking Christian communities.

By preserving these texts in both Greek and Sahidic Coptic, the Codex Borgianus serves as a bridge between different linguistic and cultural Christian traditions of the 5th century. Its diglot nature facilitates a comparative study of textual variants and helps in understanding the nuances of language translation in the early Christian era. The manuscript not only contributes to the critical task of reconstructing the original wording of the New Testament texts but also illuminates the broader historical and ecclesiastical context in which these texts were disseminated and read.

In the pursuit of establishing the original words of the New Testament, the Codex Borgianus stands out for its dual-language content, offering a direct link to the early Christian textual heritage and providing a tangible connection to the diverse linguistic landscape of early Christianity. This manuscript, therefore, is not merely an artifact of religious history but a pivotal tool in the ongoing scholarly endeavor to trace the textual development of the New Testament.

Date

Fifth century C.E.

Physical Features

The Codex Borgianus, an ancient manuscript designated as "T" or "029" in the Gregory-Aland numbering system, is a significant artifact in the study of the New Testament's textual history. This document is composed of 17 parchment leaves, each measuring 26 by 21 centimeters, and contains fragments from the Gospels of Luke and John. Its physical characteristics offer insight into the manuscript's origins and the context in which it was produced.

The manuscript's text is arranged in two columns on each page, with the Greek and Sahidic Coptic texts presented on facing pages. This layout facilitates a comparative study of the texts, highlighting the manuscript's role as a bilingual document. The number of lines per page varies between 26 and 33, which is somewhat typical for manuscripts of this period. However, the Codex Borgianus features unusually short lines, containing only between 6 and 9 letters. This brevity in line length may reflect stylistic or practical considerations of the scribe.

The script used in the Codex Borgianus is characterized by large, square letters that are compressed at the edges. This compression at the margins is a notable feature, suggesting a careful management of space on the parchment. The script's form, particularly the shapes of the alpha and iota letters, along with the overall squareness of the letters, points to a Coptic influence. Constantin von Tischendorf, a renowned biblical scholar, even suggested that the scribe might have been Coptic, based on the presence of letter forms common to Coptic writing.

Another distinctive feature of this manuscript is its lack of accents and breathings, a characteristic that is not uncommon in texts from this era but still of interest to scholars. Moreover, the manuscript does not include notation for sections or other divisions, which could indicate either an early date of composition or a specific stylistic choice by the scribe.

The physical attributes of the Codex Borgianus, from its parchment leaves to the distinctive style of its script, contribute to our understanding of the manuscript as a product of its time and cultural context. Its bilingual nature, with Greek and Sahidic Coptic texts side by side, underscores the diverse linguistic landscape of early Christianity and the efforts to make the Gospel accessible to different communities. The meticulous craftsmanship involved in its creation, from the careful allocation of space to the distinct Coptic influences in its script, reveals the dedication of its scribe to preserving these texts for future generations.

Textual Character

The Codex Borgianus holds a notable place in the study of New Testament texts due to its textual character. This manuscript, containing Greek text, is recognized for its alignment with the Alexandrian text-type, albeit with an incorporation of Byzantine text readings. This blend marks it as a secondary representative of the Alexandrian family, which is known for its early and often considered more accurate versions of New Testament texts.

Kurt Aland, a pivotal figure in biblical scholarship, classified the Codex Borgianus within Category II of his rating system. This categorization is reserved for manuscripts that, while containing a substantial portion of the early text, also exhibit later textual modifications or influences. This dual character of the Codex Borgianus makes it a rich resource for textual critics, offering insights into the transmission and evolution of the New Testament text over time.

In terms of specific textual relationships, the version of the Gospel of John found in the Codex Borgianus shows a close connection to that of the Codex Vaticanus and Papyrus 75 (P75), especially in the handling of the Alexandrian text. This affinity is significant, as both Codex Vaticanus and P75 are highly regarded for their textual integrity and their role in shaping the understanding of the Alexandrian tradition.

The manuscript exhibits certain notable textual omissions and variations:

- It omits Luke 22:43-44, a passage concerning Jesus' prayer on the Mount of Olives, aligning it with other manuscripts such as Papyrus 75, Codex Sinaiticus (ℵ*), Codex Alexandrinus (A), Codex Vaticanus (B), and Codex 1071, which also lack this text.
- Similarly, John 5:4, detailing an angel stirring the waters of Bethesda, is not found in the Codex Borgianus, consistent with its absence in some other early manuscripts.
- The Pericope Adulterae (John 7:53-8:11), the story of the woman caught in adultery, is another notable omission, underscoring the manuscript's alignment with texts that scholars believe to be closer to the original writings.

Additionally, the Codex Borgianus offers unique readings in specific passages:

- It presents the name βηθαβαρα (Bethabara) in John 1:28, as opposed to the more commonly found βηθανια (Bethany).
- Similarly, it reads βηθσαιδα (Bethsaida) in John 5:2, contributing to discussions on the geographical details in the Gospel accounts.

These textual characteristics of the Codex Borgianus underscore its importance in the field of textual criticism, providing a window into the variegated nature of New Testament manuscript traditions. Through its mix of textual traditions and specific variants, the Codex Borgianus contributes to the ongoing scholarly endeavor to reconstruct the most accurate text of the New Testament.

History of Codex Borgianus

The Codex Borgianus, an ancient manuscript of the New Testament, has a rich history that traces back to the White Monastery in Egypt. It gained its name from one of its later owners, Cardinal Stefano Borgia, reflecting the journey and the various hands it has passed through over the centuries.

The story of the Codex Borgianus is marked by a series of discoveries and reunions of its fragmented parts. These fragments, identified in scholarly circles by the numbers 029, 0113, 0125, and 0139, were found at different times and places, together comprising 23 leaves of the manuscript. A noteworthy account suggests that the monk who initially brought the manuscript from Egypt to Europe might not have recognized its significant value, leading to the loss of many of its parts.

In 1789, A. A. Giorgi undertook the careful task of editing the text of Codex 029, marking an early effort to preserve and study this manuscript. Additional scholarly work was carried out by Birch, who not only collated the Greek text of 029 but also provided a detailed description of the codex, emphasizing its uncial script on parchment, the accompanying Coptic translation, and lamenting the limited portion of the manuscript that has survived through time.

The manuscript's journey through history continued into the 20th century when Henri Hyvernat acquired two pages in 1912 in Cairo for John Pierpont Morgan, further adding to the manuscript's storied past.

Today, the Codex Borgianus is housed in several prestigious locations around the world, evidencing its dispersed nature due to historical circumstances. Parts of the codex are found in the Vatican Library, designated as Borgia Coptic 109, reflecting its connection to Cardinal Stefano Borgia. Additional leaves are preserved in the Pierpont Morgan Library in New York City (Pierpont Morgan M 664A) and in the Bibliothèque nationale de France in Paris (BnF Copt. 129). There was a brief confusion in the past where some leaves from another manuscript, Uncial 070, were mistakenly associated with the Codex Borgianus, but this was later clarified.

THE EARLY CHRISTIAN COPYISTS OF THE NEW TESTAMENT

The history of the Codex Borgianus, from its origins in the White Monastery to its current locations across the globe, underscores the complex journey of ancient manuscripts and the challenges involved in preserving and studying these invaluable links to early Christian history and biblical scholarship.

W (Codex Washingtonianus or Freer Gospels)

The Codex Washingtonianus, also known as the Freer Gospels or Codex Freerianus, is a critical piece of the puzzle in New Testament textual criticism. Identified by scholars with the symbols "W" or "032" in the Gregory-Aland numbering system, and "ε014" in the von Soden classification, this manuscript stands out for containing the four Gospels written in Greek on parchment. Through the detailed study of its writing styles, known as palaeography, experts have dated it to around the year 400 C.E., placing it in the early centuries of Christianity.

This manuscript, notable for its age and content, has experienced some loss over time, evident in the gaps within its text. Despite these missing pieces, the Codex Washingtonianus has been celebrated as a monumental discovery in biblical scholarship, particularly noted for its contributions to the understanding of the Gospel of Mark. It shares several unique textual readings with other early manuscripts, such as the Chester Beatty Papyri, which includes texts of the Gospels and Acts from the early 3rd century. This connection underscores the Codex Washingtonianus's value in tracing the textual history and variations within the earliest Christian documents.

The journey of this manuscript to modern scholarship is as intriguing as its contents. It was among a collection of manuscripts acquired by Charles Lang Freer, an American industrialist and art collector, in the early 20th century. The Codex was first published and brought to the attention of the academic world by biblical scholar Henry A. Sanders. This publication marked the beginning of its significant impact on the study of the New Testament, providing scholars with a valuable resource for understanding the textual transmission of the Gospels.

Described as one of the most important majuscule (a script style characterized by large, uppercase letters) manuscripts discovered in the 20th century, the Codex Washingtonianus is recognized for its historical and textual significance. Its contributions to biblical studies, especially in the examination of the Gospels, have made it a key manuscript for scholars attempting to get closer to the original texts of the New Testament. Positioned as the third oldest Gospel parchment codex known to the world, its value in the realm of biblical textual criticism cannot be overstated, offering a window into the early Christian era and the development of the Gospel texts.

Content

The Gospels

Date

About 400 C.E.

Physical Features

The Codex Washingtonianus, also known as the Freer Gospels, is a fascinating artifact that provides a glimpse into the early Christian era through its physical characteristics and the manner in which the Gospels were transcribed. This ancient manuscript is crafted as a codex, which is the early form of a book, predating the modern bound book we are familiar with today. It comprises 187 parchment leaves, with dimensions ranging between 20.5 to 21 cm in height and 13 to 14.5 cm in width and is encased in painted wooden covers.

THE EARLY CHRISTIAN COPYISTS OF THE NEW TESTAMENT

A notable aspect of this manuscript is the presence of replacement leaves. For instance, the section from John 1:1 to 5:11 is not original to the manuscript but was added in the 7th century, likely to replace damaged folios. This manuscript also has gaps, specifically in Mark 15:13-38 and John 14:26-16:7, indicating missing portions of the text.

The text within the Codex Washingtonianus is presented in a single column format on each page, with 30 lines per page. The script is penned in a small, slightly sloping uncial hand using dark-brown ink, characteristic of the period. Unlike later manuscripts, the words are written in scriptio continua, meaning they flow continuously without spaces between them. The manuscript does not regularly use accents, which in other texts help indicate changes in pitch, and the rough breathing marks to denote vowel emphasis are rarely applied.

Corrections within the text are evident, with most being made by the original scribe and a few others added later, around the late 5th or early 6th century. These corrections, along with the overall quality of the manuscript, suggest that the scribe was meticulous in their work, producing a text with very few errors or nonsensical readings.

The order of the Gospels in the Codex Washingtonianus is also of particular interest, as it follows the Western order: Matthew, John, Luke, and then Mark, a sequence that is different from the more commonly found order in other manuscripts.

An important feature of this manuscript is the use of nomina sacra, a practice in early Christian manuscripts where sacred names or words are abbreviated. These abbreviations are typically marked by an overline and include the first and last letters of the word. In the Codex Washingtonianus, several nomina sacra are used, representing words like God (ΘΣ for θεος), Lord (ΚΣ for κυριος), Christ (ΧΡΣ for χριστος), Jesus (ΙΣ for Ιησους), spirit (ΠΝΑ for πνευμα), man (ΑΝΟΣ for ανθρωπος), father (ΠΗΡ for πατηρ), mother (ΜΗΡ for μητηρ), son (ΥΣ for υιος), David (ΔΑΔ), and Israel (ΙΗΛ).

Through these physical and textual characteristics, the Codex Washingtonianus offers valuable insights into the practices and conventions of early Christian manuscript production, as well as the careful efforts of scribes to preserve the texts of the Gospels for future generations.

Textual Character

The Codex Washingtonianus presents a fascinating case of textual diversity. According to scholar Henry A. Sanders, this manuscript likely originated from a master copy that was itself assembled from several different manuscripts. This master copy's patchwork nature suggests it was created in a time when New Testament manuscripts were rare, possibly right after the Diocletian persecution around 303 C.E., a period known for the widespread destruction of sacred texts.

The process of compiling Codex W involved selecting fragments from various sources to create a complete Gospel codex. Sanders theorizes that for parts of the Gospel of Mark, the scribe relied on texts from North Africa, known as the "Western" text. For other parts, like portions of Matthew and Luke, manuscripts from Antioch were chosen to fill in the gaps of the older, more fragmented manuscript being copied.

The textual content of Codex W is remarkably diverse:

- In Matthew, the text aligns with the Byzantine tradition.
- The Gospel of Mark starts with a Western text-type until 5:30 and then switches to what's considered a Caesarean text-type up to the end.
- Luke begins with an Alexandrian text-type before transitioning to a Byzantine type.
- John's text is the most complex, with the initial section (John 1:1–5:11) likely added by a seventh-century scribe to replace damaged parts. This section shows a mix of Alexandrian and Western readings, a pattern that continues through the rest of John.

This blend of text-types within a single manuscript illustrates the significant liberties **some** scribes took when copying texts. They, **at times**, didn't just copy from one source; they harmonized and filled in gaps using a variety of exemplars. In doing so, they played a crucial role in the evolution of the New Testament manuscripts, especially in how individual Gospels were woven together to form a singular, fourfold Gospel codex. Codex W stands as a prime example of the dynamic and varied nature of manuscript transmission following the pivotal period of persecution, reflecting the scribes' intricate work in preserving these texts for future generations.

The Codex Washingtonianus is a pivotal manuscript in the realm of New Testament textual criticism. This codex is especially significant in the critical apparatus of the Novum Testamentum Graece, a critical edition of the Greek New Testament, where it is recognized as a primary witness of the first order. Again, its textual character is fascinating due to its display of affinities with multiple text-types, suggesting it was likely copied from several different manuscripts. This diversity is thought to possibly stem from an effort to piece together texts that survived the persecution of Christians under Emperor Diocletian.

Text-types are essentially classifications of New Testament manuscripts based on their shared readings, which differ from one group to another, helping scholars to trace back to the original text. The main text-types are Alexandrian, Western, and Byzantine, and the Codex Washingtonianus intriguingly presents sections that align with each of these text-types, as follows:

- Matthew and Luke (from chapter 8, verse 13, to the end) show a Byzantine text-type alignment.

- The beginning of Mark, up to 5:30, mirrors the Western text-type, aligning with old Latin versions.

- From Mark 5:31 to the end, the text-type is thought to be Caesarean, closely related to Papyrus 45.

- The first chapters of Luke and the latter portion of John reflect an Alexandrian text-type.

- The beginning of John, added in the 7th century, shows a mix of Alexandrian and Western readings.

The concept of a Caesarean text-type, while proposed by biblical scholar Burnett Hillman Streeter, has been a point of contention among text critics, including Kurt and Barbara Aland. Kurt Aland categorized the codex within Category III of his New Testament manuscript classification, indicating a text with a mix of early readings and significant Byzantine influence alongside unidentified sources.

Unique textual characteristics include the presence of Matthew 16:2b–3 without doubt, and the absence of passages like Luke 22:43-44 and the Pericope Adulterae, indicating careful selection or omission of certain texts. Additionally, the codex includes and omits various phrases and verses that contribute to its distinctiveness among manuscripts.

One of the most intriguing features is a subscription at the end of the Gospel of Mark, offering a personal prayer for the manuscript's scribe or owner, showcasing the intimate relationship between the text and its keepers. This codex not only illuminates the complex textual history of the New Testament but also the personal and communal reverence for these texts.

Notable readings include variations in the text that differ from the majority of manuscripts, such as specific inclusions or exclusions of phrases and verses in Matthew, Mark, Luke, and John, highlighting the codex's unique contributions to understanding the textual variances within early Christian manuscripts. These readings offer invaluable insights into the textual tradition and the meticulous work of early scribes in preserving the New Testament.

History of the Washington Codex

In December 1906, Charles L. Freer, an American art collector, acquired several ancient manuscripts in Giza, Egypt, from a dealer named Ali. Among these, a hard, blackened lump of parchment was included, seemingly from the Monastery near the Pyramid of Giza, rather than the White Monastery as Ali suggested. This lump, initially thought to be of little value, turned out to be an invaluable fifth or sixth-century codex of Paul's letters, once separated into 84 fragments.

The collection also included manuscripts of Deuteronomy and Joshua, Psalms from the Greek Septuagint, and notably, a manuscript of the four Gospels. This Gospels manuscript, written on fine parchment in Greek uncials, features an arrangement of Matthew, John, Luke, and Mark, differing from the traditional sequence. Despite significant decay at the edges, the text remains largely intact. This manuscript, now part of the Freer Gallery of Art at the Smithsonian Institution in Washington, D.C., and known as the Washington Codex of the Gospels, is identified with the letter "W."

Dated to the late fourth or early fifth century C.E., the Washington Codex is a crucial piece in the puzzle of biblical manuscripts, closely following the renowned Sinaitic, Vatican, and Alexandrine manuscripts. Its text reveals a blend of textual types, likely a composite of fragments from various sources, possibly concealed during Emperor Diocletian's persecution of Christians in 303 C.E. This theory suggests that the Codex's diversity in text types results from an attempt to preserve Scripture during times of crisis.

An intriguing aspect of the Gospels manuscript is its association with old Latin and Syriac versions and the unique, albeit discounted, addition to Mark chapter 16, suggesting it may have originated as a marginal note. Signs of use, like candle tallow blots, hint at its extensive use over time.

This remarkable preservation story of the Washington Codex, amid historical turmoil and the passage of time, underscores the endurance of biblical texts through centuries. It serves as a testament to the resilience of the Scriptures, affirming the lasting impact and perpetual relevance of these ancient texts in modern times.

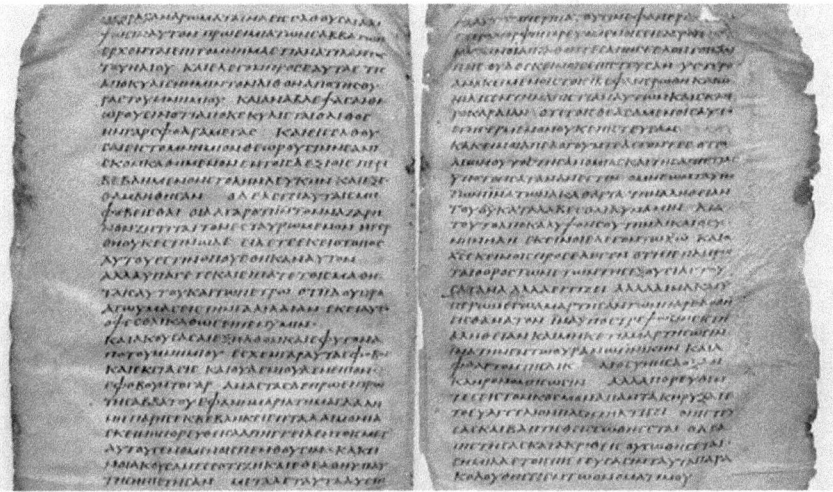

The Ending of Mark

The ending of the Gospel of Mark in the Codex Washingtonianus includes a passage that stands out because it's not found in any other known manuscript. This passage, known as the "Freer Logion," appears right after Mark 16:14 and adds a unique perspective to the discussions Jesus has with His disciples.

Κακεινοι απελογουντο λεγοντες οτι ο αιων ουτος της ανομιας και της απιστιας υπο τον σαταναν εστιν, ο μη εων τα (τον μη εωντα?) υπο των πνευματων ακαθαρτα (-των?) την αληθειαν του θεου καταλαβεσθαι (+ και?) δυναμιν. δια τουτο αποκαλυψον σου την δικαιοσυνην ηδη, εκεινοι ελεγον τω χριστω. και ο χριστος εκεινοις προσελεγεν οτι πεπληρωται των ετων της εξουσιας του σατανα, ἀλλὰ εγγιζει ἄλλα δεινα. και υπερ ων εγω αμαρτησαντων παρεδοθην εις θανατον ινα υποστρεψωσιν εις την αληθειαν και μηκετι αμαρτησωσιν ινα την εν τω ουρανω πνευματικην και αφθαρτον της δικαιοσυνης δοξαν κληρονομησωσιν.

Translation:

And they defended themselves, saying, "This age of lawlessness and unbelief is under Satan, who does not allow the truth and power of God to be understood by those under the unclean spirits. Therefore, reveal Your righteousness now," they said to Christ. And Christ responded to them, "The period of the years of Satan's power has been fulfilled, but other terrible things are near. And for those who have sinned, I was delivered to death so that they might return to the truth and no longer sin, in order to inherit the spiritual and incorruptible glory of righteousness in heaven."

This text is not found in any other known manuscript, but was partially quoted by Jerome:

et illi satisfaciebant dicentes: Saeculum istud iniquitatis et incredulitatis substantia (sub Satana?) est, quae non sinit per immundos spiritus veram Dei apprehendi virtutem: idcirco iamnunc revela iustitiam tuam.

Translation:

And they answered, saying: "This age is the essence of wickedness and disbelief (under Satan?), which does not allow the true power of God to be grasped through unclean spirits: therefore, reveal your righteousness now."

The text delves into themes of lawlessness, unbelief, and the dominion of Satan, presenting a dialogue between Christ and His followers that emphasizes the spiritual conflict of their time.

The passage reads as if the disciples are trying to justify their doubts and fears by highlighting the pervasive influence of Satan in their era, which they believe hinders the truth and power of God from overcoming the evil spirits' impurities. They plead for Jesus to manifest His righteousness immediately.

Jesus' response in this passage is profound. He acknowledges the completion of the time allowed for Satan's power but warns of more challenges to come. Importantly, He frames His own death as a sacrifice for those who have erred, offering them a chance to return to truth, avoid further sin, and ultimately share in the eternal, spiritual glory of righteousness in heaven.

Jerome, an early Christian scholar, partially quoted this passage, affirming its ancient recognition. Yet, the presence of the Freer Logion only in the Codex Washingtonianus makes it a subject of great interest and debate among scholars, providing a unique lens through which to view the theological and textual complexities of early Christian manuscript traditions. This exclusive addition to the Gospel of Mark highlights the diversity of early Christian texts and the ways in which scribes might have adapted or expanded the gospel narratives to address the spiritual and theological concerns of their communities.

Minuscule Greek New Testament Manuscripts

Minuscule manuscripts represent a critical era in the transmission of the New Testament texts. Unlike their uncial predecessors, which utilized a more formal, capital-letter script, minuscules were written in a flowing, cursive style that emerged around the 9th century C.E. This change in script not only marks a significant development in the history of biblical manuscripts but also reflects broader shifts in medieval scribal practices and the technological advances of the period.

Emergence and Characteristics of Minuscule Manuscripts

The shift from uncial to minuscule script occurred primarily because of the practical needs of copying speed and efficiency. Around the 9th century C.E., the demand for biblical texts increased significantly, partly due to the expansion of Christian monastic communities and the Byzantine Empire's commitment to religious education and liturgical uniformity. Minuscule writing, with its streamlined form, allowed scribes to produce texts more quickly and conserve parchment by using smaller, more compact letters.

Minuscules are not merely a stylistic evolution but also a technological adaptation. They demonstrate the medieval scribes' responses to the sociocultural and ecclesiastical demands of their time. For instance, minuscule manuscript 1739, known for its extensive catena, illustrates how these texts were used not only for liturgical reading but also for theological education, incorporating extensive exegetical works alongside the biblical texts.

Scribal Practices and the Accuracy of Textual Transmission

The production of minuscules involved complex scribal procedures that often included a team of scribes working under the supervision of a diorthotes, or corrector. This method facilitated rapid production but also introduced variations and errors into the texts. The transition to minuscule script did not eliminate these errors, but the role of the diorthotes was crucial in attempting to ensure the accuracy and conformity of the manuscripts to recognized standards.

For example, in Paul's epistles, variations among manuscripts might reflect different regional liturgical readings or theological emphases. Romans

5:1, where some manuscripts read "we have peace with God" (echomen) and others "let us have peace" (echōmen), shows how such variations can significantly affect the interpretation of a passage. This variant demonstrates the dynamic nature of textual transmission and the interplay between scribal practice and theological interpretation.

Theological and Canonical Implications

The use of minuscule manuscripts had profound implications for the development of the biblical canon and theological discourse. As these manuscripts were copied and recopied, they not only transmitted the textual content but also shaped the doctrinal interpretations through marginal notes, glosses, and other paratextual elements.

For instance, the Comma Johanneum, a contested passage in 1 John 5:7-8, is absent in most older and more authoritative manuscripts but appears in some later minuscule manuscripts. Its inclusion in the Textus Receptus and later translations like the King James Version shows how minuscule manuscripts could influence theological beliefs and liturgical practices, underscoring the importance of these texts in the history of Christian doctrine.

The Role of Minuscules in Modern Textual Criticism

Today, minuscule manuscripts are invaluable to scholars for understanding the textual history of the New Testament. Through comparative analysis, scholars can trace the evolution of text types and assess the influence of various scribal centers. This work is crucial for reconstructing the most likely original text of the New Testament scriptures.

In conclusion, while minuscule manuscripts introduced certain textual variations, their contribution to the preservation and dissemination of the New Testament cannot be overstated. They provide a window into the medieval church's scriptural heritage and are a testament to the enduring effort to transmit the sacred texts across generations.

f1 Designates a Family of Manuscripts Including 1, 118, 131, 209

The study of Family 1 (f1) manuscripts within the realm of New Testament textual criticism unveils a fascinating segment of the quest to approximate the original text of the New Testament. This family, comprising primarily minuscule manuscripts such as 1, 118, 131, and 209, offers a unique lens through which scholars can observe the textual variations and transmission patterns that have characterized the dissemination of the New Testament through centuries.

Origin and Characteristics

The concept of "families" in textual criticism refers to groups of manuscripts that share common textual characteristics, suggesting they originated from a common ancestor or were influenced by similar scribal practices. The designation f1 corresponds to a group of manuscripts identified by their shared textual peculiarities, which differentiate them from other manuscript traditions.

Kirsopp Lake's seminal work, "Texts and Studies 7" (Cambridge, 1902), was instrumental in defining and analyzing this family. Lake's research highlighted the shared features of these manuscripts, particularly in the Gospels, and traced their lineage back to a Caesarean archetype that could be dated to the third or fourth century. This early dating is significant as it situates the f1 family within a crucial period of early Christian textual transmission, offering insights into how the New Testament texts were copied, read, and circulated during this time.

Significance of the Caesarean Text-Type

The notion of a "Caesarean" text-type, associated with the region around Caesarea Maritima, where significant early Christian scholarship and textual preservation occurred, suggests that f1 manuscripts might represent a textual tradition distinct from the more widely recognized Alexandrian, Western, and Byzantine text-types. The agreement of f1 manuscripts with Codex Koridethi, particularly in the Gospel of Mark, reinforces the hypothesis of a unique, localized text tradition that contributed to the diverse textual landscape of early Christianity.

Manuscript 1: A Case Study

Manuscript 1, housed at the Universitätsbibliothek in Basel (A. N. IV, 2), is perhaps the most renowned within the f1 family, dating from the twelfth to fourteenth centuries. Its preservation and study provide critical data for understanding the transmission and evolution of the New Testament text.

The analysis of this manuscript and its counterparts within the family reveals both the preservation of certain textual readings and the introduction of variations, which are crucial for reconstructing the history of the New Testament text.

Methodological Implications for Textual Criticism

The examination of f1 manuscripts underlines the importance of comparative analysis in textual criticism. By evaluating the similarities and differences among manuscripts within this family and across other families and text-types, scholars can better assess the reliability of textual witnesses and make more informed decisions about the original wording of the New Testament.

This methodological approach is not without challenges, as it requires a careful balance between acknowledging the unique contributions of individual manuscript families and integrating these insights into a comprehensive understanding of the New Testament's textual history. The f1 family, with its distinctive characteristics and historical depth, exemplifies the complexity and richness of the manuscript tradition that textual critics must navigate.

The Quest for the Original Text

In the broader endeavor to approximate the original text of the New Testament, families like f1 play a pivotal role. They not only illuminate the textual and historical contexts within which the New Testament was transmitted but also contribute to the ongoing dialogue about the nature of the early Christian texts. Through the meticulous study of manuscript families such as f1, scholars can advance closer to understanding the nuances of the New Testament's textual evolution, ensuring a more accurate and faithful transmission of its message for future generations.

f13 Designates a Family of Manuscripts Including 13, 69, 124, 174, 230, 346, 543, 788, 826, 828, 983, 1689, 1709 (Known as the Ferrar Group)

Family 13, also known as the Ferrar Group, is a collection of Greek New Testament manuscripts that has significantly contributed to our understanding of the textual variations in the Gospels. This group, identified and studied extensively by Kirsopp and Silva Lake, represents a fascinating segment of the manuscript tradition that offers insights into the transmission of the New Testament text.

Identification and Composition of Family 13

Family 13 comprises a group of minuscule manuscripts including 13, 69, 124, 174, 230, 346, 543, 788, 826, 828, 983, 1689, and 1709. These manuscripts are primarily noted for their shared textual features and peculiar readings, suggesting a common origin or scribal practice. The most prominent of these, Manuscript 13, is housed at the Bibliothèque Nationale in Paris (Gr. 50) and dates from the eleventh to the fifteenth century.

The textual affinities of Family 13 with the so-called Caesarean text-type, traceable to an archetype thought to originate from Calabria in southern Italy or Sicily, mark it as distinct within the broader manuscript tradition. This identification suggests that the group's scribes operated within a specific geographical and cultural context that influenced their copying practices.

Textual Peculiarities and Their Implications

One of the notable features of Family 13 is the unique placement and inclusion of certain texts within the Gospels. For instance, in these manuscripts, Luke 22:43–44, which details Jesus' agony at Gethsemane, follows Matthew 26:39 instead of its traditional place in Luke. This rearrangement could suggest liturgical influences or theological emphases peculiar to the community that produced these manuscripts.

Moreover, the pericope adulterae (John 7:53–8:11), which recounts the story of the woman accused of adultery, appears after Luke 21:38 rather than after John 7:52. This placement is highly unusual and not found in most other manuscript traditions, highlighting the distinctiveness of Family 13 in the textual landscape.

Methodological Considerations in Textual Criticism

The study of Family 13 is crucial for textual critics aiming to reconstruct the original text of the New Testament. By examining the unique readings and textual variants found in these manuscripts, scholars can gain insights into the early transmission of the Gospel texts. Each variant and peculiarity provides a clue to how early Christians might have read and understood these foundational texts.

In dealing with Family 13, textual critics must carefully weigh the manuscript evidence against other textual witnesses. While the unique variants of Family 13 offer valuable insights, they also present challenges, as they may represent deviations from a more 'original' text rather than authentic readings. Thus, the task of the textual critic is not merely to catalog these differences but to evaluate their significance in the context of the entire textual tradition.

The Role of Family 13 in Establishing Textual Originality

Family 13's contribution to New Testament textual criticism lies in its capacity to illuminate the diverse ways in which the Gospel texts were transmitted and modified over time. Through a detailed examination of its peculiar readings and their relationships to other text-types, scholars can better understand the complex history of the New Testament's textual development.

This detailed analysis helps ensure that modern translations of the New Testament remain as true as possible to the original writings. The study of families like Family 13 is therefore not an academic exercise in isolation but a vital part of the ongoing effort to preserve and transmit the Christian scriptural heritage accurately and faithfully. The work with these manuscripts underscores the necessity of a meticulous and informed approach to textual criticism, grounded in a deep understanding of the manuscript evidence and its historical context.

Codex 33

Codex 33, often hailed as "the Queen of the Cursives," stands as a pivotal source in the field of New Testament textual criticism. This manuscript offers a unique lens through which to view the transmission of the biblical text, particularly due to its retention of the Alexandrian text type characteristics despite its later date.

Description and Historical Context of Codex 33

Codex 33 is housed at the Bibliothèque Nationale in Paris (Gr. 14) and dates from the ninth century C.E. Unlike many other manuscripts from this period, it contains almost the entire New Testament, except for the Book of

Revelation. Its comprehensive nature makes it an invaluable resource for textual critics who are seeking to understand the nuances of the New Testament text across different books and sections.

The manuscript was meticulously collated by Samuel Prideaux Tregelles, a renowned scholar in the field, during his work on the Greek New Testament between 1857 and 1879. Tregelles' collation of Codex 33 contributed significantly to the critical apparatus of modern New Testament editions, offering insights into the textual variants and the scribal habits of the time.

Textual Characteristics and Significance

Codex 33 is particularly noted for its Alexandrian text type, a textual family generally associated with older and often more reliable manuscripts, such as Codex Vaticanus and Codex Sinaiticus. The Alexandrian text type is characterized by a more concise and less paraphrastic style, which is considered closer to the original autographs of the New Testament writings.

The preservation of the Alexandrian text type in a ninth-century manuscript like Codex 33 is noteworthy because it exemplifies the continuity and the resilience of certain textual traditions even as scribal practices and manuscript production evolved over centuries. This makes Codex 33 a critical witness to the stability of the New Testament text over time, particularly in an era dominated by Byzantine text-type manuscripts.

Analyzing Textual Variants in Codex 33

The value of Codex 33 in textual criticism lies in its capacity to confirm or challenge readings found in other manuscript traditions. For example, in the Gospel of Matthew, Codex 33 supports certain readings that align with the older Alexandrian manuscripts, which might differ from those of the Byzantine tradition prevalent in later manuscripts. This alignment allows scholars to argue for a more original reading of the text based on its agreement with older, possibly more accurate witnesses.

Moreover, the study of Codex 33 assists in identifying scribal tendencies and errors that may have occurred during the transmission of the text. Understanding these tendencies enables textual critics to make more informed decisions about the original form of the New Testament writings.

Methodological Implications for Textual Critics

For textual critics, Codex 33 serves as a benchmark for comparing other manuscripts, particularly in evaluating the transmission fidelity of the Alexandrian tradition into the medieval period. Its text is often used in conjunction with other manuscripts to reconstruct a text closest to the original, using methods such as the local-genealogical principle in textual criticism. This principle involves analyzing variant readings within specific manuscript families to determine which variant best reflects the original text.

The study of Codex 33 underscores the importance of a meticulous and methodologically sound approach to New Testament textual criticism. By examining the characteristics and textual variants of this manuscript, scholars can continue to refine their understanding of the textual history of the New Testament and its transmission through the centuries. This rigorous examination is crucial in ensuring that contemporary translations of the New Testament are based on the most accurate and reliable text possible.

Codex 81

Codex 81, an important witness to the Alexandrian text type, provides valuable insights into the textual tradition of the Acts of the Apostles, Paul's Epistles, and the General Epistles. Its precise dating and geographical origin offer a unique opportunity to understand the transmission and preservation of New Testament writings in the medieval period.

Historical Background and Description of Codex 81

Codex 81 is housed primarily in two locations: the Greek Patriarchate in Alexandria, where 255 folios are preserved, and the British Library in London, which holds 57 folios. The manuscript is specifically dated to the year 1044 C.E., making it one of the few New Testament manuscripts with an exact medieval date. This specific dating helps scholars pinpoint the historical context of its production and use.

F.H. Scrivener's work, "An Exact Transcript of Codex Augiensis [with] a Full Collation of Fifty Manuscripts" (Cambridge, 1859), includes a detailed examination of Codex 81, highlighting its textual characteristics and comparing it with other manuscripts. Scrivener's collation has been instrumental in establishing the text of Codex 81 within the framework of New Testament textual criticism.

Textual Characteristics and Alexandrian Affiliation

Codex 81 is identified as part of the Alexandrian text type, known for its textual reliability and closer adherence to what many scholars consider the original text of the New Testament. The Alexandrian text type is less prone to the expansions and paraphrasing often found in the Byzantine text type, making manuscripts like Codex 81 crucial for critical textual analysis.

The textual fidelity of Codex 81 to the Alexandrian tradition is evident in its treatment of key New Testament passages. For instance, in Acts and the Pauline Epistles, where textual variation is particularly significant for theological interpretation and translation, Codex 81 offers readings that often align with older and more authoritative witnesses like Codex Vaticanus and Codex Sinaiticus.

Codex 81's Role in Textual Criticism

The significance of Codex 81 extends beyond its mere preservation of the text. As a medieval manuscript that aligns with an earlier text type, it serves as a bridge connecting the ancient Christian texts with later medieval and modern biblical scholarship. Its value in textual criticism lies in its ability to corroborate or challenge readings found in other manuscripts of the Alexandrian family.

For example, the precision of the text in Codex 81 can be seen in passages such as Romans 5:1, where the choice of a verb form can affect the doctrinal understanding of faith and justification. Codex 81 supports the reading "ἔχομεν" (we have), consistent with other Alexandrian manuscripts, providing a basis for arguing this as the likely original reading against the variant "ἔχωμεν" (let us have) found in some Byzantine texts.

Analyzing Variants and Establishing Textual Authenticity

The analysis of Codex 81 involves detailed comparison with other texts to identify and understand variant readings. This manuscript's adherence to the Alexandrian text type allows scholars to use it as a reference point for assessing the authenticity of various textual readings across the New Testament.

Through such comparative analysis, textual critics can approach a more refined understanding of the New Testament's original wording. Codex 81 contributes to this process by providing a text that, due to its historical and geographical origins, offers insights into the textual preferences and scribal practices of a specific Christian community in the 11th century.

In studying Codex 81, scholars engage with a manuscript that not only preserves but also reflects the theological and ecclesiastical milieu of its time. This engagement is crucial for developing a comprehensive picture of the New Testament's textual history, ensuring that modern translations and interpretations remain grounded in the most accurate historical text available.

Codex 565

Codex 565, a unique artifact of biblical manuscript tradition, provides crucial insights into the transmission of the New Testament Gospels. Its distinctiveness, marked by its use of gold letters on purple vellum, sets it apart in the realm of biblical manuscripts, underscoring its value for textual critics.

Description and Historical Context

Housed in the Public Library of Leningrad (Gr. 53), Codex 565 is a ninth-century manuscript written in gold letters on purple vellum, a style typically reserved for manuscripts of high ceremonial value. This luxurious treatment suggests that the manuscript was produced with significant ecclesiastical or imperial patronage, reflecting its importance within the Christian community of the time.

The work of Johannes Belsheim in "Christiana Videnskabs-Selskabs Forhandlinger" (1885) provided an initial collation of the text of Mark from Codex 565, with subsequent corrections and additional collation of the other three Gospels by H.S. Cronin in "Texts and Studies V" (4, Cambridge, 1899). These scholarly efforts have been pivotal in clarifying the textual characteristics and alignment of Codex 565 within broader manuscript traditions.

Textual Characteristics and Alignment with Codex Koridethi

One of the notable features of Codex 565 is its textual alignment with Codex Koridethi, particularly in the Gospel of Mark. Codex Koridethi, identified with the Caesarean text-type, suggests a textual tradition that may slightly diverge from the more dominant Alexandrian or Byzantine text-types. The alignment with Codex Koridethi indicates that Codex 565 likely shares this Caesarean heritage, which is characterized by unique readings and variants that can offer alternative insights into the text of the New Testament.

For example, in the Gospel of Mark, where Codex 565 aligns with Codex Koridethi, variations from the standard text might include different wordings or the inclusion/exclusion of certain passages. These variations are critical for scholars attempting to reconstruct the most accurate and original text of the New Testament, as they might represent earlier traditions or editorial revisions that have been lost in other text-types.

The Importance of Purple Vellum Manuscripts in Textual Criticism

The use of purple vellum and gold letters not only indicates the high value placed on Codex 565 but also impacts the preservation and legibility of the text. Manuscripts produced in this style are often more resilient to wear, allowing for better preservation of the text. This durability is crucial for textual critics, as it provides a more reliable witness to the early text of the Gospels.

Moreover, the distinctiveness of the manuscript's presentation may also reflect a particular theological or ecclesiastical emphasis, which could influence the choice of textual variants or the arrangement of texts. Understanding these factors is essential for fully appreciating the role of Codex 565 in the history of the New Testament text.

Textual Analysis and Scholarly Contributions

The contributions of scholars like Belsheim and Cronin to the study of Codex 565 have enabled a deeper understanding of its text and its relationship with other manuscripts. Through detailed collation and critical analysis, they have helped establish the textual character of Codex 565 within the New Testament manuscript tradition, aiding in the broader efforts to trace textual transmission and changes over time.

This rigorous scholarly work is indispensable for modern biblical studies, providing the foundation upon which current and future textual critics can build. The detailed examination of manuscripts such as Codex 565 not only aids in the reconstruction of the original text but also enriches our understanding of the historical and cultural contexts in which these texts were produced and used.

Codex 700

Codex 700, a significant eleventh-century Greek cursive manuscript, housed in the British Library (Egerton 2610), offers a wealth of textual variants that challenge and enrich our understanding of the Gospels' transmission. This manuscript's textual deviations from the Textus Receptus, particularly in passages such as the Lord's Prayer, highlight its critical role in the field of New Testament textual criticism.

Historical Context and Manuscript Description

Codex 700 dates to the eleventh century and contains the Gospels. Its importance was underscored by H.C. Hoskier in his work "A Full Account and Collation of the Greek Cursive Codex Evangelium 604" (London, 1890), which detailed the extensive differences between this codex and the Textus Receptus. Notably, Codex 700 diverges from the Textus Receptus nearly 2,750 times, indicating a rich tradition of textual variants that may reflect earlier, less standardized forms of the Gospel texts.

Textual Characteristics and Variants

The significant number of variants in Codex 700 is crucial for understanding the textual fluidity of the Gospels during the medieval period. One of the most striking variants is found in the Lord's Prayer (Luke 11:2), where the manuscript presents a version that differs markedly from that found in the majority of Byzantine texts and the Textus Receptus. Such variants are not merely scribal errors but may represent alternative textual traditions that coexisted and were transmitted alongside more familiar versions.

These variants are instrumental for textual critics in constructing a more nuanced and comprehensive picture of the New Testament's textual history. They challenge the primacy of the Textus Receptus and underscore the diversity of the textual tradition, reflecting theological, liturgical, and regional differences that influenced how the texts were copied and read.

Analyzing the Lord's Prayer Variant

In Luke 11:2, Codex 700 presents unique readings that can significantly affect the theological understanding of the prayer. For example, if the doxology commonly found in later manuscripts ("For yours is the kingdom, and the power, and the glory, forever, Amen") is absent, it could reflect a closer adherence to what might have been the original text, as the earliest manuscripts and several other ancient witnesses do not include this doxology.

This kind of variant not only affects liturgical practice but also theological interpretation, providing insights into how early Christians understood and practiced their faith. The examination of such differences enables scholars to propose theories of textual transmission and to hypothesize about the origins and movements of different text types across the Christian world.

Methodological Considerations in Textual Criticism

The study of Codex 700 illustrates the methodological complexity of New Testament textual criticism. Scholars must weigh the manuscript evidence from Codex 700 against other manuscripts, considering factors such as geographical origin, the manuscript's age, and the context of its use. This process involves detailed comparative analysis, not only with the Textus Receptus but also with other text types like the Alexandrian or Western, to determine which readings might be closest to the original texts of the New Testament.

Such analysis is crucial for creating a critical edition of the New Testament that reflects the original words as closely as possible. By examining manuscripts like Codex 700, textual critics engage in a detailed reassessment of accepted readings, challenging and refining the textual base used for modern biblical translations.

Codex 1424 (or Family 1424)

Codex 1424, also known as Family 1424, is a significant manuscript in the field of New Testament textual criticism. This manuscript, along with its related family, offers a comprehensive look into the textual variants and scribal traditions that have influenced the transmission of the New Testament text from the ninth or tenth century.

Description and Historical Context of Codex 1424

Codex 1424 is housed at the Jesuit-Krauss-McCormick Library in Maywood, Illinois (Gruber Ms. 152). Dating from the ninth or tenth century, it encompasses a wide range of New Testament books including the Gospels, Acts, General Epistles, Paul's Epistles, and Revelation. The breadth of this manuscript makes it particularly valuable for studying the textual history of the New Testament as a whole.

The manuscript belongs to a larger group of texts, designated as Family 1424, which includes several other manuscripts that share a substantially similar text. These manuscripts include M, 7, 27, 71, 115, 160, 179, 185, 267, 349, 517, 659, 692, 827, 945, 954, 990, 1010, 1082, 1188, 1194, 1207, 1223, 1293, 1391, 1402, 1606, 1675, 2191. The identification of these manuscripts as a family is based on shared textual characteristics that suggest a common source or a shared geographical and historical context.

Textual Characteristics of Family 1424

Family 1424 is characterized by specific readings and textual variants that set it apart from other manuscript families. These unique features provide insights into the scribal practices and the theological preferences of the community responsible for its production. For example, variations in the rendering of key passages, like those found in the Gospels, can reflect theological interpretations that were favored in the region or community where these manuscripts were copied.

The study of these variants is crucial for textual critics aiming to reconstruct the original text of the New Testament. Each manuscript in Family 1424 offers a piece of the puzzle, contributing to a more comprehensive understanding of the textual transmission through centuries.

Methodological Approach to Studying Codex 1424

The approach to studying Codex 1424 and its family involves a detailed collation of the textual variants found across its related manuscripts. By comparing these texts, scholars can identify common errors, omissions, or additions that may have arisen during the copying process. This comparative analysis helps in understanding the scribal habits and the degree of textual fidelity maintained within the family.

For example, the presence of a unique reading in Codex 1424 that is consistently mirrored in other members of the family but absent in other manuscript traditions might suggest that this reading reflects a local textual tradition or a scribal correction that became standardized in this particular family. Such findings are integral to debates about textual authenticity and the reconstruction of the earliest attainable text of the New Testament.

Analyzing Textual Variants in the Context of Codex 1424

One practical application of studying Family 1424 involves examining how textual decisions made by the scribes of these manuscripts influence modern interpretations of biblical passages. For instance, if a significant variant in the Epistles affects the understanding of Pauline theology, knowing the variant's origin and its prevalence in Family 1424 can provide crucial context for interpreting Paul's intent and message.

The examination of Codex 1424 within its familial context underscores the importance of manuscript evidence in resolving textual and theological questions within the New Testament. By assessing the contributions of Codex 1424 and its family to the textual tradition, scholars can better understand the development of the New Testament text and enhance the accuracy of contemporary biblical translations. This in-depth study ensures that the translations used in modern worship and study reflect the most reliable reconstruction of the original texts.

Codex 1739

Codex 1739, housed in the Lavra monastery on Mount Athos (B^42), is a tenth-century manuscript recognized for its remarkable textual integrity and its importance in the study of the Acts and Epistles. Its textual lineage offers a unique window into the early Christian scriptural tradition and provides critical insights for New Testament textual criticism.

Historical Context and Manuscript Description

Codex 1739 is a significant manuscript not only because of its age but also due to the origin of its text. According to a colophon in the manuscript, the scribe copied it from an earlier fourth-century manuscript that was housed in the library of Pamphilus at Caesarea, which is known to have contained texts corrected to conform with the Origenian (Hexaplaric) standard. This direct connection to an early and respected textual tradition enhances the value of Codex 1739 for textual critics, especially concerning the Pauline epistles.

Textual Affinities and Its Implications

The work of Morton S. Enslin, presented in "Six Collations of New Testament Manuscripts," edited by Kirsopp Lake and Silva New (Harvard

Theological Studies 17; Cambridge, Mass., 1932), and the analysis by Zuntz highlight the textual affinities between Codex 1739, Papyrus 46 (P46), and Codex Vaticanus (B). These manuscripts collectively demonstrate a clear lineage, which Zuntz argues, preserves a high-quality text form dating back to around 200 C.E., much earlier than the physical manuscripts themselves.

This relationship is particularly significant for understanding the transmission of the Pauline epistles. The alignment of Codex 1739 with such early and important manuscripts as P46 and Vaticanus supports the notion that it carries a text not significantly divergent from that of the early Christian community. This suggests that the theological content, particularly in the Pauline epistles, is well preserved and minimally altered over the centuries.

Methodological Importance in Textual Criticism

Codex 1739's affinity with known early texts like P46 and B is crucial for the methodology of textual criticism. It serves as a bridge manuscript, connecting the textual traditions of the early fourth century and later Byzantine texts. By analyzing the variants and commonalities in Codex 1739, scholars can trace how the texts were transmitted, how they evolved, and how they were preserved or altered through scribal copying practices.

For instance, examining passages such as Romans 5:1 in Codex 1739 and comparing its readings with those in P46 and Vaticanus can clarify which variants are likely to be closest to the original writings of Paul. Such comparisons are essential for constructing a reliable text of the New Testament, particularly in translations and editions used for teaching, preaching, and personal study.

Analyzing Variants in Codex 1739

The detailed study of Codex 1739 provides valuable insights into specific textual variations and their implications for biblical interpretation. For example, the treatment of key doctrinal passages in the Epistles, which discuss concepts such as justification, sanctification, and the nature of Christ, can be better understood by examining the textual witnesses of Codex 1739 alongside its related manuscripts.

By leveraging the textual evidence from Codex 1739, scholars can more confidently address questions about the original form of the Pauline epistles and other New Testament writings. This approach not only aids in the resolution of textual discrepancies but also enhances our understanding of the early Christian doctrinal landscape.

Codex 2053

Codex 2053, housed in the Messian Biblioteca Universitario (99), stands out as a critical text for the study of the Book of Revelation, particularly when analyzed within the framework of New Testament textual criticism. This thirteenth-century manuscript not only contains the text of Revelation but also includes Oecumenius's commentary, offering unique insights into the interpretative traditions and textual transmission of this apocalyptic book.

Historical and Textual Overview of Codex 2053

Codex 2053 is noted for its comprehensive authority on the Book of Revelation as asserted by Josef Schmid in his work, "Studien zur Geschichte des griechischen Apokalypse-Textes" (vol. 2; Munich, 1955). According to Schmid, this manuscript, along with others such as Codices A and C 2344, provides one of the clearest and most reliable textual witnesses for Revelation, which is crucial given the complexity and variant-rich nature of Revelation's textual history.

The inclusion of Oecumenius's commentary within Codex 2053 is particularly significant. Oecumenius's work represents one of the earliest systematic commentaries on Revelation and reflects the exegetical methods and theological concerns of the early Byzantine period. This commentary not only enriches our understanding of the interpretative context in which the Book of Revelation was read and understood but also offers insights into how the text was received and theologically engaged by early commentators.

Textual Characteristics and Contributions to Textual Criticism

The textual content of Codex 2053 provides a critical resource for scholars seeking to understand the transmission and preservation of the text of Revelation. Its value lies in its ability to corroborate or challenge other textual witnesses from different manuscript traditions. For example, in passages where the text of Revelation is known to vary significantly among manuscripts—such as the number of the Beast (Revelation 13:18), where some manuscripts read "666" while others read "616"—Codex 2053's readings can provide decisive evidence for determining the most likely original text.

Furthermore, the presence of commentary alongside the biblical text in Codex 2053 allows scholars to see how textual variants might have influenced early biblical interpretation. For instance, interpretations of symbolic numbers, imagery, and prophetic announcements in Revelation could differ based on slight textual variations, and Oecumenius's commentary provides context for understanding these variations.

Methodological Significance in Establishing Textual Authenticity

The study of Codex 2053 employs a comprehensive textual analysis, comparing its readings with those of other key manuscripts such as Codices Alexandrinus (A) and Ephraemi Rescriptus (C), as well as later manuscripts like C 2344. This comparative approach is essential in textual criticism, particularly for a text as complex and symbolically rich as Revelation.

For example, examining how Codex 2053 treats the eschatological promises and warnings found in Revelation can help establish a text that is closest to what John might have originally penned. Revelation 21:5, which proclaims, "Behold, I make all things new," serves as a poignant example. Variants in the wording and ordering of this verse across different manuscripts can significantly affect its theological emphasis and interpretative clarity.

By integrating the textual data from Codex 2053 with that from other manuscripts, textual critics can better argue for a reconstructed text that faithfully represents the original as John might have written it. This is crucial not only for academic study but also for theological application, as the text of Revelation plays a significant role in Christian eschatology.

In studying Codex 2053, scholars harness a manuscript that encapsulates both the text of Revelation and its early exegetical tradition, providing a dual lens through which to view both the history and the interpretation of one of the New Testament's most enigmatic books. This manuscript thus serves not only as a witness to the text of Revelation but also as a gateway to understanding its early theological reception and interpretative challenges.

Codex 2344

Codex 2344, preserved in the Bibliothèque Nationale in Paris (Coislin Gr. 18), stands as a significant eleventh-century manuscript encompassing Acts, the General Epistles, Paul's Epistles, and particularly the Book of Revelation. This manuscript's authority, especially for the text of Revelation, has been notably affirmed by Josef Schmid in "Studien zur Geschichte des griechischen Apokalypse-Textes" (vol. 2; Munich, 1955).

Historical Context and Manuscript Description

Codex 2344 is noted for its comprehensive inclusion of several New Testament books, making it an invaluable resource for the study of textual variations across different biblical texts. Its dating to the eleventh century places it within a period of significant manuscript production, where scribes often engaged deeply with the theological and ecclesiastical traditions that influenced their work. This context is crucial for understanding the manuscript's textual choices, especially in its rendition of the apocalyptic literature.

Textual Characteristics of Codex 2344

Codex 2344's significance in textual criticism particularly shines in its treatment of the Book of Revelation. Schmid's analysis positions this manuscript alongside Codex 2053 and others as authoritative for this complex text, known for its rich symbolic language and challenging textual history. Revelation's text in Codex 2344 is aligned with the commentaries of Andreas of Caesarea, indicating its adherence to a particular interpretative tradition which was influential in shaping the transmission of the Apocalypse.

For instance, Revelation 13:18, which discusses the number of the Beast, presents a textual variant where the number "666" is sometimes recorded as "616" in other manuscripts. Codex 2344's adherence to the Andreas commentary tradition may support the more common "666," aligning it with the majority text and differing from the textual tradition found in manuscripts like Codex Ephraemi Rescriptus (C).

Methodological Considerations in Textual Criticism

The study of Codex 2344 involves a meticulous comparison of its texts against those of other manuscripts categorized under similar traditions, such as those labeled as MA (manuscripts following Andreas of Caesarea's text) and MK (manuscripts displaying the Koine or Byzantine text type). This differentiation is crucial in textual criticism, as it helps establish a clearer lineage and textual affiliation, particularly for the interpretation of apocalyptic literature where textual stability is paramount.

The analysis of Codex 2344's text, especially within the framework of Revelation, allows scholars to discern subtle but significant variations that can alter theological interpretations. For example, the depiction of eschatological themes in Revelation can be contrasted against theological positions found in other scriptural texts, like Daniel's visions (Daniel 7-12), to provide a broader understanding of prophetic literature across the Testaments.

Analyzing Textual Variants and Theological Implications

The detailed examination of variants in Codex 2344, especially those that diverge from the Textus Receptus (TR), offers insights into the early Christian community's reception and understanding of biblical texts. For instance, variants in key passages that discuss salvation and judgment provide a richer texture to the theological debates that might have existed among early Christians, as seen in passages like Revelation 20:12-15, which speaks about the final judgment.

By considering how Codex 2344 aligns or diverges from other textual traditions, scholars can better understand the manuscript's role in the transmission and preservation of New Testament writings. This examination is not only vital for establishing the most authentic text of the New Testament but also for appreciating the depth and diversity of early Christian theological reflection.

Ancient Versions of the Greek New Testament

The translation of the New Testament from Greek into various languages has been a pivotal aspect of Christian history, allowing the spread of Christian teachings beyond the Hellenistic world. These translations have also been crucial for textual criticism, offering insights into early textual traditions and interpretations.

THE EARLY CHRISTIAN COPYISTS OF THE NEW TESTAMENT

Early Translations: Syriac and Latin Versions

The translations of the New Testament into Syriac and Latin mark significant early efforts to make the scriptures accessible to non-Greek-speaking Christian communities. The Syriac translations began as early as the second century C.E., with notable texts such as Tatian's Diatessaron, a harmony of the four Gospels. The Diatessaron, possibly first written in Greek and later translated into Syriac by Tatian himself, became influential in Syriac-speaking churches. Although the original Greek version is lost, references and quotations in other works, such as those by Ephraem in the fourth century, indicate its once widespread use.

By contrast, the Old Syriac versions of the Gospels, such as the Curetonian and the Sinaitic, provide direct translations from Greek and are believed to have originated around 200 C.E. These manuscripts are significant for showing an early stage of the text that may differ from the later Byzantine tradition preserved in the majority of Greek manuscripts. The Peshitta, emerging around the fifth century C.E., eventually became the standard Syriac Bible, including the New Testament, and integrated books that were previously omitted in earlier versions.

The Latin translations began no later than the end of the second century C.E. with the Vetus Latina (Old Latin), which represents a variety of Latin translations made before Jerome's Vulgate. These translations were crucial for early Western Christianity, especially in regions such as North Africa and later Rome. The Vetus Latina versions are diverse, reflecting a range of textual traditions that provide valuable insights into the text of the New Testament as it was known in different parts of the Roman Empire.

The Role of Jerome's Vulgate

Jerome's revision of the Old Latin text, which resulted in the Vulgate, began in 383 C.E., starting with the Gospels. This work extended over several decades and included translations of the Hebrew Scriptures directly from Hebrew texts, a novel approach at the time which aimed at improving the accuracy of the Latin text. Jerome's translation, particularly his Gospels and Psalms, eventually gained acceptance and became the standard Latin text of the Church, officially recognized by the Council of Trent in the sixteenth century.

Jerome's meticulous approach to translation, including his reliance on Hebrew and Greek texts, provides an invaluable witness to the biblical text as it was understood in the early fifth century. His work is especially important for understanding how scriptural texts were transmitted and interpreted within the Church.

Impact of Translations on Textual Criticism

The various ancient translations of the New Testament play a crucial role in textual criticism, as they often preserve readings that may be closer to the original autographs than those found in the later Byzantine text tradition. Comparisons among these versions and the Greek manuscripts can reveal variations that are critical for reconstructing the original text of the New Testament.

For instance, variations in the rendering of key theological terms and passages in the different versions can shed light on how early interpretations and doctrinal positions might have influenced the transmission of the text. Such studies are essential for understanding the development of Christian doctrine and the textual history of the New Testament.

In summary, the translation of the Greek New Testament into languages like Syriac and Latin was not merely a linguistic or cultural phenomenon but a complex process influenced by theological, ecclesiastical, and practical considerations. These translations have preserved unique textual witnesses that are indispensable for modern scholars seeking to reconstruct the most authentic text of the New Testament. Through the diligent comparison and analysis of these ancient versions, textual critics continue to gain deeper insights into the early Christian world and the transmission of its sacred writings.

The Syriac Versions

The translation of the New Testament into Syriac represents a significant development in the history of biblical texts, facilitating the spread of Christianity throughout the Syriac-speaking regions. These translations not only helped shape Christian liturgy and theology in these areas but also offer critical insights into the textual variants and the history of the New Testament's transmission.

Early Translations and Their Implications

Syriac, a dialect of Aramaic and closely related to Hebrew, became a major medium for Christian scriptures by the second century C.E. The city of Edessa (modern-day Urfa, Turkey), known for its early Christian community, emerged as a center for Syriac Christianity. This context is vital for understanding the emergence of the Syriac versions of the New Testament, which include the Old Syriac Gospels, the Diatessaron, and ultimately, the Peshitta.

1. **Old Syriac Gospels**: The earliest Syriac translations of the New Testament are found in the Old Syriac versions, specifically the Curetonian and Sinaitic manuscripts. These texts, dating from the fourth and fifth centuries but likely representing translations from around 200 C.E., are crucial for understanding the early Syriac textual tradition. They exhibit unique readings that provide alternative textual witnesses to the Greek New Testament.

2. **Diatessaron**: Tatian's Diatessaron, a second-century harmony of the four Gospels, played a pivotal role in the dissemination of the gospel narratives in a cohesive and continuous story. Although originally composed in Greek, its Syriac translation significantly influenced the Syriac-speaking churches and helped standardize Christian teachings across diverse communities.

The Peshitta: Standardization and Textual Characteristics

By the fifth century, the Peshitta became the standard Syriac translation of the Bible, including the New Testament. Its name, meaning "simple" or "clear," possibly reflects its approach to translation—straightforward and accessible to the general populace.

1. **Canonical Scope**: The Peshitta includes all the New Testament books except Second Peter, Second and Third John, Jude, and Revelation, reflecting the canonical preferences of the Syrian churches at the time.

2. **Textual Fidelity and Variants**: The Peshitta is noted for its literal approach to translation, particularly in books like the Pentateuch. However, its treatment of poetic and prophetic books, such as Psalms and the Minor Prophets, shows a freer translation style. This diversity in translation approach provides insights into the interpretative strategies of the translators and the textual preferences of the early Syriac Christian community.

Later Developments and Scholarly Contributions

In the sixth century, the Philoxenian version was commissioned by Philoxenus, the bishop of Mabbug, to revise the Peshitta based on Greek manuscripts. This version included the lesser General Epistles and Revelation, filling in the gaps left by the Peshitta in terms of canonical coverage.

1. **The Harclean Version**: In 616, Thomas of Harkel revised the Philoxenian version, creating a highly literal translation that adhered closely to the Greek text. This version is particularly valued for its adherence to the Greek source, providing a text that is often less interpretatively colored than other translations.
2. **Textual Scholarship**: The work on these Syriac versions has significantly contributed to our understanding of the New Testament's textual history. The variants and unique readings found in these texts are often used to support or challenge readings in the Greek manuscripts, helping scholars reconstruct the most authentic text of the New Testament.

In summary, the Syriac versions of the New Testament are invaluable for their witness to the early text of the Christian scriptures, their role in the Christianization of the Syriac-speaking world, and their contribution to our understanding of early Christian theology and liturgical practices. By examining these versions, scholars gain a deeper insight into the complexities of biblical textual transmission and the dynamic nature of scripture in the early Christian centuries.

The Latin Versions

The Latin translations of the New Testament hold a pivotal role in the history of Christian scripture, significantly influencing both the religious and cultural landscape of the Western world. From the earliest Old Latin versions to Jerome's Vulgate, these translations have shaped theological discourse and helped disseminate Christian doctrine throughout the Roman Empire and beyond.

Early Latin Versions and Their Development

The need for translations of the New Testament into Latin arose primarily in the Christian communities of North Africa and other non-

Greek-speaking regions of the Roman Empire. By the end of the second century C.E., Latin versions of the Scriptures were already in circulation, as evidenced by the writings of early Church Fathers like Tertullian and Cyprian. These Old Latin versions were characterized by their diversity, reflecting various local texts and theological traditions.

1. **Translation Dynamics**: The Old Latin versions were not uniform; different books of the New Testament were translated at different times by different translators, resulting in a considerable variety of textual forms. This diversity is particularly evident in the variant readings and the freedom translators took in rendering the Greek text into Latin, which often led to significant discrepancies between manuscripts.

2. **Scriptural Quotations by Church Fathers**: Tertullian and Cyprian's extensive use of these versions illustrates their widespread acceptance within the early Latin-speaking Christian communities. Their quotations from the New Testament show that the Old Latin texts they used could vary considerably, indicating that there was no standardized Latin version of the Scriptures at this time.

Jerome's Vulgate: Creation and Impact

The diversity and sometimes questionable quality of the Old Latin versions prompted the need for a revised and more consistent Latin translation. This led to Jerome's commission by Pope Damasus in 383 C.E. to produce what would become the Vulgate—destined to be the definitive Latin version of the Bible for centuries.

1. **Jerome's Methodology**: Jerome's approach was to revise the existing Old Latin text, correcting it against the best available Greek manuscripts rather than producing a completely new translation. His work began with the Gospels, prioritizing fidelity to the source texts while also considering the liturgical and doctrinal needs of the Church.

2. **Textual and Theological Influence**: Jerome's Vulgate standardized many of the key theological terms that are still in use today, such as "justification," "sanctification," and "inspiration." This standardization helped unify Christian doctrine across different regions and was instrumental in the development of Western Christianity.

Textual Variants and Their Implications

The Latin versions, particularly the Vulgate, are crucial for textual criticism due to their preservation of readings that are sometimes older than those found in the Greek manuscripts. For instance:

1. **Comparison with Greek Texts**: Variants in the Vulgate and Old Latin versions are often compared with Greek texts to help determine the most likely original reading. For example, in Matthew 3:16, the Old Latin manuscript 'a' adds a detail about a light flashing forth at Jesus' baptism, a reading not found in most Greek texts but which reflects early interpretive traditions.

2. **Theological Impact**: The translation choices made in the Latin versions have had a profound impact on Christian theology, particularly in the Western Church. The rendering of Greek theological terms into Latin influenced not only religious language but also the development of Christian thought.

In sum, the Latin translations of the New Testament, from the diverse Old Latin texts to Jerome's unified Vulgate, have significantly impacted the theological, cultural, and textual history of the Christian scriptures. Their study provides essential insights into the early transmission of the New Testament and the development of Christian doctrine, underscoring the complex interplay between text, interpretation, and community belief systems. Through these translations, the New Testament was not only preserved but also made accessible to a broader audience, facilitating the spread of Christianity throughout the Roman Empire and shaping the spiritual life of countless generations.

The Coptic Versions

The Coptic versions of the New Testament represent a crucial phase in the transmission of Christian texts, reflecting both the linguistic and theological nuances of early Egyptian Christianity. These translations are pivotal for understanding how the New Testament was interpreted and used in different Christian communities outside the Greco-Roman mainstream.

Origins and Characteristics of Coptic Translations

Coptic, which developed from the ancient Egyptian language, was adapted to use a script predominantly based on Greek letters to meet the needs of Egyptian Christians. This adaptation facilitated the translation of the New Testament into Coptic, which began in earnest by the third century C.E. and involved incorporating a significant number of Greek terms related to Christian doctrine.

1. **Dialectal Diversity**: The translations of the New Testament were conducted in several Coptic dialects, each corresponding to different regions of Egypt. The primary dialects in which the New Testament was translated include Sahidic and Bohairic, with Sahidic being the most widespread in Upper Egypt and Bohairic in Lower Egypt. Each dialect's version of the New Testament not only reflects linguistic differences but also varying theological emphases and interpretative traditions.

2. **Sahidic Coptic**: Often considered the classical form of Coptic, Sahidic was the first dialect into which substantial portions of the Bible were translated. It is characterized by its archaic and conservative features, which make it particularly valuable for textual criticism. Sahidic manuscripts are among the oldest and most important witnesses to the text of the New Testament in Coptic.

The Role of Coptic Versions in Textual Criticism

The Coptic translations of the New Testament are indispensable for scholars attempting to reconstruct the original text of the New Testament. They provide comparative material against which Greek manuscripts can be evaluated, especially in instances where the Greek textual tradition shows significant variations.

1. **Textual Variants and Alignments**: The Coptic versions often preserve readings that differ from those found in the majority of Greek manuscripts. For example, variations in the Coptic translations can illuminate how certain passages were understood in different cultural and theological contexts. These differences are crucial for understanding the development of the New Testament text and the early Church's theology.

2. **Comparative Analysis**: By comparing the Greek and Coptic texts, scholars can identify potential errors in the transmission of the text and more accurately infer the New Testament authors' original wording. This is particularly true in cases where Coptic versions align with other early versions, such as the Latin or Syriac, against the later Byzantine text type predominant in Greek manuscripts.

Theological and Cultural Implications

The translation of the New Testament into Coptic not only facilitated the spread of Christianity in Egypt but also shaped the theological and liturgical life of the Coptic Church. The use of Coptic in liturgy and theology allowed for the expression of Christian doctrine in terms that were culturally and linguistically accessible to the Egyptian populace.

1. **Integration of Greek Terms**: The inclusion of Greek words in the Coptic translations, particularly those related to Christian life and worship, underscores the deep interaction between Hellenistic culture and Egyptian Christianity. This blend of linguistic elements helped articulate Christian theology in a way that was both faithful to its origins and resonant with the local cultural context.

2. **Ecclesiastical Usage**: Bohairic, the later dialect, eventually became the standard liturgical language of the Coptic Orthodox Church, reflecting both its theological significance and its role in unifying the Coptic Christian community under a common liturgical and scriptural tradition.

In summary, the Coptic versions of the New Testament are vital for both historical theology and biblical textual criticism. They illuminate how the New Testament was received, interpreted, and used in one of early Christianity's most vibrant communities. The study of these versions continues to reveal the complex ways in which the sacred texts were adapted to meet the spiritual and cultural needs of diverse Christian populations.

The Gothic Version

The translation of the New Testament into Gothic by Ulfilas in the fourth century represents a pivotal moment in the Christianization of the Gothic tribes and the transmission of biblical texts in ancient Germanic languages. This version not only facilitated the spread of Christianity among the Goths but also offers valuable insights into the linguistic and cultural adaptations of Scripture.

Background and Impact of the Gothic Translation

The Goths, divided into the Visigoths and Ostrogoths, played a significant role in the transformation of the Roman Empire into medieval Europe. Ulfilas, a missionary bishop, undertook the monumental task of translating the Scriptures into Gothic, creating not only a translation but also an alphabet to accommodate this purpose.

1. **Ulfilas's Translation**: Born to a Gothic and Cappadocian heritage, Ulfilas was consecrated as a bishop for the Goths around 341 CE after his education and conversion in Constantinople. His translation of the New Testament excluded the books of Samuel and Kings to avoid encouraging the martial tendencies of the Goths with tales of war and conquest. His efforts produced the first and only substantial scriptural text in the Gothic language, which includes nearly half of the Gospels and some complete Pauline Epistles.

2. **Linguistic Innovations**: Ulfilas's alphabet, primarily derived from Greek and Latin characters with some runes, was crucial for the Gothic translation. This script enabled the transcription of the Gothic language and its sounds that were not present in Greek, facilitating a more accurate and accessible scripture for the Gothic people.

Textual Characteristics and Theological Implications

The Gothic version, primarily known through the Codex Argenteus, is critical for understanding early Germanic linguistic and theological contexts. This version reflects Ulfilas's Arian theological leanings, as evidenced by certain translational choices that subtly align with Arian doctrine.

1. **Codex Argenteus**: The Silver Codex, written in silver and gold ink on purple parchment, contains the four Gospels in the Western order. This codex is particularly notable for its lavish presentation and the preservation of Ulfilas's translation. The text arrangement and the inclusion of specific scriptural interpretations highlight the theological and liturgical priorities of the Gothic Christian community.

2. **Theological Adaptations**: The Gothic version's text sometimes deviates from the Greek original to conform to Arian interpretations, particularly in Christological passages. These variations are crucial for scholars studying the theological disputes and Christological understandings of the time.

Contribution to Textual Criticism and Historical Theology

The Gothic version's role in textual criticism involves its use as a comparative text against Greek and Latin manuscripts. The unique readings found in the Gothic version can sometimes support or challenge readings in other textual traditions, offering insights into the early text of the New Testament.

1. **Comparative Analysis**: By examining how the Gothic version renders certain passages, scholars can trace the textual history and transmission of the New Testament. For instance, variations in key doctrinal passages help identify how early Christians across different regions understood foundational Christian teachings.
2. **Cultural and Linguistic Influence**: The Gothic Bible also sheds light on the linguistic development of the Germanic languages and their early literary culture. The translation strategies employed by Ulfilas influenced the development of other Germanic vernacular literature.

In summary, the Gothic version of the New Testament stands as a monumental achievement in the history of biblical translation. It not only enabled the spread of Christianity among the Gothic tribes but also preserved a unique linguistic and theological heritage that continues to be of significant interest for biblical scholars and historians alike. The study of this version provides essential insights into the intersection of language, theology, and culture in the Christianization of Europe.

The Armenian Version

The Armenian version of the New Testament holds a unique place in the history of biblical translations, emerging from a context where Christianity was officially embraced at a national level early in its history. This translation not only served the spiritual needs of the Armenian people but also helped in shaping the Armenian literary tradition.

Creation of the Armenian Script and Initial Translations

The need for an Armenian version of the Scriptures coincided with the creation of the Armenian alphabet by Mesrop Mashtots around 406 CE. This development was crucial for the Christianization of Armenia and the subsequent cultural and religious consolidation.

1. **Foundational Figures**: Mesrop, aided by Sahak, played pivotal roles in translating the New Testament into Armenian. Their work began shortly after the alphabet's invention, with the translation of the Book of Proverbs, followed by the New Testament and other biblical texts. These translations were primarily based on Greek manuscripts, reflecting the strong Hellenistic influence on early Armenian Christianity.

2. **Translation Process**: The translation efforts involved sending scholars to major Christian centers to gather necessary texts, indicating a rigorous scholarly approach to ensuring the accuracy and authenticity of the translations. The involvement of Greek and Syriac sources highlights the diverse influences that shaped the Armenian biblical text.

Characteristics of the Armenian New Testament

The Armenian version is noted for its extensive manuscript tradition, which surpasses almost all other ancient versions except the Latin Vulgate. This rich manuscript culture provides significant insights into the early text of the New Testament and the theological inclinations of the Armenian Church.

1. **Textual Features**: Armenian manuscripts often include books and passages not found in the canonical texts of other traditions, such as the Third Epistle to the Corinthians and various apocryphal writings. This inclusion reflects both the cultural openness of the Armenian Church and its connections to broader Christian traditions.

2. **Affinity with Greek and Syriac Texts**: While primarily based on Greek texts, the Armenian version also shows influences from the Syriac tradition. This is evident in the inclusion of certain apocryphal books and the textual variants that align with Syriac versions. The complex interplay between these textual traditions offers valuable perspectives for textual critics studying the transmission and reception of the New Testament.

Manuscript Tradition and Historical Insights

Armenian manuscripts are invaluable not only for their textual content but also for the colophons they contain, which offer historical insights and witness to the text's transmission history.

1. **Colophons and Historical Annotations**: Many Armenian manuscripts feature detailed colophons that provide historical context, production details, and sometimes unique textual information, such as the identification of the long ending of Mark as possibly being authored by Aristion. These notes are crucial for understanding the historical and cultural context in which these manuscripts were produced.

2. **Significance of Manuscript Evidence**: The presence or absence of certain passages, such as the long ending of Mark, in over a hundred Armenian manuscripts ending at Mark 16:8, contributes significantly to debates about the original scope of the New Testament writings. Such evidence is critical for discussions on the canon and the textual integrity of the New Testament.

In conclusion, the Armenian versions of the New Testament are a cornerstone of Christian textual history, embodying the theological, linguistic, and cultural journey of the Armenian people. The translation efforts by figures like Mesrop and Sahak not only Christianized Armenia but also fostered a unique literary and religious tradition that continues to be studied for its contributions to our understanding of early Christian texts and their transmission across different cultures and languages.

The Georgian Version

The Georgian version of the New Testament is a significant testament to the early Christianization of the Caucasus region and reflects the complex interplay of linguistic, cultural, and theological factors that influenced early Christian texts.

Introduction of Christianity and Development of the Georgian Script

Christianity was established in the region of ancient Iberia, now modern Georgia, around the middle of the fourth century, largely attributed to the missionary efforts of Saint Nino. The conversion of the Georgian people led to the need for the Scriptures in the Georgian language, necessitating the creation of a unique alphabet.

1. **Creation of the Georgian Alphabet**: The development of the Georgian script was crucial for translating religious texts into the vernacular. According to tradition, Saint Mesrop Mashtots, who also

created the Armenian alphabet, was instrumental in developing the Georgian script. This new script enabled the translation of the Bible and other Christian texts, thus fostering literacy and theological education among the Georgian populace.

2. **Early Translations**: The first translations of the New Testament into Georgian are believed to have been made from Greek, although influences from Armenian and Syriac sources are also possible given the geographic and cultural proximity of these regions. These initial translations likely occurred by the fifth century, with continuous revisions and standardizations over the following centuries.

Textual Transmission and Manuscript Tradition

The Georgian manuscripts of the New Testament are valuable for their textual criticism contributions, offering unique readings and insights into the early text of the Christian Scriptures.

1. **Manuscript Evidence**: The oldest extant Georgian manuscripts of the New Testament date back to the ninth and tenth centuries, with earlier fragments indicating a robust tradition of biblical transmission. The script style used in these manuscripts, ranging from ecclesiastical majuscule to minuscule, provides clues about their dating and the textual traditions they represent.

2. **Philological and Textual Revisions**: Throughout its history, the Georgian New Testament underwent several revisions to refine the translation and align it more closely with the source texts. These revisions are evident in the varying linguistic styles and textual choices observed in different manuscripts, reflecting both the evolution of the Georgian language and the theological preferences of the translators.

St. Euthymius's Contributions and the Canonical Status of Revelation

A significant development in the history of the Georgian New Testament was the work of St. Euthymius of the Georgian monastery on Mount Athos in the late tenth century. His efforts were pivotal in translating and canonizing books of the New Testament that were previously excluded from the Georgian biblical canon.

1. **Translation of Revelation**: St. Euthymius is credited with translating the Book of Revelation into Georgian, a text that had not been considered canonical by the Georgian Church until then. His translation marked a crucial expansion of the Georgian biblical canon and reflected a broader acceptance of the full corpus of the New Testament within the Georgian Christian community.
2. **Literary and Cultural Impact**: The inclusion of Revelation and the revision of the Georgian New Testament by St. Euthymius significantly influenced Georgian spiritual and literary life. This period marked a renaissance of theological scholarship and textual criticism within Georgia, paralleling similar developments in Byzantium and the wider Christian world.

In summary, the Georgian version of the New Testament exemplifies the dynamic and complex process of scriptural translation within a unique linguistic and cultural context. The development of the Georgian script and the subsequent translations of the New Testament not only facilitated the spread of Christianity in Georgia but also enriched the Georgian literary and theological heritage. The manuscripts and their revisions highlight the ongoing interaction between text, tradition, and translation in the preservation and interpretation of sacred texts.

The Ethiopic Version

The Ethiopic version of the New Testament, known as Ge'ez, occupies a distinctive place in the textual history of biblical scriptures. This version is deeply intertwined with the religious and cultural history of Ethiopia, reflecting a unique trajectory of Christianity's spread in this region.

Introduction of Christianity to Ethiopia

The introduction of Christianity into Ethiopia is traditionally associated with the account of the Ethiopian eunuch described in Acts 8:26-39. This narrative is considered foundational, symbolizing the early receptivity of Ethiopians to Christian teachings. However, the systematic evangelization of Ethiopia is documented to have occurred significantly later, around the fourth century.

1. **Early Christianization**: According to historical accounts, notably by Rufinus, the actual establishment of Christianity took root during the reign of Constantine the Great, when two young men,

THE EARLY CHRISTIAN COPYISTS OF THE NEW TESTAMENT

Frumentius and Aedesius, began missionary work in Aksum. Frumentius, later consecrated as bishop by Athanasius of Alexandria, played a pivotal role in establishing the church and organizing missionary activities in Ethiopia.

2. **Spread and Development**: By the sixth century, the traveler Cosmas Indicopleustes observed that Ethiopia was thoroughly Christianized, indicating successful growth facilitated both by royal support and the influx of Monophysite refugees from the Byzantine Empire following the Council of Chalcedon in 451.

Translation of the New Testament into Ethiopic

The translation of the New Testament into Ge'ez is believed to have been initiated in the fifth or sixth century, associated with the broader efforts to evangelize and consolidate Christianity in the region.

1. **Role of the Nine Saints**: The Nine Saints, missionaries from Egypt and Syria, were instrumental in the Christianization of the northern parts of the Aksumite kingdom. Their work included the founding of monasteries, development of liturgical practices, and crucially, the translation of sacred texts into Ge'ez.

2. **Timeline and Translation Process**: While the exact date of the translation remains subject to scholarly debate, the most plausible period is during the fifth and sixth centuries, coinciding with significant missionary activities. The translation likely involved a synthesis of sources and influences, including Greek and possibly Syriac texts, adapted into the linguistic and cultural context of Ethiopia.

Manuscript Tradition and Cultural Impact

The Ethiopic manuscripts of the New Testament are not only religious texts but also artifacts of Ethiopia's rich cultural and artistic heritage. Most surviving manuscripts are dated much later than the original translations, reflecting ongoing scribal traditions and religious devotion.

1. **Manuscript Evidence**: While the majority of Ethiopic biblical manuscripts are from the sixteenth to the nineteenth centuries, there are notable earlier examples, such as a fourteenth-century manuscript. These manuscripts are crucial for studying the textual history and reception of the New Testament in Ethiopia.

2. **Iconography and Artistry**: The Pierpont Morgan MS. 828 of the Gospels, dated 1400-1401, exemplifies the intricate artistry characteristic of Ethiopic manuscripts. It includes full-page miniatures and ornamented folios, highlighting the integration of textual and visual art in Ethiopian Christian practice.

In summary, the Ethiopic version of the New Testament is a testament to Ethiopia's early and sustained engagement with Christianity. The translation and subsequent manuscript tradition not only facilitated the religious life of the Ethiopian Church but also contributed to the cultural and liturgical richness of the region. This version remains a vital part of the broader Christian textual tradition, offering unique insights into the adaptation and endurance of biblical texts in diverse historical and cultural contexts.

The Arabic Versions

The translation of the New Testament into Arabic is a significant aspect of Christian history, reflecting the spread of Christianity into the Arabic-speaking world and the diverse linguistic and cultural influences on biblical texts.

Early Christian Influence and Translation Initiatives

The propagation of Christianity into Arabia and the subsequent need for the Scriptures in Arabic were influenced by early Christian missionaries and theological debates within the region. The translation efforts spanned several centuries, with contributions from various Christian denominations and cultural contexts.

1. **Historical Background**: Christianity's reach into Arabia likely began by the third century, evidenced by Origen's visits for doctrinal discussions. However, the comprehensive Christianization efforts, including translations of the Scriptures, gained momentum much later, particularly with the Christian missions from Ethiopia to southern Arabia.

2. **Initial Translations**: The first known translations of the New Testament into Arabic are believed to have occurred around the eighth century, though specific details about the translators remain uncertain. These early translations were crucial for the Christian

communities in Arabia, providing access to the Scriptures in the vernacular.

Classification and Analysis of Arabic New Testament Manuscripts

The Arabic versions of the New Testament are diverse, reflecting the complex interplay of textual traditions and the multifaceted nature of Arabic dialects and scripts. Scholar Ignazio Guidi's analysis categorizes these manuscripts into six groups based on their source texts and stylistic features.

1. **Source Text Influences**: The Arabic translations of the Gospels are derived from multiple source texts, including Greek, Syriac (primarily the Peshitta), Coptic, and Latin. This diversity highlights the intertextual connections and the varied theological influences affecting the Arabic Christian texts.

2. **Eclectic Recensions and Rhymed Prose**: By the thirteenth century, the Alexandrian Patriarchate produced eclectic recensions, blending different textual traditions to create a standardized Arabic version. Additionally, some manuscripts are noted for their rhymed prose style, influenced by the classical Arabic of the Quran, which illustrates the cultural integration of Christian and Islamic literary traditions.

Modern Translations and Dialectal Variations

From the Middle Ages through the nineteenth century, further Arabic translations of the Bible were undertaken to meet the needs of different ecclesiastical groups and to adapt to the evolving forms of Arabic spoken across the region.

1. **Ecclesiastical and Dialectal Diversity**: Translations were made for Melchites, Maronites, Nestorians, Jacobites, and Copts, each reflecting specific doctrinal emphases and linguistic preferences. These translations not only served liturgical purposes but also helped in maintaining religious and cultural identities within these communities.

2. **Regional Adaptations**: Besides the classical Arabic translations, the New Testament was also rendered into the vernacular dialects of regions such as Algeria, Chad, Egypt, Morocco, Palestine, Sudan, Tunisia, and even the Maltese language. These adaptations

underscore the widespread impact of Christianity and its texts across the Arabic-speaking world, accommodating a wide range of linguistic and cultural contexts.

In conclusion, the Arabic versions of the New Testament are a testament to the dynamic and adaptive nature of Christian scripture transmission. They illustrate how religious texts are not only spiritual guideposts but also documents of linguistic, cultural, and theological exchange. The study of these versions offers valuable insights into the historical interactions between Christianity and the Arabic-speaking populations, as well as the ongoing importance of scriptural translations in fostering religious understanding and diversity.

The Sogdian Version

The Sogdian version of the New Testament holds a significant position in the study of Christian scripture transmission along the Silk Road and in Central Asia. This version offers insights into the spread of Christianity and the interaction between different religious and cultural traditions in this strategically important region.

Introduction to Sogdian Christianity

Sogdian, a Middle Iranian language, was prevalent in Central Asia around the area of modern-day Samarkand, serving as the lingua franca during the late antiquity and early medieval periods. The adoption of Christianity by the Sogdian speakers is closely linked to the missionary activities of the Nestorian Church.

1. **Linguistic and Cultural Context**: The Sogdian language's connection to the Indo-European language family facilitated the translation of Christian texts, which were primarily propagated by Nestorian missionaries. These missionaries played a crucial role in spreading Christianity to the Sogdian-speaking regions, utilizing the cultural and trade connections established through the Silk Road.

2. **Early Christian Documents**: The discovery of Christian texts in Sogdian among the ruins of Turfan in northwest China underscores the extent of Christian influence in the region. These documents include fragments from the Gospels of Matthew, Luke, and John, as well as excerpts from the Pauline Epistles, indicating an established Christian community that engaged deeply with the New Testament.

The Translation and Manuscript Tradition

The translation of the New Testament into Sogdian likely occurred in the context of the expanding influence of the Nestorian Church during the seventh century. This period was marked by significant missionary efforts extending through Central Asia, reaching even into parts of what is now China.

1. **Translation Characteristics**: The Sogdian Christian texts are characterized by a purely consonantal script that shows resemblance to Estrangela Syriac. This suggests that the translators may have used Syriac versions of the New Testament as their primary source, reflecting the strong Syriac influence on Nestorian Christianity.

2. **Manuscript Evidence**: The manuscripts, mainly dating from the ninth to the eleventh centuries, provide crucial evidence of the Christian textual tradition in Sogdian. These fragments not only help in understanding the scope of Christian scripture that was available to the Sogdian-speaking communities but also contribute to our knowledge of the textual variations present in the early New Testament manuscripts.

Scholarly Implications and Textual Analysis

The study of the Sogdian New Testament manuscripts is instrumental in piecing together the history of Christianity's reach into Central Asia. It also helps in understanding the interactions between different religious communities, such as Buddhists, Manichaeans, and Christians, who were active in this region during the first millennium.

1. **Textual Variants**: Analysis of the Sogdian fragments can reveal unique textual variants that may differ from those found in Greek and Latin manuscripts. These variants are important for textual critics as they offer alternative readings and can illuminate how scriptures were understood and used in different cultural contexts.

2. **Interreligious and Interlingual Exchange**: The presence of Christian texts alongside Manichaean and Buddhist writings in the same region highlights the rich tapestry of religious and cultural exchange facilitated by the Silk Road. This exchange influenced the development of religious texts, including how they were translated and interpreted by different communities.

In conclusion, the Sogdian version of the New Testament provides a fascinating glimpse into the spread of Christianity into Central Asia through the efforts of the Nestorian Church. The manuscripts not only enrich our understanding of the textual history of the New Testament but also illustrate the dynamic interactions between cultures and religions along the Silk Road. The ongoing study of these texts continues to shed light on the diverse ways in which the Christian faith was adapted and integrated into the fabric of Central Asian society.

The Old Church Slavonic Version

The Old Church Slavonic version of the New Testament, developed during the missionary efforts of Saints Cyril and Methodius, is a seminal text in the history of Slavic Christianity. It reflects a crucial phase in the linguistic and cultural adaptation of Christian scriptures to Slavic societies.

Missionary Beginnings and Linguistic Innovations

The missionary work of Cyril and Methodius was instrumental in introducing Christianity to the Slavic regions of Moravia and beyond. Their efforts were not only religious but also linguistic, leading to the creation of an alphabet and the initial translations of Christian texts into Slavonic.

1. **Early Missions**: The brothers Cyril and Methodius, originating from Thessalonica, were familiar with the Slavic dialects from a young age due to the presence of Slavic communities in and around the city. Their mission to Moravia in 863, prompted by the request of Prince Rostislav, marked the beginning of their efforts to create liturgical texts in the Slavic language, which was essential for the local population's understanding of Christianity.

2. **Development of the Slavic Alphabet**: Cyril's development of the Glagolitic alphabet, specifically designed for the Slavic languages, enabled the translation of the Gospels and other liturgical materials. This script was crucial for the initial evangelization efforts and the establishment of a Slavic ecclesiastical tradition.

Translation of the Scriptures and Liturgical Integration

The translation of the New Testament into Old Church Slavonic was a foundational step in the liturgical and cultural integration of Christianity into

Slavic societies. It facilitated a deeper engagement with the Christian faith and its teachings.

1. **Scriptural Translation**: The primary translation work began with the Gospel of John, specifically starting with John 1:1, to emphasize the theological depth of Christianity. This translation not only served liturgical purposes but also aimed to educate and convert the Slavic peoples by making the scriptures accessible in their native tongue.

2. **Liturgical Acceptance**: Despite initial resistance from German clerical authorities, the use of Slavonic in divine services was eventually sanctioned by Popes Hadrian II and John VIII. This approval was contingent upon the scriptures being read first in Latin and then in Slavonic, reflecting a compromise between traditional ecclesiastical languages and the vernacular.

Scriptural Transmission and Legacy

The legacy of the Old Church Slavonic scriptures is marked by the development of the Cyrillic script and the broader acceptance of Slavic liturgical practices across Eastern Europe.

1. **Evolution of the Cyrillic Alphabet**: While Cyril originally developed the Glagolitic script, the Cyrillic alphabet, thought to be developed by Cyril's follower, Saint Kliment, became more widely used. By the council of Preslav in 893, the Cyrillic script was codified for ecclesiastical and secular use throughout Bulgaria, marking a significant milestone in the history of Slavic literacy and scriptural transmission.

2. **Spread and Influence**: Following the suppression of the Slavonic liturgy in Moravia, the disciples of Cyril and Methodius dispersed across Eastern Europe, carrying with them the Slavonic scriptures and liturgical practices. This dispersion helped to establish and solidify the use of Old Church Slavonic in religious services across a variety of Slavic lands, influencing the religious and cultural landscape of the region.

In summary, the Old Church Slavonic version of the New Testament is not merely a translation of sacred texts but a monumental achievement in the cultural and religious history of the Slavic peoples. It represents the intertwined processes of religious conversion, linguistic innovation, and cultural adaptation, which collectively shaped the Christian traditions of Eastern Europe. The work of Cyril and Methodius, therefore, is foundational not only in the religious sense but also in fostering a shared Slavic literary and cultural identity.

The Nubian Version

The Nubian version of the New Testament represents a critical aspect of the Christian heritage in northeast Africa, illustrating the spread and adaptation of Christianity within the Nubian kingdoms. This version is vital for understanding the religious and cultural transformations in Nubia during the early medieval period.

Introduction to Christianity in Nubia

Christianity's penetration into Nubia is intertwined with the broader religious dynamics of northeast Africa, influenced significantly by developments in neighboring Egypt and Ethiopia.

1. **Early Christian Influence**: While the exact date remains uncertain, it is likely that Christian influences reached Nubia through Egypt during the third and fourth centuries. The establishment of the church in Upper Egypt and the Christian refugees fleeing the Diocletian persecutions would have facilitated this early introduction.

2. **Formal Missionary Efforts**: By the sixth century, formal missionary activities commenced with the arrival of Monophysite and Melchite missionaries. These groups introduced organized Christian practices and liturgical traditions, which played a central role in the religious life of the Nubian kingdoms.

The Translation of the Scriptures into Nubian

The translation of Christian scriptures into the Nubian language was a significant event, likely occurring soon after the widespread acceptance of Christianity in the region. This translation was essential for the liturgical and devotional life of the Nubian Christians.

1. **Scriptural Translation**: The precise timing of the New Testament's translation into Nubian is not documented, but based on patterns observed in similar contexts, it likely took place around the time Christianity became firmly established in the region, possibly in the sixth or seventh century. This translation enabled the local population to engage deeply with Christian doctrine in their native language.

2. **Manuscript Evidence**: The discovery of Nubian scriptural texts in the early twentieth century provided concrete evidence of the existence of a Nubian version of the New Testament. Fragments of a lectionary and other biblical texts highlight the unique characteristics of the Nubian Christian tradition.

Linguistic Characteristics and Textual Significance

The Nubian manuscripts are written in an alphabet largely derived from Coptic, with additional letters to represent sounds unique to the Nubian language. This adaptation underscores the linguistic and cultural integration of Christian texts into Nubian society.

1. **Alphabet and Language**: The use of a Coptic-based script for the Nubian language facilitated the translation and transcription of Christian texts. This scriptural adaptation was crucial for the liturgical and educational use of the Bible among Nubian Christians.

2. **Lectionary and Liturgical Texts**: The lectionary fragments for Christmastide, which include passages from both the Apostolos and the Gospel, demonstrate the liturgical use of the New Testament in Nubian worship. The choice of scriptural passages reflects both commonalities and unique aspects of the Nubian liturgical tradition compared to those of the Greek and Coptic churches.

In conclusion, the Nubian version of the New Testament is a testament to the rich and complex history of Christianity in Nubia. It reflects the dynamic interplay between religious, cultural, and linguistic elements in the region. The translation and use of the New Testament in Nubian not only facilitated the religious life of the community but also played a pivotal role in the cultural and spiritual continuity of Nubia during and after the Christian era.

Significant Editions of the Greek New Testament

This section offers an overview of the key editions of the Greek New Testament, presented in chronological order from the earliest to the latest. Most textual critics believe that these editions have improved over time, with the text's wording increasingly reflecting the original manuscripts. However, it is up to each student to explore and evaluate this progression through studying the science and art of New Testament textual criticism.

Historical Overview of the Textus Receptus

The Textus Receptus, a significant edition of the Greek New Testament, has played a crucial role in the history of biblical texts. Its development and enduring impact on New Testament studies exemplify the evolution of textual criticism and the dissemination of scriptural manuscripts.

Origins and Compilation by Erasmus

The creation of the Textus Receptus was initiated by Desiderius Erasmus in the early 16th century. Responding to the request of the publisher Johann Froben, Erasmus set out to compile a printed edition of the Greek New Testament, which would later gain prominence as the Textus Receptus.

1. **Early Manuscript Sources**: For his edition, Erasmus relied primarily on five or six late Byzantine manuscripts, dating from the 10th to the 13th centuries. Notable among these were minuscule 1 and minuscule 2 from the twelfth century. The reliance on these specific manuscripts influenced the textual character of the Textus Receptus, embedding it with the Byzantine text-type attributes.

2. **Byzantine Textual Characteristics**: The Byzantine text-type, often associated with Lucian of Antioch as per Jerome's accounts, was characterized by its readability, harmonization of discrepancies, and conflation of textual variants. Lucian's recension, developed before the Diocletian persecution of approximately 303 C.E., sought to create a standardized text that could meet the needs of the growing Christian community under Constantine's legalization of Christianity.

Dissemination and Influence

Following its compilation, the Textus Receptus underwent several revisions and reprints, each contributing to its spread and standardization across the Christian world.

1. **Publication and Revisions**: After its initial publication, the Textus Receptus was repeatedly edited and republished by figures such as Robert Stephanus and Theodore Beza. These revisions incorporated slight alterations but continued to reflect the Byzantine textual tradition.

2. **Elzevir Editions**: The pivotal moment in the history of the Textus Receptus came with the Elzevir brothers' editions in 1624 and 1633. Their declaration that this text was the "text now received by all" cemented its status as the Textus Receptus. This label signified the widespread acceptance and normative use of this edition within the scholarly and ecclesiastical communities.

Scriptural References and Theological Implications

The Textus Receptus not only facilitated a uniform New Testament textual framework but also shaped theological understanding and scriptural studies for centuries.

- **John 1:1**: "In the beginning was the Word, and the Word was with God, and the Word was God." This verse, foundational to Christian doctrine, is emblematic of the New Testament texts preserved and propagated through the Textus Receptus.

- **Impact on Translation and Doctrine**: The textual choices and the Byzantine text's characteristics influenced numerous translations, including the King James Version. This influence extended to theological interpretations and the doctrinal formulations within various Christian traditions.

In conclusion, the Textus Receptus stands as a monumental edition in the history of the Greek New Testament. Its compilation by Erasmus, based on a limited number of Byzantine manuscripts, and its subsequent adoption and revision across Europe, illustrate the dynamic and complex process of textual transmission and standardization. This edition's lasting legacy underscores the profound interconnection between textual criticism, scriptural translation, and theological construction.

Understanding the Byzantine Text and Its Historical Impact on New Testament Textual Traditions

The Byzantine text, also known by various scholars as the Syrian, Koine, Ecclesiastical, or Antiochian text, represents a critical phase in the history of New Testament textual criticism. This text type, emerging predominantly from Antioch in Syria, played a pivotal role in shaping the textual character of the New Testament manuscripts used throughout the Byzantine Empire.

Origins and Characteristics of the Byzantine Text

The Byzantine text type is generally regarded as the latest among the early Christian text types. It was meticulously crafted to enhance clarity and coherence in the scriptures.

1. **Development and Refinement**: The creators of the Byzantine text were intent on eliminating any linguistic roughness, thereby smoothing the flow of text. They often merged varying readings into a single, more comprehensive form, a process known as conflation. They also sought to align and harmonize parallel narrative passages.

2. **Propagation and Dominance**: Originating possibly in Antioch, this text type was transported to Constantinople, from where it was disseminated across the Byzantine Empire. This version of the text, renowned for its lucidity and completeness, was widely regarded as authoritative from about the sixth or seventh century until the era of the printing press.

The Role of the Textus Receptus and Erasmus's Edition

The Textus Receptus, heavily based on the Byzantine text type, became the standard text for the printed editions of the New Testament post-Gutenberg. This section explores the compilation of this influential text by Desiderius Erasmus and its implications.

1. **Erasmus's Textual Sources**: In 1516, Erasmus compiled his edition of the Greek New Testament by utilizing several late manuscripts, predominantly of Byzantine origin. His reliance on these sources meant that his edition also carried the typical characteristics of the Byzantine text, though not without some critical scholarly adjustments.

2. **Challenges and Innovations**: Lacking a complete manuscript for the book of Revelation, Erasmus resorted to translating the missing verses from the Latin Vulgate back into Greek. This action led to certain textual peculiarities in his edition, notably the inclusion of readings absent in any known Greek manuscript. For example, in Revelation 22:19, Erasmus replaced "tree of life" with "book of life," aligning it with the Vulgate but diverging from the Greek manuscript tradition.

Scriptural Illustrations and Theological Implications

The influence of the Byzantine text, particularly as solidified in the Textus Receptus, extended deeply into the theological landscape and scriptural interpretations of subsequent centuries.

- **Revelation 22:19 Example**: The Textus Receptus reads ἀπὸ βίβλου ("from the book"), a deviation found in no Greek manuscript but introduced by Erasmus. This variation underscores the complex interplay between textual transmission, scribal errors, and theological interpretation.

The Byzantine text type and its broad adoption in the Textus Receptus illustrate the dynamic processes of textual preservation, adaptation, and influence. The decisions made by textual critics and scholars like Erasmus not only shaped the scriptural texts of their own times but also set precedents that would influence biblical scholarship and religious practice for centuries to come.

The Impact of Erasmus's Greek Testament and Subsequent Editions

Erasmus's Greek Testament quickly became a cornerstone for subsequent translations of the New Testament, highlighting its significant demand and influence in early biblical scholarship.

Erasmus's Pioneering Contributions

The first edition of Erasmus's Greek Testament, released in 1516, was met with such fervor that it quickly sold out, prompting the need for a second edition. Released in 1519, this edition corrected some of the typographical errors found in the first but still retained many. It was this revised edition that Martin Luther and William Tyndale utilized as the foundation for their own groundbreaking translations into German and English, respectively. Luther's translation appeared in 1522, followed by Tyndale's in 1525, marking pivotal moments in the dissemination of biblical texts in vernacular languages.

Legacy and Standardization of Text

In the years that followed, numerous editors and printers produced various editions of the Greek Testament. Despite access to a range of manuscript sources, these editions predominantly replicated the text found in later Byzantine manuscripts. This uniformity was maintained even by notable figures like Theodore Beza, despite his access to significantly older manuscripts such as the fifth-century Codex Bezae and the sixth-century Codex Claromontanus. Beza's conservative approach highlighted a preference for the familiar Byzantine text over these older, divergent sources.

Notable Editions and Innovations

The journey of the Greek New Testament's publication saw critical contributions from other scholars as well. Notably, Robert Etienne, known as Stephanus, was a key figure in the advancement of textual criticism. His third edition, published in Paris in 1550 and known as the "editio Regia," was a lavish folio that was the first to include a critical apparatus, showing variant readings from fourteen manuscripts and the Complutensian Polyglot on its margins. Stephanus's subsequent move to Geneva and alignment with Protestant reformers underscored the intertwining of religious reform and textual scholarship.

His fourth edition in 1551 was particularly revolutionary for introducing numbered verses to the New Testament text, a practice that greatly facilitated referencing and scholarly discussion.

The Textus Receptus and Its Influence on the King James Bible

Theodore Beza's editions, spanning from 1565 to posthumously in 1611, were instrumental in popularizing what would be known as the Textus Receptus. This text became the basis for the King James Bible of 1611, illustrating how Beza's work not only preserved but also canonized a specific textual tradition in one of the most influential English translations of the Bible.

These editions and their creators played crucial roles in shaping the textual landscape of the New Testament, underscoring the dynamic interplay between textual criticism, religious tradition, and the development of printing technology.

The Evolution and Influence of the Textus Receptus on New Testament Translations

Origin and Initial Impact of the Textus Receptus

The term "Textus Receptus," meaning "received text," was first used by the Elzevir family, notable printers in Leiden, in the preface to their 1633 edition of the Greek New Testament. This phrase highlighted their claim that their text, widely accepted and unaltered, represented the authentic New Testament scripture. While this claim suggested a reliable uniformity with previous editions dating back to Erasmus's first published edition in 1516, it also inadvertently acknowledged the perpetuation of a text type laden with scribal alterations accumulated over centuries.

Challenges and Critiques of the Byzantine Text Type

Throughout the era of manual script copying, the Byzantine text type, which formed the basis of the Textus Receptus, underwent numerous minor and some significant scribal modifications. This text type dominated New Testament translations into modern languages until the nineteenth century, often obscuring the original nuances of the New Testament writings. Despite accumulating evidence of these alterations from various Greek manuscripts, versional sources, and patristic writings during the eighteenth century, few editors dared to make substantive corrections to this entrenched text form.

Breakthroughs in Textual Criticism

The nineteenth century marked a turning point with Karl Lachmann, a German classical scholar who in 1831 applied rigorous philological methods to the New Testament, methods typically reserved for classical texts. This bold approach paved the way for further critical editions, such as those by Constantin von Tischendorf and the seminal work by B. F. Westcott and F. J. A. Hort in 1881, which significantly influenced later biblical scholarship and translations.

Modern Advances and the Pursuit of Authenticity

The discovery of older New Testament manuscripts in the twentieth century has dramatically enhanced the accuracy of contemporary New Testament editions. These findings have enabled scholars to create texts that more closely reflect the original writings, moving beyond the limitations of the Textus Receptus. The United Bible Societies' edition, for instance, now utilizes these advanced resources to offer a text that is considered closer to the authentic words of the New Testament authors.

Evaluating the Textus Receptus and Majority Text in New Testament Scholarship

The Relationship Between the Textus Receptus and the Majority Text

The Majority Text, which some scholars recently attempted to validate, closely aligns with the Textus Receptus (TR). Although the TR is derived from manuscripts that largely represent the Majority Text, it does not uniformly reflect this text type. The Majority Text essentially overlaps with the Byzantine Text type, predominant during the era of Byzantium, where the Lucian recension was replicated extensively, resulting in its standardization across numerous manuscripts.

Theological versus Textual Arguments for the Textus Receptus

Advocates for the TR, such as Hodges and Farstad who authored *The Greek New Testament According to the Majority Text*, often present theological rather than textual arguments. They suggest that divine providence would prevent a corrupt text from being more prevalent and would not allow a superior text to remain obscure in a few early manuscripts, possibly buried in Egypt's sands. They also view the widespread adoption of the Majority Text by the church as a confirmation of its correctness, whereas the limited use of the "Egyptian" text indicates its rejection.

These proponents overlook the possibility that God may have guided the discovery of earlier, more accurate manuscripts in recent centuries, aiding scholars in their efforts to restore the original New Testament text.

Scholarly Consensus on Early Manuscripts

Contemporary scholarship generally holds that the earliest manuscripts, though fewer in number, likely preserve the most authentic form of the New Testament text. Defenders of the TR and the King James Version need to address why these earlier texts often contain less content than later versions.

They must provide compelling reasons for why early scribes would intentionally remove extensive passages if they were originally part of the text.

Examples of omitted sections include various verses across the Gospels and the Acts of the Apostles. The argument that these passages were excluded for reasons of readability, with scribes omitting only a few words at a time, does not typically account for the more substantial exclusions. Instead, many scholars believe these additions were later incorporated into the text due to reasons such as harmonizing Gospel narratives, inserting oral traditions, or making theological embellishments.

In summary, the Majority Text and the TR are seen by most modern scholars as compilations that include later textual additions rather than representing a purer original form of the New Testament. The ongoing recovery and analysis of older manuscripts continue to challenge the authenticity of the Textus Receptus, reshaping our understanding of the New Testament's textual history.

Evolution of Greek New Testament Scholarship: From Bengel to Alford

Pioneers of Modern Greek Textual Criticism

The progression from the Textus Receptus to more historically authentic versions of the Greek New Testament was influenced by discoveries of ancient manuscripts and the scholarly pursuit of a text that more accurately reflects the original. Around 1700, John Mill enhanced the Textus Receptus. In the 1730s, Johannes Albert Bengel, often recognized as the father of modern New Testament textual studies, published a version deviating from the Textus Receptus based on older manuscripts.

Nineteenth-Century Advances

In the 19th century, a shift away from the Textus Receptus gained momentum. Karl Lachman, a classical philologist, introduced a new Greek text in 1831, drawing on fourth-century manuscripts to more closely represent the earliest attainable version of the New Testament texts. Samuel Tregelles, an autodidact in Latin, Hebrew, and Greek, dedicated his life to producing a Greek New Testament. Published in parts from 1857 to 1872, Tregelles aimed to "exhibit the text of the New Testament in the very words in which it has been transmitted on the evidence of ancient authority."

Concurrently, Constantin von Tischendorf embarked on a lifelong mission to recover and study ancient manuscripts. His commitment is exemplified by his statement in a letter to his fiancée, expressing his dedication to restoring the original form of the New Testament. His notable discoveries include the Codex Sinaiticus and the Codex Ephraemi Rescriptus. Tischendorf's critical edition, the Editio octava critica maior (1869–1872), included a critical apparatus still in use today, underscoring the depth of his textual analysis.

Henry Alford's Contributions

Henry Alford also made significant strides in compiling a Greek text reflective of the best and earliest manuscripts. His Greek New Testament, published in 1849 with accompanying commentary, aimed to dismantle the undue reverence for the received text. Alford's work was driven by the desire to uncover the true words of God, challenging traditional views and advocating for a more critical approach to textual accuracy.

These scholars' collective efforts marked a pivotal shift towards a more rigorous and historically grounded understanding of the New Testament texts, setting the stage for future textual criticism.

Johann Jakob Griesbach's Contributions to Greek New Testament Textual Criticism

Context and Background

Johann Jakob Griesbach, born in 1745 and deceased in 1812, was a seminal figure in the development of New Testament textual criticism. His work laid foundational principles that guided later textual critics in evaluating the authenticity of manuscript readings. Griesbach's editions of the Greek New Testament were revolutionary in his time for introducing a systematic approach to analyzing textual variants.

Development of Critical Editions

Griesbach's primary contribution was his critical editions of the Greek New Testament. His approach was meticulous and innovative; he was among the first to apply rigorous textual criticism methods to the New Testament, which were akin to those used in assessing classical texts. Griesbach's editions were particularly noted for introducing a critical apparatus that listed variant readings among manuscripts. He categorized the New Testament manuscripts into three primary textual families: Alexandrian, Western, and Byzantine, which he believed represented distinct geographical areas of textual transmission.

This categorization was based on his analysis of textual agreements and disagreements, which he theorized could be used to trace the history of the text's transmission. For instance, when discussing the reliability of manuscript evidence, Griesbach might have considered principles reflected in passages like **Revelation 22:19**, which underscores the seriousness of preserving the words of the scripture without alteration.

Methodological Innovations

Griesbach is perhaps best known for his synoptic approach, which later influenced the famous "Griesbach Hypothesis." This hypothesis suggests that Matthew was the first gospel written, followed by Luke, and then Mark, who used both as sources. This theory significantly impacted subsequent synoptic problem studies, though it later gave way to Markan priority. His methodological rigor is evident in his handling of gospel comparisons, similar to the analysis one might apply to **Matthew 9:9-13** and its parallels, where the text's authenticity and consistency are critical.

In his editions, Griesbach also emphasized the importance of internal and external evidence in determining the original text. He argued that internal considerations (such as the author's style and the immediate context) and external evidence (the manuscript's age and textual family) must be balanced. This approach resonates with the biblical exhortation in **1 Thessalonians 5:21**: "Test all things; hold fast what is good," encouraging a meticulous and discerning approach to scripture.

Impact and Legacy

While Griesbach's text did not dethrone the Textus Receptus immediately, it paved the way for subsequent editions by scholars like Karl Lachmann, Tischendorf, and Westcott and Hort. His meticulous work demonstrated that a text constructed with careful consideration of both textual variants and the historical context of manuscripts could provide a more accurate representation of the "original" text than the traditionally accepted Textus Receptus.

Griesbach's editions underscored the need for a continuous re-evaluation of the textual basis of the New Testament, a scholarly pursuit that finds a parallel in **Ephesians 5:13**, "But all things that are exposed are made manifest by the light, for whatever makes manifest is light." This verse metaphorically captures the essence of Griesbach's endeavor to illuminate the New Testament text through rigorous scrutiny.

Through his life's work, Johann Jakob Griesbach significantly advanced the field of New Testament textual criticism, setting standards that would shape critical scholarship for generations. His methodical approach to the Greek text not only refined the scholarly understanding of the New Testament's textual history but also enhanced the biblical scholarship's overall rigor and depth.

The Enduring Influence of Westcott and Hort's "The New Testament in the Original Greek"

Pioneering Scholarship by Westcott and Hort

Building on the foundational research of scholars like Tregelles and Tischendorf, British scholars Brooke Westcott and Fenton Hort dedicated twenty-eight years to crafting "The New Testament in the Original Greek," published in 1881. Their work significantly advanced biblical scholarship by proposing the Neutral Text theory. According to Hort, key manuscripts such as Codex Vaticanus and Codex Sinaiticus, along with a few other early documents, closely represent the original writings of the New Testament due to their minimal textual corruption.

The Impact and Reliability of Their Work

Westcott and Hort's edition was groundbreaking, as it shifted scholarly reliance away from the Textus Receptus towards what they identified as the Neutral Text. I personally regard "The New Testament in the Original Greek" as a highly accurate reflection of the New Testament's primitive text. My own textual studies have frequently aligned with their choices, reinforcing my confidence in their methods. Even with numerous manuscript discoveries since their time, Westcott and Hort's work remains a critical reference point.

The Textual Legacy and Contemporary Confirmation

The discovery of hundreds of additional manuscripts, particularly the New Testament papyri, has only enriched our understanding of the New Testament text. If Westcott and Hort were alive today, they would likely be gratified to see that recent findings from early papyri support their views on the reliability of Codex Vaticanus and Codex Sinaiticus. Nevertheless, they might have revised some opinions in light of new evidence, such as the insights provided by P75 about the Lukan passages, which challenge some of their decisions regarding "Western noninterpolations."

In sum, the scholarly efforts of Westcott and Hort continue to influence New Testament textual criticism, validating the importance of their work in contemporary biblical studies. Their approach to the Greek text not only de-emphasized the Textus Receptus but also set a high standard for textual accuracy that has largely stood the test of time and subsequent manuscript discoveries.

Evolution of the Greek New Testament: From Nestle's Novum Testamentum Graece to the UBS Text

Establishment of the Nestle Text

Eberhard Nestle revolutionized New Testament textual criticism through his work on *Novum Testamentum Graece*. Nestle's first edition, published in 1898, was groundbreaking. It was not an original text but a compilation of readings chosen from the editions of Westcott and Hort, Tischendorf, and Weymouth, later replacing Weymouth's readings with those from Bernhard Weiss's text. His method was to adopt readings where at least two of these editions agreed, or where there was a clear preponderance of textual evidence.

Nestle aimed to produce a highly reliable Greek New Testament by synthesizing the best available texts, reminiscent of the biblical principle of "every matter must be established by the testimony of two or three witnesses" (**2 Corinthians 13:1**). Over time, Nestle's son Erwin took over and further refined the apparatus, incorporating more manuscript evidence. This methodology laid the groundwork for a text that was broadly representative of the ancient witnesses, aiming to mirror as closely as possible the original words of the New Testament.

Development and Impact of the UBS Text

The United Bible Societies (UBS) Greek New Testament, first published in 1966, built upon the foundation laid by Nestle. The UBS text was designed with a specific focus on the needs of translators. It was produced in collaboration with the Institute for New Testament Textual Research in Münster, Germany, where Kurt Aland, a significant figure in textual criticism, played a pivotal role.

The UBS text's primary aim was to provide a text critically established based on the best available manuscripts and to offer an apparatus that highlighted variant readings significant for translation purposes. This focus on translational utility reflects the practical application of scripture, as encouraged in **James 1:22**, "Do not merely listen to the word, and so deceive yourselves. Do what it says."

Methodology and Updates

Both the Nestle-Aland and UBS texts have undergone several revisions, reflecting new discoveries, such as the papyri and other ancient manuscripts, and advancements in textual criticism methodologies. The editions are regularly updated; for instance, the Nestle-Aland text reached its 28th edition, and the UBS text its fifth edition. These updates ensure that the Greek New Testament remains as close as possible to the original autographs, guided by newer findings and scholarly consensus.

The editors of these texts have made considerable efforts to be transparent about their textual decisions, often discussing the rationale for preferring certain variants over others. This process is akin to the Berean Jews' approach, who "examined the Scriptures every day to see if what Paul said was true" (**Acts 17:11**). It underscores the importance of meticulous study and verification in the pursuit of textual accuracy.

The development of the Nestle-Aland and UBS texts marks significant milestones in the field of New Testament textual criticism. By providing a critical edition that incorporates a wide array of manuscript evidence and by offering a clear apparatus for understanding textual variants, these texts serve both academic and practical needs. They facilitate a deeper understanding and more accurate translation of the New Testament, helping to fulfill the scriptural mandate to "rightly dividing the word of truth" (**2 Timothy 2:15**).

These editions exemplify the ongoing commitment to refining the text of the New Testament, ensuring that translations are based on the best possible reconstruction of the original documents. The work mirrors the biblical principle of stewardship of God's word, preserving its purity and accuracy for future generations.

Advances in Textual Criticism: Nestle-Aland and United Bible Societies' Editions

Overview of Nestle-Aland and UBS Editions

The **Nestle-Aland Novum Testamentum Graece** editions and the **United Bible Societies' (UBS) Greek New Testament** represent significant milestones in the textual criticism of the New Testament. These editions aim to reconstruct the closest possible text to the original autographs written two millennia ago, providing a more precise foundation for biblical scholarship, translation, and understanding.

Nestle-Aland Editions: 26th to 28th Revisions

The **Nestle-Aland editions** have undergone several revisions, each incorporating more extensive manuscript evidence and more refined scholarly methods. From the **26th to the 28th editions**, there has been a consistent effort to integrate findings from newly discovered papyri and other early manuscripts. Each edition has refined the critical apparatus, making it more comprehensive and helpful for scholars seeking to understand the textual variants and the decisions behind the chosen text.

- **26th Edition**: Incorporated newer findings but still relied heavily on the earlier text forms.
- **27th Edition**: Made significant strides in incorporating a wider array of manuscript evidence, improving the textual apparatus to provide clearer insights into variant readings.
- **28th Edition**: Continued to refine the text, with particular emphasis on integrating major discoveries and scholarly research from the past few decades, particularly the findings from the **Editio Critica Maior** project.

Edward D. Andrews

United Bible Societies' Editions: 3rd to 5th Revisions

The **UBS Greek New Testament**, particularly designed for translators, has evolved from its third to its fifth edition, each revision aiming to provide a text that is both textually rigorous and usable for translation purposes.

- **3rd Edition**: Updated the critical apparatus to be more user-friendly for translators, without significant changes in the text.
- **4th Edition**: Further refined the apparatus and included more manuscript evidence to assist in understanding difficult passages.
- **5th Corrected Edition**: The latest edition, which corrected minor errors and integrated more recent scholarly research and manuscript discoveries.

To provide specific examples of textual changes between the 26th, 27th, and 28th editions of the **Nestle-Aland Novum Testamentum Graece** (NA), we can look at several key passages where the Greek text was updated based on newer scholarly consensus or additional manuscript evidence:

1. **Matthew 27:16-17**:
    - **NA26**: The name "Jesus Barabbas" appeared in some manuscripts for Barabbas, the criminal. The text here in NA26 did not include "Jesus" as part of his name.
    - **NA27**: The committee chose to include "Jesus Barabbas" in the main text, reflecting the evidence from several ancient manuscripts and church fathers which mention "Jesus Barabbas."
    - **NA28**: The name was retained based on continuing support from manuscript evidence and scholarly consensus.

2. **Mark 1:41**:
    - **NA26**: The text reads Jesus was "moved with compassion" (σπλαγχνισθείς).
    - **NA27**: Continued the same reading, despite some controversy and variant readings.
    - **NA28**: Changed to "moved with anger" (ὀργισθείς) in the main text, aligning with a minority of manuscripts but considered by some scholars to reflect an original reading that might have been softened in later copies.

3. **Romans 16:5**:
    - **NA26** and **NA27**: Mention "Epaenetus, who is the first convert to Christ in Asia."
    - **NA28**: Changed to "Epaenetus, who is beloved" based on newer critical assessments and manuscript discoveries that suggest an earlier error in transmission.

These changes illustrate the ongoing process of textual criticism, where scholars continually assess and reassess the evidence from ancient manuscripts. Each revision of the Nestle-Aland editions reflects not just new findings but also deeper, sometimes revised, understandings of how certain texts might have been originally written and transmitted through the ages.

The changes between editions often involve subtle nuances that might not significantly alter theological doctrines but can enhance our understanding of the historical and cultural context of the biblical texts. These decisions are made in committee meetings of the Nestle-Aland and involve detailed discussions on the weight of manuscript evidence, internal consistency of the text, and the historical plausibility of different readings.

The progression from NA26 through NA28 highlights the dynamic nature of New Testament textual scholarship and the meticulous care with which scholars approach the task of presenting the most accurate text based on available evidence.

Challenges and Criticisms

One of my primary criticisms of the approach taken by both Nestle-Aland and UBS is the preference for "reasoned eclecticism" or the "local-genealogical method." This method tends to prioritize internal evidence (what the text likely meant or how it fits into the author's style and the rest of the text) over external evidence (the manuscript tradition itself). Critics argue, citing scholars like Westcott and Hort, that a more documentary approach should be prioritized to recover the original text. This approach considers the manuscript evidence as primary, reducing the risk of subjective interpretations based on internal consistency alone.

E. C. Colwell and other scholars have echoed this sentiment, arguing for a reconstruction of the manuscript tradition's history to better understand how textual changes might have occurred. This approach would prioritize early and high-quality manuscripts over the majority text, especially in light of discoveries like Papyrus 75 (P75), which supports the high textual quality of Codex Vaticanus.

Both the Nestle-Aland and UBS editions have significantly contributed to biblical scholarship by providing texts that reflect the earliest and most reliable evidence available. The debate over methodologies underscores the complexity of textual criticism and the ongoing quest to approximate the original New Testament writings as closely as possible. As more manuscripts are discovered and our understanding of ancient textual transmission deepens, future editions will undoubtedly continue to refine the Greek New Testament text. This ongoing process highlights the dynamic nature of biblical scholarship and the careful balance between historical fidelity and modern accessibility.

Examining Textual Choices in Nestle-Aland and UBS Editions

The approach of "reasoned eclecticism" or the "local-genealogical method" used by the Nestle-Aland (NA) and the United Bible Societies (UBS) editions of the Greek New Testament has been a subject of debate among scholars. These methods often prioritize internal evidence over external documentary evidence, potentially leading to decisions that might not align with the weightiest manuscript support. Below, we will examine several key passages to understand the decisions made in these critical texts, comparing the Westcott-Hort (WH) readings with those of the Nestle-Aland editions, and highlighting the supporting documentary evidence.

Matthew 4:24

- **WH Reading**: The text includes "paralyzed."
- **NA Reading**: Omits "paralyzed."
- **Documentary Evidence**: The omission is supported by ℵ, B, while the inclusion is found in later manuscripts like Codex Bezae (D) and Byzantine texts.

John 1:34

- **WH Reading**: "I have seen and have testified that this is the Son of God."

- **NA Reading**: "I have seen and have testified that this is the Chosen One of God."

- **Documentary Evidence**: "Son of God" is supported by the majority including ℵ, B, L, X, Δ, Θ, while "Chosen One of God" appears in variant readings.

In each case, the decision made by the NA editors to adopt one reading over another is influenced by a complex interplay of manuscript evidence, with a tendency to favor internal consistency and coherence in the narrative or theological context. This analysis underscores the necessity of considering documentary evidence to ensure that text-critical decisions are as close as possible to the original text. Nevertheless, the consistency in the readings between Westcott-Hort and the Nestle-Aland editions is 99.5% agreement, with the manuscript evidence often providing strong support for the choices made by the editors. It underscores the importance of documentary evidence in the ongoing endeavor to establish the original wording of the Greek New Testament.

Edward D. Andrews

CHAPTER 6 Dating the Earliest Manuscripts of the New Testament

The Significance of Early Manuscripts

The earliest New Testament manuscripts are crucial for textual criticism because they are presumed to be closer to the autographs in content, thus potentially providing the most accurate reflection of the original texts. Since the autographs (original writings) of the New Testament do not survive, scholars rely heavily on these early copies to reconstruct the text. The reliability of these manuscripts depends not only on their age but also on the quality and accuracy of the copying process they underwent.

Methodology in Manuscript Dating

Dating ancient manuscripts involves several disciplines, including paleography, which is the study of ancient handwriting. Paleographers examine the scripts of manuscripts to determine their age, based on comparison with other dated texts. This method, while effective, has its challenges, particularly when it comes to precision and consistency across different scholarly assessments.

One of the frequent criticisms in manuscript dating is the conservatism of date ranges assigned to manuscripts. For example, Papyrus 4 (P4), often cited in critical editions of the Greek New Testament such as the Nestle-Aland and the United Bible Societies' texts, has been subject to re-evaluation. While traditionally dated to the third century, recent scholarship suggests a late second-century origin, potentially as early as 150-175 C.E. This adjustment is based on more refined comparisons with other similarly styled manuscripts and reflects a broader call for updating the datings of approximately thirty early New Testament manuscripts.

Challenges in Paleographical Dating

Historically, paleographers like Grenfell, Hunt, and Kenyon did not always have a broad corpus of manuscripts for comparison, which sometimes led to less precise datings. Today's scholars have access to a more extensive collection of manuscripts, allowing for more accurate dating by comparing newly found manuscripts with those previously dated. This highlights a critical aspect of New Testament textual criticism—continuous refinement and correction of manuscript datings as new evidence becomes available.

Moreover, the specific styles of handwriting used during different periods of the Christian era, such as Roman Uncial or Biblical Uncial, help scholars date manuscripts more accurately. By comparing the script of New Testament manuscripts with those of dated Greek Old Testament and noncanonical Christian manuscripts, scholars can refine the dating of these crucial texts.

The Importance of Early Manuscripts

Manuscripts dated before 300 C.E. are of particular interest. These manuscripts, due to their proximity in time to the original writings, are considered potentially more accurate representations of the New Testament. Examples include Papyrus 75 (P75), which closely aligns with Codex Vaticanus, suggesting a high fidelity to earlier text forms. The study of these manuscripts involves a detailed examination of their textual and physical characteristics to understand their relationship to the texts they represent.

The process of dating early New Testament manuscripts is a complex but vital task in the field of biblical scholarship. It requires a careful analysis of handwriting, comparison with securely dated texts, and an understanding of the historical context in which these manuscripts were produced. By refining the datings of these manuscripts, scholars can better assess their value in reconstructing the original text of the New Testament, moving closer to the words as they were initially penned by the early Christian authors.

Utilizing Archaeological Evidence in Dating Early New Testament Manuscripts

Introduction to Archaeological Methods in Manuscript Dating

Dating ancient manuscripts is a complex task that relies on a variety of scholarly methods. Among these, archaeological evidence plays a crucial role, providing external and circumstantial factors that can help establish a more precise timeframe for when these manuscripts were created. This method is particularly useful when specific historical events or artifacts associated with the manuscripts can be identified, offering definitive markers for their latest possible dates of creation.

Case Studies in Archaeological Evidence

1. The Dead Sea Scrolls and the Qumran Community

The Dead Sea Scrolls, discovered near the Qumran settlement, offer a clear example of how archaeological evidence can inform the dating of ancient texts. The community at Qumran was destroyed during the Jewish war and Roman invasion around 70 C.E., which provides a terminus ante quem—or the latest possible date—for the manuscripts hidden in nearby caves. This event suggests that none of the Dead Sea Scrolls were written after the middle of the first century C.E., aligning with both archaeological findings and paleographical assessments.

2. New Testament Papyrus Manuscripts (P4+P64+P67)

Another significant example is the dating of the New Testament papyrus manuscripts P4, P64, and P67. These manuscripts were repurposed as binding strips for a third-century codex of Philo, indicating that they could not have been created later than 200 C.E. The use of these manuscripts in a codex that itself shows significant wear suggests they were in circulation long enough to be considered for secondary use, which assists in narrowing down their date of origin.

THE EARLY CHRISTIAN COPYISTS OF THE NEW TESTAMENT

3. Gospel Harmony Manuscript 0212

Manuscript 0212 offers an illustrative case where the manuscript was found in the embankment filling erected in 256 C.E. near a Christian house active between 222 and 235 C.E. The embankment's construction date provides a non-negotiable latest date for the manuscript, making it an invaluable asset in understanding the text's circulation before the mid-third century.

Challenges in Applying Archaeological Evidence

Despite the valuable insights provided by archaeological evidence, most biblical manuscripts cannot be dated this accurately due to unclear or missing contextual information. Many manuscripts were moved from their original locations, lost their associated artifacts, or lack a clear historical context that ties them to specific archaeological findings.

The Role of Paleography in Manuscript Dating

In cases where archaeological evidence is insufficient or unavailable, scholars turn to paleography—the study of ancient handwriting. This method compares the script styles and forms of manuscripts with other dated texts to estimate their age. Paleography often involves examining the stylistic and morphological features of the script, as well as the codicological aspects (study of the physical characteristics of the manuscript books).

The Integration of Multiple Disciplines in Manuscript Dating

While archaeological evidence can provide definitive dates for some manuscripts, it is typically complemented by paleographical analysis to build a comprehensive picture of a manuscript's origins. This multi-disciplinary approach ensures a more robust and reliable reconstruction of the historical context and dating of the New Testament manuscripts, bringing scholars closer to the original texts of the Scripture.

As we continue to uncover and examine both the archaeological contexts and the paleographical features of early New Testament manuscripts, we refine our understanding of their origins and the textual history of the biblical canon. This ongoing work is vital for ensuring the accuracy and integrity of biblical scholarship and for upholding the textual tradition that has been transmitted through the centuries.

Edward D. Andrews

Codicological Evidence and the Dating of Early New Testament Manuscripts

The Importance of Codicology in Manuscript Dating

Codicology, the study of books as physical objects, plays a crucial role in dating ancient manuscripts. This discipline examines the materials, structure, and format of manuscripts to provide insights into their age and origin. For New Testament manuscripts, codicology is particularly significant because the early Christian community uniquely adopted the codex format at a time when the scroll was still predominantly in use for literary texts.

Historical Context of the Codex

The codex format, essentially the book as we know it today, was revolutionary in its time for several reasons. It allowed for quicker access to specific passages, could accommodate more text, and was more portable and economical regarding materials than scrolls. The use of the codex is documented as early as the first century C.E., contradicting earlier scholarly assumptions that it was a later development. Early Christians, in particular, utilized this format extensively for disseminating biblical texts, which suggests a potential for dating some New Testament codices to the late first century.

Scriptural Example: The Apostle Paul's letters, which are among the earliest Christian writings, likely circulated initially as scrolls but were soon copied into codex form as the early church recognized the practicality of this format. This shift would have been influenced by the practical need for regular reference and study, paralleling Paul's instructions in 2 Timothy 3:16-17, "All Scripture is breathed out by God and profitable for teaching, for reproof, for correction, and for training in righteousness, that the man of God may be complete, equipped for every good work."

Advancements in Codicological Dating

During the 20th century, significant advancements were made in the field of papyrology—the study of ancient papyrus documents. The publication and analysis of numerous papyri have led to a deeper understanding of the codex's development and its early use among Christians. This knowledge has prompted a re-evaluation of the dates assigned to early Christian manuscripts. For example, many manuscripts previously dated to the third or fourth century based on the scholarly assumptions of Grenfell and Hunt have been re-assessed and dated earlier due to a more precise understanding of codicological features such as binding and page layout.

Case Study: Papyrus P4, known for containing texts from the Gospels, was re-dated to an earlier period after scholars recognized that its codicological features were consistent with other securely dated early Christian codices. The manuscript's use of the codex format, combined with its textual characteristics and comparative analysis with similarly dated manuscripts, supports a dating earlier than previously thought.

Challenges and Limitations

Despite the progress in codicological studies, dating manuscripts solely based on their physical characteristics can still be challenging. The overlap of codicological features across different periods can sometimes lead to ambiguous or conflicting datings. Moreover, the survival condition of many manuscripts can obscure or alter original features, complicating the dating process.

The Need for Integrated Approaches

To address these challenges, a comprehensive approach combining codicology, paleography, textual criticism, and historical context is often employed. This integrated method allows scholars to cross-verify the dating of manuscripts through multiple lines of evidence, enhancing the accuracy of their conclusions.

The Role of Codicology in Understanding New Testament Texts

Codicology provides essential insights into the dating of New Testament manuscripts, offering a window into the early Christian use of the codex and its implications for the transmission of biblical texts. As research continues and more manuscripts are discovered and analyzed, our understanding of the early text's physical form and its evolution will further refine our approach to reconstructing the New Testament's original wording.

Establishing Dates for New Testament Manuscripts Through Comparative Paleography

The Role of Comparative Paleography in Manuscript Dating

Comparative paleography is a critical tool for dating ancient manuscripts, particularly when explicit historical markers are absent. This method compares the handwriting styles of undated manuscripts with those of dated texts to infer their chronological placement. In the context of New Testament manuscripts, which are predominantly literary, this approach becomes invaluable due to the typical absence of direct dating within the texts themselves.

Dating Literary Texts with Documentary Evidence

Literary texts in the New Testament are rarely dated directly. Instead, paleographers often rely on indirect methods such as analyzing the handwriting on the recto side of a manuscript that bears a dated documentary text on the verso. This technique allows scholars to establish a terminus ante quem—the latest possible date the literary text could have been written. For example, if a manuscript features a literary text on the front and a dated receipt from 150 C.E. on the back, the literary text must have been created before that date.

Scriptural Connection: The meticulous care in manuscript preservation reflects the biblical exhortation found in 2 Timothy 2:15, "Do your best to present yourself to God as one approved, a worker who has no need to be ashamed, rightly handling the word of truth." This principle underlines the importance of accurately dating and understanding the manuscripts that transmit the New Testament text.

Practical Examples of Manuscript Dating

1. **P. Rylands 16**: This manuscript contains a comedic play on the recto and a dated documentary text on the verso. The extensive period the literary text was in use before being repurposed for recording transactions suggests a significant gap between its creation and the documentary text's date, possibly as much as 50 to 100 years.

2. **PSI 921 (Psalm 77:1–18)**: This Psalms fragment is written on the back of a roll containing a bank register dated 143/144 C.E. Based on the practice of reusing less valued documents for literary purposes, this Psalm fragment would likely be dated around 155 to 170 C.E.

3. **P. Michigan 130 (The Shepherd of Hermas)**: Written on the verso of a scroll with a document from Marcus Aurelius's reign (161–180 C.E.), this manuscript is dated to approximately 180–200 C.E., illustrating a shorter period between its documentary and literary uses.

Challenges in Comparative Paleography

Despite its utility, comparative paleography is not without challenges. The subjective nature of handwriting analysis, variations in script styles over time, and regional differences in manuscript production can complicate precise dating. Additionally, the condition of manuscripts, often fragmented and worn, can obscure characteristic features essential for accurate comparison.

The Significance of Paleographical Analysis

In sum, comparative paleography is a foundational method in the dating of New Testament manuscripts. By carefully analyzing the handwriting styles and comparing them with dated documents, scholars can approximate the age of these ancient texts. This process not only helps in understanding the textual history of the New Testament but also reinforces the accuracy and reliability of the scriptures as preserved through centuries. As more manuscripts are discovered and analyzed, the precision of these dating methods will continue to refine our understanding of the early Christian textual tradition.

Edward D. Andrews

Precision in Paleography: Dating New Testament Manuscripts Through Comparative Analysis

Foundations of Comparative Paleography

Comparative paleography serves as a crucial method for dating New Testament manuscripts by analyzing the handwriting styles found in undated literary texts against those in dated documents. This technique is essential in establishing the chronology of scriptural texts, given that biblical manuscripts rarely come with explicit dates.

Methodology of Manuscript Dating

The process of dating New Testament manuscripts often begins with a comparative analysis of the handwriting in these texts against that of dated documentary papyri. This approach not only includes comparing literary texts with dated documents on the verso or recto but also extends to analyzing similarities in handwriting styles across different manuscripts.

Scriptural Reference: As underscored in Luke 4:17, "And the scroll of the prophet Isaiah was handed to him. Unrolling it, he found the place where it is written," the authenticity and age of religious texts have always been paramount in religious scholarship. This principle drives the meticulous examination of manuscript handwriting to ensure faithful transmission of the scriptures.

Key Examples and Their Impact on Dating

1. **Heroninos Archive Influence**: The Heroninos Archive, dated to around 260 C.E., has been instrumental in dating several New Testament manuscripts like P17, P37, P53, P80, and P86. These manuscripts exhibit a 'documentary hand' similar to those found in the Heroninos correspondence, allowing scholars to date them to the mid-third century.

2. **Apollonios Archive and P52**: A collection of Greek documentary papyri from the archive of Apollonios, dated between 113–120 C.E., provides a foundation for dating P52. The paleographical similarities noted by Ulrich Wilcken have positioned P52 within this early second-century timeframe.

3. **Reuse of Literary Texts**: Instances where literary texts are reused for documentary purposes also provide significant dating cues. For example, P. Rylands 16, a literary text reused in the Heroninos collection, aids in dating New Testament manuscripts like P39, P45, P91, P110, and P115 to around 200 C.E. or slightly earlier.

Challenges and Considerations in Paleographic Dating

Dating manuscripts through comparative paleography, while invaluable, involves inherent subjectivity. The stylistic elements learned and used by scribes at different stages of their lives can skew the dating by decades. Additionally, the 'test-letter' theory, which focused on matching individual letter forms, has evolved towards a more holistic approach where the overall handwriting style is considered for a match.

Biblical Insight: Reflecting on 2 Timothy 3:16-17, "All Scripture is God-breathed and is useful for teaching, rebuking, correcting and training in righteousness, so that the servant of God may be thoroughly equipped for every good work," emphasizes the critical nature of accurately dating scriptures to preserve their intended teachings and integrity.

The Role of Comparative Paleography in New Testament Studies

In sum, the role of comparative paleography in dating New Testament manuscripts is a blend of art and science, requiring a nuanced understanding of ancient handwriting styles and their temporal variations. By carefully examining these styles in relation to dated documents, scholars can approximate the age of these pivotal religious texts, thereby contributing to our understanding of biblical history and its transmission through the ages. This method, while complex, continues to be a cornerstone in the field of biblical textual criticism.

Evaluating Manuscript Dates: Additional Paleographic Methods

Introduction to Ink and Punctuation in Manuscript Dating

In the quest to accurately date New Testament manuscripts, scholars utilize a variety of features beyond basic handwriting analysis. These include the analysis of ink composition and punctuation practices, which can offer additional clues about the time frame in which a manuscript was created. Such methods can refine our understanding of the manuscript's origins and help us approach the text with greater historical and textual accuracy.

Scriptural Reference: As emphasized in Proverbs 25:2, "It is the glory of God to conceal a matter; to search out a matter is the glory of kings." This verse highlights the importance of diligent study and investigation, principles that guide paleographers in their meticulous analysis of ancient texts.

Ink Analysis in Manuscript Dating

1. **Ink Composition**: The type of ink used in a manuscript can be indicative of its age. Early Christian manuscripts typically utilized carbon-based black ink, known for its durability and deep color. The shift to using brown ink, often made from iron salts and gall, became more prevalent after 300 C.E. This transition marks a significant period in manuscript history, suggesting a later date for manuscripts containing brown ink.

   - **Example**: P15 and P16, which contain black ink, are potentially older than those manuscripts where brown ink becomes apparent, aligning with the transition period around 300 C.E.

2. **Metallic Ink**: Occasionally, metallic inks were employed, particularly for special texts or significant copies. P. Oxyrhynchus 2269 is a rare example of a manuscript written in metallic ink dated to 269 C.E., challenging the notion that metallic inks were used exclusively in later manuscripts.

Punctuation and Stylistic Features

1. **Apostrophe Usage**: The introduction of apostrophes between double consonants in the early third century serves as another dating tool. This feature, initially noted by Turner, suggests a manuscript's alignment with or deviation from the practices of its purported time.

   - **Example**: The presence of a separating apostrophe in manuscripts like P52 has led to debates about its dating. Initially aligned with the Egerton Gospel, thought to be around 200 based on this feature, P52's dating has been a subject of revision among scholars. Comparative examples, such as BGU iii 715.5 (101 C.E.) and P. Petaus 86 (185 C.E.), demonstrate earlier occurrences of this feature, suggesting a need to revisit the assumed timelines for the use of such punctuation.

Handwriting Styles as Chronological Markers

The evolution of handwriting styles provides a framework for dating manuscripts. While there is overlap and gradual transition rather than abrupt changes, certain styles are predominantly associated with specific periods:

1. **Roman Uncial**: Characterized by its rounded, upright letters, this style was prevalent in early Christian manuscripts and is closely associated with the earliest phases of Christian book-making.

2. **Biblical Uncial**: Employed specifically for biblical texts, this script is an adaptation of Roman Uncial, tailored for the sacred context of scripture copying.

3. **Decorated Rounded Uncial**: Emerging around the fourth century, this ornate style was often used in manuscripts intended for ceremonial use or as luxury items.

4. **Severe (Slanted) Style**: Developing in the later centuries, this style is marked by a distinct slant and was used during a period of broader script evolution.

Scriptural Reference: In 2 Peter 1:20-21, we are reminded that "no prophecy of Scripture came about by the prophet's own interpretation of things. For prophecy never had its origin in the human will, but prophets, though human, spoke from God as they were carried along by the Holy Spirit." This passage underscores the divine origin of scripture, mirrored in the careful preservation and transmission of these texts by scribes across centuries.

Integrating Features for Accurate Dating

The integration of ink analysis, punctuation features, and handwriting styles forms a comprehensive approach to dating ancient manuscripts. By examining these elements, scholars can more accurately determine the age of New Testament manuscripts, enhancing our understanding of their historical context and ensuring a faithful transmission of the biblical text.

The Roman Uncial in Early Christian Manuscripts

Emergence and Characteristics of Roman Uncial

The Roman Uncial style of handwriting, an important script in the study of paleography related to New Testament textual criticism, is believed to have emerged shortly after the end of the Ptolemaic period, around 30 B.C.E. This style continued to be prevalent through the first two to three centuries of the Christian era. Roman Uncial is characterized by its round and smooth letterforms, which show a distinct evolution from the sharper and more compact script of the preceding Ptolemaic period. This script is larger and includes decorative serifs on several, but not all, letters, distinguishing it from other contemporary styles.

Comparison with Biblical Uncial

While Roman Uncial served as a foundational script for later developments, it is often considered a precursor to Biblical Uncial. Although some paleographers use the terms interchangeably, there are notable differences between these two styles. Biblical Uncial, unlike its predecessor, typically features minimal to no decoration and is known for its shading, which results from the deliberate alternation of thick and thin pen-strokes. This shading is closely related to the angle at which the pen is held against the paper, a technique that adds depth and texture to the script.

Notable Manuscripts and Observations

A prominent example of Roman Uncial can be seen in the manuscript P46, which dates from around 100-150 C.E. This manuscript is significant for its early style and well-formed characters, typical of the Roman period. Kenyon, the editor of the editio princeps of P46, remarked on the quality and formation of the letters, noting their classical Roman characteristics. This observation underscores the manuscript's value in studying the transition and refinement of writing styles in early Christian texts.

Evolution of the Biblical Uncial Script

The Development of Biblical Uncial

The term "Biblical Uncial" or "Biblical Majuscule" refers to a distinct handwriting style characterized by large, separate letters, which do not connect in the flowing manner seen in cursive or ligature scripts. This style was initially identified by Grenfell and Hunt in their examination of biblical manuscripts but was later recognized in various other texts as well. Notably, this script maintains a bilinear format where text aligns along imaginary upper and lower lines. In Biblical Uncial, most letters fit into uniform squares, maintaining consistent vertical heights except for a few like gamma, rho, phi, and psi. The script is marked by a deliberate contrast between thick vertical strokes and thinner horizontal ones, with right-angled and perfectly circular strokes, devoid of any connecting ligatures or ornamental serifs.

Historical Context and Emergence

The first instances of what would become known as Biblical Uncial appeared in the first century C.E. The style is thought to have originated shortly after the Herculaneum manuscript, P. Herculaneum 1457, identified by Domenico Bassi in 1914 as showing early characteristics of this script. This manuscript, predating the catastrophic eruption of AD 79, is among the earliest examples demonstrating the transition toward what would be fully realized as Biblical Uncial.

Significant Manuscripts and Chronological Development

An important document that showcases an early form of Biblical Uncial is P. London II 141, dated to 88 C.E. This manuscript is particularly valued for its resemblance to early vellum manuscripts of a similar style. By the second century, examples such as P. Hawara 24–28 and P. Tebtunis II 265 further illustrate the evolving script. P. Oxyrhynchus 20, another key manuscript from this period, features the Iliad on its recto in a distinct uncial script, demonstrating the durability and continued use of such luxurious manuscripts.

G. Cavallo, in his work "Ricerche sulla Maiuscola Biblica," argues that the Biblical Uncial style was definitively shaped in the mid to late second century AD. He bases this on several well-dated manuscripts from this period, including P. Oxyrhynchus 661, dated confidently to the second half of the second century. This manuscript, along with others like P. Oxyrhynchus 678 and P. Oxyrhynchus 2356, helps establish a clearer timeline for the popularity and standardization of the Biblical Uncial style.

The Role of Biblical Uncial in Early Christian Texts

As the style matured, it became prevalent in early Christian texts. Manuscripts such as P4+64+67, P30, and P70, among others, were composed in Biblical Uncial, demonstrating its widespread adoption for religious writings. The consistency and clarity of this script made it ideal for the transcription of important texts, facilitating the dissemination of Christian doctrines and scriptures.

The Biblical Uncial style, with its distinctive aesthetic and functional qualities, played a crucial role in the preservation and interpretation of early Christian manuscripts. Its development from the first century onward highlights its significance in the broader context of script evolution in ancient literary cultures.

The Decorated Rounded Uncial in Paleography

Defining the Decorated Rounded Uncial

The Decorated Rounded Uncial, also known as the Zierstil, identified by paleographers like Schubart, is a distinct handwriting style prevalent from the last century of the Ptolemaic period (first century B.C.E.) to potentially as late as the early third century C.E. This style is characterized by its use of large uncial letters where each vertical stroke is often finished with a serif or a decorated roundel. E. G. Turner extended its timeline, suggesting that these particular features were part of several styles spanning from the second century B.C.E. to the second century C.E., indicating a broader use and evolution of this script.

Characteristics and Manuscript Examples

Manuscripts featuring the Decorated Rounded Uncial are notably conspicuous due to their aesthetic embellishments and size of the letters. These characteristics can be seen in a range of dated manuscripts from 100 B.C.E. to 150 C.E., exhibiting variations from Formal Round to Informal Round styles. The following are some key examples:

1. **P. Rylands 586 + P. Oxyrhynchus 802 (Deed of Loan, 99 B.C.E.)** - Represents a later Ptolemaic decorated style.
2. **P. Fouad 266 (Septuagint, mid-first century B.C.E.)** - A seminal biblical text with distinctive Ptolemaic cursive notes.
3. **Greek Minor Scroll Prophets from Nahal Hever, 8HevXIIgr (50 B.C.E. to 50 C.E.) and 7Q1 (Exodus, 100 B.C.E.)** - Both showcase early forms of this decorated style.
4. **Several manuscripts from Herculaneum (first century B.C.E.)** - These are notably from Philodemus's library, giving them a pre-79 C.E. dating, crucially before the destruction of Herculaneum.
5. **P. Murabba'at 108 (early first century C.E.) and P. Oxyrhynchus 1453 (Oath of Temple Lamplighters, 30–29 B.C.E.)** - Both are significant for their clear use of Zierstil.
6. **P. London II.354 (Petition to Caius Turranius, 7–4 B.C.E.)** - An informal but slightly decorated round hand.

Analysis and Implications

These examples illustrate the widespread application and the aesthetic evolution of the Decorated Rounded Uncial from formal literary manuscripts to more informal documentary uses. Notably, the more formal versions of this handwriting style provided good comparisons for biblical manuscripts written in a bookhand, while the informal versions were often used in reformed documentary and documentary hands.

The continued discovery and dating of these manuscripts affirm the presence and stylistic continuity of the Decorated Rounded Uncial style well into the second century C.E. and, as suggested by Turner, potentially into the third century. This assertion is based on the appearance of similar serifs and decorations in manuscripts like P. Oxyrhynchus 3093, dated 217 C.E., showcasing how elements of the Decorated Rounded style persisted over time.

Contributions to New Testament Manuscripts

In New Testament textual criticism, manuscripts such as P32, P66, P90, and P104, which display the Decorated Rounded style, are critical for understanding the textual and visual context of the early Christian scriptures.

These manuscripts are generally dated to the period before 150 C.E., reflecting the style's significance in the early transmission of Christian texts.

This exploration of the Decorated Rounded Uncial not only highlights its aesthetic appeal but also its functional role in the broader historical and cultural manuscript traditions of the early Christian era.

The Severe Style in Ancient Greek Handwriting

Evolution of the Severe Style

During the Ptolemaic and Roman periods, the standard form of Greek handwriting was predominantly upright. However, as time progressed, a shift occurred where scribes began to slant their letters to the right. This change in direction emphasized the angularity of the letters and altered the appearance of curves, making them resemble ellipses rather than perfect circles. This style, characterized by a mix of narrow and broad letters, is known as the Severe style, termed "Strenge Stil" by Schubart and "Formal Mixed" by Turner. Turner noted that before the Hadrian era (117–138 C.E.), there was little emphasis on contrasting broad and narrow letters within documents. Contrarily, G. Cavallo highlighted that manuscripts exhibiting this variance in letter width were present in Herculaneum well before the second century, indicating an earlier origin for this stylistic feature.

Manuscript Examples Demonstrating the Severe Style

Several manuscripts from the second to the fourth century C.E., with well-established dates, showcase the Severe style:

1. **P. Giss. 3 (117 C.E.)**: This document celebrates Emperor Hadrian's accession and features one of the earliest examples of the broad, slanting handwriting style that gained popularity in subsequent periods.

2. **P. Michigan 3 (late second century C.E.)**: Dated firmly to the latter half of the second century due to a documentary text on the verso dated 190 C.E.

3. **P. Oxyrhynchus 2341 (202 C.E.)**: A record of legal proceedings confirming the date.

THE EARLY CHRISTIAN COPYISTS OF THE NEW TESTAMENT

4. **P. Florentine II. 108 (circa 200 C.E.)**: Part of the Heroninos archive, this manuscript of Homer's Iliad III is dated approximately 50 years prior to the archive's latest documents around 260 C.E.

5. **P. Rylands I. 57 (circa 200 C.E.)**: Contains Demosthenes' "De Corona," also part of the Heroninos archive.

6. **P. Florentine II. 259 (circa 260 C.E.)**: A letter from the same archive, written in a style common to professional literary hands of that era.

7. **P. Oxyrhynchus 2098 (first half of the third century C.E.)**: Features a text from Herodotus on the recto, with a land survey on the verso from the reign of Gallienus, suggesting a composition date for the literary text around 200–225 C.E.

8. **P. Oxyrhynchus 1016 (early to mid-third century C.E.)**: This manuscript's dating is challenging but is estimated to be no later than 240–250 C.E., based on various interpretations of the regnal years mentioned in associated documents.

9. **P. Oxyrhynchus 223 (early third century C.E.)**: Written on the verso of a document dated 186 C.E., it contains a text from Homer's Iliad.

10. **P. Herm. Rees 5 (circa 325 C.E.)**: Addressed to a government official known from the John Rylands archives to be active in the early 320s C.E.

Connection to New Testament Manuscripts

The Severe style is not only evident in classical and documentary texts but also in early Christian manuscripts. Notable New Testament papyri such as P13, P45, P48, P49, P110, and P115 exhibit this distinctive slanted handwriting, linking this stylistic evolution to the broader context of early Christian literature. This connection underscores the stylistic diversity present in early Christian texts and highlights the adaptability of script styles like the Severe style in various literary and documentary contexts across centuries.

Edward D. Andrews

Handwriting Skills of Ancient Scribes

The Professional Bookhand

In the field of New Testament paleography, the craftsmanship of scribes who produced early manuscripts is evident, particularly in those texts crafted with a professional bookhand. Among these, the Gospel codex known as P4+64+67 stands out for its exceptional calligraphy, use of paragraph markings, double columns, and punctuation. C. H. Roberts, a noted papyrologist, highlighted the structured division of this manuscript into sections, a systematic approach also seen in P75 and in notable fourth-century manuscripts such as Codex Sinaiticus (א) and Codex Vaticanus (B). Roberts pointed out that this structuring system was likely not the invention of the scribe, indicating its broader use beyond the Egyptian region where it was found.

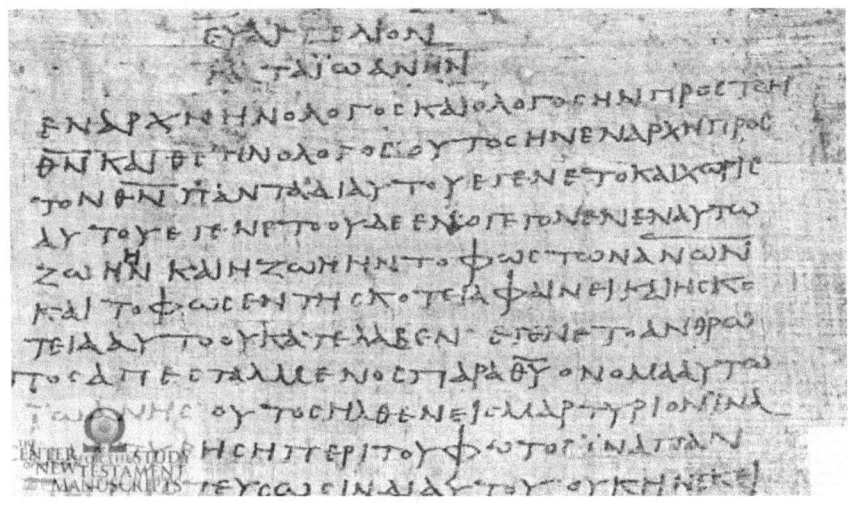

Examples of Professional Manuscripts

Several other manuscripts exemplify the high standards of professional bookhand:

- **P30**: Known for its clear Biblical Uncial script.
- **P39**: A beautiful example of early Biblical Uncial.
- **P46**: Features stichoi notations, indicative of a scribe compensated for their work.

THE EARLY CHRISTIAN COPYISTS OF THE NEW TESTAMENT

- **P66**: Likely produced in a scriptorium, reflecting organized, communal copying efforts.
- **P75**: Crafted by an exceptionally skilled scribe, showcasing meticulous attention to detail.
- **P77+P103**: Both manuscripts are noted for their refined calligraphy, standard paragraph markings, and punctuation.
- **P95**: Offers a small portion of the Gospel of John, preserved in high-quality script.
- **P104**: Celebrated as a gem among early papyri for its outstanding script quality.

These manuscripts, all dated before AD 300, provide clear evidence of the advanced skills of ancient scribes. Their ability to produce texts with such precision and beauty speaks to their professional training and the high value placed on the textual transmission of the New Testament writings during this period. Each of these examples, from P4+64+67 to P104, demonstrates that the art of bookhand was not only a technical skill but also a form of high craftsmanship, crucial for preserving some of the earliest Christian documents.

Handwriting Skills of Early Christian Scribes: The Reformed Documentary Hand

Understanding the Reformed Documentary Hand

In the study of early New Testament manuscripts, a significant number were penned in what is termed the "reformed documentary hand." This style of writing reflects a transition from standard documentary script—typically used for legal and administrative documents—to a more refined style suited for literary works. In their seminal work, *The Birth of the Codex*, Roberts and Skeat discuss the characteristics of manuscripts from the second century. They note that while these texts may not reach the highest standards of calligraphy seen in other forms, they do exhibit a competent level of writing indicative of skilled scribes. This style, referred to as "reformed documentary," suggests that the scribes involved were likely professionals who received compensation for their efforts, whether they were Christian or not.

Professional Scribes and Their Role

The transition to using a reformed documentary hand indicates a recognition of the importance of the texts being copied. This style is likely employed by scribes who, accustomed to producing legal documents, adapted their skills to the transcription of literary and religious texts. These scribes might have been hired specifically to create copies of New Testament scriptures, either for individual believers or for Christian communities. The professional background of these scribes suggests that they were capable of adjusting their handwriting to suit the specific demands of different manuscript types—shifting from purely administrative tasks to the careful copying of sacred texts.

Examples of New Testament Manuscripts in Reformed Documentary Hand

Among the papyri dating to before AD 300, at least fifteen New Testament manuscripts are identified as written in the reformed documentary hand. These include:

- **P1**: Known for its early script style that aligns with the reformed documentary characteristics.
- **P30, P32, P35, P38**: Each of these papyri shows the distinct handwriting features typical of this style.
- **P45**: One of the more famous papyri, showcasing a clear example of reformed documentary handwriting.
- **P52**: Often cited as one of the oldest New Testament fragments, demonstrating early Christian scribal practices.
- **P69, P87, P90, P100, P102, P108, P109, P110**: These manuscripts collectively exemplify the widespread adoption of the reformed documentary style among early Christian scribes.

These manuscripts highlight the adaptability of scribes who bridged their traditional documentary skills with the needs of emerging Christian literary forms. The use of reformed documentary hand in these texts not only facilitated the spread of Christian writings but also ensured a certain level of uniformity and readability across various copies, reflecting both the practical and doctrinal considerations of early Christian communities.

Edward D. Andrews

Handwriting Skills of Early Christian Scribes: The Documentary Hand

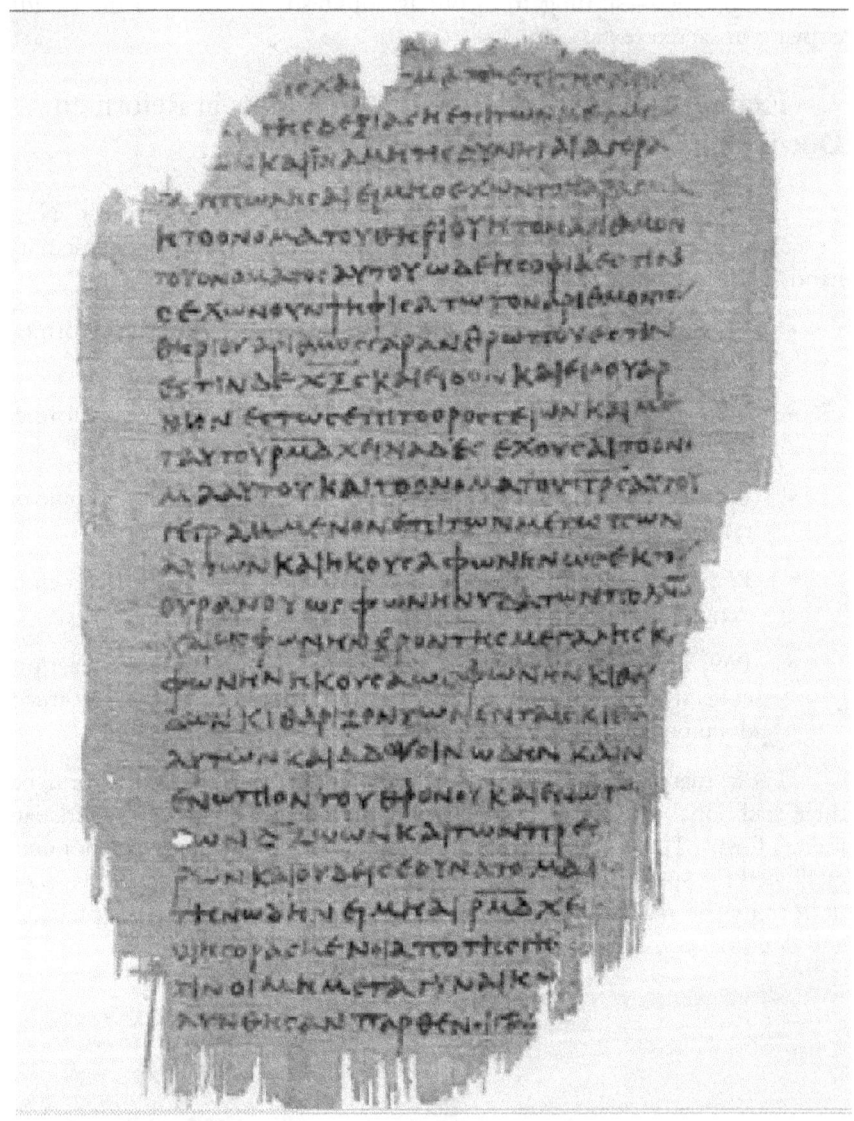

Papyrus 47

THE EARLY CHRISTIAN COPYISTS OF THE NEW TESTAMENT

Characteristics of Documentary Handwriting

In the realm of early Christian manuscripts, many of the texts were not products of a formal book trade but rather the efforts of community members with practical writing experience. These individuals, often businessmen and minor officials, were adept at creating documents and applied these skills to manuscript production. The documentary hand used by these scribes differs significantly from the more refined scripts produced by professional scribes. One notable feature is the lack of bilinearity—the consistent alignment of the tops and bottoms of letters across a line. Instead, documentary texts typically show a larger initial letter at the beginning of each line or section, a practice evident in manuscripts such as P. Bremer 5 from AD 117.

This style of script also features sporadic punctuation and frequent use of numerical abbreviations, common in practical document writing. Furthermore, spaces between words or groups of words are more prevalent, mirroring the style found in legal contracts. This spacing was uncommon in literary texts, which tended to favor a more continuous script. Examples of New Testament texts written in documentary style include Revelation manuscripts P47 and P98, which exhibit these characteristic features.

The Role of Churchmen and Women in Manuscript Production

The bulk of early New Testament manuscripts fall into the categories of documentary or reformed documentary styles. These manuscripts were often produced by church members—possibly church lectors—who were skilled in document writing. These scribes applied their practical skills to the task of copying scriptures, likely for specific patrons who commissioned their services or for use within their congregations.

Historian Gamble suggests that many of these scribes were church lectors, responsible for maintaining and reproducing copies of the scriptures. Their role extended beyond mere copying; they also prepared texts for public reading, ensuring that the scriptures were accessible and understandable to the congregation. This dual role of copying and presenting the text highlights the critical function these individuals played in the early Christian community.

Documentary New Testament Manuscripts

According to research, a significant portion of the early New Testament papyri can be classified as "documentary." This includes manuscripts like P5, P13, P15+P16, P17, P20, P23, P27, P28, P29, P37, P47, P48, P49+65, P50, P53, P70, P80, P91, P92, P101, P106, P107, P108, P111, P113, and P114. Each of these manuscripts bears the hallmarks of documentary handwriting, reflecting the practical origins of their creation.

These manuscripts collectively demonstrate how early Christian communities leveraged the existing skills of their members to create enduring religious texts. The use of a documentary hand not only facilitated the spread of Christian teachings but also ensured that the scriptures were recorded in a manner that was both practical and familiar to those within the community. This approach helped preserve the accuracy and readability of the scriptures during a formative period in Christian history.

Handwriting Skills of the Scribes: Understanding the Common Hand

Differentiating Documentary and Common Hands

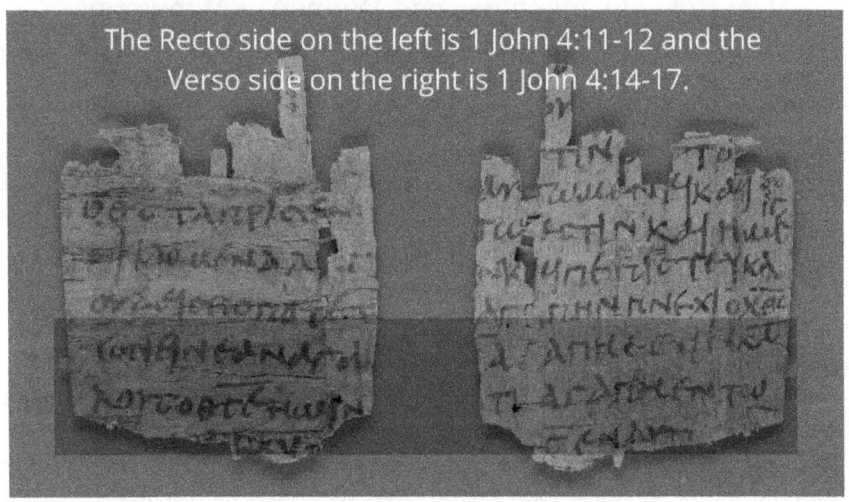

Papyrus 9

In the study of ancient manuscripts, particularly those related to the New Testament, distinguishing between a poorly executed documentary hand and a common hand can be challenging. While both may appear similar, the common hand typically represents the work of someone who may not have been formally trained in Greek writing. This style often looks more rudimentary and less structured than even a low-quality documentary script.

Examples of the Common Hand in New Testament Papyri

- **P10**: This manuscript serves as a classic example of the common hand, showing traits that suggest it was penned by someone still learning to write Greek effectively.
- **P9**: Containing a portion of 1 John, this papyrus is also clearly written in a common hand, reflecting a basic level of script competency.
- **P78**: An amulet written in a common hand, illustrating that this less formal writing style was not confined to biblical texts but extended to other types of written artifacts as well.

Common Hand in Revelation Manuscripts

Interestingly, a significant number of manuscripts containing the Book of Revelation exhibit characteristics of the common hand:

- **P18 and P24**: Both of these papyri are examples where the common hand is evident, showcasing a more rudimentary style of Greek script.
- **P98**: This manuscript is particularly noted for its common hand, displaying a very basic level of script which further emphasizes the amateurish qualities of the writer.

This prevalence of the common hand in Revelation manuscripts might indicate that these texts were not widely read in early Christian churches or that they were not often copied by trained scribes. The reasons for this could be many, including the possible private use of these texts or their less formal circulation among groups not directly connected to the main ecclesiastical authorities.

The Significance of the Common Hand

The appearance of the common hand in significant religious texts like Revelation suggests a few key points about early Christian text transmission:

1. **Accessibility**: Texts were accessible to a broad audience, including those who were not professionally trained scribes but who still engaged in the copying of texts.
2. **Variety of Manuscript Production**: There was a variety of contexts in which manuscripts were produced, not solely through professional scribe services but also by individuals with basic writing skills.
3. **Archaeological Implications**: The discovery of texts in common hand may point to differing practices of text usage and preservation, possibly indicating private ownership or use in less formal religious settings.

These insights help paint a broader picture of the early Christian world, highlighting the diversity of its textual practices and the wide range of individuals involved in the creation and propagation of biblical manuscripts.

CHAPTER 7 The Nomina Sacra (Sacred Name) in New Testament Manuscripts

English Meaning	Greek Word	Nominative (Subject)	Genitive (Possessive)
God	Θεός	$\overline{ΘΣ}$	$\overline{ΘΥ}$
Lord	Κύριος	$\overline{ΚΣ}$	$\overline{ΚΥ}$
Jesus	Ἰησοῦς	$\overline{ΙΣ}$	$\overline{ΙΥ}$
Christ/Messiah	Χριστός	$\overline{ΧΣ}$	$\overline{ΧΥ}$
Son	Υἱός	$\overline{ΥΣ}$	$\overline{ΥΥ}$
Spirit/Ghost	Πνεῦμα	$\overline{ΠΝΑ}$	$\overline{ΠΝΣ}$
David	Δαυὶδ	$\overline{ΔΑΔ}$	
Cross/Stake	Σταυρός	$\overline{ΣΤΣ}$	$\overline{ΣΤΥ}$
Mother	Μήτηρ	$\overline{ΜΗΡ}$	$\overline{ΜΗΣ}$
God Bearer i.e. Mother of God	Θεοτόκος	$\overline{ΘΚΣ}$	$\overline{ΘΚΥ}$
Father	Πατήρ	$\overline{ΠΗΡ}$	$\overline{ΠΡΣ}$
Israel	Ἰσραήλ	$\overline{ΙΗΛ}$	
Savior	Σωτήρ	$\overline{ΣΗΡ}$	$\overline{ΣΡΣ}$
Human being/Man	Ἄνθρωπος	$\overline{ΑΝΟΣ}$	$\overline{ΑΝΟΥ}$
Jerusalem	Ἱερουσαλήμ	$\overline{ΙΛΗΜ}$	
Heaven/Heavens	Οὐρανός	$\overline{ΟΥΝΟΣ}$	$\overline{ΟΥΝΟΥ}$

Introduction to the Nomina Sacra in New Testament Manuscripts

The concept of "Nomina Sacra," meaning "sacred names," represents a fascinating and significant phenomenon in the study of New Testament manuscripts. This practice involves the use of specialized abbreviated forms of certain key words that hold particular theological importance within the texts. The origin and purpose of these abbreviations provide deep insights into the religious and cultural contexts of early Christian scribes and their reverence for the sacred texts.

Origin and Development of Nomina Sacra

The practice of using Nomina Sacra can be traced back to the earliest extant Christian manuscripts, suggesting an established tradition even by the mid-2nd century C.E. Scholars speculate that this custom may have originated as a form of reverence for the divine names and titles, thereby setting these words apart from secular text. For instance, words like "God" (Θεός), "Jesus" (Ἰησοῦς), "Christ" (Χριστός), and "Spirit" (Πνεῦμα) are commonly found in their abbreviated forms in these manuscripts.

These abbreviations were not merely shorthand to save space or time. Rather, they appear to have carried a significant religious function, marking the text in a way that highlighted its sacred character. The Apostle Paul's reference to the name of Jesus, where he writes, "Therefore God also highly exalted him and gave him the name that is above every name" (Philippians 2:9), might reflect an early reverence that influenced the adoption of Nomina Sacra for the name of Jesus.

Scriptural Foundations and Usage

In the texts where these abbreviations occur, their use is remarkably consistent, suggesting a formalized system. For example, the name of Jesus is often written as "ΙΣ" rather than the full "Ἰησοῦς." This practice is not just limited to the divine names but extends to titles and other religiously significant terms.

The employment of Nomina Sacra also aligns with the Jewish tradition of showing special reverence for the name of God. In the Hebrew Scriptures, the name Jehovah appears as יהוה (JHVH) and was considered too sacred to be spoken aloud. Similarly, the Christian scribes' use of Nomina Sacra may echo this tradition of reverence and sanctity toward divine names, reflected in the New Testament manuscript tradition.

Theological Implications and Interpretations

The theological implications of Nomina Sacra are profound. By abbreviating these names, scribes indicated a theological stance that acknowledged the holiness and otherness of the divine. This practice can be seen as an early form of confessional theology in which the physical text of the Scripture itself serves as a confession of faith. As in Revelation 19:13, where it is written, "He is clothed with a robe dipped in blood, and His name is called The Word of God," the sacred names in the manuscripts highlight the divine nature of the words and the One they describe.

Differences in Manuscript Traditions

Interestingly, the practice of Nomina Sacra varies somewhat across different manuscript traditions. While the Greek manuscripts commonly employ these sacred abbreviations, Latin manuscripts, such as the Vulgate, adopt a different approach to sacred names. This variation provides valuable insights into the theological and cultural differences between these textual communities and how they viewed scriptural sanctity.

The examination of Nomina Sacra not only enhances our understanding of early Christian piety and the theological significance of the divine names but also aids in textual criticism and the reconstruction of the New Testament text. Each abbreviation tells a story of reverence, tradition, and theological emphasis that has shaped the Christian faith's foundational texts. Through these sacred names, we gain a window into the early Christian world, illuminating how they read, understood, and venerated the sacred writings that would form the New Testament.

The Presence of Nomina Sacra in Greek Old Testament Manuscripts and Other Early Christian Writings

Extending Beyond New Testament Texts

The phenomenon of Nomina Sacra, historically central to the study of New Testament manuscripts, significantly extends into the Greek translations of the Old Testament, known as the Septuagint, as well as other early Christian literary works. This extension illustrates the broad and impactful reach of this scribal practice within the early Christian communities, reflecting a continuity and consistency in their reverence for sacred texts.

Scriptural Integration and Old Testament Precedents

In examining the Greek Old Testament, the Nomina Sacra are evident in the treatment of divine names and titles, much like their New Testament counterparts. For instance, the Septuagint employs abbreviations for key theological terms such as God (ΘΣ for Θεός) and Lord (ΚΣ for Κύριος), which are analogous to the practices seen in the New Testament manuscripts. This continuity is rooted in the Jewish reverence for the name of God, as seen in Exodus 20:7, where it is commanded, "You shall not misuse the name of Jehovah your God, for Jehovah will not hold anyone guiltless who misuses His name."

Consistency in Early Christian Texts

Beyond biblical manuscripts, Nomina Sacra also appear in other Christian writings from the first few centuries C.E. These texts, ranging from theological treatises to personal letters, utilized Nomina Sacra to convey a uniform sense of sanctity and respect for the divine. Such usage underscores the integral role these sacred abbreviations played in the religious life and liturgical practices of early Christians.

The Didache, a Christian document dated to the late first or early second century C.E., incorporates Nomina Sacra in its instructions and prayers, aligning with the scribal customs observed in contemporary biblical manuscripts. This alignment across various types of Christian writings points to a widespread and recognized standard among early Christian scribes and authors, suggesting a deliberate and communal theological stance.

Theological and Cultural Significance

The adoption and adaptation of Nomina Sacra in both the Old Testament in Greek and other Christian writings signal a broader cultural and theological synthesis among early Christians. By abbreviating the sacred names, early Christian scribes linked their texts to a deeper religious tradition while also marking them as part of a distinct Christian identity. In Romans 1:16, Paul asserts, "For I am not ashamed of the gospel, because it is the power of God that brings salvation to everyone who believes: first to the Jew, then to the Gentile." The widespread use of Nomina Sacra can be seen as a textual manifestation of this theological declaration, bridging Jewish and Christian sacred traditions through the veneration of the divine names.

Manuscript Evidence and Scholarly Implications

The presence of Nomina Sacra in these diverse textual corpora provides critical insights for scholars studying the transmission and textual history of early Christian writings. The uniformity of this practice across various texts and contexts allows textual critics and historians to trace the evolution of early Christian scribal practices and to better understand the theological and liturgical priorities of these communities.

In sum, the extension of Nomina Sacra beyond New Testament manuscripts into Greek Old Testament texts and other early Christian writings illustrates the profound reverence early Christians held for the divine names. This practice not only served as a marker of sacred text but also as a reflection of the theological and communal identity of early Christian believers, emphasizing the sanctity of the divine and the unity of their scriptural heritage.

The Origin of the Nomina Sacra

Foundations in Early Christian Scriptorium Practices

The Nomina Sacra, a distinctive feature of early Christian manuscripts, reflects a profound reverence for divine names and titles through specialized abbreviations. Understanding the origins of these abbreviations is crucial for comprehending how early Christians viewed and venerated the sacred texts.

Biblical and Extra-Biblical Influences

The inception of Nomina Sacra is thought to be linked both to Jewish traditions and the unique socio-religious context of early Christianity. Jewish scribes showed great reverence for the name of God, avoiding its pronunciation and often substituting it with Adonai, or in writing, using abbreviations or symbols. This practice is evident in the preservation of the divine name, Jehovah, in the Hebrew Scriptures, demonstrating a deep reverence for the sanctity of God's name as commanded in Leviticus 22:32, "You must not profane my holy name, but I must be acknowledged as holy by the Israelites. I am Jehovah who makes you holy."

In the Christian context, this reverence expanded to include key terms associated with Jesus Christ and his ministry. The earliest manuscripts of the New Testament, dating from the second century C.E., already exhibit these abbreviations, suggesting that the practice was established quite early in Christian history. Terms such as IHΣ (for Jesus, Ἰησοῦς), ΧΡΣ (for Christ, Χριστός), and ΘΣ (for God, Θεός) are consistently abbreviated, underscoring their sacred significance.

The Role of Early Christian Theology

Theological motivations likely spurred the adoption of Nomina Sacra. Early Christians, perceiving Jesus as the fulfillment of messianic prophecies and as God incarnate, would naturally extend the Jewish practice of reverencing the divine name to the titles and names associated with Jesus. As stated in Philippians 2:9-11, "Therefore God exalted him to the highest place and gave him the name that is above every name, that at the name of Jesus every knee should bow, in heaven and on earth and under the earth, and every tongue acknowledge that Jesus Christ is Lord, to the glory of God the Father." This passage not only emphasizes the supremacy of Jesus's name but also aligns with the practice of highlighting it through abbreviation in sacred texts.

Codicological Evidence

The physical evidence from ancient manuscripts also provides clues about the origin and early use of Nomina Sacra. Papyrological findings, particularly from the Oxyrhynchus papyri and other sites in Egypt, show that Christian scribes employed these abbreviations across various types of texts, including biblical manuscripts, liturgical texts, and private letters. The widespread use across document types suggests a common standard that was widely taught and adopted within early Christian scribal schools, indicating an organized effort to maintain uniformity in the treatment of the sacred text.

Cultural and Practical Considerations

Apart from theological motivations, practical and cultural factors also played a role in the development of Nomina Sacra. In a time when materials like papyrus were costly and literacy rates were low, abbreviating commonly used sacred names could save space and enhance readability for those familiar with the conventions. This practice may have also served to visually distinguish Christian texts from other contemporaneous writings, marking them as part of a distinct religious tradition that revered Christ as divine.

A well founded observation is the practices of early Christian scribes, linking the Christian scribal practice of Nomina Sacra to earlier Jewish traditions concerning the representation of the divine name.

The use of contractions or abbreviations for sacred names, such as the Nomina Sacra in Christian manuscripts, does indeed seem to follow an adaptation of Jewish practices into the Greek-speaking Christian context. In

THE EARLY CHRISTIAN COPYISTS OF THE NEW TESTAMENT

Jewish tradition, the name of God, יהוה (Jehovah), was treated with extreme reverence. This reverence often involved avoiding the pronunciation of the name and, in written form, sometimes substituting or obscuring it, especially in contexts where non-Jews might encounter it.

In the transition to Greek, where many of the earliest Christian texts were composed or copied, this reverence was transformed into a new but related set of practices. Kyrios (Κύριος) and Theos (Θεός) were used in the Greek Old Testament (Septuagint) as common substitutes for the Tetragrammaton and other names of God found in the Hebrew Bible. Early Christian manuscripts took this a step further by abbreviating these words and others, such as ΙΣ (for Jesus, Ἰησοῦς) and ΧΡ (for Christ, Χριστός), typically using the first and last letters of each word, often with a line over them to indicate their sacred status.

This practice not only facilitated a visual distinction and reverence for the divine names but also connected the Christian texts to the broader Hellenistic cultural and linguistic practices where abbreviations were commonly used for names and terms in other contexts (e.g., personal and place names in non-religious texts). However, in the Christian manuscripts, this took on a deeply religious significance, highlighting the sacredness of the names associated with God and Christ.

Overall, this observation aligns with historical and textual scholarship that explores how religious traditions adapt and transform when they intersect with new cultural and linguistic environments. This phenomenon in early Christian manuscripts showcases an important aspect of how early Christians viewed and transmitted their sacred texts, infusing them with layers of theological and liturgical meaning.

In sum, the origins of the Nomina Sacra are deeply intertwined with early Christian reverence for the divine, drawing from Jewish traditions while innovating within their own theological and cultural contexts. This scribal practice not only highlights the sanctity attributed to the names and titles of the divine but also underscores the early Christians' intention to set apart their sacred writings as holy scripture. Through these abbreviations, early Christian scribes declared their faith in the divinity of Jesus and the sacred nature of the texts that testify about him.

Edward D. Andrews

The Use and Significance of the Nomina Sacra Lord (κυριος) ΚΣ

Historical Context and Application

The Nomina Sacra (sacred names) practice, notably the abbreviation of κυριος (Lord) to ΚΣ, holds a central place in the study of New Testament manuscripts. This abbreviation is not merely a scribal shorthand but a deliberate theological expression that underscores the divine status ascribed to Jesus within early Christian communities. The use of ΚΣ for κυριος serves as a profound instance of how textual practices reflect deep-seated beliefs.

Scriptural Foundations

The title κυριος is frequently applied to Jesus in the New Testament, signifying his lordship and divine authority. This application can be traced back to Old Testament usages where Jehovah is often referred to as "Lord." For instance, in Philippians 2:11, it is declared, "and every tongue confess that Jesus Christ is Lord, to the glory of God the Father." This passage links the confession of Jesus as Lord with the glorification of God, suggesting a direct theological and liturgical motivation behind the use of ΚΣ in the manuscripts.

Theological Implications

The abbreviation ΚΣ not only identifies Jesus as the sovereign Lord but also ties in with the early Christian recognition of Jesus's divine nature and messianic fulfillment. This usage aligns with Old Testament references to Jehovah, indicating that the early Christians viewed Jesus in the continuum of the divine revelation begun in the Hebrew Scriptures. For example, in the Septuagint, the Greek version of the Hebrew Bible, the word κυριος is used to translate the Tetragrammaton, emphasizing the continuity and fulfillment of the Old Covenant in the New through Jesus Christ.

Codicological Evidence

Manuscript evidence from as early as the second century C.E. demonstrates the widespread adoption of ΚΣ across diverse Christian texts, including the Gospels, Pauline Epistles, and other apostolic writings. This consistent use across various genres of Christian literature underscores the importance and reverence of the term within the early Christian community. Moreover, the meticulous care with which scribes applied the Nomina Sacra indicates a standardized practice that was likely taught and reinforced within early Christian scribal schools.

Cultural and Liturgical Context

The practice of using ΚΣ would have served not only as a marker of textual sanctity but also as a liturgical aid in the reading and public recitation of these texts. In the context of worship, such abbreviations would remind the reader and the audience of the sacred character of the names and titles of Jesus, enhancing the devotional atmosphere of the liturgical settings. This reflects a broader tradition of reverence for the written word of God, as commanded in Deuteronomy 12:4, "You shall not worship Jehovah your God in such ways."

Symbology and Iconography

In addition to textual use, the abbreviation ΚΣ for κυριος likely influenced early Christian iconography, where symbols and monograms such as the Chi-Rho incorporated similar abbreviations to signify Christ. These visual and textual abbreviations together played a crucial role in the expression and dissemination of key Christian doctrines, particularly the lordship and divinity of Jesus.

The use of ΚΣ in New Testament manuscripts is not just a technical detail of textual transmission but a window into the theological and liturgical life of early Christianity. It reveals how early Christians engaged with their texts not merely as literary works but as vehicles of sacred truth and divine presence, with each abbreviation serving as a testament to the profound reverence they held for the name above all names, Jesus, the Lord. Through these practices, the manuscripts themselves become a form of confession and proclamation of Jesus's divine lordship.

Edward D. Andrews

The Use and Significance of the Nomina Sacra Jesus (ιησους) IH, IHΣ

Historical Context and Scribal Practices

The use of the Nomina Sacra forms IH and IHΣ for the name Jesus (Ἰησοῦς) in New Testament manuscripts represents a critical aspect of early Christian scribal culture. These abbreviations are part of a broader system of Nomina Sacra that treated several key religious terms with distinctive reverence through specialized orthographic conventions. The usage of IH and IHΣ reflects both a theological and a practical approach to text handling by early Christian scribes.

Scriptural and Theological Foundations

The abbreviation of Jesus' name in Christian manuscripts is deeply rooted in the theological significance attributed to Jesus in early Christianity. As John 1:1 states, "In the beginning was the Word, and the Word was with God, and the Word was God." The early Christian belief in Jesus as the incarnate Word of God likely contributed to the special treatment of his name in sacred texts. Additionally, Philippians 2:9-10 emphasizes the exaltation of Jesus' name, asserting, "Therefore God exalted him to the highest place and gave him the name that is above every name, that at the name of Jesus every knee should bow, in heaven and on earth and under the earth." The reverence for the name of Jesus as instructed by Scripture likely influenced the scribal practice of abbreviating it in manuscripts.

Codicological Evidence

Evidence from New Testament papyri and codices, such as 𝔓45 and Codex Vaticanus, shows consistent use of IH and IHΣ from the earliest extant copies, dating back to the second century C.E. This indicates that the practice was well established among Christian scribes, who took great care to distinguish these sacred names from the surrounding text, often through special markings or the use of overlines to signify the sacred status of the terms.

Cultural and Liturgical Context

The use of IH and IHΣ not only facilitated a form of textual reverence but also served liturgical purposes. In the context of worship, the visible distinction of Jesus' name would have reinforced its sanctity during public readings of Scripture. This practice aligns with the didactic and confessional roles of liturgical readings in early Christian communities, where proclaiming the texts served to catechize and solidify communal beliefs.

Symbology and Iconography

Beyond the text, the abbreviations IH and IHΣ likely influenced early Christian art and iconography, where symbols associated with Christ, such as the Chi-Rho or the Iota-Eta monogram, began to appear in Christian symbols and artifacts. These visual representations, like their textual counterparts, played a crucial role in expressing and disseminating key Christian doctrines about the person and work of Jesus.

In analyzing the significance of the Nomina Sacra for the name of Jesus in New Testament manuscripts, it is evident that this practice was imbued with deep religious meaning. It was not merely a technical or aesthetic choice but a deliberate act of reverence reflecting the early Christians' theological convictions about the divine status and redemptive work of Jesus. The textual treatment of his name as a sacred element of Scripture illustrates the profound impact of Christological doctrine on early Christian textual culture, shaping how the sacred texts were copied, read, and perceived within the faith community. Through these practices, the manuscripts themselves become a form of worship and theological affirmation, attesting to the centrality of Jesus in early Christian faith and practice.

The Use and Significance of the Nomina Sacra Christ (χριστος) ΧΣ, ΧΡΣ, ΧΡ

Historical Context and Scribal Practices

The Nomina Sacra form for "Christ" (Χριστός) abbreviated as ΧΣ, ΧΡΣ, or ΧΡ, represents a key element in early Christian manuscript tradition. This abbreviation is not merely a shorthand but is imbued with deep theological significance, reflecting the early Christian community's reverence and doctrinal stance regarding Jesus as the Messiah.

Scriptural and Theological Foundations

The title "Christ" signifies "the Anointed One," paralleling the Hebrew "Messiah" and underscoring Jesus's role in fulfilling the Old Testament prophecies concerning God's anointed savior. This role is central to Christian theology, as expressed in scriptures such as John 1:41, where Andrew tells his brother Simon Peter, "We have found the Messiah" (which means Christ). Further, in Acts 2:36, Peter declares to the Jews, "Therefore let all Israel be assured of this: God has made this Jesus, whom you crucified, both Lord and Christ." These passages highlight the importance of recognizing Jesus not only as a historical figure but as the divinely anointed redeemer, a belief that is visually reinforced through the use of Nomina Sacra in manuscript texts.

Codicological Evidence

From the earliest extant Christian papyri through to later codices, such as the Vaticanus and Sinaiticus, the abbreviation of Χριστός to ΧΣ, ΧΡΣ, or ΧΡ is consistently observed. This suggests a well-established and widely recognized scribal practice by at least the second century C.E., pointing to a standardized form of textual reverence among Christian scribes. The careful treatment of Christ's title in these manuscripts not only highlights its sacred status but also serves to distinguish Christian texts from other contemporary writings.

Cultural and Liturgical Context

The abbreviation of "Christ" in early manuscripts likely served several functions beyond the theological. Practically, it facilitated the transmission of key doctrinal points efficiently and effectively in a liturgical setting. During public readings, the abbreviated forms would resonate with listeners familiar with the significance of the title, reinforcing the messianic identity of Jesus in communal worship and teaching. Such practices underscored the text's role as a living transmission of faith, where each abbreviation carried weighted significance that extended beyond the written word to the heart of Christian worship and identity.

Symbology and Iconography

Beyond the manuscripts themselves, the abbreviation for Christ likely influenced early Christian symbology, contributing to the development of symbols such as the Chi-Rho. These symbols, found in Christian art and artifacts from the early centuries, visually echo the textual reverence found in the manuscripts and are used to denote Christ's presence and authority. The integration of such symbols in both public and private worship spaces reflects the profound impact of the Nomina Sacra on the visual and cultural landscape of early Christianity.

In the examination of ΧΣ, ΧΡΣ, and ΧΡ in New Testament manuscripts, one sees a vivid illustration of how early Christians viewed their scriptures as sacred communications from God. The meticulous care in transcribing these titles as Nomina Sacra reveals a deep reverence for the identity and work of Jesus Christ as the Messiah. This practice was not merely ornamental but a fundamental expression of early Christian theology, emphasizing the divine authority and messianic mission of Jesus as central to the Christian faith. Through these sacred abbreviations, the manuscripts themselves act as theological declarations, proclaiming Jesus as the Christ—God's anointed King and Savior.

The Use and Significance of the Nomina Sacra God (θεος) ΘΣ

Historical Context and Scribal Practices

The Nomina Sacra form ΘΣ, representing the Greek word Θεός (God), is a cornerstone in the tradition of early Christian manuscript writing. This abbreviation encapsulates a profound respect and theological depth, indicating not only a space-saving technique but also a symbolic reverence for the deity at the heart of Christian faith.

Scriptural and Theological Foundations

The title Θεός in Christian scripture aligns with the Hebrew Bible's use of names for God, such as El, Elohim, and the tetragrammaton, JHVH, which early Christian Greek manuscripts translate as Κύριος (Lord) and denote with the Nomina Sacra to reflect reverence and theological significance. For example, in John 1:1, "In the beginning was the Word, and the Word was with God, and the Word was God," the use of Θεός (God) underscores the divine nature and preexistence of Christ, aligning Him with the God of Israel. The use of ΘΣ in manuscripts underscores this foundational Christian assertion with visual and textual reverence.

Codicological Evidence

The abbreviation ΘΣ is found extensively throughout Christian manuscripts from the earliest papyri, such as P{\displaystyle {\mathfrak {P}}}^52, dating as early as 125 C.E., to well-known codices like Vaticanus and Sinaiticus in the fourth century. This consistent usage across diverse texts and time periods highlights a standardized practice among Christian scribes. It was a distinctive marker that set Christian manuscripts apart, visually cueing the text's sacred content and aiding in the liturgical reading and interpretation of these passages.

Cultural and Liturgical Context

The Nomina Sacra for God (ΘΣ) served multiple purposes beyond the theological. It facilitated the transcription of the divine name in a manner that was both efficient and heightened the sacred aura of the scriptural texts during public and private readings. In the liturgical context, such abbreviations reinforced the sanctity and solemnity of the divine readings, enhancing the spiritual engagement of the congregation through the visually distinct script.

Symbology and Iconography

While primarily a textual phenomenon, the influence of Nomina Sacra like ΘΣ likely extended into early Christian art and iconography, where symbolic representations of Christian theology began to emerge. For example, symbols such as the fish (ΙΧΘΥΣ) or the Chi-Rho were used to covertly symbolize Christ; similarly, the visual abbreviation of Θεός could have subtly communicated Christian beliefs in environments hostile to overt Christian displays.

In delving into the significance of ΘΣ in New Testament manuscripts, one finds not merely a scribal shorthand but a complex, layered practice imbued with deep theological and liturgical meaning. These manuscripts are more than historical documents; they are artifacts of faith, crafted by communities who saw in Jesus not only a historical figure but God incarnate, as affirmed in Titus 2:13, "while we wait for the blessed hope—the appearing of the glory of our great God and Savior, Jesus Christ." The practice of abbreviating Θεός to ΘΣ was a way to honor and sanctify the divine name, echoing the biblical injunctions to reverence God's name and reflecting early Christian devotion to doctrinal orthodoxy and scriptural purity. Through these sacred abbreviations, the early Christian scribes declared their texts as not merely written words, but as vessels of the divine word, worthy of veneration and central to the life of the Church.

The Use and Significance of the Nomina Sacra Spirit (πνευμα) ΠΝΑ

Historical Context and Scribal Practices

The abbreviation ΠΝΑ, representing the Greek word πνεῦμα (Spirit), is a prominent feature in the system of Nomina Sacra found in early Christian manuscripts. This practice underscores the special reverence afforded to terms of significant theological import within the Christian community, particularly in relation to the Holy Spirit, a central element of Christian doctrine.

Scriptural and Theological Foundations

The concept of the Spirit is foundational in Christian theology, featured prominently from the creation narratives of Genesis, where the "Spirit of God was hovering over the waters" (Genesis 1:2), to the New Testament, where the Spirit's role is pivotal in the life and ministry of Jesus, as well as in the lives of believers. In particular, scriptures such as John 3:5-6, where Jesus teaches Nicodemus, saying, "Very truly I tell you, no one can enter the kingdom of God unless they are born of water and the Spirit. Flesh gives birth to flesh, but the Spirit gives birth to spirit," highlight the indispensability of the Spirit in spiritual rebirth and Christian living. The abbreviation ΠΝΑ in manuscripts serves not only as a textual marker but also as a theological statement emphasizing the Holy Spirit's sanctity and active presence in salvation and sanctification.

Codicological Evidence

Manuscript evidence shows the abbreviation ΠΝΑ used consistently across various types of Christian texts, including biblical manuscripts, theological treatises, and liturgical documents. This practice is observed as early as the second century C.E., indicating its acceptance and standardized use within the early Christian scribal traditions. The consistent application of ΠΝΑ suggests a wide acknowledgment of the Holy Spirit's divine status and a communal effort to honor this aspect of the Trinity appropriately.

Cultural and Liturgical Context

In the liturgical settings of early Christianity, the abbreviation ΠΝΑ would have played a crucial role during readings and public recitations of Scripture. By marking the term πνεῦμα with a special abbreviation, scribes not only highlighted the text's divine elements but also facilitated a deeper communal meditation on the Spirit's work. This practice likely enhanced the congregational understanding of and engagement with the passages concerning the Holy Spirit, reinforcing His presence and power in both the personal and communal aspects of Christian life.

Symbology and Iconography

While primarily a feature of textual transmission, the abbreviation ΠΝΑ also resonates with the broader Christian iconography concerning the Holy Spirit, often symbolized by a dove or tongues of fire. These symbols, like their textual abbreviation counterparts, serve to visually communicate the theological truths about the Holy Spirit's nature and work. The use of ΠΝΑ in manuscripts mirrors this iconographic expression, providing a textual symbol of the Spirit's dynamic and sanctifying power in the believer's life.

Through a detailed examination of the use of ΠΝΑ for the Holy Spirit in New Testament manuscripts, one can appreciate how early Christians not only acknowledged but also venerated the Holy Spirit through their scribal practices. This abbreviation was more than a convenient shorthand; it was a deliberate act of reverence, reflecting the early Church's understanding of and devotion to the Holy Spirit as a vital member of the Trinity. The careful transcription of πνεῦμα as ΠΝΑ within sacred texts denotes a deep-seated reverence for the Spirit, highlighting His divine role and ongoing work in creation, revelation, and salvation as articulated throughout Christian Scripture.

The Use and Significance of the Nomina Sacra for Father, Son, Son of God, and Son of Man

Historical Context and Scribal Practices

In early Christian manuscripts, the terms Father, Son, Son of God, and Son of Man are consistently presented as Nomina Sacra, a practice that underscores the theological importance of these titles. The usage of special abbreviations for these terms reflects their sacred status and aligns with the early Christian doctrine of the Trinity and the unique identity of Jesus Christ.

Scriptural and Theological Foundations

1. **Father (Πατήρ - ΠΡ)**: The title 'Father' for God emphasizes His relationship to Jesus and to believers, illustrating a core aspect of Christian belief in God as the creator and paternal figure. Jesus often refers to God as Father, showing a unique and intimate relationship. In Matthew 6:9, Jesus begins the Lord's Prayer with, "Our Father in heaven, hallowed be your name," highlighting the sanctity of the Father's name which is reflected in the manuscript practice of abbreviation.

2. **Son (Υἱός - ΥΣ)**: The term 'Son' primarily refers to Jesus Christ, denoting His divine filiation and messianic role. In Matthew 3:17, a voice from heaven says, "This is my Son, whom I love; with him I am well pleased." The abbreviation ΥΣ in manuscripts serves to revere and emphasize His divine sonship.

3. **Son of God (Υἱός τοῦ Θεοῦ - ΥΣ ΘΥ)**: This title affirms the divine nature and authority of Jesus. Romans 1:4 states, "and who through the Spirit of holiness was appointed the Son of God in power by his resurrection from the dead: Jesus Christ our Lord." The use of ΥΣ ΘΥ in manuscripts highlights this foundational Christian belief.

4. **Son of Man (Υἱός τοῦ Ἀνθρώπου - ΥΣ ΑΝΘΡ)**: Jesus uses this title predominantly as a self-reference, which connects Him to both His earthly mission and His heavenly glory. Mark 10:45 explains, "For even the Son of Man did not come to be served, but to serve, and to give his life as a ransom for many." The abbreviation ΥΣ ΑΝΘΡ underlines the eschatological significance of this title.

Codicological Evidence

The consistent application of these Nomina Sacra in early Christian manuscripts, dating from the second century C.E. onward, points to a standardized recognition of these terms' profound significance. The abbreviations are found across diverse textual genres, indicating their universal acceptance within the Christian scribal and theological traditions.

Cultural and Liturgical Context

The abbreviation of these titles in liturgical manuscripts likely enhanced the communal worship experience, providing visual cues to the sacredness of the texts being read or chanted. This practice would have reinforced the doctrinal teachings about Jesus and His relationship to God the Father during public readings, fostering a deeper understanding and reverence among early Christian congregations.

Symbology and Iconography

While primarily textual, the practice of abbreviating these titles may also have influenced the visual arts within early Christian communities, where symbols and icons began to reflect the theological themes found in the scriptures. These visual representations, alongside the textual Nomina Sacra, helped inculcate and propagate key doctrinal tenets throughout the burgeoning Christian world.

In exploring the use of Nomina Sacra for Father, Son, Son of God, and Son of Man, we see a clear manifestation of early Christian reverence for these titles, each of which encapsulates key aspects of Christian doctrine concerning the nature of God and Jesus Christ. These practices were not mere scribal conventions but were deeply imbued with theological significance, each abbreviation serving as a doctrinal affirmation of the Christian faith's core tenets as professed from the earliest days of the Church. Through these sacred abbreviations, the manuscripts themselves become a direct link to the theological heart of early Christianity, illustrating the profound reverence early Christians held for the divine names and titles central to their faith.

The Use and Significance of the Nomina Sacra for Cross and Crucify

Historical Context and Scribal Practices

In early Christian manuscripts, the terms associated with the crucifixion of Jesus, specifically "cross" (σταυρός) and "crucify" (σταυρόω), are often treated as Nomina Sacra. This practice not only underscores the theological centrality of the cross in Christian doctrine but also highlights the profound reverence and solemnity with which these terms are regarded in the early Christian community.

Scriptural and Theological Foundations

1. **Cross (Σταυρός - ΣΤΡΟΣ)**: The cross is the pivotal symbol of Christian salvation history, representing the instrument through which Jesus achieved redemption for humanity. Galatians 6:14 states, "But far be it from me to boast except in the cross of our Lord Jesus Christ, by which the world has been crucified to me, and I to the world." The abbreviation ΣΤΡΟΣ in manuscripts emphasizes this instrument's sacred status, mirroring its doctrinal significance as the focal point of Christian faith.
2. **Crucify (Σταυρόω - ΣΤΡΩ)**: The act of crucifixion, while a common Roman practice, holds a unique place in Christian theology as the method of Jesus' death that fulfilled Old Testament prophecies and inaugurated the New Covenant. Mark 15:24 narrates, "And they crucified him and divided his garments among them, casting lots for them, to decide what each should take." By abbreviating ΣΤΡΩ, scribes highlight the act's gravity and its central role in the narrative of redemption.

Codicological Evidence

The Nomina Sacra forms ΣΤΡΟΣ and ΣΤΡΩ appear across a range of New Testament manuscripts, from the earliest papyri to major codices of the fourth century C.E. Such consistent usage suggests a deliberate and widespread scribal convention, aimed at visually distinguishing these key theological terms. This practice facilitated both the accurate transmission of the sacred narrative and its reverential recitation during worship.

Cultural and Liturgical Context

In the liturgical practices of early Christianity, the reading of texts concerning Jesus' crucifixion would have been particularly solemn and reflective moments in the worship service. The use of Nomina Sacra for terms related to the cross would serve to enhance the congregational awareness of the sacred events being commemorated. This visual and oral emphasis helped to foster a deeper engagement with the Passion of Christ, encouraging devotion and theological reflection among the faithful.

Symbology and Iconography

The treatment of "cross" and "crucify" as Nomina Sacra likely influenced the development of Christian iconography where the cross became a central symbol in art and architecture. This textual reverence paralleled the symbol's representation in early Christian symbols such as cruciform halos, frescoes, and later, the ubiquitous use of the cross in Christian iconography. The manuscript practice of abbreviating these words reflects and reinforces the cross's profound symbolism as the sign of Christ's sacrifice and victory over death.

The use of Nomina Sacra for "cross" and "crucify" in New Testament manuscripts is not merely a textual phenomenon but a reflection of the core Christian beliefs regarding Jesus' death and its atoning significance. These abbreviations serve as a doctrinal affirmation, deeply embedded within the Christian textual tradition, underscoring the cross's centrality to Christian theology and practice. Through these sacred abbreviations, the early Christian scribes articulated a visual theology that profoundly impacted how the narrative of the crucifixion was received and venerated within the Christian community.

The Use and Significance of the Nomina Sacra for Sacred Places: Israel, Jerusalem, Heaven

Historical Context and Scribal Practices

In the tradition of early Christian manuscripts, not only are personal and divine names abbreviated as Nomina Sacra, but also certain key terms associated with sacred geography such as Israel, Jerusalem, and Heaven. These abbreviations reflect the theological and liturgical significance these locations hold within Christian belief.

Scriptural and Theological Foundations

1. **Israel (Ἰσραήλ - ΙΣΡΑ):** The term 'Israel' not only refers to the Jewish people and nation but also, in a New Testament context, symbolizes the people of God under the new covenant. As Paul writes in Galatians 6:16, "And as for all who walk by this rule, peace and mercy be upon them, and upon the Israel of God." The

abbreviation ΙΣΡΛ in manuscripts emphasizes the continued theological significance of Israel in the Christian faith, transcending its ethnic and geographic connotations to embody a broader spiritual community.

2. **Jerusalem (Ἱεροσόλυμα - ΙΕΡΣΛΜ):** Jerusalem holds a central place in both Jewish and Christian traditions as the city of David and as the site of Jesus' crucifixion and resurrection. The Gospels frequently mention Jerusalem as the focal point of Jesus' ministry, and it is symbolically portrayed as central to salvation history. In Revelation 21:2, John describes the New Jerusalem: "And I saw the holy city, new Jerusalem, coming down out of heaven from God, prepared as a bride adorned for her husband." The abbreviation ΙΕΡΣΛΜ underscores its spiritual significance as a symbol of ultimate redemption and the fulfillment of God's promises.

3. **Heaven (Οὐρανός - ΟΥΡΝ):** Heaven is repeatedly referenced in the New Testament as the dwelling place of God and as the ultimate hope for believers. Colossians 3:1 advises, "If then you have been raised with Christ, seek the things that are above, where Christ is, seated at the right hand of God." The use of ΟΥΡΝ in manuscripts highlights heaven's central role in Christian eschatology and ethics, reminding readers of their heavenly citizenship and eternal destiny.

Codicological Evidence

The consistent use of Nomina Sacra for these sacred places across various New Testament manuscripts indicates a standardized scribal practice that likely originated in the early Christian communities of the 2nd century C.E. This practice not only facilitated the transmission of texts but also visually marked the text to reflect the sacred status of these key locations, enhancing their significance during liturgical readings.

Cultural and Liturgical Context

In the liturgical setting, the reading of passages involving Israel, Jerusalem, and Heaven would have been particularly imbued with deep spiritual meaning. The abbreviations used for these terms served to enhance the listener's recognition of their theological importance, fostering a greater appreciation and reverence during worship services. This practice likely helped inculcate a sense of sacred history and eschatological hope among early Christian congregations.

Symbology and Iconography

The reverence shown through the Nomina Sacra in textual form parallels the symbolic depiction of these locations in early Christian art and architecture. For instance, mosaics and frescoes depicting Jerusalem or heavenly scenes would often accompany texts that treated these locales as Nomina Sacra, reinforcing their significance through both word and image.

In the study of Nomina Sacra for sacred places such as Israel, Jerusalem, and Heaven, we see a reflection of early Christian theology that views geography not just in physical terms but as imbued with spiritual meaning. These places, represented in the sacred texts with special abbreviations, serve as more than historical or eschatological locations; they are emblematic of God's unfolding redemptive plan, central to the Christian narrative of salvation. Through these Nomina Sacra, the manuscripts articulate a geography that is both remembered and anticipated, earthly and heavenly, woven into the fabric of Christian faith and practice.

CHAPTER 8 Textual Variants in the Greek New Testament

The New Testament Text in the First Century

Origins and Development of the Text

The composition and transmission of the New Testament texts in the first century C.E. represent a pivotal era in Christian history. During this period, the foundational texts of what would become the New Testament were written and began to be circulated among early Christian communities. These texts, including the Gospels, Acts, Epistles, and Revelation, were penned by various authors, each contributing to the burgeoning Christian canon.

Authorship and Initial Dissemination

The majority of the New Testament was written by apostles or their close associates between approximately 50 C.E. and 98 C.E. For instance, Paul's epistles, some of the earliest Christian documents, were composed between 50 C.E. and 67 C.E., beginning with 1 Thessalonians and including pivotal texts such as Romans and Corinthians. These letters were addressed to early Christian communities across the Roman Empire, instructing them in theology and ethics, responding to emerging church issues, and deepening their understanding of Jesus Christ's teachings.

The Gospels, which chronicle the life, ministry, death, and resurrection of Jesus, were written from 45 to 98 C.E.. Matthew wrote his Gospel first in Hebrew around 45 C.E., and then in Greek between 45 and 50 C.E. Mark wrote his Gospel about 60–65 C.E. Luke wrote his Gospel about 56–58 C.E. John wrote his Gospel about 98 C.E. Each Gospel provides a unique perspective on Jesus's life and teachings, tailored to their specific audiences.

Textual Transmission and Variability

As these texts were copied and recopied by hand, textual variants inevitably arose. Early Christian scribes, often working under less-than-ideal conditions, sometimes made errors of sight, memory, or judgment. Variants could include misspellings, word rearrangements, and the accidental omission or addition of words or phrases.

Despite these challenges, the core doctrines and narratives remained remarkably consistent, as evidenced by the wealth of manuscript evidence from subsequent centuries. This consistency underscores the early Christians' commitment to preserving the authenticity and integrity of their sacred texts.

Scriptural Authority and Canon Formation

From the outset, the writings that comprise the New Testament were revered as authoritative, deriving their authority from their apostolic origin and their congruence with the teachings of Jesus and the Old Testament Scriptures. For example, Peter refers to Paul's writings as Scripture in 2 Peter 3:15-16, indicating early recognition of their doctrinal authority.

The process of canon formation, while not formalized until later centuries, began with the widespread use and acceptance of these texts by early Christians for teaching, worship, and doctrine. The use of these texts in liturgical settings, particularly the Gospels and Pauline Epistles, helped solidify their status within the community as divinely inspired writings, worthy of inclusion in a distinctively Christian corpus of Scripture.

THE EARLY CHRISTIAN COPYISTS OF THE NEW TESTAMENT

Theological Implications of First-Century Texts

The New Testament texts reflect the theological diversity and the unified core beliefs of early Christianity.[99] Central doctrines such as the divinity of Jesus, the significance of his death and resurrection, salvation through faith, and the ethical implications of the gospel message are woven throughout these writings. These foundational beliefs are evident in texts such as John 1:1-14, where the divine nature of Christ is expounded, and in Romans 3:21-26, where Paul elucidates the doctrine of justification by faith.

The New Testament texts of the first century C.E. are crucial for understanding the early Christian response to the life and teachings of Jesus. The careful preservation, transmission, and reverential treatment of these texts not only facilitated the spread of Christianity across the Roman Empire but also laid the doctrinal foundations that would shape Christian theology in the centuries to follow. The commitment to textual accuracy and fidelity to the apostolic witness is a testament to the early Christian community's dedication to maintaining a coherent and faithful record of the Christian message.

Infallibility in Scripture

Infallibility refers to the complete trustworthiness of the Bible as the Word of God, free from error in matters of faith and practice. This doctrine is foundational to conservative evangelical Christianity, which holds that the Scriptures, as originally given by God, are without mistake and serve as the final authority in all matters of belief and conduct. "All Scripture is inspired by God and profitable for teaching, for reproof, for correction, for training in righteousness" (2 Timothy 3:16, UASV). The term "inspired" here

---

[99] By saying that the New Testament texts reflect both "theological diversity and the unified core beliefs of early Christianity," I mean that while the New Testament encompasses a range of perspectives and emphases due to its various authors and contexts, it also consistently affirms central Christian doctrines. For example, the writings vary in style and focus—Paul's letters address specific community issues and theological questions, while the Gospels each portray Jesus' life and teachings differently according to their audiences. This diversity enriches the New Testament, offering multiple facets of understanding and interpretation.

Despite these differences, there's a strong underlying unity in core beliefs across these texts. Key doctrines such as the divinity of Christ, salvation through faith in Jesus, His death and resurrection, and the call to ethical living under the guidance of the Holy Spirit are universally upheld. These central tenets form the foundation of Christian faith and practice, binding the diverse writings into a coherent whole that has guided Christian belief and practice through the centuries.

translates to "God-breathed," implying that the Scriptures are indeed the very words of God, imparted to human authors.

Historical Affirmation of Scriptural Authority

Historically, the church has upheld the infallibility of the Bible. The writers of the Bible themselves testify to this truth. For instance, Peter regards the writings of Paul as part of the Scriptures. "And consider the patience of our Lord as salvation, just as our beloved brother Paul also wrote to you according to the wisdom given to him, as he does in all his letters when he speaks in them of these matters. There are some things in them that are hard to understand, which the ignorant and unstable twist to their own destruction, as they do the other Scriptures" (2 Peter 3:15-16, UASV). This recognition by an apostolic witness underscores the cohesive and divine origin of the New Testament writings, aligning them with the Old Testament Scriptures.

Internal Consistency and Prophecy

The Bible exhibits remarkable internal consistency, despite being written over approximately 1,500 years by more than forty authors across various cultures and continents. This unity is compelling evidence of its divine inspiration and error-free message. Additionally, the Bible's prophetic accuracy supports its claim of infallibility. For example, the book of Isaiah, written in the 8th century BCE, predicts the coming of the Messiah who would suffer for the sins of humanity. "He was pierced for our transgressions, he was crushed for our iniquities; the punishment that brought us peace was upon him, and by his wounds, we are healed" (Isaiah 53:5, UASV). The fulfillment of this and hundreds of other prophecies in the life of Jesus Christ centuries later validates the trustworthiness of the biblical text.

Empirical Evidence and Archaeological Corroboration

Furthermore, numerous archaeological discoveries have corroborated biblical records. The historical accuracy of the names, places, and events mentioned in the Bible lends support to its overall reliability. For instance, the discovery of the Pool of Siloam in Jerusalem, exactly as described in John 9:7, where Jesus healed a man born blind, underscores the factual precision and inherent reliability of the biblical narratives.

Hermeneutical Methods: Historical-Grammatical Approach

The historical-grammatical method of interpretation is crucial for understanding the Bible in a way that affirms its infallibility. This method involves interpreting the Bible by considering its grammatical constructions and historical context. By respecting the literary genres and original languages of the Bible, this approach seeks to uncover the intended meaning of the text as conveyed by its original authors. This method stands in contrast to allegorical or subjective interpretations, which can distort the message. The historical-grammatical method aligns with the principle of "Scripture interpreting Scripture," allowing the clear parts of the Bible to shed light on the more obscure passages.

Practical Implications of Biblical Infallibility

Believing in the infallibility of the Bible has profound implications for faith and practice. It means that believers can rely on the Bible as a sure guide in all areas of life, including morality, ethics, and spiritual wisdom. It assures us that God's promises are trustworthy and that His instructions are for our ultimate good. "Your word is a lamp to my feet and a light to my path" (Psalm 119:105, UASV). This verse encapsulates the role of the Bible as a definitive guide, illuminating the path for believers and providing divine wisdom that stands above human reasoning.

The Bible's Role in Theological Formation

The doctrine of biblical infallibility is integral to evangelical theological formation. It assures that doctrines derived from Scripture are accurate reflections of God's character and will. This assurance enables a robust defense of Christian doctrine against skepticism and cultural shifts that may attempt to undermine biblical authority.

Through the consistent application of sound hermeneutical practices, such as the historical-grammatical method, believers can approach the Bible with confidence in its infallible truth. This confidence fosters a deeper understanding of God's nature and His plans for humanity, as revealed through the Scriptures, which are as relevant today as they were when first penned.

Inerrancy of Scripture

Inerrancy denotes that the Bible, in its original manuscripts, is without error in everything it affirms, whether in matters of faith, practice, history, or the cosmos. This belief is based on the Bible's self-testimony and the character of God, who is its ultimate Author. "Every word of God is flawless; he is a shield to those who take refuge in him" (Proverbs 30:5, UASV). This verse, among others, emphasizes the perfection of God's words, reflecting His omnipotence and omniscience, ensuring that the Scriptures are completely true and reliable.

Scriptural Foundations of Inerrancy

The doctrine of inerrancy is not just a theological construct but is grounded in the biblical text itself. The apostle Paul asserts, "All Scripture is inspired by God and profitable for teaching, for reproof, for correction, for training in righteousness" (2 Timothy 3:16, UASV). The phrase "inspired by God" translates from the Greek "theopneustos," which means "God-breathed." This implies that the Scriptures are not merely human words but communicated through men by God Himself, carrying His authority and truth without admixture of error.

The Nature of Biblical Authorship

Understanding the dual authorship of the Bible is crucial to grasping its inerrancy. While God is the divine Author, human authors also played a role, writing in their own styles and from their personal perspectives. However, the superintendence of the Holy Spirit ensured that what they wrote was precisely what God intended, free from error. "For no prophecy was ever produced by the will of man, but men spoke from God as they were carried along by the Holy Spirit" (2 Peter 1:21, UASV). This process of inspiration guaranteed the accuracy of the writings in the original manuscripts.

Addressing Apparent Discrepancies

Challenges to the inerrancy of the Bible often arise from apparent discrepancies within the text. A sound hermeneutical approach involves careful examination of the context, comparison with other Scriptures, and an understanding of the original languages and historical settings. Often, what appear as contradictions are differences in perspective or details that reflect the distinct purposes of the authors. A rigorous approach respects these distinctions without assuming error.

The Role of Archaeology and External Evidence

While the Bible is not dependent on external validation, archaeological discoveries and historical research have repeatedly affirmed the reliability of biblical details. For example, the existence of the Hittites, once thought to be a biblical error, was confirmed through archaeological evidence in the late 19th and early 20th centuries. Such findings lend support to the biblical record and underscore its historical accuracy.

Hermeneutics: Interpretation in Light of Inerrancy

A proper hermeneutic approach, such as the historical-grammatical method, is essential for interpreting the Bible in a manner consistent with its claim of inerrancy. This method focuses on understanding the text within its historical context and according to its grammatical structure. It seeks to discern the original intent of the biblical authors by considering the languages in which the Bible was written, the genres, and the cultural backdrop of the times.

Living Under the Authority of an Inerrant Scripture

Believing in the inerrancy of Scripture means submitting to its authority in all aspects of life and doctrine. It assures believers that the teachings of the Bible are not only true but are also applicable today. This doctrine encourages a reverent and diligent study of the Bible, promoting a life aligned with its precepts. "Your word is a lamp to my feet and a light to my path" (Psalm 119:105, UASV), indicates the guiding role of Scripture in the believer's daily walk, driven by the conviction that God's Word is both true and eternally relevant.

By upholding the inerrancy of Scripture, believers affirm their confidence in the Bible as the authoritative Word of God, foundational to all truth and righteous living. This belief not only shapes personal faith and practice but also guides the church in its mission and ministry across the globe. Through a committed and systematic study of the Bible, grounded in the conviction of its absolute truthfulness, Christians are equipped for every good work, standing firm in the truth of God's unchanging word.

The New Testament Text in the Second Century

Evolution and Transmission of the Text

During the second century C.E., the New Testament texts underwent significant transmission as the early Christian communities expanded across the Roman Empire. This century was marked by the proliferation of these texts, as well as the beginning of formal efforts to standardize and preserve the Christian scriptures. The process involved the copying of texts by hand, which was both a theological task and a practical necessity, given the lack of printing technology.

Scribal Activity and Textual Reproduction

Scribes in the second century faced the immense responsibility of preserving the accuracy of the New Testament texts amid rapid church growth and geographic spread. These scribes often worked within monastic communities or under the auspices of local church leaders. The act of copying was seen as a sacred duty, essential for the spiritual edification and doctrinal alignment of Christian believers. As 2 Timothy 3:16-17 states, "All Scripture is God-breathed and is useful for teaching, rebuking, correcting, and training in righteousness, so that the servant of God may be thoroughly equipped for every good work." This perspective underscored the scribes' meticulous approach to their task.

Textual Variants and Their Implications

With the expansion of Christianity and the resultant need for more manuscript copies, textual variants inevitably increased. Variants arose from several sources: unintentional errors such as misspellings or duplications, and occasionally intentional alterations aimed at clarifying ambiguous passages or aligning disparate accounts across the Gospels. However, it is critical to note that the vast majority of these variants are minor and do not affect fundamental Christian doctrines. The robust debate and scrutiny these variants inspired among early Christian leaders often served to strengthen the community's understanding of key theological concepts.

THE EARLY CHRISTIAN COPYISTS OF THE NEW TESTAMENT

Canonical Recognition and Regional Text Types

By the mid-second century, the formation of a recognized New Testament canon was becoming a focal point for church leaders. Figures such as Irenaeus of Lyons argued vehemently against heretical interpretations of Christianity, emphasizing the need for an authoritative set of Christian scriptures. This period saw the emergence of regional text types, such as those associated with Alexandria, Byzantium, and Western texts. Each text type represented variations in the New Testament manuscripts that reflected geographic, theological, and cultural differences within the early Church.

The regional text types highlight both the diversity of early Christian communities and their shared reverence for the New Testament writings. For example, the Alexandrian text type is known for its precise and scholarly approach to the text, often seen as closer to the original manuscripts than other text types. This reverence for the scripture aligns with Jesus' affirmation of the enduring nature of God's word in Matthew 24:35, "Heaven and earth will pass away, but my words will never pass away."

The Role of Apologists and Theologians

Second-century apologists and theologians, such as Justin Martyr and Tertullian, played a crucial role in defending and disseminating the New Testament texts. Their writings not only helped to solidify the doctrinal foundations of the Christian faith but also provided contemporary Christians with insights into the interpretation and application of the scriptures. Their efforts were instrumental in the broader recognition of the New Testament as a canonical collection, foundational to Christian belief and practice.

In examining the New Testament text in the second century, it becomes apparent that this was a dynamic period of growth, reflection, and consolidation for the Christian community. The scribes, theologians, and apologists of the time were pivotal in shaping the transmission and interpretation of what would become the bedrock texts of Christianity. Their diligent work ensured that the teachings of Jesus and the apostles would continue to guide and inspire countless generations of believers, preserving the core messages of the faith while navigating the challenges of textual variants and regional adaptations.

Canonization of the New Testament Text in the Second and Third Centuries

Contextual Overview of Early Canonization Efforts

The second century C.E. marked a pivotal era for the development of the New Testament canon. This period was characterized by both the widespread use of various Christian writings and the beginnings of formal recognition of certain texts as authoritative and normative for faith and practice within the early Christian communities.

Scriptural Validation and Apostolic Authority

The primary criterion for the inclusion of texts in the New Testament canon during this period was apostolic authority. This meant that texts were considered canonical if they were believed to have been written by an apostle of Jesus Christ or by individuals directly associated with the apostles. This link to apostolic authority is emphasized in the New Testament itself, as seen in 2 Peter 3:15-16, where Peter refers to Paul's writings as part of the existing body of scripture, thus acknowledging their authority and canonical status.

The Muratorian Fragment and Early Canonical Lists

One of the earliest known lists of canonical books is the Muratorian Fragment, dating from the latter part of the second century C.E. This document is crucial for understanding early Christian views on the canon because it not only lists the books considered authoritative but also offers insights into the reasoning behind their acceptance or rejection. The Fragment explicitly mentions the four Gospels and recognizes the Acts of the Apostles, 13 Pauline epistles, and several other writings as part of the canon, while excluding spurious works not aligned with orthodox teachings.

The significance of the Muratorian Fragment lies in its acknowledgment of the diversity of the Gospels and their harmonious testimony about Jesus Christ. This harmony and consistency were key indicators of the texts' inspired nature, as they all conveyed the fundamental truths of Jesus' life, ministry, death, and resurrection under the guidance of the Holy Spirit, fulfilling Jesus' promise in John 16:13, "But when he, the Spirit of truth, comes, he will guide you into all the truth."

Regional Variations and the Development of the Canon

During the second century, the canon was not yet uniformly recognized across all Christian communities. Different regions—such as Alexandria, Rome, and Antioch—had slightly varying lists of accepted writings, influenced by local theological concerns and the availability of texts. The core of the canon, comprising the four Gospels, Acts, and the major Pauline epistles, was broadly acknowledged, though some of the smaller epistles and Revelation were accepted more gradually as canonical.

This regional variation underscores the organic nature of the canonization process, which was influenced by the use of texts in liturgical settings, their theological coherence with the apostolic teachings, and their ability to edify and instruct the growing Christian population.

The Role of Theologians and Church Fathers

Church Fathers such as Irenaeus, Tertullian, and Clement of Alexandria played instrumental roles in advocating for and defending the canonical status of certain texts. By quoting extensively from these writings in their theological works, they not only demonstrated their scriptural fluency but also helped solidify the texts' authoritative status within the broader Christian community. Their efforts were crucial in the gradual recognition of the New Testament canon, particularly as they combated heretical movements that threatened to undermine orthodox Christian teachings.

The second-century efforts towards the canonization of the New Testament reflect a dynamic and complex interaction of theological, liturgical, and pastoral factors. These efforts were grounded in a deep commitment to preserving the apostolic teachings and ensuring that the texts used by Christians were authentic, authoritative, and conducive to the spiritual life and growth of the Christian community. The period did not see the closure of the canon but rather significant steps towards the formation of a New Testament that would guide Christian faith and practice for centuries to come.

Edward D. Andrews

Outstanding Early Catalogs of the Greek New Testament: Canonical Recognition from the Second to Fourth Century

Establishment of Canonical Texts

The process of canonization during the early centuries of Christianity was complex and evolved through various stages of recognition and acceptance by different authorities across geographical regions. This period saw a shift from an informal recognition of scriptural writings to a more formalized acknowledgment of what constituted the New Testament.

Early Catalogs and Their Significance

Catalogs such as the Muratorian Fragment, along with lists provided by early church fathers like Irenaeus, Clement of Alexandria, Tertullian, and later Origen and Eusebius, played critical roles in the development of the New Testament canon. These catalogs not only reflect the acceptance and use of certain texts as authoritative but also indicate the regional variations in the acceptance of some of the writings.

Canonical Status Across Regions and Centuries

Second Century: Foundations of the Canon

- **Muratorian Fragment (Italy, c. 170 C.E.):** This early list emphasizes the acceptance of the four Gospels, Acts, thirteen epistles of Paul, and some other books like Revelation, indicating their widespread use and acceptance in the Roman church.

- **Irenaeus (Asia Minor, c. 180 C.E.):** Advocated for the authority of the Gospels and most of Paul's epistles, reflecting a broad consensus in Asia Minor regarding the core of Christian scripture.

Third Century: Expansion and Debate

- **Origen (Alexandria, c. 230 C.E.):** Recognized most of the books currently in the New Testament but expressed ongoing debates about texts like Hebrews and James, showing that the canon was still in flux during this time.

- **Eusebius (Palestine, c. 320 C.E.):** Distinguished between universally acknowledged books, disputed books, and spurious books, which illustrates the developing criteria for canonical texts.

Fourth Century: Toward Closure

- **Athanasius (Alexandria, c. 367 C.E.):** Provided one of the first lists that corresponds almost exactly to the current New Testament canon, marking a significant step towards closing the canon.
- **Councils and Synods (c. 365-397 C.E.):** Regional synods, such as those in Laodicea and Carthage, began to formalize the canon, which helped unify the text across the Church.

Criteria for Canonical Recognition

Throughout these centuries, several criteria emerged for determining the canonicity of texts:

1. **Apostolic Origin:** Texts attributed to the apostles or their close companions were given preference due to their firsthand accounts of Jesus' teachings.

2. **Orthodox Content:** Writings that conformed to accepted Christian doctrine and accurately reflected the teachings of Jesus and the apostles were more likely to be included.

3. **Liturgical Use:** Texts used in worship across diverse Christian communities gained authority and were more likely to be considered canonical.

4. **Widespread Acceptance:** The general consensus among different regions played a crucial role in a text's canonical status.

The Role of the Muratorian Fragment and Subsequent Lists

The Muratorian Fragment and subsequent lists provided by early Church Fathers are invaluable for understanding the criteria and processes involved in the canonization of the New Testament. These documents illustrate the careful consideration given to each text, weighing historical, doctrinal, and practical factors to determine their appropriateness for inclusion in the canon.

The canonization of the New Testament was a gradual process influenced by theological, liturgical, and pastoral considerations. Early catalogs and the discernment of church leaders played pivotal roles in shaping the New Testament, ensuring that the texts included were those most suitable for guiding the faith and practice of the Christian community. Through these efforts, the New Testament was shaped into a coherent and authoritative collection of writings that continues to guide Christian faith to this day.

The View of New Testament Writings as Scripture and Its Impact on Textual Transmission

Early Views on the Scriptural Status of New Testament Texts

The recognition of New Testament writings as "Scriptural" in the early Christian community significantly influenced both the preservation and the transmission of these texts. During the first and second centuries C.E., the apostolic origin and doctrinal orthodoxy of these writings led to their increasing reverence and authority among believers.

Scriptural Authority and Canonical Recognition

As the followers of Jesus Christ sought to preserve His teachings and the apostolic doctrines, the writings that effectively communicated these truths began to be viewed with a level of reverence traditionally reserved for the Hebrew Scriptures. For instance, Peter refers to Paul's letters alongside "the other Scriptures" in 2 Peter 3:15-16, indicating an early acceptance of these texts as authoritative and inspired. This acknowledgment underscores the transition of the apostolic writings from instructive letters to holy scripture, impacting their transcription, use, and preservation.

The Impact of Canonization on Textual Integrity

The process of canonization, which gained momentum in the second century, involved discerning which writings were truly reflective of apostolic teaching and therefore worthy of inclusion in a canonical set. This discernment was based on criteria such as apostolic origin, widespread acceptance, consistency of doctrine with known apostolic teaching, and the text's utility in liturgical and pedagogical settings.

1. **Standardization of Texts:** As certain texts were recognized as canonical, there was a concerted effort to standardize and preserve these writings accurately. This led to increased scrutiny of the copies being made, promoting a higher standard of textual fidelity among scribes.
2. **Formation of Text Types:** Different regions developed slight variations in text types, which were collections of manuscripts that bore similar textual characteristics. These text types (such as Western, Alexandrian, and Byzantine) represented both the geographic diversity of Christianity and the different scribal traditions that influenced textual transmission.
3. **Theological Implications:** The recognition of writings as scripturally authoritative meant that any textual variations were subject to intense theological scrutiny. Variants were often examined not just for their grammatical or stylistic implications but for their potential theological impact. For example, variations in key Christological passages could affect how communities understood the nature of Christ.

Challenges in Textual Transmission

Despite the reverence for these texts, the manual copying process inevitably led to variations. Some of these were unintentional, caused by scribes' errors in hearing, reading, or writing. Others were intentional, where scribes made clarifications or harmonizations to address perceived inconsistencies. Ephesians 5:14, for example, which quotes a hymn or early Christian saying not found elsewhere in the Bible, shows how early Christians might integrate liturgical texts into scriptural writings.

Scriptural Interpretation and Ecclesiastical Use

As the canon solidified, the texts deemed canonical were integrated more deeply into the liturgical life of the Church. This integration further influenced the textual tradition of the New Testament, as the liturgical use required a more uniform and standardized text to avoid doctrinal confusion and maintain theological unity across diverse congregations.

The recognition of New Testament writings as Scripture profoundly affected their transcription, preservation, and doctrinal interpretation. The process of canonization not only elevated the status of these texts but also set in motion a complex interaction between theological fidelity, scribal accuracy, and ecclesiastical utility, shaping the development of the New Testament canon into the form we recognize today. This development was guided by a commitment to preserving the apostolic truth, ensuring that the teachings of Jesus Christ and His apostles would continue to instruct and inspire generations of believers across the world.

Scribal Practices and Their Influence on New Testament Textual Transmission

Alexandrian and Jewish Scribal Traditions' Impact on Early Christian Scribes

The early Christian scribes were significantly influenced by two primary scribal traditions: the Alexandrian scriptural practices, renowned across the Greco-Roman world for their meticulous attention to textual fidelity, and the Jewish scribal practices, which emphasized reverence and precision in copying the Hebrew Scriptures.

Alexandrian Influence on Christian Textual Practices

The Alexandrian Tradition of Textual Criticism

Alexandria was a hub of literary activity and textual scholarship from as early as the third century B.C.E. Its library was not just a repository of books but a center of textual study and criticism, particularly for classical texts like Homer's epics. Scholars such as Aristarchus of Samothrace and Zenodotus engaged in critical editions of texts, aiming to establish the most authentic version possible. This scholarly rigor influenced the way Christian texts were approached, particularly in terms of textual criticism and the production of archetypes for scriptural works.

Application to New Testament Texts

While comprehensive textual criticism akin to that applied to classical texts was not employed for the New Testament until later, the principles of careful textual analysis and the aim to adhere as closely as possible to the original writings were evident among Christian scribes. This approach was crucial in a time when the New Testament texts were being formalized and canonized, helping to ensure that the texts transmitted were as accurate and authoritative as possible.

Jewish Scribal Influence on Christian Manuscripts

Jewish Practices of Copying Sacred Texts

The Jewish scribes, known for their meticulous care in copying the Torah and other sacred texts, had a profound influence on how Christian scribes approached the New Testament writings. This tradition emphasized not only the accurate transmission of text but also a deep reverence for the words copied, seen as divinely inspired.

Transfer of Jewish Scribal Techniques to Christian Texts

Christian scribes likely adopted several Jewish scribal techniques, including the use of nomina sacra, a practice that may have originated from the special treatment of the divine name in Jewish texts. The respect shown to names such as Israel and Jerusalem in Christian manuscripts suggests a continuity of veneration from Jewish to Christian texts. Additionally, the layout and marking techniques used in Jewish manuscripts to denote significant sections or verses were adapted in Christian manuscripts, facilitating easier reading and interpretation in liturgical settings.

Integration and Synthesis in Scribal Work

Conscientious Copying and Correction

The dedication to producing reliable and theologically sound texts is exemplified in manuscripts like P66, where the scribe and a later corrector made numerous adjustments to improve the text's accuracy. This manuscript, along with others like P75, demonstrates that early Christian scribes were not only transmitters of texts but also engaged in a form of quality control, ensuring that what was copied conformed to the standards of textual integrity they inherited from both Alexandrian and Jewish traditions.

The Role of Christian Scribes in Preserving Textual Integrity

The early Christian scribes, influenced by Alexandrian and Jewish practices, played a critical role in the formation and preservation of the New Testament canon. Their work was not merely mechanical but imbued with a sense of sacred duty to transmit the teachings of Jesus Christ and the Apostles faithfully. This involved a balancing act of adhering to traditional scribal practices while also embracing the unique theological content of the Christian texts.

The scribal influences on New Testament scribes were multifaceted, drawing from both the rich textual traditions of Alexandria and the devout scribal practices of Judaism. These influences shaped the way Christian texts were copied, corrected, and canonized, ensuring that the scriptures used by the early Church were both accurate and authoritative. The scribes' meticulous attention to detail and reverence for the text ensured that the foundational documents of Christianity were transmitted with the highest fidelity, laying a durable foundation for Christian teaching and belief.

Assessing the Textual Reliability of Early New Testament Manuscripts

Scribal Traditions and Their Impact on New Testament Texts

The transmission of the New Testament manuscripts in the early centuries was significantly influenced by diverse scribal practices. These practices were shaped by the meticulous Alexandrian textual criticism and the devout Jewish scribal tradition, both of which played a crucial role in how early Christian scribes approached the copying of the New Testament texts.

Alexandrian Scribal Influence on Christian Manuscripts

Alexandrian Practices and New Testament Textual Transmission

The scholarly environment of Alexandria, known for its rigorous approach to textual accuracy and preservation, left a lasting imprint on Christian scribes. The practice of creating an archetype and deriving further copies from it ensured a high standard of textual fidelity, which was emulated by Christian copyists. This methodological rigor was aimed at preserving the textual integrity of literary works, a practice that early Christian scribes adapted to the New Testament manuscripts.

Application of Alexandrian Methods to Christian Texts

While full-scale textual criticism akin to that applied to classical texts like Homer's epics was not initially employed for the New Testament, the principles of Alexandrian textual criticism influenced Christian scribal practices. Early Christian scribes, aware of the sacredness of their texts, adopted methods that would ensure the accuracy and reliability of the New Testament manuscripts, paralleling the Alexandrian commitment to textual fidelity.

Jewish Scribal Traditions and Their Influence

Preservation and Transmission Techniques

Jewish scribal practices, characterized by a profound reverence for the text, also informed Christian scribal methods. Techniques such as the special notation of sacred names, precise copying methods, and meticulous correction processes were integrated into the Christian scribal tradition. These methods underscored the sacredness of the texts and the scribes' commitment to preserving their accuracy for liturgical use and doctrinal instruction.

Integration of Jewish Techniques in Christian Copying

The transition of Jewish scribes who became Christian believers potentially brought a deep respect and meticulous scribal acumen to the Christian texts. This transition might have influenced the Christian scribes to adopt and adapt Jewish scribal practices to the New Testament manuscripts, thereby ensuring a continuity of high scribal standards from the Old to the New Testament.

Edward D. Andrews

Scribal Accuracy and Textual Categories in Early Manuscripts

Refinement of Scribal Accuracy Categories in Early New Testament Manuscripts

Understanding the Alands' Textual Categories

The categorization by the Alands of early New Testament papyri into "strict," "normal," "at least normal," and "free" provides a framework for analyzing the degree of scribal control exerted during the copying process. These categories are instrumental in distinguishing the variations in how closely scribes adhered to their exemplars—the texts from which they were copying.

1. **Strict Category:** This classification includes manuscripts where scribes exhibited a high degree of control, making minimal deviations from their source texts. Such manuscripts indicate a disciplined approach to copying, where the priority was to transmit the text as faithfully as possible without introducing personal interpretations or corrections.

2. **Normal Category:** Manuscripts classified as "normal" demonstrate a balanced approach to copying. These scribes allowed for some variations, which could include minor paraphrasing or alterations that do not significantly deviate from doctrinal integrity or textual meaning. This category suggests a standard level of precision that aligns with the traditional practices of New Testament textual transmission.

3. **At Least Normal:** This intermediate category captures manuscripts where scribes were generally conservative but occasionally allowed for greater freedom than the strict category. These instances may reflect a scribe's judgment to clarify or emphasize certain aspects without substantially altering the core message.

4. **Free Category:** Manuscripts in this category show a higher degree of variability, where scribes felt more at liberty to adapt, paraphrase, or rephrase the text. This freedom could be due to several factors, including the scribe's perception of the text's needs, audience requirements, or educational background.

Application of Categories to Assess Manuscript Fidelity

The Alands' classification helps to map out a spectrum of scribal adherence that ranges from rigorous exactitude to more flexible interpretations of the text. This spectrum is critical for textual critics to understand the nature of the variations present in early New Testament manuscripts and to assess their impact on the reliability of the transmitted text.

- **Implications for Textual Criticism:** By analyzing these categories alongside individual manuscript idiosyncrasies, scholars can better understand the intentions and constraints of early Christian scribes. For instance, a manuscript categorized as "strict" might be valued for its closeness to the original, while a "free" manuscript might offer insights into early Christian interpretative traditions.

- **Case Studies:** Manuscripts like P66, which underwent numerous corrections, illustrate the dynamic nature of these categories. The original scribe might have adhered less strictly, while the corrector aimed to align the manuscript more closely with a "strict" or "normal" standard.

Enhanced Understanding of Early Christian Scribal Practices

This refined approach to categorizing manuscripts underscores the complexity of the early New Testament textual tradition. It highlights not just the variability of texts but also the meticulous care and theological conscientiousness that underpinned the early Christian scribal culture. These categories not only facilitate a deeper understanding of the textual integrity of early New Testament manuscripts but also illustrate the evolving nature of Christian scribal practices in the first few centuries C.E.

By delving into these categories and their practical implications, scholars can gain richer insights into the historical and doctrinal fidelity preserved by early Christian scribes, thus enhancing our understanding of the New Testament's textual reliability and its transmission through the ages.

Evaluation of Textual Reliability

I agree with Philip W. Comfort and suggest that textual critics could use the categories "reliable," "fairly reliable," and "unreliable" to describe the textual fidelity of any given manuscript. The use of categories such as "reliable," "fairly reliable," and "unreliable" further refines our understanding of the textual integrity of early New Testament manuscripts. By comparing manuscripts to recognized standards of textual fidelity, such as P75, scholars can more accurately determine the reliability of other texts. This comparative analysis allows for a nuanced understanding of the textual variations and the overall reliability of the New Testament manuscript tradition.

Assessing Textual Fidelity in Early New Testament Manuscripts

Definitions and Implications of Manuscript Reliability Categories

In the study of New Testament manuscripts, the classification of texts as "reliable," "fairly reliable," and "unreliable" serves as a critical tool for textual critics aiming to assess the accuracy with which these manuscripts have transmitted the original writings. These categories reflect varying degrees of adherence to the source texts, and understanding these distinctions is key to evaluating the historical authenticity of the New Testament.

1. **Reliable:** Manuscripts categorized as "reliable" are those that exhibit a high degree of textual fidelity to the most authentic form of the text available, often represented by well-established reference manuscripts like P75. These manuscripts show minimal deviations from the reference text, preserving the core message and finer details of the New Testament writings with great precision.

2. **Fairly Reliable:** Manuscripts deemed "fairly reliable" maintain a good level of accuracy but may include more variations than those found in the "reliable" category. These variations might be minor alterations in wording or order that do not substantially affect the overall integrity of the theological content but indicate a slightly less stringent adherence to the exemplar.

3. **Unreliable:** The "unreliable" category encompasses manuscripts that exhibit significant deviations from accepted textual standards. These deviations could be due to scribal errors, intentional alterations, or other factors that result in a text diverging considerably from the expected norm. Such manuscripts require careful scrutiny to distinguish core textual content from scribal interpolations.

THE EARLY CHRISTIAN COPYISTS OF THE NEW TESTAMENT

Methodology for Evaluating Manuscript Reliability

The evaluation of a manuscript's reliability often involves comparative analysis, where texts are assessed in light of a manuscript known for its high textual fidelity, such as P75. This benchmark manuscript is chosen based on both intrinsic qualities (such as the age and condition of the manuscript) and extrinsic factors (such as its acceptance and use in scholarly work). By comparing other manuscripts against this standard, scholars can gauge how closely each manuscript aligns with what is considered an authoritative text of the New Testament.

- **Example of Comparative Analysis:** In the assessment process, manuscripts like P1, P4+P64+P67, and P23 are tested against P75 to determine their fidelity. This comparison not only highlights the accuracy of the texts but also helps identify any unique readings or textual variants that may be present.

- **Scribal Motivation and Training:** The reliability of these texts is often influenced by the scribes' motivations and their training. Scribes who viewed the texts as sacred were more likely to strive for accuracy, while those with extensive training in scribal techniques were better equipped to produce precise copies. Such factors contribute significantly to the overall reliability of the manuscripts.

Detailed Examples of Reliable Manuscripts

Among the early papyri, several stand out for their reliability, including P27, P30, P32, P35, and P39. These manuscripts have been identified as particularly faithful in preserving the New Testament's original wording, thanks to the meticulous efforts of their scribes. While they may contain isolated instances of "Alexandrian polishing" or unique readings, these features are typically minor and can be critically assessed to further refine our understanding of the text.

The approach taken with these manuscripts involves rigorous examination of each variant and its implications for understanding the New Testament's original form. By systematically evaluating these variations and the contexts in which they appear, scholars can construct a more nuanced picture of the early Christian textual landscape.

In exploring these categories and methodologies, the field of textual criticism moves toward a more comprehensive understanding of the New Testament's textual tradition, aiming to reconstruct the most authentic version of the texts that have been central to Christian faith and scholarship for millennia. This process underscores the importance of meticulous scholarship in preserving the fidelity of sacred texts.

In the examination of early New Testament manuscripts, it is evident that both Alexandrian and Jewish scribal practices significantly influenced the early Christian scribes. These influences manifested in a commitment to textual accuracy that varied among manuscripts but generally adhered to high standards of copying fidelity. The early Christian scribes, equipped with methodologies from both scholarly and religious scribal traditions, endeavored to transmit the New Testament texts with a level of precision that aimed to preserve the original teachings for future generations. Through their meticulous efforts, these scribes ensured that the core messages of the New Testament were not only preserved but also transmitted with a fidelity that has stood the test of time.

Textual Integrity and Variations in Early New Testament Manuscripts

Influences on Early Christian Scribal Practices

The early centuries of Christian manuscript production witnessed a diverse range of scribal practices that significantly influenced the textual integrity of the New Testament. This period was marked by a transition from oral traditions to written scriptures, necessitating a formal approach to copying sacred texts. Influences from both Alexandrian literary traditions and Jewish scribal methods played a critical role in shaping how these texts were transcribed.

Alexandrian and Jewish Influences on Scribal Accuracy

Alexandrian Textual Criticism

In Alexandria, the rigorous scholarly environment established a tradition of textual criticism that was primarily applied to classical texts. This practice involved comparing multiple manuscripts to identify and correct errors, aiming to reconstruct the original text as closely as possible. Christian scribes, influenced by this tradition, adopted similar methods to ensure the fidelity of the New Testament manuscripts. The high standards set by Alexandrian scholars for textual accuracy greatly impacted the Christian approach to scriptural texts, promoting a careful and methodical copying process.

Jewish Scribal Tradition

Jewish scribes were known for their meticulous care in copying the Hebrew Scriptures. Their practices included precise attention to detail, such as counting letters and words to ensure that no errors were made in transcription. This reverence for the text influenced early Christian scribes, who often came from Jewish backgrounds or were converts familiar with these practices. The adoption of techniques like the use of nomina sacra and special markings for sacred names or phrases shows the continuation of Jewish scribal traditions in Christian manuscript production.

Textual Variations and Their Implications

Origen's Observations on Textual Divergence

Origen, a third-century theologian, noted the diversity in manuscript quality and fidelity, attributing discrepancies to factors such as scribal negligence or deliberate alterations. His observations highlight the challenges faced by early copyists who balanced the preservation of textual accuracy with the interpretation of doctrinal points. Origen's critique underscores the complexity of early Christian textual transmission, where the integrity of manuscripts could be compromised by both accidental errors and intentional changes.

Celsus's Critique and the Harmonization Efforts

Celsus, a second-century critic of Christianity, accused Christian scribes of altering the Gospels to harmonize discrepancies and defend against critiques from non-Christians. This accusation points to a practice of modifying texts to present a unified narrative, reflecting concerns over doctrinal consistency and the persuasive power of the Christian message. Such practices likely contributed to the emergence of harmonized Gospel texts like Tatian's Diatessaron, which sought to create a single, cohesive Gospel account by blending the four canonical Gospels.

Early Efforts to Standardize Textual Content

The Role of Harmonization in Textual Standardization

The second century saw attempts to standardize the Gospel accounts through harmonization, driven by the desire to resolve contradictions and simplify the Christian narrative for easier dissemination and teaching. Tatian's Diatessaron is a prime example of this effort, eliminating differences to produce a singular, continuous Gospel narrative. While this approach was initially popular, particularly in regions like Syria, it eventually gave way to a preference for the four distinct Gospels, as church leaders like Theodoret sought to preserve the unique perspectives and teachings of each original text.

Impact of Marcion and the D-text on Canonical Texts

Marcion's radical separation of Christian doctrine from Jewish scriptures led him to create a highly edited version of Luke and Paul's epistles, which aligned with his theological views but deviated significantly from other early Christian texts. Similarly, the creation of the D-text, likely in response to theological and ecclesiastical needs, introduced additional narrative details and adjustments favoring certain theological perspectives. These efforts highlight the dynamic nature of early Christian text production, where doctrinal interpretation often influenced textual content.

The early New Testament manuscripts exhibit a spectrum of textual reliability, shaped by a complex interplay of scribal practices, doctrinal influences, and external criticisms. The efforts to harmonize and modify texts reflect the early Christian community's struggle to define and defend its doctrinal boundaries through scriptures. Understanding these early textual practices provides valuable insights into the development of the New Testament canon and the foundational texts of Christianity.

Evolution and Impact of Textual Alterations in Early New Testament Manuscripts

The Dynamics of Textual Transmission from the Second to Fifth Centuries

The process of copying and transmitting New Testament texts from the second to the fifth centuries was characterized by a range of scribal practices, leading to both intentional and unintentional textual alterations. These changes provide insight into the evolving nature of scriptural texts and the varying degrees of accuracy maintained by scribes during this period.

Early Textual Variations and Their Causes

Initial Observations by Early Theologians

Origen, a prominent third-century theologian, noted significant diversity among the manuscripts available to him, attributing the discrepancies to scribal errors or deliberate emendations. His observations underscore the challenges faced in maintaining textual fidelity, highlighting issues like scribal negligence or the boldness of some copyists to alter texts according to their judgment. Origen's critique reflects a broader concern with the accuracy of scriptural transmission, echoed by other early Christian scholars and critics.

Criticisms and Challenges Highlighted by Celsus

Celsus, a second-century critic of Christianity, argued that Christians altered the Gospel texts to shield against criticisms and contradictions pointed out by secular or opposing religious observers. His observations suggest that some early scribes engaged in harmonizing the Gospels to present a unified narrative, a practice that became more pronounced as the Church sought to establish doctrinal consistency across different communities.

The Trend Towards Harmonization

Integration of Gospels in Codex Form

By the late second century, the physical compilation of the Gospels into single codex volumes began to influence how scribes viewed and copied these texts. The act of placing all four Gospels together led to increased efforts to harmonize discrepancies among the accounts, particularly as these texts were being used more centrally in liturgical and doctrinal instruction. The transition to codex form also facilitated the combination of the New Testament with the Old Testament, further impacting scribe practices by elevating the New Testament to the status of sacred scripture.

Quantifying Gospel Harmonizations

Research into the major Gospel papyri—such as P45, P66, and P75—shows that while harmonizations to remote Gospel parallels were infrequent, they nonetheless occurred. This trend intensified by the fourth century, with manuscripts from around 350–400 C.E. exhibiting a significant increase in harmonizations. This shift illustrates the growing tendency among fourth and fifth-century scribes to align the Gospel accounts more closely, influenced by the physical and theological positioning of the texts within a unified Christian canon.

The Canonization Process and Its Effects

Canonical Recognition and Textual Standardization

The official recognition of the twenty-seven books of the New Testament as sacred scripture had profound implications for textual practices. This canonization, which aligned the New Testament with the revered Old Testament, prompted scribes to ensure that the texts not only conformed to each other but also reflected established ecclesiastical teachings and practices. This period saw insertions that aligned with church rituals and oral traditions, indicating a move towards an ecclesiastically standardized text that supported the institutional needs of the Church.

The Role of Lucian and Alexandrian Texts

The late third and early fourth centuries witnessed significant textual recensions, such as those attributed to Lucian of Antioch, whose work aimed to create a more fluent and harmonized Greek New Testament. In contrast, the Alexandrian text type underwent less substantive editing, relying instead on a selection of variant readings to refine the text. The efforts of figures like Hesychius, and later Athanasius, in Alexandria, contributed to the development of a textual standard that balanced fidelity to older manuscripts with the needs for clarity and accessibility in liturgical and doctrinal use.

The period from the second to the fifth centuries marked a crucial phase in the textual history of the New Testament, characterized by evolving scribal practices influenced by theological, ecclesiastical, and cultural factors. These changes, from early variations noted by Origen to more systematic harmonizations in later centuries, highlight the dynamic interplay between preserving scriptural integrity and adapting texts to meet the growing and changing needs of the Christian community. The study of these developments sheds light on the complex process of how sacred texts were transmitted, altered, and ultimately canonized in the formative years of Christianity.

Fourth-Century Shifts in the Transmission and Preservation of the New Testament Text

Contextualizing the Fourth Century: Persecution and Protection

The early fourth century marked a pivotal era in the history of early Christianity, characterized by severe Roman persecution under Diocletian and the eventual legitimization of Christianity by Constantine. This period profoundly influenced the textual transmission of the New Testament, both through the destruction of texts and the subsequent efforts to preserve and standardize what remained.

Diocletian's Persecution and Its Impact on Christian Texts

The Intensification of Persecution

Diocletian's reign heralded the most intense persecution of Christians to date, with specific directives to dismantle Christian congregations and destroy their scriptures. The edict issued at Nicomedia on February 23, 303, explicitly commanded the destruction of Christian texts, aiming not just at suppressing the religion but at eradicating its doctrinal foundations. Eusebius, an eyewitness and the first church historian, vividly documented the destruction of churches and the burning of sacred scriptures, marking this as a dark period of loss and devastation for the Christian community.

Responses to the Persecution

Despite the widespread destruction, many Christians went to great lengths to protect their sacred texts. In regions like North Africa and particularly in Egypt, some believers chose martyrdom over surrendering their scriptures. Others employed deception, handing over non-sacred texts or hiding their scriptures in secure locations. This period of persecution inadvertently led to the preservation of some of the most important early

Christian documents, including several New Testament manuscripts found in places like Oxyrhynchus and the Fayum region.

The Role of Codex Form in Textual Transmission

Codex Format and Scriptural Integration

By the end of the second century and into the third, the physical compilation of the Gospels and other New Testament writings into the codex format (a precursor to the modern book) began to influence textual transmission significantly. The inclusion of the Gospels, along with the Old and New Testaments in single volumes during the fourth century, facilitated a more unified view of these texts as collectively sacred scripture. This physical and conceptual integration played a crucial role in the efforts to harmonize and standardize the texts.

Harmonization and Standardization of Texts

Increasing Harmonization Efforts

As the Gospels were increasingly read and interpreted together, scribes felt a growing compulsion to resolve discrepancies among the accounts. This led to a notable increase in harmonization efforts, particularly from the fourth century onward, as Christian scribes aimed to present a coherent narrative in their sacred scriptures. The phenomenon of harmonization was not merely a response to internal desires for consistency but also a defense mechanism against external criticisms from opponents like Celsus, who accused Christians of textual inconsistency.

Preservation and Canonical Formation Post-Persecution

Recovery and Reconstruction Post-Diocletian

The aftermath of Diocletian's persecution saw a concerted effort to recover and preserve surviving Christian texts. This period was crucial for the survival of many early Christian writings, which were later used as archetypes for new copies. The preservation efforts in rural Egyptian communities, far from the administrative reach of Alexandria, played a particularly significant role in maintaining the textual tradition of the New Testament.

Canonical Recognition under Constantine

The legalization of Christianity under Constantine not only ended the persecution but also initiated a new era of textual proliferation and standardization. Constantine's commission of fifty Bibles for the new Constantinople churches marked a significant moment in the history of the New Testament, promoting the circulation of texts that adhered to emerging orthodox standards. These efforts were likely influenced by contemporary textual scholars like Lucian of Antioch, whose works contributed to what would become the Byzantine text type.

The fourth century was a transformative period for the New Testament text, marked by severe challenges and remarkable resilience. The efforts to preserve, protect, and standardize these texts in the face of persecution and destruction underscored the community's commitment to maintaining the doctrinal integrity and continuity of Christian scripture. This era not only ensured the survival of these texts but also set the stage for their canonical recognition and the standardization that would dominate Christian scripture in subsequent centuries.

The Evolution and Influence of New Testament Textual Traditions Post-Fourth Century

Shifting Centers of Scriptural Scholarship and Textual Production

Following the tumultuous fourth century, the landscape of New Testament manuscript production saw significant shifts, largely influenced by geographical, linguistic, and theological changes. The transition from the third to the fifth century marked a pivotal era in the consolidation and standardization of New Testament texts, with major contributions from centers like Alexandria, Antioch, and later, Constantinople.

Alexandria and Antioch: Early Centers of Textual Traditions

Alexandrian Contributions to Textual Scholarship

In Alexandria, a rigorous approach to textual accuracy continued to influence the production of New Testament manuscripts. This center was known for its critical approach to texts, often striving for a purer form of the scriptures through careful examination and correction of manuscripts. However, as the regional language preferences shifted from Greek to Coptic, the production of Alexandrian Greek manuscripts gradually declined. This shift significantly reduced the influence of Alexandrian textual traditions in the broader Christian world.

Antioch's Role in Textual Development

Conversely, Antioch became increasingly influential in shaping the New Testament text. Lucian of Antioch's work, characterized by a more harmonized and accessible version of the Greek New Testament, gained prominence. His editions reflected a pragmatic approach to scripture, aimed at both doctrinal clarity and liturgical utility. The text from Antioch, noted for its smooth language and coherent presentation, began to dominate the Christian East, laying the groundwork for what would become the Byzantine text tradition.

The Rise of Constantinople as a New Scriptural Hub

Constantinople and the Byzantine Text Tradition

By the fifth century, Constantinople had emerged as a major center for Christian scholarship and manuscript production. The strategic relocation of political and religious authority to Constantinople under Constantine and his successors catalyzed the city's development as a hub for Christian texts. Manuscripts produced in this period predominantly reflected the Byzantine text type, which was directly influenced by Antioch's Lucianic text. This tradition prioritized textual consistency and uniformity, aligning with the empire's emphasis on doctrinal unity.

The Byzantine Text: Dominance and Standardization

Proliferation of the Byzantine Text

From the sixth century onward, the Byzantine text type became the most widely produced and used form of the New Testament text across the Greek-speaking parts of the Christian world. This text type was characterized by its homogeneity, with manuscripts showing remarkably consistent readings across centuries. The predominance of the Byzantine text lasted well into the Middle Ages, fundamentally shaping the theological and liturgical landscape of Eastern Christianity.

The Textus Receptus and Its Historical Irony

The Emergence of the Textus Receptus

The term "Textus Receptus," literally meaning "received text," was coined in the seventeenth century to describe the Greek New Testament edition published by the Elzevir brothers, which was based largely on late Byzantine manuscripts used by Erasmus, Stephanus, and Beza. This text, while declared as the standard, ironically embodied a culmination of the textual variances that had been ironed out over the centuries. It was not until the advent of modern textual criticism, fueled by discoveries of older and more diverse manuscripts, that the true extent of the Textus Receptus's departures from earlier textual forms was fully understood.

The Impact of Linguistic and Regional Shifts

Decline of Greek and Rise of Local Vernaculars

As the Greek language's dominance waned in regions like Egypt, and as Latin took over as the lingua franca of the Western Mediterranean, the production of Greek manuscripts concentrated increasingly in Byzantium. This concentration ensured the survival of the Greek New Testament through Byzantine scribes, even as other regions transitioned to different languages and scriptural traditions.

The post-fourth-century development of New Testament texts illustrates a complex interplay between regional centers of power, shifting linguistic landscapes, and evolving theological needs. The transition from diverse early Christian textual traditions to a more uniform Byzantine text encapsulates both the desire for doctrinal consistency and the practical realities of scriptural production in a changing world. This period not only solidified the Byzantine text's dominance but also set the stage for future debates and developments in biblical scholarship.

Edward D. Andrews

Understanding Textual Variants Through Reader-Reception Analysis

Introduction to Reader-Reception Analysis of New Testament Variants

This method investigates how scribes, in their role as readers and not merely copiers, might have introduced changes into the text. Initially, scribes worked alone, manually copying from source documents. During this solitary work, some variations arose from mere copying mistakes, while others stemmed from the scribes' interpretations and engagements with the text. These adjustments indicate that scribes often interacted with the text more actively than merely duplicating it; they sometimes reshaped it according to their personal insights or even unconsciously.

Currently, no unified theory in New Testament studies fully explains how the way scribes perceived texts influenced their transcription. It might seem obvious that a diligent scribe should focus solely on accurate reproduction, down to every letter. Yet, regardless of their meticulousness or professionalism, scribes inevitably infused their personal interactions into their work. They internalized and occasionally modified the text during copying, especially when they regarded the text as sacred and divinely inspired.

The concept of reader-reception, emphasized by literary theorists like Gadamer, illuminates the dynamic interaction between the scribe as a reader and the manuscript. Gadamer introduced the notion that each reader approaches a text with a blend of unfamiliarity and familiarity, shaped by their historical and cultural background. He discussed an "intermediate area" where the text is understood as belonging both to its original context and to the reader's interpretative traditions. The closer a scribe's context is to the original setting of the text, the more their interpretations are likely to resonate with its intended meanings.

Gadamer contended that our historical backgrounds inevitably influence our comprehension, suggesting that our initial biases about a text are crucial to our interpretation. These biases are not obstacles but rather starting points for engagement, which can lead to a deeper understanding and a "fusion of horizons"—the merging of the reader's and the text's perspectives.

This fusion is not merely a direct assimilation of the text's intended message but a complex interplay where the reader's preconceptions and the text's challenges lead to a continuously evolving understanding. According to Gadamer, this process involves the reader projecting their interpretation onto the text as they begin to understand its meaning, continually refining this projection as they delve deeper.

The Role of Scribes as Interactive Readers in Textual Criticism

Textual critics need to account for the historical context of the scribes who produced the manuscripts we study today. These scribes were more than mere copyists; they were engaged, interactive readers. This perspective shift—from viewing texts as static to seeing them as interactive—mirrors modern trends in literary criticism that emphasize the reader's role in shaping text interpretation. Likewise, textual critics should consider variant readings in ancient manuscripts as reflections of each scribe's unique interaction with the text.

Wolfgang Iser's theories shed light on this idea. Iser suggested that scribes didn't simply read texts passively; they played an active role in forming their meanings. He proposed that a text's meaning is not fixed but comes to life through the reader. Scribes, acting as readers, co-create the text by interpreting its "gaps" or ambiguous parts. These gaps challenge readers to use their imagination to complete the text, turning reading into a creative act.

While typical readers engage imaginatively, scribes often went a step further by physically adding to the texts. Historical evidence suggests that each scribe, in creating a copy, effectively produced a new version of the text. These changes weren't just the result of errors or misinterpretations; they also arose because texts actively invite readers to fill in missing details.

For instance, consider how a literary work is not merely a self-contained object but something that comes to full realization only with the reader's participation. During the reading process, readers—or scribes—must complete the text using their imagination to expand on parts that the text merely suggests. This active engagement can lead to variations in how the text is reproduced. Take the example from the Gospel of Luke, where after Jesus' crucifixion, the crowds return home "beating their breasts." Some scribes, imagining a more intense scene, added details like the crowds also "beating their foreheads" or lamenting, "woe to us for the sins we have committed this day, for the destruction of Jerusalem is imminent!"

Iser called these underdeveloped parts of the text "blanks," which act as catalysts for interaction by compelling the reader to actively fill them in. These blanks disrupt the narrative flow and enhance the reader's engagement, playing a critical role in how texts communicate. Iser believed that filling in these blanks is essential to understanding and appreciating texts.

This active participation by scribes illustrates that the history of the New Testament's textual transmission is characterized by gradual expansions and modifications as successive scribes incorporated their interpretations into the text. This process highlights that scribes were not simply transcribing words; they were deeply engaged in a complex interaction with the text, interpreting and sometimes expanding on it according to their understanding and the expectations of their religious communities.

Understanding Ancient Textual Vocalization and Its Impact on Manuscript Production

In ancient times, creating written texts was a vocal process. Authors typically dictated their writings to an assistant called an amanuensis. After dictating, the author would often read the text aloud again to make edits and adjustments. If the author wrote the text personally, he would usually speak the words as he wrote them. This method ensured that all writing, whether dictated or personally penned, was spoken aloud during its creation.

Paul Achtemeier highlighted how pervasive this oral practice was, noting that no writing occurred without vocalization. This was evident not only in dictation but also in personal writing, where authors would speak the words as they wrote. This tradition continued with scribes who reproduced manuscripts, who would also read aloud the texts they were copying.

Bruce Metzger described the vocalization process as consisting of four steps:

1. Reading the text to oneself, usually out loud, to grasp a line or a clause.
2. Memorizing this snippet of text.
3. Dictating it back to oneself for transcription, which could be silent or spoken softly.
4. Physically writing down the text.

This process reveals that scribes typically read and processed texts in chunks—larger units of meaning rather than word by word. This method meant that scribes might not replicate the exact words of the text but rather its overall sense. They usually vocalized the text twice during this process—once when initially reading and again when writing it down.

The dynamic interaction involved in this method meant that reading and writing were interconnected activities that influenced each other. Scribes did not just passively transfer text from one page to another; they engaged with the text, interpreted it, and sometimes even altered it as they wrote.

Furthermore, the process of decoding a text during reading involves understanding chunks of information that correspond to the natural breaks in sentences, not just individual words. This chunk-based processing can sometimes lead to errors in transcription. For example, a scribe might accidentally skip over sections of text—a mistake known as haplography—because his eyes might jump from one familiar word to the same word a few lines down without realizing some text was missed.

This method of chunk-based reading and writing challenges a scribe's ability to copy text verbatim. As they read ahead mentally, scribes might struggle to copy each word precisely as their attention is divided between understanding the text and transcribing it accurately. This can lead to various transcription errors if the scribe does not carefully review what has been written.

Overall, the process of vocalization and chunk-based reading significantly influenced how ancient texts were transmitted and can explain some of the variations and errors found in manuscript copies. This method required a delicate balance between accurate transcription and the scribe's interpretation of the text's meaning.

Understanding the Role of Reader Interpretation in Scribal Errors and Creativity

Scribes could be influenced by their own thoughts or previous readings of a text, which sometimes led to errors in copying. A well-known example occurred with the scribe of P66 during the transcription of John 5:28, which reads, "An hour is coming when all who are in the graves will hear his voice." Distracted, the scribe initially wrote "wilderness" instead of "graves." This mistake was likely due to the phrase "hearing his voice" reminding him of John 1:23, where John the Baptist is described as "a voice crying in the wilderness." Upon noticing the mistake, the scribe corrected "wilderness" to "graves."

Reading involves a complex interaction between the reader and the text. Wolfgang Iser, a literary theorist, emphasized that reading is a dynamic activity where the structures of the text and the reader's engagement with it are crucial for communication. Successful comprehension of a text depends on the text's ability to engage the reader's interpretive skills. Iser proposed that this interaction is an active and creative process shaped by the reader's background and expectations. While the text invites interpretation, it does not command it, allowing the reader's inputs to influence their understanding and, for scribes, the final outcome of their copying.

Ideally, a New Testament scribe should copy the source text accurately. However, historical evidence from manuscripts shows that scribes often interpreted the texts as they read, leading to various textual variants. Their active involvement and personal interpretations during the copying process produced unique and sometimes creative versions of the scriptures. This type of participation should not be viewed as negligence but as a natural aspect of how texts were historically transmitted. Scribes were not merely mechanical copiers; they were engaged readers who actively made sense of the texts, sometimes introducing new elements or altering existing ones in the documents they produced.

Kurt and Barbara Aland categorized early New Testament manuscripts into four levels of textual fidelity: "normal," "free," "strict," and "at least normal." Although I have some concerns about their specific classifications, their approach to categorizing manuscripts based on how faithfully scribes copied texts is insightful. According to the Alands, a "normal" text has a limited amount of variation, typical for the New Testament tradition. Examples of these are manuscripts like P5, P15+16, P18, P20, P29, P46, and P66.

A "strict" text closely follows the source with minimal deviations and includes manuscripts like P1, P4+64+67, P23, P27, P35, P39, P65, P70, and P75. On the other hand, a "free" text, such as those in P9, P37, P45, P69, and P78, shows more considerable variations. Manuscripts labeled "at least normal," like P22, P32, P72, and P77, are mostly normal but tend towards stricter fidelity.

The "strict" manuscripts, often produced by professional scribes or those adhering to Alexandrian scribal practices, represent the highest fidelity in copying, though they make up only about a quarter of early manuscripts. The majority of manuscripts fall under "normal" or "at least normal," indicating that while New Testament scribes generally aimed to preserve the essence and meaning of the texts, exact wording was not always a priority.

THE EARLY CHRISTIAN COPYISTS OF THE NEW TESTAMENT

The sacred nature of the content allowed for some flexibility in expression to improve readability or clarify meaning, akin to modern translation practices that might add nouns or glosses for clarity.

Scribes' subjective interactions with the texts meant their copies could differ from the originals for various reasons: correcting perceived errors, aligning the text with oral traditions, enhancing expressiveness, or theological motives. Such alterations were typically not viewed as tampering but as enhancements to the text's presentation.

This subjective engagement often led scribes to produce versions that conveyed the thought of the text rather than its exact words, favoring a thought-for-thought over a word-for-word approach. For example, manuscript P45 often paraphrases, leaving out less essential details for brevity and clarity, such as simplifying descriptions in the multiplication of the loaves or omitting the time of night in Mark 6:48.

Similarly, P66 adds phrases to improve understanding or fill perceived gaps, like including "taking away the sin of the world" in John the Baptist's declaration in John 1:36, or adding "yet" in Jesus' statement about attending a feast in John 7:8 to prevent misinterpretation of His intentions.

These instances show that scribes were not just replicating text; they were actively engaging with it, interpreting and sometimes expanding it to fulfill what they perceived as its intended purpose or to make it resonate more clearly with contemporary audiences. Therefore, the history of New Testament text transmission is characterized by gradual changes, with each generation of scribes leaving their mark on the sacred texts.

Scribes often acted as co-creators while copying texts, which sometimes affected the accuracy of their transcriptions. The most precise copies typically came from scribes who devotedly focused on the original texts, copying them word for word. For instance, the scribe of P75 tried hard to minimize errors but couldn't entirely suppress his creative instincts. In the Gospel of Luke, the story of Lazarus and the rich man leaves the rich man unnamed, but in P75, this scribe initially names him "Nineveh," which Priscillian later changed to "Finees." Bruce Metzger theorized that a tendency to avoid empty narrative spaces, known as 'horror vacui,' might have compelled the scribe to give a name to the rich man.

Major textual additions in the Gospels often arose from perceived gaps in the narratives. For example, the earliest versions of the Gospel of Mark end abruptly at 16:8, likely confusing readers expecting a more detailed resurrection account like those in other Gospels. To provide closure, many scribes created various endings, resulting in five different conclusions across various manuscripts.

Early Christian scribes, who frequently also served as church lectors, had to balance textual fidelity with the listening needs of their congregations. This dual role, coupled with the significant influence of oral tradition regarded as authoritative as written texts, led them to weave well-known oral stories into the written Gospels to fill perceived gaps.

One notable example is the addition of an episode where Jesus is strengthened by an angel in the Garden of Gethsemane, included in some manuscripts but not others, highlighting its controversial status. Early church fathers disagreed on its inclusion; some omitted it because it suggested Jesus showed human weakness, while others added it from oral traditions.

Another significant oral addition is the story of the adulterous woman in the Gospel of John, absent from early manuscripts and consistently appearing only in texts from the ninth century onward. Known from the Syriac Peshitta and later the Latin Vulgate, this story likely moved from oral recitation to the Greek manuscript tradition before being incorporated into later copies. This narrative, while debated among scholars, shows how oral traditions could influence the textual content of the Gospels.

Overall, the interplay between oral and written traditions played a crucial role in how texts were copied and preserved, especially in places like Egypt, where scribes might have been more successful at maintaining the integrity of the written word compared to their Western counterparts, who were more prone to blending oral traditions into the manuscripts.

CHAPTER 9 Modern Theories and Methods of New Testament Textual Criticism

The Primary Task of Textual Criticism: Recovering the Original Wording of the New Testament

Introduction to Textual Criticism

Textual criticism of the New Testament is an academic discipline dedicated to recovering the most accurate text of the New Testament as originally penned by its authors. This process involves a meticulous examination of the surviving manuscripts to identify and correct alterations, whether accidental or intentional. The discipline relies on principles and methods developed to discern the original words of the biblical texts amidst the variations found in the extant copies.

Variants and the Witness of Manuscripts

At the heart of textual criticism is the comparison of textual variants. These variants arise from numerous factors including scribal error, theological emendations, or simple misinterpretation. For instance, in the Gospel of Mark, the verse Mark 1:1 in some manuscripts includes the phrase "the Son of God," while others omit it. Determining which of these reflects the original text requires an analysis not only of the manuscripts themselves but also of their historical context and the scribal practices associated with them.

Scripture supports this careful scrutiny; as Proverbs 25:2 states: "It is the glory of God to conceal a thing: but the honour of kings is to search out a matter." The meticulous work of textual critics honors this divine principle by seeking to unveil the original words as inspired.

Methodological Approaches

One key method in textual criticism is the categorization of manuscripts based on shared textual characteristics, which can indicate common geographic or historical origins. Manuscripts are grouped into text-types, such as the Alexandrian, Western, Byzantine, and Caesarean. Each text-type represents a different transmission history, with the Alexandrian text-type often considered the closest to the original due to its older manuscripts and more restrained scribal alterations.

For example, Codex Sinaiticus and Codex Vaticanus are pivotal witnesses of the Alexandrian text. Their significant agreement with older papyri lends weight to their readings, especially in contentious passages. As Romans 15:4 notes, "For whatsoever things were written aforetime were written for our learning," underscoring the importance of accessing the most original form of the text for true understanding.

Evaluating Variants

The evaluation of textual variants often involves external and internal criteria. External criteria look at the manuscript evidence itself—the age of the document, the quality of the text, and its geographical spread. Internal criteria involve the examination of the text, considering which variant best explains the others. This might include looking at which reading might have given rise to the others or which is least likely to be the result of intentional alteration.

An example of applying these criteria can be seen in John 7:8, where some manuscripts include "yet" in Jesus' statement about not going up to the Feast of Tabernacles. Including "yet" resolves apparent contradictions with later verses where Jesus does go to the feast, suggesting a scribal addition to clarify Jesus' intentions and maintain doctrinal consistency.

The Role of Divine Providence

While engaging in textual criticism, it is also acknowledged that divine providence has played a role in preserving the scriptures through centuries of transmission. As Isaiah 40:8 declares, "The grass withereth, the flower fadeth: but the word of our God shall stand for ever." This belief underpins the confidence that, despite human errors in transcription, the essential truths and teachings of the New Testament have been reliably preserved.

The primary task of New Testament textual criticism is not merely an academic exercise but a profound responsibility to restore the original words of the scripture as faithfully as possible. This endeavor not only deepens our understanding of the sacred texts but also strengthens our faith in the reliability of the Bible as the word of God, ensuring that what is taught and preached is as close as possible to what was originally inspired. This aligns with the commitment in Nehemiah 8:8, "So they read in the book in the law of God distinctly, and gave the sense, and caused them to understand the reading."

The Role of Divine Providence in Textual Criticism

Divine Providence and the Preservation of Scripture

In the realm of textual criticism, the role of divine providence is critically acknowledged as a guiding force in the preservation of the scriptures through the centuries. This belief is rooted in scriptural assurances like Isaiah 40:8, which proclaims, "The grass withereth, the flower fadeth: but the word of our God shall stand for ever." Such passages underpin the confidence that, despite human errors in transcription, the essential truths and teachings of the New Testament have been reliably maintained. The concept that God has not only preserved but also restored the scriptures is a profound testament to the divine oversight believed to guide the textual tradition of the Bible.

Historical Phases of New Testament Textual Transmission

The transmission of the Greek New Testament can be viewed as occurring in three distinct phases, each underpinned by divine providence:

1. **The Apostolic Era**: In the first century, the authors of the New Testament, under divine inspiration moved by the Holy Spirit, wrote the 27 books that constitute the New Testament. This period was marked by the direct impartation of divine wisdom and truth through the apostles and their close associates, ensuring that the foundational texts of Christianity reflected God's will and teachings accurately.

2. **The Era of Textual Variants**: Following the Apostolic Age, the manuscripts underwent a period characterized by both intentional and unintentional textual variants. The copying process, carried out by scribes over centuries, inevitably introduced variations. Some of these were due to human error, while others were the result of deliberate alterations. Despite these challenges, many scribes endeavored with great diligence to produce copies that were as faithful as possible to the originals. Their efforts were seen as part of a broader divine plan to ensure the preservation of scripture.

3. **The Restoration Era**: This period marked a significant phase in the history of biblical scholarship. Starting with the Renaissance and gaining momentum through the Reformation and into the modern era, a multitude of renowned textual scholars devoted their lives to recovering the original wording of the New Testament texts. Armed with evolving methodologies and increasingly sophisticated tools, these scholars sifted through the myriad of manuscripts to identify the most authentic readings. The dedication of these individuals to restoring the text is viewed as a continuation of God's providence, using human agency to reclaim the purity of scripture.

The Interplay of Human Effort and Divine Oversight

The interplay between human effort and divine oversight in textual criticism highlights a dynamic relationship where scholarly rigor is complemented by a theological acknowledgment of God's sovereignty over scripture. Just as 2 Timothy 3:16-17 states, "All Scripture is breathed out by God and profitable for teaching, for reproof, for correction, and for training in righteousness," so too is the work of textual critics seen as part of God's plan to equip the faithful with a reliable text.

By recognizing the divine hand in guiding the preservation and restoration of the New Testament, believers can engage with the biblical text with both intellectual rigor and spiritual reverence. This dual approach ensures that the text not only remains historically and philologically accurate but also theologically vibrant and alive, capable of imparting the divine truths it was originally intended to convey.

In this context, divine providence does not negate the need for meticulous human scholarship; rather, it empowers and necessitates it, offering reassurance that the ultimate truth and integrity of the scriptures are maintained, not by human will alone but through the grace of divine guidance.

Principles of Internal Evidence for Establishing the Original Reading

Determining the Original Reading

The Objective of Textual Criticism

Textual criticism of the New Testament seeks to ascertain the most accurate text as originally written by the New Testament authors. This scholarly discipline involves a detailed comparison of the textual variants found in ancient manuscript copies to reconstruct a text that is as close as possible to the original. The ultimate goal is to identify what the New Testament writers penned, under divine inspiration, ensuring that the message conveyed is faithful to their intent.

Methods in Textual Criticism

1. **External Evidence**: This method examines the age, geographical distribution, and textual lineage of various manuscript traditions. External evidence helps to trace the historical path of a text, discerning which readings might have originated earlier and which are likely later additions or alterations.
2. **Internal Evidence**: This involves looking at the text itself to determine the most likely original reading. It includes two sub-categories:

- **Intrinsic Probability**: This pertains to what the original authors were more likely to have written, considering their style, vocabulary, and theological context.
- **Transcriptional Probability**: This focuses on understanding the changes scribes might have introduced, intentionally or unintentionally. It explores whether a scribe might have omitted or altered words, simplified text, or harmonized passages with other scriptures.

Scriptural Support for Textual Criticism

The practice of textual criticism, though modern in some of its methods, aligns with the biblical injunction to seek truth and understanding diligently. As Proverbs 25:2 states, "It is the glory of God to conceal a matter; to search out a matter is the glory of kings." This pursuit of biblical accuracy not only honors the text but also the divine message it conveys.

The Role of Divine Providence

In textual criticism, there is also an acknowledgment of divine providence in preserving the scriptures. Isaiah 40:8 reminds us, "The grass withers and the flowers fall, but the word of our God endures forever." This verse supports the confidence that despite human errors in transcription over the centuries, the core truths and divine instructions of the New Testament have been maintained through God's sovereign will.

Challenges in Textual Criticism

While the aim is to recover the original text, several challenges arise:

- **Variants**: With thousands of manuscripts and numerous variants, deciding between them can be complex.
- **Lost Manuscripts**: The earliest manuscripts are incomplete, and none of the original autographs have survived.
- **Subjectivity**: Decisions can be influenced by the scholars' theological and cultural perspectives.

The Use of Critical Editions

To address these challenges, scholars use critical editions of the New Testament, such as the Nestle-Aland and the United Bible Societies' editions, which include detailed apparatuses showing the most important variants and the evidence supporting each reading. These tools are indispensable for anyone engaging in serious study of the New Testament text.

Maintaining Textual Integrity

In ensuring the integrity of the New Testament text, it is crucial to balance a rigorous scholarly approach with a reverence for the text's divine origin. While human efforts in textual criticism seek to clarify and correct the text, it is ultimately understood that the preservation of Scripture is governed by Jehovah's providence. As such, every attempt to recover the original wording is conducted with an acute awareness of the text's sacredness and its pivotal role in conveying divine truth to humanity.

In this task, textual critics act as stewards of Scripture, using all available means to ensure that the New Testament we read today reflects as closely as possible the inspired writings of the apostles. Through this meticulous work, scholars not only preserve the historical and literary integrity of the New Testament but also affirm its ongoing spiritual authority and reliability.

The Practice of Textual Criticism: Assessing the Merit of the Shorter Reading

The Principle of Brevity in Textual Decisions

In the discipline of New Testament textual criticism, scholars engage in the meticulous task of reconstructing the most authentic text of the New Testament scriptures as originally penned by the apostles and their contemporaries. This task is foundational, for as Paul asserts in 2 Timothy 3:16, "All Scripture is given by inspiration of God, and is profitable for doctrine, for reproof, for correction, for instruction in righteousness." Hence, establishing the original reading is not just an academic exercise but a theological imperative to preserve the words inspired by the Holy Spirit.

One of the guiding principles in this endeavor is the preference for the shorter reading. This principle is predicated on the understanding that scribes, throughout the history of textual transmission, were more likely to add material to a text—either as a clarification, harmonization, or embellishment—than they were to omit it. The shorter reading, therefore, is often considered closer to the original text unless other factors suggest otherwise.

Illustrative Examples from New Testament Manuscripts

The Evolution of the Lord's Prayer's Conclusion: Examining Matthew 6:13

Matthew 6:13 features a well-known variant sequence that concludes the Lord's Prayer, with various endings proposed across different manuscripts and traditions. This analysis seeks to determine the most probable original form of this biblical text, emphasizing the documentary evidence and its historical context.

Main Reading (WH NU):

- **Text:** Text omits the doxology at the end of the prayer.
- **Support:** Codices ℵ*, B, D, Z, 0170, f1

Variant Readings:

1. **Variant 1:** Addition of αμην ("amen")
   - **Support:** Manuscript 17, Vulgate Clementine (vgcl)
2. **Variant 2:** Addition of "because yours is the power forever."
   - **Support:** Itala (itk), Syriac Peshitta (syrp)
3. **Variant 3:** Addition of "because yours is the power and the glory forever. Amen."
   - **Support:** Coptic Sahidic (copsa), Didache (omits αμην)
4. **Variant 4:** Addition of "because yours is the kingdom and the glory forever. Amen."
   - **Support:** Syriac Curetonian (syrc)
5. **Variant 5/TR:** Addition of οτι σου εστιν η βασιλεια και η δυναμις και η δοξα εις τους αιωνας. αμην.
   - **Text:** "because yours is the kingdom and the power and the glory forever. Amen."

- **Support:** Codices L, W, Δ, Θ, 0233, f13, 33, Majority Text, Syriac

6. **Variant 6:** Addition of οτι σου εστιν η βασιλεια του πατρος και του υιου και του αγιου πνευματος εις τους αιωνας. αμην.

    - **Text:** "because yours is the kingdom of the Father and the Son and the Holy Spirit forever. Amen."
    - **Support:** Manuscript 157 (1253)

The earliest extant witnesses primarily support the omission of any doxological ending, suggesting that the prayer originally concluded with the petition for deliverance from evil. The variations found in later manuscripts and versions likely reflect liturgical embellishments, which were incorporated into the text from external sources such as the Didache.

The Didache, an early Christian document, is pivotal for understanding the liturgical use and expansion of the prayer's conclusion. Its form of the doxology, emphasizing "power and glory," likely influenced later textual additions, which further elaborated this ending to include "kingdom," aligning with traditional Jewish blessings.

From a textual critical standpoint, the simplest reading—omitting the doxology—supported by Codex Sinaiticus (ℵ*), Codex Vaticanus (B), and others, is typically considered the most likely original. This assertion aligns with the principle of lectio brevior (the shorter reading is preferred), especially in the absence of compelling reasons for the omission of a well-established doxology.

Historically, the expansion to include "kingdom," "power," and "glory" reflects the evolution of Christian liturgical practice, particularly within Syrian traditions, as noted by Westcott and Hort. This liturgical embedding likely catalyzed the integration of these elements into the textual tradition observed in the Textus Receptus and subsequently the King James Version.

In conclusion, the original form of Matthew 6:13 likely did not include a doxology, as evidenced by the earliest and most reliable manuscript traditions. The varied longer endings that emerged in different textual witnesses highlight the dynamic interaction between scriptural texts and communal worship practices, illustrating the development of Christian liturgical and theological expressions over time. This investigation not only clarifies the textual history of the Lord's Prayer but also enriches our understanding of early Christian piety and its scriptural foundations.

Mark's Ending (Mark 16:9-20)

Evaluating the Concluding Verses of Mark's Gospel: A Textual Inquiry

The conclusion of the Gospel of Mark is one of the most intriguing puzzles in New Testament textual criticism. This analysis seeks to discern which of the varied endings most likely reflects the original intent of Mark's narrative. The gospel is notable for its abrupt and enigmatic style, particularly in how it concludes, with several different endings found in various manuscripts.

The Five Main Endings of Mark 16:

1. **End at 16:8**

    - **Text:** καὶ ἐξελθοῦσαι ἔφυγον ἀπὸ τοῦ μνημείου, εἶχεν γὰρ αὐτὰς τρόμος καὶ ἔκστασις· καὶ οὐδενὶ οὐδὲν εἶπαν· ἐφοβοῦντο γάρ ("So they went out and fled from the tomb, for terror and amazement had seized them; and they said nothing to anyone, for they were afraid.")

    - **Support:** Codices ℵ, B, along with versions such as syr, cop, arm, geo, and some church fathers like Eusebius, Jerome, and Severus.

2. **Shorter Ending**

    - **Text:** πάντα δὲ τὰ παρηγγελμένα τοῖς περὶ τὸν Πέτρον συντόμως ἐξήγγειλαν. Μετὰ δὲ ταῦτα καὶ αὐτὸς ὁ Ἰησοῦς ἀπὸ ἀνατολῆς καὶ ἄχρι δύσεως ἐξαπέστειλεν δι' αὐτῶν τὸ ἱερὸν καὶ ἄφθαρτον κήρυγμα τῆς αἰωνίου σωτηρίας. ἀμήν.

    - **Support:** Codex itk and cited in several modern versions.

3. **Traditional Longer Ending (Mark 16:9–20)**

    - **Text:** Detailed narrative including appearances of Jesus and the Great Commission.

    - **Support:** Manuscripts A, C, D, Δ, Θ, and many others across various regions, also cited by early church fathers from the second century onward.

4. **Traditional Longer Ending with Additional Postscript**

    - **Text:** κακεινοι απελογουντο λεγοντες... ("And they excused themselves saying..." followed by dialogues concerning unbelief)

THE EARLY CHRISTIAN COPYISTS OF THE NEW TESTAMENT

- **Support:** Codex W (Freer Gospels).

5. **Both Shorter and Traditional Longer Ending**

    - **Text:** A combination of endings found in a minority of manuscripts.
    - **Support:** Manuscripts L, Ψ, and versions syr, cop.

Analysis of the Textual Variants: The primary evidence suggests that the earliest and most reliable manuscripts (ℵ, B) conclude at Mark 16:8. This abrupt ending aligns with Mark's often terse and enigmatic style, emphasizing the fear and amazement of the women, which resonates with the thematic elements of secrecy and the unexpected nature of Jesus' messianic kingdom throughout the Gospel.

The longer endings, particularly the Traditional Longer Ending, introduce a narrative style and theological emphases that are somewhat divergent from the earlier sections of Mark. These verses (9–20) contain vocabulary and theological motifs that are uncharacteristic of Mark's usual diction and thematic focus. This has led many scholars to consider these additions as later expansions meant to harmonize Mark's account with the other Gospels, reflecting the liturgical and doctrinal development of the early Christian community.

Therefore, the evidence leans heavily towards Mark originally ending at 16:8. The earliest and most reliable manuscripts conclude at this verse, and the additional endings are not found consistently across the earliest textual witnesses. The abrupt ending at 16:8 is thematically consistent with the Gospel's portrayal of fear and misunderstanding, which permeates Mark's depiction of the disciples' and others' reactions to Jesus's actions and teachings.

Moreover, the longer ending, while rich in post-resurrection narrative common to other Gospels, displays significant stylistic and vocabulary differences from the rest of Mark, indicating it was likely a later ecclesiastical addition to provide closure missing from the earlier, more ambiguous conclusion.

The most plausible original ending of Mark's Gospel appears to be at verse 16:8. This conclusion is supported by the weight of the earliest manuscript evidence and the stylistic and thematic coherence of the Gospel as a whole. The additional endings likely emerged as early Christian communities sought to provide a more resolved conclusion to the Gospel, incorporating elements from the broader Christian tradition and other New Testament writings.

In summary, the original ending of Mark likely concluded with the women's fearful silence in 16:8, a challenging and theologically provocative ending that invites the reader to wrestle with the implications of the resurrection and the response of Jesus's followers. This conclusion maintains the integrity of the narrative style and theological themes of the Gospel as established by the most ancient textual evidence.

The analysis of these endings illustrates the dynamic process of scriptural transmission and the ways in which early Christians engaged with the text of the New Testament. It also highlights the importance of textual criticism in helping modern readers understand the complexities and the historical development of the biblical texts.

Determining the Original Reading of 1 John 5:7-8: A Textual Analysis

Textual Variants of 1 John 5:7b-8

1 John 5:7b–8 presents two primary variants in its textual tradition, which significantly impacts the theological interpretation particularly concerning the doctrine of the Trinity.

Primary Textual Evidence (WH NU):

- **Greek**: ὅτι τρεῖς εἰσιν οἱ μαρτυροῦντες, 8 τὸ πνεῦμα καὶ τὸ ὕδωρ καὶ τὸ αἷμα, καὶ οἱ τρεῖς εἰς τὸ ἕν εἰσιν.

- **Translation**: "because there are three testifying: 8 the Spirit and the water and the blood, and the three are for one [testimony]."

- **Supporting Manuscripts**: ℵ (Codex Sinaiticus), A (Codex Alexandrinus), B (Codex Vaticanus), (Ψ) (Codex Athous Lavrensis), Majority of Byzantine texts, Syriac, Coptic, Armenian, Ethiopian, and some Old Latin manuscripts.

Variant Reading (Textus Receptus):

- **Greek**: οτι τρεις εισεν οι μαρτυρουντες εν τω ουρανω, ο πατηρ, ο λογος και το αγιον πνευμα, και ουτοι οι τρεις ἕν εισιν. 8 και τρεις οι μαρτυρουντες εν τη γη, το πνευμα και το υδωρ και το αιμα, και οι τρεις εις το ἕν εισιν.

- **Translation**: "because there are three testifying in heaven: the Father, the Word, and the Holy Spirit, and these three are one. 8 And there are three that testify on earth: the Spirit and the water and the blood, and the three are for one [testimony]."

- **Supporting Manuscripts**: Late manuscripts such as 61, 88, 221vr, 429, 636vr, 918, 2318, Vulgate (in part), Speculum, and quotations by Latin Church Fathers such as Priscillian and Fulgentius.

Historical Context and Scholarly Opinion

The variant including the "heavenly witnesses" (the Father, the Word, and the Holy Spirit) appears predominantly in later Latin manuscripts and is absent from the earlier and more widely distributed Greek texts. This passage is known as the Comma Johanneum. The earliest explicit evidence of this reading appears in the writings associated with Priscillian, who was active in the late 4th century C.E., and it gradually entered the Latin textual tradition. Noted textual critics, including Bruce Metzger and Kurt Aland, argue that this variant likely originated as a marginal gloss explaining the Trinitarian symbolism of the water, blood, and Spirit mentioned in the original text. This gloss was later incorporated into the body of the text in some Latin manuscripts, influencing the Textus Receptus and consequently the King James Version.

The scholarly consensus, particularly among those adhering to a documentary approach and favoring Alexandrian witness, is that the shorter reading without the "heavenly witnesses" is likely original. This view is supported by the manuscript evidence and the absence of this passage in the writings of early Greek Church Fathers and the most ancient Christian texts.

Conclusion on the Original Reading

After considering the manuscript evidence, the historical transmission of the text, and the scholarly perspectives, it is reasonable to conclude that the original reading of 1 John 5:7-8 did not include the Trinitarian formula found in the Textus Receptus. The passage was originally understood to reference the earthly witnesses — the Spirit, the water, and the blood — which testify to the identity and mission of Jesus Christ without explicit reference to a heavenly testimony by the Father, Word, and Holy Spirit.

These examples underscore the principle of preferring the shorter reading as a useful heuristic in textual criticism, especially when supported by the weight of manuscript evidence. In seeking to determine the original text, textual critics are guided by such principles, combined with a comprehensive examination of the manuscript tradition.

Edward D. Andrews

The Practice of Textual Criticism: Evaluating the Harder Reading

Establishing the Original Reading

Textual criticism of the New Testament is a scholarly pursuit guided by several key principles aimed at recovering the most authentic texts as they were originally inspired. Among these principles is the preference for the "lectio difficilior" or the more difficult reading. This principle is based on the assumption that scribes were more likely to simplify or harmonize difficult passages than to make them harder. Therefore, a more challenging version of a text, particularly when supported by older and diverse manuscript evidence, is often considered closer to the original.

Exploration of Challenging Readings in New Testament Manuscripts

Determining the Original Reading of Luke 22:43-44: An Examination of Textual Variants

Textual Analysis of Luke 22:43-44

In the documentary method of textual criticism, the documents themselves often provide the most significant insights into the original text. This approach, which somewhat prioritizes documentary evidence over internal evidence, is particularly relevant in examining the textual variants of Luke 22:43-44.

Documentary Evidence for Luke 22:43-44

1. **Main Textual Evidence (TR, WH, NU):**

    - **Greek:** ὤφθη δε αὐτῷ ἄγγελος ἀπ' οὐρανοῦ ἐνισχύων αὐτόν. 44 καὶ γενόμενος ἐν ἀγωνίᾳ ἐκτενέστερον προσηύχετο· καὶ ἐγένετο ὁ ἱδρὼς αὐτοῦ ὡσεὶ θρόμβοι αἵματος καταβαίνοντες ἐπὶ τὴν γῆν.

    - **Translation:** "43 And an angel from heaven appeared to him, strengthening him. 44 And being in agony, he prayed more earnestly, and his sweat became like great drops of blood falling down on the ground."

THE EARLY CHRISTIAN COPYISTS OF THE NEW TESTAMENT

- **Supporting Manuscripts**: ℵ*, D, L, Θ, Ψ, 0171, 0233, f, Majority of Greek manuscripts, Latin manuscripts, and translations according to Church Fathers such as Justin, Irenaeus, Hippolytus, Eusebius.

2. **Variant 1 – Placement of Verses after Matthew 26:39:**

    - **Supporting Evidence**: Family 13 and some lectionaries with additions.

    - **Observation**: This transposition in some manuscripts suggests that the verses were known and variably placed, reflecting their contested presence in the textual tradition.

3. **Variant 2 – Omission of Verses:**

    - **Greek Evidence**: P69Vvid, P75, ℵ¹, A, B, N, T, W, itf, syrs, copsa.

    - **Church Fathers and Scholars**: According to Anastasius, Jerome, Hilary, Marcion, Clement, Origen.

    - **Significance**: The omission in significant early manuscripts such as P69 and codices like B (Vaticanus, circa 300-330 C.E.) and ℵ (Sinaiticus, circa 330-360 C.E.) indicates that these verses might not have been part of the original text. Their absence is noted across a geographically and theologically diverse set of early Christian writings.

Scholarly Interpretation and Conclusions

The textual evidence for Luke 22:43-44 presents a complex scenario. The presence of the verses in later manuscripts and their inclusion in the writings of several Church Fathers suggest that these verses became integrated into the Lucan narrative early in the history of the text's transmission. However, their absence in earlier, significant manuscripts and versions, along with their variable placement in the text by different scribes, underscores their dubious authenticity as part of the original Gospel of Luke.

The documentary method, particularly with an emphasis on Alexandrian manuscripts, leans towards the omission of these verses as the more likely original scenario. The scholarly consensus, including opinions from figures like Bruce Metzger and the influential work by Westcott and Hort, aligns with the hypothesis that these verses were added to the text from an early, extracanonical source of Christian tradition. This addition likely served to enhance the depiction of Jesus' human suffering and divine mission, resonating with the theological inclinations of the communities using these texts.

In conclusion, while the verses of Luke 22:43-44 hold significant traditional value and provide a profound insight into the human aspects of Jesus' passion, the weight of the documentary evidence suggests that they were not part of Luke's original Gospel. The inclusion of these verses in major critical editions of the New Testament, albeit within double brackets, indicates their disputed nature but also acknowledges their enduring impact on Christian doctrine and liturgical practice.

Jesus' Family's Perception (Mark 3:21)

In Mark 3:21, some manuscripts convey that Jesus' own family said, "He is out of His mind." This portrayal of Jesus being regarded as out of mind by His relatives could be seen as disparaging or irreverent, making it a difficult passage for early Christian scribes and readers. The easier alteration found in some manuscripts is that "people" said this, not His family, potentially to shield the sanctity of Jesus' familial relationships. The more difficult reading, preserved in significant early texts, likely reflects the original more accurately, emphasizing the human misunderstandings Jesus faced, even among His closest kin.

The Anointing of Jesus (John 12:1-8)

John's Gospel presents an account where Mary of Bethany anoints Jesus' feet with costly perfume. A variant exists in the wording concerning Judas Iscariot's objection to this act; some manuscripts highlight his concern for the poor, while others emphasize his greed more bluntly. The harsher critique of Judas' character, found in older and more diverse manuscripts, might have been softened in later copies to either mitigate the portrayal of his betrayal or to focus on the moral teaching about the poor. The more difficult reading, which portrays Judas negatively, aligns with John's generally stark depiction of his character, suggesting its originality. These examples illustrate how the principle of preferring the more difficult reading aids scholars in piecing together the most probable original texts of the New Testament.

The Practice of Textual Criticism: Identifying the Reading from Which Other Variants Could Have Developed

Textual criticism, the academic discipline dedicated to recovering the original wording of texts, particularly those as significant as the New Testament, uses several methodologies to evaluate the vast array of manuscript evidence. A core principle among these methodologies is identifying the reading from which other variants likely developed. This principle is based on the understanding that some textual variations serve as the root from which other deviations can be logically derived, making these readings potentially closer to the original text.

Case Studies in Variant Genealogy

The Beatitudes (Matthew 5:3-12)

In the Gospel of Matthew, the Beatitudes offer profound insights into the kingdom of heaven. However, variations exist among manuscripts regarding the blessings pronounced. For instance, the phrase "Blessed are the poor in spirit" is sometimes found simply as "Blessed are the poor" in other early texts. By analyzing the semantic and thematic contexts, scholars can infer that the more specific "poor in spirit" could easily have been generalized to "poor" by a scribe seeking to broaden the teaching's applicability, thus suggesting that the more specific phrase is likely original.

The Woman Caught in Adultery (John 7:53-8:11)

The passage of John 7:53-8:11, often referred to as the Pericope Adulterae or the story of the adulterous woman, has been a topic of significant scholarly debate due to its textual variations and questionable presence in the earliest manuscripts. This article aims to scrutinize the documentary evidence and weigh the internal and external textual data to ascertain the originality of these verses within the Gospel of John.

Textual Variants and Manuscript Evidence

1. Manuscripts Omitting John 7:53-8:11

- **Early Papyri and Codices:** P39vid, P66, P75, ℵ (Sinaiticus), Avid (Alexandrinus), B (Vaticanus), Cvid, L, N, T, W, Δ, Θ, Ψ, 0141, 33.

- **Versions and Translations:** it,f, syrc,p, copsa,ach2, geo.

- **Patristic Citations**: Not referenced in Origen, Chrysostom, Cyril; mentioned by Tertullian and Cyprian as absent in some manuscripts they knew.
- **Significance**: The broad absence in early and geographically diverse manuscripts suggests these verses were likely not part of the original Gospel of John. Notably, the Diatessaron, a second-century harmony of the Gospels, does not include this passage.

2. Manuscripts Including John 7:53-8:11

- **Codex Bezae (D)**: The earliest Greek manuscript including this passage, dating around 400 C.E.
- **Later Manuscripts**: F, G, H, K, M, U, Γ, and others from the Byzantine text-type.
- **Lectionary Evidence**: Inserted in various locations, indicating uncertainty about its placement—e.g., f1 places it after John 21:25, and f13 after Luke 21:38.
- **Marginal Notes**: In some manuscripts, the verses are marked with asterisks or obeli, indicating the scribes' awareness of their dubious authenticity.

3. Patristic and Scholastic Observations

- **Didymus the Blind**: Acknowledges the existence of manuscripts containing the story, indicating early but sporadic inclusion.
- **Augustine**: Suggests the passage might have been omitted in some circles to avoid seeming to condone adultery.

Textual Analysis and Contextual Considerations

The narrative content and style of John 7:53-8:11 differ markedly from the surrounding Johannine text. The vocabulary and syntax show dissimilarities with the rest of the Gospel, suggesting a different authorial hand. The pericope disrupts the narrative flow from the Festival of Tabernacles discourse in John 7 to the declaration of Jesus as the Light of the World in John 8:12, which seamlessly continues the thematic developments of chapter 7.

Furthermore, the story's placement varies across manuscripts, sometimes appearing in Luke's Gospel, which supports the theory that it was a floating tradition, incorporated into John's Gospel at different points by later scribes.

THE EARLY CHRISTIAN COPYISTS OF THE NEW TESTAMENT

Considering the weight of documentary evidence, the internal stylistic discrepancies, and the lack of early patristic support, it is reasonable to conclude that John 7:53-8:11 was not part of the original text composed by the Evangelist John. The passage likely originated from an early Christian oral tradition that sought to exemplify Jesus' teachings on mercy and justice, which was subsequently incorporated into the textual tradition of the Gospels by well-meaning scribes influenced by its edifying content.

Despite its profound theological and moral value, the documentary method, with a preference for Alexandrian witnesses, suggests these verses were later additions to the Gospel of John. The inclusion of the passage in modern editions, marked with double brackets, acknowledges both its historical influence on Christian thought and its dubious origin within the Johannine corpus.

Variant Origin in the Description of Jesus' Baptism (Matthew 3:16-17)

In the account of Jesus' baptism in the Gospel of Matthew, variations occur in how the voice from heaven is quoted. The majority of texts present the voice saying, "This is my beloved Son, with whom I am well pleased." However, some ancient sources, including variant readings found in other Gospels like Mark and Luke, frame this declaration differently, such as "You are my beloved Son; with you I am well pleased."

The variation between "This is my beloved Son" and "You are my beloved Son" offers an interesting case for textual critics. The first version, as a third-person declaration, might be seen as directed more toward an observing audience, aligning with Matthew's frequent emphasis on Jesus' identity being revealed to others. The second version, using the second person, creates a more intimate communication between the Father and Jesus. Scholars hypothesize that the second-person address could be the original saying, which was later adapted to the third person in Matthew to emphasize the public affirmation of Jesus' divine sonship to the gathered crowds, thus serving an instructional purpose for the Gospel's readers.

By examining the contexts in which these variations appear, textual critics suggest that the second-person form of the declaration might be the root from which the third-person variant in Matthew developed. This adaptation would be a natural evolution within the text to enhance the narrative's teaching moment for its audience, illustrating how theological emphases shaped the transmission of the Gospel texts. In these examples, the principle of identifying the reading from which other variants could have developed aids scholars in understanding the historical development of the New Testament text.

The Practice of Textual Criticism: Identifying the Author's Characteristic Readings

Textual criticism of the New Testament involves meticulous analysis to determine the most authentic text as originally written by the authors. The process includes evaluating variations among manuscript copies to discern which readings most closely reflect the original intent and style of the New Testament writers. This task is foundational for preserving the integrity and accuracy of Scripture as conveyed in manuscripts such as those found among the Dead Sea Scrolls and other ancient codices.

The Criteria of Authorial Characteristic

One of the key principles in textual criticism is selecting the reading that best aligns with the known style and theological content of the author. This method is rooted in the understanding that each New Testament writer had a unique voice and theological perspective, which can guide critics in their decision-making process.

Example: The Style of Paul

Paul the Apostle, known for his theological depth and rigorous argumentation, exhibits a distinctive style in his epistles. For instance, Paul's use of the phrase "in Christ" is prolific throughout his writings. When encountering a textual variant in passages of his epistles, a reading that includes a theological reflection on being "in Christ" might be more characteristic of Paul compared to a more generic alternative. Consider Galatians 2:20, "I have been crucified with Christ. It is no longer I who live, but Christ who lives in me." The depth of relational theology centered on Christ reflects Paul's characteristic style and theological emphasis.

Example: The Vocabulary of John

John's writings are marked by a high degree of theological reflection on the nature of Jesus as the Logos, the Light, and the Life. His gospel and letters frequently utilize unique terms such as "logos" (Word) and "zoe" (Life), which are less common in other New Testament writings. In evaluating variants within John's texts, readings that employ these specific terms and reflect this high Christology are likely more authentic to John's style. An example is found in John 1:1, "In the beginning was the Word, and the Word was with God, and the Word was God." The use of "logos" aligns closely with John's theological vocabulary and thematic focus.

Theological Consistency as a Guideline

Beyond linguistic style, the consistency of theological themes also serves as a critical criterion in textual criticism. This principle helps in identifying readings that are congruent with the broader theological context of an author's known works.

Example: The Eschatological Themes in Thessalonians

Paul's letters to the Thessalonians are deeply eschatological, reflecting a focus on the return of Jesus Christ and the resurrection of the dead. A textual variant in 1 Thessalonians 4:16 that more explicitly mentions the coming of the Lord would be considered more characteristic of Paul in this context because it aligns with the thematic elements prevalent throughout both epistles.

Manuscript Evidence Alignment

In addition to stylistic and thematic considerations, the support of a reading by early and diverse manuscript traditions can reinforce its authenticity. This principle is not isolated but works in conjunction with understanding the authorial style and theological consistency.

Example: The Comma Johanneum

The Comma Johanneum in 1 John 5:7-8, which appears in later manuscripts but is absent in the earliest and most reliable Greek manuscripts, provides an example where manuscript evidence does not support its authenticity. The reading does not align with the stylistic and theological patterns of John's writings and is absent in the oldest manuscripts, suggesting that it is not original.

In practicing textual criticism, scholars must carefully balance these criteria—authorial style, theological consistency, and manuscript evidence—to best approximate the original text of the New Testament. This disciplined approach ensures that the translations and interpretations of Scripture remain as true as possible to the intentions of the original authors, providing a reliable foundation for faith and practice.

Principles for Establishing the Original Reading: Contextual Coherence and Theological Alignment

In the field of New Testament textual criticism, ensuring the authenticity of the text involves more than analyzing manuscript age or textual variants. A critical principle is the preference for readings that best fit the overall context of a passage and align with the author's known theological perspectives. This approach is vital for a holistic understanding of Scripture, affirming that the text not only reflects historical authenticity but also theological integrity.

Coherence with Literary and Historical Context

Textual decisions often depend on how well a variant reading integrates with the surrounding literary and historical context. A reading that seems out of place or interrupts the flow of a narrative or argument is less likely to be original.

Example: The Agony in the Garden (Mark 14:34)

Consider the account of Jesus's emotional turmoil in Gethsemane. Mark 14:34 reads, "My soul is exceedingly sorrowful unto death." This expression of deep distress fits seamlessly into the narrative's context, which portrays Jesus confronting his impending death. It aligns with the psychological and emotional descriptions found elsewhere in the Synoptic Gospels, making it a plausible original reading over any variant that might underplay the intensity of Jesus's emotions.

Alignment with the Author's Theological Framework

A variant's authenticity is also evaluated based on its consistency with the author's theological views as expressed throughout the text. This criterion helps in distinguishing between readings that may have been altered to fit later theological developments versus those that truly reflect the author's original intent.

Example: Paul's Justification by Faith

Paul's letters frequently emphasize justification by faith apart from works of the Law (e.g., Romans 3:28, "For we hold that one is justified by faith apart from works of the law."). This theological stance is a cornerstone of Pauline doctrine. Therefore, a textual variant that supports this view within the context of Paul's arguments about the Law and grace is likely authentic. Conversely, any variant suggesting justification by adherence to the Law would contradict Paul's established theological framework, indicating a later interpolation rather than original content.

Scriptural Harmony

Another aspect of assessing the context is determining how well the reading harmonizes with other scriptural passages. This does not mean forcing agreement but recognizing the continuity of themes and teachings across the texts.

Example: The Harmony of the Gospels

In the Gospels, teachings and events involving Jesus are presented from different perspectives but should fundamentally convey consistent theological messages. For instance, the concept of the Kingdom of God is central in the Synoptic Gospels. A variant that depicts this Kingdom in terms completely at odds with the shared view of Matthew, Mark, and Luke would require careful scrutiny. A reading that integrates well with the synoptic presentation of Jesus's teachings on the Kingdom is more likely to be original.

Theological Motivations in Variants

The influence of theological motivations on textual alterations cannot be overlooked. Variants may arise from scribes' intentional or unintentional insertions that reflect their theological biases or attempt to clarify what they believed was the correct doctrine.

Example: The Baptism and Genealogy of Jesus (Luke 3:22-23)

In Luke 3:22, following Jesus's baptism, a variant exists in the voice from heaven. The majority of manuscripts read, "You are my beloved Son; with you I am well pleased." However, some ancient sources, including Codex Bezae, read differently: "You are my Son, today I have begotten you." This variant echoes Psalm 2:7, a messianic psalm traditionally associated with royal enthronement and adoption.

The majority reading fits better within Luke's theological framework and narrative style. Luke consistently presents Jesus as the Son of God from the moment of conception (as seen in Luke 1:32-35, where the angel tells Mary, "the child to be born will be called holy—the Son of God"). This is reinforced throughout Luke's narrative, which emphasizes Jesus's divine sonship established prior to his public ministry.

The variant "today I have begotten you," while theologically significant and echoing the messianic psalm, introduces a notion of Jesus achieving or being granted sonship at the time of baptism, which diverges from the theological continuity presented in Luke. It suggests a moment of adoption rather than pre-existing sonship. This reading, while intriguing, might reflect a theological interpretation aligned more closely with adoptionist Christology, which was not the author of Luke's intent based on the broader context of his Gospel.

Luke's portrayal of Jesus's identity from conception to baptism consistently supports the reading where Jesus is affirmed as the beloved Son who has always been in this relationship with the Father, not entering into it at baptism. Therefore, the more fitting reading for Luke's theological narrative and Christological emphasis is "You are my beloved Son; with you I am well pleased."

This example highlights how textual critics must weigh the fit of a variant not only with the immediate context but also with the theological themes and narrative consistency across a biblical book. This approach ensures that the text reflects the original author's intent and the theological message they sought to convey to their audience.

In textual criticism, preference is thus given to readings that are congruent with the immediate literary context, consistent with the author's theological views, and in harmony with the broader scriptural witness. These principles guide scholars in making informed decisions that strive to faithfully reproduce the original texts of the New Testament.

Principles for Establishing the Original Reading: Valuing Less Harmonious Readings in Parallel Passages

In New Testament textual criticism, one of the guiding principles is the preference for less harmonious readings when dealing with parallel passages across different texts. This principle is predicated on the notion that scribes were more likely to alter texts to make them align more closely with similar passages in other books, thereby inadvertently creating harmonizations that might not reflect the original text. Preferring the less harmonized version helps maintain the distinct voices and original intents of the individual authors.

Understanding the Principle of Lectio Difficilior Potior

The principle often referred to as "lectio difficilior potior" (the more difficult reading is to be preferred), underlies this approach. It suggests that scribes were more likely to simplify or adjust difficult passages to make them more understandable or consistent with other familiar texts, rather than complicate a straightforward text. Therefore, a reading that appears less harmonized or more challenging in the context of similar biblical passages might be closer to the original.

Example: The Death of Judas (Matthew 27:5 vs. Acts 1:18)

In Matthew 27:5, it is recorded that Judas "went away and hanged himself." However, Acts 1:18 provides a different detail: "Falling headlong, he burst open in the middle and all his intestines spilled out." These accounts of Judas's death are seemingly discordant, with each gospel presenting a different aspect of his demise. The preference in textual criticism would be for the original texts to maintain these distinct details as the initial act of hanging as described in Matthew 27:5 led to an eventual fall that resulted in the gruesome details given in Acts 1:18. A harmonized version that attempts to combine these two descriptions into a single coherent narrative might represent a later editorial attempt to reconcile the accounts.

The Role of Independent Attestation

Independent attestation supports the authenticity of less harmonious readings by showing that multiple independent sources align with the more challenging or divergent versions of the text. This reinforcement by independent lines of tradition strengthens the case for a reading's originality.

Here's how this interpretation aligns with conservative biblical scholarship and the principles of textual criticism:

Integrating Accounts of Judas's Death: A Textual and Theological Analysis

Sequential Interpretation of the Events

The passage in Matthew 27:5 succinctly states, "And throwing down the pieces of silver into the temple, he departed, and he went and hanged himself." This description provides a clear account of Judas's initial method of suicide. Turning to Acts 1:18, the text adds, "Now this man acquired a field with the reward of his wickedness, and falling headlong, he burst open in the middle and all his intestines gushed out." When read in sequence, the narrative can be understood as follows: Judas hanged himself, and either the rope or the branch from which he was suspended broke, causing him to fall and suffer the injuries described in Acts.

Theological and Literary Considerations

From a theological perspective, both accounts contribute to the narrative of Judas's tragic end, reflecting his despair and the consequences of his betrayal of Jesus. The details in Acts might also serve a theological function, emphasizing the severity of Judas's fate as a warning against betrayal and wickedness.

In terms of textual criticism, this interpretation respects the integrity of both texts by taking them at face value while allowing for a narrative that logically connects them. This approach avoids the need for assuming textual corruption or significant harmonization efforts by later scribes, which would be suggested if the texts were seen as outright contradictory.

Manuscript Evidence and Tradition

The manuscript evidence for both passages does not show significant variations that would suggest an attempt to harmonize these accounts in the early textual tradition. This consistency across manuscripts indicates that early copyists transmitted what they received without substantial alteration to align the accounts of Matthew and Acts more closely.

By viewing the events as sequential—Judas hanging himself and then the rope or branch breaking leading to his fall and subsequent injuries—the accounts in Matthew and Acts can be reconciled. This perspective maintains the textual integrity of each account and aligns with a conservative approach to Scripture interpretation, which seeks to uphold the authenticity and historical reliability of the biblical texts. This interpretation also illustrates how different gospel accounts of the same event can provide complementary rather than contradictory details, enriching our understanding of the narrative and its theological implications.

Example: The Beatitudes (Matthew 5:3-12 vs. Luke 6:20-23)

The Beatitudes are presented in both Matthew and Luke, but with notable differences. Matthew's version is more spiritualized ("Blessed are the poor in spirit"), whereas Luke's version is more direct and physical ("Blessed are you who are poor"). The less harmonious nature of Luke's account, which is more stark and lacks the spiritualizing language of Matthew's version, might suggest it is closer to the original sayings of Jesus, reflecting an unadulterated form of the teaching. Preferring Luke's less harmonized version in this case could point to its authenticity, especially given Luke's tendency to emphasize the material and social aspects of Jesus's teachings.

The Impact of Contextual and Thematic Consistency

While the preference for less harmonious readings is a useful principle, it must be balanced with considerations of contextual and thematic consistency within each gospel or epistle.

Example: The Lord's Prayer (Matthew 6:9-13 vs. Luke 11:2-4)

The Lord's Prayer is recorded in both Matthew and Luke, with Matthew's version being more extended and liturgically developed compared to Luke's simpler and more abrupt version. Luke's version does not include the doxology "For yours is the kingdom and the power and the glory forever. Amen," which is present in some manuscripts of Matthew but absent in the earliest and most reliable ones. The simpler form in Luke, and its absence of the doxology in the most ancient witnesses of both gospels, suggests that the less harmonized, more austere version in Luke may be closer to the original form of the prayer as Jesus taught it.

These examples illustrate the principle of preferring less harmonious readings in textual criticism. By valuing these readings, scholars aim to preserve the distinctiveness and authenticity of the biblical texts, reflecting a closer adherence to what the original authors might have written and the original audiences might have heard. This methodological approach helps in constructing a text that is as close as possible to the original manuscripts, maintaining the diversity of perspectives and theological nuances in the New Testament.

PRINCIPLES OF EXTERNAL EVIDENCE FOR ESTABLISHING THE ORIGINAL READING

Principles for Establishing the Original Reading: Valuing the Oldest Manuscript Evidence

In the discipline of New Testament textual criticism, determining the most authentic text often revolves around the age and reliability of the manuscript evidence. The axiom "prefer the reading attested by the oldest manuscripts" plays a crucial role in this analytical process. This principle rests on the understanding that earlier manuscripts, being closer in time to the originals, are less likely to contain the cumulative errors or alterations that can appear in later copies.

The Significance of Early Manuscripts

The value of the oldest manuscripts lies in their proximity to the original writings of the New Testament. The closer a manuscript is in time to the original autographs, the fewer the generations of copying and the lower the potential for transmission errors. Manuscripts from the second and third centuries C.E., for example, are considered particularly significant in this regard.

Example: Papyrus 75 (P75)

Papyrus 75 (P75), dating to around 175-225 C.E., contains large portions of Luke and John. Its importance is highlighted when compared to later manuscripts that show variations not present in this papyrus. For instance, in Luke 11:2, P75 omits the doxology "For yours is the kingdom, and the power, and the glory forever, Amen," a reading that is absent in many other early manuscripts and is considered by many scholars not to have been part of the original text of Luke. The consistency of P75 with other early and reliable manuscripts supports the omission as closer to the original text.

Aligning Manuscript Evidence with Authorial Style

While the age of a manuscript is a critical factor, the principle does not operate in isolation. The characteristic style and theological consistency of the author also play integral roles. This multidimensional approach ensures that the oldest manuscript's reading aligns with what we know of the author's linguistic and thematic patterns.

Example: Codex Sinaiticus and Codex Vaticanus

Both Codex Sinaiticus and Codex Vaticanus, dating from the fourth century C.E., are among the oldest and most complete manuscripts of the Bible. Their readings often take precedence in textual criticism due to their age, quality, and the textual tradition they represent. For example, in Mark 1:1, the phrase "the Son of God" is present in later manuscripts but is absent in Sinaiticus and Vaticanus. This omission is significant because it aligns with the more abrupt and terse style of Mark's Gospel, suggesting that the simpler form of the text may be original.

Evaluating Manuscript Agreement

Another aspect of utilizing the oldest manuscripts is assessing the degree of agreement among them. When several of the earliest manuscripts concur on a particular reading, this consensus is taken as strong evidence of its authenticity.

Example: The Ending of Mark

The ending of the Gospel of Mark presents a famous case where the most reliable early manuscripts, including Sinaiticus and Vaticanus, end at Mark 16:8. This abrupt ending is absent in later manuscripts that include additional verses (Mark 16:9-20). The agreement of the oldest manuscripts on ending at verse 8 suggests that this may reflect the original conclusion of Mark's Gospel, despite the more extended ending's presence in the majority of later texts.

Through careful analysis of the oldest manuscript evidence, in conjunction with considerations of authorial style and manuscript consensus, textual critics aim to reconstruct the New Testament texts as faithfully as possible to their original form. This meticulous approach not only preserves the textual integrity of the Scriptures but also ensures that the teachings within them are transmitted accurately for future generations.

Principles for Establishing the Original Reading: Geographic Diversity in Manuscript Evidence

In the field of New Testament textual criticism, one critical principle is to prefer readings supported by manuscripts originating from widely separated geographical areas. This principle stems from the understanding that broader manuscript dissemination across diverse regions suggests a reading's early and widespread acceptance, thereby potentially reflecting a closer approximation to the original text.

Significance of Geographical Distribution

The distribution of manuscript evidence across different geographic regions plays a pivotal role in assessing the authenticity of textual variants. When a particular reading appears in manuscripts found across a range of locales—from Asia Minor to North Africa to Europe—it strengthens the argument that this reading is not the product of localized scribal error or alteration but represents the original text more faithfully.

Example: The Text of John 1:18

John 1:18 offers an example where geographic distribution is key. The verse has two main variant readings: "the only begotten Son" (monogenes huios) and "the only begotten God" (monogenes theos). The variant "the only begotten God" is supported by key manuscripts including Papyrus 66 and Papyrus 75, early texts from Egypt, and Codex Vaticanus and Codex Sinaiticus, which, though found in Egypt, are thought to reflect a text from a wider region due to their textual characteristics. The widespread early support for "the only begotten God" in both Alexandrian and Western text-types, and its presence in early papyri, suggests this may be the more original reading despite the theological complexities it introduces.

Evaluating Manuscript Families

Textual critics also consider the agreement among different manuscript families when evaluating variants. Manuscripts are often categorized into families or text-types that represent a particular scribal tradition. The agreement of readings across these diverse traditions is particularly persuasive.

Example: The Ending of Mark's Gospel

The ending of Mark's Gospel (Mark 16:9-20) is absent in some of the earliest and most geographically widespread manuscripts, including Codex Sinaiticus and Codex Vaticanus (both associated with a text-type thought to originate in the Alexandrian region) and in the writings of early church fathers from different regions who do not mention the longer ending. The geographic spread of manuscripts omitting these verses across different text-types suggests that the shorter ending of Mark might more closely represent the original composition of the Gospel.

The Role of External Evidence

While internal evidence such as context and authorial style is crucial, the external evidence of manuscript dispersion provides an essential counterbalance. It ensures that readings are not only theoretically plausible but also historically grounded in the early transmission of the text.

Example: The Pericope Adulterae (John 7:53-8:11)

The story of the woman caught in adultery, found in John 7:53-8:11, is absent from all early Greek, Latin, Syriac, and Coptic manuscripts. Its presence in manuscripts from more isolated regions or later manuscripts suggests it was a later addition, despite its wide acceptance in later tradition. The geographic distribution of the earliest manuscripts lacking this passage supports the conclusion that it was not part of John's original Gospel.

The principle of preferring readings supported in manuscripts from widely separated geographical areas is a robust method in textual criticism. It leverages the breadth of manuscript evidence to mitigate the impact of localized textual alterations, ensuring the selected text reflects a reading that has withstood the complexities of early Christian text transmission across diverse cultural and regional contexts. This methodological approach helps in reconstructing a New Testament text that is as faithful as possible to what the original authors penned, ensuring that the scripture remains a reliable and authoritative foundation for faith and practice.

Edward D. Andrews

Principles for Establishing the Original Reading: Assessing Textual Concordance Across Manuscript Traditions

In New Testament textual criticism, one of the principles for determining the most authentic text is to prefer readings that are supported by the greatest number of text types, particularly when one of these text types is the Alexandrian. The Alexandrian text-type is often considered among the most reliable due to its age and close adherence to a more "literal" transcription tradition.

Importance of Text Types in Textual Criticism

Text types, or text families, are groups of manuscripts that share similar textual characteristics, likely due to common geographic or historical origins. The primary text types include the Alexandrian, Western, Byzantine, and Caesarean. Each text type provides insight into how the New Testament text was transmitted and possibly altered over time in different regions.

Alexandrian Text-Type: A Benchmark for Authenticity

The Alexandrian text-type is valued for its antiquity and relative purity. Originating from the region around Alexandria, Egypt, this text-type is represented by some of the oldest extant manuscripts, such as Codex Sinaiticus and Codex Vaticanus, which date back to the fourth century C.E. The textual tradition of Alexandria is noted for its rigorous scholarly approach to manuscript copying, which was less prone to paraphrastic expansions common in other text types.

Evaluating Textual Concordance: The Case of Matthew 6:13

In the Lord's Prayer, the doxology "For yours is the kingdom and the power and the glory forever, Amen," appears in many later manuscripts, particularly of the Byzantine text-type, which became the dominant text-type in the medieval Greek Orthodox Church. However, this doxology is absent in the most reliable Alexandrian manuscripts, such as Codex Sinaiticus and Codex Vaticanus, as well as in early versions and Church Fathers' writings from diverse regions.

The presence of the doxology in multiple text types but its absence in the Alexandrian manuscripts presents a compelling case. The principle would lean towards the exclusion of the doxology as part of the original text of Matthew, since the Alexandrian, noted for its conservative copying tradition, along with early diverse witnesses, does not support this addition.

The Role of Diverse Manuscript Evidence

The support of a reading by multiple text types, especially when including the Alexandrian, is significant because it indicates that the reading was widely accepted across different geographic and cultural contexts in the early Christian world. This broad acceptance enhances the probability that the reading is original.

Example: John 7:8

In John 7:8, there is a variant where some manuscripts have Jesus saying, "I am not going up to this feast," while others include an additional "yet" ("I am not yet going up to this feast"). The reading with "yet" is supported by a range of text types, including Alexandrian, Western, and some Byzantine manuscripts, suggesting a broader and earlier acceptance. This variant, by being supported across multiple text types and including the conservative Alexandrian tradition, is considered more likely to reflect the original wording intended by John.

Integration of Textual Data

In assessing textual variants, the integration of data from different manuscript traditions, particularly when they converge with the Alexandrian tradition, provides a robust basis for determining the text closest to the original. The principle of favoring readings supported by the greatest number of text types, as long as one is Alexandrian, helps ensure that the chosen reading has not only wide but early attestations, making it the strongest candidate for authenticity.

By adhering to these principles, textual critics aim to reconstruct a New Testament text that reflects the truest form of the original writings, grounded in a careful and comprehensive evaluation of the manuscript evidence across diverse traditions. This methodological rigor supports the transmission of a text that remains faithful to the apostolic witness and doctrinal purity as originally recorded.

MODERN APPROACHES TO NEW TESTAMENT TEXTUAL CRITICISM

Modern Approaches to New Testament Textual Criticism: Understanding Radical Eclecticism

In the field of New Testament textual criticism, radical eclecticism represents a contemporary methodological approach that seeks to evaluate each textual variant on its own merits, independent of a strict allegiance to any particular manuscript, family, or text type. This method emphasizes a case-by-case analysis, relying on both internal and external criteria to determine the most probable original text.

Principles of Radical Eclecticism

Radical eclecticism combines elements of earlier criticism methods but does not bind itself to the traditional categories of text types such as Alexandrian, Western, Byzantine, or Caesarean. Instead, it assesses each variant independently, considering a wide range of evidential bases from manuscript traditions to linguistic and historical contexts.

Focus on Manuscript Evidence

Unlike more conservative approaches that might prioritize the text of the earliest manuscripts or specific text types, radical eclecticism looks at the broadest possible spectrum of textual witnesses. This includes papyri, majuscules, minuscules, lectionaries, and translations into other languages, as well as patristic citations. Each piece of evidence is weighed to ascertain its contribution to reconstructing the original text.

For example, in examining a passage like Romans 5:1, where there is a variant between "we have" (echomen) and "let us have" (echōmen), radical eclecticism would not automatically favor the Alexandrian reading just because of its source. Instead, it would evaluate the variant in light of its theological implications, syntactical coherence, and how it fits within Paul's argument in Romans, as well as its attestation across a variety of sources.

Theological and Contextual Considerations

Radical eclecticism also places significant emphasis on the coherence of a reading within the theological and literary context of the New Testament writings. This involves a detailed analysis of the authorial style, vocabulary, and theological themes, alongside an understanding of historical and cultural backgrounds.

Example: Philippians 2:6

In Philippians 2:6, the phrase "who, being in the form of God, did not consider equality with God something to be exploited," presents variants around the translation of the Greek word "harpagmos" (exploited, grasped, or held onto). Radical eclecticism would look at Pauline theology, the usage of Greek terms, early Christian understanding of Christ's nature, and how different readings might alter theological nuances, supported by diverse manuscript evidence.

Independent Evaluation of Variants

A key characteristic of radical eclecticism is its independence from the traditional constraints of text types. Each variant is judged on its own merits, which allows for a potentially more objective assessment but also requires a highly nuanced understanding of multiple disciplines, including linguistics, paleography, and history.

Example: Mark 16:9-20

The long ending of Mark's Gospel is absent in some of the oldest and most reliable Alexandrian manuscripts (e.g., Codex Sinaiticus and Codex Vaticanus) but appears in many later manuscripts across different text types. Radical eclecticism would analyze the early patristic commentary on the Gospel of Mark, the stylistic differences between this ending and the rest of Mark, and the theological content of the verses to make a decision about its originality.

Applying Radical Eclecticism in Practice

Radical eclecticism's strength lies in its flexibility and comprehensive approach, drawing on a wide array of textual witnesses and scholarly disciplines to make informed decisions about the text of the New Testament. While this approach can lead to less predictability in its conclusions, it strives for the most historically plausible and textually coherent restoration of the original writings. By considering each variant in its full context—linguistic, historical, theological, and manuscript evidence—radical eclecticism offers a robust framework for navigating the complex landscape of New Testament textual criticism.

Modern Approaches to New Testament Textual Criticism: Exploring Reasoned Eclecticism

Reasoned eclecticism represents a balanced and widely accepted approach in New Testament textual criticism, especially among conservative scholars. This method combines rigorous analysis of external manuscript evidence with internal considerations such as context and authorial intent, seeking to ascertain the original wording of the New Testament texts through a reasoned evaluation of all available data.

Principles of Reasoned Eclecticism

Reasoned eclecticism, also known as reasoned criticism, carefully assesses both external and internal evidence, avoiding the extremes of relying solely on either the oldest manuscripts or the text type with the broadest attestation. It acknowledges the necessity of understanding the historical and cultural context in which the texts were copied and the theological biases that may have influenced scribes.

External Evidence: Manuscript Quality and Distribution

The evaluation of external evidence involves an examination of the quality, age, and geographical distribution of manuscripts. High-quality manuscripts that are older and come from a variety of geographical areas are typically given more weight, as they are less likely to have been subjected to localized textual corruption.

For example, in examining a variant such as in Ephesians 1:1, where some manuscripts include "in Ephesus" and others do not, reasoned eclecticism would consider which manuscripts omit this phrase. Notably, important manuscripts like Papyrus 46 and Codex Vaticanus (both from around the 4th century C.E.) omit "in Ephesus," suggesting that the original might have been more general in addressing a wider audience, rather than specific to Ephesus.

Internal Evidence: Contextual and Stylistic Consistency

Internal evidence examines the consistency of a textual variant with the broader literary and theological context of the book, as well as the specific style and vocabulary of the author. Reasoned eclecticism critically evaluates whether a variant fits an author's typical usage and the immediate narrative or theological context.

For instance, in Philippians 4:13, various manuscripts display slight differences in the wording of Paul's declaration, "I can do all things through Christ who strengthens me." Reasoned eclecticism would look at Paul's usual expression of reliance on Christ throughout his epistles to determine which variant most likely reflects his original wording and theological intent.

Applying Reasoned Eclecticism: A Case Study in the Gospels

Example: The Beatitude Variants (Matthew 5:3 vs. Luke 6:20)

Matthew's Gospel reads "Blessed are the poor in spirit," whereas Luke simply states "Blessed are you who are poor." Reasoned eclecticism would not only consider the manuscript evidence for these readings but also evaluate the theological themes of Matthew and Luke, recognizing that Matthew often spiritualizes his account to emphasize moral and spiritual lessons, while Luke focuses more on literal and social aspects. The difference in wording reflects the distinct theological emphases and audiences of the two Gospel writers, suggesting that both readings are original to their respective texts.

The Role of Patristic Citations

The use of writings from the early Church Fathers can also inform reasoned eclecticism by providing additional insights into how early Christians understood and transmitted the New Testament texts. Citations of New Testament passages in patristic literature can offer valuable external support for or against certain textual variants.

Example: The Comma Johanneum (1 John 5:7-8)

This passage, which includes a reference to the Trinity, is absent in nearly all Greek manuscripts before the sixteenth century and in the writings of the early Church Fathers. Reasoned eclecticism would assess both the lack of early and widespread manuscript support and the theological implications of the passage's inclusion or exclusion, likely concluding that it was a later addition to the text.

Through a balanced analysis of external and internal evidence, reasoned eclecticism seeks to reconstruct the New Testament text as faithfully as possible to the original. This approach ensures that textual decisions are not merely based on the oldest or most widespread evidence but are supported by a comprehensive evaluation of all relevant data. By applying these principles, scholars can provide a text that is both historically credible and theologically consistent.

Modern Approaches to New Testament Textual Criticism: Aland's Local-Genealogical Method and Classification of Manuscripts

Kurt Aland's local-genealogical method offers a nuanced approach to New Testament textual criticism by emphasizing a detailed examination of textual variations on a case-by-case basis, supplemented by a genealogical analysis of manuscripts. This method aims to determine the original text by considering both external (documentary) and internal (textual context and content) evidence, though with a pronounced emphasis on the documentary side when possible.

Fundamentals of the Local-Genealogical Method

The local-genealogical method acknowledges the complexity of the textual tradition of the New Testament, suggesting that no single manuscript family consistently preserves the original text across all passages. Therefore, it rejects the notion of constructing a simple stemma (manuscript family tree) that could inaccurately simplify these relationships.

Assessing Variants Independently

Each textual variant is analyzed independently, recognizing that the original reading could be preserved in any manuscript or group of manuscripts, regardless of their classification into traditional text types. This approach is meticulous and requires a comprehensive understanding of both the textual data and the historical manuscript context.

Integration of External and Internal Evidence

While external evidence (manuscripts' historical and geographical data) usually takes precedence, internal evidence (contextual and stylistic coherence) is also crucial, particularly in cases where the documentary evidence is ambiguous or conflicting.

Example: Variant Analysis in Mark 6:51

In Mark 6:51, the critical apparatus might show differing manuscript support for multiple readings within the same verse. The local-genealogical method does not automatically favor the textual variant supported by the majority or even the oldest manuscripts. Instead, it evaluates each variant's origin, considering how and why each variant might have arisen, looking at transcriptional habits, and contextual appropriateness.

Documentary Approach Versus Eclecticism

The documentary approach advocated by Aland and others stresses the importance of manuscript evidence as the foundation of textual criticism but allows for internal evidence to play a decisive role when manuscripts do not provide clear answers. This method contrasts with pure eclecticism, which might overly favor internal consistency over the harder external evidence.

Example: Textual Decisions in Matthew 16:20 and 16:21

In Matthew 16, discrepancies in manuscript testimony regarding the phrases "the Christ" versus "Jesus Christ" illustrate how textual critics must balance documentary and internal evidence. The documentary method would start with the strongest manuscript evidence but also consider the internal narrative and theological coherence of each variant, assessing which reading best fits the immediate context and the broader Gospel narrative.

Challenges and Criticisms of the Local-Genealogical Method

One challenge of the local-genealogical method is its complexity and the intensive nature of its application, requiring detailed knowledge of manuscript histories and the capacity to evaluate internal evidence without bias. Critics argue that this method can lead to inconsistencies in the text, as decisions made on a verse-by-verse basis may result in a final text that no single manuscript group originally contained.

Application in Textual Criticism

The application of Aland's method involves a meticulous, multifaceted analysis that goes beyond simple comparison of textual variants. It includes understanding the historical context of each manuscript, the specific scribal practices that may have influenced textual transmission, and the theological or liturgical traditions that may have impacted how texts were copied and used.

Aland's local-genealogical method represents a sophisticated blend of traditional textual criticism and modern analytical techniques. By carefully balancing documentary and internal evidence, this approach seeks to reconstruct the New Testament text with a high degree of historical fidelity. It highlights the complexity of the textual tradition and the necessity of a meticulous, evidence-based approach in the quest to recover the most original text of the New Testament.

Modern Approaches to New Testament Textual Criticism: Metzger's Judgment of Variants According to Text Types

Bruce Metzger's approach to New Testament textual criticism through the classification of manuscripts into text types serves as a cornerstone for understanding variant judgments in biblical scholarship. His method emphasizes the critical evaluation of textual variants by categorizing the extant manuscripts into primarily four text types: Alexandrian, Western, Caesarean, and Byzantine. Each text type reflects distinct scribal practices and geographical origins, influencing how textual critics assess the authenticity of variant readings.

Understanding Text Types

Text types are classifications that help scholars organize and evaluate manuscript evidence based on common characteristics shared among groups of manuscripts. This categorization is crucial for understanding the genealogy and geographical distribution of textual variants.

THE EARLY CHRISTIAN COPYISTS OF THE NEW TESTAMENT

Alexandrian Text Type

The Alexandrian text type is characterized by manuscripts that are generally considered to have been produced by highly skilled scribes in Alexandria, known for their rigorous scribal practices. This text type is often viewed as the most reliable due to its age and the conservative nature of its scribal transmissions. Proto-Alexandrian manuscripts like P45, P46, P66, and P75, and codices such as Codex Vaticanus (B), are prized for their textual fidelity and minimal scribal intervention.

Western Text Type

The Western text type is marked by a tendency towards paraphrasis and harmonization, often incorporating explanatory additions or harmonizing discrepancies among parallel texts. This text type is predominantly found in manuscripts from regions like North Africa, Italy, and Gaul, and is also reflected in Old Latin translations and writings of early Western Church Fathers.

Caesarean Text Type

Identified by scholars such as Burnett Hillman Streeter, the Caesarean text type is seen in a limited group of manuscripts, primarily affecting the Gospels. This text type is thought to represent a mixture of Alexandrian and Western readings and is associated with manuscripts that might have circulated in Caesarea and influenced by Origen's scholarly activity.

Byzantine Text Type

The Byzantine text type, forming the basis of the Textus Receptus and the majority of medieval manuscripts, is characterized by a high degree of uniformity but is often considered less reliable due to its later origin and tendency towards smoothing over textual difficulties. Despite this, it remains a critical component of the textual tradition, especially in the book of Revelation where some Byzantine manuscripts preserve a comparatively purer text.

Metzger's Evaluative Approach

Metzger's methodology involves a detailed examination of each variant independently, considering both external manuscript evidence and internal consistency. He advocates for a balanced approach where no single text type is inherently superior, but rather, each is evaluated for its contribution to understanding the original text.

Integrating Internal and External Evidence

While Metzger emphasizes the importance of external evidence from manuscripts, he also carefully considers the internal evidence of readings. This includes examining the context within which a reading appears, its coherence with the broader scriptural narrative, and its theological plausibility.

Practical Application in Textual Criticism

Metzger's work, particularly his detailed commentary in the United Bible Societies' Greek New Testament, illustrates how judgments on variant readings are made. He frequently notes that readings supported by a combination of Alexandrian and Western witnesses are typically more authentic. However, he also acknowledges that true readings can occasionally be found preserved uniquely within one text type, emphasizing the necessity of a comprehensive evaluation that includes transcriptional and intrinsic probabilities.

Metzger's approach to textual criticism through the local-genealogical method and his careful classification of manuscripts into text types provide a framework for evaluating the vast array of textual variants in the New Testament. By balancing the strengths of external manuscript evidence with the insights provided by internal analysis, Metzger's method aims to reconstruct the New Testament text with a high degree of historical and textual accuracy. His legacy in textual criticism underscores the complex, yet profoundly meticulous, nature of determining the most authentic text of the New Testament.

Modern Approaches to New Testament Textual Criticism: Assessing Reasoned Conservatism

Reasoned Conservatism is a methodological approach within New Testament textual criticism that treats all main manuscript traditions—Byzantine, Alexandrian, Western, and Caesarean—as potentially reliable witnesses to the original text. This perspective challenges the preference for the Alexandrian text by emphasizing that no single text type inherently carries more historical authenticity than the others.

Principle of Textual Equality

Reasoned Conservatism holds that every main text type should be evaluated without presupposing the superiority of one over others. This approach suggests that biases towards a particular text type could overlook valid textual evidence from other traditions.

Independent Development of Text Types

Advocates of Reasoned Conservatism argue that each text type has developed independently and possibly traces back to origins as early as the second century C.E. They propose that these text types have been preserved through separate transmission lines that have not necessarily mixed, supporting the idea that each line could independently preserve the original readings.

Example: Early Byzantine Readings

The discovery of Byzantine-like readings in early papyri such as Papyrus 46, dating around 200 C.E., suggests that some aspects of the Byzantine text type could be earlier than previously thought. This evidence challenges the assumption that the Byzantine text type is purely a product of later standardization.

Evaluating Consensus Readings

Reasoned Conservatism values readings that have broad support across multiple text types, considering such consensus as a stronger indicator of a reading's authenticity.

Example: Variants in the Lord's Prayer

The doxology of the Lord's Prayer, "For yours is the kingdom and the power and the glory forever, Amen," found widely in Byzantine manuscripts and some Western texts, is absent in the earliest Alexandrian manuscripts. While Reasoned Eclecticism might discount this reading due to its absence in older Alexandrian texts, Reasoned Conservatism would argue for its inclusion based on its prevalence across other manuscript families, suggesting it might reflect an original reading that was lost in the Alexandrian tradition.

Critiques of Reasoned Conservatism

Critics of Reasoned Conservatism often point out that this approach might lead to the re-admission of readings from the Byzantine text type that were previously considered later additions. They argue that the method could reintroduce elements that were not part of the original text but became widely disseminated through the Byzantine tradition.

Objective Overview

Reasoned Conservatism challenges the predominance of the Alexandrian text type in modern critical editions of the New Testament. By advocating for an egalitarian approach to manuscript evidence, it seeks to ensure that textual criticism does not favor one tradition over others without sufficient grounds. While this method faces criticism for potentially embracing readings from historically later text types, it underscores the complexity of textual transmission and the need to consider all evidence in reconstructing the New Testament text.

Perception of the Byzantine Text and Textus Receptus: Almost all textual critics, especially since the time of J. J. Griesbach (1745-1812), have viewed the Byzantine text type, which heavily influences the Textus Receptus, as less reliable than other text types like the Alexandrian. The reason for this view is largely due to its later manuscript evidence and the perceived accumulation of scribal alterations through centuries. It is viewed as "corrupt" by the leading textual scholars.

Use of the Textus Receptus: Karl Lachmann was pivotal in moving away from the Textus Receptus towards older manuscripts that were believed to better represent the original text of the New Testament. Since then, most critical editions of the New Testament, such as those by Westcott and Hort (WH), Nestle-Aland (NA), and the United Bible Societies (UBS), have relied on a broader and older manuscript base than the Textus Receptus. These texts generally prioritize older manuscripts which often belong to the Alexandrian text type, considered more reliable due to their age and closer proximity to the original autographs.

Modern Bible Translations: Since the emergence of the Revised Version (1881) and the American Standard Version (1901), most modern Bible translations have indeed moved away from the Textus Receptus in favor of these critical editions (WH, NA, UBS). These translations aim to incorporate the latest scholarly research and manuscript discoveries to provide a text that is as close as possible to the original writings of the New Testament.

King James Version Only Movement: The King James Version Only movement advocates for the exclusive use of the King James Version, arguing that it is the most accurate or divinely approved translation. This movement favors the corrupt Textus Receptus and, by extension, the Majority Text, which shares much in common with the Byzantine text type predominant in the TR. It's important to note that while this view is held by an extreme minority within the broader Christian community, they have a very loud voice and have mislead many.

Modern Approaches to New Testament Textual Criticism: Coherence Based Genealogical Method

The Coherence Based Genealogical Method (CBGM) is a sophisticated approach to New Testament textual criticism that has gained prominence in recent years. It combines quantitative analysis with traditional qualitative methods to determine the most probable original text of the New Testament. This method focuses on understanding the relationships between textual variants through a genealogical network of manuscripts, assessing both the external support and the internal coherence of readings.

Principles of the Coherence Based Genealogical Method

The CBGM operates on the premise that the history of the New Testament text can be best understood by examining the coherence and genealogical relationships among all known variants and manuscripts. This method seeks to reconstruct the history of the text by mapping out these relationships to identify which variants are most likely original.

Genealogical Linkages

The core of the CBGM involves creating a "global stemma," which is a kind of family tree that maps the relationships between different manuscripts based on shared textual readings. This involves an analysis of both prior agreements (where manuscripts agree before a split in transmission) and posterior agreements (where manuscripts converge after a divergence).

Example: Analysis of Variants in Romans 5:1

In Romans 5:1, there is a textual variant between "we have" (ἔχομεν, echomen) and "let us have" (ἔχωμεν, echōmen). By applying CBGM, scholars can examine how this variant appears across different manuscript lineages and assess which reading shows greater coherence and fewer anomalies in its transmission path.

Internal Coherence Evaluation

The CBGM also assesses the internal coherence of a reading by evaluating how well it fits with the surrounding text and the broader theological context of the passage. This aspect of the method requires a detailed analysis of the narrative or argumentative structure of the text, as well as linguistic and stylistic considerations.

Example: The Comma Johanneum (1 John 5:7-8)

The Comma Johanneum is a famous case where the CBGM has been applied. By analyzing the internal coherence of the passage, scholars noted that the trinitarian formula included in some late manuscripts does not cohere well with the style and theology of the rest of the Epistle, suggesting its later addition.

External Evidence Assessment

In addition to internal coherence, the CBGM evaluates the external evidence by considering the age and reliability of the manuscripts that support a particular reading. This includes analyzing the geographical spread and the textual quality of the manuscripts.

Example: The Ending of Mark's Gospel

For the controversial ending of Mark's Gospel (Mark 16:9-20), CBGM helps determine which manuscripts most reliably represent the original ending of Mark by analyzing their genealogical relationships. The oldest and most reliable manuscripts, such as Codex Sinaiticus and Codex Vaticanus, do not include these verses, suggesting that the shorter ending may be closer to the original text.

Applying the Coherence Based Genealogical Method in Practice

The application of CBGM involves both computer-assisted analysis and traditional scholarly judgment. It allows scholars to visualize the complex relationships between textual witnesses and to make informed decisions about the text's history based on comprehensive data.

Steps in Applying CBGM

1. **Collection of Variant Data**: Gather all known variants for a specific passage.
2. **Construction of a Preliminary Stemma**: Map out the initial relationships based on direct manuscript comparisons.
3. **Assessment of Coherence**: Evaluate how well each variant fits within the textual and historical context.
4. **Revision of the Stemma**: Adjust the genealogical tree based on findings from the coherence analysis.
5. **Final Evaluation**: Decide on the most likely original text based on the combined evidence.

By integrating rigorous statistical analysis with traditional textual criticism, the Coherence Based Genealogical Method offers a powerful tool for uncovering the most reliable form of the New Testament text. It represents a significant advancement in the field by providing a more nuanced understanding of textual transmission and the dynamics of variant development.

Modern Approaches to New Testament Textual Criticism: Emphasizing the Documentary Method

The Documentary Method in New Testament textual criticism is an approach that prioritizes historical and manuscript evidence over internal conjectures when determining the original text of the New Testament. This method has been reinforced and refined over time, emphasizing the importance of documentary evidence as a more reliable indicator of the text's historical authenticity than solely internal analysis.

Foundation of the Documentary Method

The Documentary Method rests on the principle that the text of the New Testament should primarily be reconstructed based on the physical evidence provided by manuscripts. This approach aligns with the views of early textual critics like Westcott and Hort, who argued that "documentary evidence has been in most cases allowed to confer the place of honour against internal evidence" (Hort, 1881). It is rooted in the belief that a thorough examination of the manuscript tradition can yield a more objective understanding of the New Testament text.

External Evidence as Primary

The central tenet of the Documentary Method is that external evidence—manuscripts, their dates, provenances, and textual character—should be the primary factor in textual decisions. This is because manuscripts are tangible artifacts of the text's transmission and provide direct insight into its history.

Case Study: The Role of P75

The significance of the Documentary Method is exemplified by the discovery and analysis of Papyrus 75 (P75). Found in the 20th century, 𝔓75 is a key witness to the gospels of Luke and John and dates to around 200 C.E. Its high textual agreement with Codex Vaticanus (B), estimated at 83% similarity, suggests a very early and reliable type of text, reinforcing the credibility of the Vaticanus text. This discovery has been pivotal in demonstrating that the texts of some early papyri were not as fluid or independent as previously thought.

Implications for Textual Criticism

The findings related to P75 have led to a reevaluation of the approach to textual criticism that overly relies on internal evidence, such as conjectured authorial style or perceived theological motifs. The close relationship between P75 and Vaticanus challenges the notion that the high quality of

Vaticanus was the result of a fourth-century scholarly recension and suggests instead that it reflects a text type already in circulation by the second century.

Historical Contextualization of Manuscripts

Understanding the historical and geographical context of manuscripts is crucial in the Documentary Method. It allows scholars to trace the transmission paths of textual variants and to assess the influence of regional textual practices on the New Testament.

The Alexandrian Context

The scholarly environment of Alexandria is often cited as a hub for textual preservation and transmission. Early Christian scribes in Alexandria were noted for their scholarly rigor, which likely contributed to the preservation of a relatively stable and pure text, exemplified by manuscripts like P75 and Codex Vaticanus. This context supports the notion that some regional manuscript traditions maintained a high fidelity to the original texts.

Reassessing the Documentary Method

The Documentary Method in New Testament textual criticism provides a robust framework that prioritizes manuscript evidence while still valuing internal textual analysis. This approach does not disregard internal evidence but rather integrates it in a balanced way, with a slight emphasis on the more objective documentary evidence. This method is particularly useful when external evidence is strong and consistent, but it also allows for a shift towards internal considerations when the manuscript evidence is less conclusive or when it presents anomalies.

Importance of Balanced Evidence Assessment

The Documentary Method recognizes that while external manuscript evidence often offers more objective insights into the text's history, internal evidence, such as linguistic patterns and contextual coherence, is also crucial for understanding the intent and integrity of the text. The method advocates for an initial reliance on the tangible data provided by manuscripts but does not ignore the insights that can be gained from examining the text's internal features.

Challenges of the Documentary Method

While this method has greatly enhanced our understanding of the textual transmission of the New Testament, it faces the inherent challenge of any historical inquiry based on physical artifacts: the incompleteness of the evidence. No single method, including the Documentary Method, can fully reconstruct the original text due to gaps in the manuscript tradition and the complex history of textual transmission. However, by prioritizing manuscripts while judiciously using internal evidence, this method strives for the most historically grounded reconstruction possible.

Integration with Broader Textual Criticism Practices

Integrating the Documentary Method with reasoned eclecticism creates a comprehensive approach that leverages the strengths of both methods. This synthesis allows for a dynamic evaluation process where external evidence is typically prioritized, but internal evidence is also critically assessed to resolve textual questions.

Complementary Approaches

This integration is particularly effective in cases where manuscript evidence is ambiguous or where multiple textual traditions present compelling but conflicting readings. By employing both external and internal criteria, textual critics can navigate these complexities more effectively, making decisions that are informed by a fuller spectrum of evidence.

Enhancing Textual Reconstruction

By combining the Documentary Method's emphasis on manuscript evidence with the nuanced analysis of text internal to reasoned eclecticism, scholars can approach the New Testament text in a manner that respects its historical transmission while also considering the literary and theological nuances that may influence textual variants. This combined approach seeks to reconstruct the New Testament text as faithfully as possible to its original form, acknowledging both the physical transmission history of the documents and the literary context of the writings.

The Documentary Method underscores the need for a meticulous and evidence-based approach to New Testament textual criticism. By focusing on the documentary evidence and supplementing it with a careful analysis of internal textual evidence, scholars can navigate the complex history of the New Testament's transmission and make more informed decisions about its text. This method not only respects the historical integrity of the New Testament writings but also enhances our understanding of their textual development over time.

Modern Approaches to New Testament Textual Criticism: Assessing Manuscripts Through a Study of Singular Variants

Bruce Metzger's approach to New Testament textual criticism incorporates an insightful method of categorizing manuscripts into text types, each defined by distinct scribal characteristics and geographical origins. This method is particularly valuable when combined with a detailed analysis of singular variants within these manuscripts, providing deep insights into the scribal habits that influenced textual transmission.

Classification of Manuscripts by Text Types

Metzger's method organizes manuscripts into four primary text types—Alexandrian, Western, Caesarean, and Byzantine. Each type represents a different scribal tradition, with the Alexandrian text typically regarded as the most reliable due to its association with early and well-trained scribes of Alexandria who are known for their careful and conservative copying practices.

Alexandrian Text Type

The Alexandrian text type, often deemed superior in textual criticism circles, is exemplified by its early manuscripts like P45, P66, P75, and codices such as Vaticanus (B). These manuscripts are valued for their textual purity and minimal scribal alterations, reflecting a high fidelity to the original texts.

Western Text Type

In contrast, the Western text type is characterized by a tendency towards expansion and harmonization, often incorporating additional explanatory material. This type is prevalent in manuscripts from Western locales like North Africa and Europe and is mirrored in the Old Latin and certain Syriac translations.

Caesarean and Byzantine Text Types

The Caesarean text type, less widely recognized, is noted for its blend of Alexandrian and Western readings, while the Byzantine text type, forming the basis of the Textus Receptus, is marked by later manuscript evidence and a uniformity that suggests extensive standardization.

The Role of Singular Variants in Textual Criticism

Singular variants—readings found in only one manuscript or manuscript group—offer a unique window into the scribal practices and textual interactions of early Christian copyists. The study of these variants can reveal the individual tendencies of scribes and their responses to the texts they were reproducing.

Scribal Habits and Singular Variants

The analysis of singular variants, as advocated by scholars like Ernest Colwell and James Royse, helps to identify the specific scribal habits that may have led to unique textual readings. For instance, Royse's examination of early papyri like P45 and P66 provides insights into the scribal culture of early Christianity, highlighting how scribes might have interacted with their texts not just as copyists but as engaged readers.

Reader-Reception Methodology

Applying reader-reception methodology to the study of singular variants allows scholars to consider how scribes, as readers, might have understood, interpreted, and consequently altered the text based on their cognitive and cultural contexts. This approach considers the scribe as an active participant in the creation of textual meaning, potentially introducing changes that reflect personal interpretations or community doctrines.

Implications of Singular Variant Analysis

Studying singular variants does more than just illuminate individual scribal practices; it also provides critical data for reconstructing the history of the New Testament text. By examining these unique readings, scholars can gain a better understanding of the diversity of textual traditions and the complex processes of textual transmission in early Christian communities.

THE EARLY CHRISTIAN COPYISTS OF THE NEW TESTAMENT

Textual Transmission and Scribal Creativity

The examination of singular variants sheds light on the dynamic nature of textual transmission, revealing that the text of the New Testament was not static but was subject to the interpretative and sometimes creative inputs of its copyists. This realization challenges the notion of a singular "original" text, instead presenting a more nuanced picture of early Christian scriptural traditions.

Bruce Metzger's classification of manuscripts into distinct text types, combined with a detailed study of singular variants, offers a comprehensive framework for understanding the complexities of New Testament textual criticism. This approach not only helps identify the most reliable readings but also enhances our understanding of the historical and cultural contexts in which these texts were copied and transmitted. By recognizing the role of the scribe as both a copier and an interpreter, this method enriches our appreciation of the New Testament as a living document, continually shaped and reshaped by the communities that preserved it.

Edward D. Andrews

CHAPTER 10 How Scribes Influenced the Text of the New Testament

An Introduction to Scribal Practices and Textual Transmission

The transmission of the text of the New Testament has been significantly influenced by the practices and peculiarities of scribes who copied these sacred texts throughout the early centuries. Understanding scribal tendencies is essential for any study in New Testament textual criticism, particularly as we aim to discern the most authentic form of the text that was likely original to the authors.

The Dual Nature of Textual Evidence

Textual criticism employs a robust approach involving both external and internal evidence to evaluate and determine the originality of textual variants. External evidence includes manuscript origins, textual families, and the geographical and historical context of these documents. Internal evidence is subdivided into intrinsic probabilities—which speculate what the author most likely intended to write—and transcriptional probabilities, which focus on the copying practices of scribes.

Understanding Transcriptional Probabilities

The primary focus here is on transcriptional probabilities, a category that delves deep into how scribes interacted with the texts they copied. This analysis is crucial because understanding the types of errors scribes were prone to, this can lead us to more accurate conclusions about the likely original readings of the New Testament.

Common Scribal Errors

Scribes often introduced variations into the text unintentionally through common errors such as confusion of similar-sounding letters, misspellings, or accidental omissions and additions.

Phonetic Confusions and Their Implications

For example, the similarity in pronunciation between certain Greek letters led to frequent confusions such as between ο and ω, or αι and ε. In Romans 5:1, the difference between ἔχομεν ("we have") and ἔχωμεν ("let us have") could stem from such a phonetic confusion. Similarly, in Luke 22:40, προσεύχεσθαι ("to pray") could be easily mistaken for προσεύχεσθε ("you pray") due to the similar pronunciation of αι and ε.

Scribal Leaps: Homoeoteleuton and Homoeoarcton

Scribes might also omit text by accidentally skipping from one occurrence of a word or phrase to another similar one. This phenomenon, known as homoeoteleuton, occurs when the scribe's eye jumps from one end of a phrase to the same ending of another phrase further down the text, skipping all intervening words. Conversely, homoeoarcton describes a similar skip but at the beginning of lines or phrases. These errors can lead to significant textual variations, where either a portion of the text is lost (haplography) or mistakenly duplicated (dittography).

Scribal Additions and Harmonizations

Scribes not only omitted but also added text, often harmonizing accounts between Gospels or adjusting language for stylistic consistency. These additions can sometimes reflect a scribe's attempt to clarify or enhance the narrative but may also introduce discrepancies between manuscripts.

Doctrinal Adjustments

While early textual critics like Hort believed that doctrinal motives rarely influenced textual alterations, more recent scholarship suggests otherwise. Studies indicate that some scribes might have altered texts to align with prevailing theological views or to address contemporary doctrinal debates. This is particularly noted in the so-called Western text of Acts, which appears to exhibit anti-Judaic tendencies, possibly reflecting the theological inclinations of the scribe or the community for which the manuscript was produced.

The study of scribal tendencies not only reveals the human element in the transmission of the New Testament but also underscores the complexity of determining the original text. Each variant must be examined critically, considering both the possible scribal practices that could have introduced changes and the broader textual context that might support one reading over another. As we analyze these singular variants and the patterns they reveal, we gain invaluable insights into the early history of the New Testament text and the meticulous work of its earliest transmitters.

A Deep Dive into Scribal Variations

In understanding how scribes influenced the transmission of the New Testament text, it is crucial to explore the full range of scribal activities that have shaped its textual history. This examination is based on both the external evidence of the manuscripts and the internal dynamics of the text as it was copied and recopied through generations.

Exploring Scribal Activity Through Metzger's Insights

Philip W. Comfort's NEW TESTAMENT TEXT AND TRANSLATION COMMENTARY is an important tool for such a study. However, we focus on Bruce Metzger's *Textual Commentary on the Greek New Testament* serves as an essential resource in this study, providing detailed analysis of significant textual variants along with evaluations of transcriptional probabilities. Metzger's commentary sheds light on the scribal practices that likely contributed to these variations, offering insights into the external and internal factors that influenced scribal decisions.

Case Studies from Metzger's Commentary

1. **Pruning Unnecessary Words**: In Matthew 13:44, Metzger discusses the Alexandrian scribes' tendency to omit superfluous words, suggesting a disciplined approach to text transmission that valued conciseness.

2. **Scribal Embellishments**: Acts 5:37 highlights how scribes sometimes added words like πολὺν or ἱκανόν to enhance the narrative, indicating a move towards a more detailed and elaborative text.

3. **Expansion of Sacred Names**: In Acts 20:21, the expansion of the names of the Lord reflects a common scribal practice aimed at expressing reverence and clarifying subjects within the text.

4. **Clarification Through Addition**: Ephesians 2:21 shows how scribes would insert terms like ἡ to make the text clearer to readers, reflecting their role as intermediaries who often sought to facilitate understanding of the scriptures.

Principles Guiding Textual Evaluations

Critics have long debated the application of common sense versus established canons of criticism when evaluating textual variants. These canons, while helpful, often conflict in practice and require careful application to avoid contradictory conclusions.

Conflicting Applications of Textual Principles

For example, in Mark 10:7 and John 5:17, scholars debate whether the presence or absence of certain words results from scribal error or intentional modification for stylistic reasons. These discussions highlight the ongoing tension between internal logic and external manuscript evidence in textual criticism.

Edward D. Andrews

The Role of Transcriptional Probabilities in Textual Criticism

Understanding transcriptional probabilities involves recognizing the types of errors scribes were likely to make and using this knowledge to make informed judgments about the original text. This approach is critical for deciding among possible readings and reconstructing the most authentic version of the text.

Common Scribal Errors and Their Implications

- **Homoeoteleuton and Homoeoarcton:** These errors occur when scribes accidentally skip over similar endings or beginnings of words, often resulting in omitted text. Recognizing these patterns is essential for identifying which readings might represent the original text.

- **Harmonization and Doctrinal Adjustments:** Scribes often altered texts to align them with parallel passages or doctrinal expectations. Such changes, while informative about the scribe's context and intentions, complicate efforts to recover the original wording.

Evaluating Scribal Tendencies: Between Theory and Practice

The theoretical framework for analyzing scribal tendencies must be robust enough to accommodate the diverse and complex nature of manuscript evidence. Critics like Griesbach and Hort have provided guidelines, such as preferring shorter or more difficult readings, but these rules must be applied judiciously to avoid oversimplification.

Challenges in Applying Critical Principles

The principles of preferring shorter (lectio brevior potior) or more difficult readings (lectio difficilior potior) often lead to practical dilemmas. Critics must balance these guidelines with other considerations, such as the possibility of unintentional omissions (homoeoteleuton) or the scribe's tendency to clarify or elaborate on the text.

The study of scribal tendencies in the transmission of the New Testament is a complex field that requires a nuanced understanding of both the physical manuscript evidence and the internal dynamics of the text. By carefully examining how scribes interacted with the texts they copied, scholars can gain deeper insights into the historical transmission of the New Testament and better reconstruct the original writings. This detailed approach not only illuminates the technical aspects of textual criticism but also enriches our understanding of the early Christian world and the meticulous work of its scribes.

Navigating Complexities in Scribal Variations - Advanced Analysis

As we delve deeper into the intricacies of scribal practices that shaped the transmission of the New Testament, it becomes crucial to explore the advanced methodologies and critical debates that influence modern textual criticism. This exploration not only expands our understanding but also refines our approaches to deciphering the most authentic text possible.

Advanced Methodologies in Textual Criticism

Modern textual criticism employs a variety of advanced methodologies to address the challenges presented by scribal variations. These methodologies involve a combination of historical-critical analysis, quantitative data assessment, and contextual interpretation to form a comprehensive view of the scribal landscape.

Utilizing Quantitative Data

Recent advancements in digital humanities and computational analysis have allowed textual critics to utilize quantitative methods to assess manuscript variants. These techniques enable scholars to detect patterns and anomalies in scribal behavior that might not be evident through traditional qualitative analysis alone. By quantitatively assessing variants across multiple manuscripts, scholars can better identify common scribal errors and unique readings.

Critical Debates and Scholarly Discourse

The field of textual criticism is marked by ongoing debates that challenge conventional understandings and methodologies. These debates often focus on the interpretation of scribal intentions and the impact of external influences on the text.

The Debate Over Scribal Intentions

One major area of debate concerns the intentions behind scribal changes. While some scholars argue that most scribal variations result from unintentional errors or simple oversight, others contend that many changes are deliberate, influenced by theological, doctrinal, or cultural factors. For instance, the discussion around the Western text's anti-Judaic tendencies highlights how scribes might consciously alter texts to reflect prevailing theological sentiments.

External Influences on Scribal Practices

Another critical debate revolves around the extent to which external influences, such as ecclesiastical doctrines or local liturgical practices, shaped scribal decisions. This debate challenges the notion that scribes operated in isolation, suggesting instead that they were part of broader communities that influenced their copying practices.

Applying Theories in Practical Textual Criticism

In practical terms, applying theories of scribal behavior to actual textual criticism involves a careful balance of multiple considerations. Scholars must navigate between respecting the manuscript evidence and acknowledging the potential for scribal creativity and bias.

Case Study: Analyzing Complex Variants

Consider a complex variant in John 7:53-8:11, the Pericope Adulterae, which is absent in many early manuscripts but appears in several later ones. Critics must decide whether its absence in early manuscripts indicates that it is a later addition, or whether its inclusion in later manuscripts reflects a restoration of an original passage that was perhaps omitted due to its controversial content. This decision requires a careful analysis of both the external manuscript evidence and the internal narrative and theological coherence of the passage.

Enhancing Scribal Studies Through Interdisciplinary Approaches

Finally, enhancing our understanding of scribal tendencies benefits greatly from interdisciplinary approaches that incorporate insights from linguistics, history, and even psychology. These disciplines can provide deeper insights into the cognitive processes of scribes and the historical contexts in which they worked.

Integrating Linguistic Analysis

Linguistic analysis can help clarify why certain scribal errors, such as the confusion of homophones, were more likely to occur, given the linguistic context of the time. Understanding these linguistic factors is crucial for accurately interpreting the reasons behind specific variants.

The study of scribal tendencies in the transmission of the New Testament continues to be a dynamic field, enriched by both traditional methods and modern innovations. By integrating rigorous historical scholarship with cutting-edge analytical techniques, textual critics can provide more precise and nuanced reconstructions of the New Testament text, thereby offering richer insights into the early Christian world and its textual legacy. This ongoing work not only illuminates the past but also informs contemporary interpretations of these foundational texts.

Unpacking Scribal Behaviors

Understanding the meticulous work and distinct characteristics of early Christian scribes is pivotal in the field of New Testament textual criticism. This segment delves deeper into the groundbreaking studies by Ernest C. Colwell, particularly his 1965 examination of the scribal habits observed in Papyri P45, P66, and P75. Colwell's approach to isolating specific scribal tendencies through singular readings has significantly advanced our understanding of how individual scribes contributed to the textual variations we encounter in early New Testament manuscripts.

The Methodological Approach of Ernest C. Colwell

Colwell's pioneering work focused on discerning the unique habits of scribes by analyzing their singular readings—those variants that a scribe shares with no other known manuscript. This method provides invaluable insights into the scribal process, revealing the individual tendencies that can significantly affect the text.

Key Findings from Colwell's Study

1. **P75 - The Disciplined Scribe**: This manuscript showcases a scribe whose careful and deliberate approach aimed to reproduce the source text with high fidelity. The variants in P75 largely reflect a disciplined effort to maintain textual integrity, showcasing minimal deviation from the source.

2. **P45 - The Free Scribe**: Contrasting sharply with P75, the scribe of P45 exhibited a freer approach, often harmonizing, smoothing, and even whimsically substituting text. This scribe's liberal handling of the text suggests a less controlled copying environment and a greater degree of textual freedom.

3. **P66 - The Supervised Scribe**: The work on P66 appears to reflect a scribe who aimed to produce a good copy but fell into occasional errors, possibly due to fatigue or lapses in concentration. However, the presence of what might be termed supervisory oversight suggests a dual-layer of scribal activity, where a foreman or a second scribe corrected or guided the primary scribe's work.

4. **Comparative Analysis of Controlled vs. Uncontrolled Traditions**: P75 and P66 represent controlled scribal traditions with oversight and a clear intention to limit deviations from the source text. In contrast, P45 represents an uncontrolled tradition, where the scribe felt free to modify the text according to personal judgment or community needs.

Broader Implications of Colwell's Findings

The detailed profiles of these three scribes reveal that scribal activities can vary significantly, which challenges the traditional generalizations about scribal practices. Instead of broad statements about scribal tendencies, Colwell's approach suggests that each scribe may exhibit unique behaviors that should be considered when evaluating textual variants.

Harmonization and Word Loss Trends

- **Harmonization Practices**: Colwell found that harmonizations made by these scribes were typically in response to the immediate context rather than to parallel texts or general usage. This insight helps in understanding how scribes interacted with the text as they copied, often modifying it to better fit the narrative or theological context they perceived.

- **Tendencies to Omit Words**: Interestingly, all three scribes studied tended to lose more words than they added. This finding was confirmed by a subsequent study that extended the analysis to six early papyri, reinforcing the idea that early textual transmission was characterized more by omissions than by additions.

Reevaluating Textual Principles Based on Scribal Tendencies

The tendency of scribes to omit rather than add text suggests a revision of the common textual criticism principle that shorter readings are preferable (lectio brevior potior). Colwell's findings imply that, in many cases, the longer reading might be closer to the original, especially if the shorter reading can be explained by common scribal errors such as homoeoteleuton.

The meticulous study of singular readings and scribal habits offers profound insights into the complexities of New Testament textual transmission. Ernest C. Colwell's methodological innovations provide a more nuanced framework for understanding individual scribe's contributions to the text, challenging simplifications and urging a more detailed consideration of each scribe's impact. This approach not only enriches our comprehension of the textual history of the New Testament but also enhances our ability to reconstruct the most authentic text possible.

Detailed Analysis of Early Scribal Practices

In this section, we continue to explore how early Christian scribes influenced the text of the New Testament, focusing on the seminal work of scholars like Peter M. Head and the nuanced studies of specific early manuscripts. These studies provide critical insights into the scribal tendencies that shaped the earliest stages of New Testament textual transmission.

Advances in Understanding Scribal Practices

Peter M. Head's research on the singular readings of smaller gospel fragments further substantiates earlier findings about scribal tendencies, particularly regarding the prevalence of omissions over additions. This pattern is crucial for understanding the dynamics of textual changes in early Christian manuscripts.

The Significance of Singular Readings

Head's study underscores that singular readings—unique to individual manuscripts—often arise from spelling variations, transpositions, and harmonizations. Such singular instances are instrumental in revealing how scribes interacted with the text, whether through conscious modification or unintentional errors.

Scribal Habits in Specific Manuscripts

Detailed studies of manuscripts like P46, P66, P72, and Codex Bezae have shed light on the varied scribal behaviors and their implications for textual criticism:

- **P46**: G. Zuntz's analysis highlights a scribe's approach in transcribing Pauline epistles, revealing tendencies toward both preservation and alteration of the text.
- **P66 and P75**: Gordon D. Fee's work provides insights into the scribal habits present in these papyri, illustrating a spectrum from careful copying to more liberal textual interpretations.
- **Codex Bezae**: D.C. Parker's comprehensive study showcases the extensive scribal corrections and variations, illustrating a complex history of textual transmission.

Early Versus Later Scribal Traditions

The transition from a relatively uncontrolled to a more rigorously controlled scribal tradition marks a significant shift in the manuscript history of the New Testament. Early scribes operated with more freedom, which often resulted in a "wild" or "unedited" text, while later scribes, especially from the ninth century onwards, adhered to stricter standards of accuracy and consistency.

Implications for Textual Criticism

- **Early Scribal Freedom**: The freedom early scribes enjoyed allowed for a diverse array of textual variants, reflecting a dynamic and evolving scriptural tradition.

- **Later Scribal Precision**: The increase in scribal precision over the centuries underscores the evolving nature of textual transmission and the increasing importance of fidelity to a perceived original text.

The Role of the Papyri in Modern Textual Criticism

The discovery of early papyri has been pivotal in refining the canons of criticism, particularly by providing a clearer view of the earliest stages of textual transmission. These manuscripts offer a window into the scribal practices that prevailed during the initial centuries of Christianity.

Reevaluating Canonical Rules

- **Refining Canons of Criticism**: Studies of the papyri suggest that traditional rules of textual criticism, such as preferring shorter or more difficult readings, may need refinement to accommodate the complexities revealed by early scribal practices.
- **Influence on Modern Editions**: While the papyri have not drastically changed the printed editions of the New Testament, they have enriched our understanding of the text's early history and supported existing readings with earlier evidence.

The meticulous examination of early manuscripts and the singular readings they contain has fundamentally enhanced our understanding of how the New Testament text was formed and transmitted. These studies not only challenge our preconceptions about scribal practices but also provide a more nuanced foundation for textual criticism. By delving into the details of how individual scribes worked, we gain invaluable insights into the intricate process of scriptural preservation and transformation across the centuries. This ongoing analysis continues to refine our approaches to reconstructing the most authentic text of the New Testament, highlighting the intricate balance between preserving a sacred tradition and adapting to the practical realities of textual transmission.

Advances in Understanding Scribal Practices: 1995 to 2024

Since the foundational studies of the mid-20th century, the field of New Testament textual criticism has seen significant advancements, particularly with the integration of digital technologies and the discovery of new manuscript evidence. These developments have deepened our understanding of how scribes influenced the text of the New Testament and have introduced new methodologies for analyzing scribal behaviors and textual variants.

Technological Advancements in Manuscript Analysis

1. **Digital Imaging and Spectroscopy**: The use of multispectral imaging technology has allowed scholars to recover previously unreadable text from damaged manuscripts. This technology has revealed corrections, marginalia, and under-text that were not visible to the naked eye, providing new insights into the scribal practices and the history of specific texts.

2. **Online Manuscript Collections**: Platforms like the Virtual Manuscript Room (VMR) of the Institute for Textual Scholarship and Electronic Editing (ITSEE) and the Leon Levy Dead Sea Scrolls Digital Library have made high-resolution images of New Testament manuscripts available to researchers worldwide. This accessibility has democratized the field, allowing a broader spectrum of scholars to engage in textual criticism and to share findings more rapidly.

3. **Collaborative International Projects**: Initiatives like the International Greek New Testament Project (IGNTP) have facilitated collaborative work across institutions and countries, focusing on creating comprehensive digital editions of New Testament manuscripts. These projects often include transcriptions, translations, and detailed commentaries on scribal features.

Manuscript Discoveries and Reevaluations

4. **New Manuscript Finds**: Since 1995, several significant manuscript finds have continued to inform textual criticism. For instance, the discovery of additional papyri fragments has occasionally added to existing codices, offering more complete understandings of certain books.

5. **Reevaluation of Known Manuscripts**: Recent scholarly work has led to a reevaluation of the dating and provenance of many important manuscripts. Changes in these foundational aspects can

alter our understanding of the development of text types and the geographical spread of textual traditions.

Methodological Innovations in Textual Criticism

6. **Quantitative Analysis and Stylometry**: The application of statistical methods and computational stylometry has enabled more objective analysis of textual variations. These methods can, for example, help in distinguishing between scribal errors and intentional alterations, or in identifying stylistic patterns that may indicate a particular scribe's work.

7. **Interdisciplinary Approaches**: Increasingly, textual criticism has embraced insights from other fields such as cognitive psychology and cultural studies. These perspectives have enriched our understanding of the scribal culture and the cognitive processes behind textual transmission and errors.

Theoretical Developments in Understanding Scribal Behavior

8. **Scribal Culture Studies**: Recent scholarship has placed greater emphasis on understanding the socio-cultural context of scribes. This includes studies on the educational background of scribes, their role within their communities, and how these factors might have influenced their approach to copying texts.

9. **Shift in Canons of Criticism**: Theoretical discussions have increasingly questioned traditional canons of criticism, such as lectio difficilior potior (the harder reading is to be preferred) and lectio brevior potior (the shorter reading is to be preferred). Scholars advocate for more nuanced criteria that consider the broader manuscript context and the specific scribal culture.

The last three decades have significantly advanced our knowledge of how scribes influenced the New Testament text. With ongoing technological advancements, new manuscript discoveries, and innovative methodological approaches, the field of New Testament textual criticism is better equipped than ever to understand the complexities of textual transmission. These developments continue to refine our approach to reconstructing the original text and understanding its early history, ensuring that our interpretations are grounded in the most comprehensive and precise evidence available.

Bibliography

Aland, K. a. (1987). *The Text of the New Testament.* Grand Rapids: Eerdmans.

Andrews, E. (2019). *Misrepresenting Jesus: Debunking Bart D. Ehrman's Misquoting Jesus [Fourth Edition].* Cambridge: Christian Publishing House.

Andrews, E. D. (2016). *THE COMPLETE GUIDE to BIBLE TRANSLATION: Bible Translation Choices and Translation Principles [Second Edition]* . Cambridge: Christian Publishing House.

Andrews, E. D. (2016). *YOUR GUIDE FOR DEFENDING THE BIBLE: Self-Education of the Bible Made Easy.* Cambridge, OH: Christian Publishing House.

Andrews, E. D. (2016). *YOUR WORD IS TRUTH: Being Sanctified In the Truth.* Cambridge, OH: Christian Publishing House.

Andrews, E. D. (2018). *THE KING JAMES BIBLE: Do You Know the King James Version?* Cambridge, OH: Christian Publishing House.

Andrews, E. D. (2019). *400,000+ SCRIBAL ERRORS IN THE GREEK NEW TESTAMENT MANUSCRIPTS: What Assurance Do We Have that We Can Trust the Bible?* Cambridge, OH: Christian Publishing House.

Andrews, E. D. (2019). *INTRODUCTION TO THE TEXT OF THE NEW TESTAMENT: From The Authors and Scribe to the Modern Critical Text.* Cambridge, Ohio: Christian Publishing House.

Andrews, E. D. (2019). *THE READING CULTURE OF EARLY CHRISTIANITY: The Production, Publication, Circulation, and Use of Books in the Early Christian Church.* Cambridge, OH: Christian Publishing House.

Andrews, E. D. (2020). *INERRANCY OF SCRIPTURE: How Can We Believe Inerrancy of Scripture In the Originals When We Don't Have the Originals?* Cambridge, OH: Christian Publishing House.

Andrews, E. D. (2020). *THE NEW TESTAMENT DOCUMENTS: Can They Be Trusted?* Cambridge, OH: Christian Publishing House.

Andrews, E. D. (2020). *THE P52 PROJECT: Is P52 Really the Earliest Greek New Testament Manuscript?* Cambridge, OH: Christian Publishing House.

Andrews, E. D. (2022). *THE ORIGINAL TEXT OF THE NEW TESTAMENT: Ascertaining the Original Words of the Original Greek New Testament Manuscripts.* Cambridge, OH: Christian Publishing House.

Andrews, E. D. (2023). *A JOURNEY THROUGH ANCIENT LETTER WRITING: A New Look at New Testament Letters in the Greco-Roman World.* Cambridge, OH: Christian Publishing House.

Andrews, E. D. (2023). *BIBLICAL EXEGESIS: Biblical Criticism on Trial.* Cambridge, OH: Christian Publishing House.

Andrews, E. D. (2023). *DISCOVERING THE ORIGINAL BIBLE: Accuracy, Authenticity, and Reliability.* Cambridge, OH: Christian Publishing House.

Andrews, E. D. (2023). *HOW WE GOT THE BIBLE.* Cambridge, OH: Christian Publishing House.

Andrews, E. D. (2023). *THE BIBLE AS HISTORY: A Historical Journey Through the Bible.* Cambridge, Ohio: Christian Publishing House.

Andrews, E. D. (2023). *THE BIBLE ON TRIAL: Examining the Evidence for Being Inspired, Inerrant, Authentic, and True.* Cambridge, Ohio: Christian Publishing House.

Andrews, E. D. (2023). *THE NASB: Preserving Truth or Compromising Accuracy?: A Critical Look at the Shift from the 1995 to 2020 Editions of the New American Standard Bible (NASB).* Cambridge, OH: Christian Publishing House.

Andrews, E. D. (2023). *THE SCRIBE AND THE TEXT OF THE NEW TESTAMENT: Scribal Activities in the Transmission of the Text of the New Testament.* Cambridge, Ohio: Christian Publishing House.

Andrews, E. D. (2023). *THE TEXT OF THE NEW TESTAMENT: A Beginners Handbook to New Testament Textual Studies.* Cambridge, OH: Christian Publishing House.

Andrews, E. D. (2023). *THE TEXTUS RECEPTUS: The "Received Text" of the New Testament.* Cambridge, OH: Christian Publishing House.

Andrews, E. D. (2023). *Unlocking the Bible: A Beginner's Guide to the Coherence-Based Genealogical Method (CBGM): Understanding How Scholars Piece*

Together the New Testament. Cambridge, OH: Christian Publishing House.

Andrews, E. D., & Farnell, F. D. (2017). *BIBLICAL CRITICISM: What are Some Outstanding Weaknesses of Modern Historical Criticism?* Cambridge, OH: Christian Publishing House.

Bagnall, R. S. (2009). *Early Christian Books In Egypt*. Princeton, NJ: Princeton University Press.

Bagnall, R. S. (2009). *The Oxford Handbook of Papyrology (Oxford Handbooks)*. Oxford, NY: Oxford University Press.

Bagnall, R. S. (2012). *Everyday Writing in the Græco-Roman East*. Berkeley and Los Angeles, CA: University of California Press.

Black, D. A. (2002). *Rethinking New Testament Textual Criticism*. Grand Rapids, MI: Baker.

Bruce, F. (1984). *The Books and the Parchments: How We Got Our English Bible*. Ada, MI: Fleming H. Revell Company.

Bruce, F. (1988). *The Canon of Scripture*. Westmont, IL: InterVarsity Press.

Bruce, F. F. (1951, 1990). *The Acts of the Apostles (3rd edition)*. Grand Rapids, MI: Eerdmans.

Comfort, P. W. (1992). *Early Manuscripts & Modern Translations of the New Testament*. Wheaton, IL: Tyndale House Publishers.

Comfort, P. W. (1992). *The Quest for the Original Text of the New Testament*. Eugene, Oregon: Wipf and Stock Publishers.

Comfort, P. W. (2005). *ENCOUNTERING THE MANUSCRIPTS: An Introduction to New Testament Paleography and Textual Criticism*. Nashville, TN: Broadman & Holman.

Comfort, P. W. (2008). *New Testament Text and Translation Commentary*. Carol Stream, IL: Tyndale House Publishers.

Comfort, P. W. (2008). *New Testament Text and Translation Commentary*. Carol Stream: Tyndale House Publishers.

Comfort, P. W. (2008). *New Testament Text and Translation Commentary: Commentary on the Variant Readings of the Ancient New Testament Manuscripts and How They Relate to the Major English Translations*. Carol Stream, IL: Tyndale House Publishers.

Comfort, P., & Barret, D. (2019). *THE TEXT OF THE EARLIEST NEW TESTAMENT MANUSCRIPTS: Papyri 1-72, Vol. 1* . Grand Rapids, MI: Kregel Academic.

Comfort, P., & Barret, D. (2019). *THE TEXT OF THE EARLIEST NEW TESTAMENT MANUSCRIPTS: Papyri 75-139 and Uncials, Vol. 2.* Grand Rapids, MI: Kregel Academic.

D., E. B. (2012). *The Text of the New Testament in Contemporary Research: Essays on the Status Quaestionis. Second Edition (New Testament Tools, Studies and Documents, 42).* Boston, MA: BRILL.

Finegan, J. (1974). *Encountering New Testament Manuscripts.* Grand Rapids, MI: Eerdmans.

Gamble, H. Y. (1997). *Books and Readers in the Early Church: A History of Early Christian Texts.* New Haven and London: Yale University Press.

Greenlee, J. H. (2008). *Introduction to New Testament Textual Criticism (Revised ed.).* Peabody, MA: Hendrickson Publishers.

Greenlee, J. H. (2012). *The Text of the New Testament: From Manuscript to Modern Edition.* Grand Rapids, MI: Baker Academic.

Hodges, Z. &. (1985). *The Greek New Testament According to the Majority Text.* Nashville, TN: Thomas Nelson Publishers.

Hurtado, L. W. (2019). *TEXTS AND ARTIFACTS: Selected Essays on Textual Criticism ans Early Christian Manuscripts.* New York, NY: T & T Clark.

McKenzie, J. L. (1975). *Light on the Epistles: A Reader's Guide.* Chicago, IL: Thomas More Press.

Metzger, B. M. (1994). *A Textual Commentary on the Greek New Testament (2nd ed.).* New York: United Bible Society.

Metzger, B. M., & Ehrman, B. D. (2005). *The Text of the New Testament: Its Transmission, Corruption, and Restoration (4th Edition).* New York: Oxford University Press.

Myers, A. C. (1987). *The Eerdmans Bible Dictionary* . Grand Rapids, Mich: Eerdmans.

Pickering, W. (1980). *The Identity of the New Testament Text (rev. ed.).* Nashville: Nelson.

Porter, S. E. (2013). *HOW WE GOT THE NEW TESTAMENT: Text, Transmission, Translation.* Grand Tapids, MI: Baker Academic.

Sturz, H. A. (1984). *The Byzantine Text-Type & New Testament Textual Criticism.* Nashville, TN: Thomas Nelson Publishers.

Wasserman, T. &. (2017). *A New Approach to Textual Criticism: An Introduction to the Coherence-Based Genealogical Method.* Atlanta: SBL Press.

Westcott, B. F., & A., H. F. (1882). *The New Testament in the Original Greek, Vol. 2: Introduction, Appendix.* London: Macmillan and Co.

Westcott, B. F., & Hort, F. J. (1882). *Introduction to the New Testament in the Original Greek: Appendix.* New York, NY: Harper and Brothers.

www.ingramcontent.com/pod-product-compliance
Lightning Source LLC
Chambersburg PA
CBHW050546160426
43199CB00015B/2554